11-1-63

(63-14013)

This is a volume in
THE UNIVERSITY OF MICHIGAN HISTORY OF THE MODERN WORLD
Upon completion, the series will consist of the following volumes:

The United States to 1865 *by Michael Kraus*
The United States since 1865 *by Foster Rhea Dulles*
Canada: A Modern History *by John Bartlet Brebner*
Latin America: A Modern History *by J. Fred Rippy*
Great Britain to 1688: A Modern History *by Maurice Ashley*
Great Britain since 1688: A Modern History *by K. B. Smellie*
France: A Modern History *by Albert Guérard*
Germany: A Modern History *by Marshall Dill, Jr.*
Italy: A Modern History *by Denis Mack Smith*
Russia and the Soviet Union: A Modern History *by Warren B. Walsh*
The Near East: A Modern History *by William Yale*
The Far East: A Modern History *by Nathaniel Peffer*
India: A Modern History *by Percival Spear*
The Southwest Pacific to 1900: A Modern History *by C. Hartley Grattan*
The Southwest Pacific since 1900: A Modern History *by C. Hartley Grattan*
Africa: A Modern History *by Ronald Robinson*

THE SOUTHWEST PACIFIC SINCE 1900

A Modern History

The University of Michigan History of the Modern World
Edited by Allan Nevins and Howard M. Ehrmann

The Southwest Pacific Since 1900

A Modern History

AUSTRALIA   NEW ZEALAND   THE ISLANDS   ANTARCTICA

BY C. HARTLEY GRATTAN

Ann Arbor: The University of Michigan Press

TO MY WIFE
Marjorie Campbell Grattan

MY THREE DAUGHTERS
Rosalind, Jacqueline, Jennifer

AND

MY SON
John

Contents

MAPS

AUSTRALIA

CHAPTER I

Commonwealth and Common Welfare

The history of federated Australia up to World War I was essentially a story of an effort to continue general economic development along lines already laid down: the emphasis on the land industries, industrial enterprise secondary, urbanization still very vigorous, the task largely left to the states and private enterprise, while the several governments endeavored to define a social policy which would guarantee the common welfare. Until 1910 decisive direction was in the hands of political Liberals, with political Labor a supporting and pressuring associate, while after about 1910 Labor, now politically mature, tried to overstep the limits of state action laid down by the Liberals and proceed toward its version of socialism. While economic progress and social reform obviously played large roles, the dominant state of mind among both Liberals and Laborites was nationalistic. World War I violently interrupted this effort to build a national commonwealth and provide for true common welfare.

Commonwealth politics started off with a monumental "blunder" by Queen Victoria's governor-general, the Earl of Hopetoun. Hopetoun had had earlier experience of Australia as governor of the Colony of Victoria, where he was immensely popular. His first political task in his new office was to "send for" and commission someone to form the first government of the Commonwealth and this had to be done before the people had declared their views in an election. It was assumed that the first election would confirm Hopetoun's choice in office and that he would, therefore, actually launch the Commonwealth on its career. To the inner circle of federalists, the obvious choice was Edmund Barton. On landing at Sydney, where the Commonwealth was to be ceremonially launched on January 1, 1901, Hopetoun had it suggested to him that it would be in line with Australian precedent if the premier of New South Wales, the Mother Colony, were selected as the first prime minister. Hopetoun accepted this and "sent for" William Lyne.

Hopetoun's choice both offended and alarmed the inner circle of the federalists. They were offended because Edmund Barton had been passed by; they were alarmed because they feared for the future of the Commonwealth in Lyne's hands. The inner circle felt strongly that the Commonwealth could be properly launched only by a man who was a protectionist and a stout federalist, possessed of a continental vision, able and willing to give thought to laying sound foundations for the new government. William Lyne possessed, in their eyes, only one of these qualifications: he was a protectionist. Otherwise he was an antifederalist, possessed of a circumscribed provincial outlook, and was thought very unlikely to rise above these handicaps and offer an adequate Commonwealth policy. He would get the adventure off on the wrong foot. The inner circle, therefore, with Alfred Deakin in the lead, launched an elaborate, ramifying intrigue to make it impossible for Lyne to get a representative cabinet. Barton refused to serve. Deakin refused to serve. Deakin persuaded Cameron Kingston to withhold his co-operation and he also persuaded the still influential David Syme to refuse the services of "his" Victorians—notably Sir George Turner—unless Deakin was included, while knowing full well that Deakin could not be persuaded. So Lyne could not form a cabinet of any substance, had to return his commission to the governor-general, and Barton was then sent for. Lyne took his rebuff with dignity, though he all but pointed a finger publicly at Deakin as the agent of his frustration. Yet it cannot be questioned that Deakin employed intrigue in the higher interests of the Commonwealth.

Barton formed a cabinet that held office from January 1, 1901, to September 24, 1903. It was formed on two principles—to assemble in the service of the central government tested political talent of the colonies and take into account the political geography of the federation. The seven ministers allowed by the constitution were, as first appointed and assigned, two from New South Wales, Barton himself as prime minister and minister for External Affairs and William Lyne as minister for Home Affairs; two from Victoria, Alfred Deakin as attorney general and Sir George Turner as treasurer; one from Western Australia, Sir John Forrest as postmaster general; one from South Australia, Charles Cameron Kingston as minister for Trade and Customs; and one from Queensland, Sir J. R. Dickson as minister for Defence. Tasmania was represented by a minister without portfolio, briefly by N. E. Lewis, a former premier, more lengthily by Sir Philip Fysh, who eventually succeeded to the portfolio of postmaster general when Sir John Forrest was reassigned in a cabinet adjustment.

The first Parliament—seventy-five representatives, thirty-six senators —was elected in March 1901 and opened in Melbourne on May 9. Before Queen Victoria's death on January 22, she had agreed that her grandson the Duke of York (later George V) should visit Australia to perform the opening ceremonies. This arrangement was reluctantly confirmed by King Edward VII, only after he had perused a skillful memorandum from Arthur Balfour arguing the case in terms that vaguely foreshadowed his imperial formula of twenty-five years later. The visit became a move in intra-imperial politics. Accompanied by his wife and a large suite, the Duke performed the ceremony and then made a tour of the new Commonwealth, visiting every state. He detected a "strong feeling of loyalty to the Crown and deep attachment to the Mother Country," sentiments which, he was told, had not been universal a few years earlier and which he suggested to Joseph Chamberlain should be assiduously cultivated. (The Duke afterward visited New Zealand, South Africa, and Canada before returning to England.) The new Parliament proved a magnet for political talent; there was a general migration from state to federal politics; and the drainage of political talent out of the states abruptly became a problem. It proved perennial.

The party divisions were far from precise. The followers of Barton, the ministerial majority, were ostensibly united on protection, but not on the other issues. The opposition, gathered behind George Reid, was ostensibly a free trade group, but had disagreements on other questions. Both parties had liberal and conservative wings. Only the Labor party gave any appearance of being monolithic, but Labor, then officially agnostic about the fiscal question, had a free trade and a protectionist wing. The fiscal question loomed so large that it obscured from all except the most foresighted the fact that Labor held, at least potentially, the key position in party politics. It was not, as was widely assumed at this time, simply a minority party whose existence could be ignored while the larger parties shifted office back and forth. That this was true was not made too clear during Barton's prime ministership.

Edmund Barton was fifty-two years old when he became prime minister. Of urban middle-class origin, he was born in Sydney in 1849 and educated at the University of Sydney (B.A. and M.A.), where he distinguished himself in classics under Charles Badham. For a career he turned to the law and obtained his training by "reading," first under a solicitor and then under a barrister. He practiced as a barrister, specializing in commercial law; he "took silk" in 1889. Although Barton was capable of hard work when aroused, he had the reputation of being unsystematic, dilatory, even lazy. A clubman, he was very fond of good living. He first entered politics in 1879 as a supporter of Sir Henry Parkes and free trade, but later became a moderate protectionist and a supporter of Sir George Dibbs. Discontinuously a member of the lower house, he held cabinet office only briefly—under Dibbs—and his most distinguished political position was the speakership (1883–87). He was not a skillful politician, being disdainful of the bickering and personalities inherent in the political process and, like so many Australian lawyer-politicians, appears not really to have understood the game. He was thought a rather ponderous, though lucid, speaker. His one great political passion was federation, a cause he fervently embraced when Parkes raised the issue again in 1889. This was the kind of large question that aroused him to the full use of his powers and to which he could give sustained devotion. It brought him the prime ministership and a knighthood. There was a marmoreal quality about Barton that made him seem something of a public monument rather than an accessible man.

At the opening of the first Parliament the governor-general read a speech outlining a comprehensive legislative program; only a fraction of it was enacted into law while Barton was prime minister, and some of the items have never been legislated. Alfred Deakin was the policymaker of the administration. Barton himself appears to have been less interested in commonweal than Commonwealth, and when a proposal of a social nature proved contentious, it was either laid aside or was allowed to become lost in the mazes of politics. This approach caused the resignation of Charles Cameron Kingston over a failure to support his position on conciliation and arbitration. But the legislative record was good on "machinery" measures, the acts needed for the establishment of the seven ministries provided for in the constitution—both those such as customs and the post office, which were taken over from the states as going concerns, and those which had to be newly established—and the judiciary act establishing the High Court. A first step was taken toward the assumption of responsibility by the Commonwealth for the British colony of Papua in New Guinea, an expression of the "islands policy" developed in the colonial period. A democratic bias was shown in legislation providing that universal suffrage, male and female, be the rule in federal elections and making it clear that while entry into the public service would be by examination, the service would be staffed throughout by promotion from the ranks, and not by a specially recruited, highly educated, administrative elite.

The fiscal issue was compromised. While the debate over Barton's tariff was protracted, it was quite obviously seized upon as an opportunity for defining positions rather than as an occasion for definitive decision. Reid, although now self-committed to a tariff for revenue, rather than to outright free trade, insisted that in no instance should the tariff be covertly used to protect existing industries or to bring into existence new ones. A drift toward protection was perceptible, but decision was postponed, with the feeling that provision had been made to insure adequate revenue. On only one major social issue was decision decisive—the governing of the composition of the Australian population, and that was in effect before the Commonwealth was established. The Parliament acted to insure that there should be continental uniformity. It legislated the White Australia policy in two acts, one defining general policy, the other dealing specifically with the situation on the sugar fields of Queensland. Although there can be no question that xenophobia and race prejudice played a role in the definition of policy, the leaders of Parliament—notably Alfred Deakin—were careful to expound the point that the objective was not to asperse the character of, say, the Chinese or Japanese, but to insure that the population be European, preferably British. To avoid proscribing specified races, the Barton ministry adopted a suggestion of Joseph Chamberlain and provided for a "literacy test" for immigrants with the tacit understanding that it would be so administered as to exclude black, brown, and yellow peoples as permanent settlers. The fear was that these peoples, if numerously represented in Australia, would offer competition with European labor which could not successfully be met and would be unassimilable—in effect, a permanent body of second-class citizens. In this view the White Australia policy was socioeconomic rather than racial, and by and large this approach became the orthodox defense of the policy—hence the frequent allegation that it was unfortunately named. However, the name was vigorously exploited by the xenophobes and the racially prejudiced, and the policy was wide open to distortion both by Australians and foreigners, as soon became unpleasantly apparent. The Australians no more escaped the problems inherent in a legislative determination of the racial and national composition of a people than have the Americans or any other peoples embarked on this necessary, but inherently invidious, enterprise. The special legislation with regard to Queensland was designed to clear the sugar industry of colored—kanaka—labor and bring about a shift to the use of white labor. This was clearly required if White Australia was to apply continentally. But the policy involved a decision on whether or not the Australian tropics could be developed and its industries carried on by white labor, a question even more open at that time than now. The legislators decided that white men could do both jobs, essentially an act of faith in defense of an ardently held ideal. But more or less recognizing that the economic argument in favor of colored labor ran strongly against them, the legislators covered their position by providing that sugar grown by white labor should be "assisted," first by excise remission, later by a bounty, thus in effect making the cost of White Australia a charge upon the taxpayers, as it has ever since been in one way or another. The support for White Australia cut across party lines, with the Labor party especially convinced of the absolute rightness of the policy. Objections were voiced chiefly by laissez-faire Liberals and the planting interests of the sugar country. A larrikin note was struck when voices were insistently raised against Chamberlain's euphemistic subterfuge and in favor of straight-out proscription, regardless of international repercussions.

When Alfred Deakin became prime minister in succession to Barton in September 1903, he was forty-seven years old and at the peak of his powers. He was a strikingly different person from his old friend and political associate. Melbourne born and bred, of middle-class origin, he was educated at a public school and took a law degree at the University of Melbourne. As complex and elusive, but attractive, a personality as ever flourished in Australian politics, his temperamental bent was toward literature. He was sensitive to poetry, emotionally rather than theologically religious, given to brooding, with a strong liking for solitude, and with a spectator's view of the world of action, while by the accidents of life a participant in it. He acted good fellowship—he was "Affable Alfred"—but he evaded intimate political friendships. He was a brilliant, emotive speaker, "silver-tongued," and a fluent writer. These were his prime political assets. He led by persuasive conciliation rather than by prestigious assertion of a point of view. Though trained for the law, he was not a particularly successful lawyer, but rather approached politics through journalism, in which the greatest single influence upon him was David Syme. He had the journalist's gift for improvising rationalizing justifications for his policies, as in a leader or editorial—as Vogel of New Zealand had, for example. He entered Victorian politics in 1879 and held a seat in the lower house continuously for twenty years, rising to ministerial office, but never accepting the premiership, though offered it several times. From 1890 his primary concern was federation. He had in full measure the essential armor of the politician: a high sense of his rightness. A liberal protectionist and a nationalist, he was also an imperialist—an "Australian Briton." Far more sensitive to popular Australian nationalist aspirations than Barton, he shared with Labor a strong belief in social reform through institutional change, but drew a line—well this side of Labor socialism—beyond which he would not go. It was his political tragedy that he failed to establish in the public mind, even in the minds of his natural followers—least of all in the minds of Labor voters—just where the line ran and what justified placing it at that particular point. He suffered many of the disabilities of the literary man manqué in politics; his political life was more that of a character in a novel of his own composition than of a politician in the ordinary understanding of the term. He had the habit of standing back and looking critically at himself and his fellows, as in his secret political correspondence to the London *Morning Post* and in the manuscripts found among his voluminous private papers and published many years after his death. Yet he *was* a politican, capable (in his own words) of "all the tactics, contrivings, plots, and counterplots and personal relations involved." He was the greatest middle-class politician in Australian history.

As prime minister, Deakin inherited the political insecurities latent in Barton's Parliament. These found open expression in the election of December 1903 from which the Deakin following emerged as a minority group. In the House Deakin had twenty-five followers, Labor twenty-five, and the Reid group twenty-four, with one independent member; in the Senate he had but nine followers, Labor fourteen, and Reid thirteen. It was painfully plain that Commonwealth politics was to be a three-party affair, with Labor holding the bargainer's advantage and encouraged by events to suppose that it could, in the not too distant future, gain a majority and office. The only obvious way to stop Labor, considering the drift of opinion in the country, was for the two non-Labor groups to join forces, and this would work only if Labor gained no more ground at the expense of its rivals. In the immediate situation, however, Deakin, in possession of the prime ministership (with a cabinet consisting largely of carry-overs from Barton's administration), could retain office only if he could command the support of Labor. He made the tentative assumption that he could, but was quickly disillusioned. When Parliament met in March 1904, he introduced a conciliation and arbitration bill—a measure which in Barton's time had been the cause of Cameron Kingston's resignation—which excluded the workers in state undertakings. This was a challenge to Labor. It had declared in favor of including state employees, with railway workers particularly in mind. This Deakin resisted as an unwarranted intrusion into the affairs of the states. Labor pressed its point, won the vote on its amendment, and Deakin promptly resigned. But Labor won only because certain of Deakin's followers voted with it, as well as some of Reid's, thus underlining the fluidity of party politics at that moment.

Labor, triumphant, formed its first Commonwealth government. Its prime minister was John C. Watson, born in Chile, educated in the state schools of New Zealand, and resident in Australia since the 1880's. A printer by trade, he entered politics through the trade unions of Sydney.

Quite willing and able to defend Labor's socialism, he was nevertheless a very moderate Laborite, personally gracious in parliamentary manner, and widely liked as a man. His two strongest ministerial associates from the Labor ranks were William Morris Hughes of New South Wales and Andrew Fisher of Queensland. As the parliamentary party had at the moment no experienced lawyer in its ranks, Henry Bournes Higgins, the dissident Victorian Liberal, associate of Deakin, was co-opted to become attorney general. The government had the tolerance but not the guaranteed support of Deakin. It lasted only four months, and it fell when outvoted on the mechanics of granting preference to unionists under the conciliation and arbitration bill which it had reintroduced. The defeat was administered by a mixed group of conservative protectionists and free traders, with Reid in the forefront, feeling he had the sympathy of Deakin.

With Watson's fall another minority government, a coalition of protectionists and free traders led by Reid, came into office. George Reid, Scottish-born in 1845, was the son of a Presbyterian minister. The family arrived in Australia when Reid was seven. Reid was a public servant and lawyer when he turned to politics in New South Wales in 1880, already a convinced free trader. He succeeded Parkes as leader of the free trade group and was premier, with Labor support, 1894–99. This was Reid's most radical phase. An erratic, unpredictable, and somewhat shallow man, he was capable of good legislative work. In New South Wales he passed creative educational legislation, good land legislation, and wrestled manfully to insure sound finance, including equitable taxation. He was not reactionary, although he became progressively more antisocialist (that is, anti-Labor) and went about talking of the danger from the socialist tiger. Enormously stout, with an uncannily walrus-like face, punctuated with an appropriately droopy mustache, he sported a monocle which he handled as a stage prop. He was an excellent speaker, a first-class debater, and one of the few Australian politicans with a reputation for wit, though some stories about him are also told of other politicians in England and America. ("If you were my husband, I'd put poison in your tea." Business with the monocle. "If you were my wife, I'd drink it.") He was fond of good living and women.

Reid's government lasted ten months, from mid-August 1904 to early July 1905, and it survived as long as it did only because the House was not in session for six months of his term of office. His cabinet was a mixture of former members of the Barton-Deakin entourage—Sir George Turner was treasurer, for example—and new faces, mostly free traders. After Reid, the dominant figure was Allan McLean, one of the most ardent of the few Victorian antifederalists, a protectionist, and in Parliament an associate of Deakin. It is alleged that McLean was there to see that the truce arranged between Deakin and Reid with regard to fiscal policy was observed. The avowed opposition to the government was Labor and a group of radical Liberals—Deakin followers, such as William Lyne, Isaac Isaacs, H. B. Higgins, and Littleton Groom. Deakin, however, extended to this government, as he had extended to the Watson government, tolerance but only conditional support. Though Reid managed, in spite of his handicaps, to put through some useful legislation, no act had larger implications than the Conciliation and Arbitration Act of 1904. It emerged from Parliament as a compromise suiting nobody. Accepting the extension of coverage to state government workers, Reid swapped with Labor the exclusion of agricultural and domestic workers for a clause allowing unions to contribute to the support of political activities, and he managed to retain the cumbersome provision about preference for unionists over which the Watson government had resigned. Reid thus took legislative responsibility for a measure which logically supported a rapid growth of politically oriented trade unions—the workers had to be organized in unions to approach the court—and this in turn provided political Labor with indispensable voting strength, though at the cost of a union influence on the party which was never to be satisfactorily controlled or even explicated. The unions also provided from their leadership a strategically important contingent of Labor politicians. It was ironic that Reid, a most vocal anti-Labor man, should have done this, but Australian politics is full of ironies.

Reid did not *settle* the conciliation and arbitration question, and probably consoled himself with the realization that he had not. It turned out to be a hardy perennial, troubling to the minds and emotions of all sides in politics. He guaranteed, however, that the determination of wages, hours, and conditions should be a quasi-judicial and quasi-political as well as an economic and labor-market question; that the government should inject itself into the marketplace in an attempt to control and direct the inevitable "higgling" and, hopefully, head off the use of the strike weapon. As was the case with legislation of similar character in the states, this legislation was a middle-class effort to moderate and control class warfare, welcomed by Liberals, acceptable at this stage to labor. Yet in spite of this accomplishment, Reid's government fell on Deakin's initiative. Even before Deakin moved in Parliament, he gave Reid an oblique glimpse of his intent in a political speech at Ballarat which Reid interpreted, with an assist from *The Age* newspaper, as "notice to quit." Deakin had found, or had had found for him, the way back to office and political stability.

Deakin's road back to office was pioneered by the radical Liberals who had refused support to George Reid. They had held discussion with the parliamentary Labor group in which common policies had been defined and even the possibility of a coalition government discussed. At this time the Labor parliamentarians, under Watson's leadership, were prepared to consider coalition with Liberals, but there was rising objection to this course in the party organization in the states, especially if it involved granting "immunity" from Labor opposition in general elections. Any arrangement between parliamentary Labor and the Liberals was to be for the life of the particular Parliament only; and sentiment was rising against even such limited deals. While the radical Liberals were ready to enter into written agreements with Labor, Deakin himself was a good bit more coy. He personally objected to the tight organization of the Labor party, especially the influence on parliamentary policy of the general organization outside, to the pledge which in his view compromised the representative's independence, and to caucus rule which he felt confirmed the destruction of that independence. His position with regard to Labor was that if he was to be prime minister with its support *he* would lay down policy—it would be *his* policy—and if then Labor was willing to support him and his party, he would be glad of the support. It was possible for Labor to accept this position because in many respects Deakin was moving in the same general direction as Labor. Moreover, in the parliamentary situation of that moment, it was more profitable for Labor to support Deakin than to have George Reid, or some similar figure, in office.

In any event, Deakin upset the Reid government before he had come to any agreement with Labor. An agreement may have been anticipated, but none was actually made until after Deakin was prime minister and had found places in his cabinet for such radical Liberals as Isaacs, Lyne, and Groom. Deakin then submitted to Watson a brief summary of his legislative program, and Labor in caucus returned to him a promise of "general support during this Parliament in the transaction of public business." The promise was that of the Labor parliamentarians not of the party at large, which viewed the move very critically and intended to fight the Liberals at general elections. However, recalling that the Deakin group was a minority in Parliament and therefore only able to retain office because of Labor support, the agreement was open to the interpretation that Deakin and his followers were subject to Labor dictation. This charge was freely made at the time and has been repeated since by historians, particularly those with a bias in favor of Labor and interested in establishing that it was powerful at as early a date as possible. Actually, it appears from the record that Deakin successfully maintained the interpretation he placed upon the arrangement until such time as Labor began to press him to go beyond the line he drew between left liberalism and laboristic socialism. When it became apparent that Deakin was adamant at this point, Labor withdrew its support and Deakin fell. This rather dramatic denouement came when Labor felt that its political strength was rising and Deakin's falling. The judgment was in general correct, but Labor failed to time the moment of action correctly and left the way open for Deakin to play a final card that momentarily took a trick that Labor expected to have.

Essentially, what Deakin aimed to do was to provide a legislated social context for private enterprise capitalism under a federal constitutional structure in which regard was to be shown for state rights—with a clear recognition that the paramountcy of the federal government was inevitable, desirable, and, within limits, to be promoted. Under the protection of these generalizations, a wide variety of tactical moves was possible. Labor, while equally as interested in the legislative definition of a social context as Deakin, wanted to concentrate socio-economic powers in the federal government at the expense of the states and to put limits to private capitalism by systematically nationalizing all enterprises that were, or might become, monopolies—monopoly to be what Parliament said was monopoly. And whereas with regard to the social context, Deakin hoped to keep the emphasis on equality of opportunity, Labor's bias was in favor of an egalitarianism of condition.

Deakin's chosen instrument for promoting economic development was the tariff, supplemented by bounties. His first political problem was how to get Parliament committed to a truly protective tariff. In the political situation in which he immediately found himself, he had to find a way of inducing Labor to embrace protection as the party policy. Up to this point Labor members had been free to be either free traders or protectionists.

Deakin had long regarded protection as a people's policy in that it created jobs, but he was well aware that sweating was possible, even likely, behind tariff barriers if no provision was made for insuring somehow that wages were fair and reasonable. What he now proposed was to tie together tariff and state fixation of wages. The idea was in the air; it had been suggested recently by Sir John Quick, protectionist member of a royal commission on the Tariff. In his presentation of the case, Deakin proposed to use an excise tax on goods manufactured in Australia behind a tariff to control wages, levying the tax or remitting it according to the state of the wage scale in the industry as ascertained by the arbitration court. This he called the New Protection and it was this version of his policy that he sold to the Labor party. However, the High Court declared this use of an excise tax unconstitutional. It was soon perceived, however, that the arbitration court could by itself effectively deal with the wage problem. Accepting this, though yearning for the excise tax approach also, Labor was able to confirm its acceptance of protection, and in time it became more protectionist than were the Liberals, and as such often an ally of the manufacturing interest. The classic wage-fixing case that confirmed Labor's allegiance to protection was the Harvester judgment of 1907, given by the great rationalizer of court regulation of industrial relations in Australia, Mr. Justice Henry Bournes Higgins. In that judgment Higgins laid down the principles of the "basic" wage, the foundation of the wage structure of Australia. In the specific case his calculations resulted in a wage increase of 27 percent. Deakin thus managed at once to commit Labor to protection and to confirm its acceptance of the arbitration court. In 1908 he had his triumph when his people for the first time put a thoroughgoing protective tariff on the statute book. The free traders were finally and decisively routed. At the same time preference for goods from the United Kingdom was instituted, but with care that domestic production was amply protected. The precedent here was the preference granted South Africa in 1906. Preference was the imperialist phase of Deakin's economic policy, as New Protection was the nationalist phase.

The Deakin government also turned to bounties to stimulate development. As to rural industries, it sought to encourage the production of semitropical products: cotton, flax, rice, tobacco, and dried fruits, while it also extended bounties to iron and steel production. The old ironworks at Lithgow, New South Wales, at this time passed under the control of Charles Hoskins, who had lobbied for the bounty. In line with the Deakin approach, provision was made that payment of fair and reasonable wages be a condition for receiving the bounty. Labor, looking forward, saw to it that the act provided that the ironworks could be taken over by the government if it decided to legislate to that effect.

Further to fortify the position of the people, Deakin in 1908 legislated old-age and invalid pensions on a Commonwealth-wide basis, superseding the schemes of the states. A measure strongly favored by Labor, it was also quite acceptable to Deakin as a Liberal. To facilitate such a use of public money the Deakinites invented the Trust Account system and established that money voted to such an account could be regarded as "expended" and need not be considered part of "surplus revenue" to be distributed to the states. This encouraged the growth of federal spending. But whereas Labor thought of old-age pensions as somehow "socialistic," to Deakin they were contributions to the general welfare under free enterprise capitalism. Either way, they were a move toward the Welfare State.

By late 1908 the Deakin government had been in office for over three years, an unprecedented term. The Labor members and the party followers outside Parliament, who had never been very favorably disposed to keeping the Liberals in office, found the favors increasingly in the nature of fringe benefits rather than centrally important installments of their program. They felt, moreover, that Deakin was just about played out. This made them restless to take office and get on with *their* job. Watson, the most convinced exponent of Labor-Liberal collaboration, had retired from the party leadership in 1907. His successor, Scottish-born Andrew Fisher of Queensland, by repute a solid, slow-thinking, blunt, and honest man, was a coal miner by trade. Deputy leader was, fatefully, W. M. Hughes. Fisher had arrived in Australia in 1885 at the age of twenty-three. Self-educated, he had approached politics through the trade unions, had entered the Queensland lower house in 1893 and had transferred to the federal house in 1901. He was a member of Watson's government of 1904. Rather than being a brilliant figure who won leadership by self-assertion, Fisher exemplified a theory of Labor party leadership. The party believed in closely disciplining its parliamentary representatives and thought of the leader as simply *primus inter pares,* not as a headman of the prima donna kind. The leader, when prime minister, could not even select his own cabinet; it was elected by caucus. He was simply an expression of the movement and the party, not a self-directing charismatic figure in his own right. When Labor prime ministers have developed such characteristics, they have caused trouble for themselves with the party. Fisher was the first Labor leader to try to operate according to the Labor theory of leadership. It was his luck to have as his first task to execute a caucus decision to turn Deakin out too soon.

The restless Laborites were not the only ones dissatisfied with Deakin. His prestige with the voting public was declining. In the 1906 election Deakin's committed following had been reduced to seventeen; he was obviously being squeezed between the left of Labor and the right of the avowed antisocialists, with the heft of the pressure coming from the left. In mid-1907 Sir John Forrest, feeling himself to have been a long-suffering man, resigned from the Deakin cabinet, alleging that he could no longer tolerate the association with Labor. He had been strenuously opposed at the polls by Labor and he had strenuously fought back. Forrest took a small following with him from the Deakin ranks, and his "corner" became a kind of fourth party in Parliament, leaning toward

Reid's following but not yet of it. Perceiving the way the wind was blowing, Reid late in 1908 tried to bring Deakin down, but not succeeding he passed his party leadership to his deputy, Joseph Cook. An English-born coal miner who had arrived in Australia in 1885 at the age of twenty-five, Cook had entered politics in New South Wales as a free-trade Labor member in 1891, but left the party in 1894 rather than sign the pledge and joined Reid's party. He was several times a minister. In 1901 he went to the federal Parliament. A vigorous but unimaginative man, he was aggressively combative, glorying in the roughest rough and tumble of parliamentary warfare. He was the first ex-Labor man to make a substantial career on the other side of politics. He defended his shift of position as growth of understanding.

The second Labor ministry held office only seven months and hardly got beyond announcing the party program. Its accession to office was a signal for the opposition, divided three ways into followers of Deakin, Forrest, and Cook, to begin exploration of the possibilities of fusion. Deakin, though the obvious leader of any fusion, did not take the initiative in the discussions. Rather, by a speaking tour, he sought to strengthen the bargaining position of himself and his group. He especially aimed to establish the point that if fusion was to come with Alfred Deakin as leader, it would be to bring into existence a *liberal* anti-Labor party. In effect he proposed to swallow the conservatives, not to be swallowed by them. It was his belief that only a decisively liberal party could successfully win elections and rule Australia against a Labor opposition. Forrest made a bid for leadership, a case of ambition outrunning discretion, but expectedly got nowhere. This threw the decision to move into the hands of Joseph Cook. Knowing Deakin would not approach him, and fully realizing that the status quo was impossible politically—likely to lead all three groups to ruination—Cook decided to approach Deakin. The result was an agreement for the fusion of the Deakin, Forrest, and Cook groups under Deakin's leadership to oppose Labor.

This was an odd—many thought it an utterly outrageous—conglomeration of politicians. It emerged, without a doubt, from as craftily *political* a deal as any in Australia's history, but unavoidable if Commonwealth politics was not to degenerate into chaos. As Deakin wrote, he now found behind him "the whole of my opponents since Federation." But who had swallowed whom? There were more conservatives to be swallowed than Deakin liberals to swallow them. Worse still, only one of the strong-minded radical liberal followers of Deakin was with him in the new combination—Littleton Groom. Before fusion Isaac Isaacs and Henry Bournes Higgins were appointed to the High Court. William Lyne, when fusion took its bow in Parliament, denounced Deakin as

"Judas"—an imputation which Laborite William Morris Hughes iron-ically repudiated as unfair to Judas—and became an independent (only to have his career ended at the polls by Labor). What was created in 1908 was a party in which the internal balance was tipped in favor of conservatism. Deakin's political legacy to the anti-Labor group in politics was not a liberal party but a party in which liberalism and conservatism were perpetually at war, a party which carried the seeds of its own periodical disruption and destruction. Yet it was an inevitable, or in-dispensable, party, and as often as it destroyed itself it was reconstituted under one name or another—sometimes as the Liberal party—for years into the future. It was an authentically Australian political creation, the secret of which had been discovered in the colonial period when men as disparate in views as Robertson and Parkes in New South Wales, or Griffith and McIlwraith in Queensland, or Deakin and Gillies in Victoria, had joined together to secure and hold office. It was as head of this imperfect fusion, this Lib-Con substitute for Lib-Lab, that Alfred Deakin returned to the prime ministership for the third time on June 2, 1909. He held office only ten months.

Deakin's third term as prime minister was a finger-in-the-dike opera-tion. It was more obviously marked by preliminary, often infirm, defini-tions of basic policy—definitions taken up and recast later by Labor—than by enduring legislation. Policy was defined with regard to defense, the Northern Territory, the transcontinental railway that was to integrate Western Australia with the eastern states, and Commonwealth-state financial relations. Essentially, in the few months he was in office, Deakin tried to continue to impose his liberal, nationalistic, continental views on the new party grouping and the country. What he was seeking to frustrate and defeat was Labor's "socialism." Unfortunately for him, the tide of public opinion was running against his moderation. The majority of the voters were becoming ever more convinced that Deakin, especially as leader of fusion, was too moderate for their taste—that Labor repre-sented their sentiments more accurately. From about 1910 to 1915 the Australian voting public appears to have reached a kind of peak of radicalism. How radical it really was is hard to say, but it was certainly in a mood to give Labor its chance to govern. As the official opposi-tion—the voters' alternative to fusion—Labor was the inevitable re-cipient of all protest votes. It was obviously gaining ground, not only in the Commonwealth, but in most of the states as well. The only real question was when Labor would win a decisive victory at the polls.

It was the election of April 1910 that brought Labor to office and power in the Commonwealth. Labor won forty-one seats in the House to Fusion's thirty-one, and of the three Independents, two favored Labor and one Fusion. In the Senate, Labor held twenty-two seats—it won all eighteen contested in the election—and Fusion held fourteen, all hold-overs. Among the Laborites of enduring fame who took office were Andrew Fisher, prime minister and treasurer; William Morris Hughes, attorney general; George Pearce, minister for Defence; Frank Tudor, minister for Trade and Customs; and King O'Malley, minister for Home Affairs. Although these men and their fellows in the cabinet and legis-lature in most instances considered themselves in some sense socialists, there was a good deal of uncertainty about the exact sense in each instance. The Labor party had not yet officially adopted a straight-out socialist objective—it would not do so for another decade—but in 1908 was satisfied to declare its objective as follows: "(a) The cultivation of an Australian sentiment, based upon the maintenance of racial purity, and the development in Australia of an enlightened and self-reliant com-munity. (b) The securing of the full results of their industry to all pro-ducers by the collective ownership of monopolies and the extension of the industrial and economic functions of the State and Municipality." From its platform at this stage the party was strongly nationalistic (with racist overtones) and prepared to accept the burdens of defense as it had long been argued in Australia—by George Higinbotham for ex-ample—that true nationalists should. It was now protectionist with do-mestic safeguards. The arbitration courts were one safeguard, unions—legislatively fostered—were another, social services a valuable assist, and manipulated excise taxes were yearned for. Whether it saw the policy clearly or not, the party patently supported the redistribution of the national income in favor of the workers. It was anti *big* capitalist (though not inimical to small capitalists) as shown by its positions on monopolies, which it would nationalize, its land policy—it proposed taxation designed to break up large estates—the proposed entry of the government into banking and insurance, and its dubiety about overseas borrowing and nonresident bondholders. It favored direct over indirect taxes because it believed the latter were disadvantageous to the poor. It still clung to the populist democracy that had ruled its attitudes during constitution-making, hence its emphasis on initiative and referendum. It leaned to-ward a unitary, as contrasted with a federal, Commonwealth—its pro-posals for constitutional amendments illustrated this. It favored the supremacy of Parliament; it was critical or uncomprehending of judicial review. Many of its positions it shared in general, though not in the details of application, with the Deakin liberals, especially the more radical. However, it was by no means always the case that the exponents of Labor policies and proposals—even the leaders—always saw the full implications of the positions. Where Labor clearly diverged from Deakin liberalism was in favoring a unitary Commonwealth and in its anti-capitalism.

The Commonwealth Labor platform both expressed the ideas of the party at large—it was not the creation of the parliamentary politicians alone—and concealed the differences of opinion in the labor movement, particularly in the trade unions. As the party waxed in political strength, so the unions multiplied in numbers and membership. Indeed, the political strength of the party was, in some degree not easy to determine, derived from the increase in union membership. In 1906 there were 300 unions with about 150,000 members, a considerable increase since the turn of the century; in 1914 there were 712 unions with 523,000 members. The trade unions harbored the radicals and received the most direct impact of those radicals in the labor movement who were outside the unions and the party. Many of the trade unionists were not as devoted to arbitration as the politicians were becoming, and some politicians, while favorable to arbitration, were still prepared to defend strikes in certain circumstances. In Australia as in New Zealand the courts were one of the rocks on which labor tended to split into arbitrationist moderates and direct action radicals. There were important, bitter strikes on the Victorian railways in 1903, in the metal mines of Broken Hill in 1908–9, in the coal mines of northern New South Wales in 1909, and on the Brisbane tramways merging into a "general strike" in Brisbane in 1912. Radical, sometimes antipolitical, positions were constantly being propagated among the workers, as by the small Socialist and Socialist Labor (Daniel De Leon's group) parties. From 1902 to 1909 the famous English agitator Tom Mann, then in his socialist phase, was active on the left in Australia, particularly in Victoria. He wielded considerable general influence as well as particular influence on radical trade unions and on men then in their most radical phase but later to be Labor party politicians, such as John Curtin and Frank Anstey, as well as on leftist intellectuals like R. S. Ross (1875–1931), the brilliant agitator and labor journalist. And beginning in 1907 the American I.W.W. infiltrated Australia via Adelaide, advocating the One Big Union idea, "direct action," the "general strike," and a strongly antipolitical approach. On the left the Labor politicians were regarded as functioning as a brake on "the revolution." They were accused of doing nothing to stay the coming of the situation depicted in Jack London's *Iron Heel* (1907), which had a vogue in Australia. When William Morris Hughes wrote his long series of newspaper articles under the general heading of "The Case for Labor"—a selection from which became a famous pamphlet of that title (1910)—he was much concerned to combat the extreme left while presenting the party position as a mixture of liberalism, nationalism, and governmental collectivism, with emphasis on the "inevitability of gradualness" (though that phrase was not yet invented). The existence of the extreme left, however, intensified the insecurity felt by liberals and conservatives about the true or ultimate intentions of political Labor because it was impossible to explicate at all exactly the influence of the far left on the parliamentarians.

The point was that the Labor party was integrally an expression of a labor movement that was anything but monolithic in its thinking. It was rather a congeries of dissident groups, and any search for its point of view could only result in uncovering a miscellany of dissidence. If this was unquestionably true on the left of the movement, it was just as true on the right. On the right, for example, were the Roman Catholics. Because of the traditional social position of the bulk of the Roman Catholics in Australia, and the predominance of the Irish among them, the Catholics had a strong tendency to support protest movements in politics and to support Australian nationalism to fend off imperial influences. A proportion of them—exactly what proportion cannot be exactly ascertained—early identified with the labor movement and, when it appeared, the Labor party. Pope Leo XIII's *Rerum Novarum* (1891) greatly encouraged this and so did the sympathetic view of the labor movement and party taken by the Catholic bishops, notably, as pioneer of the attitude, Cardinal Moran, archbishop of Sydney.

There were, however, several issues dividing the Catholics from Labor. In the early years, the articulate Catholic politicians favored protection as against free trade when Labor did not, they were far keener about federation (as a nationalistic move) than the Labor politicians, they were at odds with Labor over the question of the state schools, and they were suspicious of Labor's "socialism." The latter question was actively debated in 1905 and Catholic fears were quieted by "glosses" suggested by Labor spokesmen which in effect differentiated Australian Labor socialism from continental European socialism of a far more strongly Marxist flavor. The Catholics accepted the allegation that Australian Labor was trying to humanize the social order rather than to introduce continental-style socialism. For this reason the Catholic voters were not much influenced by George Reid's campaign against the Socialist Tiger. By the election of 1910, when federal Labor triumphed, it was widely believed that Labor's success was to be attributed in large part to the vote of the "Catholic bloc." Yet it could not be alleged that Labor was a Catholic party, and it stood to reason that the Catholics must be a conservative influence. The existence of a sizable Catholic contingent among the Labor party's supporters was additional proof that the Labor movement was a congeries of dissidents. But the majority of Labor's representatives in Parliament up to World War I were actively or nominally Protestants or agnostics.

The Fisher Labor government of 1910–13 completed the Deakin liberal program (with some recasting of details in application) and made a start on its own more radical program. It was one of the two most successful administrations of the pre-World War I period—equaling Deakin's of 1905–8—and was probably the best Labor performance in peacetime ever. Nevertheless, it was marked, and, in Labor's eyes, marred by a failure to amend the constitution so as to remove limitations on the federal power that frustrated Labor's socio-economic ambitions.

Labor made two tries at amending the constitution, the first in 1911, the second in 1913. On both occasions the objectives were to transfer to the Commonwealth the power (a) over *all* trade and commerce (as against interstate trade and commerce only), (b) over *all* commercial and financial corporations, including those formed in the states and abroad, (c) over "wages and conditions of labor and employment in any trade, industry, or calling" plus the specific extension of the federal arbitration power to the state railways, and (d) over "combinations and monopolies" with the provision for their nationalization. On the first occasion the voters were confronted with a single "proposed law" in the referendum, this requiring acceptance or rejection en bloc, while in the second they could pick and choose among six proposed laws, but either way they rejected all the proposed extensions of federal powers, though less decisively on the second than on the first occasion. On the one hand the Labor proposals were centralizing—forecasting a definitely unitary system—while on the other they were designed to open the way to Labor socialism, particularly through the nationalization of industries. Both tendencies were strongly resisted by Alfred Deakin in 1911, his last important political act, and his success deeply gratified him. Here, he said, was the final dividing point between his liberalism and Labor socialism; here he found the opportunity to make it clear that he was a liberal capitalist, not a conservative socialist.

The double rejection of Labor's proposals was not the final occasion for public decision on the questions at issue, least of all taken separately and outside the particular interpretative context in which they were placed in 1911 and 1913. Almost every matter dealt with was to come up again later in one connection or another, for the problems arising out of the distribution of powers between the Commonwealth and the states were both pervasive and enduring. The limitations on federal power were to prove seriously handicapping to efficient government of an increasingly complex and increasingly integrated economy. It was a genuine misfortune that, as was shown so clearly in 1911 and 1913, it was almost impossible to consider constitutional changes on these and related points calmly, because in the Australian political context they were inevitably immediately entangled with allegations, true and false, about the socio-economic intentions of the two great political groups, Labor and anti-Labor. Often, as a result, problems requiring to be dealt with entirely escaped rational handling. Because Labor mixed the monopoly question—and the Australian economy unquestionably had and continued to have a tendency to monopoly—with one particular way of dealing with monopolies, namely nationalization, monopoly was not faithfully dealt with at all, and Australia ended up worse off in this respect than the United States, which at least began to tackle this great problem in 1890. That Australia was not much worse off than the United Kingdom with regard to this matter was hardly much compensation.

Since the Fisher government failed to modify the constitution to facilitate progress toward Labor socialism—it was blocked, interestingly and significantly enough, by the same voting constituency that put it in office—the question arose as to what installments of socialism it was able to put on the law books. Looking at the record, a sympathetic commentator has selected three items: the Commonwealth Bank, the transfer of the note issue—the issuing of paper money—to the federal government as a monopoly, and a land tax.

A good deal of antibank sentiment found expression in Australia at the time of the bank crashes of 1893 and during the subsequent depression. It was early suggested in colonial labor circles that "national"—that is, colonial government—banks be established to circumvent the private banks. The most elaborate and carefully considered scheme for a government bank was worked out by King O'Malley (c. 1858–1953), a Canadian who after extensive and highly miscellaneous experience in the United States arrived in Australia in the late 1880's and brought his banking ideas with him to the federal Parliament in 1901. He promoted the idea of a government bank within the Labor party and by 1908 was able to outline his ideas in detail and commit the party to the general idea. What O'Malley had in mind was a government-capitalized bank which would engage in trading and savings bank business, handle government (federal, state, local) banking business, manage the public debt, hold a monopoly of the issue of paper money, and serve as a central bank. He proposed to associate the federal and state governments in ownership, but the management was to be nonpolitical. O'Malley's bank was to be competitive with the private banks, and the state savings banks too, but whether it would by intent drive all the private banks out of business, as some Laborites hoped, was an open question. When Labor came to power in 1910, O'Malley became a cabinet member, but he found his associates unenthusiastic about his bank. He therefore organized a secret cabal, called the "torpedo squad," to push the cause in caucus. He eventually won out, but the bank that was finally established by legislation in 1911 and opened for business in 1913 was a much more modest affair than O'Malley had in mind. It was, in effect, a trading and savings bank, capitalized by the federal government, which was to do a lot of business with governments and be competitive with private banks. Its management, though appointed by the government, was independent of the government—it turned out stubbornly independent. It was not concerned with debt management or the note issue; it was not a central bank—and did not begin to become one for over a decade after establishment.

While the federal government took over the note issue, a separate body, unconnected with the bank, was established to deal with the matter and the associated gold reserve. O'Malley himself was well aware that the bank actually established fell far short of what he had in mind. It was socialist only in the sense that a government-capitalized bank was socialist, especially one established by a Labor party. As a matter of fact, the Commonwealth Bank was in reality no more socialist than the United States Federal Reserve System (established 1913). In its first phase, it was a rather unaggressive example of state capitalism. However, by its existence it provided a focus for an intense and enduring political controversy over banking and the role of government in banking which never died down for long and has not died out to the present day.

The Labor party's land tax was an even more ambiguous example of socialism. Taxation of land values was a policy of the Australian liberals long before Labor took it up. It was pioneered by Sir Graham Berry in Victoria in 1877; it became mixed up with Henry George's ideas at a later stage. As the Labor party saw it, a land tax was to serve two purposes: to produce revenue and, by its impact, to encourage the breaking up of large privately owned estates. In the latter respect it was a weapon in the long war over the land that has marked Australian history; specifically it was a contribution to a battle over the land going on in the states at the time. Labor at this stage believed fervently in the richness of the Australian land resources; William Morris Hughes declared that acre for acre Australia's land was as rich as any in the world.

The discussion of the tax in the federal Parliament revealed that Labor took a rather physiocratic view of the land as the ultimate source of wealth, but that it differed from a physiocrat like W. C. Went-worth in aiming to disperse the land to as many small holders as pos-sible—a policy called in Australia the promotion of "closer settlement." It believed that "closer settlement" was the only way of establishing a soundly founded increase in the population of the country: its vision was of a rural Australia, in spite of the already characteristic urbaniza-tion and its own political dependence on an urban vote. Labor's land tax was therefore an attack on big-capitalist landholders in the interest of potential small-capitalist landholders, a paradoxical undertaking for socialists of any definition. But its tax was not criticized and resisted because of its rationale, its objective, or because it was an inefficient means to the end sought, but because it assaulted a vested interest and was an invasion of the province of the states in whose hands, since the rejection of Parkes's suggestion to the contrary, the land and the respon-sibility for its development remained.

Labor was more obviously left liberal than socialistic when it ex-tended the federal social services by legislating for maternity allow-ances (a move which inspired the radical Liberal, Littleton Groom, to raise for the first time the question of a comprehensive national in-surance scheme) and liberalized the old-age pensions. Labor's favor for noncontributory services, as against the insurance approach, was made plain. It also extended the coverage of federal arbitration to federal government, domestic and agricultural workers, and made some tech-nical adjustments suggested by H. B. Higgins to facilitate the court's operations. It put through what was in essence Deakin's scheme for making per capita payments (25 shillings per head) to the states as a substitute for the system under the Braddon Blot, with special addi-tional grants to Western Australia and Tasmania, laying more firmly the foundations of the Commonwealth's financial supremacy in the federation on which in time a towering structure was to be built. It was carrying forward established national undertakings to which the Com-monwealth was committed when it accepted the transfer of responsibility for governing and developing Northern Territory from South Australia and provided for the government of the federal capital territory carved out of New South Wales, which the third Deakin government had finally settled upon after a great deal of shilly-shallying over the exact site.

In 1912 Walter Burley Griffin of Chicago, U.S.A. (a pupil of Frank Lloyd Wright), won an international competition for the design of the proposed capital city—Eliel Saarinen, then of Finland, was runner-up—and in 1913 the proposed city was officially named Canberra (pro-nounced Canbră) after the alternatives of Myola and Shakespeare had, luckily, been rejected. The key figure in these moves was King O'Malley as minister of Home Affairs; the responsibility finally rested with Fisher's Labor cabinet. Thus was implemented George Reid's constitutional amendment designed to save Sydney's pride from the dreadful affront of having Melbourne permanently the national capital city; but there remained the tremendous tasks of not only building the city but also of making it a popularly acknowledged symbol of Australian nationality. While the former proved difficult and long drawn out, the latter, since it involved the mastery of subtle imponderables, was even more difficult and protracted. In men's emotions, sectional loyalties continued to outweigh national loyalties, and Canberra long served as a butt for frustration and exasperation rather than as an expression of national pride.

The election of 1913 resulted in a stalemate. Alfred Deakin retired from politics on the eve of the election, sadly because of failing memory and physical disabilities, and Joseph Cook, as though in tribute, formally renamed the Fusion group the Liberal party. The Laborites in the campaign reached the high point in the devotion to populist democracy by advocating initiative and referendum for *all* legislation; and it proposed as a forward step in socialization a Commonwealth coastal and overseas shipping line. But the campaign was really a fight over Labor's constitutional amendments, and it was probably the Liberal party's success in opposing these that accounted for its narrow victory in the struggle for seats in the House. It won thirty-eight seats to Labor's thirty-seven. In the Senate, however, Labor held twenty-nine seats and the Liberals but seven. Labor's losses of seats in the House were largely in rural electorates, a fair warning that appeasement of the rural voters must be part of its stock-in-trade. If Cook and the Liberals had won, they could not easily govern. Cook therefore set about to "manufacture" a "double dissolution"—of House and Senate complete and simultaneous —as provided in the constitution. This he did by provoking the Labor-dominated Senate twice to reject his proposals for prohibiting the practice of "preference for unionists" on government undertakings. In the elections that ensued on September 5, 1914, Cook suffered a sharp defeat. Labor won forty-two seats in the House and Cook thirty-two, while in the Senate Labor won thirty-one seats to the Liberals' five. On the hustings Labor had talked to the farmers about cooperative marketing and the extension of government credit to them. Cook suggested carrying out in a liberal fashion through federal-state collaboration many of the things Labor wanted to do in its fashion after constitutional amendment. However, the election was overshadowed by the outbreak of World War I, the consequences of which to Australia nobody could, at that time, take the measure.

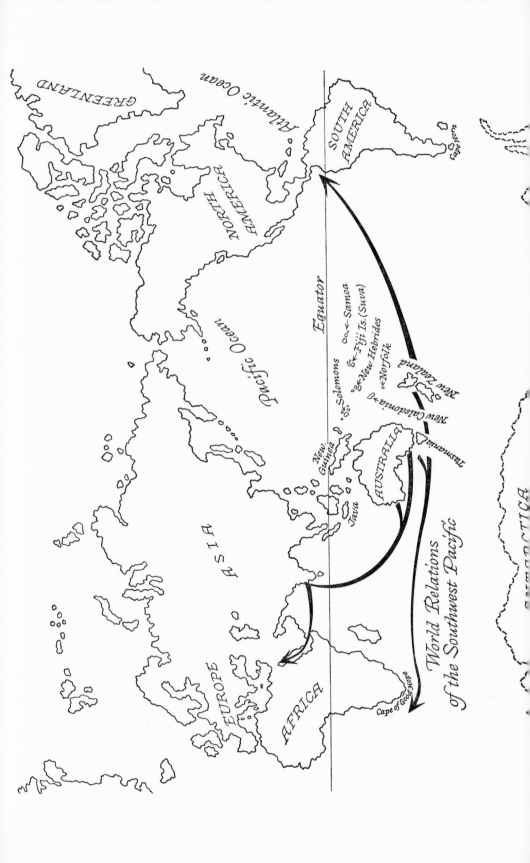

GREENLAND

Atlantic Ocean

NORTH AMERICA

SOUTH AMERICA

Cape Horn

Equator

Pacific Ocean

←← Samoa
Solomons ←Fiji Is. (Suva)
←New Hebrides
←Norfolk
New Caledonia
New Zealand

New Guinea
Java

AUSTRALIA

Tasmania

ASIA

EUROPE

AFRICA

ANTARCTICA

Cape of Good Hope

World Relations of the Southwest Pacific

Writing anonymously in the London *Morning Post* in 1903 Alfred Deakin remarked that "we are still a loosely allied set of communities divided from each other by vast distances and preoccupied by parochial aims." When war broke out in 1914 this was still true in spite of the accumulation of national legislation and the implementation of national policies by the federal government. Unity was implicit rather than actual, better expressed than when Australia was a congeries of colonies, but very far from perfect. What Deakin called "a unity arising out of circumstances so general in their scope and so potent in their effects that they force into the same paths even the apparently uncontrollable waywardness of the purely local policies of the several states" certainly existed, as it had existed indeed in colonial times, but Queensland was different from Victoria, New South Wales from both, Tasmania was *sui generis,* not only because it was an island, and South Australia was hardly to be confused with Western Australia.

There was a slackness in the economies of all the states except Western Australia until around 1905. Western Australia, shaken out of her protracted lethargy by gold discoveries in the 1880's and 1890's, continued to progress by encouraging the expansion of a wheat-wool complex in the economic heartland of the state, the southwestern portion. It supported continuing expansion by a liberal land policy, state financial assistance to farmers, and close attention to the problem of water supply in country deficient in surface and underground resources. A scheme originally designed to supply water to the gold city of Kalgoorlie by piping and pumping it from a source near the Indian Ocean coast was subsequently tapped for the benefit of farmers settled near the pipe line; and other water supplies were obtained by wisely conserving the limited rainfall.

Around 1905 economic conditions in the eastern states changed for the better, partly because of the return of good rains, partly because of rising prices for exports. From around 1905 to 1914 the states generally were encouragingly prosperous but not booming.

As early as they individually could after the depression of the 1890's, the states resumed borrowing for development, this indicating a faith in the future, but to 1914 borrowing was not on such a scale as in the 1880's. Whereas in the earlier period the colonies had borrowed almost exclusively in London, in this period the practice of floating government loans locally was instituted in the more advanced states. At the same time there was some withdrawal of British investment on private account and a substitution of locally owned capital. Public expenditure continued to be heaviest on railways, but quite large sums were invested in some states on harbor works (for example, South Australia), water supply and irrigation schemes, and the purchase of land to be broken up into small parcels for closer settlement. New South Wales continued to have the largest gross debt, but Western Australia came to carry the largest per capita debt of all the states, followed by Queensland and South Australia, Tasmania and New South Wales, with Victoria—her lesson learned?—least burdened. When World War I broke out, the states were spending loan money at a rate of about £4 per head per annum.

From 1900 to 1915 the total population of the Commonwealth increased by 1,200,000 to 4,970,000. Over-all increase was at a rate of about 2 percent per annum, a good figure. In most states natural increase was running about 15 per 1000 per year. Around 1911 about eighty out of every hundred Australians were native born. From 1901 to 1905, when the country was depressed, there was a net loss through emigration of 7000 persons, but at the same time there was a redistribution of people within the Commonwealth. New South Wales and Western Australia increased their populations, but Western Australia alone made a really brave showing. "T'othersiders"—people from the eastern states —at first concentrated on the gold fields around Kalgoorlie but soon scattered through the developing wheat country, had a considerable political influence, as was noted in discussing the adoption of the constitution and as continued to be the case for some years. The "internal migrants" came mostly from Victoria, which lost population most heavily, but Tasmania was already in the business of exporting its young people to the mainland in search of "a living" and careers.

When the eastern state economies revived, the question of increasing the population by induced and assisted immigration arose once more. Alfred Deakin and the other leaders on his side of politics were pro-immigration—believing that development was definitely a function of numbers and having defense considerations in mind also—so too were Labor leaders like William Morris Hughes, but other labor spokesmen were skeptical, fearing the effects on the labor market, especially that in the cities. Although the Commonwealth governed over-all immigration policy, stimulation, subsidization, and direction of immigration was an affair of the states. In consonance with the focus of their developmental policies, the states placed the emphasis upon the introduction of laborers for their public works, farm laborers, and farmers with small capital. Along with self-moving immigrants, all states financed assisted immigrants. Starting cautiously in 1906, the states introduced about 40,000 assisted migrants in the next five years, but, optimism mounting, 150,000 persons were assisted 1911–15. All states participated in the activity, but New South Wales, naturally enough, absorbed most people, with

Victoria close behind, followed at a distance by Queensland, Western Australia, and South Australia, with Tasmania taking less than 500 and not even attempting to compensate for her losses to the mainland. But if the policy was to direct the assisted newcomers into rural occupations and onto the land, urbanization was not successfully controlled and the capital cities continued to grow.

By natural increase, "internal" migration, unassisted and assisted immigration, New South Wales increased its population by over half a million to 1,893,000, Victoria recovered her depression losses and added close to a quarter million to her population for a total of 1,425,000, Queensland added 192,000 for a new total of 686,000, Western Australia's population boomed up by 136,000 to 316,000, while South Australia added only 89,000 for a total of 446,000, and Tasmania only 25,000 for a total of 198,000. Northern Territory had a practically stationary population.

Wool remained Australia's prime product and continued to be the principal money-earning export. Production rose from 408,000,000 pounds in 1902 to 735,000,000 pounds in the 1914–15 season, but these figures conceal a good deal of irregularity of production, mostly caused by drought. 1914 was a dry year. In 1902 there were 52,675,000 sheep in Australia; by 1914 the total had risen to 82,491,000, but this figure was still well below the peak reached in 1891. The great drought of the turn of the century, by showing up the weaknesses of the stations developed in the very low rainfall country during good seasons, and underscoring the recalcitrant problems of such country, demonstrated that most of the sheep of Australia were going to be run in future in the heartland of the southeast of the continent on the wheat-sheep country and the drier lands contiguous to and just beyond it. The very low rainfall country would, of course, continue to be occupied—optimism about it would probably rise in good seasons; the area of stations in it would be romantically large because it would be a matter of how many acres it would take to support a sheep; the flocks spread over the huge acreages would be large; but total number of sheep run would all told be but a fraction of the grand total of the state or nation, though the number would be far higher in good years than in years of drought.

New South Wales maintained its position as the premier sheep and wool state—it had about 44 percent of all sheep in 1914—but Queensland was making rapid progress, increasing its numbers from 7,214,000 in 1902 to 23,130,000 in 1914. Western Australia showed the profit of its wool-wheat complex by almost doubling its sheep in the period. On the other hand, Victoria increased its flocks comparatively little, and in South Australia and Tasmania the numbers actually declined. At this stage, while flocks of 500 sheep were now most numerous, most of the sheep were accounted for by the flocks in the 2000 to 5000 range. Very large flocks—that is, 20,000 to 100,000 and beyond—were now mostly found in western and central Queensland. Most of the sheep were held on stations of 1000 acres and up. The average weight of the fleece continued to rise. The old pests of the sheep country were still not under control, and a new one was added in this period, the sheep blow-fly, which came in from either South Africa or India in the late nineteenth century and spread widely over the inland pastures. The price of wool, while moving very irregularly upward, increased by about 50 per cent between 1900 and 1914. Aside from the impact of the spread of the wool-wheat complex (not only in Western Australia), the most important change in the pastoral industry was brought about by the increasing demand for mutton and lamb for the frozen meat trade. At the outbreak of war, exports were running around 20,000 tons annually, with the United Kingdom overwhelmingly the most important market. This development, which required for success the breeding of dual purpose animals, was most important to pastoralists whose stations were in well-watered country where fattening paddocks could readily be developed and access to a port by railway was easy. A consequence of breeding dual purpose animals was a rise in the production of cross-bred wool and a decline in the proportion—it still remained very high—of fine merino. However, the Australian industry was less important, both relatively and absolutely, than New Zealand's.

The cattle industry, still decidedly subordinate in the pastoral economy to sheep and wool, was changing its character under the impact of demand for beef for freezing and export. The industry had suffered severely from the ravages of the cattle tick and then from the great drought. In Northern Territory and northern Western Australia times were hard indeed. Queensland was ovewhelmingly predominant in the production of beef for export. Around 1906 the prospect of increasing sales of animals to the freezing works stimulated interest in breeding better stock. The favored animal in the northern cattle country was the Shorthorn. In the southern states, where animals were slaughtered chiefly for local consumption, other breeds, for example the Aberdeen Angus, were favored as better suited to their specialized environments—for example, in the mountainous country. The range animals of northern and north-western Queensland were over-landed to the railways and carried to conditioning paddocks in the southeast of the state, butchered in abattoirs at coastal points, frozen, and exported to Britain. From 40,000 tons of frozen beef exported in 1900–1901, the total rose to 130,000 tons in the 1914–15 season. However, Australia long continued to be but a minor contributor to the world's beef supply.

Dairy cows increased in numbers during this period, rising from 1,250,000 in 1900–1904 to 2,000,000 in 1910–14. The production of milk, butter, and cheese for local sale and consumption was, of course, an ancient Australian industry, though because of the scarcity of adaptable country a difficult one to establish, and not until 1897 did exports of dairy products exceed imports. (New Zealand was the principal supplier.) The Commonwealth early attempted to assist by laying a duty on imported cheese. The establishment of dairying as an export industry was associated with experimentation in the making of artificial pastures, the breeding of animals adapted to Australian conditions, notably the Milking Shorthorns, the Illawara (N.S.W.) Milking Shorthorns—the Illawara (south coast) district was the first important center of dairying in Australia—and Jerseys, and especially technological innovations. The dairy industry succeeded almost in proportion as it was mechanized.

It is significant that the expansion into the export trade in the early Commonwealth years came after the introduction of refrigeration in the 1870's, cream separators, pasteurization, and cooperative dairies in the 1880's, and the Babcock test in the 1890's. The building of railways connecting the dairying districts with the capital cities and the principal ports was a notable assist. At this stage the outstanding problem of the industry was a slackness about sanitation on the farms and in the factories, resulting in the production of a high percentage of low quality butter. Standards began to be imposed by law during World War I. In the prewar period New South Wales ran the most dairy cows, with the principal dairying districts the Illawara and the Northern rivers, Victoria was second with Gippsland as its principal district, and Queensland was a rising third with the industry concentrated in the southeast of the state. The drought of 1914 and the war had depressive effects on the dairy industry.

Expansion of the acreage devoted to wheat was most marked in New South Wales and Western Australia. Whereas Victoria and South Australia increased their acreages by 500,000 acres each, the New South Wales increase was 1,800,000 acres and Western Australia's 1,280,000 acres. Over the Commonwealth as a whole the increase was 4,171,000 acres; New South Wales and Western Australia therefore accounted for about three-fourths of it. This was plowing virgin soils. At the same time the average production per acre was rising, with sharp variations caused by drought, largely attributable to better culture methods, such as more intelligent use of fallowing (which was now better understood), the increased use of fertilizers, and the adoption of strains of wheat better adapted to Australian conditions. Increases in yields per acre were most marked in Victoria and South Australia, but this was in fact a period of rising yields generally; it had begun around 1895. The great Australian wheat-breeder, William Farrer (1845–1906), had his impact at this time. English born and educated, Farrer arrived in New South Wales in 1870 and became a government surveyor. He retired in 1886 on an inherited annuity to a station called Lambrigg, near Tharwa, New South Wales, on the banks of the Murrumbidgee River. Here he set about his wheat experiments, cross-breeding on an extensive scale, and corresponding with wheat experts the world around. The great enemy of Australian wheats was rust; to avoid rust, an early maturing breed was needed; but there was also need for wheats of better milling qualities. Farrer's particular interest was in rust-resistant varieties, but he also experimented in other directions; his contributions were various; he was a great pioneer; but it is now accepted that ultimate success eluded him. However, he set the direction of Australian wheat research. He was anxious to make a contribution to the industry, and in 1902 he released a variety called Federation which was not wholly rust-resistant but a good deal more so than any then known. Federation, soon established as the variety most widely grown, continued dominant for a quarter century. In 1910–14 Australia was producing about 90,000,000 bushels of wheat annually, of which perhaps 60 per cent was exported, 8 per cent of the wheat entering world trade.

The growth of factory industry, what the Australians customarily call secondary industry, was chiefly in New South Wales and Victoria, the established locales. The industrial structures of the two centers continued closely comparable. In Victoria in 1901 there were 3249 factories with 66,529 employees, while by 1915 there were 5413 factories with 113,-834 employees; whereas in New South Wales in 1901 there were 3367 factories with 66,135 employees and in 1915 5269 factories and 116,611 employees. However, Victoria with the smaller total population had a higher proportion of its workers in factory industry.

It is difficult to get a clear understanding of these industrial structures, but they were founded in the preliminary processing of raw materials, the preparation of food and drinks, and the production of commodities for personal and domestic use. In 1907 when Alfred Deakin was busy with the New Protection, he called attention to the continued predominance of small units. It appears that around three-fifths of all employees worked in factories having ten hands or less, while a lesser proportion worked in factories having one hundred hands or more. In both states the factories fell most numerously into the category "clothing, textile, etc.," but Victoria had half as many again of these as did New South Wales—including clothing, hat and cap, boot and shoe, and hosiery factories and woolen mills. The emphasis was on light industry, but most decidedly so in Victoria. This is borne out by the fact that whereas in Victoria about thirty out of every one hundred workers were females, in New South Wales the proportion was twenty out of a hundred; Victoria also had more children under sixteen working in factories, and it had twice as many outworkers. Victoria had a clear predominance in the production of agricultural implements, but New South Wales had a more impressive development of metal-working industries in general. Victoria had the larger "export" trade—that is, sales of factory-made goods beyond its borders within the Commonwealth, but New South Wales was the chosen seat of the great portent of things to come. The Broken Hill Pty. Ltd. had in 1911 decided to move out of metal mining and refining into steel production. This would give New South Wales clear predominance in the heavy industry indispensable to the creation of a full-blown industrial structure.

From the record it is apparent that the states had been, speaking generally, developing along roughly parallel lines. At the outbreak of war, New South Wales had the most expansive economy, followed in order by Victoria, Queensland, Western Australia, South Australia, and Tasmania. The pace-setters were New South Wales and Victoria; the laggard state was Tasmania.

Politically, they were also running parallel, though no more exactly than in development. The principal political task in all was the assimilation of the Labor party to the political world. The effects were different in every state.

In New South Wales, where Labor first gained political strength, the party became the official opposition in 1904 after thirteen years in Parliament, but it did not gain office for another six years. In 1910 J. S. T. McGowen (1855–1822) took office as premier, but in 1913 he resigned in favor of W. A. Holman (1871–1934), the driving force and intellectual leader of his cabinet. McGowen, a skilled tradesman (boilermaker) and long-time trade unionist, a devoted Anglican, was an honest but undistinguished man, but Holman, a self-educated intellectual with legal training, a brilliant orator, was perhaps the most distinguished state Labor leader in Australian history. He was born in England and had arrived in Australia in 1888 with his parents, who came out to fulfill a theatrical engagement. Holman thought of himself as a socialist; his government made ventures into state-owned and managed industry; but by an odd fatality when the chance to undertake a basic industry presented itself in 1911 it was muffed, and the government assisted the Broken Hill Pty. Ltd. to establish itself in steel at Newcastle. Thus, a government "socialist" in principle and action opened the way to an outstandingly important private capitalist enterprise. This circumstance clearly illustrated that Australian Labor's socialism in its classic expression was a socialism of a preindustrial sort—a socialism related to an agrarian society and not clearly thought out in relation to a society which would be industrialized. The Holman administration also showed how intense state loyalties still were within the labor movement, for it was this Labor government that played an important role in defeating federal Labor's referenda of 1911 and 1913, designed to augment federal powers at the expense of the states. Nevertheless, Holman's administration was, with all its vagaries, an excellent example of what Labor could do as a government—and was so viewed by the voters.

On the other side of politics, the most significant government was that of Sir J. H. Carruthers (1857–1932), born in New South Wales, educated in arts and law at Sydney University, in office 1904–7. Carruthers identified himself with the promotion of "closer settlement" by breaking up large estates into smaller units, either after government purchase or by the voluntary action of the owners, and by moving the state into irrigation—specifically by obtaining authorization to build the Burrinjuck Dam on the Murrumbidgee River. Up to that time irrigation agriculture in New South Wales had been a private undertaking only, notably by Sir Samuel McCaughey on his estate at Yanco. (Contemporaneously, the states of New South Wales, Victoria, and South Australia, with Commonwealth collaboration, were studying the utilization of the Murray River waters, a development which reached the point of agreement in 1914 but had its impact later.)

The Victorian Labor politicians had no success in winning office before World War I. The Liberals held their established position. The most important premier was probably W. H. Irvine (1858–1943), an Irish-born teacher and lawyer, educated at Trinity and Melbourne, who was in office 1902–4, after which he went to the Federal House. He eventually became chief justice of Victoria. It was not the duration of Irvine's regime that made it important, but the fact that he, a Liberal of conservative leanings, firmly entrenched state socialism in Victoria by turning state enterprises over to incorporated nonpolitical "authorities." He was no friend of Labor; he fought it bitterly in the Victorian railway strike of 1903, which had such significant repercussions on federal Labor's policy with regard to arbitration. In institutionalizing state socialism, he showed that he, like Deakin, was prepared to move in the same direction as Labor. What differentiated Irvine's approach from Labor's was that

Labor wanted to go forward into the production of commodities, whereas Irvine and those who thought like him provided services helpful—sometimes absolutely indispensable—to private enterprisers engaged in commodity production, the "mixed economy" approach. By the circumstance that so many of Labor's ventures into commodity production were discarded as failures or liquidated and disposed of by their opponents, Australian state socialism became *identified* with the kind of enterprises Irvine was interested in. To reiterate, he was not in any sense a laborite socialist.

In Queensland the situation was different again. Queensland was the most purely pastoral state in the country—its sugar, wheat, and dairying were decidedly secondary, and manufacturing was insignificant. When coupled with Labor's doctrinaire inheritance from William Lane, this made the situation seem unpromising for Labor. Yet by 1903 Labor had so far adapted itself that it entered a coalition government under the Liberal, Sir Arthur Morgan (1856–1916). However, this was but a brief interlude at a moment of political crisis. Not until 1908 did it become the official opposition, and not until 1915 was it able to win office in its own right. But when it did gain office it stayed a long time, as we shall see, and its experiments in "socialism" proved even more various than those of New South Wales and by and large of an even more decidedly fringe character.

The South Australian Liberals and conservatives were only a little less successful than the Victorians in holding onto political power. In 1905–9 a Labor-Liberal government led by the Laborite Tom Price (1852–1909) emphasized land settlement; it was succeeded by a government led by a Liberal, A. H. Peake (1859–1920), who had been Price's treasurer. Peake was shortly succeeded (1910–12) by J. Verran (1856–1932), Price's successor as leader of the Labor party, but Verran's fall brought Peake back to office (1912–15).

The first Labor premier of Western Australia was Henry Daglish (1866–1920), a Victorian t'othersider, in 1904–5, but his advent hardly disturbed the conservatives and liberals, for when he resigned office he also quit the Labor party and entered politics on the other side. Not until John Scaddon (1876–1934), also a t'othersider, achieved office in 1911 —and held it until 1916—was there provoked that great indicator of political change, a fusion of the conservatives and liberals.

In Tasmania the first Labor premier, John Earle (1865–1932), held office for but seven days in 1909. Otherwise, the conservatives and liberals ruled until Earle climbed back to power in 1914.

Thus before the outbreak of World War I Labor had gained office in its own right in four of the six states and the Commonwealth. Victoria and Queensland had yet to be conquered. But in no instance had it won power so easily and securely that it had eroded the political confidence of the conservatives and liberals. Labor's most drastic effect on its opponents was to convince them that they could no longer take the risk of fighting separately; that it was the best political wisdom to combine to fight Labor. Labor's significant accomplishment, aside from that just mentioned, was first to establish itself as the official opposition and then to demonstrate that it was indeed the voters' alternative to the older ruling groupings and was able to form a government. Once that was accomplished, the old and exhilarating days of "auctioneering" were over and the sobering tests of power were at hand. It turned out that Labor's best chances of gaining effective power and office were in the states, though not all of them. The crucial date in the rise of Labor as a political force was 1910, when Labor gained power in New South Wales (and the Commonwealth.) A close study of politics and opinion *circa* 1910 would illuminate much about the prewar Australian mind.

The cultural history of Australia has not yet been studied in enough detail to support confident generalizations about either the apparent continuities, the apparent discontinuities, or the status and orientation of the intelligentsia, academic and lay, with regard to cultural activities in Australia in the successive periods. It is fairly clear, however, that in literature and painting a tradition which was first given clearly discernible shape in the 1880's and 1890's continued dominant up to World War I when it began to weaken.

Essentially, the period from the coming of the Commonwealth to World War I was a continuation of "the 1890's." But as careers begun in the 1890's carried through this period into the postwar era and as many new figures who were to be the characteristic writers and artists of the 1920's and 1930's began their careers before the war, one has a sense of both continuity and change. It should not be overlooked, however, that the cultural workers continued throughout to consider themselves marginal men and to complain about their condition. The centers for writers and artists continued to be Melbourne and Sydney, with reciprocated dubiety characteristic, but a sense of isolation in a hostile world was general. The social focus was still on economic activities—production and development, including the politics of these—and even the reformers were preoccupied with the economic welfare of their constituents but not particularly their cultural or spiritual condition. The material standard of living was a widespread preoccupation. And the conflict between devotion to the cultural development of Australia and to personal participation in the cultural life of the mother country continued in full force. The export of talent continued; and significant Australian careers were often broken by extended residences overseas.

In the novel, the period began with Miles Franklin's (1879–1954) *My Brilliant Career* (1901), the first fruit of a career almost immediately interrupted by a protracted residence in the United States and England, during which she published only occasionally or published under an unpenetrable pseudonym. William Hay (1875–1945) also initiated his career in 1901 and continued it in Australia, but in a self-imposed isolation that was unbroken by "discovery" until after his death. In 1955 what was alleged to be his best novel, *The Escape of the Notorious Sir William Heans* (1918), was revived, and there was a controversy about its merits. Barbara Baynton (1862–1929), who won the approbation of Havelock Ellis (himself briefly a resident in Australia, the fictional record of which is *Kanga Creek* [1922]), contributed a small book of acerb short stories, *Bush Studies* (1902) and a novel, *Human Toll* (1907), but published no more and spent most of her life in England. But the climactic book of this period was Tom Collins' (Joseph Furphy, 1843–1912) *Such is Life* (1903), the work of a lifetime, a novel organized in diary form and carrying a vast deal of ideological freight drawn directly from the 1880's—undoubtedly an Australian classic. It is indicative of the situation that it took many years to find any appreciable number of readers for it, in spite of the fact that it became a talismanic Australian book for several literary generations'. Collins, however, ranks at least on a par with Henry Lawson in the Australian canon and above him for those whose taste embraces ideological concerns. In 1903, also, Mrs. Aeneas Gunn (1870–1961) published her classic children's story *Little Black Princess,* followed in 1908 by *We of the Never Never,* a brilliant invocation of pioneering in the Northern Territory, after which she fell silent. Louis Stone published *Jonah* (1911), a novel of ambition set in the slums of Sydney, an early example of a genre strangely undercultivated in Australia—the "city novel" as contrasted with the "bush novel." And in 1913 Norman Lindsay opened the literary phase of his career. But by far the most important *career* initiated in this period was that of Henry Handel Richardson (Ethel Richardson Robertson, 1870–1946), who published *Maurice Guest* in 1908, a very impressive study of life among the students of music in a German city, and in 1910 *Getting of Wisdom,* an account of life in a girls' school in Melbourne. H. H. Richardson, who lived the greater part of her life in England, brought a current of continental psychological realism into the Australian novel, a unique contribution, the influence of which, however, is impossible to define, and she achieved something rarely accomplished by Australian writers of fiction of any quality: a substantial number of substantively significant novels. She became the outstandingly important novelist of Australian origin to her time, and by personal choice and declaration she wished to be considered an Australian novelist, thus countering by psychological identification her physical expatriation.

Among the poets the same pattern of completion and initiation of careers was to be found. Furnley Maurice (Frank Wilmot, 1881–1942), a bookseller, began his career in 1903; his verse was founded in a complex moral vision of a disillusioned socialist utopian. Simultaneously, Bernard O'Dowd (1866–1953) began to publish. In ideas he was very much in the ethos of Lawson and Tom Collins, a laboristic radical democrat with affinities to Walt Whitman, with whom he had corresponded. However, O'Dowd, a lawyer by profession, wrote verse with a high ideological content, a "poetry of purpose," but his bent was for rhetoric and his weakness was for burdening his poems with a comprehensive assortment of classical references, being especially beset with the notion that the bare Australian bush—ignoring the aboriginal mythology—was a proper habitat for the mythological creatures of the Greeks. This was also characteristic of Hugh McCrae (1876–1958), a whimsical lyricist who began to publish in 1909, and of Norman Lindsay and his admirers, writers otherwise unsympathetic to O'Dowd's outlook. The probable meaning of this essentially "escapist" note in Australian poetry—and painting—has never been fully and intelligently explored, but it appears to be a reaction to the assessed or imagined poverty of the Australian cultural scene, a kind of desperate effort to attach to the richer culture overseas. Implicitly, these men raised the question of on what meat an Australian Caesar of the pen should feed. Allied to O'Dowd by the use of poetry to communicate an ideology, but otherwise very different—even antipathetic—was William Baylebridge (1883–1942), who began publishing privately in 1908. In 1913 C. J. Dennis (1876–1938) began his career as a popular but sociologically significant versifier, of which the classic result was *The Sentimental Bloke* (1915). And early in 1914 Christopher Brennan published the most substantial single volume of his troubled lifetime, *Poems*.

The professional theater continued under the domination of J. C. Williamson until his death in 1911, and "the firm," which soon after came under the control of the Tait brothers, was dominant for a good many years after. Probably the most famous Australian-born actor of this time was Oscar Asche (1871–1936), trained for the theater in Norway, who divided his energies as actor, producer, and popular playwright between London and Australia. About 1912 the movies began to have a depressive effect upon the live theater. The Australians early took up movie-making, and characteristically one of the locally made full length features was a film about Ned Kelly. (This may be the earliest full-length feature made in the world.) This threw the burden of the preservation of the live theater for anything more than light entertainment—that is, the frothy musicals of London and New York—on the "little" and repertory theaters. The problem of Australian plays even for the "little" theaters continued still to be unsolved. The commercial theater made but one memorable contribution, a stage version of *On Our Selection* in 1912, described by a connoisseur as the "nearest approach to an authentic [Australian] folk-drama." The strongest repertory theater was that in Adelaide, but the most important little theater was that under the direction of Gregan McMahon in Melbourne. The theoreticians of an indigenous Australian drama drew heavily upon the example of the Irish theater and several Australians, notably Louis Esson (1879–1943), discussed the problem with W. B. Yeats. Although many of those who wrote about an Australian drama and theater did not stay to wrestle with the problem—for example, Spencer Brodney who abandoned the task for a career in New York journalism—Louis Esson continued an enthusiast all his life long and went on to write, publish, and have produced *Australian* plays to the point that he became a key figure in the slow, hesitant, uneven rise of the Australian drama.

Music-making, but not composing, continued in full vigor up to the war. Not only was there a great deal of amateur music-making, both instrumental and vocal, but there was a good deal of professional instruction available to aspirants, both in and out of the conservatoria. A state-supported conservatorium was established in Sydney in 1914, with the enthusiastic backing of the Labor premier, W. A. Holman. In Melbourne a symphony orchestra was founded by Albert Zelman in 1906, and one was founded in Sydney two years later by W. Arundel Orchard. Composing lagged a good deal behind performance. Probably the most accomplished composer of this period was Alfred Hill, an Australian with a New Zealand family background, who brought the Maoris into music and musical plays, as well as Australian, but not aboriginal, themes.

The prestige of Australian painting was greatly and enduringly enhanced by a boom in demand and prices which first showed itself in Melbourne in 1907 but which did not influence Sydney until a decade later. The first beneficiary of this acceptance of Australian painting was Sir Arthur Streeton. Although this did not mean that henceforth new painters had an easy time of it, it did establish painting and painters of readily identifiable quality in a more secure position than their fellow artists of literature, a position they have since maintained. The new position was sustained not only by casual purchasers, but by liberal patrons, such as Sir Thomas Elder of Adelaide and Howard Hinton of Sydney, who bought for later presentation to public institutions. At the same time there was encouragement to produce color-illustrated books about Australian artists, and this led to the establishment of the most lushly illustrated and pretentious art periodical Australia has ever known, *Art in Australia,* founded in 1916 by S. Ure Smith. While the established artists profited greatly by these favorable changes, new figures appeared and slowly established themselves to become the "masters" of the next period, notably Hans Heysen (1877–), who first came to notice in 1908 and Elioth Gruner (1882–1939), whose first important exhibition was held in 1913. This was the time also when the numerous brothers Lindsay made their first impact on the public, especially distinguished among them Lionel (1874–1961), an etcher and woodcut maker, and Norman (1879–) who became best known for illustrative etchings, pen-and-ink drawings, and oils. Norman was also a cartoonist for *The Bulletin* and a novelist. His penchant for the earthy and the bawdy, elevated into a philosophy of life and art, insured him an exhilaratingly stormy career in a country where to shock the bourgeoisie hardly qualifies as hard work. In 1911 David Low left New Zealand to join *The Bulletin* as political cartoonist; during the war he established a reputation which allowed him to migrate to London and world eminence in his field. On the gallery side, by far the most important development was the Felton Bequest, of which the Melbourne National Gallery was the beneficiary. Alfred Felton (1831–1904), a wholesale and manufacturing druggist, left a net estate of £378,000, one-half of the income to go to charities annually, the other half toward the purchase of pictures for the Gallery. This benefaction insured that the Melbourne Gallery was to be the richest in all Australia and a respected gallery of the world.

The forward impetus given to state education in the 1870's and 1880's, when the systems became free, compulsory, and secular had been exhausted by the early 1900's. It had left the schools not wholly free, though the surviving fees were minimal and easily avoided, not wholly secular because various arrangements were made for religious instruction —though with a careful avoidance of any strictly sectarian teaching by the regular staffs—and not compulsory for the entire school-age population because of the scatter of the dwellers in the outback country. The state systems were also but slowly feeling their way toward the establishment of high-schools accessible to all prospective students, and technical education (which had developed mostly around mining) was of uneven quality and coverage. The Catholic Church had adopted the tactic of the American Catholics of complaining about the "injustice" of having to pay taxes in support of state schools while also being liable for fees in support of the parochial schools. The decade before the war was a period when there was much discussion of reform and a good deal of creative action, as in curriculum, maintenance of instructional standards, and teacher training. The coming of the Labor party into politics was helpful to the schoolmen, for Labor saw in education a prime benefit to its working-class constituency.

At this stage, however, Labor's interest tended to stop at the school-leaving age of fourteen and extend beyond it only with regard to technical education. There was a feeling that the universities had isolated themselves from their communities—except perhaps for their professional schools, from which there was a steady flow of trained personnel—an opinion vigorously rebutted by some of the academics. It is clear, however, that there was no educational ladder up which more than a minority could climb to the university level and certainly no great body of opinion in favor of extending university education to everybody capable of benefiting, regardless of family circumstances. The aspiration to establish universities was still active. The University of Queensland was established and endowed at Brisbane in 1909 and began its first term in 1911 with four faculties (classics, chemistry, engineering, and mathematics) and eighty students. Western Australia followed suit in 1911, after a decade of constant agitation, and formally inaugurated university work in 1913 with three faculties, arts, science, and engineering. The Queensland university had grown out of extension work from Sydney, inaugurated in 1893, while the University of Adelaide had had an examination center at Perth from 1898. Thus, by the outbreak of war all six states had a university, but the impulse to establish them was now exhausted, for no more were established for over thirty years. Although university extension, important as a method of bringing a university into the community, was at this time adjudged a failure, the W.E.A. was introduced into New South Wales in 1913 by Albert Mansbridge, who had established it in England.

Taking education in its largest sense, the Felton bequest was an educational contribution of immense importance. By the same token, and with a nationalistic overtone besides, the benefaction of David Scott Mitchell (1836–1907) was also of high educational importance. The difficulty he had in making it casts a glare of light on the Australian mind of the time. Mitchell, a wealthy bachelor (B.A. and M.A. of the University of Sydney), a lawyer by profession though he never practiced, spent his life in book collecting. For many years before his death his sole occupation and consuming passion was collecting Australiana in its widest possible definition and with no other purpose, apparently, than to strive toward comprehensiveness. In the end he possessed the richest Australiana collection in existence anywhere; this he proposed in 1898 to give to the trustees of the Public Library of New South Wales, together with an endowment for maintenance and expansion, provided a separate corporation was formed to control the resulting library. This was done the following year and 10,000 books and fifty pictures were given into the corporation's care. But another condition was that suitable housing be provided by the state for the entire collection which would become available to the public on his death. This the politicians were slow about doing, and Mitchell laid down the requirement that if the housing was not available within one year of his death, the collection would go elsewhere. Thus spurred on, the Library trustees induced the state to reserve a desirable site for the Mitchell library and in 1906 the foundation stone was laid. The influence of Sir J. H. Carruthers on the politicians was decisive. Mitchell thereupon set the endowment at £70,000 and on his death the next year 61,000 books, manuscripts, maps, views, and portraits passed to the Library. It was opened for public use in 1910. Although other great Australiana collections have been built up, notably at Melbourne and Canberra, the David Scott Mitchell collection, with increments by purchase and gift, retains its pre-eminence.

Sport continued to be pre-eminently the popular preoccupation. "For Victor Trumper is today / Our one Australian hero." Victor Trumper (1877–1915) was a renowned cricketer, the "world's greatest batter." And in this period Australia, teamed with New Zealand, emerged into world tennis. The Australasian team won the Davis Cup in 1907, 1908, 1909, 1911, and 1914. The pre-eminent Australian player was Norman Brookes of Melbourne.

CHAPTER II

World War I

World War I was Australia's war because the country was British—in relation to questions of war and peace *colonial* British. As recently as 1911 it had been informed, along with the other dominions, by British Prime Minister Asquith that foreign policy was the exclusive responsibility of the United Kingdom Foreign Office speaking for the Empire as a unity and that the dominions could not of right claim participation in its formulation, particularly the taking of ultimate decisions. This was not well received in Australia, for it blocked the Australian aspiration for fuller participation in running the Empire. When in 1916 Andrew Fisher, lately Australian prime minister, arrived in London to be high commissioner, he declared: "If I had stayed in Scotland, I should have been able to heckle my member [of Parliament] on questions of Imperial policy, and to vote for or against him on that ground. I went to Australia. I have been Prime Minister. But all the time I have had no say whatever about imperial policy—no say whatever. Now that can't go on. There must be some change." The only qualification that Fisher might have made was that the dominions could and did on occasions of their own selection seek to move the imperial authorities on foreign policy issues by pressure designed to promote their own interests. Australia had done so, particularly with regard to Islands questions. But imperial decisions were nevertheless binding upon the dominions whether or not they conformed to their conceptions of what was right and proper. Australia was committed to participation in World War I by the decision of Sir Edward Grey and those of his colleagues who accepted his position.

The commitment to war was fervently accepted. Whatever understanding of the foreign political situation existed in Australia was British, founded on such official expositions as that of Grey at the Committee of Imperial Defence in 1911, newspaper dispatches of London origin, or discussions in British magazines and books. The Australians responded as

Australian Britons even when they were also nationalist Australians.

It was one of the paradoxes of Australian nationalism that while responsibility for self-defense was accepted, it was accepted with recognition that it could not by any manner of means be achieved in full measure. A conspicuous element of Australia's sense of dependency upon the British imperium was—and long remained—a dependence in the ultimate for its defense. What could be done by way of self-defense was conceived of within the strategic conceptions of imperial defense, as a contribution to the sinewing of imperial defense. This reliance upon imperial defense was accompanied by a sense of obligation to contribute to imperial defense, in effect to participate actively in British wars. The decision on the latter point was first made at the time of the Sudan episode in 1885 and reiterated at the time of the South African War of 1898. It predated the Commonwealth. The Australians interpreted their automatic commitment to belligerent status when Britain went to war as also committing them to the fullest possible participation in the war. They did not, as did the Canadians, accept the commitment to belligerent status but propose to debate the nature and extent of their participation. Yet in the end they fell out most violently among themselves precisely over the question of how their commitment to participate should be implemented.

The Australian experiment in self-defense within the imperial system involved preparations by sea, land, and later, air. Defense by naval power was the essence of the Pax Britannica in the shade of which Australia had been since its foundation, but as World War I approached the British deliberately concentrated on naval power in the North Atlantic, with lesser attention to the far reaches of the Empire. They argued that if the center of Empire held, all else was safe. By the time the Commonwealth was formed, Australia's "enemies" were thought to be Germany and Japan. From 1902, however, the United Kingdom was in alliance with Japan, and the alliance was renewed in 1911. While Australians differed as to how absolutely this association tempered the possibilities of Japanese action menacing to them—they never wholly lost their suspicious fear of Japan (viewed in terms of the Yellow Peril), and there was some apocalyptic writing about the Japanese—it was of Germany that they became officially most fearful as World War I approached, both because Germany was the identified opponent of the United Kingdom in Europe and on the high seas and because of German activity in the islands neighboring Australia. The Australians tended to exaggerate German naval strength in the Pacific and its military strength in the Southwest Pacific islands. The Australian navy was a direct expression of Australian nationalism and of the fears about her security, intensified by a sense of remoteness from the concentration of British power in the North Atlantic Ocean.

The founding of a navy was mooted by Sir John Forrest when he was the first Commonwealth defense minister, in Sir Edmund Barton's cabinet, but rejected by him and Barton in 1903 in favor of a ten-year renewal of the traditional system of British ships on an Australian station, toward the maintenance of which the Commonwealth was to make an annual contribution. This dated back to 1887. The British naval authorities were then most fervently devoted to the thesis that the defense of the Empire was best to be achieved by a single fleet centrally controlled and directed. They strongly deprecated dominion national navies, being most positive about their capacity to guarantee security from the center around 1906–9. After the great naval "scare" of 1909 they were more amenable to arguments in favor of dominion forces, and the effect of the 1909 "scare" in Australia intensified the wish for a national navy. The visit of Theodore Roosevelt's Great White Fleet to Sydney in 1908 was also a stimulus to action. The arrangement of 1903 was never popular in Australia; it was stringently criticised by Sir John Quick of the Deakin Liberals and W. M. Hughes of Labor. In 1906 Alfred Deakin began a series of tentative but largely frustrate moves toward a national navy and continued them in 1907 and 1909, while Andrew Fisher took decisive steps to translate proposals into ships in 1909 and 1910. An agreement with the imperial authorities was then worked out under which the Commonwealth would have full control of its ships in time of peace, but would transfer control of them to the imperial authorities when war broke out. The Australian navy was chiefly to be confined to operations within the boundaries of the Australian station, defined on the north by a line so drawn as to touch the coasts of Papua in New Guinea but to exclude the British Solomon Islands, on the east by a line running south to the Antarctic Circle, taking in the New Hebrides, New Caledonia, and Macquarie Island but excluding New Zealand, along the circle westward to a point well to the west of the continent and then northward through the Indian Ocean until it joined the northern line south of the westernmost islands of the Netherlands East Indies. The first units of the Australian fleet arrived in Australia from the United Kingdom on October 4, 1913. The previous March a naval college had been set up, the site of a Commonwealth naval base had been selected at Jervis Bay, eventually annexed to the landlocked capital territory, and the previous June the administration of the Australian station had passed to a Commonwealth Naval Board. The new navy was designated the Royal Australian Navy, the ships HMAS. Enlistment was voluntary; the officers were assigned from the British navy. At the outbreak of the war the principal ships were a battle cruiser, two light cruisers, three destroyers, and two submarines.

Land defense had a history running back to the beginnings of settlement when British marines were employed, but since 1870, when the British garrisons had been withdrawn, land defense had been a responsibility of the colonies. One motivation of federation was to correct the disabling fragmentation of the land forces which colonial particularism involved, but while central control was achieved through federation, acute problems remained. A central question was how an army should be raised. The tradition was that it should be a voluntary service. However, it was the conviction of men like W. M. Hughes that service should be compulsory. In 1905 Hughes and other like-minded people of various political outlooks formed an Australian National Defence League to advocate compulsory training more or less on the Swiss model; it was largely in this guise that Hughes first came to the attention of the Establishment in England. Starting from the proposition that every citizen of a democracy had a duty to defend his country, Hughes and his associates advocated a system under which training would start in school and be continued into the middle twenties of adult life. This general approach had been, as a matter of fact, adopted by the Commonwealth as early as 1903, but for one reason and another was not implemented until 1911—then by a Labor administration—after the land defense problem had been studied by Lord Kitchener as visiting expert. Under Kitchener's influence, with Lord Haldane's thinking about army organization in mind, Australia adopted compulsory military training, the principle of compulsory service for home defense in time of war, but the principle of voluntary overseas service, the overseas forces of Australian origin to operate in close co-operation with the British army. The compulsory training features of this system met with widespread resistance and prosecutions for noncompliance quickly rose into many thousands. The Australians worked actively with the Committee of Imperial Defence. They also, in 1911, set up a Royal Military College at Duntroon, Australian Capital Territory, on the model of West Point. To insure their indoctrination with the imperial point of view, it was assumed that graduates would take tours of duty in England, India, Singapore, or Hong Kong before appointment to the Australian army. Thus at the outbreak of World War I Australia had a system of compulsory army service for home defense, voluntary service in close association with the imperial forces for overseas action, *and also* a tradition of resisting compulsion.

The Australian interest in aviation seems ex post facto to have a measure of inevitability about it, given the importance of the conquest of distance to Australians, both domestically and globally. While Lawrence Hargrave (1850–1915) was a pioneer of aerodynamics important enough to give his name to the chair in the subject at Sydney University, all the pioneering in actual flight was done in Europe and America. Australians, however, were in the field in England well before World War I, and the first flight in Australia occurred in 1909. Nevertheless, it is remarkable that the Commonwealth government set up a flying school at Point Cook, Victoria, in August 1914 and that it was able to supply flyers (but not planes) for military duty early in 1915.

When Andrew Fisher, as leader of Labor, declared that Australia was with Britain in the war to "the last man and the last shilling," he was speaking as a patriot, not as a man with an understanding of international politics, the national war potential, or the likely nature of the conflict then opening. As a matter of fact, Australia as a primary producing country with a population of only 4,500,000 had a low industrial war potential, a decisive handicap; its strength lay quite elsewhere. Clear-sighted understanding of its true position was impeded by the prevailing flamboyant conception of the Australian economic potential; eyes focused on rosy illusions about the future could hardly be expected to see the realities of the present. A reality was that its capacity to supply even small arms fell short of the manpower it could mobilize, and it was able to do far less about heavy fighting equipment. Once its men were dispatched overseas their supply, maintenance, and movement was the responsibility of the British government, though at Australian expense. Efforts to reorganize and expand Australia's capacity as an arsenal were largely frustrated by the unavailability of equipment for importing from overseas sources. At maximum the Defence Department's factories producing woolens, clothing, harness, cordite, and small arms employed but a few thousand hands. It is an index to the situation that Australia sent 6000 workers, skilled and unskilled, to the war factories of England. Such useful industrial expansion as took place was with regard to production for civilian use, involving in the end 400 different articles—the most notable event was the coming into production in 1915 of the BHP steel works at Newcastle, N.S.W., an American-style plant built by an engineer from Philadelphia. The effort was to produce locally, largely regardless of cost and quality, goods hitherto imported, and here again the effort was frustrated from going as far as opportunity allowed by the inability to get the required machinery overseas. In pursuit of indispensable supplies there was also a temporary shift in the origin of imports. As imports from England declined of necessity, those from the United States, for example, rose from 12 to 25 per cent of the total. The basic

Australian contribution to World War I was in terms of fighting man-power, foodstuffs, and raw materials, and the greatest of these was manpower.

Since the Australians as a people never suffered such a disillusion with World War I as overtook the American people, pride in the exploits of their fighting men proved a durable inheritance. To Australian leaders, participation in war was an indispensable stimulus to national matura-tion. It was necessary to be "blooded" in order to grow up. Therefore, an inheritance of World War I was a strong and enduring conviction that Australia came of age on the battlefields, especially and particularly at Gallipoli. Fully exploiting the distinctively British capacity for extracting glory out of signal defeat, the Australians built the Gallipoli experience into a prime item of proof of their distinction as a people.

Following the Canadians and the New Zealanders, the Australians offered a force for overseas service with the imperial army. Enlistment voluntary, building upon the body of compulsorily trained, but not con-fining themselves to them, the Australians organized 20,000 men in the first instance, mostly foot soldiers, but some as mounted infantry. Briga-dier General William Throsby Bridges (1861–1915), son of an English naval officer and an Australian mother, educated militarily in Canada, founding commandant of Duntroon, inspector-general of Common-wealth military forces, and identified with New South Wales, was given the task of organizing and commanding the force. His chief of staff was Major C. B. B. White (1876–1940), a Victorian-born Queenslander. (The state-identification of military men of all grades was important throughout the war.) Brigadier General Bridges named the force the Australian Imperial Force—the A.I.F.—thus emphasizing that it would operate with the imperial army. It was during World War I that the policy became established—effectively so at Gallipoli—of keeping the Australian troops in identifiable military units immediately in the charge of Australian commanders responsible to the Australian government. The avoided alternative was that they be attached to British forces in a fashion that reduced or obliterated their identity and transferred their immediate governance to British officers—which overtook the New Zealanders in France. Originally intended for England and France, momentarily under orders to go to South Africa to assist in suppressing the Boer rebellion, the Australians eventually were directed to Egypt for their war training, arriving in the same convoy as the New Zealanders with whom they were soon closely associated under the collective name Anzac. Before the war was concluded Australia had raised by voluntary enlistment over 400,000 troops, of whom 332,000 were dispatched over-seas. Three-fifths of those enlisted fell in the categories clerical, tradesmen, and laborers, the foundation of the allegation that Labor voters manned the army (an allegation important in relation to the fight over conscription). Only 4 per cent were classified as "professional," but 14 per cent were listed as following "country callings," these including owning farmers and graziers as well as "hands." About 80 out of every 100 volunteers were native born, this was argued to show the depth of the imperial patriotism of the Australian people. Of the states, New South Wales and Victoria, in that order, contributed the highest proportion of their males of military age, while Western Australia contributed the largest proportion of its total population. Australia contributed about the same proportion of its male population of military age as did Canada, 6 per cent less than did New Zealand, and almost 10 per cent less than the United Kingdom. Casualties were very high, running to 65 per cent, largely because the soldiers were assessed and used as front-line shock troops. Deaths on active service exceeded 60,000.

Both the Australian army and navy first saw action in the Pacific in connection with the dislodging of the Germans from the islands, but the earliest major action was at Gallipoli, where both the foot soldiers and the mounted troops without their horses were employed with British, New Zealand, Indian, and French forces. The Australians were under the immediate command of Bridges (who was killed by a sniper). Over Bridges was the British-Indian soldier Lieutenant General Sir William Birdwood leading the Anzac forces. The senior officer in charge of the expedition was the Briton Sir Ian Hamilton. Gallipoli was essentially an effort to relieve the Russians from Turkish pressure, open up communications with south Russia via the Dardanelles, and change to the advantage of the Allies the constellation of political forces in the Balkans. The Russians had asked that something be done about the Turkish pressure upon them, and it was the idea of Winston Churchill, then at the Admiralty, to attempt to meet the need by opening up the Dardanelles to Allied uses. Originally, this was conceived as a naval action, but trial resulted in a rather costly failure, and the next step was to devise a combined naval and military effort to the same end, the military effort to be sited on the peninsula of Gallipoli. The Turkish opposition to the Allied invaders was led by the German Liman von Sanders, among whose subordinates was the subsequently great Mustapha Kemal. Participation in this their first adventure in Europe, brought the Australians, a young overseas people, into collision with the Turks, an old Asiatic people with a long-established but shrinking foothold in Europe. The Australians were landed on the peninsula, by accident at an extremely disadvantageous point, on April 25, 1915; after enduring fantastic hardships, participating in the bitterest of trench and position fighting, and suffering stalemate, the last of them were withdrawn on December 19, 1915. Losses by death totaled 7600, and 19,000 were wounded. "Blooded" they were indeed, but in a campaign that, however brilliant in conception, was in execution a failure. Little about it compared in skill to the withdrawal from it.

Returned from Gallipoli to Egypt and joined there by additional men from Australia, where recruiting had been stimulated by the delayed and censored news from Gallipoli, the forces were divided into two groups: the foot soldiers were soon dispatched to France and eventually joined to units brought directly to England from Australia; the mounted troops were sent against the Turks again, this time in Palestine.

The Australians in France, as front-line shock troops, experienced to the full the horrors of trench warfare and the terrible slaughter for limited territorial gains characteristic of warfare in World War I. Out of this inhuman combat was generated the manpower demands upon Australia which eventually triggered the bitter wartime domestic controversy over conscription for overseas service. The Australians, inducted into France to replace the losses at Verdun, were in the summer of 1916 associated with actions on the Somme River, in 1917 with actions at Bapaume, Bullecourt, Messines, and the third battle of Ypres, and in 1918 with the struggles over Villers Bretonneux (where later an Australian war memorial was erected), leading on to the final assault on the Hindenberg Line. Australian dash and fierceness in the last phase of the war in France inspired their victim, General Erich Ludendorff, to a tribute to their fighting qualities. Assembled at Charleroi in France, the Australians were withdrawn to England, demobilized, and repatriated to Australia. From the fighting in France emerged one of the greatest "civilian soldiers" of the war and of the Australian forces, General Sir John Monash.

Meanwhile, the mounted troops campaigned in Palestine under the leadership of Lieutenant General Sir Harry [Henry George] Chauvel, in what was in composition an Anzac force—in France Anzac had ceased to exist. Later, under General Allenby not only the Australians and New Zealanders but also cavalry of Britain, India, and France were combined to rout the Turks from the Holy Land. These actions of the war were not only the ones most comparable to those of the Boer War, so important in the Australian military experience, but also among the last spectacular cavalry actions in modern warfare. The Palestine campaign also brought the Australians into association with one of the most enigmatic and enduringly controversial of contemporary Englishmen, Colonel T. E. Lawrence of *Seven Pillars of Wisdom* (1926).

The war did not induce a boom in production in Australia; there was a decline in productivity. Comparing production by value at 1911 prices, agriculture, dairying, and manufactures increased, but pastoral and mining decreased. A central wartime problem was to market the production available for export. Aside from insuring that there was no trading with the enemy, a phase of which was Hughes's bravura performance in breaking the German grip on the metals trade, the outstanding problem was the transportation of exports to legitimate, war-supporting points of consumption. In the course of the war practically all commodities came under government control, in the end mostly in intimate relation to schemes whereby the British government purchased everything available for export. It was the states that ordinarily took the initiative in dealing with the marketing problems of the producers (and in regard to price also the local consumers), the Commonwealth acting collaboratively at particular points, sometimes at a relatively late stage in the war. 1916 was the year in which the export trade became most elaborately organized and fixed in relation to the United Kingdom market. Control of commodities ordinarily passed to "boards" or committees, forecasting the way in which much marketing was eventually to be organized in the postwar period. However, the classic success of the time—the marketing of wool—proved not to be a precedent for the industry. The Commonwealth authorities had the initiative in the government-to-government dealings with the United Kingdom, and thus a primary influence on the all-important question of price; they also had the initiative with regard to the shipping which provided the indispensable link between the producers and their export markets. Because of a shortage of shipping, the British authorities had a natural preference for drawing supplies from the Americas. The outward and inward voyages thence were shorter, the turn around quicker, and one ship could do the work of two or three sent on the long voyage to Australia. Australia suffered considerably from this geographically dictated administrative decision, and quantities of commodities piled up in the country, some under conditions which allowed deterioration or destruction, for example, much wheat was destroyed by plagues of weevils and mice. Prime Minister Hughes finally took action to assist the Australian exporters by purchasing a fleet of steamers from under the noses of the British shipping authorities, establishing a Commonwealth Shipping Line. The line's fleet was augmented by ships built in Australia—this being regarded as a wartime industrial triumph. Labor had favored a government-owned line before the war, but Hughes's action, while a clear expression of Labor's Fabian collectivism, was actually taken after he had left the Labor party.

The general effect of the war was to increase the power and authority of the Commonwealth at the expense of the states. In large measure this was made possible by the enormous elasticity the High Court found in

Part V, section vi, of the constitution: "The naval and military defence of the Commonwealth and the several States . . ." The Court decided, for example, that concealed in the defense power was a power of the Commonwealth to fix the price of bread within a state if that contributed to the efficient management of defense. However, the principal legislative source of Commonwealth power during the war was the War Precautions Act of 1914 (comparable to Britain's Defence of the Realm Act). Especially by the employment of regulations under the act, this was a very powerful support of orders and schemes for getting things done or prohibiting them from being done. Passed when Labor was in office, the act tempted an aggressive prime minister with a strong wish to exercise power to dictatorial proceedings. William Morris Hughes was such an aggressive prime minister, grasping of power, troubled hardly at all about the rights and wrongs of his procedures and none too scrupulous about means if the ends struck him as valid. The war brought out Hughes's autocratic tendencies and his hysterical tendencies in equal measure. It was said, either in admiration or criticism, that Hughes governed Australia "with a fountain pen."

In retrospect, however, it is apparent that the most effective augmentation of Commonwealth power occurred in the field of finance, although it took some years after the war for the Commonwealth to consolidate its war-won power. The tendencies set going in World War I continued between the wars and found their fullest expression in World War II. Alfred Deakin, for one, had foreseen that it was through finance that the Commonwealth was likely to achieve dominance, but the development actually occurred as a pragmatic response to pressing necessities, not as a consequence of anybody's theoretical forethought, least of all as a phase of a move toward unitary government for Australia. Early and late the development had very unpleasant side-effects of which much political capital was made.

Although Commonwealth taxes were multiplied in kind and intensified in incidence and the revenue thereby augmented—a Commonwealth income tax on top of the state income taxes (pioneered by South Australia in 1885 and adopted by all states by 1908) was instituted in 1915, fatefully it turned out—the principal reliance for war finance was on loans. Labor instituted this financial policy, and though its great faults were pointed out by Labor and anti-Labor spokesmen, it was never given up during the war. The net result was to saddle the Commonwealth with a huge debt, fatten the rentier class—$4\frac{1}{4}$ to $5\frac{1}{2}$ per cent was paid for the money—and to run up postwar debt charges to a sum larger than the Commonwealth's prewar budget. At least 85 per cent of the Commonwealth's wartime expenditure was obtained from loans; and a remarkable

70 per cent of this was obtained within Australia in seven war loans progressively more widely subscribed to. The balance of the borrowings came from London. In managing the domestic loans, the then new Commonwealth Bank played a strategic role; and the process vastly strengthened the emerging domestic money market. At the outbreak of war the states were borrowing for development at the rate of about £20 millions per annum. This borrowing was continued during the war, tapering off only slightly in the later years but, except for New South Wales, the borrowing was done by the Commonwealth on behalf of the states, a radical innovation; it was borrowing for the states that eased the Commonwealth into borrowing for its own purposes.

The effort of the states to keep up their development works was not peculiar to them, however, for the Commonwealth itself carried one great work to completion during the war—the East-West railway linking Western Australia to the eastern states—and provided the machinery for a Commonwealth-state cooperative scheme to utilize the waters of the Murray River on a large scale. A consequence of the war, which the method of war finance undoubtedly intensified, though this was unperceived at the time, was a steep rise in prices. Economics being largely absent from the political mind, a devil and scapegoat was found in the "war profiteer." He was given a hard run. Resort was had to price fixing, first by the states with some attempt at planned uniformity among them, from early 1916 by the Commonwealth. But it was impossible for the arbitration courts to keep abreast of the pressures on the cost of living, and real wages declined. This, with war weariness and political Labor's disadvantageous position after its dislodgment from office, led to much labor unrest, especially in 1916 and 1917.

Labor's return to office in September 1914 with strong majorities in both the House and Senate seemed to forecast political stability. This proved to be an illusion. All was not easy within the Labor cabinet and caucus. Fisher was leader and prime minister, and Hughes as attorney-general and George Pearce as minister for Defence were the strong cabinet members—Hughes being the most aggressively ambitious. In October 1915 Fisher stepped down as prime minister in favor of Hughes and went to London as high commissioner in succession to Sir George Reid. Allegedly, Fisher's health had weakened under the strain of war leadership—also a critical component of the strain had been constant needling from Hughes—and even more sinister explanations have been covertly circulated down the years. The episode awaits critical study. At any rate Hughes became prime minister by inheritance—Labor prime minister.

William Morris Hughes, a London-born Welshman, was fifty-one years old in 1915; he had landed an unregarded immigrant in Brisbane in 1884 at twenty. Scrawny of body like so many descendants of victims of the Industrial Revolution, early a chronic sufferer from dyspepsia and from deafness, he was nevertheless mercurially active of mind and body, seemingly and mysteriously gifted with resources of energy denied men of better physical endowment. After adventures outback in Queensland, which he later inextricably mixed up as to fact and fiction, he settled in Sydney in 1886. Earning a scanty living as petty shopkeeper, he entered the fringes of politics as a leftist preaching "socialism" and Henry George-ism and step by step established himself as a Labor party and trade union organizer, specializing in the latter connection in the water-front occupations.

In 1894 he entered the New South Wales Parliament as a Labor member, convinced of the possibilities of social reform by parliamentary methods, favoring arbitration over direct action in industrial affairs, a Fabian collectivist, but above all a nationalist and an imperialist. The great psychological division in him was between his laboristic views of domestic affairs and his nationalist-imperialist chauvinism in foreign affairs. Once in political office, he was never out again as long as he lived (he died in 1952); he transferred to the federal parliament in 1901. His keen, sharp but inadequately furnished mind—"ignorant" and "small minded" are words that occur in assessments of the Hughes of the World War I period, by Walter Hines Page, Wilson's ambassador to London, and Nitti, the Italian prime minister—was underlain and too often directed by a perfervid Welsh emotionalism that, tinged as it was by a bitterness that stemmed from an uneasy sense of inferiority, led him into extravagances of vituperative rhetoric that made him famous but not loved. Something of a natural oddity, he was delightfully caricaturable in person and manner, and it was the New Zealander David Low, then of *The Bulletin,* who pinned Hughes the wartime leader to paper for all time, not without malice.

Exceptionally possessed of the great political asset of conviction of his own exhaustive rightness, he was by nature a prima donna leader, player of a lone hand, secretive, power grasping, ruthless with critics, dissenters, and oppositionists. Dignity was simply not in him; he was a stranger to moderation. He could lead, but he could not permanently command warm and sacrificial loyalty; he was a public hero whom his closest associates inevitably came to dislike, even to fear, as they got to know him. His complexity as a man, intricately related to parallel complexities in the Australian character and mind, did him in: what he did in one guise pleased, what he did in another angered. Few contemporaries could consistently admire him whole (for what was the whole?); some could admire him in one part, some in another, and contemporaries might both like and abhor him. In speaking or writing of him, the Australian tendency was to cover dislike with a glaze of praise for what he had done that had pleased. A complex, wonderful, exasperating, disastrous man and politician, he became by his own hand and the contributions of contemporaries a vast, overlooming complex of legends. The man got lost among them. There was no single "Billy" Hughes, but a bewildering multiplicity of Billy Hugheses.

Hughes directed the completion of the organization of the Commonwealth for war with notable assists from nonpolitical administrators; and it was he who, in pursuit of a more intensive exploitation of Australia's prime contributory strength—the manpower—cracked the unity of the country. Hughes the dreamer of dreams about domestic and imperial felicity was fated always to destroy even while he most passionately believed he was creating.

His view of the war was hardly original and certainly not laboristic; it was familiarly Manichaean, the good British versus the bad Germans, light against the darkness inhabited by demons called Heinrich von Treitschke, Friedrich von Bernhardi, and Wilhelm Hohenzollern (forgotten to be Victoria's grandson). What it lacked in interpretative originality was made up for by the emotional fervor of its exposition on public platforms, and what gave Hughes's utterances their decisive cutting edge was the fierce advocacy of "total" organization and exploitation of imperial resources for absolute victory in the war and the ensuing peace. His early exploit of ousting the Germans from the Australian metals trade was not to him simply a necessary move to free the imperial economy from a now embarrassing international entanglement the better to fight the war, but a permanent expulsion of devils from the imperial economic Eden. Hughes's vendetta with the Germans was intensely personal; he was an Australian Theseus fighting the German Minotaur.

But it was not at home that he achieved his apotheosis—though it was there that it was temporarily of most political use to him—but in the United Kingdom, where he went in 1916, as Labor prime minister of Australia, to become the darling of his fellow jingos, a public hero, a Privy councillor, the recipient of the freedom of nine cities and of numerous honorary doctorates, including the Oxford D.C.L. The ranting passion of his speeches—was he not a new Demosthenes rousing the sluggards?—and the drift of his thought, however, complemented and intensified not what was great and admirable in Britain or honorable to her in her current predicament, but the mounting war hysteria. His admirers were the Lloyd Georges, the Northcliffes, the Maxses, the obsessed militarists. To them he appeared an exhilarating gale out of "the colonies"; a prophet from the outer marches of the imperium, especially if his laboristic ideas were ignored, as they so readily could be when Hughes the reactionary nationalist-imperialist was dominant. He stood in startling contrast to such thoughtful but less colorful colonial leaders as Smuts of South Africa and Borden of Canada. He took home from Britain not only vociferous praise which echoed well in wartime Australia, not only honors signifying his acceptance by the British powers-that-be, not only ships to carry Australian produce to market, but the idea conveyed to him by his friends among the British military—who saw a use for this frenzied man—that only if Australia adopted conscription for overseas service could it properly signify its allegiance to the cause and the victory to which Hughes had declared his devotion.

Although Hughes was an architect of compulsion for home defense, he was acutely aware that volunteering for imperial service was the Australian dogma, held to by none more firmly than the supporters of Labor. He did not precipitate conscription into the Australian arena; that honor appears to belong to Sir William Irvine, who remained the most single-minded conscriptionist of them all. Hughes was aware that the proposal had been ill received. He knew that any step by him to introduce conscription would probably divide his Labor cabinet and caucus, and perhaps the country. This he did not want. He hoped, on the contrary, that he could contrive to get majority Labor support, sacrificing only a recalcitrant minority, either by exposition of the case (supported by figures supplied to him which were later proved to be false), by cajolery, or by exploitation of war-generated emotion. He surveyed the position carefully, consulting the federal caucus and leaders in the states such as Holman of New South Wales. He found, apparently, that while many leaders would support him, many would not. How the rank and file would go was uncertain. He concluded that he could manage it, not by parliamentary action as Canada and New Zealand had done, or by regulations under the War Precautions Act, but by boldly submitting the question to the people at a referendum (or plebiscite)—an interesting example of Labor populism. He concluded, in short, that he could lead the country to a "yes" vote regardless of what the leaders might do or say. He was wrong.

The conscription campaign of 1916 was a traumatic experience for Australia. The question at issue—not the defense of Australia, for that conscription was already allowed, but the way in which a proper contribution of manpower to imperial defense was to be made—was of the very highest character, a question of public policy which should have been decided in the calmest atmosphere manageable. That it was raised in wartime probably made this impossible. But any remnants of calm and judiciousness that existed were destroyed by Hughes himself. His native incapacity to be calm, to be conscientiously scrupulous about means when an end in view seemed to him indisputably right, did in both him and his cause. He loaded the question on the ballot paper, he abused the censorship to the disadvantage of his critics, he manipulated permissions for libel actions to the hurt of his opponents, he cast his wounding invective broadside, he equated *his* position with "loyalty," he systematically debased the currency of discussion and by a kind of Gresham's law caused its general debasement. What should have been a dignified, dispassionate debate degenerated into a brawl which distressed many—even of those on his side. What dishonored Australia was, therefore, not the "no" vote that carried the day even against Hughes's desperate measures, as the conscriptionists tried to argue, but the fetid atmosphere generated by the controversy before and after the vote was taken. And Hughes, having lost the first effort but having survived politically as prime minister, compounded the damage by trying again for an affirmative vote in 1917, only to lose more decisively than the first time.

Why the Australians voted "no" must remain a mystery—in the absence of a critical history of this time—or at least a point subject to a variety of explanations. While the small group of people against war as an instrument of national policy, and therefore against the war going on, advocated a "no" vote, it cannot be argued that the national "no" majority expressed a rejection of the current war. Many of the most ardent proponents of a "no" vote, including conspicuous Labor party leaders, were prowar, but insisted upon the voluntary principle, arguing that it had produced all the soldiers Australia had, on any reasonable showing, any obligation to supply. Nor is it at all certain that any determining number of people voted "no" because of politicized war weariness, which found clearer expression in the strikes of the coal miners in 1916 and the railway workers of New South Wales in 1917. To be sure there were in the labor movement men suspicious of the war and more, like Frank Anstey of Victoria, critical of a war policy that dealt more gently with wealth than with men, but these people were peripheral and never got much further than to engineer the passing of fractionally supported resolutions in favor of a negotiated peace. Perhaps there was a measure of true disaffection from the British cause among the Irish, both Catholic and non-Catholic, who listened to the anticonscription speeches of Bishop Mannix of Melbourne and other Irish-Australians rightly disturbed by the British treatment of the leaders of the Easter Rebellion in Dublin. Probably more significant than any readily identifiable anticonscription group was the "silent vote" cast by people who either felt that conscription was wrong in principle or unnecessary in the light of the heavy voluntary enlistments. These people felt that Australia had been sufficiently "blooded"; it was wrong and unnecessary compulsorily to bleed it white. And how is one to interpret the "no" vote of the men on active service? Allegedly more people voted "no" in the second referendum than the first because they felt that by then the enormous American manpower pool was available and to draw more men from Australia was not justifiable.

The immediate political impact of the campaign on the Labor party was catastrophic. The conscription proposal intensified, but was not the sole generator of, all the intraparty hostilities to Hughes; had the question not arisen Hughes might have stayed with Labor to the end of the war. As soon as it was clear that Hughes was going through with his referendum scheme, the cabinet began to break up. F. G. Tudor, Hughes's minister for Trade and Customs, an office he had held in every Labor administration since Fisher's first—a native-born Australian, a hatter who had come into federal politics in 1901 via the Victorian trade union movement—led the way by resigning. Hughes nevertheless held the party in line for the support of the legislation authorizing the referendum, his last and most disastrous success as Labor leader. The day before the first referendum was held, three more cabinet members quit, specifically in protest against Hughes's lack of scruple in the conduct of the public debate and the arrangements for the vote. After the referendum was over, two more ministers—one was King O'Malley—resigned. This left Hughes with but three of his old Labor cabinet associates. At the first caucus meeting after the vote, a motion of "no confidence" in Hughes was submitted. It was immediately amended to effect a compromise; but before a vote could be taken, Hughes walked from the room saying, "Let all who support me follow me." Of the sixty-five Representatives and Senators present, only twenty-three followed Hughes. But the party was irrevocably split. A similar purging of the ranks took place in the states. Holman of New South Wales, Earle of Tasmania, and Scaddon of Western Australia, all representative of the prewar political upsurge of Labor, were cast out. Old-timers like J. C. Watson and W. G. Spence departed. The federal parliamentary party reorganized under the leadership of F. G. Tudor. Back of Tudor's parliamentarians in the country were many anticonscriptionists, more or less obscure, who in due course rose high in the party—including James Scullin of Victoria, E. G. Theodore of Queensland, Joseph A. Lyons of Tasmania, John Curtin of Western Australia, and Ben Chifley of New South Wales. On election posters Labor's opponents set going the canard that Labor had blown out its brains, an amusingly self-regarding image of the defectors. This partisan verdict can only be taken as not proven.

What really happened was that while Labor was cast into the political wilderness, this was not specifically because it had opposed conscription but because the war induced a conservative mood in Australia in the face of which the labor movement could not easily establish the legitimacy of its postwar radicalism at the Commonwealth level; it did better in the states. Hughes kept himself in office by riding the conservative tide, but he was eventually cast out by a surge of this tide when his laboristic radicalism became offensive. Labor's anticonscription position was actually the last popularly ratified expression of its widely accepted pre-World War I radicalism, not the effective cause of its subsequent failures in federal politics.

Hughes hung onto the prime ministership, but not only was his group, which he styled the National Labor party, a minority vis à vis both Labor and Cook's Liberals, but it did not muster the talent required to staff a strong government. After Hughes, only George Pearce was a man of stature. National Labor lasted only three months—and that long only because it commanded the reluctant support of the Liberals. Then came a call to attend Lloyd George's Imperial War Cabinet in London. Obviously, only a prime minister in a strong political position could leave the country. Joseph Cook, an experienced hand at such dickering, proposed after discussions with his Victorian supporters—such as W. A. Watt and Sir William Irvine—that the Liberals and National Labor form a joint administration with him, as leader of the larger group, prime minister with a majority of the cabinet posts at his disposal. Hughes refused and, with an assist from J. C. Watson, tried to form what he called the National party, significant items in its program being winning the war, industrial arbitration, and White Australia—National Labor being its nucleus. The Liberals refused to join. Cook countered with the suggestion that a three-party government be formed. This Tudor rejected. Finally after Parliament had met and the political difficulties of the status quo were made even more painfully obvious, Hughes and Cook devised a government in which Hughes was prime minister—his *sine qua non*—with five cabinet members of national Labor background, including the indispensable Pearce at Defence and Cook as minister for the Navy, with five other Liberals in the cabinet, including such established political figures as Sir John Forrest, Littleton Groom, and W. A. Watt. The name of the combination was the National party. The word Labor was handed back to Tudor.

This was a characteristically Australian political creation, a carefully negotiated combination of disparate individuals and points of view carrying the seeds of its own destruction, the largest seed being Hughes. However, when it went to the polls in May 1917, it thoroughly trounced Labor, taking fifty-three seats in the House to Labor's twenty-two and twenty-four in the Senate to Labor's twelve. Paradoxically, Hughes the war leader was thus strongly endorsed by the same electorate that had repudiated Hughes the conscriptionist. In the campaign Hughes, who left his old pro-Labor anticonscriptionist constituency in New South Wales for a Victorian constituency, addressed himself to praising his own attitude toward winning the war while rubbing corrosive salt into what he regarded as the national sore of Labor's attitude toward the war (which, he now began to allege, was imposed on it by sinister outside forces), thereby widening the breach between himself and his old associates, and to praising "war socialism" (for which he took great credit), thus alarming his more conservative new associates by implicitly indicating that once the war was over he would probably revert to his laboristic outlook in domestic affairs. Yet at this moment the win-the-war gambit provided Hughes with an apparently unassailable security, as was curiously illustrated when late in 1917 he made his second try to get conscription endorsed by referendum. If he failed, he said, he would resign. He did fail and he did resign, but Labor was not in a position to form a government, and Hughes was at the moment the only man on the other side of the House who could do so, so the governor-general commissioned him again and he remained prime minister. He still had six years to go.

In May 1918 Hughes, accompanied by Sir Joseph Cook, went to England. As he stayed on for the Peace Conference at Paris, he did not get back to Australia until August 1919. W. A. Watt, the treasurer, was in charge while he was away.

When Hughes had been in London in 1916 he had, as Australian prime minister, attended meetings of the British War Cabinet. In 1917, when Hughes was detained in Australia by political difficulties, an Imperial War Cabinet met in London, a device of Lloyd George's to that time constitutionally unknown to the British system. It provided a kind of top-level directorate for the Empire. As Sir Robert Borden of Canada pointed out at one of its sessions: "We meet . . . on terms of equality under the presidency of the first Minister of the United Kingdom; we meet . . . as equals; he is *primus inter pares.*" The body was executive in function, not merely consultative; it made decisions about the conduct of the war and issues of foreign policy (a reversal of Asquith's position of 1911). This suited the Australians and Hughes very well indeed. It appeared to give them that voice in the running of the Empire for which they had long pined. A great negative merit was that it secured this objective with none of the difficulties many Australians found in imperial federation, contemporaneously being promoted again by Lionel Curtis, the great hierophant of the imperial mystique of his time. What was not perceived by the Australians was where minds like Borden's were trending. Hughes himself—the cabinet at home had strong reservations—was eagerly in favor of Borden's extension of the principle to support separate representation of the dominions at the peace conference, the dominions' representatives to be members of the British Empire Delegation (in effect the Imperial War Cabinet with a different hat), and he accepted Borden's further extension of the principle to justify separate dominion signatures of the treaty and individual dominion membership in the League of Nations. But beyond this neither Hughes himself nor any other Australian wanted to go. They tended to dig in their heels on the status quo of 1919 and to resist the Canadian, South African, and Irish developments in thought about the status of the dominions that came to expression in the 1920's. The Australians argued that they could do all that they wanted to do and that it was legitimate for a dominion to do on the constitutional basis then implicit. They failed to understand the strength and nature of the nationalism at work in South Africa, Canada, and Ireland.

What Hughes accomplished at the Peace Conference won him the approbation of a greater variety of Australians over a longer period of time than almost anything else he did in his long career. Although before he left for England parliamentary Labor attempted to deny that he could speak for Australia, chiefly because his conscription proposal had lately been rejected again but also because he was against Labor's hankering for a negotiated peace and in any case a peace which should be Wilsonian in temper, there can be no doubt that he did fairly faithfully represent the predominant outlook on those matters which chiefly engaged his attention at Paris: reparations, the disposition of German New Guinea, and defense of the White Australia policy. Few Australians of his time fully understood that he figured at Paris as an extremist, reactionary nationalist, more sympathetic to Clemenceau than to anybody else, least of all that he warranted any condemnation on that account. His crude methods as exponent of a point of view might be deplored and his larrikin bad manners, especially in his relations with President Woodrow Wilson, deprecated, but this was by the way and did not necessarily imply any repudiation of his positions. It was, however, an outrageously incongruous image of progressive Australia that he projected on the international screen. Yet such is the vanity of human wishes that every substantive accomplishment of Hughes at Paris was sooner or later

eroded away, redefined in a fashion favorable to the position of his opponents, or brought under severe domestic and international criticism as
a consequence of changed world circumstances, and it was characteristically apt that one of his brilliant Paris staff became an implacable enemy
who went into politics with the primary purpose of pushing Hughes out.

Hughes went to the Peace Conference with a rancorous distaste for the
Wilsonian world-view and, since with him a difference of opinion led inevitably to a personal feud, for Woodrow Wilson himself. Already he
had protested against the way in which the British had allowed Wilson's
Fourteen Points to be made the basis of the prospective peace settlement
without consultation of the dominions. It was not only that Hughes
rejected some of the Points out of hand; it was also that he rejected the
thinking implicit in the Points and, chiefly by invoking the "blood and
treasure" argument, denied the right of the American spokesman to
forecast the character of the peace. He strongly felt that other countries
—for example, Australia—had fought longer at greater porportionate
cost in "blood and treasure" and had a better right to insist that their
wishes be met. At Paris his task as he saw it was to insure that Australia's wishes be met even if it meant that he had to defy the world.
Basing his position upon the proposition that Germany was guilty of
starting the war as charged in the propaganda, he argued that she should
be punished for her crime against civilization in a *"diktat"* handed down
by her vanquishers. In his judgment the peace as made at Paris was
"spoiled," not by the haggling and the element of vengeance in it but by
the Wilsonian corruption that survived in it. In international outlook,
Hughes was something of a social Darwinist, long teeth, sharp claws, and
all.

In one of Lloyd George's moves that can only be explained by reference to which way he thought the political wind was blowing in Britain,
the British delegation to the Reparations Commission was packed with
men of no understanding of international economics but with a known
disposition to push Germany under as a trading nation and at the same
time to "make her pay." One of the three appointees was William Morris
Hughes; he became chairman of the British group and vice-chairman of
the Commission. To his exasperation, the whole question was immediately entangled in Wilsonian dogma, firmly supported by the Americans
on the Commission (including Bernard Baruch and John Foster Dulles).
Hughes wanted to collect the whole cost of the war, widely interpreted,
from Germany. "The crime is theirs, and they must pay." The Australian
bill as he presented it was for £464,000,000; the Wilsonian approach
automatically reduced the claim by at least three-quarters. In the end the
Commission's proposals were rejected by the Council of Four, and a

different scheme for reparations—begging the question of quantity—was written into the Treaty. When Hughes reported on the Treaty to the Australian House of Representatives, he sadly said that Australia could not hope to get more than £100,000,000. When the system collapsed finally in 1932, Australia had received £5,571,720, or a little over 1 per cent of what Hughes had at first hoped for. Amusingly enough, in the light of the later great popularity of Keynesian economics in Australia, not least of John Maynard Keynes's concerns in his world-famous *The Economic Consequences of the Peace* (1920) was to denounce the Hughesian approach to reparations.

Hughes came off rather better in his struggle to gain control of German New Guinea, though his aspiration to put it on the same footing as Papua by annexing it to the Commonwealth was frustrated. Here Hughes was giving clear expression to Australia's traditional "islands policy." Although in this particular circumstance he threw the emphasis on the significance of New Guinea to Australia's security—he who controls New Guinea controls Australia—a variant of the old thesis that the islands were a protective screen for Australia and therefore must be British controlled, he also on other occasions had expressed keen interest in the economic exploitation of the islands through trading, planting, mining, and other activities profitable to the intruding British whites. In London in 1907 as a member of an Australian committee on shipping problems he had said: "I do not think the Conference realizes that the Islands of the Pacific ought to be (if they are not) our exclusive monopoly, as far as trading is concerned. I do not mean to say excluding Great Britain; I mean excluding Foreign Powers." By annexing German New Guinea to Australia he would, therefore, be taking a step toward the wished-for British monopoly. If he annexed it he also would be in a position to implement the White Australia policy and keep out the feared Asiatics. On the other hand he had no interest in the concept of mandates, then in circulation, or in the cluster of ideas later summed up in the term "trusteeship"; he was concerned only with Australian welfare, not native welfare or native progress. Hence his rather crude jokes about missionaries as food supply; hence his personal acceptance of forced native labor.

The New Guinea question at Paris was entangled in the circumstances of Australia's presence in German New Guinea and the arrangements between the United Kingdom and Japan with regard to the disposition of German possessions in the Pacific (see Chapter IX). Hughes's wish to effectuate the Australian position in New Guinea by annexation was paralleled by the New Zealand wish to obtain possession of German Samoa and the South African wish to get German Southwest Africa.

Massey of New Zealand and Smuts of South Africa therefore supported Hughes's position—Smuts a bit ambiguously because he was an architect of the mandates idea, while Lloyd George for the United Kingdom and Borden for Canada supported the Hughes position on the ground of imperial solidarity, justified expediently by reference to the smallness, remoteness, and limited importance of the territories in question. In taking their stand for annexation these men were knowingly in conflict with Wilson's point of view on the disposition of conquered colonial territories set out variously in the "points," "principles," "ends," and "particulars." And since Hughes wanted annexation to be able to "close" the territory economically (to achieve a trading monopoly) and, with regard to immigration, to enforce White Australia, he was at the same time in conflict with other Wilsonian ideas than those directly bearing upon the colonial territorial question.

It was because these conflicts were obvious that Lloyd George contrived to have the dominions' representatives—"your savages" as Clemenceau called them; Hughes, whom he liked, he once suggested was a former cannibal—and their claims brought in early at Paris with a view to committing Wilson to the desired disposition of the territories before the covenant of the League of Nations was fixed and the mandate principle and procedures—later embodied in Article 22—were operative, thus imposing a tactical *fait accompli*. However, the general idea of mandates had wide acceptance among the British and dominion delegations—Smuts did not stand alone—and in the Australian delegation itself Lieutenant Commander J. G. Latham (as he then was)—one of several staff members to achieve distinction, others being Robert Garran, Frederick W. Eggleston, and Henry Gullett—believed that a mandate would be in Australia's best interest if the Australian conditions of control could be met. It was Latham who in general discussion with the British delegates and with the help of Sir Maurice Hankey devised a formula for a C-class Mandate which satisfied Hughes's concern for the governing of a territory under the restrictive laws of the mandatory power as to trade and immigration. This was not the same as annexation, though it was, in a phrase later used, like a ninety-nine-year lease as compared to freehold. After Hughes had, in spite of this easy way out, proposed to fight the matter through on the dogma of annexation, even in the face of Lloyd George's withdrawal of support on the ground that New Guinea was not worth a decisive break with Wilson, the compromise was accepted. (See Chapters IX and X.)

But Hughes gave his most larrikinish exhibition in connection with the third item on his agenda, defense of White Australia. The White Australia policy was implicitly at issue in the New Guinea contention, but it was promoted to centrality when the Japanese (who had applauded Hughes's fight for annexation) raised the proposal that a declaration favoring the principle of racial equality be incorporated into the League Covenant. Though the proposal was important in itself, to the Japanese it involved national pride and honor as Baron Makino made clear, and the way in which it was handled would inevitably have an influence upon Japan's attitude toward other aspects of the peace settlement, notably in the Pacific.

While there was reason to doubt the wisdom of incorporating such a declaration in the Covenant at that juncture of history and genuine uncertainty about exactly how such a declaration would affect immigration legislation which operated to exclude intending migrants on ground of race, it was far from certain that such a declaration would absolutely destroy the well-established and generally conceded right of nations to determine the racial composition of their people. To Hughes, however, White Australia was a sacred item of belief, and of the many things in which he strongly believed (true and false), in none did he believe more passionately. And, by and large, his countrymen were at one with him. His reaction was therefore not to voice doubts, to hesitate, to canvass the proposition in all its perplexing implications, to try to balance the spiritual satisfaction of recognizing a moral imperative against the probable practical consequences to the relations of nations in a still strongly racist world, but to resist it violently à outrance as poisonous nonsense, firmly rejecting all of Baron Makino's conscientious glosses, interpretations, and efforts to devise a compromise formula. Hughes was not disposed to consider anything, least of all this, which might by any possible subtlety of logic or turn of unpredictable circumstances lead to a challenge to White Australia, to tolerate for one moment a proposition which forecast the breakdown of White Australia and the flooding of the country with Asiatic immigrants. He fought Baron Makino's proposal tooth and claw, as if in defense of Australia's holiest grail. He fought, also, without scruple.

Woodrow Wilson, under whose chairmanship the question was debated, tried hard to take a statesman-like, world citizen's view of the situation—well aware though that his own people, particularly his Californians, would take the Hughes line if they came to believe that acceptance of the fateful words would lead inexorably to the destruction of bars against Asiatic immigration. Realizing this, Hughes attempted to build a fire under Wilson, whom he regarded as his real opponent in the matter, by "leaking" his interpretation to the American press. This was dirty fighting indeed. But Wilson was not moved by this resort to gutter tactics; he was determined to accept the Japanese proposal until he was told by Colonel House that the British would not support him. When the proposal was put to a vote it was carried eleven to six, showing that Hughes had lost his fight in world opinion, but Wilson then ruled that as a substantive change in the Covenant it required a *unanimous* vote and hence had failed. In this curious fashion White Australia won a victory on the world stage, and Hughes was its triumphant paladin. But the consequence was that Wilson had to concede the Japanese position on Shantung—a concession which he deeply deplored and regarded as his most disgraceful. It probably helped on that disintegration of the situation in the Western Pacific out of which World War II, so costly to the Australians, eventually flowed.

Four months after his return from Paris with the Peace Treaty, Hughes took his party to the country in a general election. He hoped for a victory comparable to that won by Lloyd George in Britain just after the armistice, but this eluded him. It was later than he thought, for the forces which were within three years to eliminate him from the prime ministership were already actively at work. It was not easily possible at the time to formulate postwar policy, least of all one that fitted into the idea of a "closed" Empire, of which Hughes was a partisan, so his proposals were rather in general reminiscent of those of his old days as a Labor man, a politically dangerous hand for him to reveal. Nevertheless, he did distinguish some of the durable issues of the between-wars repertory, such as the government's role in labor relations— he proposed to emphasize conciliation, to look into the adequacy of the basic wage, and to tackle price inflation, marketing, and shipping. He proposed to continue his "war socialism," while in a simultaneous referendum—also laboristic in tone—he proposed to increase Commonwealth powers over trade and commerce, corporations, and labor relations by rewriting existing provisions, and to add the power to deal with monopolies by nationalization. Furthermore, he proposed to call a constitutional convention to carry out a complete review of the constitution. He also proposed to carry on in foreign affairs in the aggressive manner he had illustrated at Paris. He emphasized Australia's membership in the League; he assumed the Imperial Cabinet approach would continue to give Australia a role in determining a common imperial foreign policy. But if he was generally laboristic in outlook, he was fiercely hostile to the Labor party, which had recently resolved that neither Hughes nor any who had followed him should ever be readmitted. He attacked Labor as under the influence of the Irish Catholics, the I.W.W., and, in forecast of things to come, "Bolshevism." It was a curious exhibition of the art of denouncing the party whose ideological clothes one had appropriated, but it conciliated neither the traditional conservatives of his following nor the rural conservatives who now emerged in force as the Country party.

The election produced a House in which the Nationalists had thirty-five seats and the support of one independent member, Labor twenty-six and one supporting independent, while the Country party had ten seats and two supporting independents. The referendum was defeated. Political strength was obviously with the conservatives, but the Nationalists were not only a minority in a House of seventy-five—they were were weakened by the constantly increasing anti-Hughes sentiment within the party, while the logical ally for purposes of security in office, the Country party, was wholly anti-Hughes. The Country party was formally established in January 1920 under the leadership of W. J. Mc-Williams of Tasmania, but its origins could be traced back at least to 1913, when rural organizations in New South Wales began to endorse candidates who, if successful, sat in Parliament with the conservatives. Thus, the new party—rurally oriented ideologically as contrasted with the urban orientation of the conservative politicians who were dominant —began as a "corner" of the conservative party.

What kept Hughes in office as prime minister for the ensuing three years was the hard political fact that the Country party could with reason tolerate the Nationalists in office but could not with reason either assist Labor to office or help keep it there if it gained the position. Moreover, it was clear even at this early stage that the Country party could not hope ever to be a majority party itself; it would have to function as a pressure group and gain office through coalition—by coalition with whom but the Nationalists from whose womb it had issued? The politics of the situation was for the Country party to bide its time until it was possible to "dump" Hughes at a moment when the Nationalists had to share the cabinet posts with it to retain office themselves. That time came right after the 1922 election.

Hughes had to survive after the 1919 election on the basis of the Nationalist parliamentary membership, riddled though it was by disaffection. He might have succeeded in maintaining himself had he not had a run of bad luck not wholly self-induced. He had to absorb the postwar slump of 1921. While continuing to identify with reasonable assurance the persistent issues of the between-wars period, he no longer had a sure touch in policy with regard to them and was unable to get credit of political use even when he was essentially right. Failure to carry the referendum while simultaneously winning the election was bad luck rather characteristic of Australian politics, but failure to bring off the promised constitutional convention was a new variety of failure in constitutional affairs. The only break Hughes got in the constitutional field was a shift in the High Court's outlook toward a very kindly view of the scope of Commonwealth powers under the constitution. His emphasis on conciliation in labor relations was not the answer, for unrest continued; by persisting in it he drove the vastly prestigious Mr. Justice Higgins to resign from the court. His Royal Commission on the basic wage showed that the wage—as calculated on Justice Higgins' old principles—even when the housewife utilized every device of economy, clever and shabby, should be far higher than it currently was. This was politically embarrassing to Hughes, for it was impossible in the inflationary situation then existing to raise the wage and close the gap disclosed.

"War socialism" for which Hughes took great credit and regarded as a model for peacetime policy came under heavy attack, especially from the very farmers alleged by Hughes's friends to have profited substantially from it, and this occurred before it was entirely clear that the same farmers were going to plump for a kind of producer syndicalism (called by Labor "farmer socialism") to improve their position in a disappointing market. Thus in effect they enjoyed the fun of attacking Hughes's position while preparing to accept a comparable approach. And his effort to devise a new approach to socialism by arranging government collaboration with private enterprise in capitalization and top management displeased both sides, the conservatives because it took the government deeper into "trading," Labor because the capitalists were in it. His protectionist position gave him no personal prestige; the position was common to too many of the politicians of varying party allegiance. His support of immigration and an active development program did him no good, since it could be alleged that these were conservative positions he took up for protective coloration. He favored the building of Canberra as the national capital, but there was no political profit for anybody in the enterprise—too many believed that it symbolized the irrelevant absurdity of overambitious politicians, not maturing nationhood. He started a trend toward seeking the advice of experts, but nobody believed that Hughes would follow expert advice if it contradicted his own opinion.

Even Labor's lurch further to the left was of more use to his enemies than to him. He could not even put together a strong cabinet or conduct an efficient, economical administration. Not only did his disposition to play a lone hand make cooperation with him difficult and promote administrative insecurity, but the Nationalist parliamentary group was not rich in human resources for cabinet posts. The indispensable Pearce was still at hand, but cabinet changes became numerous—even Pearce was shifted around—and strength eluded. The most hopeful recruit was Stanley Melbourne Bruce who had come into Parliament in 1918 in place of Sir William Irvine on his translation to the Supreme Court of Victoria. Bruce, it appeared, was a man of strength and destiny. In 1921 Hughes made him treasurer in place of Sir Joseph Cook, who went off to London to be high commissioner. Bruce went into the election of 1922 as a Hughes loyalist.

It was macabre that Bruce should carefully make the point during his campaign that he was a Hughes loyalist, because when the showdown came after the election he profited from the negotiations to oust Hughes from the prime ministership and finally became his successor in the office. The election produced a House in which no party had the numbers to support a government by itself. There were thirty Labor members, twenty-eight Nationalists, fourteen Country party members, two Liberals, and one independent. In the Senate the position was twelve Labor, twenty-three Nationalist, one Country party. Only by coalition in the House could a government be formed. The Liberals would unquestionably vote with (and eventually join) the Nationalists, but this strength was unimportant unless the Country party was disposed to team up with the Nationalists. That party made it clear it would not "play" if Hughes continued as prime minister. Its leader now, its principal ideologist and a very ruthless politician, was Dr. Earle Page, native-born Australian of New South Wales, educated at Sydney University, a surgeon by profession, who had served in the A.I.F. Page was aggressive in his attempt to eliminate Hughes. The aim was not peculiar to him and his party; it was also the aim of the Liberals, of whom the strongest, J. G. Latham of Victoria, sometime member of Hughes's staff at the Peace Conference, had come into politics to achieve precisely his elimination. He closely collaborated with Page to that end. (Latham was a native-born Australian, educated M.A. and LL.M. at Melbourne University.) There were also the anti-Hughes Nationalists who were glad to be spectators of a regicide by party outsiders.

The pressure was against Hughes in favor of Bruce, for he was acceptable to Page as a political collaborator. Bruce was thus jockeyed into the invidious position of having to tolerate the elimination of the man to whom he had just lately ostentatiously declared his loyalty. Page undoubtedly perceived that if he could thus alienate Hughes from Bruce and vice versa, this would intensify the isolation of Hughes from political influence. Essentially, that is how it worked out. Hughes soon saw the jig was up; he resigned on February 9, 1923, never to be prime minister again, even though he had thirty years in politics still to go. He advised the governor-general to send for Bruce. There then came into existence the Bruce-Page government which stayed in office continuously until 1929. Hughes retired to a back bench as a private Nationalist member, a "dangerous political Cerberus," bidding his time until a sop to his injured feelings should come to hand. It came.

The Nationalist party, senior in the coalition as it ever subsequently remained, was a lineal descendent of the "fusion" Deakin and Cook had arranged in 1909 to counter Labor's mounting strength. Its history to this time was a section of the curious story of liberal-conservative collaboration in Australian politics. It had already with a change of name been able to absorb Hughes and his National Labor following at the price of conceding the leadership to an ex-Labor man, a tactic of survival it was to repeat. It was at the moment strong enough to depose this anomalous leader; it was not strong enough to form a government unassisted. By fusion it had been born, by fusion it had recaptured office after having been defeated by Labor, but now office was attainable only by coalition, a very different thing. It was at last up against an organized political minority which it was impossible to absorb. For decades into the future the Nationalists—under whatever name they chose to function—were to have to deal with the Country party as a symbiotic but indigestible associate, rather more stable organizationally than they were. And this in spite of the fact that the Country party was simply a hiving off of rural conservatives from the general body of conservative supporters of the Nationalists, an unwonted consequence of the realization of the colonial dream of establishing a "sturdy yoemanry" on the Australian land. As an indispensable minority led by tough bargainers, the Country party proved able to command more than its proportionate share of seats in the cabinet and thus to have a heavier influence on public policy than otherwise was attainable. Not that the Country party could ever impose its ideology in its successive formulations, but it certainly achieved great influence behind the scenes and hence in detail impossible as yet to describe. In dealing with Bruce, Earle Page exacted five cabinet posts, including the treasury for himself, and left Bruce six and the prime ministership. In proportion to its seats in the House, the Country party had title to no more than three cabinet posts.

CHAPTER III

Insecurity, Uncertainty, Depression

Stanley Melbourne Bruce was forty years old when he became prime minister (born 1883), but he already had a physical ripeness and a mature manner. His presence was impressive, he had dignity, and he was friendly though a trifle remote. A native of Melbourne, his family was well-to-do, identified with the importing business. An updated version of colonial politicians of the order of James Service, he appears to have had no affinity with Alfred Deakin, the paragon of the Victorian Liberals. He was a conservative. A graduate of the Church of England Grammar School of Victoria, a cachet of social position, and from Cambridge in England, he had been called to the English bar. In the war he had served in the British army, not the A.I.F., first with the Worcester Regiment at Gallipoli, where he had been severely wounded, and then with the Royal Fusiliers in France, where he had been wounded again. Invalided out in 1917, he had been awarded both the British Military Cross and the Croix de Guerre. He returned to Australia to enter politics the next year. Colonial-born, his patina was English; he was obviously less Australian than his immigrant predecessor Hughes and his associate Page. So decidedly English was his patina that he easily irritated the "dinkum Australians," to whom any suggestion of the English toff was offensive. He was not popular, and he was never allowed to forget that he had once appeared in the House wearing, of all un-Australian things, spats!

The most cultivated, best-educated, Australian politician of his time, he could quickly master the intricacies of "problems," but his tactical grasp of the politics of situations was unsure and his strategical conceptions vague. He was a man of intelligence, but did not give the impression of "brains," as did his associate J. G. Latham. It is doubtful that he had any clear conception of the predicament of the Australian nation in the 1920's. He certainly did not see how to deal successfully with the predicament in which he found himself. Like the comparable politicians of the other democratic countries, he was a prisoner of his time. Bruce's later career was in the service of Australia in England and then of England in England. After World War II he became Viscount Bruce of Melbourne. By title and disposition he maintained an attachment to his natal land.

In the phrase of a later prime minister, Bruce was a king's man. Like his economic orientation, his political outlook was "colonial"; he was less nationalist-colonial than was William Morris Hughes, but, as became a time of peace, less stridently imperialist also. Like his opposite numbers in New Zealand, Bruce was little disposed to argue points of foreign policy, but was prepared to be critical about economic policy. In order of importance, Bruce's foreign policy was based on maintenance of the unity of the British Empire, which in practice meant that Australia would, after consultation, follow the British foreign political line; the achievement and maintenance of close friendship between the British and the Americans, both tasks to be left to the British with no particular Australian participation; and support of the League of Nations conceived of as a complement to a strong British Empire, again as to line in close conformity to British policy in League affairs. Under Bruce Australian nationalism was in abeyance, as though a casualty of the war or a victim of the prevailing conception of Australia's international position. Under Bruce Australia was neither repelled by Chanak, which emphasized dominion responsibility for London policy, nor heartened by Locarno which contracted the dominions out of responsibility. The country's position in the Pacific was generally defined by the treaties which emerged from the Washington Conference of 1921–22, at which Australia had been represented by Sir George Pearce. These arrangements left Australia fairly complacent, though there was a continuing undercurrent of suspicion about Japanese purposes especially because of Japan's near approach to Australia as mandatory of the Micronesian islands.

At the Imperial Conference of 1921 Mr. Hughes had put up a stiff fight for the renewal of the Anglo-Japanese alliance (which the Washington treaties superceded), chiefly on the grounds that it suited Australia for Britain to have a presumably moderating influence on the Japanese policy. He fiercely resisted the Canadian-sponsored United States position that the alliance be dropped as implicitly hostile to her. Hughes with characteristic recklessness did not hesitate to affront the Canadians by alleging that they were responding to pressure from the anti-British forces in the United States, as if Hughes knew anything in particular about the meaning of American opinion.

However, Australia's position in the Pacific was rarely disentangled, even for purposes of discussion, from her position as a British country on the outer marches of the Empire whose ultimate defense was seen as dependent upon British seapower. It was, for example, not considered that Australia could better her position by any special relation with the United States, and all moves made in that direction came to nothing. The prevailing opinion was that in her exposed position in the Pacific, she must depend at any time of crisis upon British assistance, which would be forthcoming, and would be decisive. Hence the conservatives of Australia were persistently keen about the development of the Singapore base, though unlike the New Zealanders, they contributed no money toward building it. Rather, the Australians continued to maintain their national navy and compulsory military training, while keeping the permanent army small. In essence there was little shift from the prewar position. Australia did not develop foreign relations at this stage. Her external relations were imperial relations, and to keep close to Britain was the operative idea.

Unlike the exuberant Hughes, who was profoundly irritated by the British failure to fortify the 1919 position by developing a satisfactory machinery of "consultation" with the dominions on foreign policy questions, Bruce's quieter reaction in 1924 was to send a "liaison officer" —it was Richard Gardiner Casey—to London as his personal representative in matters of foreign policy, with a view to getting closer to the Foreign Office. His position was that discussions with London about such matters should take place behind the scenes, not in public (hence little is known about them). No effort was made to use the League of Nations as a forum for the expression of independent political views. In the discussions of the status of the British dominions that marked the 1920's, Australia took her stand essentially on the status quo of 1919, but interposed no obstacle to the realization of the aims of the dominions differently disposed, however much she disapproved of those aims. When they were given legal form in the Statute of Westminster, she took no action to adopt the Statute, but arranged that its general application to her be blunted. It was General J. B. Hertzog's observation at the 1926 Imperial Conference, when he spearheaded the drive for a new definition of status, that Mr. Bruce, once he had voiced his strongly "loyal" imperialist sentiments, was prepared to take his cue from a British leader like Lord Birkinhead, who saw clearly what Hertzog was after and was prepared to go along. Hertzog saw Bruce as no help and no hindrance. Australian nationalism between the wars was predominantly economic in expression. Labor's economic nationalism was much stronger than that of the conservatives, isolationist in essence, symbolized by its consistent devotion to high tariffs. Politically, the conservatives confined their weak nationalism to domestic self-government, while with regard to imperial and foreign affairs they were imperialist-colonial. Labor, on the other hand, tried to combine an antiwar idealism with a nationalistic isolation in extra-Australian affairs. Culturally, the nationalistic impulse was weak in the 1920's but began to pick up strength in the 1930's.

The Bruce-Page era suffers in evaluation from its association with the Great Depression to which, ex post facto, it seems to have been the prelude. It is difficult to recover how it seemed to the leaders and followers of the time who, of course, had no prevision of the future. The essential item on the agenda was development, the persistent Australian national purpose. Since the Bruce-Page government was conservative, development was understood to be on the basis of the traditionally validated means of private enterprise with equally traditional assistance from the governments of the Commonwealth and the states, the focus on the land industries. The effort was to increase established and new types of production by using more intensively land hitherto only exploited extensively or hardly at all, some of which proved to be marginal, and by increasing productive efficiency on land already fairly intensively used. The idea and purpose of "closer settlement" ruled. The way forward was conceived to be a further development of the country as a producer of foodstuffs and raw materials, and, since the domestic market was small and fairly easily outrun, export markets were an essential factor in ultimate success.

The Australian purpose was complemented by an imperial purpose. The British imperialists had come out of the war convinced that the way to repair and eventually augment the Empire's strength, obviously eroded by war, was by the development of the imperial estate more or less on a closed Empire basis—meaning in practice Imperial assistance in filling the unoccupied (or lightly occupied) lands of countries like Australia with immigrants from Britain. Imperial capital was also to be made available to facilitate the establishment of the immigrants in their new situations. The immigrants were by policy to be directed onto the land, away from the cities and urban factory industries. It was no part of the imperial purpose to complicate the trading relations of the United Kingdom and the dominions and colonies, but rather to confirm the traditional nineteenth-century pattern as the British understood it. The Australian economy was, that is, to remain "colonial."

Bruce summed up his government's policy in three words, "Men,

Money, Markets"—plentiful assisted and self-moving immigration, ample capital imports, increasing commodity exports.

But general strategy was one thing and actual tactics another. It was impossible to ignore that the Bruce wing of the coalition represented urban interests, a significant fraction of which, like that assemblage of mine magnates associated with Collins House, Melbourne, and the steel-masters of Broken Hill Pty., also with headquarters in Melbourne, had a stake in domestic industrial development which it proposed to increase. The Page or Country party wing, on the other hand, was straight-forwardly rural in outlook. Political contention over policy was thus implicit between the two wings of the government. In practice each conceded something to the other, but instead of a lucid compromise based on a recognition of the fact that Australia should seek to develop industries as well as foodstuffs and raw materials, the compromise was something of a muddle. In large part the muddle was supported and intensified by the fact that the third word of Bruce's trio—"markets"—was impossible to translate creatively in practice. The result was that instead of an expanded viable economy, Australia achieved a "propped up" economy, superficially progressive and prosperous, but vulnerable.

It was attempting to carry out the Bruce-Page policy when the basic trend in Australia, as in all comparable countries, was—because of technological and scientific change—for rural pursuits to give employment to a diminishing proportion of the total population, though perhaps more workers numerically. As measured by percentage increases in numbers employed, Western Australia and Queensland made the greatest progress in farming. Within farming, protected industries such as dairying and sugar did better than staple industries such as wheat and wool. A "drift to the cities," or "from the land," or urbanization was an ineluctable consequence. The great capital cities continued to grow. By logic, employment should have been found for the additional urban workers in, for example, manufacturing. In Australia in the Bruce-Page era, in spite of the continuation of efforts to use tariffs and bounties to promote factory industry and the encouragement of English companies to invest in Australia, while the numbers employed in factories increased, the proportion of the total national work force so employed in the 1920's was only infirmly steady. Australian factory industry was not, therefore, expanding fast enough to perform its logical socio-economic function satisfactorily, even in New South Wales and Victoria, the states in which factory industry made most progress. The tertiary industries were more dynamic, but the persistence of substantial unemployment was a warning of maladjustment. It seems reasonable to suppose that one reason for this was the failure to perceive accurately the vital role of factory industry in Australia's current and future development. In Bruce's mind, apparently, factory development was merely a tactical factor in a campaign fundamentally intended to promote the rural industries. But even if he had favored the promotion of factory industry as a primary task, it is doubtful that he could have done so. The Country party was hostile to the cities and factory industries, regarding the drift to the cities as deriving from wrong-headed "urban" policies which were to be fulminated against and fought. The party might compromise its positions with its partner in office, but it was not prepared to abandon them.

Until 1925 it looked as though the broad strategy was absolutely correct and, given Australia's obvious national need for development, there is warrant for saying it was fundamentally correct, assuming a capacity for quick tactical shifts, straight through the piece, but after 1925 it was increasingly obvious that something was wrong, and within two years there were clear signs that a depression was at hand.

Men—immigrants, predominantly *British* immigrants since Australia was then at its most xenophobic and the Italian immigrants were virulently abused as "semi-coloured"—could be found, but unemployment persisted at about 10 per cent of the work force; during the Bruce-Page years the excess of arrivals over departures ran about 40,000, while in 1927 it exceeded 50,000. Capital could be obtained, but how it could best be used with certain economic justification was increasingly unclear to critical students. Australia was disadvantaged not so much because of mistaken domestic policies, though costs were patently too high, as by the weakness of the external markets, on which it was heavily dependent. Particularly, it was disadvantaged because of its heavy dependence on the United Kingdom market, a dependence which was lessening by the development of outlets in the East, notably Japan, but not fast enough and not in a fashion that inspired universal confidence in Australians who cherished their dependence on Britain.

During the 1920's the trend was toward higher and higher tariffs, the Country party resisting, Labor supporting the Nationalists, but a distinction was made between reasonable protection for industry and prohibition of imports. However, there was a difference of opinion over how exacting the government should be in demanding of protected industry a standard of efficiency high enough to "justify" protection, as measured by prices for domestically produced goods compared with identical imported goods. The tendency was for the domestic industries to be high cost and high price and hence vulnerable to imports unless heavily protected. The Country party spokesmen, practically the only passionate critics of tariff policy, believed that the high cost factory industries imposed a burden on rural industries which was especially embarrassing to them as exporters. There was unquestionably something in this, but instead of fighting it out on this line, and getting the problem of costs threshed out (as it never was), the rural producers eventually adopted the tactic of "protection all around," or the extension of the principle of protection to rural industries. While remaining antitariff they sought to balance the protection given the factory producers by protective devices designed to secure weak positions of their own. This inevitably allowed the development of "soft spots" in the rural economy, as the tariff had in the urban. As high costs in urban factory industry burdened the rural producers, so the protection of rural production forced urban costs to still higher levels, particularly as wages were automatically adjusted to a cost-of-living index.

Productivity was lower in manufacturing than in the land industries, and various other fundamental factors of the Australian situation unfavorable to the development of factory industry, such as the smallness and excessive scatter of the market, were pointed out. Overcapacity, costly to maintain, rather quickly developed; factory layout was often inexpert; finance and marketing were ill-understood. A case could unquestionably be made for the point of view that any decided shift of policy emphasis toward factory industry development was dubious. Whether all the obstacles identifiable were irremediable was another question, and whether Australia could hopefully go forward economically without factory industry development was still another. In price terms the consumer goods industries were doing much better than heavy industry and engineering, not a heartening situation if fundamental industrial progress was wanted.

The drift toward industrialization was, nevertheless, ineluctable, whether the problems were faced frontally or evaded. By the end of the 1920's a rationalization of it, at first in terms of factory industry's capacity to support population beyond what could be expected of land industries, began to be developed. And in spite of difficulties, it was clear that steel, for instance, was finding its feet. The steel industry, after the competition of imports had practically closed it down in 1922–23, resumed production in 1923. An intensive going-over to achieve technological efficiency helped make reopening feasible, but it was nevertheless finally supported by heavy protection against imports. From then on, however, there was steady progress in productive efficiency, in systematically gaining direct control of raw materials, and in the establishment, ordinarily in collaboration with British capital, of steel-using industries, the first of which was a "wire rope" works. A great horizontal and vertical "trust" was in the making. On the demand side, orders from governments bent on "Buying Australian" were fundamental—steel for the railways and for public works was more important than were orders from private enterprisers. The vigor of steel was nevertheless a major indicator of a probably secure future for Australian industrial development. It is characteristic of the situation that in 1928 it was thought feasible to establish a second steel works, at Port Kembla, known as Australian Iron & Steel Ltd., a mixed Australian and British venture— the old firm of Hoskins of Lithgow working with Baldwin's Ltd., and Dorman, Long of England.

The critical moment in the development of rural industry was when it could fully satisfy domestic demand for its product and had to export to sustain its position and expand further. The Australians were firmly convinced that their task was to produce; they were little disposed to limit production for any reason; the philosophy of "a little less" as applied to production (as distinguished from work) did not appeal. When production in any line exceeded domestic requirements, the tendency was not only to go on producing, but to go on expanding production. Because of this emphasis, there was small interest in critically examining industries with export surpluses in order to eliminate excessively high-cost marginal producers; the solution of the problem was sought at the marketing end. The objective was so to manipulate the market as to sustain the producers. Resort was usually had to schemes to control the flow of supplies onto the domestic market in order to maintain a "home consumption" price while forcing the rest of the production onto the export market where, inevitably, it fetched a lower price. By juggling the two ranges of returns the producers would, it was hoped, receive in the end a remunerative return for the total production. In effect this was to sustain producers by a tax on the Australian consumers. By one scheme or another this technique of survival in a difficult marketing situation during the 1920's was applied to dried fruits (chiefly produced under irrigation along the Murray River), butter (the chief producer being New South Wales), and sugar (almost wholly produced in Queensland). These industries had begun to develop exportable surpluses either immediately before or just after World War I.

However, the older and economically more important exporting land industries, while taking their chances in the free market, contributed very significantly to making this export subvention feasible. Some effort was made to increase returns to the wheat growers by developing producers' pools, most successfully in Western Australia, while the New South Wales government pioneered the cheaper technique of "bulk handling," as contrasted with the marketing of wheat in bags. The wool growers, whose exports were the most fundamentally important of all, returned to their tradition of marketing through competitive auctions once the accumulated wool stocks of the war period had been successfully marketed by the British Australian Wool Realization Association. In this they were encouraged by a "strong" world market for their product. Obviously, if prices for wool and wheat declined, Australia would be in serious trouble.

The trend of production in the agricultural and pastoral industries was upward. The production of wool rose from 663,000,000 pounds in 1923–24 to 938,000,000 in 1928–29. New South Wales continued to be the premier wool producing state by a wide margin, contributing around 40 percent of total production. While stations of huge acreages and large flocks continued to exist in dry western New South Wales and in western Queensland, most sheep were run on properties of 1000 to 5000 acres, and there was a strong bias in public policy, especially where the Labor party was influential, in favor of smaller production units, most effectively applied where stations were on land leased from the government. The wheat-sheep combination continued to be developed; it was most clearly dominant in the southwest of Western Australia. As the export trade in frozen lamb and mutton failed to grow, in contrast to the New Zealand experience, merino sheep continued overwhelmingly (90 per cent or better) the favored type. Increasing attention was given to pasture improvement where this was climatically feasible, but none of the menacing pests of the industry was mastered. In the middle 1920's, however, important steps were taken to bring science to bear on pastoral problems. Not only were new plants of foreign origin and domestic breeding brought into use, but the study of the missing "trace elements" in certain soils was initiated, leading off with the discovery of the significance of manganese in 1928.

The beef cattle industry, after 1921, became dependent on the domestic market, fortunately active, absorbing 85 per cent of production. After the price collapse in frozen beef in 1921, the British market declined, and while exports increased to Belgium and the East, they did not compensate for the losses. Beef as an export marked time indifferently in the 1920's.

In wheat farming progress was in terms of acreage planted, the introduction of new and more productive varieties, and mechanization of production, especially the increasingly wide use of tractors instead of horses. The farmers became dependent upon two basic imports, petrol and phosphate rock for fertilizer. There was a tendency toward larger cultivation units, with 1000 acres still a kind of accepted justifiable maximum for a farm. But unless the wheat grower was in a definitely marginal area (usually defined in terms of low and uncertain rainfall but also of soil deficiencies not yet thoroughly understood), his problem was more apt to be economic than agronomic (though scientific research had much to contribute even here), chiefly expressed as the debt load caused largely by inflated land values or high development costs. He was attempting to carry on an industry characterized by exceptional "risks," climatic and otherwise. It is indicative of the situation in which the wheat farmer found himself that his home and the towns that serviced him were markedly short of amenities.

For mining the 1920's were also a time of insecurities and uncertainties. The value of gold produced precipitately declined. The black coal industry lost its export trade, long important to it, not to be recovered for thirty years. It became dependent upon the domestic market, luckily improving. On the other hand, the fabulous brown coal deposits of Victoria, convenient to Melbourne, began to be successfully exploited for the production of electricity as the basic power resource for the state's various industries. General Sir John Monash, in his capacity of engineer, added new luster to his reputation in the Victorian development. New South Wales, the heavy industry state, was dependent for power on black coal. Iron ore production, based wholly on the domestic market, increased as the steel industry found its feet. But the price fluctuations of the international metal market, on which it was so very largely dependent, caused silver-lead production to follow an erratic course, while zinc did well only as long as the British Board of Trade was paying a higher than world market price for it.

Like the other industries, mining became a high-cost enterprise, in the opinion of students, with regard to labor, materials, and freight, and as in the other industries, but perhaps with more intensive attention, an effort was made to meet the situation by pursuit of technological progress, as at the mines of the great Broken Hill field. If times were tough, the dynamic ambition of the mine masters was not diminished. As the Broken Hill Pty. had moved from base metal mining into steel before the war, so the remaining mines of the field sought through collaborative action to fortify their positions as great capitalist companies utilizing both Australian and British money. From a headquarters at Collins House in Melbourne, led by men like the Ballieus and W. S. Robinson, the associated mines began in 1915 by purchasing and developing the complex of smelters at Port Pirie, South Australia, and then building works to treat or fabricate base metals at Risdon, Tasmania, where the island's relatively great resources of hydroelectric power could be tapped, and Port Kembla, on the south coast of New South Wales, proliferating specialist companies as they went. Through by-products of the operations they moved toward chemicals (eventually in collaboration with the British ICI) and, in the 1930's, went further afield into paper production from eucalyptus stock.

Thus if mining qua mining had a rather unhappy time in the 1920's, the mine masters were clearly on the road forward in Australia. They even added to their numbers and their bases, for it was in the 1920's that the struggle to develop the vastly rich mines at Mt. Isa in western Queensland—related to the derelict copper field of Cloncurry—was initiated. This eventually involved the American Guggenheims. While world market conditions were certain to continue determinative of the health of Australian mining, it was obvious by the 1920's that treatment and fabrication in Australia were also basic to its future.

Transportation, consistently a problem in Australia and an important component of the complex of high production costs, had a difficult time in the 1920's. The railways came under the competitive pressure of the automobile. By the end of the decade over half-a-million motor vehicles were in use, four-fifths of them passenger cars, and the country was well on its way to being one of the most intensively motorized countries of the world. American cars dominated the roads, fed largely by American-vended gasoline.

Extension of mileage of railways ceased to be the goal, though significant work was done, such as the completion of the north-south coastal line in Queensland, the completion of the line from Sydney to Broken Hill, and the building of a Commonwealth-owned line from Port Augusta to Alice Springs in the center of the continent. The railways absorbed capital at a faster rate than profitable traffic increased. But the great creative task, unification of the variously gauged state systems, was not seriously tackled, largely because of the provincialism of the states. In 1920 Mr. Hughes initiated a campaign for unification which led to a Royal Commission. Hughes's motivation was partly economic, partly concern for defense needs. However, neither Hughes nor his successor Bruce was able to get the states to implement any program. The state leaders lacked the continental vision, and the South Australians worked hard to "keep the 4' 8½" gauge as far from Adelaide" as they could. However, New South Wales and Queensland collaborated with the Commonwealth in building a standard gauge line into Brisbane that linked the Queensland capital with Sydney. As the 1920's wore on, losses on the state railways mounted and in the depression contributed heavily to unbalancing budgets. Efforts to deal with the situation often took the form of control of road-rail competition in favor of rails. Paradoxically, however, the governments were at the same time assisting the motorcar by improving the roads. In the 1920's the states

began to assume direct responsibility for principal arteries, leaving subsidiary roads to the localities, while the Commonwealth began in 1923
to make grants to the states for road building and maintenance. Funds
were found by licensing cars and taxing petrol.

Commercial aviation was begun in 1918 by flyers returned from
the war, but almost all the pioneer companies were short lived. To
regulate the activity a federal air navigaton act was passed in 1921, and
a Controller of Civil Aviation began to provide and equip airports,
designate who should serve defined routes, and provide mail contracts
and subsidies. Until 1926 an effort was made to keep the air services beyond the railheads, noncompetitive with the railways and confined
chiefly to the outback to shrink the enormous distances and the time
consumed by surface transportation. A rationalization of government interest was that commercial aviation contributed to defense by developing pilots, facilities, and knowledge of air conditions over routes useful in defense, an argument curiously analogous to the ancient British
argument for a strong mercantile marine. The pioneer lines were in
Western Australia from Geraldton north to Derby (1929), in Queensland from Charleville north across the railheads to Cloncurry (1922),
and cross-country from Sydney to Adelaide (1924). The Queensland
line, in which Hudson Fysh was the moving spirit, was named Queensland and Northern Territory Air Service, or Qantas, and was to develop
into the federal government's chosen instrument. After 1926 the rule
of noncompetitiveness with the railways was gradually abandoned. In
1929 Qantas was allowed into Brisbane, and a Perth-Adelaide line
parallel to the transcontinental railway was established. Australia was
one of the leading air-minded countries of the world.

Coastal and ocean shipping began in a burst of optimism founded
in the high freight rates of wartime and gradually subsided into un-
profitability. On the coastal services the rate of profit on shipping operations became trivial, and the companies survived only on the basis of
earnings on outside investments. By 1926 the British services to and from
Europe via Suez were in financial difficulties, and the Australian exporting interests had shipping high on their agenda of problems. The transpacific service was passing to the heavily subsidized American ship-
operators. W. M. Hughes's famous wartime government-owned shipping
service was put under an independent operating board by Bruce in 1923
and at maximum was successfully operating fifty-four steamers, but by
the middle 1920's it was unprofitable, and in 1928 was sold, a casualty
of the difficulties of the shipping industry as much as of the free-enter-
prise prejudice of the Bruce-Page government.

Like the "men" of Bruce's trinity, "money" was freely available during most of his administration. A contemporary referred to the government's "open-handedness." The incomes of the several governments rose as the economy and the population grew, and so did expenditures. More indicative of the kind of money available is the fact that large sums were borrowed, so large as to suggest to critics a reversion to the situation of the 1880's. A boom sustained by borrowed money developed. However, it was the aspiration of Earle Page, the federal treasurer, to reduce Commonwealth expenditures to the proportionate volume of the prewar period, for his bias was against big government. He was a proponent of that variety of decentralization favored by the rural-oriented politicians, especially of New South Wales, known as New States, a gambit that got nowhere in particular but served admirably over many years as a stick with which to beat the centralizing dogs, whether federal or state. Page's dependence for revenue was, paradoxically for him, primarily upon customs, secondarily upon income and excise taxes. His experiments in tax cutting, again paradoxically, chiefly involved the income tax, not the tariff. Page was considerably handicapped in his campaign to cut down federal spending by irreducible obligations such as the interest on debt, price increases, and the assumption, not always wisely, of new obligations.

Actually, Commonwealth expenditures which had been £16,000,000 in 1913–14 were £58,000,000 in 1920–21 and £78,000,000 in 1929–30, but in 1929 after six years of Page as treasurer, the proportionate distribution of expenditures was federal 35 per cent, state 54 per cent, and the small balance representing the spending of independent authorities and the underdeveloped local governments within the states. The states spent more than the Commonwealth by necessity, and they necessarily borrowed more because their responsibilities were money-eaters and the federal government at this stage was only marginally interested in proposing ways of helping with these burdens.

Development, through the core of federal policy, was in execution a state policy. The federal government's principal direct responsibility for development on the continent was with regard to Northern Territory. It remained, as by established tradition, both recalcitrant and enigmatic. Its secret, though apparently not utterly vacuous, eluded the politicians and the "practical" men alike, as it had since the early days. Feeble government, disastrous trade union policies, and continuing diagnostic failures of the policymakers compounded the difficulties of the Territory, inherently a problem area. There was, as ever, much talk of developing the North, a proportion of it hopelessly misguided, but little creative planning and less sound action.

The states spent money for development by buying up land, subdividing it and selling it off on terms for more intensive use to returned soldiers and immigrants, by extending irrigation works to bring land into use, by building railways and roads, by lending borrowed money at low rates, all—in the circumstances of the times—ways of making losses. Western Australia had an especially costly failure in land settlement. The failures were attributable to misjudgment of soils through failure to obtain or heed scientific advice, overcapitalization of the production units burdening the occupants with impossible loads of debt, fundamental inadaptability or undertraining of the settlers, failure of markets to develop, or several such factors in combination. Public works were overcapitalized primarily because of overoptimism about growth possibilities, but also because they were used to relieve unemployment, especially rife among the un- and semiskilled workers usable on them. (Responsibility for unemployment rested with the states.) State losses on "development" began to be embarrassing by the middle 1920's; budget deficits began to appear; the debt load was heavy. Between 1923 and 1929 the total debt of Australia rose from £923,000,000 to £1,093,000,000, showing a substantial increase every year. By 1929 the states owed about two-thirds of the total. Interest was running at £55,000,000 annually, and half of it was payable in London.

While the situation reflected a maldistribution of responsibilities and of financial capacity to meet responsibilities, as between the states and the federal government, historically arising from the effort to preserve the integrity of the old colonies in a federal structure, the nub of the problem was considered to be federal-state financial relations. This was taken to be the unanswered question of Australian federalism. The Bruce-Page government slowly moved toward a new effort at solution, Page as treasurer being the responsible agent. Oddly, in the light of his bias, his solution involved an augmentation of federal power. He consolidated a position that had been adumbrated in World War I, but he left a loose end to be tucked in later and he failed, naturally enough, to anticipate how another war would throw the system badly askew to the disadvantage of the states once more.

Essentially, what the Bruce-Page government proposed was to discontinue the established policy of making per capita grants of twenty-five shillings to the states, to take over the management of the accumulated state debts, and to make a federal contribution toward meeting the interest on them and a contribution toward a sinking fund to extinguish them, as the *quid pro quo* for the discontinued grant. Debt management was assigned to a National Debt Commission established in 1923. Additionally, the Commonwealth proposed a Loan Council composed of representatives of state and federal governments to pass annually on the total loan to be raised for their joint and several purposes and to allocate the agreed total among the governments. This would at once avoid competition among the governments in the money markets, currently rather embarrassing, solidify Australia's credit, and perhaps allow the disciplining of unthoughtful borrowers. All new debt would be handled by the National Debt Commission like old debt, but under a formula that made the Commonwealth responsible for half the annual contribution to the sinking fund. This was a major and on the whole sensible tidying up of a very untidy situation. The states, however, fought hard to retain their financial independence, none more persistently than New South Wales. The loose end not tucked in at this time was the matter of special federal compensatory grants to certain states claiming a disadvantageous impact of federalism, especially the tariff, upon them. The states involved were the "outer" states of Western Australia from 1910 and Tasmania from 1912. South Australia was shortly to be added (1929). This problem was settled later. Page began his campaign for changes in federal-state financial relations in 1923 and, by a process of adapting his proposals to meet objections and by coercion, carried it to a successful conclusion in 1929, even though it involved the considerable feat of obtaining a yes-vote for a validating constitutional amendment (105a) in a referendum.

But if Page brought borrowing and debt management under better governmental control, with a specially strong position for the Commonwealth government, he was also largely responsible for placing the Commonwealth Bank effectively outside government control. This step was taken in 1924. It was in harmony with the Bruce-Page policy of placing government enterprises in the hands of independent boards, as contrasted with Labor's preference for ministerial control. However, it is not clear that Page's primary objective was the "independence" of the Bank, though a Board to control it was set up. Rather, the obvious objective was so to reconstitute the Bank that current difficulties with regard to finance, domestic and international (that is, relations with London), could be dealt with better. The aim was to make the Bank a central bank. In harmony with this, the note issue was at long last to be transferred to it. But the legislation did not establish a central bank, for nobody then knew just how a central bank should be constituted under Australian conditions. Nevertheless, Page's legislation opened the way toward the development of central bank functions over the next twenty years. Fundamentally, however, the reconstituted Bank remained pro tem a state-owned trading bank, and in this form its attention was in 1925 specifically directed, under Country party pressure, to the provision of rural credits. Its relations with the private trading banks, less as a competitor than as a central bank, remained ambiguous and often difficult. What was perhaps marginal in Page's mind—its planned independence of the government—proved to be crucial, for instead of being close to the federal Treasury it was removed from it and in time of crisis proved to be hostile to it; this was a crippling obstacle to effectuating any Treasury initiative with regard to fiscal policy.

The Labor party was the opposition to the Bruce-Page regime, at minimum in the sense that it was the only available party to which voters could turn as an alternative to the coalition, at maximum as the exponent of a vision of a desirable social order different from that implicit in the Bruce-Page orientation. Labor was the inevitable recipient of "protest" votes; it was also the recipient of the "socialist" vote. However, what "socialism" meant to Commonwealth parliamentarians (or the state Labor politicians) was still unclear, and how it would influence their actions if elevated to office was also still unclear. In the political situation of Australia, the maximum oppositionist character of the Labor party was the basis of its formal version of itself and the source of its mystique, but its minimum oppositionist character was the most probable explanation of any Commonwealth electoral victory it might achieve.

While Labor was protractedly in opposition at the federal level, it had important political successes in the states. The state politicians tended to take on "protective coloration" suitable to the general atmosphere of their states. The three states in which Labor was strongest politically were Queensland, New South Wales, and Western Australia, while in Tasmania it was consolidating its power preliminary to a long run in office. Its fortunes in Victoria and South Australia were less exhilarating. In Queensland Labor was continuously in office during the Bruce-Page era, as it had been since 1915. The most vigorous Queensland Labor premier of the decade was E. G. Theodore (1919–25), who had been in Parliament since 1909. In New South Wales, while Labor did not develop a Queensland-like tenacity, it was in office under John Storey (1920–21), James Dooley (1921–22), and John Thomas Lang (1925–27). In Tasmania the successful Labor premier of the time was Joseph Aloysius Lyons (1923–28).

While all these men were reformers, their political colorations differed. Often they were personally hostile to one another, not least because of their differing interpretations of the Labor outlook. Theodore, for example, while known as Red Ted, emphasized "closer settlement," state marketing, irrigation, and small-scale mining, gave some attention to social services (unemployment insurance, 1923) and to changing the political machinery—he got the Queensland upper house abolished in

1922, the only man ever to succeed in gaining this ancient Labor objective. Essentially, he was conservative, biased toward the small capitalist and against the big capitalist. He dropped all but a few of the considerable array of "socialist" ventures in state trading, all of which were in any case peripheral to the economy, while he raised the rents of the holders of leases of government-owned land, thus illustrating Labor's bias against the Big Man. In Western Australia, under Philip Collier, who had succeeded to leadership at the time of the anticonscription breakup, Labor came to office in 1924 and remained in power until 1930, when the depression temporarily displaced it. Collier's regime was closely based on trade union support, but it was moderate in policy. He was consistently against any left extremism of objective or method. Similarly, Lyons' outlook was conservative, as became a man whose purpose was to manage intelligently the affairs of a rural state feeling itself at a disadvantage under the federal system and soliciting financial assistance from the federal authorities.

J. T. Lang, by contrast, was oriented toward the urban unionized working class, fittingly as Labor leader in the most important industrial state in the country. He concentrated in the 1920's on elaborating the social services and legislating innovations favored by the trade unionists, for example, the forty-four-hour week and compulsory unionism. He failed in his attempt to abolish the upper house. He showed characteristic Labor bias by increasing the land tax in an attempt to break up large estates and by establishing some state commodity industries of peripheral economic significance and some state financial institutions. Yet Lang was hostile to any party objective *he* regarded as extremist and to the communists. How these men behaved in the 1930's will emerge shortly and clearly illustrate their characters.

The general economic situation of the workers was reasonably favorable during the 1920's, their position organizationally was strong, but labor was restless and the Bruce-Page government had great difficulty with labor relations. Money wages went steadily upward from 1923 to 29, and real wages also rose, though not to the same extent as money wages and if correction was made for unemployment, less impressively still. Prices consistently went up faster than wages. The workers held that wages were always vainly chasing prices and that unemployment was all too common. While the number of unions declined, total union membership increased, from 700,000 in 1923 to 900,000 in 1929, at the latter date including 59 per cent of all male and 41 per cent of all female employees; 86 per cent of all members belonged to unions formally involved in the arbitration system. In 1927 a central organization of trade unions was formed, the Australian Council of Trade

Unions. It was not entirely inclusive, but it represented the majority of the principal unions. The workers believed that the Bruce-Page government was antilabor (as well as anti-Labor). The unionists regarded Bruce's attitude as strongly class-angled and oppressive, a reaction natural to minds dominated by the class-struggle outlook. During the period, between 70 and 80 per cent of all strikes were in mining, a very large proportion in the black coal mines of New South Wales. However, some of the most exasperating strikes were on the waterfront, in base metal mining, among the timber workers, and on the railways. Persistent unrest in the black coal industry in New South Wales supported the conclusion that New South Wales was the most turbulent state in the country. Yet with the coal fields removed from the picture, the conclusion is that however uneasy labor relations may have been, they were not, as measured by number of strikes—even in New South Wales—really bad. It is interesting that the communists have candidly admitted that they gave a lot of attention to the coal fields and to the Miners' Union in this period.

The Labor party had lurched to the left ideologically in 1921, impelled by news from Europe of revolution, including revolution in Russia, apparently indicating that the days of capitalism were numbered. However, the effective immediate influence leading to a new "objective" and a complementary statement of "methods" for the party was not communist but rather the position taken up by eclectic socialist intellectuals like R. S. Ross. What was central in Ross's mind was control of industry by the workers and of industry comprehensively by some kind of national economic council, parallel in position to the federal Parliament.

The movement for a redefinition of the party objective was initiated by E. J. Holloway of Victoria, who at the time stood close to the unions but who ended up a Commonwealth parliamentary politician and a member of Labor cabinets. Holloway turned to the unions for advice, which gave the radicals their chance. The union proposals were dealt with by the party at Brisbane in 1921 and caused a primary clash between the political moderates, of whom E. G. Theodore was the most effective, and the trade-union radicals. Theodore's line was that the proposed objective and the accompanying statement of methods was a mixture of I.W.W. and communist ideas, alien to Australia, and calculated—this was the nub of the matter—to drive voters away from the Labor party. Oddly, one clash that might have been expected did not eventuate—a clash between the Catholics, since the conscription purge even more important in the party than hitherto, and the leftists. It just happened that the Catholic politicians were at this time more Labor party than Catholic and hence at their least sensitive about ideological issues between the Church and the radical theorists. J. H. Scullin of Victoria, a devout Catholic, later to be a Labor prime minister, was an impassioned defender of the new objective and of the new methods.

The objective, finally accepted by conference twenty-two votes to ten, was: "The socialization of industry, production, distribution and exchange." It got more solid support from the delegates of the predominantly rural states than from states beginning to feel the impact of industrialization. New South Wales was solidly against it. The "methods," safeguarded by a declaration in favor of legal procedures, were: "Socialization of Industry by—The organization of workers along the lines of industry; The nationalization of banking and all principal industries; The municipalization of such services as can best be operated in limited areas; The government of nationalized industries by Boards upon which the workers in the industries and the community shall have representatives; The establishment of an elective Supreme Economic Council by all nationalized industries; The setting up of Labor research and Labor information bureaux and of Labor educational institutions, in which the workers shall be trained in the management of the nationalized industries." All this was to be done through Parliament and the trade unions. Then Maurice Blackburn of Victoria submitted an interpretative "declaration" which, though never incorporated into the platform, was accepted; it effectively reduced the head of steam the leftists had generated and indicated how the moderates could live with their new objective and "methods": "That the Australian Labor Party proposes collective ownership for the purpose of preventing exploitation and to whatever extent may be necessary for that purpose; that wherever private ownership is a means of exploitation it is opposed by the Party; but That the Party does not seek to abolish private property, even of an instrument of production, where such instrument is utilized by its owner in a socially useful manner without exploitation."

Even with the Blackburn tempering, the new objective and schedule of methods never achieved universal acceptance in the party, and at Canberra in 1927, while the objective, having acquired fetishistic significance, was retained, the methods were drastically restated: "Socialization of Industry by—The constitutional utilization of the Federal, State and Municipal Government Parliamentary and administrative machinery; The extension of the scope and powers of the Commonwealth Bank until complete control of banking is in the hands of the people; The organization and establishment of cooperative activities . . . ; The cultivation of Labor ideals and principles . . . ; The setting up of Labor research and . . . information bureaux and . . . educational institutions;

Progressive enactment of reform as defined in the Labor Platform . . ."

Thus, within six years of reaching their farthest left, the Labor politicians decided to play down the threat of nationalizing the "principal industries," the organization of unions on industry lines, and worker participation in industry management. They reverted to the reform of the social order, de-emphasized socialism, and toyed with the idea that "banking" was *the* key to social change. Nationalization of banking had been in the platform since 1919, but now it was given greater pride of place. However, Labor still professed to be socialist, at least on state occasions, and an important consequence of its highly generalized propaganda for socialism was the wide diffusion of a fairly malign version of capitalism as a conspiratorial racket and of capitalists as profiteering racketeers. The contemporaneous capitalists did a remarkably feeble job of projecting any different image of themselves. The maintenance of the "fiction" that it was socialist deflected Labor's attention from the crucial point that in office it would have to manage a capitalist society and would have to understand capitalism if it was to achieve even its marginal ends. In spite of pious gestures toward research and education, Labor steadily failed to do its homework on these lines. This had disastrous political consequences. One cause of the failure was Labor's suspicion of intellectuals.

Just as the Labor party swung left, the communists were struggling to their feet organizationally. The first move to form a party was made in 1920 by the Australian Socialist party, a sect and not a party, when it called a conference on the matter in Sydney. Aside from its own following the participants were leftist trade unionists closely associated with the contemporaneous One Big Union movement inspired by the I.W.W. The conference resolved on the formation of a Communist party, but the Socialists soon balked at terms and conditions unfavorable to them, and as a result two parties appeared, one composed of Socialists and the other of the O.B.U. crowd and the I.W.W. remnants. In 1921 the Communist International, with which both parties were in touch, ordered unity, and this was achieved the next year, but at the expense of the loss of most of the Socialists and all of the true-believing I.W.W. But even after this purge of dissidents the party had not achieved internal harmony. The leadership was heterodox about organization and tactics. Orthodoxy raised its head; orthodoxy was slavish subservience to the positions of Moscow. Not until 1931 did the orthodox group triumph. Then a thoroughly Stalinist party emerged. The Comintern agent who directed the Stalinization of the party was an American known to Australians as Herbert Moore, his real name being Harry M. Wicks. The principal figure in the party thereafter was Laurence Louis Sharkey.

In the early stages of its career the Communist party wanted to join the New South Wales Labor party—communism was then largely a Sydney phenomenon—but as a distinct organization to be permitted to carry on its self-determined activities. It was so accepted early in 1923 by the casting vote of the chairman of the conference. J. T. Lang immediately launched an anticommunist campaign and before the end of the year had the communists out of the party. This action was confirmed federally, and the communists never got back as a party, though they continued to penetrate the trade unions, the traditional stamping grounds of the dissident left in Australia, and through the trade unions they found their way close to and into the governing apparatus of the Labor party.

The Bruce-Page government approached labor relations through the arbitration courts. By 1923 the court system had become enormously complex, consisting as it did of a series of different set-ups in the states and the federal court. Inherently rather disorderly, the complexity was further disordered by the union practice of shopping around between state and federal courts in search of the award at the moment most favorable to it as to wages, hours, or conditions. While almost all the significant unions were registered with the courts and "accepted" them—only on the extreme left and the extreme right was there any anticourt sentiment— the unions generally asserted their right to strike including the right to strike against an award of a court. As they believed in the class-struggle version of labor-capitalist relations, the strike was their ultimate weapon either to enforce their will or resist the employer's (or the court's) will. As Bruce-Page saw it, the federal government's tasks were (1) to bring order into the system to eliminate conflicts between awards, state and federal, and (2) to discover and apply ways and means of disciplining strikers and strike leaders, with special attention to leaders given to injecting political elements into ostensibly economic strikes. The worst offenders in the latter respect were eventually identified as the communists; the classic case against the communists as holding views and promoting actions incompatible with the Australian system of labor relations was made by Attorney General J. G. Latham in 1926. One way and another these tasks occupied Mr. Bruce's attention from 1923 to 1929, but the critical years were 1926 and 1929.

Since the forum of decision about Bruce's proposals was the federal Parliament, the attitude of the Labor party was important, although the unions were Bruce's opponents in the country. Political Labor was generally unanimous in defense of the court system, but it was always divided on specific measures of reform proposed by Bruce, especially about schemes for making the federal or the state courts dominant in the system. Labor refused to follow the logic that acceptance of the courts meant abandonment of the strike weapon, no matter what precedents Bruce's legal officers might cite. Labor's position was that while some strikes might be questionable, most of them were "just" and that it was no business of the government's to determine which were which. Labor defended the right to strike. On disciplinary measures against strikes and strike leaders, Labor's position was that this clearly involved questions of civil liberties and as it took up a civil libertarian stand, it resisted the legislating of such measures and supported challenge of them in the courts. The courts sustained the labor position often but not always; it was in fighting such cases for labor that Dr. H. V. Evatt of New South Wales first came into prominence and J. T. Lang first revealed his strong opposition to federal pretentions. Labor made the argument that in seeking to deal severely with a minority of extremists, Bruce was jeopardizing the rights of the vast majority who were loyal to the courts. As to the communists, Labor rejected the position that they should be singled out for oppressive treatment. In part this was a reflection of Labor's civil libertarian view; in part a reflection of the view that the communists expressed a legitimate leftist criticism of the social order which, while not Labor's, should not be proscribed; and in part a reflection of Labor's position that the political party had no right to interfere in union affairs and how the unions handled the communists was strictly union business. (This illustrated a facet of the hopelessly ambiguous relation of the party and the unions, for if the party kept out of union affairs, the unions did not keep out of party affairs.) By and large, the positions assumed in the 1920's became the Labor orthodoxy of the ensuing decades.

Bruce began in 1923 by offering, more or less seriously, to reduce the jurisdiction of the federal court in favor of the state courts, but in 1926 he sought by constitutional referendum to lodge primary jurisdiction in the federal court and to reduce the state courts to the status of delegates of the federal authority. However, he confused the issue by also seeking in the same referendum to amend the constitution (1) to give the federal government full power to deal with "trusts and combinations . . . in restraint of trade, trade unions, and associations of employers . . ." and (2) to give it authority to protect the public interest in strikes jeopardizing an "essential service." This array of proposals, all calculated to increase the power of the federal government (which was, of course, a Labor party policy) provoked a wide array of reactions on both sides of the political fence. The referendum was defeated.

The defeat of the 1926 referendum solved nothing; it did not even indicate that the status quo was acceptable to the nation. At this time both the political and the economic situations were running against the Bruce-Page regime. This was reflected in the results of the 1928 general election when Labor bounded forward to thirty-one seats in the House, while the Nationalists fell back to thirty, the Country party sustained its position but, very significantly, two independents, both agrarian radicals, won seats. The agrarian radicals were chiefly concerned to register a confused protest against developments with regard to the tariff and the arbitration system, linked together in their minds and inimical to rural interests. At the same time discontent was mounting in the Nationalist camp both in Parliament, for a variety of reasons associated with the budget and proposals for new taxes, and outside, where the special interest pressure groups, enormously influential in Australian politics, were becoming increasingly arrogant in their antigovernment stands. At this time export prices (but not domestic prices) and profits were falling and unemployment was rising. Certain employers sought to mount a wage-cutting drive; an arbitration court ordered a wage cut in the timber industry. The timber workers struck against the award. Labor intensified its resistance to the deflationary moves. Bruce moved to apply and even extend his disciplinary measures against strikers. Ill-advisedly he also moved to suspend the prosecution of John Brown, a coal magnate, for locking out his miners to enforce a wage cut. He thus stood convicted of class-angled action.

It was in this variously disturbed situation that Bruce again moved to deal with the political hot potato handed to the Commonwealth government by Sir George Reid. In May 1929 Bruce delivered an ultimatum to the state premiers: either the states should hand over their powers with regard to labor relations legislation to the Commonwealth or the Commonwealth would withdraw from the field except for the maritime industries, to be treated as a special case. The premiers refused to hand over. Bruce then proposed a bill taking the federal government out of the field, except for the maritime industries, a reversal of his 1926 position. It passed.

Bruce's action provided his opponents with the opportunity to destroy him. The principal agent of his destruction turned out to be William Morris Hughes. Hughes was, of course, anxious for revenge; he was also a firm believer in the arbitration system and assumed the voters were also and would take Bruce's proposals as effectively ruining it. At the moment Hughes was not a member of the Nationalist party; he had recently been expelled for voting against Bruce on the John Brown case. Neither was he leader of any group of his own, but he counted on the Independents and certain of the Nationalist and Country party dissidents to follow his cue. To force Bruce out Hughes moved that the new act not be brought into force until it had been submitted to the judgment of the people either in a referendum or a general election. This motion was accepted by the House by a majority of one, and the speaker, Littleton Groom, refused to use his vote to produce a tie and thus defeat the motion. Bruce responded to the rebuff by resigning. A general election ensued. But if the occasion of Bruce's fall was arbitration, the cause of it was mounting discontent in the country. Nobody realized how deep the discontent was or how rapidly it was increasing. The election showed.

The election of 1929 was a great triumph for Labor; it won forty-six seats in the House. The Nationalists were reduced to fourteen seats with three irregulars additionally, the Country party had ten seats with one irregular, and there was one entirely independent member; the Nationalist-Country party coalition was broken; the anti-Labor forces were thus not only weak but disadvantageously fragmented. The election had indeed dealt harshly with the Nationalists who had not only dropped sixteen seats but also had suffered the unprecedented disaster of the defeat of their leader and prime minister, S. M. Bruce. Bruce was defeated by a Labor candidate, E. J. Holloway, only lately heavily fined for encouraging strikers. Four other Bruce-Page ministers also suffered defeat. By excluding W. M. Hughes and and other anti-Bruce survivors of the election from their ranks, the Nationalists had further reduced their strength. Leadership of the Nationalist rump passed to J. G. Latham. The Country party had shown a greater power of resistance to adverse pressure than the Nationalists. Earle Page continued as leader.

However, the Labor victory was sadly alloyed, and its period in office was destructive of party cohesion. The Senate had not had to go to the country and, victorious in the House, Labor was faced with a Senate in which it held but seven seats as against twenty-nine held by an implacably hostile opposition. This forecast a rough time for Labor legislation. Labor had been materially advantaged in its bid for the House by the general recognition that the economic situation was worsening, this supporting a heavy protest vote against the Bruce-Page government undoubtedly more important than the vote against its arbitration proposals, but once in office Labor was definitely disadvantaged by further and rapid economic deterioration with which it was ill-prepared to deal and which it was disposed to try to handle in ways that inspired fierce conservative opposition both in and outside Parliament. Labor thus profited in the short run and lost in the long run from economic developments. Its difficulties were compounded by the fact that there was no cluster of

Labor policies specifically designed for use in the situation in which it found itself. Not only was there no comprehensive established party orthodoxy to help insure the cohesiveness of the parliamentarians under pressure, but equally importantly the Labor leadership was in a poor position to establish, even in the minds of its own people, the legitimacy of the new policies it proposed, let alone in the minds of the people outside Parliament. The opposition was in a strong position to profit greatly from the apparent legitimacy of the policies its supporters, open or concealed, chose to promote. The great Labor victory thus occurred in an economic-political context certain to stimulate the fissiparous tendencies indigenous to the Labor party as it had already depressed and fragmented the opposition. But whereas Labor took the unprecedented depression-generated punishment in office, the conservatives had already taken it in an election. Therefore, as Labor disintegrated in office, the opposition consolidated its strength in the country. The result was that within two years Labor was turned out of office.

James Henry Scullin of Victoria became the Labor prime minister, the first since W. M. Hughes had left the party in 1916, fated to preside over a tragedy of almost Grecian lineaments. This gave him the appearance of weakness as leader which as a verdict upon him personally was strikingly unjust. Scullin (1876–1953) was born near Ballarat, Victoria, the son of a railway worker. He was the first native-born Labor prime minister. He was a Roman Catholic. Formally educated only through primary school, he had attended night school while working as a "shop assistant" and was additionally self-taught to an undefinable extent. He had active literary interests, especially in the Australian writers, and a keen interest in public finance from the "socialist" angle. His facility with words was great; he was extraordinarily articulate; his oratory commanded the admiration of even his political opponents. Converted to "socialism" by Tom Mann, Scullin joined the Labor party in 1903 and first tried to enter the federal Parliament in 1906, standing unsuccessfully against Alfred Deakin. In 1910, riding the Labor upsurge of that year, he won a seat which he retained until 1913. From 1906 to 1910 his principal occupation had been organizer for the Australian Workers' Union, but after his parliamentary experience he turned to journalism and became editor and part owner of the Ballarat *Echo,* an afternoon pro-Labor daily. He was an anticonscriptionist and pro-Irish during the war. His support of the radical party objective of 1921 was strong and, in the debate about it at Brisbane, perhaps crucial. Like the numerous other Roman Catholics in the Labor party at the time, he appears to have been able to ignore or suppress any sense of conflict between his Catholicism and his "socialism." In 1922 he returned to the federal

House, taking the seat just vacated by F. G. Tudor who had resigned as party parliamentary leader. Five years later Scullin was elected deputy leader to Matthew Charlton and on Charlton's retirement in 1928 became leader, with E. G. Theodore, who had entered the federal House from New South Wales in 1927, as his deputy. Within a year he led his party to victory.

What actually had happened to Australia economically was that the basic exports of the country, wool and wheat, had suffered precipitate price declines and at the same time it had become extremely difficult to borrow any more money in London. Thus, two principal props of the Australian economy had been shaken at once. The national income, a concept now widely publicized by the economists, declined by one-third over four years. For the wayfaring Australian the most immediately observable effect was a steep rise in unemployment to a probable maximum of 30 per cent and thus the placing of numerous people in a position where they were rapidly impoverished. At a higher level of awareness it was also noticeable that dangerously large deficits were occurring in the budgets of the states and the federal government, the former being proportionately and in money aggregates the more important—New South Wales being the worst offender. As the value of exports declined not only were the producers placed in financial jeopardy but the trade balance assumed a menacing shape, and this raised the complex question of foreign exchange. The vital importance of sound "sterling balances" in London to Australia's economic health was emphasized as never before. The Australian economy was suffering a sharp deflation which was hitting some people harder than others. The questions were how far this deflation would go—most guesses were wrong on the side of optimism—or should be allowed to go, what established economic positions should be defended or allowed to erode or be eroded by plan, and whether and how the deflation could or should be countered.

In the situation economic policy was obviously more than ordinarily the essence of politics. As the situation developed it was clear that economic policymaking in Australia was an exceedingly difficult business. This was so not only because of the differences in political complexion of the House and Senate but because of the existence of extra-parliamentary bodies capable of making policy decisions of fundamental importance— not to notice the bodies that could advocate policies with good hope of influencing the politicians and the extra-parliamentary bodies. During the two years of Labor government the significant extra-parliamentary policy-making bodies were the Commonwealth Bank, the Loan Council, the federal arbitration court, and the conference of state premiers. A very significant aspect of both the Loan Council and the conference of state premiers was that they included by right representatives of state governments of an anti-Labor political complexion. Of the bodies exerting influence but not in a position to make firm policy decisions, the most important were the trade unions, a close group of professional economists, and the private trading banks.

During its twenty-four months in office, the Labor government passed through four phases. It began by pushing the tariff sharply upward to cut down imports and, with a rather absurd disregard of the time factor and of the country's weakness as a producer of factory equipment, to revive existing industries and force into existence new industries to relieve unemployment. Further to relieve unemployment it cut off immigration: 9000 more people left Australia in 1930 than arrived. To the wheat farmers it proposed that they increase production as rapidly as possible —they responded by a vast increase in acreage planted—and that they market through a national pool that would save them the middleman's cut. The woolgrowers were offered—but refused—a similar pool. And Labor attempted to legislate a change in banking, not to nationalize it but to bring into existence a Reserve Bank of a shape useful in implementing the government's proposed use of credit to finance public expenditures, while also remodeling the Commonwealth Bank. It proposed a repertory of constitutional amendments of a centralizing import designed to facilitate the execution of Labor policy. Meanwhile, the depression was worsening.

Labor came up against the opposition of the Senate, an unreasoning political opposition which clearly showed that while the conservative Senators were largely bankrupt of ideas they were rich in a capacity to obstruct. They did not reject all Labor proposals, but they picked out for rejection those which savored of unorthodoxy and which were crucial to Labor's program. In effect, the Senate boxed Labor into the status quo, disregarding both the manifest inadequacies of the existing machinery of economic government, many of which conservatives had pinpointed earlier, and the equally manifest necessity for experimentation in policy under the unprecedented conditions. At the same time the Commonwealth Bank, under the leadership of Sir Robert Gibson, strongly supported by the Melbourne banks, taking its stand on the independence granted it in 1924, took a firm position which proved to be a hard-faced, traditionalist banker's orthodoxy hostile to Labor's ideas. It was early borne in on Labor's leaders that they had made a mistake in not taking Frank Anstey's advice to force an early double dissolution of the House and Senate, preferably on a banking question, in the expectation of being carried into power with a favorably disposed Senate in the ensuing election. It was now too late. The Laborites, particularly the trade unionists, felt too strongly that a Labor government in office was a more certain guarantee of protection against wage cutting and in favor of an inflationary policy than the possibility of a Labor government in power after the great gamble of an election in such disturbed times—a "bird in hand" argument.

Meanwhile, there was strong pressure on the governments through the Loan Council to balance their budgets, this argued to involve the cutting of salaries, wages, and social security benefits. Pressure to this end was exerted by Sir Otto Niemeyer of the Bank of England, in Australia to survey the financial position at the request of the federal government. The Commonwealth Bank complemented and reinforced the pressure and assumed the role of prime mover in the campaign for it. Orthodoxy, with which Labor's political opponents strongly identified themselves, was on the side of deflation. In the situation the pro-inflationist Laborites could not but regard Niemeyer as a British financial pirate waving the black flag of antiworker reaction.

In this unhappy situation Labor lurched into its next period. By great bad luck Mr. Scullin had to go to England to attend an Imperial Conference (and to defend successfully the selection of an Australian, Sir Isaac Isaacs, just lately made chief justice of the High Court, as governorgeneral), while Mr. Theodore had to retire as treasurer because of an accusation of corruption, alleged to have occurred in his Queensland days, now inopportunely and probably maliciously raised by his Queensland political opponents. The two strongest men were thus absent from government counsels at a critical time. Joseph A. Lyons, hitherto postmaster-general, was sent to the Treasury, while his rather weak Tasmanian associate, J. E. Fenton, became acting prime minister. Lyons' conservatism was plain; he was suspicious of Theodore as an experimentalist, anything to the left of him was anathema. Lyons and Fenton were quite unable to dominate the Labor caucus. Pressure in favor of inflation was playing upon it from the radical trade unionists, especially from the unionists of New South Wales, whose spokesman in caucus was John Beasley. Scullin was hostile to J. T. Lang, the New South Wales party boss, and Theodore was actually at odds with him on his home grounds. Overriding the objections of Lyons and Fenton—indeed the opposition of Scullin and Theodore also—caucus resolved in favor of a rather simplistic inflationary policy and also, on motion by Anstey, in favor of compelling the retention of maturing government securities by their holders. These resolutions gave notice that the rank-and-file Laborites saw in reflation *the* alternative to the conservatives' deflation —interpreted by Labor largely in terms of wage cuts—and had their eyes on the bondholders as villains of the piece. (The New South Wales radicals also defied Scullin at this time by engineering the appointment of H. V. Evatt and E. A. McTiernan of their state to the High Court.)

While Lyons was thus being alienated from the party, he performed his most radical act. He used his influence as treasurer in support of a campaign by the Bank of New South Wales in favor of raising the exchange rate. He did this in response to pressure from the farmers. The Commonwealth Bank, which had reluctantly seen Australia go off the gold standard in November 1929 after only four years "on" it, had dug in its heels on maintaining the par value of the Australian pound. Nevertheless, the situation was such that a black market in exchange had developed and the trading banks, in whose hands the matter was, were losing control of the regular market. Whether or not because of Lyons' help, the Bank of New South Wales won the argument. Exchange went to £A 130 = U.K. 100 in January 1931. This eased the situation of the exporting industries. At the same time the federal arbitration court cut the basic wage of that segment of the workers under its jurisdiction by 10 per cent, a triumph for the deflationists. In December 1931 the Commonwealth Bank took charge of exchange and established the rate as £A 125 to U.K. 100; when the United Kingdom went off gold in 1932 Australia immediately experienced material benefits. A favorable balance of trade was achieved. The exchange rate was continued.

At this juncture Scullin returned from England and a new act of the drama began. He decided to bring Theodore back into the cabinet: caucus agreed, even though he was not yet clear of the charge of corruption in Queensland. This completed the alienation of Lyons and his friends, for it appeared to signify Scullin's acceptance of inflation. Lyons left the party and went to sit with the opposition, where in due course he was joined by Fenton and three other right-wingers. The stage was then set for the so-called "battle of the plans" for easing Australia out of its crisis. The bottom of the depression had not yet been reached, but the situation was desperate enough to demand decisive action as the only alternative to collapse. Scullin himself was extremely uneasy about the apparent drift toward chaos, but whereas many Australians were being driven left by developments, Scullin himself was in search of a middle ground between the knowing-nothing right and the extremist inflationists of the left, a remarkable development in a man who only a decade before had been on the far left of his party. His emerging position, essentially a matter of placing country above party, was sure to alienate some of his supporters in the House and country and extremely unlikely to gain him any credit from his political opponents. The difficulty was to find a plan (a word widely but loosely used at the time) that was economically sound—in the light of current knowledge and understanding—and politically viable—the ignoring of party lines assumed.

Scullin first allowed Theodore to unfold his "plan." It was radical, in the context of its time and place, but a long way from reckless. Although it dealt with all aspects of the problem—policy in regard to bank credit was to be liberalized, interest rates on credits were to be reduced, a tax was to be levied on interest on government securities, the exchange rate was to be flexible under government control, etc.—but the politically fatal element was the proposal of a fiduciary currency issue of £18,000,-000 to be spent by the federal government on relief for wheat growers and state-initiated public works to absorb the unemployed. This was enough to brand the whole plan "inflationary." But as Theodore made plain, he had only turned to fiduciary currency after the Commonwealth Bank had refused cooperation in any alternative reflationary proposals. Theodore's plan was anything but viable. Labor was in no position to establish the legitimacy of the ideas it embodied. It was anathema to the Commonwealth Bank and the trading banks; it was rejected by a Premiers' Conference; implementation by the Senate was impossible to achieve.

Theodore's "plan" was seen in its earlier developmental phrases in contrast to the proposals of the orthodox deflationists. Suddenly, in February 1931 J. T. Lang of New South Wales injected a "plan" into the discussion which, if it did not make Theodore's look acceptable to the orthodox, did make it look a good deal less radical than formerly. In the final formulation of his plan Theodore was able to help himself by attacking Lang. Lang had recaptured the premiership of New South Wales late in 1930 from T. R. Bavin, an enthusiastic deflationist. His campaign position had been that no cuts should be made in wages and social security benefits, which meant implicitly that he was against deflationary budget balancing. His victory was attributable to a combination of two factors, tight control of the Labor machine, of which from 1927 he was effectively dictator, and his standpat attitude regarding wages. He was under strong pressure from the radical unionists to embrace straightout inflation and to "do something" about the exactions of the bondholders. An attack upon the bondholders was congenial to Lang, in his character as demagogue, in that his rationale of the depression was that it was a conspiratorial assault by the London bankers, the Australian bankers working hand-in-glove, upon the standard of living of the Australian working class. He kept his "plan" carefully under wraps until he dramatically unveiled it at a Premiers' Conference. It consisted of three points: that Australian governments should pay no more interest to British bondholders until the rate was reduced to 3 per cent; that interest on all domestic borrowings be reduced to 3 per cent; that a "goods standard" currency be set up for Australia. In the original presentation the British-held debt was alleged to be war debt which, in the light of Britain's arrangement about war debt with the United States, it was unjust that Australia be held to pay. This factually incorrect allegation about the nature of British-held Australian debt was made irrelevant when Britain offered Australia a moratorium on war debt in June, but the 3 per cent demand still stood. What Lang was saying was that he would not pare his budget, would not cut wages and other payments to individuals, would cut interest domestically, and would repudiate interest due in London to force a reduction to a rate of 3 per cent.

This was the most extreme radicalism at the government level during the depression. And Lang went through with his "plan." He repudiated in April, and, since the responsibility for payment then fell on the federal authorities, was promptly sued by them for the recovery of the money. There was a flight of capital from New South Wales. The New South Wales State Savings Bank, refused support by the Commonwealth Bank, suspended payment under pressure of a run. (It was eventually absorbed into the Commonwealth Savings Bank. The rural credits operations of the old state savings bank were set up as the Rural Bank of New South Wales. By the late 1940's this bank was strong enough to enter the general banking field.) The Lang state Labor party had in March been expelled from the federal Labor party on the issue of whether federal parliamentarians owed their final loyalty to federal caucus or to the state party directorate—in this case J. T. Lang. The motion of expulsion was made by John Curtin of Western Australia. A clutch of New South Wales Labor members of the federal House, loyal to Lang, then completed the break with the federal party by setting up a separate caucus under the leadership of John Beasley. As Lyons had taken away conservative federal Labor party people, so now Beasley took away the radicals of New South Wales.

Following up its established initiative in policymaking, the Loan Council about this time set up a committee of economists to devise a comprehensive plan for submission to a conference of premiers. The focus was to be the budgetary problem, but a wide latitude for suggested action was allowed. The economists were D. B. Copland, L. F. Giblin, L. G. Melville, and E. O. G. Shann. These men worked out a scheme which, after it had been debated by the assembled premiers and Mr. Scullin, took the following form: Focusing on the budget deficits, a reduction of one-fifth from the 1930 level was to be made in all adjustable government expenditure (except for invalid and old-age pensions which were to be reduced only one-eighth). Focusing on the burden of debt service (to which Lang had so dramatically directed attention), all internal government debt—external debt not being touched—was to be converted on the basis of a 22½ per cent reduction in the interest rate. Focusing on increasing government income, the sales tax (introduced in 1930) was to be raised to 6 per cent and primage on imports to 10 per cent. Focusing on bank policy, interest on advances and deposits was to be reduced, this being expected to loosen up credit and bring idle money into use. And focusing on the situation with regard to mortgages, "relief" was to be given by the states acting individually.

This "plan," dubbed the Premiers' Plan, Scullin and Theodore accepted. A great merit of it in their eyes was that a sacrifice was demanded of bondholders. They took the lead in implementing it, thus encouraging the states to act complementarily. Since they had been able to assure the Latham-Lyons opposition that conversion would be voluntary, not compulsory, its legislative support was guaranteed. A further conservative objection that the scheme was "the Lang Plan plus hypocrisy," voiced for example by R. G. Menzies of Victoria, was ignored. It was accepted that some of the parliamentary followers of Scullin would be alienated—their argument was that Labor should not implement a plan patently not its own but that of its political opponents—and that Beasley's group would be hostile. It was accepted, too, that the Labor party executive was extremely uneasy about the position Scullin had taken, particularly his acceptance of budget cuts involving wages and other payments to persons. It was, therefore, rather gratifying that in the critical voting on implementing measures but sixteen Labor members, including Lang Laborites, voted against, yet it was disquieting that the measures were only carried with the support of the Latham-Lyons opposition, for on the figures it meant that if the Lang Laborites ever voted solidly with the opposition on any issue, Labor would be defeated. Labor now held office, it seemed, only by grace of Lang Labor support. For several months Scullin clung to office on this basis until in November the Beasley forces engineered his defeat by a surprise parliamentary maneuver on the occasion of what appeared to be an innocuous debate over the distribution of employment on relief works in New South Wales. Beasley alleged that federal Labor, specifically Theodore, was manipulating such employment to Lang Labor's hurt. For the first time in history a Labor government of the Commonwealth was defeated by the votes of Labor members. The exploit brought Beasley the unlovely sobriquet of Stabber Jack.

There is a disposition among critical Australian writers to apply such words as "sterile" and "mean" to the cultural life of the 1920's but to emphasize a renewed vitality and creative expansiveness in the 1930's which led on through the war into the postwar period. A debilitating odor of complacency often mistaken for the sweet smell of success is alleged to have pervaded Australia in the 1920's, while the challenging disorders of the 1930's uncovered not only the inadequacies of the status quo but also energies which the complacent had ignored or resisted in the previous decade.

In his evaluation of Australian democracy published in 1921 Lord Bryce returned several times to the point that "intellectual interests play no great part in" the lives of the citizenry. In his own way and terms, D. H. Lawrence, who visited Australia in 1922, perceived this also and gave it characteristically vivid expression in letters and fiction. "Men of high scientific and literary attainments are found among physicians, journalists, engineers, and in the Universities," Bryce said, but, he added, they "take less part in public affairs than does the corresponding class in the United States, France, or Britain" and indeed "contribute less to the formation of a national opinion than was to be expected." Bryce found that the intelligentsia qua intelligentsia (though not necessarily as professional specialists) were still the marginal men they had always been. They themselves, and particularly the people of aesthetic interests, felt themselves isolated from Australian life and from one another, and many of them felt in the 1920's that the cultural life was, in a nationally appropriate image, "drought-stricken." The 1920's appeared to be the nadir of a downswing from a peak of cultural enthusiasm reached in the 1880's and 1890's, and they felt that few cared. In the middle of the 1920's the distinguished Australian-born explorer, Sir George Hubert Wilkins, recorded the verdict that "most Australians are well off in regard to creature comforts, and many of them soon reach independent means; yet the absence of the expressed desire for culture and for higher things, and their contentedness with the mediocre, make them perhaps the poorest rich people in the world today." In public interest and esteem, sport retained its predominance over the intellectual life in any of its phases, and swimmers, prize fighters, race horses, cricketers, and tennis players were the popular heroes.

In education, the feeling throughout the 1920's was that the pressing task was to consolidate the gains lately made, leaving the mass of the population educated to the primary level, but with the way open for the more energetic to achieve a high-school education. Essentially, this meant consolidating on the basis of the contributions of two remarkable directors of education, Frank Tate (1863–1939) of Victoria and Peter Board (1858–1945) of New South Wales. Both men had dealt and were still dealing creatively with public education in almost all its aspects: teacher training, the syllabus of pupil instruction, and the development of high and technical schools. All progress was made under a system of control centralized at a single point in each state, except for the separate parochial system of the Roman Catholics and the variously sponsored private schools at the grammar school level. This left education to a peculiar degree the concern of the schoolmen, not the parents, least of all the general public. While this approach equalized educational opportunity between city and bush and insured identical standards in all of the state's schools, the system was operated in an environment in which a school-leaving age of fourteen was accepted and the popular disposition was to regard the education obtained by the fourteenth year as enough. The high and even the technical schools rather than the universities tended to be seen as the top of the educational ladder which only a minority could aspire to reach. Any popular pressure pushing the level of expected formal educational achievement beyond the fourteen-year level was weak. This meant that high-school graduates were in effect an elite, and since only a minority of them went on to the universities, university graduates were a superelite. However, during the 1920's and through the 1930's the size of both elites steadily increased, though as late as 1937 Frank Tate was able to say that "the greatest hindrance to Australian education" was "too early admission into wage-earning occupations." "It is not unfair to point out, as one of the serious handicaps to Australian progress," he went on, "the fact that the greater proportion of our leaders in public life, in commerce, and in industry, have had little more than an elementary school education."

By the middle of the 1930's, however, the educators were abandoning their fixation on "consolidation" and were actively seeking ways and means of improving the system. It had been borne in on them that a changing Australia required a changed educational program. Simultaneously, they became aware that the proportion of public expenditures allotted to education was declining, a peculiarly discouraging indication of misunderstanding of the situation among the politicians. The cuts in the appropriations during the depression weighed heavily. In 1930, with funds supplied by the Carnegie Corporation of New York, an Australian Council of Educational Research was established in Melbourne with Frank Tate in charge. The Council examined current problems, surveyed the past, and projected a future, all of which tasks produced a flood of publications. In 1938, the New Educational Fellowship held a conference in Australia at which the views of educators from the United Kingdom, Europe, and the United States were fervently laid out for public inspection. Thus, by the end of the 1930's, the complacency of the 1920's was almost wholly dissolved and changes impended in both the high and technical schools.

As in the case of public-school education, the leaders in university education felt much better about their situation in the 1920's than they did in the 1930's. In these decades the universities grew in numbers of students, faculty, and coverage of subject matter. However, not until 1925, when Sydney established the post, did any Australian university feel it necessary to have a full-time vice-chancellor. The universities remained basically teaching, not research, institutions with little graduate education. There was more general approval and support of the schools for professional training than of the "arts" course. An extraordinarily high proportion of students were part-time. Degree hunting overwhelmed cultural adventure. Students proceeding beyond a first degree still almost invariably went to the United Kingdom for further higher education. The proportion of Australian-born personnel on instruction staffs progressively increased; chairs embracing several related subjects were broken up into their component parts; the place in the academic hierarchy of teachers of established but not traditional subjects was improved; and new fields ranging from anthropology to Japanese language and literature were introduced. In 1927 the first academic course in Australian history was given at Melbourne by Professor Ernest Scott (1867–1939). Melbourne also established the first university press; its first publication was, with symbolic appropriateness, a monograph on the white Australia policy. No new universities were established but two "university colleges" were set up, one at Canberra in 1929, associated with the University of Melbourne, the other at Armidale in New South Wales in 1938, associated with the University of Sydney.

As the 1930's wore on, the university leaders, like their associates in the state schools, began to recognize that the era when Australia could be run on elementary education was passing and that a high-school educated elite would not do either. To succeed, Australia also required a large contingent of university-educated people. Like comparable democracies, Australia not only had the problem of making all citizens literate but the problem of creating a successful society—for which it was obligatory to raise an ever-increasing proportion of the citizens to a first-degree standard. This would require not only the expenditure of more money on higher education but also the expansion of the instructional staff, the widening of the range of subject matter, and probably the founding of new universities.

In 1935 it became apparent also that something had to be done about the country's libraries. In that year, Ralph Munn, an American, and Ernest Pitt, an Australian, using funds supplied by the Carnegie Corporation, published a report on the Australian libraries which, while carefully giving credit where credit was due, generalized that: "In the widespread establishment of free public libraries as an essential part of the nation's educational plan, Australia ranks below most of the other English-speaking countries... Australia was better provided with local libraries in 1880 than it is today." While there were admittedly substantial general libraries and a few good specialist libraries, such as the Mitchell, particularly in Sydney, Melbourne, Canberra, and Adelaide, library systems were lacking, and no single general collection was, by the standards of the English-speaking world, distinguished. Where large and well-supported special purpose libraries might be assumed to exist, as at the universities, this was not so, for "no Australian university appears to regard the development of its library as ... a vital factor in its progress ..." This adverse verdict had the immediate consequence of stimulating Geoffrey C. Remington of Sydney to establish a Free Library Movement, a propaganda organization aiming at the establishment of a modern library system in New South Wales involving state and local government collaboration. Thus, at the outbreak of World War II, a forward movement as to the libraries was imminent.

Looking back, it is obvious that an important development between the wars was a gradual improvement of the position of specially informed persons. This is not to say that these socially indispensable persons immediately established themselves in impregnable positions, either personally or institutionally, least of all that they won easy acceptance either from the general public or the men of social power, but at least it is fairly clear that in the 1920's they began to say their several says with ever-increasing effectiveness. Resistance to them was sometimes discouragingly violent, but over the long pull they did surprisingly well. As a segment of the population they were increasing in numbers, probably a derivative effect of that high porportion of so-called "tertiary" occupations long characteristic of Australia, and they were keen to redeem themselves from the reproaches leveled at them by Lord Bryce.

A classic example of resistance and seeming rejection was the case of Griffith Taylor and his efforts at a scientific definition of the true character of the Australian continent in climatological terms. Based in the Commonwealth Bureau of Meteorology, Taylor had begun his studies as far back as 1908 and had published findings in 1911, but in the 1920's, when he was teaching at Sydney University, his work really began to make an impact on the public mind, and there was an angry resistance to it. Taylor's vision of the continent was in implicit contradiction to the ruling popular image of an entirely rich continent only awaiting man's exploitation to gush forth its lush bounties in support of a probable resident population of 100,000,000. He sought to cut Australia down to a more rational potential, and although his general conclusions won acceptance in informed circles, his reaction to public abuse was to go to North America in the late 1920's to continue his career as a geographer.

On the other hand the economists had a more exhilarating time. In 1924, a School of Commerce was established in the University of Melbourne with Douglas Berry Copland (1894—), a New Zealander in Australia from 1917, in charge. Copland was a man of immense assurance, with a marked bias in favor of the application of economics, as successively understood, to business and governmental affairs. In 1927 he was joined by L. F. Giblin (1872–1951), the English-educated son of a Tasmanian premier, a man of more diverse culture and more philosophical turn of mind, as first occupant of a newly endowed research chair in economics. Copland initiated a drive to improve the position and influence of economics and economists academically, in business, and in government. In 1925 an Economic Society of Australia and New Zealand was founded, and it sponsored a professional journal, *The Economic Record,* the first issue of which was published in November 1925. Copland's activities influenced all Australia (and New Zealand) and economics became the queen of social sciences. In business, the banks were the first to appoint staff economists; in government the states made use of economists before the federal government did so.

At the federal level the absorption of university-educated personnel directly into the regular public service was considerably impeded by the established prejudice against deliberately recruiting anything like an elite. The preference was for taking in new young people with minimum formal educational achievement and promoting from the ranks. After World War I the service was considerably diluted educationally by "soldier preference." Aside from scientific personnel, usually dealt with outside the regular public service rules, university-educated personnel in the service consisted almost wholly of ambitious ordinary recruits who obtained university degrees by attending courses part-time while holding down public service jobs. As to the politicians, they were, if professionally qualified at all, more apt to be lawyers than anything else. After Barton no Australian prime minister until Bruce was a B.A. graduate. Bruce was the first prime minister to take any marked interest in "experts"; he used them rather freely on special and royal commissions; but his selections were not always good and for political reasons he made very uneven use of their findings.

It was he, however, who first tried to get economists into the federal service, apparently on the theory that rough economic times were ahead.

In 1929 he had an act passed for a bureau of economic research. Labor opposed the legislation on the ground that if the economists were to find facts they would be duplicating the work of the statisticians and if they were to enunciate policy they would be intruders on the preserves of the politicians. On coming to power, Labor simply avoided implementing the act. As R. S. Ross said in 1930: "We, as a party, write no books, produce no pamphlets and set up no research—yet we think we can safely bring Australia through all the currents of action into the Eldorado." However, the economists established a strong position as consultants during the depression; they devised the Premier's Plan which, ironically, was eventually implemented by federal Labor. Following the return of the conservatives to power, economists began to infiltrate the public service via statistics, to serve the Commonwealth Bank, to man the Grants Commission, etc. Procedures for recruiting university-trained people—chiefly economists—were established in the 1930's. Discovering latent talent for public administration, economists rose rapidly to senior public service positions and after the war also appeared as diplomats, academic administrators, and even as candidates for the honorary post of elder statesman.

Whereas in economics the forward movement chiefly stemmed from Melbourne and eventually affected the whole country, the expert study of public affairs came most vigorously to life in Sydney to affect the whole nation. Unlike economics, however, the study of public questions was largely a collaboration of academics and laymen. An Australian Institute of Political Science was founded in Sydney in 1932 at the instance of a lawyer, R. W. G. Mackay (1903–60). In the next year it began a series of "summer schools"; from the papers delivered volumes were compiled that by 1939 had covered the constitution, economic planning, party politics, education, immigration, foreign policy, and the social services—a fair conspectus of the current interests of the intelligentsia. In 1935 the Institute became sponsor of *The Australian Quarterly* (No. 1, March 1929), a substantial and valuable journal of opinion of an even wider range of concerns, established and emergent.

Closely allied to the Institute's interest was public administration, the academic study of which was pioneered at the University of Sydney by F. A. Bland, who began to publish on his specialty in the early 1920's and continued to do so in the 1930's. Geoffrey C. Remington, a Sydney lawyer, associated with the Institute and a friend of Bland, took the initiative in getting the public servants to form branches of the British Institute of Public Administration, beginning in New South Wales in 1937 and spreading throughout the country. Its publication, *Public Administra-*

tion, began the same year. By inducing public servants to take a serious interest in the problems of their profession, it was possible considerably to upgrade the bureaucrats not only in their own eyes but in the eyes of the informed public. However, this did not resolve the paradox that while Australians rely heavily on the bureaucracy and ask a very great deal of it, they normally take a dim view of its size and quality.

The Political Science Institute's practice of issuing collections of papers by various hands covering a given subject was inherited, not initiated. The first volume of the kind appeared in Melbourne in 1920 under the editorship of Meredith Atkinson, appropriately dedicated to Lord Bryce. Atkinson justified his volume by observing that Australia had thus far made astonishingly few contributions to "sociological" literature. The practice was followed not only by the Institute but by the Australian Council of the Institute of Pacific Relations, founded in the 1920's. The strength of this organization was in Melbourne. It gave close attention to the problem of peopling Australia, publishing its results in books of multiple authorship. The IPR was later absorbed into the Australian Institute of International Affairs which, begun in Sydney in 1924, became a nation-wide organization in 1932 with its first chairman the New South Wales politician Sir T. R. Bavin. A characteristic "art form" of the IPR and the AIIA was the "data paper" prepared for use at international conferences instituted by the parent bodies; "data papers" were at once vehicles for information about Australian policies of international implications and for Australian thinking about international questions. In 1937 the AIIA launched a journal, *The Austral-Asiatic Bulletin,* the first periodical devoted to international affairs in Australian history.

These activities, evidence of considerable intellectual vigor, throve, insofar as they throve, on the collaboration of academics and laymen. (An aptly illustrative monument to what academic-lay intellectual collaboration could accomplish was a two-volume *Australian Encyclopedia,* published in Sydney in 1927.) Among the laymen, lawyers were conspicuous; among the academics, economists. The academics also included, appropriately enough, several whose particular preoccupation was or had been adult education, at the time most vigorous in New South Wales and Western Australia. There was a great deal of overlapping of active personnel, and the body of interested persons was really embarrassingly small. All in all, probably the most distinguished lay intellectual involved was F. W. Eggleston (1875–1954), who had been in Victorian politics and was to complete his career in the diplomatic service.

The home-staying intellectuals who engaged in these enterprises were heroes laboring in a fairly stony vineyard which many Australians were disposed to acknowledge barren and to abandon. The export of talent continued (balanced to an unknown extent by the import of talent from Britain). At the outbreak of World War II the impression was that the number of Australians in London was on the increase. A study of Australian Rhodes Scholars made at that time revealed that of those graduated by 1927 or earlier, 34 per cent had chosen to make careers outside Australia; and this was only a partial measure of the leakage, for it was also stated that "more than 200 graduates from one Australian university alone are more or less permanently settled in England . . ." The situation is further illuminated by the fact that after lauching the Australian Institute of Political Science, R. W. G. Mackay expatriated himself to London; that after producing the most influential interpretive study of Australia ever written by an Australian, W. K. Hancock left his professorship at Adelaide for a protracted period of expatriation in England; and that the cartoonist and etcher Will Dyson (1880–1938), returning to Australia after his triumphs in wartime London, comparable to Low's during World War II, finally gave Australia "away" and returned to London to end his days.

It should be kept in mind that Australian governments had for some years employed scientifically trained persons such as geologists, astronomers (who often doubled as meteorologists), and specialists in sciences relevant to the land industries, and that there were scientists in the universities from their establishment—of whom in this period perhaps the most distinguished was the physicist T. H. Laby (1880–1946) of Melbourne. In the 1920's the federal government put its scientific establishment on a sounder footing and fostered the research that was to become of central importance not only in Australian development but also with regard to the place of science and scientists in Australian life. During the war Mr. Hughes had in 1916 set up an Advisory Council to deal with science and industry questions; in 1920 this became the Institute of Science and Industry. In 1926, under the Bruce-Page regime, it was reconstituted as the Council for Scientific and Industrial Research, in which form it continued for two decades. On the industry side the emphasis was at first on agricultural and pastoral problems, the industries themselves often contributing funds in support of the work, but in 1937, conforming to the shift in the conception of Australia's future development, work on the problems of factory industry was begun.

Australian manufacturers proved slow to establish their own research facilities. While CSIR did not control all the scientific research in Australia, under the direction of Sir David Rivett (1885—) it came to dominate the activity both in its pure and applied aspects. It soon overshadowed the work in the universities—in spite of the strengthening it had had from the founding of the Australian National Research Council in 1919, and the private laboratories—to an extent that caused complaint and ill-feeling within the scientific community. Nevertheless, it did not do everything, not even when full account is taken of its cooperation with the other agencies. It did not obscure by collaboration the fundamental work in agriculture of the Waite Institute of South Australia (founded in 1925), or overshadow the work of the Walter and Eliza Hall Institute (founded in 1916) in Melbourne which shifted from clinical research to fundamental research in the medical sciences in 1923. Far from doing everything creditable or remarkable even in applied science, it was not wholly responsible for the feat most widely publicized overseas, the adventure in applied entomology that resulted in the clearance of the prickly pear pest from thousands of acres of useful land in Queensland and New South Wales.

There can be no question but that interest in serious Australian writing suffered from a downswing during the 1920's that gave literature the appearance of greater marginality than ever before. The volume of publications declined. No literary magazine was able to maintain publication for any extended period. Able men and women who had begun careers before the war continued their work but with a diminished *élan* as they grew older. New careers were opened. The literary lamp flickered badly, though it did not go out. A significant aspect of the situation was that most writers suffered from isolation from the fructifying literary currents running overseas, and to too many—confusing a proper concern with being Australian with a debilitating intellectual isolationism, the besetting sin of Australian intellectuals—this was a cause not of alarm but of congratulation. Too many writers valued the accumulated cultural capital, meager though it was, rather more highly than any imaginable new investment from overseas, as if they thought that literature was a static enterprise turning out a "made-in-Australia" product the form and content of which had long since been satisfactorily fixed. Those who recognized that the artist's task was perpetually to see and assess the world anew, recognizing that only to the sun is there nothing new under it— so that even "Australia" was a concept perpetually to be reexamined and reevaluated—got on with the job.

While no really significant literary career is to be identified with the 1920's, H. H. Richardson completed in it her trilogy *The Fortunes of Richard Mahoney,* the complex story of a life-fighting Protestant Irishman in Australia and England and the personal hell he was doomed to make, which she initiated in 1917, with a second volume in 1925, and a final volume in 1929. In the 1920's also, Katherine Susannah Prichard, a romantic realist, a flawed artist who saw man as a labor-cursed victim of social forces, was second only to Richardson among the novelists of her generation. She had begun publishing in 1915, producing such characteristic books as *Black Opal* (1921), *Working Bullocks* (1926), and her very best *Coonardoo* (1929). She continued on into the succeeding decades until defeated as her weakness for the didactic became a weakness for communist didacticism. It was in this decade that Brent of Bin Bin (long an impenetrable pseudonym, now known to be that of Miles Franklin) began to publish the volumes of a vast panorama of the squatting life, a full-throated paean to Australia, rooted, with personal variations, in the outlook of the 1890's—first with *Up the Country* (1928), and continuing with three more volumes in the 1930's and ending with three in the 1950's. Vance and Nettie Palmer in the 1920's settled down to a literary career under Australian conditions that was to become exemplary for its devotion to a cause. And it was then that the gentle, delicate, simply phrased lyricism of Shaw Neilson (1872–1942) found expression in books, a miniscule but unique contribution to the canon of Australian poetry.

Yet however viewed, the 1920's had the appearance of a time when literature was more than usually an eccentric concern. Few of the books here mentioned immediately won any considerable public in Australia itself. All except Neilson's poems were published in the United Kingdom. Richardson was an expatriate; Brent of Bin Bin had long been abroad (but was soon to return as Miles Franklin); Prichard spent most of her time in effective isolation in Western Australia; the Palmers moved restlessly about eastern Australia and to Europe, finally to settle in Melbourne; and only Neilson, an unskilled laborer by trade, was firmly rooted in Victoria.

The 1930's were different, not so much because of any change in the terms and conditions of the literary life as because more books of quality, begging the question of relative and ultimate merit, were published. Whatever it is that makes men write was actively at work. In the 1930's, Vance Palmer, who had been writing fiction for two decades, firmly established himself as a subtle analyst of character; Miles Franklin published a novel, *All That Swagger,* a "chunk" from Brent of Bin Bin's mine, the first brought out by her in Australia in over thirty years; Richardson and Prichard continued to produce, though with diminishing energy; and Norman Lindsay contributed a stream of characteristic novels, including his amusing account of boyhood, *Saturdee* (1933).

New writers also enlivened the literary scene: diversely talented women like Barnard Eldershaw (pseudonym for two women schoolteachers), who produced several novels pleasantly touched with irony, and Eleanor Dark who, beginning in 1932, produced five brilliantly written psychological studies of the moderately cultivated life on the coastal fringe. Kylie Tennant in 1938 burst upon the scene with a clever sociological novel of the Australian small town. There were expatriate, highly professional writers like Helen Simpson and Christina Stead. Gifted men, new and old to writing, contributed, including Leonard Mann and his loosely written character studies of urban types, Brian Penton (1904–51), a rousing political journalist, with two novels of the pioneers as brutalitarians, Frank Dalby Davidson, a stylist as Mann and Penton were not, bringing the animal story to perfection, Seaforth Mackenzie (1913–55), a most penetrating psychologist, Xavier Herbert who at the end of the decade provided *Capricornia* (1938), an undisciplined outpouring of energy picturing and scandalizing life in Northern Territory, and, barely noticed in Australia at the time, Patrick White in London offering the dour *Happy Valley* (1938).

There was also more significant poetry published in the 1930's than the 1920's. This was peculiarly the decade of William Baylebridge (1883–1942) and Furnley Maurice (1881–1942), while Robert Fitzgerald and Kenneth Slessor established themselves. It was the time, too, of the Jindyworobaks, a school of nationalistic poets who sought somehow to attach themselves to the aboriginal culture, or it to them, and to be as Australian as possible. Baylebridge, a solitary who confirmed his isolation by publishing his work privately and distributing it sparingly, was a poet of purpose who advanced an ideology which was astonishingly contrary to the unexamined assumptions of Australian democrats. Stylistically, he was syncretic and his syncretism was of unfashionable elements. Above all—to those who knew his work at all—he was controversial both qua poet and qua ideologist, and controversy, not all of it literary in substance, has pursued him down the decades. Only in the 1960's is his work to be openly published. Furnley Maurice in 1934 suddenly found himself (rather than grew into a manner) and published *Melbourne Odes,* modern in form and substance, enlivened by a sardonic humor common enough among Australians but uncommon in their poetry. Fitzgerald and Slessor were relics of a strange outburst of "normanlindsayism" guided by Lindsay's sons in the 1920's, basically an effort to establish that it was *the* philosophy of life and letters for Australia. In the end it failed even to satisfy its promoters. The younger Lindsays retired to London to become skilled literary carpenters and one, standing his erstwhile philosophy on its head, became a Marxist. Fitzgerald and Slessor settled down to pursue their own courses and to become distinctive and admirable poets, ornaments of their generation.

Most of the novelists wrote short stories, some wrote poetry, several wrote plays, and some did all four—Palmer and Prichard for example. Palmer was also a skilled essayist, an all-around man of letters, unique in Australia. The 1930's produced writers whose primary vehicle was the short story, such as Dal Stevens, Gavin Casey, and Peter Cowan. But whereas the short story throve, the drama did not. Louis Esson attempted to establish a theater for the Australian drama in Melbourne in the early 1920's; the effort failed after a few hectic seasons. So, too, Gregan McMahon's effort in Sydney to establish a repertory theater willing to do Australian plays also failed about the same time. By the middle 1920's the noncommercial theater appeared dead and the commercial living theater continued under heavy pressure from the movies. The commercial theater in the 1920's produced musical comedies and latter-day melodrama from London and New York, often played by mixed Australian, British, and American companies. The depression completed the wreck of the theater, not least because of a heavy tax levied on admissions, but phoenix-like, it rose again from the ashes in the 1940's. The point here is that the Australian drama got nowhere on the boards between the wars, and the theater was heavily under the shadow of the cinema (which was an import, mostly from Hollywood). In the 1920's, however, the Australians, always excellent dancers and stimulated by a tour by Pavlova, discovered that they were intensely interested in the ballet. The radio had but a slight impact on literature, but it had a strongly creative impact on music as a performing art. The diffusion of good music was a net gain for the nation, and while Sydney had had trouble keeping its symphony orchestra going and Melbourne's survived largely because of generous patronage by a department-store owner, the government radio proved to be a principal agent of a musical revival.

Among the painters there was a clash between tradition and experimentation which began to simmer about the time of World War I, rose to a boil in 1937, and continued into World War II. Tradition was the Australian version of impressionism, marked by a high reverence for academic drawing, carried on by a numerous company of epigoni of the "old masters"—Streeton and Lambert—of whom Elioth Gruner and Hans Heysen were in the 1920's and 1930's the most substantial. Painting embraced landscape, portraiture, and still life, all representational and rather obviously satirized as "look and put." The most distinguished pictorialist photographer of the time, Harold Cazneaux (1878–1953), was closely linked with the traditionalist painters.

The experimentalists exploited new ideas of both color and form, and while some had had direct experience of "modern" painting overseas, many received their impulse indirectly from color reproductions. In 1929

Basil Burdett was saying that "although not modern in the true sense of the word," the experimental painters "have differed sufficiently from the accepted [Australian] modes to appear so to many people." Burdett's reference was to such painters as Roland Wakelin (1887—) and Grace Cossington Smith, pioneers, and to John D. Moore (1898—), Kenneth Macqueen (1897—), and Margaret Preston. Wakelin and Smith were decorative painters, Moore and Macqueen landscapists, while Margaret Preston specialized in still life, particularly flower pieces of the indigenous flora, and pioneered the adaptation of aboriginal design. While the modernist note became progressively more obvious, particularly in the work of Melbourne painters to be noticed shortly, it was sufficiently muted in the painters just named to allow their ready assimilation to the Australian tradition, as can be illustrated by their acceptance by a principal collector of the traditionalists, Harold Herbert, as well as by the fierce antimodernist, Sir Lionel Lindsay. The Melbourne group was more aggressively modern, conspicuously George Bell (1878—) and Arnold Shore (1897—), painters and teachers of painters. From their studios in the late 1930's began to emerge younger men to whom the new mode was their fundamental art, notably Russell Drysdale (1912—), Albert Tucker (1914—), and Sidney Nolan (1917—). These men also learned much from color reproductions of the work of the overseas avant garde. In 1938 William Dobell (1899—) returned to Sydney from a long stay in England and was almost immediately recognized as the most accomplished modernist in the country. His specialty was portraiture. George Finey, the most brilliant caricaturist of the 1920's and 1930's, also responded to the modernist impulses.

The simmering controversy between the traditionalists, still unquestionably dominant but feeling themselves challenged, and the modernists erupted around two public events. Seeking to consolidate their position the traditionalists in 1937 enlisted R. G. Menzies, then Lyons' attorney-general, to spearhead a drive for a national academy which they would dominate to the effective definition of public taste. This brought the modernists out full cry. The battle was largely fought in the Melbourne newspapers with Sir Keith Murdoch's *Herald,* in politics impeccably conservative, of which Basil Burdett was art critic, supporting the modernist cause. When finally formed, the Academy, while weighted on the traditionalist side, also included some modernists. It by no means dominated the world of painting or the public taste.

Since the middle 1930's shows of "modern" painting had been percolating into Australia, though no comprehensive show had been undertaken. Indicative of the drift toward modern was the purchase of examples of post-impressionism by a bastion of traditionalism, the

National Gallery of Victoria: Degas and Cezanne in 1938, Van Gogh in 1939. Burdett and Murdoch followed in 1939 by staging a show, known as the *Herald* show, consisting of French and British pictures painted since 1880 which included works by Cezanne, Van Gogh, Gauguin, Leger, Modigliani, Matisse, Picasso, Braque, Dali, and others. The English section included works by Steer, Tonks, Sickert, John, Nash, Wadsworth, and Matthew Smith. The impact was tremendous and all in favor of the modernists. If the traditionalists still had oppositionist tricks in their bag, like a lawsuit against a prize-winning Dobell portrait which, they alleged, violated the terms of the bequest in that it was caricature not art, the door was nevertheless opened to the modernists, and they poured joyously through.

In the late 1930's there was a quickening of interest in the condition of the aborigines accompanied by a clearer realization of the complexities of the situation. As settlement had spread the aborigines, it will be recalled, were pushed aside and their numbers rapidly diminished. The colonial governments often took feeble steps to assist the survivors, but failure of anyone to find a satisfactory rationale of aboriginal adjustment to the new situations gave a sense of the hopelessness of the effort. The aborigines would, it was anticipated, gradually fade away. To some people this was a terrible tragedy, to others a grimly inevitable accompaniment to white man's progress, to others a "good thing." Hardest on the aborigines was the period from 1830 to 1890, when the geographical pattern of white settlement reached stability. The net effect was to leave the surviving aborigines, perhaps one-sixth of the number living on the continent in 1788, isolated from the great concentrations of European population on the sea coasts, on or beyond the outskirts of bush settlement. Out of the sight of most people, they were also out of mind of most.

Apart from the purblind great majority, there were at least three special-interest points of view about the "abos": those of the missionary, the "protector," and the anthropologist. The question of the aborigine was not as general a challenge to the Australians as the question of the Maori was to the New Zealanders. It was, rather, the concern of specialist minorities who, unluckily, did not see the problem in the same light. This made the making of government policy difficult. The missionaries and the protectors had been active practically from the earliest days, while the anthropologists with some claim to being modern in outlook only began to make an impact about 1870.

A keen intellectual interest in the aborigines had characterized such explorers as Flinders, Grey, and Eyre; Grey and Eyre had also had experience as protectors, but the intellectual interest had been decidedly quickened as modern anthropology developed after Darwin's ideas were circulated. Almost all the pioneer modern anthropologists of Europe and America were, for one reason or another, keenly interested in the Australian aborigines, notably Lewis H. Morgan and J. G. Fraser. Both addressed many questionnaires to Australian correspondents, the former to Lorimer Fison and, particularly, A. W. Howitt, the latter to Baldwin Spencer. Spencer himself used the questionnaire method in his relations with his "protector" collaborator, F. J. Gillen, who spent his time in the field in central Australia while Spencer was at his professorial post in Melbourne. Fison and Howitt produced a joint book, *Kamilaroi and Kurnai* as early as 1880 and Howitt his classic study, *The Native Tribes of Southeast Australia,* in 1904. Spencer and Gillen published their first joint book, *The Native Tribes of Central Australia,* in 1899.

Although modern anthropology as applied to the aborigines established itself early in Australia, no chair of anthropology was established in any Australian university until 1925, when A. R. Radcliffe-Brown, who had been studying the aborigines for over a decade, was appointed professor at Sydney University. A journal of anthropology, *Oceania,* was established five years later. A. P. Elkin, a successor of Radcliffe-Brown's at Sydney, published a most influential study of the aborigines in the late 1930's. In the 1930's the three principal interests were all quite strong, though it would appear that the protector interest, neither religious nor anthropological, was dominant, chiefly because the protectors were the principal executants of government policy in the states, upon which responsibility for aboriginal welfare chiefly rested. The federal government's concern was with the aborigines of Northern Territory.

In 1937 a formal conference of state and Commonwealth "aboriginal authorities"—mostly protectors—was held at Canberra, the first national conference at the government level ever held. From the discussions it clearly appeared that the aboriginal problem weighed more heavily on Queensland and Western Australia and on the Commonwealth because of its responsibility for Northern Territory, than on such states as South Australia, Victoria, and New South Wales. (Tasmania, of course, no longer had any aborigines.) With regard to full-blood myall, or wild, aborigines, most of them were to be found in the far north of the continent, in the Kimberley country of Western Australia, Arnhem Land of Northern Territory, and on Cape York in Queensland. It was also clear that the aboriginal problem was not single but several, and the several problems were complexly intertwined. There were the wild blacks, largely but not wholly removed from contact with white "civilization." There was the problem of the detribalized full bloods, usually closely associated with mixed bloods, who had traditionally been and still were the principal labor supply for the outback cattle stations, and who hung around the outskirts of the outback towns when out of employment. And there were the mixed bloods, mostly European-aboriginal mixtures, who were rapidly increasing in numbers and likely to continue to increase both by continued miscegenation and by marriage among themselves. Their status was very complicatedly ambiguous. All told there were upwards of 50,000 full bloods, of whom perhaps half were still living the traditional nomadic life, and perhaps 25,000 mixed bloods. At the conference it was the general disposition to favor the isolation on reserves of the still tribalized, nomadic full bloods, to concentrate upon improving the conditions and rewards of work of the detribalized blacks, and to propose that somehow the assimilation of the mixed bloods to the general population be managed. The problems of the detribalized full bloods and that of the mixed bloods were obviously socio-economic in character and to be handled by the protectors and the missionaries, but the problem of the still tribalized full bloods was different. The anthropologists, though not unanimous on the point, felt that protectors and missionaries were not the best people to deal with them, at least not until a much greater effort to study aboriginal life and culture had been made. While no state proposed to shrug off its responsibilities for the welfare of the aboriginal and part-aboriginal people, there was nevertheless a strong feeling that the Commonwealth should play a larger role in the work. The states simply couldn't find enough money to do what they thought should be done.

While it can thus be variously demonstrated that Australia by the outbreak of World War II had begun to move off an uncomfortable dead center toward which it had trended for forty years, as though deciding that while downhill was indubitably easier and nation building in its cultural aspects decidedly uphill work, it had nevertheless to be tackled, it was still very noticeable in the late 1930's that here was a country without a focus. It was rather a nation with six foci, among which Sydney and Melbourne jousted for first place, a nation acutely beset by regionalism to the point that foreigners often wondered whether there were any Australians or only Sydney-siders, Victorians, South Australians, Queenslanders, Tasmanians, and Western Australians. Most Australians, it seemed, knew little of Australia beyond their parishes, though they were reaching out: a popular commodity of the time was the book of internal travel, supplied by Ion Idriess, Frank Clune, *et al.* In spite of the fact that a favorite political gambit of the intellectuals was denunciation of the state parliaments as nests of bumbling mediocrities with parish pump outlooks—*écrasons l'infame!*—the people thought differently. As the results of referenda showed, most voters were against reducing state powers by increasing federal powers and deaf to the siren songs of the theorists, Labor or conservative, politician or academic, who expounded the thesis that federalism had failed and only a single parliament and bureaucracy could properly govern the land.

And, as a matter of fact, the only available national political focus was widely scorned, often by people who otherwise sought to aggrandize it. This was Canberra, the federal capital. In 1927, construction deplorably delayed by World War I and shortly to be delayed again by the Great Depression and World War II, Parliament was for the first time opened there, with appropriate ceremonies, by the Duke of York (later King George VI). But the bureaucracy, the real government of the country perhaps, was only very slowly transferred to the bush capital. During the depression angry disgruntled pessimists demanded that Canberra, seemingly remotely removed from all that mattered, be shut down for a hundred years. In 1939 the continental ideal it represented was still frustrate. During World War II federal Australia was in effect run from *three* cities: Melbourne, Sydney, and Canberra, the angles of a mystic triangle of which the significance was not universally apprehended.

CHAPTER IV

Into and Through World War II

While the Scullin government moved toward the acceptance of a moderate recovery program, the conservatives stirred themselves to mend their political fences in anticipation of regaining control of Commonwealth affairs. The key figure in the enterprise proved to be Joseph Aloysius Lyons. On leaving Labor, Lyons accused his old associates of favoring inflation, refusing to balance the federal budget, and seeking political control of banking. His positive program was to restore the public credit by balancing the budget through strict economy in public expenditures. This was enough to gain him the leadership of the urban conservatives, but it was hardly enough to fortify the conservative forces against their internal disagreements. It was indicative of probabilities that the Country party refused to cooperate with Lyons and his friends in creating a new conservative party.

To get control of the badly fragmented conservative forces—a fragmentation even worse outside Parliament than in—Lyons and his new-found associates began by forming an All for Australia League in Melbourne. J. G. Latham was authorized to negotiate with the League on behalf of the Nationalist parliamentarians. As a result, the League transformed itself into the United Australia party and on the absorption of the Nationalists into the party, Latham, in an unparalled gesture of self-abnegation, resigned all claims to party leadership in favor of Lyons, largely in recognition of the fact that while he was the abler man, he lacked the popular appeal that Lyons possessed. Assuming the leadership of the new party in Parliament, Lyons automatically became leader of the Opposition and immediately launched a no-confidence motion against Labor. It was defeated. The reconstituted and renamed conservatives than settled down to await Labor's inevitable demise, once more under the leadership of an ex-Labor man.

Joseph Aloysius Lyons (1879–1939) was the son of a Tasmanian farmer poor in health and circumstances. He was a Roman Catholic, the first to lead a non-Labor party in federal history. Lyons went to work at the age of twelve. Given a home by two of his aunts, he was sent to school and at the age of seventeen had qualified as an elementary school teacher and blossomed out as an educational reformer. In 1909 he quit teaching and entered politics as a Labor party man keenly interested in improving educational opportunity by the establishment of high schools. He held various cabinet posts, including that of treasurer in the Earle Labor government of 1914–16, but unlike his leader he was anti-conscriptionist and, on Earle's expulsion from the party, succeeded to the leadership. In 1923 he took office as premier, with his party a minority in the House, but proving a success as treasurer he gained a majority for Labor for the first time in Tasmanian history and continued in office until 1928, when his party was defeated. Lyons was a conservative Laborite chiefly interested in sound finance and the encouragement of the entrepreneurs of farming, mining, and that factory industry which was firmly based on Tasmanian natural resources.

In 1929, at the solicitation of J. H. Scullin, he stood for and won a seat in the federal House. Lyons' response to the pressures generated by the depression showed that his ideas were more strongly negative than positive in the support of a conservative course. As an innovator he seems early to have exhausted himself in the field of education. His Catholicism, which was devout, was plainly more devotional than a support of his political and economic positions. At no stage was he a man of ideas. His conventional negativism dominated his career on the anti-Labor side as shown in his general "don't rock the boat" policy, complemented by opportunist action to appease boat-rockers. To the conservatives he was a reconciling symbol of what was allegedly sound and sane. They exploited his personality, and when he had served his turn, they made his life difficult after the precedent established in dealing with their other ex-Labor leader, W. M. Hughes. The quintessence of Lyons' personality was a warm and kindly geniality. His appearance suggested the koala, and the cartoonists fully exploited the indeed uncanny resemblance—the koala, too, is lovable. His outstanding political talent was as a conciliator. This was the man whom Lionel Curtis hailed in 1938 as the only man in the world who ruled a continent.

In the election of 1931 the U.A.P. won thirty-seven seats in the House and held twenty-two in the Senate, the Country party took seventeen in the House and held four in the Senate, the Australian Labor party under Scullin won fourteen in the House and held eight in the Senate, Lang Labor took five in the House and held two in the Senate, and there were two independents in the House. Lyons negotiated for a coalition, but finding the Country party terms unacceptable, formed a government from his own followers. He became his own treasurer, appointed J. G. Latham attorney general, Sir George Pearce minister of Defence, J. E. Fenton postmaster-general, and S. M. Bruce, triumphantly returned to Parliament, a minister without portfolio. This illustrated both the very mixed heritage of the U.A.P. and the continuity on the right in spite of recurring disciplinary troubles.

The conservatives returned to office for a run of ten years, of which Lyons was to serve for eight as prime minister. In 1934 the U.A.P. lost seats in the House, thus requiring that a coalition be formed with the Country party. The election brought Robert Gordon Menzies of Victoria, a distinguished conservative lawyer who had had a meteoric rise in Victorian state politics, into the House on the U.A.P. side. He was immediately advanced to cabinet rank as attorney general in place of J. G. Latham, who had not stood for re-election. (Latham was appointed chief justice of the High Court in 1935.) The Lyons cabinet now began to exhibit great instability and the comings and goings of ministers became confusing even to the compilers of the official parliamentary handbook. Lyons not only took in new faces, he brought old faces back, including that of the durable William Morris Hughes. In 1935 he transferred the Treasury to Richard Gardiner Casey of Victoria, in Parliament since 1931. Menzies, however, proved to be the most "fiery particle" in the successive combinations, though Hughes continued to have his moments, and by 1937 the internal incohesiveness to which the conservatives were subject was far advanced.

While the conservatives took the majority of the seats in the House and Senate, Labor still commanded a large popular vote and was consistently stronger than its record indicated. Probably because of the way the federal electorates were determined in relation to concentrations of working-class votes as much as because of voter suspicions about its program, Labor had difficulty in translating its strength into federal seats. There was, too, the assumption that voters were not willing to give Labor federal power while quite willing to vote it into office in the states and maintain it there. Or state electorates may have been bounded more favorably to Labor. Gerrymandering was not unknown in Australia. Since compulsory voting had been applied to federal elections since 1928 (since 1915 in Queensland), political apathy expressed in failure to vote was not a factor.

While Labor clearly had difficulty in capitalizing its strength at the federal level, it did far better in the states. It returned to office in Queensland in 1932 under Forgan Smith, in Western Australia in 1933 under Philip Collier, and in Tasmania in 1934 under A. G. Ogilvie, for exceptionally long runs in power. Thus, Labor achieved enduring political supremacy in all the agrarian states except South Australia. There, after it had split disastrously over the Premiers' Plan and expelled its pro-Plan premier, it lost the election of 1933 and was kept from office for many years by conservatives with agrarian support who set out to transform the state's economy by an industrialization program. The climactic figure in this campaign was Thomas Playford, who held office from 1938 for over a quarter century.

In the two states which were the seats of industrial development Labor had poor political luck. In Victoria this was largely because of the tactical power of the Country party in state politics and the State Labor party's strong reaction against the Premiers' Plan which led it to expel the Labor premier, E. J. Hogan, who had implemented it—he went over to the Country party. In New South Wales Labor was troubled by a protracted intraparty brawl over Langism. In 1932 Lang, in resisting the efforts of federal authorities to collect the money they had laid out in payment of interest on the state's overseas debts, resorted to very dubious expedients to frustrate them and was adjudged by the governor to be acting illegally. Being evasive about mending his ways, Lang was dismissed from office, raising a debate among constitutionalists about the reserve powers of the Crown. In the ensuing election, Lang's forces were defeated, and he was displaced as premier by B. S. B. Stevens, leader of the U.A.P. forces and supported by the Country party. Stevens maintained himself in office for nine years, during which he made a particular point of selling off state enterprises in commodity production.

Lang, however, continued to boss the Labor party, but after the 1937 federal election there began a bitter struggle to dislodge him. This involved both the "regulars" of the federal Labor party, of whom the best known was J. B. Chifley—who after being one of Scullin's ministers had lost his federal seat in the debacle of 1931—and a heterogenous group of state laborites, including communists, led by R. J. Heffron. This became perhaps the most extraordinary of all the many intraparty fights in the history of Australian Labor. It did not reach its conclusion until 1939, when Lang was finally driven from the state party executive. Ironically, however, Heffron did not immediately succeed to the state parliamentary leadership; it went to W. J. McKell, who will appear in another role. New South Wales Labor under McKell got back into office in 1941 for the longest continuous run in its history. Heffron did not gain the leadership and the premiership until after World War II. By that time he had moved to the right.

Scullin remained leader of the federal parliamentary forces until

1935, when he was succeeded by John Curtin of Western Australia, newly returned to the House after his defeat in 1931. Scullin continued in Parliament until 1949. Curtin had been in Parliament while Scullin was prime minister and had strongly objected to Labor's implementation of the Premiers' Plan. This now counted greatly in his favor in dealing with Labor dissidents, but he was elected by caucus by a margin of only one vote over his rival, F. M. Forde of Queensland. It was Curtin's task to reunify Labor at the federal level where, of course, Langism, divisive in New South Wales, obtruded itself. This was not accomplished until 1941. Curtin's larger and—from the standpoint of Labor's federal future—more important task was to help the party evolve policy positions which would make it acceptable to the voters as an alternative to U.A.P.-C.P. rule.

When the Lyons government took office in 1932 the country was near the bottom of the depression. It based its policy largely on the Premiers' Plan, emphasizing budget balancing and giving attention to trade, marketing, and, as the international situation began to assume a prewar shape, defense. It founded its hopes for Australia's recovery chiefly on improved prices for exports, recognizing the crucial importance of world market prices in Australian affairs. Avoiding acceptance of the restrictive policies fashionable elsewhere, it continued to place emphasis upon increasing production. Production continued its upward trend. In the Lyons era, survival as an economically viable country was the ruling idea.

Sheep numbers and wool production moved slowly and uncertainly upward, New South Wales maintaining its premier position. Price per pound, a trifle over fourteen pence in 1932-33, rose irregularly to a peak of twenty-five pence in 1934–35 and then settled back to twenty-one pence in 1939–40. The wool-growing industry again proved to be the strength of the country. The wheat industry continued in severe crisis and became a prime political problem. Scullin's grow-more-wheat proposal of 1930 was a success on the production side but a failure on the marketing side, only partly because the suggested national pool was rejected by the Senate. Labor's subsequent efforts to rescue the industry were also largely frustrated because the money it proposed to spend was regarded as inflationary. The industry sank into intensifying disorder. Bankruptcy and dispossession harassed the growers; those who stayed on the land were commonly barely solvent. In dealing with the situation the Lyons government and the states, on which rested primary responsibility for much of the uneconomic expansion of the past, became involved in complicated rescue operations. A shrinkage of the area planted took place, particularly in marginal regions of low yield occupied in recent years. The area which had reached 18,000,000 acres under the Scullin stimulus in 1930 sank to a low of 12,000,000 in 1935, rose about 2,000,000 acres in the relatively good year of 1938, and then began to sink again toward the deep lows of World War II. The wheat industry became a ward of the governments, kept going by debt-adjustment schemes, subventions, government-guaranteed prices, and Commonwealth participation in the international schemes for regulating the world wheat market, the required money obtained by a tax on flour. While low world prices allowed increased wheat consumption in the Far East, and this benefited Australia, no factor emerged to insure the steady viability of the industry in a free market. Nevertheless, in the familiar paradox of farming, while the economic position was bad, agronomic progress continued. Butter, sugar, and dried fruits, earlier involved in protective marketing schemes, continued in them.

Manufacturing, after a retreat in the early depression years, regained its drive beginning in 1933, assisted by the devaluation of the currency and the tariff, and in the later 1930's made genuine progress, even though a shift in tariff policy slightly increased import competition, particularly in the engineering, chemical, and paper industries, and costs continued a challenge. In steel, which had great success in reducing costs, the BHP showed its continuing vitality by absorbing the Australian Iron & Steel works at Port Kembla in 1935, thus resuming its monopoly position in the industry. The number of steel-using industries associated with it increased. It now began to be commonly but not universally accepted that factory industry must be a central reliance in Australia's economic future, particularly as a support of any increase in the population. However, between 1930 and 1939 the country lost a good many people through emigration, the rate of national increase declined, and the annual population increase dropped below 1 per cent. In the late 1930's unemployment was still running about 9 per cent. At the outbreak of World War II the total population stood at 7,000,000.

In dealing with trade and marketing, in large measure two names for the same thing, that is, the disposal of Australia's production, the Lyons government had an uneasy time.

At the Imperial Conference of 1930, attended by Scullin, there had been discussion of imperial trade problems, but the questions had been referred to another conference to be held later at Ottawa, Canada. This conference took place in 1932. S. M. Bruce led the Australian delegation. From Ottawa Bruce proceeded to London, where in 1933 he became high commissioner and began a long term in office. He had found his métier. Ottawa proved to represent an effort to integrate the dominion economies more closely with the United Kingdom's by molding the United Kingdom trade policy into a shape favorable to the dominions as exporters of primary products.

Made supple by the stresses and strains of the world depression, Britain was persuaded to continue "free entry" for commodities in that category and at long last to reciprocate the preferences she had enjoyed in the dominions' markets, thus strengthening the positions of the dominions in her markets, while her position in theirs was to be improved by continuing "free entry" and new preferences. This meant protection of Australia's share of the British market for certain commodity exports, notably wheat, sugar, dried fruits, canned fruits, butter, and processed milk, a position guarded, moreover, by an understanding that if supplies from British domestic agriculture, at this time being encouraged to expand and granted first place in the market, crowded the Australians, their share would be protected at the expense of foreign suppliers (the Argentines, the Danes, etc.). In the case of meats, the complications of the British position required some limitations on supplies, an unwelcome restriction to the production-conscious Australians. These arrangements were made on the assumption that prices of agricultural products would rise and, from the dominion side, that the British market was, evidence to the contrary notwithstanding, bottomless. To Britain was left the task of reconciling her position as a world trader, investor, and ship owner with her position as a protected market for the dominions' farmers, as well as an agricultural producer in her own right. In her trade negotiations with the United States in 1938, she required some minor sacrifices from the Australians. The net effect was to intensify Australia's integration into the imperial trading system. The percentage of Australian exports going to Britain rose, in the case of some commodities, to the point that the British seemed the only market. Wheat and wool were the only commodities still clearly in the world market category.

On the Australian side, Ottawa required a revision of the tariff. This led the Lyons government to bring forward an extraparliamentary policy-making body Labor had pretty much ignored, the Tariff Board. Although Parliament did not legislate all the Board's recommendations, its record of concurrence was quite good. The ostensible effect was to reduce the tariff on some imports from Britain, eventually not only as reflected in the schedules but also with regard to such protection as was given by the devalued Australian currency and primage. The avowed purpose was to improve the competitive position of British suppliers in the Australian market. The purpose—and its translation in practice—alarmed both Labor and the Australian manufacturers, who insisted that "competition" not be so competitive as to destroy existing industries or prevent the establishment of new ones. Thus, while the British could be given a preferred position as against foreigners, they should not be able to take unimpeded advantage of the disabilities to which Australian factory industry was heir, for example, "costs." The government's own commitment to industrialization now strengthening, this was a compelling argument. The Tariff Board interpreted Article IX of Ottawa in the light of it. A consequence was that prior to granting Britain an increased preference, the general tariff applicable to foreigners was kept high, leaving Australian industry substantially protected against both British and foreign competition.

To be able to grant favors to foreigners an "intermediate" tariff was introduced, the rates above British preference but below the standard level. In 1938 Australian negotiators, as a *quid pro quo* for acknowledging Britain's difficult economic position, persuaded the British to acknowledge the Australian position in the following terms: "That in the interests of both countries and of the British Empire as a whole it was desirable for Australia to endeavour to bring about as soon as possible a substantial increase in her population; That it was impossible to achieve this objective solely or principally by an expansion of Australian primary industries; That there was therefore a necessity to combine with such expansion the sound and progressive development of Australian secondary industries."

The Australian efforts to diversify their trading outlets after Ottawa were made difficult by the way in which Ottawa agreements applied in regard to the increases in tariffs on goods from outside the Empire—which reduced sales in the Australian market—and by the general intensification of bilateralism and control of trade and exchange in the world. Although negotiations were conducted in 1935 with Belgium, Czechoslovakia, France, Germany, Italy, Poland, and Switzerland, agreements were made only with Belgium, Czechoslovakia, France, and Switzerland, and in no instance did any decisively fruitful consequences follow, though at the time even limited results were important. As the 1930's wore on there was a growing conviction that the Far East was Australia's hope for her future as a trading nation. The difficulties and confusions about trade from which Australia was then suffering came to a climax in 1936. In that year reflationary spending in Australia generated a financially embarrassing increase in imports not compensated by satisfactory export prices. The response was an adventure in bilateralism called "trade diversion," an excellent example of Lyons' opportunism.

Under financial stress and pressure from British traders to "do something" for them in the Australian market, the Lyons government—R. G.

Casey the treasurer and H. S. Gullett the minister for Trade taking the lead—undertook to deal with vexing trading relationships with the United States and Japan, the latter in a promising stage of rapid development, the former essentially in the shape it had had since it had begun in 1792 and hitherto dealt with as the machinery of mutilateralism made possible. In the American case the ostensible objective of the policy was to redress a perennially unfavorable trade balance, which far outran Australia's bilaterally earned dollar resources, about which the Americans were not then disposed to negotiate, by radically reducing the Australian imports of automobile chassis in the expectation that this would open the way to the establishment of an Australian motorcar industry and would improve sales of British cars. In the case of Japan, with which Australia had a very favorable trade balance founded upon exports of wool, the objective was to cut down the swelling inflow of Japanese piece goods to preserve the Australian market for British suppliers principally, other suppliers incidentally. Both efforts to mold trade to the heart's desire did more harm, economically and politically, than good. Clearly, this was not a way forward, and the policy was abandoned. H. S. Gullett resigned. By 1938 Australia's extra-imperial trade policy was rather obscure, though it leaned toward "freer" trade and "Ottawa" was widely considered uncomfortable. Only events could clarify the situation.

In its marketing phases, the disposal of Australia's production had begun to be "organized" in the 1920's in one way or another to fortify the position of producers by differential pricing for "home consumption" and "export" sales. The Lyons government added wheat to the list of commodities so handled. In their earlier phases the schemes had been based on voluntary cooperation of producers, and noncooperators had had to be tolerated, but in the more difficult situation of the 1930's tighter control seemed required and, since most of the commodities were produced in more than one state and Commonwealth-wide control was wanted, Commonwealth legislation was required. If blocked from selling beyond the quota on the market of one state, a man could then sell on the market of another instead of sending the surplus overseas, obviously control of the domestic market was impossible, and it was there that the vital compensatory returns were to be obtained. In the 1930's it was estimated that the home price of sugar was at one time 200 per cent above the world price, while for butter it varied from 25 to 50 per cent above. Committed to production as it was, and unwilling to let any industry go under, the Commonwealth was disposed to legislate—even at a high cost to consumers—in the hope that this was temporary. Decisions of the High Court led it to suppose that it was within its constitutional powers in doing so. Nevertheless, Section 92 of the Constitution said "trade, commerce and intercourse among the States . . . shall be absolutely free." The legislation was, therefore, challenged. The climactic case was carried beyond the High Court to the Privy Council in 1936, and the Privy Council declared the legislation in question was in violation of Section 92. The Lyons government then attempted to salvage the situation by proposing a constitutional amendment which would make Section 92 specifically inapplicable to "laws with respect to marketing." In March 1937 the voters rejected it by majorities in all states. This made the future of Commonwealth participation in "orderly marketing" uncertain.

As the general economic situation began to improve, with wool prices leading the way, and Lyons began to talk recovery, as he was to do in the 1934 election, the emphasis of interest began to shift from economies and budget balancing to liquidating unemployment. Union labor pressed for shorter hours and restoration of the wage cuts, but the state governments, which still had responsibility for unemployment, threw the emphasis on public works. B. S. B. Stevens, the U.A.P. premier of New South Wales, which in 1933 had the highest rate of unemployment in the country, and Forgan Smith, the Labor premier of Queensland, in which the rate was more moderate but still high, took the lead in pressing the Loan Council for ample loan money for works, with the support of Labor premiers coming to office in Tasmania and Western Australia.

In a surprisingly short time, though with hesitations reflecting business opinion, the Council and Prime Minister Lyons, who had all along been favorably disposed personally, accepted and even suggested that the unification of the railway gauges should at long last be carried out, to which Labor agreed. It wasn't. The actual works undertaken were more modest: railway electrification, roads, bridges, sewers, hospitals, schools, afforestation. And as the states multiplied their works, so also did the Commonwealth which, for instance, resumed a slow-paced spending on the construction of Canberra. Far from advancing socialism, distorting the structure of production, or competing with private enterprise, as businessmen alleged they would, the works had a stimulating effect on the economy. The success of the loans floated to finance them was an indicator of recovery. The loans were not, however, ordinarily obtained for works only but in combination with loans largely used to fund the accumulation of floating debts, which had the form of Treasury bills. This was a contribution to financial order and a deflationary complement to the inflationary spending on works.

Probably stimulated to action by unrest in Western Australia, Lyons also moved to deal with the loose end Earle Page had left dangling in the area of Commonwealth-state financial relations. As the depression bore heavily in on their overwhelmingly agrarian state, the Western Australians felt that their troubles, which stemmed from disabilities suffered from federation, had been strongly reinforced. A movement active for at least ten years now proposed to solve the troubles by major surgery: Western Australia was to secede from the Commonwealth and resume her status as a separate self-governing colony. This was really an extreme expression of that provincial particularism which all states continued in some measure to exhibit; it was obviously related to Lang's attempt to go it alone in New South Wales. On April 8, 1933, the Western Australian electors voted by a margin of 68,000 to secede, and while the federal authorities formally rebutted their case, the movement did not collapse until the imperial authorities advised that for constitutional reasons they could do nothing. Lyons, a citizen of a state also allegedly suffering disabilities, was naturally sympathetic to the Western Australian difficulties, though not to the radical solution of secession, and to get the special grants which had been going to Western Australia, Tasmania, and South Australia on a sound and continuing footing, he established a Grants Commission to determine annually just what sums the federal government should pay. The Commission, particularly in the hands of its founding members, F. W. Eggleston and L. F. Giblin, not only performed this function but in studying the problem and rationalizing criteria and procedures contrived a distinguished contribution to the vexing problem of federal-state relations indigenous to all federations.

While thus adapting its economic policies in response to political pressures, the Lyons government managed to evade changes in banking policy. Late in 1932, digesting recent experience, the A.L.P. Banking Committee stated that, while social ownership and control was of course "the one complete and permanent remedy for the ills of the social system," the most important step toward that end was "the establishment of the social ownership and control of the banking system which controls and operates the monetary system." Two years later in the general election of 1934 Scullin, while substantially outbidding Lyons on all specific spending proposals such as public works and the guaranteed price for wheat, tried to make banking and monetary reform the main issue, but with no very obvious political profit. However, there was sentiment within the government favoring legislation to develop the central banking functions of the Commonwealth Bank and a sufficiently widespread response to Labor's criticism of banking to support the idea of a Royal Commission "to inquire into the monetary and banking systems." Such a Royal Commission was appointed at the end of 1935, Justice Mellis

Napier of the Supreme Court of South Australia, chairman, with Professor [of Economics] R. C. Mills of Sydney University and J. B. Chifley,
the A.L.P.'s man, conspicuous members. The Commission's work was
done as Keynesian economics was infiltrating Australia, and Professor
Mills was its carrier on the Commission. His most receptive pupil was
Chifley. At the same time the example of New Zealand was before the
members. The intellectual climate was changing.

In its Report, which was rendered in 1937, the Commonwealth Bank
and the trading banks were both criticized for their depression-time
policies, proposals for developing the Bank's powers as a central bank
and for tightening its controls over the trading banks were elaborated,
and the need for a clear definition of Bank-Treasury relations to insure
that final authority over monetary policy rested with the Treasury (and
beyond it with Parliament, i.e., the currently dominant government
party) was admitted, though not detailed. It was possible for both
the government and Labor to claim that the Report supported their general positions. The Lyons government, R. G. Casey in charge, slowly
moved to implement the Commission's recommendations as it read
them, but in the end no legislation was actually passed, partly because
of difficulties created by the trading banks, led by the Bank of New
South Wales seeking to avoid central bank control, partly because of increasingly urgent political exigencies. In historical perspective it turned
out that as significant as anything in the Report was J. B. Chifley's
"Dissent, Reservation and Addenda": "In my opinion, the best service
to the community can be given only by a banking system from which the
profit motive is absent [i.e., without private trading banks], and, thus,
only by a system entirely under national control." This forecast things
to come.

Running parallel to the Lyons government's struggle to define and
implement an economic policy was its effort to meet the challenges of
the changing international scene. From 1916 to 1935 not only were
external relations in the hands of the prime minister, as traditionally,
but there was no separate department of External Affairs. W. M. Hughes
had taken External Affairs into the prime minister's department, and
Bruce and Scullin had seen no reason for a change. By 1935, however,
external affairs had become important enough to warrant the recon-
stitution of a separate department and the appointment of a minister
in charge. This did not mean that from 1935 the minister made policy or
that he carried out policy made by the prime minister. Rather, policy
appears to have been made by the cabinet and both the prime minister
and the minister for External Affairs enunciated cabinet policy when they
dealt with the issues as they arose. The policy in any case was founded

on the dogma of the diplomatic unity of the British Empire and in substance was in agreement with and in support of British policy.

The Lyons government supported British policy through its involutions during the 1930's, including the Chamberlain government's appeasement policy and its sequelae. Unlike New Zealand, Australia essayed no independent action in foreign policy in the decade. As traditionally, the Australians put a higher value and more emphasis on the diplomatic unity of the Empire than did many of their imperial associates. The Australians conceived their relation to the Empire as organic, not merely functional. The motivation for this derived from an acknowledgment of Australia's strategical weakness standing alone, which it was hoped would be compensated for by close association and collaboration with the British—and, possibly, the League. However, there had been since before World War I an ever-intensifying sense in the official mind that there was a greater urgency and somehow a more immediate national relevance about Pacific Basin than about European policy. There was no strong conviction that to deal faithfully with the Far Eastern issues an Australian national policy different from British policy was required, but rather that Australia should pay special heed to getting its voice heard in consultations with Britain when Pacific policy was up for discussion. Even with regard to Pacific policy the dogma of the diplomatic unity of the British Empire ruled, and to the outside view an Australian influence on British Pacific policy was no more obvious than an Australian influence on European policy.

Such debate as took place between the conservatives and Labor over political foreign policy turned upon differing conceptions of what impact of British policy back upon Australia was tolerable. The conservatives, while hoping that the crises of the 1930's could be weathered successfully, were nevertheless prepared to accept war. In their book, if Britain was at war, Australia also was at war. Labor on the other hand constantly sought for ways and means of contracting out of British policies which promised to bring on war even by inadvertence and whether or not the League was a factor in them. The A.L.P. was anxious to keep Australia out of war, including British war. It was neither enthusiastic about collective security through the League nor much influenced by the prowar strain in the antifascism of the left. With regard to its attitude toward Italy (the Ethiopian war and sanctions) and Spain (the Civil war), it was suspected that a Roman Catholic influence was important. The A.L.P.'s position was in some measure "isolationist," and Lang Labor was more decisively isolationist still. Labor's position largely derived from the circumstance that after the party split over conscription in 1916 anti-imperialist, antiwar, prodisarmament, pro-League-as-conciliator (not as wielder of war-risking sanctions) views dominated the party mind. Labor's real concern, however, was with domestic questions, not external affairs; it did not think too deeply about Australia's world position, least of all in terms relevant to the world situation in the 1930's. It was John Curtin's great contribution that with a personal background of thinking practically identical with that of his party he was able to present a case that, given the assumptions, made so much sense.

The preoccupations of the parties were such that neither made any striking contribution to the debate carried on by the intellectuals over the possibility of developing a fully adequate strictly national Australian foreign policy, to be justified fundamentally by reference to Australia's position in the Pacific. An interesting aspect of all the discussions—which, in spite of the fact that the national welfare was at stake, were remarkably desultory and low-pressure—was, in the light of the future, the small part calculations about the United States played in them. In 1930 the Australian professor W. K. Hancock, in a vastly influential book about his country, heavily discounted the significance of the United States to Australia, and this was also in substance the official position. Not until the late 1930's did Australian publicists really try to alter that verdict. In 1936 the architects of "trade diversion" were oblivious to the unfortunate political implications of a quarrel with the United States at that moment in history. It was a minority of the Australian intelligentsia, not the politicians, who led the way to a more balanced assessment of the significance of the United States. When the politicians decided that the United States did matter—particularly in the Pacific—they found themselves embarrassed by the State Department's active memories of the trade dispute.

More heat was engendered by the simultaneous debate over the closely related matter of defense. Here also the differing basic orientations of the conservatives and Labor determined their positions. Both were deeply impressed with the strategic isolation of Australia. As the conservatives were imperially oriented, they saw Australian defense within the framework of imperial defense from which Australia would profit—which would be its ultimate reliance—and to which as a *quid pro quo* it must therefore contribute to the best of its ability. They held to the thesis that the defense of Australia followed from defense of the Empire and should be conducted as far away from Australia as possible, priority being given to the defense of the United Kingdom as the center of the Empire which must hold if anything was to hold. The Mediterranean and Suez and Singapore were other focal points of imperial resistance also commanding close Australian collaboration. As a nation in the Pacific, Australia had a particular stake in Singapore as a center of imperial power in the East and the point on which imperial collaboration in Australia's defense would turn. Singapore would keep an enemy away from Australia. In this "appreciation," if Australia were directly attacked, presumably in the form of raids, imperial forces would help repel the aggressor. Naturally, this emphasis on imperial cooperation deeply influenced the specifics which were the substance of Australian defense policy. Official policy followed from imperial thinking, epitomized at such imperial conferences as those of 1923 and 1937, especially as enunciated by the Committee of Imperial Defence. Although the Australians had only intermittent and marginal influence on the Committee's thinking, the Lyons government chiefly derived its fundamental ideas about defense from it. As in foreign policy, it followed Britain.

Labor, as became its orientation, seized upon the established Australian responsibility for its national defense and placed its emphasis there rather than on collaboration in imperial defense. It asserted that the most important contribution Australia could make to imperial defense was to develop as far as possible its power to defend itself. While Labor did not deny the axiom—much less repudiate it—that imperial assistance was Australia's final reliance, it threw the emphasis toward the fullest development of Australia's defensive powers. This was an alternative answer to the problem of its strategic isolation. The difference of emphasis worked itself out as a different program of the specifics of defense preparation. An odd effect of the debate was that while the conservatives appeared to be reiterating a ready-made, externally supplied argument, supported by fervent invocations of "loyalty" to Britain, Labor appeared to be trying to think out an admittedly difficult problem anew. The conservatives accorded Labor little credit for its effort, but there was considerable sympathy for the Labor position in the country, often in rather surprising places.

The Lyons government initiated a rearmament program late in 1933. In its time the Bruce-Page government had carried out a five-year defense program—the emphasis had been on the navy, the principal concern as to the army being with compulsory military training. In 1928 as a preliminary to the formulation of a new program, the government had a British expert examine the problem of developing the air force, but before a program could be unveiled the government lost office. The depression drew a heavy line between the Bruce-Page program and the Lyons rearmament program. The Scullin government abolished compulsory military training in accordance with a standing electoral promise, thus saving money, and practiced strict economy in defense expenditures otherwise, putting a part of the fleet into mothballs and doing nothing to develop the air force. On its accession to office the Lyons government, still preoccupied with budget-balancing, followed the Scullin precedents in its first budget, but for 1933–34 provided for an increase in defense spending to continue over the ensuing three years. It returned in substance to the Bruce-Page program, but did not restore compulsory military training, though it did assist the air force, and, especially, the navy. Expenditures were stepped up in the second three-year program announced in 1937. Traditionally, Australia had spent more than any other dominion on defense by any measure (per capita, per cent of budget, per cent of national income) and did so once again. There was some opinion that Australia was still not, in the light of its predicament, directing enough of its available resources to defense, but the real argument was over how the money should be spent.

In the collision over the specifics of defense the conservatives, oriented toward imperial cooperation, inevitably placed the emphasis on the navy and, while not ignoring the army, the air force, and matériel production, gave them lesser public emphasis. Labor, oriented toward national defense as the primary task, advocated shifting the emphasis to the air force and domestic matériel production. Labor did not improvise this line as an opportunist oppositionist gambit; it had been feeling its way toward this solution of Australia's defense problem since the end of World War I, when Frank Anstey directed attention to the fact that while Australia could not afford a navy big enough to defend itself, it might succeed in doing so with airplanes, submarines, and domestically produced matériel. John Curtin, a protégé of Anstey's, used this thinking—dropping out submarines—to support his proposals in the late 1930's. Interestingly enough, he drew some support from a school of theorists in the Australian armed forces who were dissatisfied with the thinking of the Committee of Imperial Defence. He also drew implicit support from industrialists interested in building airplanes in Australia.

While the Lyons government rejected Labor's emphasis on air power for defense, it was not indifferent to aviation. It strengthened the air force, encouraged those who proposed to build planes in Australia, and pursued a vigorous civil aviation policy in which defense considerations played a part. A good deal of progress was made in domestic civil aviation during the 1930's, and in the middle of the decade international links began to be established. At the Imperial Conference of 1926 a program for the development of an "all red" imperial air service, comparable to the shipping services and cable and wireless communications, was decided upon. Australia was to cooperate in developing this not only as a terminus distant from Britain but as a staging area on the United Kingdom-New Zealand route. This made it necessary that routes linking the great Australian cities be developed and required that the rule keeping airlines beyond the railheads and noncompetitive with the railways be abandoned, a change first implemented in 1929. The obvious port-of-entry for a line from England was Darwin in Northern Territory, which became the focus for the domestic lines up the west coast from Perth, those linking the cities of the southeast, and the line north from Adelaide. This had the incidental effect of revealing how small and shabby the northern gateway to Australia really was, six decades after its founding by the South Australians. Its sorry condition symbolized the much deplored, vigorously discussed failure of the Australians to master the intricate problems involved in the settlement and exploitation of the North.

The United Kingdom-Australia service was initiated in 1934. Flying boats were placed in service in 1937. The Singapore-Darwin link, via Netherlands East Indies, was placed in the hands of Qantas Empire Airways, Ltd., a mixed British-Australian stockholding company. At this stage Qantas, still a private company, was beginning to be regarded by the government as its "chosen instrument" in aviation. While Labor insisted on Australian participation in the international service because it feared that otherwise the British might try to get control of Australian domestic aviation, the government reasoned that experience in flying the Darwin-Singapore run was a useful contribution to defense. When the time came to establish a line across the Tasman Sea to New Zealand it was arranged, after tortuous negotiations, that a company called Tasman Empire Airways be formed, with stockholdings by British Overseas Airways Corporation (after 1940 wholly owned by the British government), Qantas, and Union Airways of New Zealand, in which the New Zealand government was a stockholder. The line, known as TEAL, began operating in April 1940.

The British and the Australians accepted competition in the service to Europe when they allowed the Dutch—who had established an Amsterdam-Batavia line—into Australia in 1938. This provided a much faster service to Europe than the British could then supply. On the other hand, the Australians resisted the efforts of the Americans, represented by Pan-American, to establish a line from the United States west coast to Australia. The Pacific had first been crossed from California to Queensland by a mixed Australian-American team led by Kingsford-Smith in 1928. The point at issue with the Americans was the question of reciprocation of landing rights in Hawaii to any transpacific British line that might be established. Whereas New Zealand, then not yet linked to Australia and the British service to England, allowed Pan Am into Auckland on a contingent basis pending a settlement of reciprocation, the Australians refused any such accommodation. Pan Am's activity led directly to the establishment of the TEAL service. It is also indicative of the Australian attitude toward the Americans that not until 1935 were any other than British planes imported into Australia.

Involved in Labor's position on defense, as also in that of the armed forces' theorists, was a skepticism about Singapore—the turntable of imperial cooperation—on two grounds: (a) because in the defense of Australia it was too far away from the probable line of approach of a likely aggressor, and (b) because it seemed improbable that Britain could reinforce Singapore as required if the menace to Australia came while Britain was heavily engaged in a war in Europe.

This skepticism obviously derived from a judgment on who was likely to direct hostile forces against Australia. Threading its way through the arguments about both foreign-political and defense policy was the question of against whom should Australia prepare for defense. The Japanese were obvious nominees. However, Australia had also to prepare itself against the European enemies of Britain. Her predicament was like New Zealand's.

It contained many variables, not least of which were that the Japanese might never attack as far southward, but satisfy or exhaust themselves on the continent of Asia—a possibility the Australians cherished for a few years after the Manchurian incident of 1931—and that if the Japanese did turn southward they might be stopped north of the equator —by Singapore?—well short of any direct attack on Australia. There was, too, the incalculable influence of the United States on developments. By 1937 the Australians were convinced that Japanese policy was becoming menacing to them, chiefly because of the resolute Japanese rejection of restraints upon themselves—including a pact of non-aggresson which in that year Australia proposed—but nevertheless the Australians continued to look for a settlement or accommodation that would appease Japan. The Australian suspicion of the Japanese was, of course, of long standing, and it had never been stifled by such arrangements as the Anglo-Japanese alliance in its successive forms, by the Washington treaties of the 1920's which supplanted the alliance, or by the very helpful increase in trade with the East in the 1920's and 1930's to which Japan was a principal contributor.

Japan, indeed, was in large measure the Far East (or Near North) to the Australians, and in their tradition it was a menace. They knew their white Australia policy was objectionable to the Japanese, who were assumed to resent W. M. Hughes's affronts to them in its name at

Paris. The Australians early and continuingly suspected what the Japanese might be doing to their hurt in the mandated Micronesian islands, they were periodically alarmed about Japanese activities on the pearl-shell beds in the waters to the north of the continent, and they complained about the aggressive Japanese trading in the islands south of the equator. While the Australians had sent a goodwill mission to the East in 1934 to encourage trade, headed by J. G. Latham, in 1936 they had not hesitated to apply "trade diversion" to the damage of trade with Japan. And while a little later the Australian government was prepared to displease the Australian left by insisting that a trade union ban on export of pig iron to Japan from Port Kembla be lifted, that same government, shortly after, acted to stop the export of iron ore to Japan from Yampi Sound in the northwest of Western Australia.

It was Japan's southward ambitions that really alarmed the Australians. Their suspicions, deductions, and forecasts about the probable southward movement convinced them that their defenses should be prepared against the Japanese. This factor directed men's minds to the problems of continental defense while Australia was—hopefully temporarily—beyond British help. It set the Australians wondering about American policy. They could not, however, calculate a defense policy exclusively in relation to probable Japanese intentions and actions, or one based exclusively on defense of their continent, for they were also committed to support the United Kingdom in Europe. Only ex post facto did it become clear what should have been done.

The 1937 general election, far from quieting the contention within the Lyons government, intensified it. Cabinet reorganization did not stifle it. The U.A.P. lost a few seats, Labor gained a few as had been anticipated, but the U.A.P.-C.P. coalition was put in no danger of displacement from office. Election discussion had ranged over a variety of continuing issues including banking, marketing, and defense and attention had been given to a new question, the social services.

In the 1920's progress in the social services was, by default of conservative action, left in the hands of state Labor. The Bruce-Page government had carefully studied a variety of proposals for new legislation in the field, but had not legislated a single one of them. Its sole positive contribution in the field of welfare was the development of the Department of Health (established in 1921 by Mr. Hughes). As the depression lifted, interest in the social services mounted. Intellectuals pointed out that far from being a world leader in the field any more, Australia was now one of the laggard nations. John Curtin as federal Labor leader, like his party fellows always interested in the redistribution of the national income to promote equality of material condition, spoke earnestly about the need for forward steps in the field. Thus, under pressure from several directions the Lyons government responded by making elaborate studies of a National Insurance plan covering sickness, medical treatment, pensions for widows and orphans, and an extension of the coverage and value of the old-age pensions. In further response to pressure it additionally promised to better the existing maternity allowances, to cooperate more alertly with the states on unemployment relief (though still maintaining that unemployment was a state responsibility) and on children's health measures. The Lyons proposal was contributory—an insurance scheme. Labor favored the scheme in general, but asked that a program of unemployment benefits be incorporated and reiterated its traditional position in favor of a noncontributory scheme paid for out of general revenue.

The Lyons cabinet accepted the National Insurance bill after some internal bickering for which the Country party members, who resisted endorsing it, were chiefly responsible. It was legislated. But then the legislation was not brought into operation. This caused a political explosion.

On March 20, 1939, R. G. Menzies resigned from the cabinet in protest, he said, against the abandonment of the National Insurance scheme to which, he alleged, he had the strongest personal commitment. He blamed the abandonment on the Country party. Lyons said it was caused by financial troubles associated with heavy spending on defense. However, Menzies was a devoted practitioner of the art of politics—not a flaming idealist. His personal identification with the social services was not clearly established (nor did it ever become so). Rather, it was the case that for the previous five years he had been deeply implicated in the intracoalition dissension. He had not only feuded constantly with the Country party members, but he had lately—by strong implication—indicated that he took a highly critical view of Lyons as a leader. Other members of Lyons' cabinet had caused trouble, hence the instability that had characterized it since 1934, but Menzies was persistently and presumably purposefully troublesome. He had refused appeasement. He appeared to be the spearhead of a Victorian effort to recapture the leadership of the principal conservative party and the prime ministership. Resignation from the cabinet therefore appeared to be intended to signalize the final breakup of the Lyons government to which it was no longer politically profitable to belong. All that was unique about this public disarray of a conservative government was that the man who appeared to want to profit most from the incoherence had chosen to leave the government instead of staying inside to collect his reward.

By this time the strain of try.ng to keep dissident conservatives in some kind of line was telling on Lyons' health. There were strong rumors that he wanted out of his high but uncomfortable post. However, it was not his fate to find refuge in some prestigious sinecure, for on April 7, 1939, still prime minister, he died of a heart attack while on an Easter visit to Sydney. Earle Page, as leader of the Country party, succeeded pro tempore to the prime ministership. A fierce struggle for the leadership of the U.A.P.—which carried with it final succession to the prime ministership—then ensued. William Morris Hughes (dropped from the cabinet in 1935 by Lyons for his dissident views on foreign policy but returned shortly after), R. G. Casey, allegedly Lyons' favorite for the succession, Thomas W. White (soldier, businessman, politician, cabinet member recently resigned, son-in-law of Alfred Deakin), even the absent S. M. Bruce as a likely conciliator, and R. G. Menzies—all but Hughes Victorians—entered the battle. On April 18 Robert Gordon Menzies emerged the victor by five votes. W. M. Hughes had proved his strongest opponent. Earle Page, violently opposed to Menzies, had to be pushed out of the prime ministership to let Menzies in, and he signalized his reluctant departure by a ferocious and extremely personal attack on Menzies as a disloyal colleague. Menzies had to select a cabinet from the U.A.P. parliamentary minority of twenty-six.

When Robert Gordon Menzies became prime minister the conservatives had already been in office for over seven years. Since the change of leadership took place during the parliamentary term which had begun in 1937, and therefore without the clarification of the political position an election might have represented, Menzies inherited unalloyed the weaknesses of the Lyons administration and added some peculiarly his own. His accession caused a split in the Country party between those who agreed with Earle Page's attack—and the consequent withdrawal of support from the U.A.P. and from cabinet offices—and those who regarded a personal feud as an inadequate reason for foregoing the kudos of cabinet posts, but the Page group ruled party conduct, so the significance of the support Menzies had from C.P. dissidents was difficult to estimate. Worse still, he did not command the unswerving loyalty of all his U.A.P. people; there was an especially critical faction in New South Wales of which the voice was the *Sydney Morning Herald*.

Menzies was commonly believed to have an excessive sense of his intellectual superiority to his associates which found exasperating expression in allegedly arrogant speech and conduct. His ability to command popular support in the country was openly doubted. And if his support was tepid and divided, his official opposition was strengthening. While the Labor party had not as yet been able either to absorb or eliminate the dissident Langites of New South Wales, it was, under Curtin's astute leadership, obviously improving its political position and prospects. It was indicative of the drift that a Labor man won Lyons' old seat at the by-election. An untried leader, Menzies faced a difficult prospect, whether it was federal politics, national economic affairs, or the international situation that was in question.

Economically the country was feeling the effects of the downswing of 1938. Wheat after two years of relatively successful marketing without financial assistance from the government had in the 1938 season again become an acute problem because of a decline in price. An experiment in "home consumption" pricing was initiated to provide a subvention for the wheat growers, and long-term stabilization schemes were under discussion. Wool prices were down. Manufacturing seemed to be in a fairly good position, but its structure, its strengths, and weaknesses in relation to general and defense demands were not well understood. Its technological resources appeared better than its competitive economic position. Imports were up and government action to curb the flow was under consideration. Like New Zealand, though less acutely, Australia faced the problem of dangerously diminishing sterling balances in London. The states were again experiencing budget deficits. The set of things appeared to be toward a renewal of deep depression. Unemployment was above 10 per cent, involving almost 300,000 workers.

The international situation was menacing. Although what was happening in Europe was in the forefront of the government's mind and it was understood, once the Munich euphoria had evaporated, that a war in which Britain would be involved was an imminent possibility, it was also the general opinion that war in the Pacific was a certainty either simultaneously with an outbreak in Europe or very shortly after. Although obviously working on a higher intellectual plane than Lyons, and employing a greatly superior rhetoric, it was not apparent that Menzies' basic assumptions were very different. He was "a King's man"; he proposed to follow and support Britain. But how wisely to prepare for "the worst" in coordination with Britain was still unclear, and the obstinacy with which history followed a mystifying pattern peculiarly its own, proving once again that it was more subtle than any "argument," was no help. Menzies proved rather good at the rhetoric of purposes but realizing them in actuality was another matter, largely because he was unable to master the resistances of politics and public opinion. Nevertheless, he led

Australia into the war and through its first two years when he finally fell, a victim of the confusions of politics and public opinion more than of his personal inadequacies.

As the continuator of Lyons' policies it was his fortune actually to carry out certain decisions about international policy made before Lyons' death which were, in the Australian context, significant innovations, pregnant with unwonted possibilities. On the assumption that Australia's peculiar national destiny was in the Pacific "where we have primary responsibilities and primary risks"—a world region which is *Far East* to Europeans and *Near North* to Australians—but emphasizing that Australia was a British dominion in the Pacific and that he was "little given ... to encouraging the exaggerated ideas of Dominion independence and separatism" current elsewhere, Menzies announced in April 1939 that his government proposed to establish diplomatic relations with the United States, Japan, and China. The diplomats, however, would so act as not to involve "any departure from the diplomatic unity of the Empire," and would therefore not act as from a separate and independent country but as representatives of a loyal British dominion. A pause of a year ensued before the appointees began to arrive in the foreign capitals.

War finally came on September 3, 1939. As a traditionalist, believing fervently in the indivisibility of the Crown, Menzies held that if Britain was at war, Australia also was at war. There was in his mind none of the ambiguities and reservations that plagued Canadians such as Mackenzie King, leading them pointedly to emphasize that a declaration of war by Canada was strictly a Canadian act by letting Canada stand neutral a few days until a formal Canadian declaration could be made. In 1937, when Lyons' attorney general, Menzies had made clear his attitude toward the Statute of Westminster. While leading an attempt to have adopted certain sections (2, 3, 4, 5, 6) of the Statute to bring Australia in line with Canada, South Africa, and Ireland, he had said:

I know that quite a number of responsible people are troubled about the proposal to adopt the Statute of Westminster for the reason that they feel it may give some support to the idea of separatism from Great Britain ... I think that the business of devising the Balfour Declaration in 1926, and the business of devising and drafting the preamble of the Statute of Westminister in 1931 were both open to grave criticism ... I believe that the 1926 declaration ... was, in substance, a grave disservice. But that does not prevent me from saying that these things have been done ... I want to suggest [that] those who are troubled about this legislation, are now too late. That is why I said I was referring to them as a matter purely of historical interest, because for better or worse we have the Balfour Declaration and the history of 1926 and 1930 ... I think, and I suggest to the House, that having regard to these circumstances, we ought at this stage to recognize the facts and to come into line uniformly with the other dominions. I think that on all these matters of constitutional doctrine and practice, as much uniformity as possible throughout the British world should be aimed at.

However, the House refused to recognize "the facts," and the states protested any change on the ground that their constitutional positions might be adversely altered. Therefore, in 1939 Menzies was where he always had been without even the benefit of the technical uniformity he had been prepared to accept. Although Australia was not consulted about the British guarantee to Poland, it was strongly committed to British policy. Shortly before war actually broke out Menzies in a broadcast enunciated a traditionalist formulation of the position: warning that war appeared imminent, he said, "We in Australia are involved because, in plain English, the destruction or defeat of Great Britain would be the destruction or defeat of the British Empire and would leave us with a precarious tenure of our own independence." When war between the United Kingdom and Germany finally came, Menzies and his cabinet awaited only for official confirmation before announcing that Australia was also at war. Menzies told the people: "It is my melancholy duty to inform you officially that, in consequence of a persistence by Germany in her invasion of Poland, Great Britain has declared war upon her and that, *as a result, Australia is also at war.*" (Italics added.)

The Menzies government made a cautious approach to the war. In September 1939 it obtained the passage of a National Security Act— counterpart of the War Precautions Act of 1914—which purported to allow it to do almost anything which could be related, even if only contingently, to the defense of the Commonwealth, including things the central government was debarred from doing in peacetime by the constitution. This gave the government a free hand in bringing the resources of the country to bear on the war, except as it was stayed by regard for established conventions, such as no conscription for overseas service, the condition of parliamentary and public opinion, and its own inhibitions. These limiting factors governed the Menzies government's actions. Significantly, the act had to be strengthened in June 1940. Parliamentary Labor was cooperative in all connections demonstrably related to the prosecution of the war. Outright opposition to the war was confined to the Communist party and its fellow-travelers as a result of the Nazi-Soviet Pact of 1939. Strong in certain trade unions the communists tried hard to impose their antiwar line on the Australian Council of Trade Unions and suffered only a shamefully narrow defeat. More important than communist influence on public opinion was the tactic of politicizing the economic strikes that occurred, notably in the New South Wales black coal mines. Finally, in May 1940 the Party was banned, but since it was well prepared for this contingency, it continued to function strongly underground.

The Menzies administration took up defense where the Lyons' government had laid it down and carried on from there, increasing money expenditures but, more significantly, seeking an improvement of organization as the context of the effort changed—as by the coming of the war and the fortunes of war overseas. The disasters in Europe in 1940 had their repercussions. However, the mental climate of "business as usual" carried over into wartime and was impossible to dissipate wholly as long as the war remained far away in Europe.

Organizationally, the characteristic move was to break up the omnibus ministries of peacetime into their component parts or functions and to constitute each part or function a separate ministry. One of Menzies' earliest moves, for example, was to set up a ministry of Supply and Development (a characteristically Australian association of functions) to deal with the task of organizing industry to meet the supply requirements of the armed services and to be responsible for the supply itself. Hitherto, the armed services had governed supply themselves, but in 1939 it was apparent that the task was getting beyond them. As the number of ministries and some more or less independent subordinate organizations concerned with defense production multiplied, Menzies sought to control and guide them by establishing a ministry of Defence Coordination, of which he himself took charge, thus emphasizing his sense of the prime minister's responsibility. In 1939, to man the upper echelons of the organizations, the government brought into its service economists and businessmen—at first on an advisory basis. It was beginning to be obvious that the permanent public service, in spite of the presence of men of very great ability, did not have the human resources to meet fully the needs of the time. Among the economists, Douglas Copland, who became prices commissioner in 1939, had perhaps the greatest personal prestige and exerted an influence on policy beyond his special province within the government, but as time passed other economists made their marks. Among the businessmen, none brought greater personal prestige to the government service than Essington Lewis (1881–1961) of the Broken Hill Pty., Ltd., and none rendered greater service to his country, first as an adviser (1939), later (1940) as responsible director of industrial production. By example and command he brought into the war effort the best available production administrators of Australian industry.

Under Menzies the war effort, in spite of his personal sense of the necessity for stepping it up to an ever-higher level—which was much stimulated by a visit to the United Kingdom early in 1941—while well organized in relation to the objective of "total" war, never reached anything like "total" intensity. It was carried to about the point where no intensification was possible without a frontal invasion of the civilian economy and the standard of living, but not beyond. In large part this was because the Australians, neither in terms of parliamentary politics nor public opinion, saw at all vividly the need for total commitment. Until Pearl Harbor the civilian economy was very little disturbed, largely for political reasons which now it appears very unwise to have let rule, though how Menzies could have done differently is hard to show. Yet it was demonstrated that Australia's resources for war were greater than anybody had hitherto imagined. By the fortunes of politics it was left to Labor to divert resources to war in the fullest possible measure. Labor was able to do this partly because of the coming of war in the Pacific, partly because it was better situated to deal ruthlessly with the issues. In an atmosphere of high risk, the people would take from a Labor administration what they would not accept from a conservative administration in an atmosphere of low risk.

From the standpoint of resources for war a distinguishing difference in the Australian situation in 1914 and 1939 was the much higher level of industrialization that had been achieved by the outbreak of World War II. It was no longer true that Australia's primary significance to the imperial war effort was as a source of manpower, foodstuffs, and raw materials. It was still important for these, but in the second war it could go far toward equipping its own forces and toward supplying other forces of its area—for example, as a member of the Eastern Group Supply Council those of India and New Zealand. However, it was far from a fully mature industrial structure that the Australians had. In addition to fully exploiting its resources for war production by carrying out conversion and to extending those resources by new factories and by additions to existing ones, which all countries found necessary, it also faced special problems deriving from its stage of industrial development. Most of the plant extensions and new plants were built in the most intensively industrialized states, New South Wales and Victoria, but the greatest proportional additions were made in South Australia, thus confirming the South Australian ambition to industrialize. And since most of the existing plants, including the fundamentally important steel works, were on or near the seacoast and theoretically highly vulnerable to enemy raids, a special effort was made to disperse new plants inland in order to reduce vulnerability and to tap resident manpower resources.

The problems special to Australia, however, were of a different order.

Even in relation to the existing industrial structure, Australia had but a miniscule machine tool industry, and some branches of industry, such as heavy chemicals, were imperfectly developed. The supply of skilled labor was inadequate to support expansion, and even in New South Wales, where most improvements had recently been made, the technical schools were underdeveloped even in relation to the prewar demand, let alone the suddenly expanded demand of wartime. However, as remarked earlier, the technological ingenuity of Australian industry was greater than its strictly economic strength, and the ability to improvise was an outstanding quality of its workers. Economically, an important strength was the relative cheapness of its steel, of which it was now producing a million tons a year, essentially an Essington Lewis achievement. The consequence was that, competitive price not being a determining factor, the Australians were able to improvise in relatively short order a rather remarkable machine tool industry and to fill some of the more unfortunate gaps in its industrial structure—though not, of course, all of them. For example, it made new kinds of alloy steels but no tin plate and while it came to fabricate aluminum it produced none. It built airplanes. It also succeeded in the long run, by improvisation of facilities, in training a very respectable number of skilled tradesmen, thus acquiring a strong sense of the importance of technological education to Australia's probable future, which had significant consequences after the war. In carrying out this deployment and expansion of industrial resources, it relied principally in Menzies' time on the scientists already in government employ, like those with CSIR and the government's munitions works. The great deficiency of Menzies' war effort was its lack of intensity, not irrelevance of plan.

If in his time the problem with regard to secondary industry was conversion and extension to achieve greater and more varied factory production for war, the problem with regard to the land industries was essentially one of disposal of the supplies certain to come forward. Agriculture, 1939–41, faced neither the task of increasing production nor, except in minor particulars like flax, of varying production, but of getting rid of the commodities that would normally be produced. The land industries were not seriously affected during the first two years of war by the redeployment of manpower, because workers could be replaced from the unemployed; nor by diversion of production from agricultural machinery to war matériel, for they were reasonably equipped for normal production; nor by interference with basic supplies such as petrol and superphosphate. All these would later embarrass the land industries, but not yet.

It was the disorganization of the overseas markets that caused difficulty, particularly the planned redefinition of what the British market would receive or attempt to provide shipping to receive. Agriculture and grazing were related to the war through those foodstuffs and fibers which were in demand by Britain, by the Australian armed forces, and by Australian civilians, but the combined demand from these did not, under the circumstances, insure markets for *all* Australian production. Any failure to dispose of production fully might entail reducing it in future seasons—where that was at all feasible, as with regard to wheat, a most unwelcome possibility to the production-conscious Australians—or extensive waste (at government expense) of perishable commodities whose production could not easily be inhibited. Since marketing production was an established Australian problem, it was, even in wartime, simply a familiar problem in a rather different guise, involving, until Pearl Harbor, less an adaptation to war—such as factory industry was undergoing—than a struggle to keep going along familiar lines. In short, the problem in wartime appeared to be the same as in the different conditions of peacetime: to insure somehow the stability of the various land industries. Thus, the wheat farmers, for instance, tended to pursue a line in Parliament which differed hardly at all from that they had been pursuing since 1930; and by an unlucky accident of politics a wheat farmer-politician gained a strategic position of power between the conservatives and Labor, with fateful consequences for the conservatives.

Australia's predicament at the outbreak of war in Europe justified a cautious approach to the problem of how best to deploy its fighting strength. The character of the combat in Europe in its early stages made Australia's brief hesitation quite unimportant in the larger perspective, but it had significance in indicating the awareness of the leadership of a very exasperating problem. When a course was determined upon, it was to support Britain in Europe. This was to honor a traditional patriotic obligation. The earliest Australians to go directly to the aid of Britain were airmen, at first either long-term or short-term members of the Royal Air Force, then the Australians fed into the R.A.F. through the Empire Air Training scheme centered in Canada. Airmen, indeed, constituted the principal Australian contribution directly to the defense of the United Kingdom throughout World War II. As to the navy, at the outbreak of war Australia delayed for two months, until November, before releasing its ships for service outside Australian waters—save the cruiser "Perth" which went immediately to the Mediterranean—except as specifically authorized. Compulsory military training was reinstituted in the army in October, but an overseas force recruited from volunteers, with Lieutenant General Sir Thomas Blamey in command, was not dispatched until January 1940. It was sent to Palestine to be readied for such use as developments might require in defense of the Suez Canal, oil, Turkey, Iraq, or India. Actually, it did not not engage in combat until after Italy entered the war in June 1940, when it fought variously in the Mediterranean theater. That this disposition had seriously weakened the Australian position in the Pacific was painfully clear to the leadership by the beginning of 1941.

At the entry of Italy into the war there were two Australian divisions in Palestine. A third was later supplied. They constituted important elements of an imperial force scattered over Palestine, Egypt, Sudan, and Kenya, to which New Zealanders, Indians, and Africans also contributed elements. The imperial commander was General Sir Archibald Wavell. Australian troops first entered battle against the Italians under the field direction of General R. E. O'Connor as replacements for an Indian division withdrawn for service against the Italian army in Abyssinia. At that stage the Italians were in retreat after a drive toward Egypt from Tripolitania. The Australians first encountered them at Bardia and continued in the forefront of operations as they were driven from Bardia, Tobruk, Derna, and Benghazi in turn, out of Cyrenaica back into Tripolitania. Then, instead of making plans for O'Connor to pursue the Italians immediately into Tripolitania and finally destroy them, at Churchill's instance the British leadership decided to halt the campaign at the Cyrenaica frontier and divert forces to the support of the Greeks. Hitler, for his part, decided to send Rommel and German troops to North Africa to renew the drive on Cairo and the Canal.

The British decision to go to the support of the Greeks was a Churchillian inspiration comparable to that of Gallipoli in World War I—in intent essentially a "political" act undertaken with insufficient military means to insure success. As the best troops available at the time, the burden of executing the operation fell to the Australians and the New Zealanders. The operation in April 1941 inevitably failed, and an evacuation ensued which was not nearly so well executed as that from Gallipoli. Moreover, it was immediately succeeded by disaster in Crete in May. What was equally unfortunate was that the adequacy, efficiency, and candor of the consultations between the imperial authorities and the Australians with regard to the employment of their troops was pointedly questioned. The verdict was that the Australians had not been properly consulted as they had every right to expect, by precedent and current instructions to their commander of troops, Sir Thomas Blamey. He, it emerged, had challenged the proposed operation on military grounds at an early stage, but his opinion had been suppressed by the imperial command. Prime Minister Menzies, who was in the United Kingdom on a visit, was at no stage fully informed about the matter, and neither were his cabinet colleagues in Canberra. Menzies felt it necessary to raise the whole business of "consultation" in the War Cabinet in London; on his return to Australia he told his colleagues that the great difficulty was "that Churchill had no conception of the British Dominions as separate entities." In any case there was clear evidence that this was no way to run a war, but that this revelation disaffected any considerable number of Australians of influence was nonsense. The popular reaction to the disaster was shown by a marked rise in recruitments for overseas service. Sequentially in June-July, the success of Australian troops in a campaign from Palestine into Syria and Lebanon, equally badly managed from the standpoint of consultation and equally political in intent, plucked up the spirits of the depressed.

Meanwhile, Rommel, who had arrived in Africa in February, began operations against the British in late March with his mixed Italian and German army. He forced the British, including Australian troops, into retreat from the Cyrenaica-Tripolitania border, took Benghazi on April 4, and shortly the struggle was focused on Tobruk. Here the British, including a large number of Australians, took a strong stand in the expectation of being besieged. The siege lasted 242 days from April 11. After Tobruk was isolated by Rommel's forces, the British retired to the Egyptian frontier. Wavell made two attempts to relieve Tobruk—one in mid-May, the other in mid-June—but both failed. He was relieved of command and replaced by Sir Claude Auchinleck. In July, at the instance of Sir Thomas Blamey, it was requested that the Australians in Tobruk be taken out by sea on the ground that they were becoming physically deteriorated; this was resisted by the imperial officers immediately concerned and by Churchill, but it was successfully insisted upon by Prime Minister Fadden, Menzies' successor, with the result that only a single Australian battalion actually saw the siege to its conclusion. The British finally forced Rommel to give up the siege on the day the Japanese bombed Pearl Harbor, and, indeed, he was forced to retreat out of Cyrenaica altogether. Opportunely receiving strong reinforcements, Rommel counterattacked on January 21, 1942, and Tobruk was in his hands by June 21. The British were forced back to a stand at El Alamein.

Like the first British failure to gain a conclusive victory in North Africa by pursuing the enemy into Tripolitania and destroying it, the second failure to secure victory was attributable also to the weakening of the forces at the disposal of the command. Earlier, they had been diverted to Greece; now the Far East called them. Because of the menace under which their homeland now lay, the sixth and seventh Australian divisions were returned to Australia. Nor was this all. Other elements were also sent to the Far East, and to complicate matters the responsibilities of the command were increased to encompass much of the Near East beyond North Africa. However, the Australian ninth division, based in Palestine, was brought to El Alamein, where it participated in stopping Rommel and in establishing the position. Auchinleck was relieved of command and replaced by General Sir Harold Alexander, with Lieutenant General Bernard Montgomery as field commander. The Australians made a distinguished contribution to Montgomery's successful battles at El Alamein which started Rommel on the road to destruction. As active pursuit toward Tripolitania got underway, the ninth was withdrawn for return home, and thus only the New Zealanders of the troops from the Southwest Pacific participated in the final triumph in North Africa and went on to fight in Italy. Unlike the New Zealanders, the Australians had left before American-British cooperation resulted in the ejection of the enemy from North Africa. The ninth division arrived in Australia in March 1943. Australia had suffered 18,700 casualties—3150 dead and 6800 prisoners—5000 in Greece and Crete. The Australian navy was also active in the Mediterranean theater against the Italians.

The decision to deploy Australian forces primarily in support of Britain in Europe was a calculated risk. The essence of the calculation was the gamble that the position in the western Pacific would not become directly menacing to the Australian homeland, that if it did deteriorate into warfare, this would be kept to the north away from Australia, and imperial assistance would be forthcoming at the moment of crisis in amply sufficient measure to keep the Australian homeland secure. The symbol, and in some proportion difficult to define the actuality, of imperial support in the defense of Australia was Singapore, and much attention was given at this time, actual and prospective, to strengthening it. The defensive position in the Netherlands Indies was also kept actively in view.

In the larger perspective the determination of Australia's security was not in Australian or imperial, least of all Dutch, hands. The ultimate decision on whether or not war would develop in the western Pacific, particularly directed toward Australia, was in the hands of the Japanese. To a very great extent British reassurances to Australia about the state of Singapore were composed of the persistent British doubt that Japan would risk war by a southward move at all and a striking underestimate of what Japan could accomplish by such a move. Japan's decision for war was certain to be a product of domestic forces difficult to weigh and interpret: Japanese calculations about the way in which the war in Europe was going for the Axis powers and their enemies, particularly in terms of the effect upon their colonial possessions in the East, and the likely ultimate response of Japan's opponents in the East to a southward thrust on her part. This tangled situation was further complicated by the fact that both what Japan would do would be determined in large measure by the outcome of Japanese-American diplomacy with regard to the issues in the western Pacific, and, assuming American failure to appease or deter Japan, that what Japan would accomplish to the menace of Australia if it then opted for a southward thrust would depend on how the United States responded to the challenge of armed force. As the Australians saw it, their tasks were to try as far as possible to keep on the good side of the Japanese, as by closing the Burma Road and sending Sir John Latham to them as minister, to help maintain the American and Japanese diplomatic conversations, and to endeavor to commit the Americans to cooperation with the British and themselves with regard to bases and sea and air power in the western Pacific—conceived both as deterrents to Japanese southward moves and as of vital importance in case of actual warfare. Why the Menzies government in the face of its undoubted knowledge of the risks it was taking in the Pacific allowed "Europe" to claim so high a proportion of its defensive power-in-being is a complex question involving judgment of the weight properly to be given in a potentially perilous situation to traditional imperial loyalties and to nationalistic considerations. A short answer is that the Menzies government chose not to try for a carefully calculated balance between the two but to overweigh traditional loyalties in a traditional fashion until it was too late to rectify the situation effectively.

Between the outbreak of war in Europe in 1939 and the coming of warfare in the western Pacific in 1941, when Australia was heavily involved in the Near East and otherwise in the British Europe-oriented strategy, it was also concerned with protecting its position in the Pacific. This involved moves at the highest diplomatic levels that could be reached to try to make Singapore serve its intended purpose, and efforts in the islands and on the continental mainland. All were well intentioned, none was sufficient nor successful.

With regard to diplomacy, conceived of as a means of influencing the course of events in the western Pacific, Australia was at a disadvantage. In 1941, when Prime Minister Menzies told his cabinet colleagues that Churchill had no proper understanding of dominion status, he also told them that "the more distant the problem from the heart of Empire the less he thought of it." That meant that Churchill thought relatively little about the western Pacific as compared to Europe. As the position in the western Pacific assumed a more menacing shape, the Australians became ever more concerned as it appeared about to impinge on their national security. Their conception of prospects and of dealing with developments did not at first differ materially from that of the British, but as the months of 1940 passed and their insecurity about Japanese intentions became greater, they developed a keen sense of urgency. To a marked degree the problem of obtaining reinsurance within the British community focused on Singapore and included gaining assurance that Britain would honor its promise to reinforce Singapore in all respects—manpower, air power, sea power—if Australia were menaced.

The European situation after the fall of France in mid-1940 lessened the possibility that Britain could do anything adequate about Singapore, as Churchill frankly declared—to the consternation of the Southwest Pacific dominions—ironically, just as the repercussions of the European crisis worsened the position. Although willing to assist in strengthening Singapore, the Australians thus ran against formidable obstacles in their campaign to get the job done even in the measure defined as adequate by the imperial service chiefs on the scene, let alone the measure apparently required: the British—or Churchill's—inability to see the situation, whether this involved thinking of Singapore as a determent to war or in war; the Churchillian failure to understand the actual condition of Singapore as a stronghold, partly explainable by faults in British communications; and in largest part the inability of Britain to act because of poverty of resources. When in London early in 1941 Menzies played for the final time and in the face of his cabinet's skepticism the card of deterring Japan from an adventurist course by diplomatic "firmness" and got nowhere, he came to the realization that "nothing [in any respect] could be achieved without the United States of America." The British had reached this conclusion with regard to themselves a year earlier.

Australia by that time had exchanged ministers with the United States. The first Australian minister to the United States, Richard G. Casey, had taken up his appointment in March 1940; the first American minister to Australia, Clarence Gauss, reached Canberra in July. However, the Australians found themselves as much at a disadvantage with the United States as with the United Kingdom, though for different reasons, and they accentuated their disadvantage by insisting that the presence of their minister in Washington did not imply "any departure from the diplomatic unity of the Empire." Since the Roosevelt administration was insecure about how to deal with the dominions (except for Canada and Eire) the tendency in Washington was to try to deal with them through the United Kingdom, an approach seemingly supported by the Australian emphasis on "diplomatic unity . . ." In dealings with Secretary of State Cordell Hull the Australians suffered a special handicap because of Hull's unfavorable memory of the trade dispute of 1936. But the fundamental difficulty was that Australia appeared to the Americans chiefly as an associate of the British in the Western Pacific, not as an independent factor. It was assumed that Australian power was at British disposal and that in some proportion decided in consultation with the British it would be brought into play, with British power, *north of the equator,* where the issues between the Americans and the Japanese had their focus and where, in the thinking of the armed forces, war would take place if it took place anywhere.

There appeared to be no urgent reason for the Americans to investigate and evaluate Australia in relation to the United States, least of all in relation to an armed conflict not likely to reach her or her vicinity. Australia was therefore seen as an ancillary, not a primary, factor in the equation in the western Pacific. The Americans had already defined a strategic approach to the war, epitomized in the slogan "Europe first." The first job would be to defeat Nazi Germany as the *fons et origo* of aggression, including in some fashion possible Japanese aggression. If the Japanese went to war no fundamental redefinition of policy would be required, because only such forces would be assigned to the Pacific as were necessary to "hold" them in check until Hitler was defeated and resources became available to finish them off. While the American position, established in substance by 1940, involved support of the British Empire against the Nazis, its exponents were very unclear about what they meant by the British Empire, for their minds were focused on the United Kingdom and they did not clearly see the possible predicament of an outlier of the Empire, such as Australia, if the Japanese actually attacked, especially since they failed to consider that the Japanese might at an early stage carry the war south of the equator. The Australians were in a remarkably poor position to campaign against this orientation in order to bring their own position into better perspective, since it closely conformed to their own view as an imperial associate, but it obviously lowered their visibility to the Americans and could deeply jeopardize their security.

With regard to protecting their position in the western Pacific, it must be emphasized that because of their heavy involvement in the Near East, the Australians had relatively little force to deploy, and that although Prime Minister Menzies made an effort to increase the intensity of the domestic war effort on his return from Britain in 1941, his effort to increase the deployable resources was largely frustrated by the political context in which he found himself. He was shortly to be forced out of office by his own nominal supporters.

Essentially, what the Menzies government tried to do was to support

Britain's Europe-oriented strategy while deploying the resources left over as advantageously as possible in the defense of Australia. It was not that the scheme of deployment was wrong but that the resources were insufficient. Since the British were unable, also because of poverty of resources, to strengthen Singapore adequately, the Australians were in the dangerously ambiguous position of having most of their defensive resources in "Europe" while unable to command any satisfactory support from "Europe" for their own defense in the western Pacific. This situation had been forecast by those students of British affairs who, since World War I, had alleged that Britain could no longer meet her imperial defense obligations in full. The Menzies government, by placing support of Britain in Europe ahead of national self-defense instead of in balance with it, had landed Australia in a precarious position. Thus, both the British and the Australians, seeking compensation for their inadequacies, mounted a campaign to commit the Americans to an intimately collaborative program involving bases and armed forces. Since the British were the principal British actors on the Washington stage and the Australians by choice but supernumeraries, the consequence was that the British focused attention on Singapore as their principal factor in the western Pacific equation, while the Australians could only call attention to possibly useful sites for bases in their territory, island and continental.

In this fashion the Australians were jockeyed, with an assist from their own version of international relations, into appearing to support the British thesis about Singapore when, as a matter of fact, they had been skeptical of Singapore at least since 1934, and their skepticism was at the time rightly on the increase. The British campaign to commit the Americans to collaboration in the western Pacific, always involving American use and support of Singapore, was conducted at all possible levels of approach but without success. The Americans stoutly resisted commitment to Singapore, doubting its usefulness as a base and rejecting the theses about its value as a deterrent and in actual warfare. Nor did the Americans respond favorably to the Australian suggestions about their sites for bases. Both had different ideas of what actual warfare in the western Pacific would be like. Both were wrong, and that reasonably accurate forecasts were made by bystanders was an irrelevancy. As a result, when war finally came all parties were at a disadvantage, and a collaboration in resistance to Japan had to be improvised among spreading ruin. The Australian primary commitment to "Europe" was still being honored to the debilitation of their national defense in the western Pacific. By the fortunes of domestic politics the Australian Labor party was then in office in the Commonwealth.

The tortuous course of Australian domestic politics from Menzies' accession to the prime ministership in 1939 until that of John Curtin in 1941, just two months before Pearl Harbor, was remarkable. Not the least remarkable aspect of the situation was the failure of the electorate in the election of 1940 to give either side that majority in the House which was indispensable if there was to be a government securely in office as the times required. The effect of the 1940 election was to pass the balance of power in the House to two crotchety independents, one inclined toward the conservatives, the other toward Labor. A solution would have been to form an all-party, or national, government, but Labor rejected this in accordance with its long-standing policy of ruling alone or not at all. In this situation Labor, led by Curtin, came to office with the political stalemate unresolved, met the Japanese challenge head on, and finally won the indispensable support of the electors in the general election of 1943.

Once installed in office in 1939 Menzies had somehow to fortify his position. Lacking charisma he had to attempt this by strictly practical political means, such as admitting to his cabinet men of doubtful reliability. As the leader of a minority in the House he had to do this sooner or later, especially since pro-Labor sentiment appeared to be on the rise in the country. An indicator was the fact that the seat in the House vacated when R. G. Casey was appointed minister to Washington was taken by Labor at the by-election. Anti-Laborism is the prime cement binding Australian conservatives together, even though it can, under the strain of factionalism, exhaust its cohesive virtue. In March 1940 Menzies came to an accommodation with the Country party, though only after Sir Earle Page had been replaced as leader by A. G. Cameron of South Australia—a man of violent emotions given to putting the hardest words on critics and opponents. Cameron brought Arthur W. Fadden of Queensland and John McEwen of Victoria with him into the Menzies cabinet. Sir Earle Page stayed well outside. W. M. Hughes, Menzies' erstwhile rival for the prime ministership, who entertained a fierce dislike of him, remained inside. Ambitious P. C. Spender of New South Wales received a promotion in the hierarchy. The Menzies position was strengthened. But in August three cabinet members, all able and all particularly loyal to Menzies personally, lost their lives in an airplane accident at Canberra. This materially weakened the security of Menzies' position.

Menzies had little cause for complaint about the parliamentary attitude of John Curtin, or indeed of the Labor party, toward him, particularly when the prosecution of the war was in question. There were obvious policy differences, notably over how to balance imperial and national defense commitments, how to govern banking and credit policy, and the specifics of social policy affecting the civilian population, but on the war as war there was substantial agreement. Curtin's parliamentary manner was benign, not aggressive. In June 1940 the Labor party formally defined its attitudes in a long resolution: "Complete and indissoluble unity with the Allies"; control of the "entire resources" of the country by the Commonwealth government; a strong and accelerating domestic war effort; trade union rights to be safeguarded; and an excess profits tax to take the profit out of war for the capitalists. But adumbrating a more serious difference with the Menzies government was the declaration, "the extent of European participation . . . to be determined by circumstances as they arise, having regard to the paramount necessity of Australia's defence." Not only did this refer to Labor's earlier attitude, but Menzies' failure to interpret the point as Labor would have interpreted it led to Labor's bitterest criticism of him and his associates. Labor, however, accepted "European participation"; indeed, in the resolution it accepted the policy of sending divisions to the Near East and reinforcing them. It simply wanted a different balance. Then turning to the political situation it reiterated that "the Labor Party should maintain its integral identity" and proposed "that a National War Council, including representatives of Labor, should be established to advise the Government in respect to the conduct of the war and in preparing for postwar reconstruction." Curtin communicated all this to Menzies, who countered by once more putting the case for a "national government." This was considered by the Labor parliamentarians and rejected.

On the eve of the 1940 general election the state of the parties was: United Australia party twenty-five and Country party sixteen, giving the government forty-one supporters; Labor led by Curtin twenty-seven and so-called Anti-Communist (i.e., Lang) Labor led by John Beasley five; and one independent (the dissident wheat farmer). In the Senate the government coalition had twenty seats to Labor's sixteen. After the polling the line-up was United Australia twenty-three, Country party thirteen, Labor thirty-two, Anti-Communist Labor four, and two independents—the wheat farmer and a wealthy Melbourne retail merchant close to the U.A.P. but critical of it. The Senate remained in the government's hands. This was regarded as an "unworkable" Parliament. Menzies told a foreign journalist, "If my fools had had longer they would have done worse." In hard fact he had not acquired any new supporters of substance—he had to go on with the same crowd—while Labor had added to its parliamentarians two able men, J. B. Chifley, returned to Parliament for the first time since the debacle of 1931, and Dr. H. V. Evatt, returned to politics after nine years on the High Court bench. Ironically, both were from New South Wales where Menzies had suffered his worst misfortunes.

In immediate sequel Menzies was given a vote of confidence by the U.A.P. members, securing the prime ministership, but things went curiously in the Country party. After the election A. G. Cameron had arranged a meeting between Menzies and Sir Earle Page at which they had composed their seemingly irreconcilable differences, but when the Country party discussed the leadership question, there was an obvious reluctance even to nominate Cameron for the post, although in the end this was done. When it came to a vote the members divided equally between Sir Earle Page and John McEwen and no way to break the tie could be discovered. In desperation the members voted unanimously to elect Arthur W. Fadden deputy leader and instructed him to act as leader. Actually, Fadden was leader for some years thereafter. Cameron walked out and eventually joined the U.A.P. When Menzies announced his cabinet it was revealed that he had found places for Fadden (the senior post of treasurer), McEwen, and Page, but not for Cameron. From the U.A.P. Hughes and Spender were still with him and Harold Holt had been found a place. The conservatives had achieved a simulacrum of unity by ostentatiously papering-over the well-known cracks.

The unsatisfactory character of the election results immediately brought the question of parliamentary cooperation to the fore. The negotiations were complex, involving spokesmen for all four parties and the independents. Along the way Curtin and Beasley tried to compose party differences but failed. The skirmishing was around the price the Menzies government could be persuaded to pay in terms of acceptance of Opposition policies for Opposition participation in the National War Council Labor had proposed. Dr. Evatt wanted to push harder for office than Curtin, in the adverse parliamentary circumstances, was willing to do. Labor's proposal for a Council was accepted, but how far Menzies committed himself to Labor's policies, and to which, was unclear. The Council was to consist of the prime minister and two U.A.P. ministers, one Country party minister, three representatives of the A.L.P., and one of the Beasley group. The Council was consultative, not executive. With vicissitudes, it lasted out the war.

It was this precariously balanced situation that Menzies left behind him when he went to London early in 1941 to take part in the councils of Empire. It then emerged that he made a much more favorable impression as a man and political leader in Britain (and, when he crossed the Atlantic, in America) than he did at home. Participation in affairs at the highest level keyed Menzies up; he was challenged to do his best, which was very good, as he rarely felt he was in Australia. He carried this overseas inflatus back to Australia with him in April, and his first impact was forceful. His prestige was enhanced. His message was that Australia must be committed to an unlimited war effort across the board, military and civilian, not only to support the existing deployment of forces but to achieve that balanced deployment which would fortify Australia's position in the Pacific. During Menzies' absence Curtin had become progressively more concerned about the worsening position in the western Pacific and was in a mood to support Menzies. While Menzies was away Labor had proposed to recall some of the troops in the Near East to correct the obvious imbalance. Menzies reorganized and improved the administrative structure to step up war-related production, added ministers to the cabinet and ungraded others, and appeared to be about to achieve his full stature as a national war leader.

He had, however, miscalculated, not what should be done, but the strength of his personal political position. Although it was still plain that Labor's power was increasing—in March 1941 the Beasley Labor faction had joined the Curtin-led parliamentary party, closing Labor's ranks, and in May, W. J. McKell had led New South Wales Labor to a resounding triumph—it was not Labor that threatened him. It was his own cabinet. While he had been away Arthur Fadden had been acting prime minister. Fadden, leader of the Country party by default, was very ambitious. A bustling, cocky man, unpolished but conventionally genial, formerly a town clerk, and by trade an accountant, Fadden found the position of prime minister decidedly to his taste. He got along very well with John Curtin and mistook Curtin's instinctive courtesy for political ascendancy over him. He found he was popular with the cabinet, as Menzies was not. Menzies' absence released the inhibitions of the cabinet, revealing to Fadden allies in the U.A.P. He believed that he was popular with the people, as Menzies was not. The idea came to him that he, although leader of the minority party of the coalition, should, against all precedent and political reason, displace Menzies and thus solve the problem of an insecure government led by an "unpopular" prime minister. Fadden's calculations were right up to the point of displacing Menzies, but he soon found that there was more to being prime minister than being "popular" personally. To lend dignity to the proposed regicide the cabal first suggested that Menzies be "kicked upstairs" by being returned to London as Australian spokesman at the imperial level, leaving Fadden in charge in Canberra. Labor vetoed this on the ground that the times required the presence of the prime minister in Australia. (Sir Earle Page was sent to London instead.) The cabinet then set about to convince Menzies that he was not wanted and after three stormy cabinet sessions he resigned. Not only did Fadden and his Country party associates openly show their hostility but W. M. Hughes and P. C. Spender (expressing the view of the anti-Menzies New South Wales faction) showed that they were of the same mind. Even Harold Holt concurred. Unlike the deposition of Hughes in 1923, which was a consequence of pressure from outside, Menzies' deposition was an inside job. It was, said a horrified witness, "a lynching." Fadden became prime minister on August 29, 1941. Menzies, with striking magnanimity, and supported by his strong sense of responsibility, accepted the post of minister for Defence Coordination in Fadden's cabinet. On October 7 Labor, with the support of both independents, defeated the Fadden government on its budget, and Curtin was called upon to form a Labor government.

John Curtin was a seemingly mild, sensitive, normally soft-spoken, gentle-mannered, earnest man, basically of a retiring disposition. He was temperamental, had a quick temper, and lacked the anodyne of humor. He never troubled to develop a "public image." Elevation to the prime ministership challenged him to transcend himself—and he did.

He was born in Creswick, Victoria, near Ballarat, in 1885. Creswick had been the locale of a rich alluvial gold field where there had been some deep mining, but in Curtin's youth it was a small, third-rate service town for farmers and graziers. Curtin was the son of a policeman, but during the boy's early youth the father was crippled by rheumatism and this adversely affected the family fortunes. Of Irish stock, the Curtin family was Roman Catholic, but Curtin himself, coming under the influence of the rationalists, lapsed as a very young man. He attended state schools, but left at fourteen to go to work. Beyond his basic schooling he was self-educated; early in life he acquired the habit of wide and reflective reading. Going to Melbourne in search of work, Curtain became an apprentice printer. There he came under the influence not only of the rationalists but also of the English socialist agitator Tom Mann, and he became warmly friendly with Frank Anstey, a key figure in establishing Labor's hostility to "the Money Power" and its fixation on gaining governmental control of banking and credit. Anstey's influence was deeper and more enduring than Mann's. At twenty-one in 1906 Curtin joined Mann's Victorian Socialist party, organized as a "vanguard" group dedicated to pushing Labor toward a more radical program. In the service of socialism Curtin became a soapbox orator on the Yarra Bank. But Curtin was not simply a self-educated socialist intellectual; he also found great satisfaction in the basic constituent of Australian popular culture, sport. He played Australian-rules football and cricket, he walked, and he swam. He was devoted to billiards. His weakness, however, was drink, and at one stage of his life it almost ruined him. He suffered severely from frustration and self-doubt.

From the heady but febrile excitements of radical agitation he moved to the stern practicalities of trade unionism. He became secretary of the Victorian Timber Workers' Union and thus the union's key official. He edited the union's journal and as far as a trade went, he was always thereafter a journalist. His trade union work taught him to manage men by speech and pen. Curtin developed clarity of utterance but not concision; he tended to be wordy. He got his points across, but he did not make them economically. The striking verbal epitome that carried conviction in a flash eluded him.

A conspicuous opponent in Victoria of Hughes's conscription proposal of 1916, Curtin went to Western Australia early in 1917 to edit the weekly *Westralian Worker*. Allegedly, he did so on the advice of Anstey, who sought to shelter him for fuller development than seemed likely in the hectic environment of Melbourne. Curtin fought the Hughes 1917 conscription referendum and then settled down to party work in the west. He stayed with *The Westralian Worker* until 1928. His job was to build up the party after the anticonscription debacle. As a proselytizer he was enabled to sort out his ideas and to develop his writing and speaking abilities. Like most successful Laborites he became at once a sound party man of a leftist tinge and strongly nationalistic. Bypassing state politics, he won a seat in the federal House in 1928, but lost it in the Labor debacle of 1931. As an Anstey man, he opposed Scullin's acceptance of the Premiers' Plan, stigmatizing it as dirty-bottle washing for the conservatives and advocated resignation if no alternative to implementation could be found. He was re-elected to the House in 1934 and in 1935 became leader of the parliamentary party in succession to Scullin. At this stage he was, even to the parliamentary newspapermen, simply "that bloke from the West." His constituency was Fremantle, a constituency gerrymandered to counterbalance the Labor stronghold at the port by including some of the middle-class suburbs of Perth. It was a rather unsafe seat from the Labor point of view, but Curtin stuck to it, resisting transfer elsewhere. In 1940 he held it only by virtue of the votes of the soldiers overseas. He was the first Western Australian to become prime minister.

Labor took office with a consciousness that Australia's defense position was weak and with a determination to strengthen it by intensifying the war effort in spite of public apathy. Curtin had given a lead in that direction even before ousting the conservatives from office. It had been behind his support of the Menzies attempt to engineer an unlimited war effort. But even though Labor was, through the War Council, better informed about the situation than would have been the case in the normal course of politics, it did not have a perfect understanding. Above all it did not realize that within two months the situation in the Western Pacific would come to a frighteningly thunderous climax which would confront Australia with the challenge of war in a historically unprecedented shape. Hitherto war had been a challenge far away. Now it was suddenly to be a challenge at the gates. It was not certain that it could be kept at the gates. It might come into the front yard.

When that war broke out in December 1941 the Australians expected that it would be fought to the north, focused on Singapore, and that their peculiar risk was Japanese raids into the Tasman Sea, either to interfere with shipping or to attack vital points on the continental coast. While it was recognized that Pearl Harbor was a disaster to the Americans, the details of the disaster only belatedly became known. For the moment the most important conclusion was that the Americans would fight and the long-sought Anglo-American collaboration in the western Pacific would become a reality. The Australians, already implicated in Malaya, did what they could to strengthen their position; indeed, they extended their thin resources of men and matériel into the islands in relation to the Malay Barrier. They welcomed the establishment of the ABDA command under Sir Archibald Wavell by Roosevelt and Churchill, for it represented a collaboration they had long sought, but they were annoyed that they were not invited to participate directly at the highest level of decision at Washington. They then began their protracted campaign for status in the top leadership of the war and the diplomacy flowing from it. Labor's position was far more nationalistic in genesis and expression than anything the conservatives had ever essayed.

The rapidity with which the situation deteriorated under the impact of the Japanese thrust was a great shock not only because it was utterly disproportionate to earlier estimates of the Japanese strength, in general and in detail—Japanese strategical and tactical ability, capacity in the air, on the sea and on the ground, with regard to weapons, and with regard to personal fighting qualities—but also, conversely, because of the revelation that they and their associates were weaker than had yet been candidly admitted. They began to fear an invasion of their continent, and a plan was made for the defense of the "heartland" on the continent itself. Their resources for this were frighteningly limited.

The continent was drawn into the geography of the ABDA command when the northwestern portion was included. The continental focus at this stage was Darwin in Northern Territory. Both sides in the struggle recognized the importance of Darwin as a point from which forces could be sent in support of the Malay Barrier, though it was weak in itself not only because of its isolation but because of its underdevelopment for wartime uses. Darwin was first attacked from the air by the Japanese on February 19, 1942, the first occasion in history on which shots fired by an external enemy had been directed against the Australian continent. During the course of the war more than sixty air raids were suffered by the town.

By the time Darwin was raided not only was it already serving the Australians, the British, and the Dutch, but also the Americans. The Americans tried to support their own position in the Philippines against the Japanese and to participate in the defense of the Malay Barrier. When the possibility of implementing the American strategy of an approach to the western Pacific north of the equator disappeared, the possibility of an approach to the combat area from the south was explored. In December General Dwight Eisenhower suggested an approach to the Philippines via Rabaul on the island of New Britain; and shortly the use of the northern continental mainland of Australia for air or sea bases was suggested. It was too late to do anything constructive about these proposals, and in fact it was Darwin which first importantly served American combat purposes. American troops intended for the Philippines but diverted to Australia were sent to Darwin via Brisbane and found American aviators and navy units already there. The aviators had pioneered the use of Australia as a base, and an American aviator, Lieutenant General George H. Brett, was deputy to the commander in chief of ABDA. The Americans suffered heavily in the first Japanese raid on Darwin.

The portent of collapse in the north was the loss of the "Repulse" and the "Prince of Wales" by a Japanese air bombing attack on December 10, 1941. These ships symbolized the British promise to reinforce Singapore in an emergency, and the absence of air cover for them on their journey to the north along the peninsula against Japanese landing parties symbolized that what the British could do was too little. However, the effort to strengthen Singapore, Malaya, and the Malay Barrier in terms of troops, planes, and ships continued after this disaster, and the Australians participated in it. Singapore fell, victim of an approach down the Malay Peninsula to its unfortified backdoor, on February 16, 1942. Java fell on March 12, 1942. Both disasters cost the Australians heavily in terms of prisoners of war—14,972 at Singapore, 5000 in the Netherlands Indies. The sufferings of these prisoners, and others taken later, strongly fortified anti-Japanese sentiment in Australia. Australians were numerously involved in the dreadful Burma Railway affair. On the other hand, epic escapes were made from beleaguered Singapore and from Java which gilded the horror of war with adventurous heroism. To the naval defense of Java the Australians contributed not only seagoing day labor but also such a tragic epic as that of the destroyer "Perth."

The inexorable unfolding of disaster was not without its controversies between the Australians and the British. Once again Churchill disagreed with the Australians, this time with John Curtin, over the disposition of Australian troops. Churchill sought not only to divert Australian troops recalled from the Middle East for the defense of their homeland to Ceylon, Singapore, and Java, but more controversially to Burma. Curtin, backed by his military advisers, wisely resisted the Burmese diversion, to Churchill's annoyance—both for technical and strategic reasons in the later judgment of the Australian military historians. In the final phases Churchill was preoccupied with trying to keep the Japanese out of the Indian Ocean, the Australians with trying to keep them off their continent. Churchill never really believed that an invasion of Australia was likely; hence he put British assistance to Australia on the rather gruesome basis that it would be supplied after invasion had actually taken place. At this stage Roosevelt, apparently still thinking of Australia as ancillary to British power in the East, supported Churchill by offering to supply American troops for the continent if the Australians would agree that their troops remain in the Middle East and accept transfer in part to the Malay Barrier area. Roosevelt pressured Curtin to accept this arrangement through Minister Casey in Washington.

The dispersion after the collapse of the Malay Barrier was westward to Burma, India, and Ceylon and southward to Australia. Early in February the Australian chief of staff suggested to his government that in the situation then emerging Australia was bound to be the principal base for any counterattack on the Japanese in the western Pacific. Its preservation for this role was vital. However, the direct Japanese menace to Australian security was not conceived as arriving via Darwin, the significance of which remained its relation to the Malay Barrier, but via the islands to the northeast of the continent from the Japanese mandate of Micronesia. The focal point there was Rabaul. The Japanese first attacked Rabaul on January 4, 1942; and on the twenty-third they took possession of it, capturing or dispersing the Australian defenders. This seemed to portend an invasion of the continent by way of New Guinea and down the tropical coast of Queensland to breach the defensive line of the "heartland"—called the Brisbane Line—in the southeast. This approach of an enemy had been envisioned by Kitchener years earlier, even before the coastal railway had been built. While in the inevitable ignorance of wartime the Japanese intention was read as continental invasion in force, what the Japanese actually had in mind was to isolate and blockade the Pacific Coast "heartland" and let it wither away by gaining possession of strategic islands and cutting the lines of communication with the Panama Canal and the west coast of the United States. Their eyes were on New Guinea, the Solomons, New Caledonia, Samoa, Fiji . . . (see Chapter XI).

As the fighting lines moved toward Australia the government acted, in the face of much popular apathy, to put the country on a war footing. Late in December Prime Minister Curtin released a startling statement of his government's conclusion about how the war would have to be fought. Stating the opinion that "the war with Japan is not a phase of the struggle with the Axis Powers, but a new war," Curtin declared:

The . . . Government . . . regards the Pacific struggle as primarily one in which the United States and Australia must have the fullest say in the direction of the democracies' fighting plan. Without any inhibitions of any kind, I make it quite clear that Australia looks to America, free of any pang as to our traditional links or kinship with the United Kingdom. We know the problems that the United Kingdom faces . . . But we know . . . that Australia can go and Britain can still hold on. We are . . . determined that Australia shall not go . . .

These were fighting words in a multiple sense, for they appeared not only to be a rousing assertion that "Australia shall not go" but also a repudiation of the traditional loyalty to Britain at a moment of mutual peril. What Curtin meant, however, was nothing so drastic as that—two days later he was declaring that "our loyalty to the King goes to the very core of our national life. I . . . consider . . . Australia an organic part of the whole structure" of the British Empire. He intended a dramatic assertion of Labor's intentions (a) to continue the campaign for equality of status and certain participation in the highest direction of the war, and (b) to realize to the full on that reinsurance of Australia's security by the Americans toward which the conservatives had been feeling their way—if they had had any clear purpose—perhaps since 1940 and certainly since Menzies had "caught on" in London early in 1941. But what neither the Labor government nor the critics of Curtin's unfortunate formulation were clear about was how it was to operate and how it would influence the positions and actions of Australia, the United Kingdom, and the United States. In any event Curtin's hyperbole was shown to be unnecessary. The Labor government also at this time expected that help in the Pacific would be forthcoming from the U.S.S.R., apparently on the assumption that the Russians would ignore or denounce the Soviet-Japanese nonaggression pact. The pact was not denounced until April 6, 1945.

What the Australians primarily sought was defense against the Japanese and the opportunity to collaborate with the paramount friendly power in the Pacific in repelling the Japanese. What the Americans sought was to preserve Australia as a base from which to mount resistance to the Japanese. They accepted Australia as a base before they had any clear idea of her strength as an ally; in fact her strength was one of the most rewarding surprises the Americans had in the Pacific war. The Australians were clear about the desirability—indeed the indispensability—of collaboration, but they were not clear about the thinking of the high directors of the war, which was in implicit contradiction of the Australian thesis that the war in the western Pacific was a new war to be fought aggressively from the beginning. To them it was a phase of the Europe-centered war against the Axis. Months before war had broken out in the western Pacific, they had decided that the ruling consideration must be to defeat the enemy in Europe and that if a Pacific war broke out the strategy should be to fight a low-pressure war—to contain and harass the Japanese but to reserve an all-out assault on them until victory had been attained in Europe. As the Australians saw the situation their position was practically identical with that of the New Zealanders, who reciprocated the opinion (see Chapter VIII). The Australians and the New Zealanders, therefore, tried to approach the United States jointly, as illustrated by their agreement in February 1942 that they would accept an American commander in chief.

The Americans appeared briefly to accept this position, as is illustrated by the short-lived Anzac naval arrangement during the life of ABDA. But when the British and the Americans faced the radically deteriorated situation in March 1942 and the British passed responsibility for the western Pacific war to the Americans, the Americans put Australia and New Zealand into complementary but different areas. Australia was placed in a Southwest Pacific Area, which was oriented north through New Guinea toward the Philippines and Japan, while New Zealand was placed in a South Pacific Area, the focus of which was the islands north of New Zealand and eastward of the Australian area. The Australians were thus within an area in which their primary relations were with the United States Army and the New Zealanders within an area in which their primary contacts were with the United States Navy. The first naval task was to guarantee the viability of the lines of communication between Australia, New Zealand, the United States west coast, and the Panama Canal through the islands. To command the area of which Australia was the fundamental part, the Americans assigned General Douglas MacArthur, arranging, in view of the delicately dangerous position in the Philippines, that the Australians appear to have asked for him. Mac-

Arthur arrived by air at Darwin in the midst of a Japanese air raid and proceeded via Alice Springs to Melbourne. He formally assumed his command on April 19. Almost immediately he decided that the defense of Australia should be mounted in New Guinea and that the push against the Japanese should proceed north from there. This conformed equally with the traditional opinion that Australia's defense was best conducted "away from" the continent and with the current position of the Labor government. The Brisbane Line thereupon became a mare's nest out of which the politicians drew fearful and wonderful things.

But while this represented important progress with regard to Australian-American collaboration, it left both the Australians and the United States command with the problem of dealing with the consequences of the Europe-first emphasis in the western Pacific. What both parties wanted was the allocation to the western Pacific of manpower and matériel sufficient not only to stop the Japanese but to begin rolling them back from their achieved "frontiers" toward their homeland. That MacArthur saw the situation in terms practically identical with the Australian view was a lucky circumstance and that the naval authorites in the Pacific also agreed was additional good luck. The task was not easy, however, but because focus of the argument was in Washington and was conducted in a characteristically American context, it was easier than if British ideas had ruled, if the evidence in the diaries of Lord Alanbrooke is to be taken seriously.

The Curtin government slightly modified the inherited administrative structure, introduced new personnel, shifted the policy emphasis to conform with its social bias, and about the time the "Prince of Wales" and the "Repulse" were sunk began to step up the pace of action toward what Curtin was to call a "work or fight" regime. Necessarily, this was not a cautiously or exhaustively planned effort and, given the very fast pace, it was an effort inherently liable to bottlenecks and disbalances. Under the prick of fear of invasion of the continent the pace was at its briskest during 1942 and the first six months of 1943, when the progress of the war in New Guinea made it possible to announce that the pressure directly on Australia had been effectively relieved. However, the war was still going on in Europe, and the war in the Pacific still had a very long way to go. But the government's reassessment of the position allowed a shift of resources in order to carry on at a stiff pace during the remainder of the war, however protracted it might be.

The Curtin government sought to manage the country's manpower and capacity for production as would best enable it to meet four basic responsibilities: first, the defense of Australia; second and integrally related to the foregoing, its responsibility for supply to the American forces under Reciprocal Lend-Lease, for which an agreement was signed in September 1942; third, its responsibility to keep up the flow of food-stuffs and fibers to the United Kingdom; and fourth, its responsibility for the supply of the civilian population. The understanding was that all responsibilities had to be judged in relation to the war and therefore any seeming priority of one over another had to be determined by reference to the total war context. The responsibilities had to be met in largest measure by a redeployment of the resident manpower and the existing production facilities. Though the contribution of the Americans through Lend-Lease to the facilitating of production in Australia was important, their primary contribution was military manpower and military hard-ware.

A major move, therefore, was to reduce civilian factory production and sharply to "rationalize" what was allowed to continue, this not only reducing the flow of supplies to the civilian market but also the varieties within the supply, thus releasing facilities for war work or preventing their absorbing materials vital in war production. While there was capital investment in new facilities, with emphasis on those for munitions pro-duction, aircraft production, and shipbuilding, there was no likelihood that the pressure for war production could be eased in any considerable part by bringing into being a vast range of new plants, as in North America. From 1942–43 private investment became negative. The greater proportion of the construction work passed into the hands of an Allied Works Council, with E. G. Theodore in charge, which not only built new factories and facilities but also constructed the facilities needed by the Australian and American armed forces and built strategic roads for internal transport, notably in northern Queensland and Northern Ter-ritory. To support the Council's work, machines and manpower were transferred from state public works except as they could be related to wartime needs. The Council reached its manpower peak at the end of 1942.

In its impact the Curtin program involved a frontal invasion of the civilian-serving economy to divert resources to war-serving ends, some-thing Menzies had never found possible to undertake. The trend from the beginning was toward "austerity"; it was reached before the end of 1942. The standard was that of Britain, not of North America, where resources were so monumentally greater. The cherished amenities of peacetime life suffered sharp restriction, and when the pressure on food supplies coming forward became acute, there was no hesitation about submitting the Australian civilians to rationing even with regard to commodities of which Australia was normally a considerable exporter, let alone such imported items as tea, without which life in Australia is hardly supportable.

Integral to the new disposition of the production facilities and the building up of the armed forces was the redeployment of the manpower resources. Working in close relation to those charged with the direction of industry and the armed forces, a manpower directorate undertook this task, using compulsion. It shifted manpower from nonessential industry into war-related industry, from retail trade, banking, insurance, etc., to more vital use elsewhere, not impeding a drift out of agriculture. It trained and placed hosts of new technicians, and recruited women not only to fill certain places vacated by men but also to make a strikingly large net addition to the supply of labor. Since any moves having to do with labor and its utilization involved the trade unions and their elaborate structure of controls over terms and conditions of employment, the directorate of manpower could only function in close collaboration with trade union representatives. Fortunately, they exhibited an unexampled flexibility. By September 1942 the bottom of the manpower barrel was clearly in sight, but there was almost a year yet to go before another redeployment could be undertaken. At this stage the most disadvantaged segment of the economy with regard to manpower was agriculture. In spite of mounting pressure to step up production of, for example, vegetables for the American and Australian armed forces, which created a manpower problem, the ruling view was that agriculture was to be seen chiefly in terms of awkward surpluses.

In another phase, shifting the labor force brought into being a large army of conscripts for the defense of Australia and its territories—formed without too active a reference to the needs of the production apparatus. The troops returning from the Middle East, who would form the hard core of the expanded army, were, of course, volunteers, available for service anywhere in the world. So also were the airmen and the sailors. The question arose as to how the expanded army could be used successfully in defense of the Commonwealth with part of it employable only within fixed geographical limits and part of it employable anywhere. A considerable proportion of the conscripts showed their spirit by volunteering for overseas service, one motive, interestingly enough, being to get into a more prestigious branch of the service. The difficulty nevertheless remained, and it became acute as 1942 wore on, for it became obvious that the defense of Australia could not be conducted entirely within the continental limits and portions of New Guinea and well might involve sending troops into the Netherlands East Indies, the Solomon Islands, and perhaps farther afield to the north. The obvious tactic was either to abolish the restriction on the use of conscripts which, after all, was not rooted in a conception of responsibility for the defense of Australia as such but in a conception of a proper participation in imperial defense, or redefine the area in which conscripts might be employed. Before all Australian eyes was the American conscript force deployed in the defense of a foreign country of which it knew very little. Prime Minister Curtin was deeply committed to opposition to conscription for overseas service and so was his party, but at this stage only a minority in the party was likely to take a stubbornly doctrinaire position in opposition to change. In fact, opposition to full Australian participation in the war was currently at a heavy discount; in December 1942 the ban on the Communist party was lifted and as a prowar party it began its period of most rapid growth and most ramifying influence. Curtin was able to gain support for change not only outside Parliament and the Labor party but inside the party and the parliamentary caucus. In January 1943 the area in which conscripts might serve was redefined as from the equator in the north and the 110th and the 159th meridians on the east and west. This did not free the conscripts for use over the entire area likely to be determined as relating to the defense of Australia, but it considerably enlarged it. The restriction never became embarrassing in the prosecution of the war.

In financing the gigantic war effort significant changes were made by Treasurer J. B. Chifley. He operated within a context in which the national income was rising rapidly (national income produced £935 million in 1940–41 and £1283 million in 1943–44) but in which the Commonwealth's defense expenditures were rising still faster both absolutely and as a proportion of total expenditures. The concentration on war was constantly intensifying. He could avoid neither increases in taxes nor the widening of the gaps which had to be closed by borrowing. He paid for as much of the war out of current income as he could, in accordance with Labor's policy, but he simply could not pay for all of it that way. The loan program was carried out domestically. With regard to taxes he showed Labor's bias by proceeding to intensify the incidence on the higher income brackets and companies first and only then, and under the cover of the need to sop up excess purchasing power in the hands of wage earners, proceeded to deal severely with the recipients of the smaller incomes. With regard to taxes Chifley early made a move which was the outstanding contribution of World War II to that aggrandizement of the Commonwealth in relation to the states which had marked World War I. Early in 1942 he sponsored legislation that in effect required the states to vacate the field of income tax. The objective was to achieve a uniformity in the incidence of the tax throughout the Commonwealth which it was illegal to do by discrimination to meet the problem of varying state rates, as well as to gain Commonwealth control of taxes on income regardless of their level. The states were given compensation by grants roughly equivalent to the income taxes they had been collecting. The scheme was challenged in the High Court, but the verdict went to the Commonwealth on more secure grounds than its defense power and what was ostensibly a wartime expedient became a permanent fixture.

Chifley also took early steps to bring banking and credit policy into line with Labor's conceptions, largely in terms of Labor's reading of the report of the Royal Commission of 1937. This was done by regulations under the National Security Act and did not become politically arguable until 1945, when the scheme was legislated. Also within Chifley's purview or influence, though not directly his administrative responsibility as treasurer, was price control, which it was hoped would become a permanent part of the Commonwealth's economic powers, and social security which he regarded as a necessary support (rather than a thing-in-itself) to the then but faintly adumbrated central postwar Labor policy of "full employment." The significant change in price control administration was a shift from allowing price rises as costs demonstrably rose to the use of subsidies to fudge the rises on the ground of blocking inflation. Wth regard to social services, their elaboration in wartime had been initiated by Menzies, who in 1941 had added child endowment. In 1943 Labor, after its electoral victory, added widows' pensions, invalid pensioners' wives' benefits, and funeral benefits for all pensioners, and in anticipation of the further and more fundamental elaboration now forecast, established a National Welfare Fund, in the Commonwealth's financial system a trust fund. A welfare state was in view.

While Chifley's attention to war finance was exemplary, the tilt of his mind was definitely toward postwar reconstruction. When in December 1942 a Ministry of Postwar Reconstruction was established, he was put in charge of it with Dr. H. C. Coombs as the director-general. What nourished Chifley's keen interest in reconstruction was his determination that never again should the Australian working class suffer as he felt it had suffered in the Great Depression. Chifley was determined not to return to those days. Australia's postwar planning was permeated with antidepression thinking of a Keynesian character. The ideal toward which he looked was what he came to call, with surprising sentimentality and surpassing vagueness, "the light on the hill"—symbolizing a socialist society. But if the beckoning ideal was vague and in the Australian context rather bedraggled, it was shared by his prime minister, most of his cabinet associates, and a large proportion of his countrymen. The means chosen for reconstruction were a mixture of the modish and the traditional.

Labor had accepted that it should not deliberately pursue socialism under the cover of putting the country on a war footing—the allegation that it *was* so doing was a favorite ploy of its conservative critics. But Labor was committed, and had been since its important war resolution of June 1940, to the planning of reconstruction while the war was still on. It could not fail to be heartened to perceive how much of what had to be done to mobilize a country for war, whether its peacetime stance was capitalist or socialist, savored, in its book, of socialism. The problem was how much of what had to be done to which Labor was highly sympathetic could be carried forward and retained in peacetime. Labor found the directed economy congenial to its long-term purposes, and there inevitably arose the argument that if the economy could be so successfully directed in wartime, even if to an economic equivalent of Lord Keynes's famous postholes, why could it not be successfully "directed" in the same fashion to peacetime ends? As it turned out the answer, especially with regard to significant aspects, was found not so much in terms of war economy or socialism as constitutionality. The constitutional criterion proved lethal to some of the devices Labor most cherished.

The key idea in the reconstruction plan that evolved was "full employment." With this key a door was to be opened on a new and inspiriting perspective on the ancient Australian preoccupation of development, or what the economists came to call "growth," envisioned to consist in a high degree of industrialization, though the rural industries were also a prominent concern. To turn the key in the social lock, emphasis was placed on banking and credit policy, that old Labor concern, and around this were arranged contributory or ancillary policies designed to make life and labor better—from a very considerable extension of the social services to housing and town planning, railway unification and extension in the "permanent frontier" areas of the north, road building, expansion of electricity supply, more irrigation, and a revivified educational system with much facilitated access to largely expanded opportunities up to the university level. Although the primary responsibility for the promotion and execution of development would remain constitutionally with the states, the federal government would by an extension of its constitutional powers undertake enlarged responsibilities, govern general economic policy, and participate more variously than ever before both administratively and financially. The Commonwealth bureaucracy would necessarily be enlarged. The use of nationalization (a term used interchangeably with socialization) as a weapon was not precluded either for commodity production or services or either for established industries or new industries to be set up, but the ideal was in actual fact a mixed economy, as Labor defined the mixture from time to time, with factory industry peculiarly the province of the private entrepreneurs. In accordance with Labor tradition, a tenderness for small-scale private enterprise was forecast. And a steady job at good wages as man's ultimate boon in this world was not merely to be for men already in Australia; there was to be a vigorous promotion of immigration, a surprising note for Labor to strike, to build up the population to a size more compatible with Australian resources and the now painfully obvious defense needs. And "full employment" was to be advocated internationally as the proper policy of all nations. What was good for Australia was good for all mankind. How this program worked out in actuality became a significant aspect of the substance of Chifley's postwar prime ministership. Here it can be said that to a surprising extent it forecast the general tone, though not every note of the postwar Australian symphony. Perhaps because of the close association of so many Labor-sympathetic intellectuals with the Reconstruction Ministry and the Treasury, this was by far the most sophisticated program Labor had ever evolved.

Labor's well-established bias was, of course, in favor of the aggrandizement of the Commonwealth, especially in terms of its powers in socio-economic matters, and it had clearly demonstrated what it conceived this to mean in terms of constitutional change thirty years earlier. The vast enlargement of the Commonwealth's effective power under the defense power allowed a foretaste of what could be done by a strong Commonwealth, but the taste was wry insofar as it was recognized that with the coming of peace the constitutional support of the wartime structure would be withdrawn. Labor had no real choice but to face the question of constitutional revision while the war was going on, even though there might be question of the wisdom of attempting to achieve it in wartime. It did so with considerable optimism, fortified by the knowledge that thoughtful men on both sides of the political dialogue recognized the need for an enlargement of Commonwealth powers in the interest of effective and efficient government in an integrating nation, but the optimism was tempered insofar as it was recognized that state governments of any political complexion were fairly sure to be balky about changes which reduced their powers and that the people, on the record of the referenda, were plainly more inclined to say no than yes to proposals for change.

In the wartime context Labor's favor for change was first demonstrated by its course in declaring war on Japan. Instead of accepting the

United Kingdom's declaration of war as involving also an Australian declaration, as Menzies had done with regard to the declaration on Germany, Labor arranged that royal instruments authorizing the governor-general to declare war on behalf of the king be obtained through the high commissioner in London and sent out to Australia by picture-gram. Then acting on the Commonwealth's right to offer separate advice to the king with regard to Australia's external affairs, a separate Australian declaration of war on Japan was made, all documents counter-signed by Prime Minister Curtin. In the reasoning of Curtin's attorney general, Dr. H. V. Evatt, whose constitutional expertise had been established during his nine years on the High Court, this change of method was in line with Australia's indisputable status in the Empire which, he said, had been determined "once and for all" in the Balfour Declaration of 1926. However, Australia had not adopted a number of the provisions of the subsequent and consequential Statute of Westminster 1931.

The next step Labor took was, therefore, an attempt to persuade Parliament to accept those sections of the Statute (2 to 6 inclusive) which Mr. Menzies had asked it to adopt in 1937. This Labor did late in 1942. But unlike Menzies, who had based his case on the desirability of constitutional uniformity among the dominions, Evatt—as voice of the government—argued that since status had been settled a quarter of a century earlier, all he was asking for as a matter of urgency was certain legalistic adjustments of Australia's powers now required to facilitate administrative action in prosecuting the war. He posited no change of status but argued for power the better to act in the international context in which Australia now found itself. However, it was impossible to keep the discussion at this innocuous level, for Labor's opponents inevitably raised not only the question of status which they saw being modified in a fashion distasteful to them but also the whole inflammable question of loyalty to Britain. They flatly denied that the matter had any urgency. This being their view, it was not surprising that William Morris Hughes, in leading the opposition to Labor's case, after stating his view of status in terms that now had no standing outside Australia and New Zealand, and defining the implications of the Declaration and Statute in a highly prejudiced fashion, should have ended in a burst of frenzy: "There is no urgency in the matter, and because this statute was enacted to serve the purposes of men and communities who have proved themselves disloyal," he moved the reference of the bill to committee (where presumably it would be killed). However, the Parliament adopted the allegedy disloyal bill, and in 1942 Australia achieved that "uniformity with the other dominions" for which Menzies had pled in vain five years earlier.

Concurrently, Labor also moved to deal with constitutional questions in their more strictly domestic phase. A bill entitled Constitutional Alteration (War Aims and Reconstruction) was introduced in the House by Dr. Evatt on October 1, and a constitutional convention was held in Canberra in November. The preparatory document of the convention was titled, "Post-War Reconstruction: A Case for Greater Commonwealth Powers." The range of matters discussed under this head was very wide, including not only the case for greater powers but also the problem of legal support of Commonwealth-wide primary producers' "syndicates" or marketing boards, an inheritance from the peacetime past, the problem of constitutional validation in the next peacetime of the powers over the economy and the labor force presently resting on the defense power, anticipatory validation of the powers necessary to carry out Labor's but dimly adumbrated reconstruction program, and even the provision of constitutional status for the celebrated "four freedoms" of Roosevelt's wartime propaganda. However, the method of constitutional alteration recommended by the convention was not the frontal approach to the people in a referendum as Labor's strong populist orientation supported, but a resort to the alternative method of "referral" of powers by the states to the Commonwealth. Though tried, this method did not succeed, and the constitutional problem had to be dealt with otherwise at a later stage.

If the constitutional questions brought Dr. Evatt as attorney general to the center of the stage, his handling of "external affairs"—foreign affairs—as minister for External Affairs chiefly insured his continued presence there. Although he was known among the interested intellectuals—foreign affairs in the Australian context was definitely an elite concern—to be sympathetic to the idea that Australia should have a foreign policy peculiarly its own, founded on its dominion status and its geographical position, Dr. Evatt began his career by stating that Labor contemplated no changes in the established line. He and Labor were, however, driven forward by events into the most elaborate independent venture in foreign policy Australia had to that time ever known. To support it the Ministry for External Affairs was much expanded, and diplomatic representation abroad was steadily increased, using both career men and prestigious individuals of no particular diplomatic background, as did other democracies. However, from the outbreak of war in 1941 to well into 1943 Dr. Evatt and his coadjutors were preoccupied not so much with foreign policy as conventionally understood as with the problems arising from Australian-American collaboration in the prosecution of the Pacific war.

Dr. Evatt arrived in Washington early in 1942, in his own image, to "pound on doors." He belligerently sought entry for Australia into the ruling circles of the war wherever they might be meeting, and he assumed on good grounds that the vital meetings were, or should be, in Washington. It appeared in the existing circumstances to be more important that Australia's voice be clearly heard in Washington than, at the moment, in London where in any case it was more familiar and, indeed, accepted. Evatt was determined not to have Australian participation in the direction of the Pacific war conducted from behind any British arras in London, as Churchill proposed, but at the center of vital decision as he identified it. Once installed at the significant tables his job would be to present the pro-Pacific view of the war that Australia so inevitably took and which MacArthur and the American naval leaders in the Pacific shared. Dr. Evatt was neither by disposition nor training a diplomat; he was an advocate, a lawyer supporting a brief. Since to him it was self-evident that what he was advocating was designed to insure Australia's survival, this engaging his deep patriotic nationalistic emotions, and because his temperament was authoritarian, his advocacy was hard hitting and often rather sharp-pointedly angular—not in the diplomatic convention. At the moment Australia was without a minister in Washington because R. G. Casey, not choosing to serve a Labor government, had resigned to join the British service as minister of State in Cairo (and later to become governor of Bengal in India). This move generated another testy correspondence between Churchill and Prime Minister Curtin. However, Evatt managed only a conditional success. A Pacific War Council was set up in Washington with Australia a conspicuous member—the other members were the United States, the United Kingdom, Canada, China, the Netherlands, and New Zealand—but Evatt was unable to place Australia firmly in those places where the executive decisions on the prosecution of the war were being made. He achieved an advisory position only, as he candidly informed Parliament. The problem of establishing Australia's right to representation at the very highest levels abided. Imperceptibly, it merged into the problem of achieving a properly regarded voice for a small, or middle, power in a big power world.

Labor consolidated its political position in the general election of 1943 and won not only a ratification of party policy but also of Curtin's war leadership. It won forty-nine seats in the House of seventy-four, and from July 1944 would have twenty-two of thirty-six seats in the Senate. It was over a quarter-century since it had been in such a strong position. The U.A.P. dropped back to fourteen seats in the House and twelve in the Senate, while the Country party had but eight in the House and two in the Senate. There were three independents in the House, two of whom were favorably disposed to Labor, and two in the Senate. By this time the U.A.P. was obviously disorganized. There was a good deal of uncertainty about whether Menzies or Hughes was the party preference for leader, but Menzies in fact was elected to the position. Hughes publicly exercised on Menzies his terrible talent for vituperation. The quarrels within the U.A.P. had their impact on the War Council in which whatever national political unity there was achieved expression. Both Menzies and Hughes resigned. Fadden and his Country party associates stayed on and so did P. C. Spender, nominally a U.A.P. member. Hughes was soon induced to return, but Menzies stayed away. The Council was not disbanded until August 1945.

The redeployment which began after the election was a continuing effort to rebalance the war effort in the light of global changes as they bore on Australia. It was soon apparent that they were likely to become frequent and of major import. This involved the reallocation of the labor force between the armed forces at their maximum size, and the industries—factory and land—and between production for war and for civilian supply. The redeployment merged into demobilization, and long before that point was reached in 1945, the many questions associated with reconstruction were raised ever more insistently. The postwar slant became more and more pronounced. However, the labor situation remained tight as long as the fighting continued, and it became apparent that even after demobilization Australia would have a labor shortage if full employment was achieved.

Not only were men drawn out of the armed forces by the normal processes of release, but targets for special releases to meet the manpower needs of industry were defined. At the same time new recruits continued to be taken into the armed forces as new classes came of age. Within factory industry some manpower was directed out of war production, which passed its peak in 1943, in spite of the fact that new ranges of munitions and equipment were still just coming into production, thus reversing the flow initiated in 1941. Manpower from war production was directed in 1943 chiefly into civilian factory production, but in 1944 also into house building where the situation was desperate.

This shifting about soon raised the question of what was to be done with the government factories when they were no longer needed for war production and implicitly the larger question of the industrialization program. As enunciated by Prime Minister Curtin in the light of studies then in progress, the government's policy involved a much larger permanent munitions production program than any hitherto, a ratification of Labor's prewar position, this involving the retention of many of the war-built factories, but nevertheless many of the factories would be leased (and some sold) to private enterprise for incorporation into the private sector of the economy. This did not mean, however, that the government intended to keep out of other commodity production, for in September 1944 it was announced that the Commonwealth in collaboration with the state government of Tasmania would set up an aluminum ingot plant at Bell Bay, Tasmania, eventually to be based on domestic bauxite. At about the same time it began to transfer to private control the aluminum-processing facilities in Victoria and New South Wales. The Labor government plainly intended to keep on defining the mixture of the economy it had in view, but it also anticipated that Australian private enterprise would undertake a program of industrial expansion and that British capital, and possibly United States capital also, would flow abundantly to Australia in the postwar period. In facilitating the establishment of an automobile manufacturing industry it repealed a monopoly agreement made by the Lyons government before the war, opening the way not only for General Motors–Holden's, an American enterprise, but also for possible competitors, American and British. Labor's objective was plainly a strongly competitive, rapidly expanding economy and, while the idea of self-sufficiency was in the air, it was apparent that Labor did not interpret this as requiring the cutting of traditional overseas ties or the preventing of the enlargement of the economic ties, hitherto rather thin, with the United States. Furthermore, Labor recognized that the course it was plotting made it improbable that reliance could be placed wholly upon established sources of export income in the future. It therefore gave notice that factory industry should think of developing export outlets. It proposed to assist by expanding the trade commissioner service. Labor emphasized the need for the Australian factories to be competitively efficient to win a place in the world market for manufacturers.

In the same moving context the government had also to deal with agriculture, understood as including the pastoral industry. At first the task was to assure that supplies matched war demand, but as the war situation changed and the demand pattern changed, the task was to match the new pattern, as to care for overseas relief and rehabilitation requirements laid on Australia, for example, by UNRRA. The distribution of production became: (1) to the Australian and (2) American armed forces, (3) to the United Kingdom, (4) to the Australian civilian population, and (5) to other proper recipients. Administratively, the task involved getting agriculture into a better position than hitherto for a clear sight of its problems in a national-international perspective. By law and tradition agriculture was a state responsibility. The federal Department of Commerce had drifted into a relation with agriculture through marketing; it now became the Department of Commerce and Agriculture, the first occasion on which agriculture had been specifically recognized in the title of a Commonwealth department. A federal Bureau of Agricultural Economics was transferred to it from its place of origin in Postwar Reconstruction. A Food Executive was formed at the cabinet level and a Food Control within the Department, the activities of the latter embracing production, processing, defense foodstuffs, and civilian supply. (The food processing industry had been expanding and not only the better to prepare foodstuffs for export in wartime as by deboning meats, dehydrating vegetables and eggs, etc., but by a considerable elaboration of canning, an established industry, involving the local making of tin cans, though no tinplate was produced domestically.) However, decisions and administrative actions affecting agriculture continued to be taken in a variety of places, federal and state.

In mid-1943 the manpower situation in agriculture was difficult; the permanent labor force was down by one-fifth, the seasonal force by over one-half. The fertilizer supply was less than one-third of normal (largely because of the Japanese possession of Nauru—see Chapter XI), and all other necessary supplies, including machinery and petrol, were scarce. There were then shortages, sometimes of a seasonal character, of dairy products, meat, eggs, some vegetables (especially in processed form), sugar, rice, and dried vine and citrus fruits. There were surpluses only of apples and pears and the export staples, wheat and wool. However, wheat production as measured by acreage sown was decreasing; the wartime low came in 1943 with 7,875,000 acres, the smallest acreage since 1912. The total agricultural situation was further complicated by the very severe, almost continent-wide drought of 1943–45, the worst in forty years. In 1944, for example, the wheat yield fell to 1.63 bushels in Victoria, 5.7 in South Australia, and 6.02 in New South Wales, while the national average was only 6.25 bushels. Sheep numbers which had reached 125,000,000 in 1942 declined by 29,000,000 in the ensuing four years with the worst losses in 1944 during which New South Wales alone lost 10,200,000 sheep. In this context the rationing of food in Australia becomes entirely understandable, and it is also plain why agriculture was chosen to be the prime beneficiary of the new deployment of manpower. Of the 20,000 men specially directed out of the services into industry during 1943–44 no less than 15,000 were sent into agriculture, while late in 1944 a further 20,000 began to move into it. A larger number of female harvest workers was recruited. Nevertheless, agriculture continued to be short of labor to the end of the war; nor were there enough supplies of materials and machines necessary for maximum production. However, better seasonal conditions and other encouragements such as a £7,000,000 subsidy for dairying in lieu of a price increase led to a rise in production all around. The Americans eased the pressure of demand somewhat by taking over the supply of their troops in the Pacific, no longer based on Australia in significant numbers.

The idea now began to emerge that in the postwar years there would probably be a return to the familiar troubles with regard to the disposal of production. Wool was thought likely to be more menaced than ever by synthetics. The government set up a wool publicity and research program. In this context of doubt the long-term contracts with Britain for all wool, meat, and dairy products available for export, announced in 1944 to extend beyond the expected end of the war, were highly welcome. Nevertheless, additional commodity marketing boards were set up. What was not clearly seen was that the Australian land industries—as the principal suppliers of exports—would, in a period of rapid industrialization, take on a role in the emergent economy roughly analogous to that of agriculture in America in the late nineteenth century, when domestic manufacturing was getting stronger but had not yet relieved agriculture of much of the burden of providing the external strength of the economy by its exports. Needless to say, the shape of the postwar world economy and Britain's place in it was not very accurately foreseen.

Between 1943 and 1945 the reconstruction program moved forward from broad generalizations through studies of the particulars of the several segments of the economy involved—primary industry, secondary industry, housing, the railways, etc.—to increasingly specific proposals. Anticipating demobilization, provision was made for preference for ex-servicemen in employment, and while the way was opened for the men to go on the land according to historical precedent, more indicative of the emerging picture of postwar Australia were the provisions for giving ready access to technical and higher education. The key idea of full employment, though discussed as a fundamental both at home and at international conferences, was not set out in a White Paper until May 1945. Meanwhile, a vast federal-state public works program was developed under the supervision of a National Works Council, established in January 1944. To be launched when the war was concluded, it involved tremendous public investment, principally by the states as usual. The housing studies, posited on federal-state financial collaboration, not only revealed the staggering dimensions of the shortage which had been cumulating since depression times but the extent of the slum areas in the cities and the urgent need for slum clearance. The building of no less than 50,000 units of housing by public agencies per annum for some years was believed to be necessary. While the owner-occupied single-family cottage-style house with a garden was taken to be the proper standard, forecasting the still wider extension of the already marked urban sprawl, the erection of several-storied, multiple-unit housing was also proposed, not least for the areas from which the old single-story, single-unit slum housing was to be removed.

The scheme for the standardization of the railway gauges, on the agenda since colonial times but given new urgency by the inland transport troubles of wartime, was not only significant in itself but incidentally gave an idea of how the geography of development was then conceived. The 4′ 8½″ gauge selected as standard obtained only in New South Wales and on the Commonwealth's transcontinental line. Under the scheme all the Victorian lines and the South Australian lines east of Spencer Gulf would be converted. The transcontinental line would automatically be linked to the heartland lines of the east, while in the west it would be extended from Kalgoorlie to the Indian Ocean, linking the Western Australian "island" more effectively to the east. To tie "permanent frontier" country to the heartland, a line would be provided from Bourke in New South Wales north through central Queensland to Hughenden, partly by building new line, partly by converting existing Queensland lines. From Hughenden east to Townsville existing line would be converted to give the north lateral access to the Pacific littoral, while the same line in its existing western extension would be converted from Hughenden to its terminus at Djarra (including the spur to the rich mining center of Mount Isa). From Djarra a new line would be built northwest into Northern Territory which would join the existing line (to be converted) leading up to Darwin from its current inland terminus at Birdum. Postwar emphasis on developing "the north" was thus forecast. In this comprehensive plan the Queensland lines north and south of Townsville, including the north-south coastal line, the South Australian lines on Eyre Peninsula, the Western Australian lines north and south of the standard gauge line Kalgoorlie-Indian Ocean, and the line running up to Alice Springs in the center of the continent would not be converted and thus would stand outside the new continental network. Whether this implied a judgment on the national significance of the development potentials of the areas served was not made clear, but that the plan could be so read was quite obvious.

Early in May 1945 discussion began on what was to become known as the Snowy River scheme, whereby the waters of that eastward-flowing river in the mountains of southeastern New South Wales would be diverted under the mountains—generating great quantities of electricity as they went—into the Murrumbidgee-Murray river system to support irrigation. This scheme, too, promised to support the intensive development of the heartland, not least by linking electrically the industrial complexes in Victoria and New South Wales but also by making possible more intensive exploitation of the Murray Valley region. It was thus amply clear by the war's end that public spending for development was to be as integral to full employment as it had characteristically been to the less sophisticated economic policies of earlier times. It was also clear that the southeastern portion of the continent would be most intensively developed because it was indisputably the richest portion of the continental inheritance. Development in "permanent frontier" areas might be brought to a higher level than hitherto, but they would nevertheless retain their established character of contributory areas.

The welfare state idea continued to be pursued. In 1944 unemployment and sickness benefits were legislated and free medicines for all were provided for under a pharmaceutical benefits act which, however, was challenged in the courts and declared unconstitutional. The federal government also provided for free beds for all in the public wards of the hospitals. Since the hospitals were under the control of the states, this was done by paying subsidies to the states on a per day per bed basis.

In 1944, too, the struggle to secure the constitutional basis of reconstruction was resumed, this time by resort to referendum, some of the states having failed to refer the required powers as requested in 1942. Essentially, the effort was to fortify powers which the federal government had taken under the National Security Act but which would automatically expire on the coming of peace. The government argued that since the powers it was asking were in fact constitutionally available to the states in peacetime this meant that they would not be dangerous in the hands of the federal government in peacetime but would enable it to serve the people's interests on a national basis. A special play was made of the point that the powers were needed to combat postwar inflation. Apparently to dissipate the fears of those who feared, or might fear, an all-powerful central government, the powers asked for were specified to expire five years after the war, whereupon they would revert to the states to which they belonged. A particular fear the government had to combat was that it was asking for the power to continue labor conscription in peacetime. But no matter how the case was argued it failed to impress an adequate number of voters. The government's case was rejected in the referendum by 350,000 votes. Queensland, New South Wales, Victoria, and Tasmania voted no, South Australia and Western Australia voted yes.

In March 1945 Chifley introduced into the House a Commonwealth Bank Bill and a Banking Bill, embodying regulations under the National

Security Act. In the treasurer's own words, the purpose of the Commonwealth Bank Bill was "to strengthen the central banking functions of the Commonwealth Bank; to ensure that the monetary and banking policy of the Commonwealth Bank will be in harmony with the main decisions on matters of government policy and in the interests of the people of Australia; to ensure the development and expansion of its general banking business by active competition with the trading banks; to return the control of the Commonwealth Bank to the governor [from whose hands the Bruce-Page government had removed it] who will be assisted by an advisory council; and to assist in developing small industries and in enabling the people to secure homes." Policy should be to contribute to "(a) the stability of the currency of Australia; (b) the maintenance of *full employment* [italics added] in Australia; and (c) the economic prosperity and welfare of the people of Australia." In introducing the Banking Bill Chifley began: "The purpose of this bill is to regulate banking and make provision for the protection of the currency and the public credit of the Commonwealth. The regulation of the banking system [i.e., the trading banks] is an essential accompaniment of the revision of Commonwealth Bank powers." The bills initiated a heated controversy over banking and credit policy which was carried on inside and outside Parliament and in the courts during the ensuing six years and was to contribute importantly to putting an end to Labor's longest continuous tenure in federal office. However, the bills of 1945 were enacted as presented to Parliament in the face of the adamant opposition of Menzies and the slightly less rigid disapproval of Fadden.

As the progress of the war in the Southwest Pacific and South Pacific areas freed the Australians from their sense of imminent peril the way was opened for the development and enunciation of foreign policy. As it unfolded, as much in response to events as in relation to any comprehensive prior theoretical formulation, it proved to be a mixture of nationalistic, internationalistic, and socio-economic elements. Nationalistically, it was an effort to guarantee Australia's sovereign independence both in terms of military security and freedom to pursue its self-selected socio-economic policies, including White Australia. Internationally, the progression was conceived to be from a close regional association with New Zealand, to a close association with the Empire, to important participation in whatever substitute for the League of Nations might be evolved. The chosen socio-economic policy was full employment, accompanied by a strong tendency to make Australian laboristic policies generally the test of virtue. While Dr. Evatt was the spokesman for the policy, it was not, as was sometimes alleged, his creation, though the mode of its expression was frequently his choice, particularly since improvisation to meet specific challenges was rather frequent. As a lawyer, Evatt naturally gave policy a legalistic flavor and as a combative person an aggressive expression.

There were in the policy traditional elements that could be traced a good distance back in Australian history, such as the concern about the environing islands, as well as traditional Labor party elements, raised now to a higher level of sophistication than hitherto. In any case the ideas, whatever their derivation, were ratified beforehand by the Labor government. The most devastating criticism of the policy—Menzies was the keenest critic, with P. C. Spender not far behind—was not so much that it often violated the diplomatic unity of the Empire, though to make this point undoubtedly gave the imperialists great emotional satisfaction, as that since it was usually grounded on assumptions to which the relative power of the nations was tangential, it constantly overbid Australia's hand in terms of relative power.

Prime Minister Curtin took the lead in reasserting Australia's devotion to the Empire. Although he apparently did so for his own private reasons and with regard for purely domestic currents of emotion and opinion, he also appeared to initiate a discussion of the future of the Empire that spread widely in 1943 and 1944, to which Lord Halifax contributed a famous speech at Toronto, Canada, and Field Marshal Smuts contributed an equally impressive speech at London, and which was taken up vigorously by the press of the Empire. Curtin's proposal was in effect an updating of an Australian (and New Zealand) position of at least sixty years' standing. It was, while a trifle odd for a Laborite, of an impeccable orthodoxy. To insure the cohesiveness of the Empire in the future, Curtin proposed to establish a continuously functioning Imperial secretariat to facilitate the formulation and carrying out of common imperial policies which would regularly be discussed and agreed to at meetings of the prime ministers at London and, on occasion, at the capitals of the dominions.

Although it was very obviously not on Curtin's mind that he was doing so, he actually "bought into" the standing and currently intensifying dispute between the integrationists, of whom he was one, and the devolutionists who, it happened, were on the side of history, as was soon to be shown by what occurred in the Empire after the war. Curtin was asking for something it was impossible in the circumstances to obtain; he was, however, voicing a strongly founded Australian aspiration: to give institutional expression to Australia's organic relation to the

Empire. Events were to continue to deny the Australians any chance to do this; that their relation was conceived to be organic continued to be reflected in their imperial policy. Dr. Evatt, as a member of the Curtin cabinet, was formally committed to the Curtin view, but it was plain that he himself was a devolutionist, though of the kind that posited constant and intimate collaboration with the Empire associates, especially Britain, to advance common policies whenever and wherever possible and to expect from the associates support for Australian policies in Australia's area of special responsibility, the Pacific Basin. His statements on imperial relations—after the Curtin proposal at the Prime Ministers' conference of 1944 had obviously ceased to be meaningful—showed no regret that the integrating imperial secretariat had been consigned to the constitutional lumber room.

The first substantial expression of Labor's foreign policy was a regional pact, the Australian-New Zealand Agreement of January 1944. The original spur to forcible expression of the attitudes, opinions, and policies which found a place in the Agreement was worry about what might happen in the Pacific by way of disposal of territories and other questions, contrary to Australia's interests and wishes. It was to explore attitudes toward "the islands" that Dr. Evatt first approached the New Zealanders. Although before the outbreak of war the Lyons government had been little interested in New Zealand, the Australians and New Zealanders had been in intermittent touch about war matters since 1939, and the consultations had become more frequent after the outbreak of war in the Pacific. They had agreed in February 1942 to an American commander in chief and a little later that a Pacific War Council in Washington was a necessity. The assignment of each to a different area for war purposes had not dampened their sense of common interests in the international sphere. Late in 1943 they exchanged high commissioners for the first time. There was a feeling that force would be lent to their contentions if they were closely associated in backing them. Related to this was Dr. Evatt's feeling that the time had come for a reiteration of the demand for representation in the highest councils, specifically in the light of the fact that neither country had been represented at the Cairo conference at which decisions with regard to the prosecution of the Pacific war and the postwar disposition of Pacific territories had been made. Australia and New Zealand had not even been consulted. Dr. Evatt found that the New Zealand Labour government was in agreement with him about a wide variety of matters, though not always as to expression or illustrative application when agreed.

A formal conference at Canberra was opened by Prime Minister

Curtin. A last minute improvisation was to turn the "agreement" into a treaty, something unprecedented in the relations of British dominions, but assumed by Evatt to be within the powers of dominions. (As seen from the New Zealand angle, see Chapter VIII.)

The substance of the treaty-agreement was:

(a) A forceful assertion of the right to representation at the highest level in executive bodies running the war, planning armistices, or planning and establishing a future "general international organization."

(b) "Within the framework of a general system of world security, a regional zone of defence comprising the Southwest and South Pacific areas shall be established that this zone should be based on Australia and New Zealand, stretching through the arc of islands north and northeast of Australia, to Western Samoa and the Cook Islands."

(c) "The two Governments accept as a recognized principle of international practice that the construction and use, in time of war, by any power, of naval, military and air installations, in any territory under the sovereignty or control of another power does not, in itself, afford any basis for territorial claims or rights of sovereignty or control after the conclusion of hostilities."

(d) "The two Governments declare that the interim administration and ultimate disposal of enemy territories in the Pacific is of vital importance to Australia and New Zealand, and that any such disposal should be effected only with their agreement and as part of a general Pacific settlement." "The two Governments declare that no change in the sovereignty of system of control or any of the islands of the Pacific should be effected except as a result of an agreement to which they are parties or in the terms of which they have both concurred."

(e) An elaborate definition of postwar policy with regard to the islands within the Southwest and South Pacific areas. (See Chapter XI.)

(f) A case for an International Air Transport Authority to operate services on "international air trunk routes."

(g) An assertion of the national right to control immigration and emigration (i.e., to uphold White Australia and White New Zealand).

(h) A description of the machinery for continuing consultation on foreign policy in all its aspects.

The Agreement was not, however, an exhaustive conspectus of the foreign policies of either nation. It was, in spite of the references to the matter of representation at the highest levels and to the Pacific at large, primarily focused on the region and designed to bring it closely under the control of Australia and New Zealand. In this latter respect, Dr. Evatt was of a more particularistic frame of mind than the New Zealanders and left to himself would have produced an even more particularistic and brusquely phrased document. It was the New Zealanders who saw to it that it was modulated and that the fact that both countries were dominions of the British Empire was definitely mentioned. The Agreement was unclear about the role of other nations, notably the United States, in the defense of the region against external aggression, the only aggression at all likely to occur. It said nothing about full employment, the primary policy of the socio-economic phase of Australia's foreign political program which was to be given clear expression at the International Labor Organization conference at Philadelphia in April and at the Monetary and Financial Conference at Bretton Woods in July 1944. And although there were very pointed references to changes in the "sovereignty or system of control" of the islands of the Pacific, north as well as south of the equator, there was no specific reference to possible changes in South and Southeast Asia, although what would happen there was certain to have a powerful impact on the region's international position. The only reference at all relevant, and it was veiled, was to White Australia, probably the most provocative of all possible policies having relevance to relations with Asia. Nor was anything concrete said about policy toward Japan.

The second great forward step in foreign policy was the participation in the San Francisco conference to write a United Nations charter, April–June 1945. Dr. Evatt's—and presumptively Labor's—general attitude toward the charter, much less specific than New Zealand's but closely complementary, had been made clear early in 1944. To borrow Mr. Justice Higgins' phrase for the arbitration courts, the aspiration was to bring "law and order" to a "new province"—the relations of the nations. Dr. Evatt wanted an organization which would "contain" the implicit and all too often open war of nation against nation as he believed the court contained a domestic class war. He hoped for an organization in which the emphasis would be on the sovereign equality of the states (with domestic jurisdiction amply defined to include tariffs and the determination of the racial composition of the people) which were seeking to maintain international law and order. Labor had a strong tendency to "shun [or try to evade] the ugly facts of power." It sought to emphasize justice, social and political, and to think in terms of democratic machinery for supporting that value. Seeking as always to make Australia's weight felt at the highest levels for its own and the world's good, it appeared obvious that this could not be done if considerations of relative national power were to rule but might be achieved if the participating nations were taken as sovereign equals. Thus, from Australia's conception of its necessities as a small (or middle) power in a big power world and with an intense conviction of clear insight into what was just, politically and socially, a program for a charter was evolved. The subject was canvassed with the New Zealanders at a consultative conference under the

Agreement held at Wellington November 1–6, 1944. A large area of agreement was established.

At San Francisco Dr. Evatt was not only dominant in the Australian delegation, in spite of the fact that Prime Minister Curtin had tried to set up a countervailing force within the delegation, but was the principal spokesman of the small powers against the big powers (Britain, the United States, the U.S.S.R., and China). At a preliminary conference of the representatives of the British dominions held at London, the most important differences that emerged between Australia and New Zealand on the one hand and Britain on the other proved to be with regard to the big power possession of a veto and with regard to the program of trusteeship for dependent territories. The veto question was intimately involved with the power question which so preoccupied Dr. Evatt because the right to veto was to be held by the Big Powers occupying permanent seats in the upper house, or Security Council, of the organization and was thus a challenge to the Australian emphasis on the sovereign equality of all nations. (Involved here may also have been Australian Labor's well-established hostility to upper houses of legislatures.) A large part of Dr. Evatt's considerable energy went into the campaign against the veto. This cause was lost and the way left open for the destructive veto-ing that has marked the U.N.'s career. Otherwise much was gained. Not only as members of the executive committee of the Steering Committee of the conference but also as indefatigable advocates of presumptively creative changes, the Australians, with Dr. Evatt's tireless participation, had considerable influence on the shaping of the charter. As the official report of the Australian delegates put it, "out of some 38 distinct amendments of substances originally filed by Australia, 26 were either adopted without material change, adopted in principle or made unnecessary by other alterations." The Australians helped to strengthen the General Assembly in which all nations were equal against the Security Council where, by virtue of the veto, some were more equal than others, and to strengthen the Economic and Social Council, presumptively the forum for discussion of the cherished social reform policies. They gained a conspicuous declaration in favor of full employment, obtained—this was the special task of the New Zealanders—a progressive Trusteeship Council, and generally saw to it that an organization serviceable for Australia's purposes was evolved. Dr. Evatt, it became plain, proposed to center Australia's foreign relations in the United Nations insofar as it was an avenue of escape from the power politics of a world prospectively to be dominated by Big Powers. In that kind of world Australia was unquestionably a weak, peripheral nation. In the contrary kind of world —a rule-of-law world under a strong United Nations—it would be the sovereign equal of all and could hope to wield influence. The U.N. was a refuge in a flight from power politics which Australia could not hope effectively to play.

On July 5, 1945, Prime Minister John Curtin died. Joseph Benedict ("Ben") Chifley was elected his successor by caucus and took office on July 13.

CHAPTER V

A Middle Power in the Pacific

When he was elevated to the prime ministership Ben Chifley was sixty years old, a well-tempered veteran of the wars of the labor movement—trade union and political—and unlike his predecessors, Scullin and Curtin, took office after accumulating considerable experience of federal cabinet office. Chifley was born of Irish Catholic stock in Bathurst, New South Wales, in 1885. His father was a blacksmith. Although a towns-man born and a town dweller all of his life, his formative years from five to thirteen had been spent on a grandfather's farm. In closely identifying himself with the inland town of Bathurst he differed significantly from most of Australia's prime ministers who, even if provincials by origin, have usually acquired close identification with a city of the littoral. Chifley also differed from his fellows in having had considerable experience of local government and none of state government. His schooling was meager, but was pieced out with part-time and evening study and he showed an obvious capacity to learn from experience and from better-educated men with whom he came into contact. By trade he was a rail-way worker and until he lost his seniority by participating in the railway strike of 1917, he was an engine-driver. He had a good deal of experi-ence in the railway workers' union.

After failing in earlier attempts to gain a seat, he was elected to the federal House in 1928. He was a member of Scullin's cabinet. Losing his seat in the debacle of 1931, he was out of the House until 1940. Much of his political energy in the intervening years went into the fight on J. T. Lang in New South Wales. As a trade unionist and Labor politician he felt a strong moral identification with his mates of the labor movement. He tended to give a moral significance to the policies he embraced, and he found a high moral value in fighting for what he had decided was right. While he was formed in his younger days by the labor movement, he was reformed intellectually during the Great Depression which left a deep mark upon him. He strongly felt that he had found an escape from the policy dilemmas of that time through Keynesian economics as understood in a context of laboristic beliefs. As prime minister he appeared to the public to be a homespun philosopher of Labor, not an elusive intellectual like Curtin. It is indicative of the enduring strength of his loyalties that while his marriage to a Protestant woman by a Protestant clergyman deprived him of the sacraments of his Church for years, he persistently attended mass. The Church graciously unbent to give him Catholic burial. The cultivation of a Chifley "legend" began even before his death in 1951. While it was Curtin who led Labor to office and power and Chifley who was in charge when it met defeat once more, it was Chifley who was chosen for idolization. This was a triumph of personality.

The Chifley administration took up the task of government between the end of combat in Europe (May 8) and the end of combat in the Pacific (August 15). As it retained office until the end of 1949 it ran its course under postwar but certainly not peacetime conditions. Anything resembling peacetime only occurred after Labor was out of office. Both in its domestic and foreign aspects the context was peculiarly difficult. In its domestic aspects, while demobilization and reconversion were carried through without depression and full employment was achieved almost without effort on the government's part, progress toward a satisfactorily balanced distribution of the labor force, a proper balance between heavy and light industry, between the factory and the land industries, and proper provision of basic supply (e.g., coal, electricity, steel, petrol) to support production in all fields—let alone orderly economic growth—proved elusive. The Chifley government congratulated itself that it had achieved economic stability, but this was an illusion and the full employment in which it took such pride was too obviously based on a boom in consumer demand. Undeniably, the situation looked good: the national income steadily rose, and the percentage of the gross national product invested was increasing. In some part the troubles arose because of the impossibility under the circumstances of taking corrective actions in any logical sequence or with reasonable promptitude, in some part because of fogginess about what needed to be done, and in some part because the economic disorder overseas, especially in the United Kingdom and Europe, was reflected in Australia's import-export trade and external financial relations, including relations with the dollar. All this not only caused domestic disorders of one kind and another but also cramped efforts to correct them. How far different policies would have eased the situation was the essence of the political argumentation of the time.

The overseas troubles centrally involved the United Kingdom, head of the "sterling area" of which Australia was a part—its principal trading partner, the focal point of its politico-cultural loyalties. The Chifley administration calculated its course to render all possible support to Britain, but whether in a fashion that served Britain's and Australia's interests best was the question. The situation was dramatized as a "dollar shortage." Australia was normally "dollar short" in that it normally earned fewer dollars by exports to the United States and the dollar area generally (including Canada) than it needed to pay for the imports from dollar sources or which contained a high dollar content. Traditionally, it had been able to supplement its own dollar earnings by buying dollars with sterling, but when sterling became inconvertible its access to dollars was limited to what was allocated to it from the dollar pool of the sterling area, controlled by the United Kingdom. (The more than $100,000,000 that had been spent in Australia by the Americans during the war had gone into the dollar pool in exchange for sterling and hence was unavailable for postwar needs.) In the postwar situation Australia wanted many things from the United States, not least capital equipment for new industries as well as things like oil which did not come from the United States but which had a high dollar content. As long as she could draw freely on the sterling area dollar pool everything was all right, but when the pool became inadequate to the demands upon it, the Chifley government saw nothing for it but to conform to the British request that dollar imports be cut. An obvious way to ease the pain was for Australia to borrow dollars on her own account, gambling upon her ability to service and repay the loan in due course. It also could have actively encouraged the flow of dollar capital investments into Australia. These things the Chifley government was hesitant about doing.

Although it was internationalist enough to push through membership in the International Monetary Fund and the Bank for Reconstruction and Development in the face of the opposition of the economic primitives in its own ranks, the Chifley government was reluctant to borrow dollars from either institution or in the American money market, beyond an inescapable minimum ($20,000,000) needed for times of crisis. Chifley entertained the traditional Labor suspicion of the overseas bondholder, which had been intensified during the Great Depression, and he had a special suspicion of dollar obligations as traditionally the most difficult for Australia to service. His skepticism about obligations to the dollar area even extended to a doubt about the wisdom of acquiring American machinery because of the future need to maintain it with spare parts only obtainable with dollars. He hesitated to assume servicing obligations for American capital investments. He was in fact pessimistic not only about the future of Australia's relation to the dollar but the world's rela-

PAPUA

Thursday Is.

GREAT BARRIER REEF

Weipa

ek

Cooktown

arroloola
ly Waters

Cairns

Rankine

Normanton

Townsville

RRITORY

Mount Isa
Cloncurry

ARUNTA
DESERT

Mary Kathleen

Mackay

PACIFIC
OCEAN

lice Springs

Winton

Longreach

Rockhampton

QUEENSLAND

Bundaberg

USTRALIA

Maryborough
Gympie

Oodnadatta

Charleville

Brisbane

Toowoomba

Farina

Lismore

rcoola   Woomera

Bourke

Walgett

Grafton

duna

NEW SOUTH WALES

Whyalla   Port Pirie

Cobar   Tamworth

Port   Wallaroo
icoln   Renmark

Port Augusta   Broken Hill

Nyngan

Newcastle

Dubbo

Hay

Parkes   Orange

Adelaide   Mildura

Bathurst

Sydney
Wollongong

Wagga Wagga

Swan Hill

Albury

Port Kembla

Horsham

Canberra

Kingston

Bendigo

Cooma
Bombala

VICTORIA

Ballarat
Geelong

Melbourne

Portland
Warrnambool

Wonthaggi

Bell Bay

Burnie

Launceston

TASMANIA

Hobart

tion to it. He was querulous about the rapid exhaustion of the American loan to the United Kingdom, blaming it wholly on price rises in the United States; he was dubious about benefits from the Marshall Plan; he anticipated an early depression in the United States and disastrous world-wide consequences, and he held to the idea to the end of his term of office. He felt safer as to the future in expanding Australia's external financial obligations to a minimum extent and in any case keeping within the sterling area. If he could maintain the status quo—and one of his acts to do so was to devalue the Australian pound when the pound sterling was devalued—he felt that he could, given control of banking and credit, maintain full employment in Australia. Too ample and ill-considered a link to the dollar might increase Australia's vulnerability.

When the war ended there were 31,000 factories in Australia. Before Labor went out of office 9000 more were added. Employment in factories rose from 565,000 at the beginning of the war to 890,000 in 1948–49. Except for the time of transition from war to peace, when there was a slight drop, there was an annual increment of factory workers all during Labor's term of office. The growing point of this increase was in the "engineering" category. Not only was "engineering" thus identifiable by the number of factories added and number of workers but also by the figures on "new capital expenditure." The increase in the number of factories and factory workers did not change the concentration of industrial development in New South Wales, Victoria, and South Australia —fundamentally around Sydney, Melbourne, and Adelaide. Growth of factory industry thus meant intensified urbanization, and, while an effort was made to decentralize, the factors ruling location of industry hampered that development. The factories were mostly the traditionally small establishments, the proportion employing twenty persons or fewer remaining constant at about four-fifths, while factories employing 101 and upward stayed constant at about one-twenty-fifth, leaving the middle group at one-sixth. While the factory growth conformed to the regnant idea of Australia's future it was not planned, nor was it well supported by the basic heavy industries or the services. It was heavily dependent on overseas imports not only for basic machinery but also for technical know-how, innovation, and research. While much was made of the idea that Australia was aiming at self-sufficiency, this was really remote and improbable, and if a new industry "replaced" an import, the changes in the pattern of domestic production caused a change in the character of the imports required to keep it going and expanding, not diminishing their total volume or value but increasing both. Unless and until factory industry became a heavy exporter, Australia was dependent on its traditional exports—those supplied by the land industries—for the imports it required to keep going and growing.

This being the case it was remarkable that while in office Labor did so little to formulate a forward policy for the land industries in their new economic context. The wartime performance of the land industries, which had been good, had been carried out at the cost of a steady erosion of their capital equipment, not least soil fertility, and in the face of a decline of the labor force below a level necessary to maintain efficiency. In the latter years of the war, drought and wind erosion had taken a heavy toll, which dramatized the need for soil conservation measures. While production had, as noted earlier, rebounded from the lowest levels reached, sheep did not recover to prewar numbers in this period. The prospect at the end of the war was thought not to be so much a resumption of expansion in terms of acres in use, though it was not assumed that the final pattern of cropland in use had been determined, as the continuance of advance agronomically on the best acres already identified.

The truly difficult problem, however, was believed to be economic: how was the production to be marketed at remunerative prices? The ruling idea was that production beyond the level of domestic requirements was inherently speculative, except possibly for wool—which was menaced by synthetics. A rise in the resident population was the only visible *plus* in the emergent situation, for this promised to absorb a larger proportion of the production domestically. For the surpluses, the best solution seemed to be to accept the bulk purchase contracts offered by Britain for such commodities as she wanted. The contracts offered at least temporary security, even if at prices below the levels reached in the free markets of the world. (This price sacrifice could be rationalized as assistance to Britain in her time of troubles.) Wheat could be similarly protected by entering into the International Wheat Agreement, and sugar likewise. Wool, once the accumulated stocks of wartime had been disposed of, would return to the free market auction system.

All this would tend to make agricultural prices "administered" and turn them into political questions, but better this than a bankrupting chaos. As a matter of fact, the administered prices put the land entrepreneurs into a fairly good financial position. But this was to deal with the land industries in a fashion more reminiscent of the 1930's than in that suggested by their emergent economic role—to provide exports to buy the imports to support industrialization. Not that the farmers and graziers saw their economic significance in any such terms. They saw themselves not as servants of industrialization but as the truly creative producers of the Australian economy; in terms of exports they were indeed the prime contributors to economic health. Wool was still the most important commodity produced in and exported from Australia.

The irony was that the acceptable financial position of the land entrepreneurs at this time was not exploitable in full to their and the country's benefit because of the imbalance of the industrial sector and the maldistribution of the labor force, not least as evidenced by the inability of the steel industry to work to full capacity. It was impossible for the land industries to obtain all the labor and materials (fertilizer, wire, galvanized iron, wire netting, and machinery) needed to support agronomic progress. Public works of benefit to agriculture were very slowly undertaken. Under Labor, then, the problems of agriculture were not dealt with forthrightly because of the concentration of attention on industrialization as the only possible support for an expanded population. On occasion there was difficulty about meeting the commitments to Britain. Agricultural production rose but 10 per cent over prewar, less than the percentage increase of population, as compared to 28 per cent in the United States.

In January 1946 Labor signaled that it intended to follow its established policy of aggrandizing the Commonwealth by announcing that the uniform income tax which had been established in 1942 would be permanent. A new formula for reimbursing the states was devised, and under it the flow of funds to the states steadily rose, though never to a level at which the states were satisfied. Combined with earlier arrangements with regard to federal-state relations, this consolidated the Commonwealth's predominant position. A consequence was a further development of Commonwealth-state collaboration in meeting both common constitutional responsibilities and state responsibilities in which there was a discernible Commonwealth interest or concern. This was shown to be a fundamental development rather than a party-political development when the conservatives continued to elaborate the collaboration on their return to office. The development involved the continuation of old collaborations and the experimenting with new ones, involving land and factory industry assistance, roads, housing, health, scientific research, and education.

More controversial were Labor's experiments in public enterprise. Here it was almost certain at some point to collide with the private enterprise dogma of its opponents. It was safe enough when it provided services to private producers, but it was taking a risk if it went into commodity production or tried to set up a state monopoly of a basic service in which competition was adjudged feasible. Thus, when Labor in implementing the aviation policy enunciated in the Australia-New Zealand Agreement sought to create a Commonwealth-owned monopoly of air services, domestic and overseas, it was prevented by a constitutional decision from absorbing the intrastate services and had to accept continuing private competition on the interstate lines. It achieved monopoly only of the overseas service and, taking over Qantas as its chosen instrument, it set the stage for building up a globe-encircling nationalized service. On cue from British Labour it nationalized the Australian stake in imperial cable and wireless services, an arrangement unlikely ever to be disturbed. It provided, without seeking monopoly in any aspect, for the continuance of shipbuilding, so vital an activity in wartime, and for the retention in government ownership of ships used in coastal and overseas services. Although clear on the importance of improving land transport by standardizing railway gauges, it failed to do so, even though it continued to negotiate with the states about the matter. Recognizing the vital importance of expanding electricity generation and irrigation, its most spectacular action was to launch in collaboration with certain of the states the Snowy River scheme, a truly mammoth venture in hydroelectric and irrigation development that was estimated to take twenty years to bring to completion. Labor continued with its project for aluminum production in collaboration with Tasmania, but at the risk that the government stake in the project would one day be sold off to private enterprise. It confirmed the Commonwealth's predominance in scientific research for the benefit of the land and factory industries.

Labor supported the Commonwealth's entry into Antarctic exploration and scientific research and arranged for Commonwealth participation in coastal whaling (see Chapter XIV). It initiated and established international collaboration in scientific and socio-economic research in the islands. And although delayed and hindered by obstacles beyond its control, it planned and initiated—in contravention of its own tradition—an immigration program of a size and scope that insured that immigration would have an enormous impact on the Australian scene. Rationalized by reference to the manpower needed for defense and development and thus at once an effort to insure Australia's future and a vote of confidence in it, the program was designed to put the emphasis on British immigrants, as earlier, and to involve no modification of the White Australia policy. In execution, while the British emphasis was achieved, though not to the extent hoped for, the exigencies of the international migration situation led to unprecedented immigration of other European nationalities, including displaced persons, raising the probability that Australia would in time become as mixed as to national origin as, say, Canada if not the United States. This promised to have an almost revolutionary effect on the tone and savor of Australian life.

Australia's economic and political external relations remained more those of a country reacting and adapting to overseas forces and initiatives than a country that was itself an initiator. When it enunciated external policies designed to serve its interests it could not hope to impose them but could only seek to effectuate them by advocacy and maneuver. While the Big Powers jockeyed to protect their positions, Australia jockeyed to protect its position in the context the Big Power policies and maneuvers created. The status of Australia had unquestionably been upgraded by the war, especially in the Pacific, but in the emerging superpower world its position both as to recognition and power (the one being to an extent a function of the other) was still precarious. It was because of this that Dr. Evatt put so much emphasis on the United Nations and hoped so fervently for a rule-of-law world. Dr. Evatt's greatest triumph was thus his elevation to the presidency of the United Nations General Assembly in 1947. But as the superpower antagonism mounted, the problem of how best to relate Australia to the new and distasteful power situation became exacting, not least how best to relate to the United States as the predominant power in the Pacific if not the whole world.

Unable to establish the validity of the Curtin proposal for the governance of the British Commonwealth, Labor had to adapt to whatever might happen in the postwar period. Its general policy was to maintain the status quo in its own relation to the United Kingdom, not agreeing that the changed relations of others made any difference to the Australian relation. The country had derived great satisfaction from the arrival of the British fleet in the Pacific to participate in the war on Japan. The fleet was at first based in Sydney and later the Labor government gave the United Kingdom £25,000,000 toward its expenses incurred in Australia. It was the Labor government also that in 1946 resumed active collaboration in imperial defense activities and with the United Kingdom established in the desert country at Woomera, South Australia, a weapons development and testing center for rockets and other equipment, including a testing "range" that was eventually extended to the Indian Ocean coast. Australia's financial and other commitments to this project were very heavy.

It was Labor also, in the person of Prime Minister Chifley, that participated in the discussions arising from the withdrawal of Ireland from the Commonwealth and the decision of India to become an independent republic. The Labor position was to deplore withdrawals from the Commonwealth but to recognize that the decision was for the people involved to make and to accept the redefinition of relation the Indian intention involved but to maintain that it made no difference to Australia's relation. Labor therefore accepted that the Crown had no role in India's government (as by a governor-general) and that the Crown to India was simply the head of the Commonwealth. This left Australia one of the monarchical nations of the Commonwealth and an effort was made to derive some special quality from this as to her relationship to the Commonwealth. Chifley deprecated any formal dropping of "British" from the title of British Commonwealth. On the other hand, it was Labor which, when the term of His Royal Highness the Duke of Gloucester as governor-general expired, proposed the appointment of William McKell, Labor premier of New South Wales, in the face of conservative criticism of selecting an Australian at all, let alone a man with a strong party-political identification.

As spokesman in foreign policy Dr. Evatt was still under the necessity to assert Australia's status and to try to fortify it by fending off the veto whenever possible. To insure that Australia be a party to the formal surrender of Japan he felt it necessary to make what President Harry Truman later called "strong public statements." They gained Australia the right to representation at the ceremonies in Tokyo Bay, when the documents were signed on her behalf by Sir Thomas Blamey. Evatt was similarly concerned to insure that Australia be able to play what he re- garded as a proper role in the making of peace treaties in Europe, this involving a campaign to curb the powers the Council of Foreign Ministers had assumed. But the real center of his interest was not Europe, however important it was, but the Pacific. The focus here was Japan, but Evatt also dealt with the changes occurring or impending elsewhere in Asia. These raised problems different from those inherent in the Japanese situation. Conceiving that the Pacific was the area in which Australia's position was special, Evatt felt that Australia should be supported by the Commonwealth countries as the Commonwealth's spokesman, not least because effective United Kingdom power in "the East" was declin- ing. By combining Australian strength with Commonwealth prestige, he felt he could wield considerable influence.

Until World War II Australia had felt isolated from Asian affairs and to a great extent insulated from them by British power and prestige as well as in lesser degree by the power and prestige of other friendly colonial powers such as France and the Netherlands. Neither in the British-dominated or the other colonial areas did the Australians have any special relations with the indigenous peoples or any particular under- standing of their aspirations. While Asia at large was long viewed as a potential menace, the most specifically identified menace was Japan. World War II appeared to the Australians to confirm that they had been right about Japan, and this conclusion dominated their postwar policy positions toward it.

The war triggered off long-brewing changes in Asia beyond Japan, and complicated questions about how Australia's relation to the Asian countries should now be defined were inexorably raised. In essence the change was a revolt against rule by the European colonial powers, a struggle for national freedom. In assessing a given situation it was hard to decide what weight to give to the two conspicuous constituent elements of anticolonialism, nationalism and communism, not least because a vulgar Marxism was usually the economics of the anticolonialists. In harmony with its domestic orientation, Australian Labor tended to put the emphasis on the nationalistic element and discount, without ignoring, the communist element, thus allowing a favorable view of developments at the risk of alienating or annoying the resisting colonial powers. The conservatives were more inclined to want to keep in the good graces of the colonial powers if only because they had always been friendly to Australia in the past. Labor, however, saw no particular risk in its course and indeed a positive gain if its attitude inspired a friendly view of Australia in the minds of the emerging Asian leaders.

Labor's policy found clearest expression in its favor of the Indonesians against the Dutch in the tangled situation in the Netherlands East Indies. Labor proposed to follow up after independence was achieved by offering assistance in achieving economic and political stability and to support the positions of the new Asian nations *and Australia* with a regional pact embracing them all which would perhaps have the United States as an associate. What Labor wanted was friendly relations with the new Asia. It did not believe this would involve any dilution of the European character of Australia, for it intended to keep the White Australia policy. When White Australia was challenged in this or any other context, Labor stoutly defended it. Labor made it clear that in its view while Australia should make deliberate efforts to gain the friendship of the Asian nations it nevertheless should not hesitate to support policies serving its own national interests even in the face of possible Asian criticism or resentment.

With regard to Japan, Dr. Evatt's task was more urgent, more complicated, and more frustrating. Essentially, what he set out to do, with as near to national support as he ever achieved, was to see to it that a "hard" but just peace was imposed on Japan. Not only had Japan been the focus of Australian suspicions before the war but the fact that the Japanese had made aggressive war on Australia was resented, a resentment intensified by the criminality of Japanese conduct in combat and in the treatment of prisoners. The Australians not only actively pursued the business of trying Japanese for war crimes in their own military courts—they tried almost a thousand individuals and sentenced 148 to death and 39 to life imprisonment—but an Australian justice was president of the International Military Tribunal for the Far East which sat in Tokyo to try the "major" war criminals. It was regretted by the Australians that the Emperor was not tried by the Tribunal. They founded their case for a "hard" peace on their fierce hostility to the Japanese and rationalized their view by reference to the necessity they felt to guarantee that Japan should never again be in a position to make aggressive warfare to the menace of Australian security. Specifically, they founded their case on the Potsdam Declaration with regard to Japan (though they resented their exclusion from the Potsdam Conference) and the early policy definitions of the United States government and the Far Eastern Commission which sat in Washington.

Australia was one of the eleven members of the Far Eastern Commission (and made a characteristic effort to exclude the veto from its machinery) and one of the four members of the Allied Council in Tokyo which had an advisory relation to the supreme commander in charge of the occupation, General Douglas MacArthur. On the Council the Australian member also represented New Zealand, India, and the United Kingdom, thus illustrating what the Australians meant by their claim to primary British responsibility in Pacific Basin affairs. The Australians also assumed primary responsibility for the British contribution to the occupation forces.

At the start of the occupation the Australians were in essential harmony with the Americans who assumed and were granted principal responsibility for the way in which it was carried out. Progressively, the relation became less harmonious and on occasion became cacophonous. While there was disagreement about procedures, the Australian objective being to keep the Americans as closely under the authority of the Far Eastern Commission as possible, the more significant disagreements were over ends. The latter tended to find expression in such questions as the quantity of reparations to be exacted and their distribution among the claimants, the permissible level of industry especially in relation to war-supporting potential, the permissible structure of control of the Japanese economy, centering on the question of the *zaibatsu,* Japan's economic and political foreign relations in the occupation period, questions of trade and its rehabilitation, the role to be played by trade unions, and generally the large problems of democratization and its effective progress. The Australians sought to prevent the revival of Japan's war-making capacity and to impose upon the country something resembling the Australian laboristic social ideal as contrasted with the version of democratic capitalism which they saw the Americans imposing.

The disagreements arose in large part out of the shifting American definition of Japan's role in the world of nations, epitomized as a shift from considering Japan an enemy to considering it an ally of a special kind. Involved in this was the American effort to return Japan to self-support to relieve the American taxpayer of the burden of large dollar contributions to the country's support. From the Australian point of view MacArthur and the United States government in asserting and implementing policy to achieve their ends radically departed from the original policy declarations on which Australia founded its case. It also appeared to the Australians that the Americans in executing their policy were in effect making a piecemeal peace with Japan. Therefore, after a time during which they criticized and opposed American policy, they arranged during a face-to-face discussion between Evatt and MacArthur in Tokyo a general reconciliation with American actions; they decided that the best tactic to assure achievement of the ends they had in view was a peace treaty with Japan. In a peace treaty they might gain a victory for at least the essence of their point of view, a guarantee that Japan would not again develop its war-making power. For various reasons beyond Australia's control, it proved impossible to get a peace treaty written before Labor went out of office. As we shall see, Labor opposed the treaty finally prepared.

Crucially involved in the Australian-American disagreements over Japan was the question of the Cold War. Dr. Evatt held the view that the questions at issue between the Soviet Union and the United States and the West generally were not symptomatic of an irrepressible and unavoidable conflict but could be composed by rational compromise. He therefore had but limited sympathy with the American view that a re-definition of Japan's role was required by the exigencies of the Cold War in its Pacific-Asiatic expression. In the American perspective Japan was no longer the source of rational anxiety; the true source of anxiety was aggressive communist power in Asia, first the Soviet Union's power, a little later the Red Chinese power. Dr. Evatt, however, defended the position that Japan, the demonstrated menace to Australia's security, was still the identifiable menace to its security. While quite capable of opposing the Soviet Union on specific points, Dr. Evatt refused to accept as valid the American thesis that communism was the overriding menace either in the Pacific Basin or, indeed, elsewhere.

Yet with all the contention between Australia and the United States—and contention over Japan was not the whole of it—Dr. Evatt kept it in view that somehow the United States should be committed to the support of Australia's security. In his time, however, no opportunity arose to nail down such a commitment. Allegedly—because the point has never yet been demonstrated—he attempted to obtain such a commitment when the United States in determining its security program for the Pacific sought the use of the great base that had been built at Manus Island at the time of MacArthur's progress from New Guinea to the Philippines. If this was the case, Dr. Evatt failed. And it seems more likely that he failed because he held too firmly to the policy about bases enunciated in the Australia-New Zealand Agreement. He was roundly criticized by those Australians who felt strongly that the United States must at almost any price be committed to the support of Australia's security. It was left for Labor's conservative successors to deal with this problem.

The Chifley government took the full impact of postwar trade union unrest in which communism was a constituent element of undefinable dimensions. Prime Minister Chifley believed that a Labor government was in effect a workers' government and should command the consideration of the trade unionists, not least because they contributed so largely to the votes that had put it in office. He therefore resented, not strikes as such, but strikes in defiance of, or aimed at the destruction of, the established machinery for dealing with issues between employees and employers, to the support of which the party was committed. He himself favored conciliation over compulsory arbitration, but he held that the arbitral machinery should be used in good faith and the strike resorted to only when no other remedy was left. He was hostile to "direct action." A strike designed to wreck the arbitral machinery was a challenge to the government. The Chifley government was anticommunist. As Chifley put it: "The Australian Labor party is entirely opposed to the principles of communism, including its economic theories for the management of the country, and its attitude toward religion." But he added, echoing a position first formulated by Labor two decades earlier: "I shall never support any policy which is designed to deprive minorities of the right of expression." Communism was interpreted as a foreign faith without good works, which nevertheless should not be proscribed.

The communists were at their maximum strength in the postwar period. Once restored to legality during the war and having taken up a prowar position, they had thrived as never before, exploiting the role of the U.S.S.R. in the war and extending their influence in the trade unions and among the intelligentsia. In the postwar period they attempted to exploit their power and, since by a tradition based on some contemptuous remarks Lenin had made in 1912 they had no particular regard for a Labor government, they had no scruples about exploiting it to Labor's detriment. The strike was, of course, an established means of Australian trade unions in pursuit of their ends. The use of direct action instead of resorting to the courts was a well-established minority position more talked about than used. The communists tried to make direct action the majority policy, at least for the unions they controlled.

Although the communists were strong in the management of important unions, notably in coal mining, land and sea transport, and engineering and construction, there was never an equivalence between union membership and the number of communists. Even within unions that were communist controlled the presumption was that the communists were a minority and that the communist officers were in effect a "junta." In theory the communist officers could be eliminated from their positions by democratic means. Actually, this was easier to say than to carry out because the Australian communists were like overseas communists in employing corrupt means—rigged elections, physical intimidation of opponents, the slanting of the contents of union papers—to gain and retain office.

In the immediate postwar period organized opposition to the communists and their stooges in the unions was largely in the hands of the Labor party's so-called Industrial Groups and the Catholic Social Studies Movement, both specially organized for the purpose, but much depended upon finding strong and durable anticommunist candidates for the strategic offices, particularly the office of secretary. Although the Catholic organization notably strengthened the anticommunist forces in the unions, its presence had fateful consequences later on, not least because of the Catholic impact on party politics. At this time both Catholic laymen and the Catholic bishops revived once again the ancient discussion of how far Catholics could in good conscience support the socialist objective of the Labor party. The chief contribution of the Labor government directly to the support of the anticommunists in the unions was legislation to be administered by the arbitration courts to protect union elections from communist manipulation. As the communist-led unions brought about more and more strikes which could be interpreted as efforts to disorganize the Australian economy for political ends, the conservative politicians began to pressure the Labor government to do something drastic about the communists. Mr. Menzies pressured Labor as hard as he could short of asking for proscriptive legislation. Prime Minister Chifley held to his refusal to proscribe a minority. The conflict over what should be done reached its climax after Labor had left office.

The communist and communist-inspired activities of unions were, of course, carried on at a time when the unions in general were exceptionally active in asserting claims, making it difficult for the unsophisticated to know just what was communist and what was not. The general union objectives were shorter hours and increases in wage rates beyond the automatic adjustment to the cost of living index, hopefully to win for the workers a larger share of the national income. The unions did win some wage boosts, and in 1948 they won the universal forty-hour week.

As far as the Labor government was concerned the climactic communist-inspired strike was that in the New South Wales black coal mines in 1949. Traditionally the greatest contributors to turbulence in labor relations in the nation, the miners had long been communist led. In some part this was explainable by reference to the bad conditions of life and labor in what had been a sick industry for at least twenty years. During the war black coal production, of which New South Wales contributed around 80 per cent, was constantly less than demand, and this continued to be the case after the war, when demand went on rising as industrialization proceeded. The inadequate coal production was a principal handicap to the achievement of full and continuous production in all instances where coal for power was the immediate or ultimate reliance. In 1946 the federal Labor government in collaboration with the Labor government of New South Wales set up a Joint Coal Board to carry out a basic reorganization of the industry to "ensure regular production of coal to meet the needs of the Australian economy," to distribute the coal in its proper kinds to the proper consumers, to develop the extensive coal resources further, and "to promote the welfare of the workers." This was a substitute for nationalization for which the miners were asking. Labor relations were placed in the hands of a Coal Industry Tribunal, a special arbitral authority.

In mid-June 1949 just as the Tribunal was about to announce a favorable decision on "long service leave" for the miners and when the miners had just had the Tribunal's hearings on a thirty-five-hour week adjourned and inexplicably had withdrawn their application for a wage increase, the miners struck, ostensibly to enforce their version of all three claims by direct action. This strike was interpreted by the federal Labor prime minister and the state Labor premier as a strike to destroy the Tribunal. It was stigmatized as "a wholly unreasonable and unjustifiable repudiation" of the arbitration system on which Labor took its stand. "The whole economic and social life of the nation" had been placed in extreme jeopardy by the action. Living conditions for many became intolerable and 500,000 workers were thrown into unemployment. "It has been suggested," Chifley said, "that this stoppage has been planned by a communist section of the miners' officials for some months. I hesitate to believe that any citizen could be so callous as to plan deliberately for the holding up of the life of the community and the imposition of the intolerable hardships ... But this is what has happened." Why Chifley should "hesitate to believe" was obscure, for the strike was in fact an Australian phase of the general communist effort to disrupt postwar recovery in the Western countries and the Australian communists believed that it would, when spread by sympathetic and supporting strikes, lead to a "revolutionary situation" from which they would profit enormously.

The Chifley government, with some internal dissension over means, set about to wean the rank-and-file miners away from their communist leaders by speech and publication and to hamper the leadership by such means as a law to freeze union funds to prevent their use to support the strike. And it sought to get coal production going again by sending troops to operate the open-cast mines, an utterly unprecedented antistrike action by a Labor government. The Chifley pressure and harassing tactics were designed to force the rank-and-file to repudiate their communist leaders and, in meetings they themselves called, to vote the end of the strike, and return to the Tribunal for redress of grievances. This approach involved the gamble that a majority of the miners were moderates and fundamentally loyal to political Labor and its policies. Whether or not this was true, the strike was ended after lasting seven weeks. Political Labor's victory was thus a tremendous setback for the communists and forced the abandonment of the direct action tactic. It ushered in a period of comparative peace in labor relations generally. It did not, however, guarantee the displacement of the communist leaders either in the miners' or any other union and politically it was hardly at all useful to Chifley in the ensuing general election. The voters, it seemed, were more impressed by the disastrous disorder the communists had created than by Chifley's tactical victory over them.

With the experience of operating a controlled economy which had been gained in wartime, Labor believed it had the means of achieving socialism. However, the failure to consolidate the basic powers constitutionally in the referendum of 1944 was a disturbing development. While exploitation of the distinction between the ending of combat and the formal making of peace might enable the government to prolong its grip on the coveted powers, it could not retain a permanent grip on them or even for as long as economic conditions might seem to warrant. It was, then, disastrous to the Chifley government that in only one instance was it possible to consolidate constitutionally the wanted powers: in 1946 after a bad scare from the High Court it was by referendum that the social security power was put on a sound constitutional basis. But all the other constitutional amendments that the Chifley government proposed were defeated: that needed to support Commonwealth-wide marketing legislation—for wheat, flour, butter, cheese, and milk products, dried fruits and other fruit products, and sugar—the power needed for the Commonwealth to deal with the terms and conditions of employment, and to deal with prices, rents, and charges. The last was defeated in

June 1948, which caused something of a crisis, for while price, rent, and charges control could be passed to the states and the states could achieve a measure of uniformity by negotiation, the Commonwealth decided when it relinquished the controls that it would abolish most of the subsidies it had been paying to sustain its chosen price levels. Since the states could not afford to pay the subsidies, they would have to set their prices at higher levels than the Commonwealth had established. An upward movement of prices over a fairly wide front was therefore inevitable. But this was less disturbing to the Chifley government than the prospect that it might lose control over banking. The struggle over banking was the climactic struggle for controls over the economy.

The architect of the controls over banking which had first been imposed under National Security regulations in 1942 and had been formally legislated in 1945, had been Mr. Chifley as Curtin's treasurer. Chifley's objective had been to place banking and credit firmly in the hands of the government of the day working through the Commonwealth Bank in its aspect as a central bank. In Chifley's eyes the 1945 legislation was an experiment to determine whether by such controls Labor's objective could be achieved or whether in the end it would be necessary to nationalize banking as he had declared in 1937. Either way it was Chifley's purpose to guarantee continuous full employment. The effect of the 1945 legislation on the private trading banks was to shrink their policy-making functions drastically, particularly with regard to credit, and to reduce their economic role and their profitability. The private banks had accepted the situation with reasonable grace as long as the war lasted, but when the war was over they looked around for ways to strengthen themselves. One way was amalgamation of banks. The Chifley government showed no hostility to this. What it feared was a concerted attack in the courts on the legislation. The banks had shown their hand when they had propagandized against Labor's intentions as deducible from the National Security regulations. Actually, however, the attack upon the 1945 legislation in the courts came from an unexpected quarter. Section 48 of the 1945 Act provided in effect that the accounts of states, state authorities, and local governments held by the private trading banks should at a specified date be transferred to the Commonwealth Bank. This section was challenged in the High Court by the Melbourne City Council, and in August 1947 the High Court ruled that the states, state authorities, and local governments could, in fact, bank where they chose. While this did not defeat an absolutely vital section of the Act, such was the nervousness about what would now happen—it was assumed that the trading banks would move to attack vital sections—that Chifley's response on August 16 was: "Cabinet today authorized the Attorney-

General (Dr. Evatt) and myself to prepare legislation for submission to the Federal Parliamentary Labour party for the nationalization of banking, other than state banks, with proper protection for shareholders, depositors, borrowers, and staff of private banks."

By this surprisingly curt announcement Chifley told the country that what had been Labor's policy since 1919 and to which he had declared his personal allegiance in 1937 was at last to be implemented. The die was cast as a tactical move to protect the vital controls over the economy and to insure full employment. Then ensued the greatest and bitterest political battle since the battle over conscription in World War I. To an astonishing extent the fight was not over the idea of central banking or over to what extent banking and credit had to be controlled by government to ensure full employment but over nationalization (equated to socialism) versus free enterprise. Chifley's choosing to nationalize the banks before his 1945 legislation had been seriously challenged was assumed to represent not a defense of full employment, but a first step toward full socialism and in any case a long stride away from a rationally mixed economy. The trading banks, the conservative parliamentarians, and the newspapers therefore fought the legislation as socialism. Chifley's defense of his legislation in Parliament was unfathomably weak. (The strongest defense of it was a pamphlet prepared by a private organization of academics.) Chifley's remarks revealed once more that he was still fighting the Great Depression, and that he was still anticipating another depression, presumably to come from the United States. He concluded: "Full public ownership of the banks will ensure control of banking in the public interest. It will enable effective steps to be taken against the dangers of secondary inflation. It will assist us to stave off depression and to avoid a repetition of the miseries of 1930. Beyond this, it will open a long-locked doorway to the development of a monetary and banking system truly adequate to our national requirements and wholly devoted to the service of Australia." (The last remark was an oblique reference to the common Labor thesis that the Great Depression was made by bankers in service of non-Australian interests.)

The legislation was quickly and easily passed by a Labor-dominated House and Senate. It was equally promptly challenged in the High Court by the trading banks and the three states which currently had anti-Labor governments (Victoria, South Australia, and West Australia). On August 11, 1948, the High Court declared certain sections of the Act vital to carrying out nationalization constitutionally invalid. The Labor government, violating its tradition, appealed to the Privy Council in the United Kingdom. It was now particularly concerned to know whether or not Section 92 of the constitution—"trade, commerce and intercourse among the States, whether by means of internal carriage or ocean navigation, shall be absolutely free"—was an insuperable obstacle to nationalization. In the appeal the Commonwealth government was joined by the Labor governments of New South Wales and Queensland. In July 1949 the Privy Council dismissed the appeal on the ground that it had been made without the permission of the High Court and in October published its reflections on the case. These reflections made it quite clear that section 92 was indeed a formidable obstacle to nationalization when interstate transactions were an integral part of the activity in question. However, since the question was not faced frontally but approached tangentially with much emphasis on the facts of particular cases, the issue was apparently left open. Nevertheless, it looked as though the constitution stood as an insurmountable obstacle between Labor and socialism insofar as socialism meant nationalization.

As Chifley seems to have misread the political meaning of the public reaction to his handling of communism, especially in the coal strike, so also he seems to have misread the political meaning of his constitutional misadventures. Failure to carry referenda was such a normal happening in Australia and apparently so disconnected from voting behavior in elections that Chifley appears to have overlooked that it could be interpreted as indicating a majority opposition to Labor's program. Failure to carry bank nationalization was a constitutional failure of a slightly different character, but Chifley seems not to have properly weighed the anti-Labor sentiment the effort inspired nor to have noticed how effective the propaganda of the banks had been. He leaned far too heavily on the assumption that the majority in Australia favored Labor and, adding up its record sympathetically, would keep it in office. At the time the most widely accepted theory of politics in Australia cast Labor in the leadership role and denominated the opposition as parties of resistance to Labor. However, the political history of the Commonwealth since World War I showed that the voters had come to favor the conservative parties of resistance at the polls and turned to Labor only when the conservatives had declined in effectiveness for one reason or another. Labor was the beneficiary of the fluctuating protest vote—and it stood to be victimized by it also. It had been demonstrated conclusively that Labor could not safely consider itself the "natural ruler" of the Commonwealth, however it might view itself in some of the states. In the Commonwealth it was simply the voters' alternative to conservative rule and it inevitably suffered in popularity when it had been long in office and had alienated the so-called "floating voters" who controlled election results. The man who read the political signs aright at this time was Robert Gordon Menzies.

The election of 1943 had reduced the U.A.P. to an unimpressive rump party of twelve in the House (six from Victoria, four from New South Wales, two from Tasmania). Menzies' grip on the leadership was insecure. The rejection of Labor's comprehensive proposals for constitutional change in the referendum of 1944 suggested to Menzies that the time had come to perform the hallowed conservative maneuver of liquidating the established party and forming a new one. In the election of 1943 the opposition to Labor had been more fragmented in terms of a multiplicity of *ad hoc* parties than ever before in history. In proposing to liquidate the U.A.P. and launch a new party, Menzies therefore faced a situation analogous to that faced by J. A. Lyons in bringing the U.A.P. to birth in 1931. His problem in fact was more difficult than Lyons' in that Lyons' personal political position had been strong, whereas in 1944 Menzies' personal political position was at its lowest point. Moreover, Lyons faced a Labor government that was obviously tottering, whereas Menzies faced a strong Labor government—which lasted, in fact, five years more. Like Lyons, he could command no assistance from the Country party.

Nevertheless, Menzies succeeded in forming his new party. He transformed the U.A.P. into the Liberal party and announced his success in the House in February 1945. It was a party more democratically organized than the U.A.P. and less dependent upon a self-appointed Victorian oligarchy for finance, but it was a national party only in that it came to have alliances with more or less autonomous groupings in Queensland, South Australia, and Western Australia. Its basic strength was in Victoria. Ideologically, it had discernible connections with Alfred Deakin's fusion in that while emphasizing concern for the welfare of the people it proposed to support that welfare by relying upon the dynamic forces in Australian capitalism instead of turning to socialism. It was also like the old Liberal party in including numerous conservatives. It was in the tradition of amalgamating the liberals and the conservatives to draw the support of every anti-Labor voter and politician not likely to support the Country party. It was an old crowd doing business under a new name and charter, as became obvious when it finally achieved office. In the 1946 general election which returned the Chifley government to office, Menzies, while reducing Labor's seats by but three, increased his following by 50 per cent, or from twelve to eighteen. Further progress was obviously dependent upon a swing to the right in the electorates, probably to be induced by disillusion with Labor.

Preliminary to the general election of 1949 Labor took notice of the great increase in population since federation and arranged an increase in the number of seats in the House and Senate. The constitution provided that seats in the House never exceed twice the number in the Senate, so the new arrangement was for 121 seats in the House and 60 in the Senate, or ten for each state. In the election Chifley waged a passive campaign. He showed more optimism about links to the dollar than hitherto, but emphasized that he expected more from an inflow of British capital. He told the people that only by a constitutional amendment could banking now be nationalized. But essentially he stood on the record: "My colleagues and I ask that you judge us on our record and on our ability to go on with the job of building Australia into the nation we all want it to be." The opposition waged an aggressive antisocialist campaign, though Menzies was appreciably more temperate than Fadden of the Country party; and Menzies now at last joined Fadden in demanding that the Communist party be proscribed. The Opposition gamble was that the country was ready to swing right. In the election the Liberals gained fifty-five seats in the enlarged House and the Country party nineteen, while Labor had but forty-eight. In the Senate, Labor retained control and from July 1950 would have thirty-four seats to twenty for the Liberals and six for the Country party. Mr. Menzies was once again prime minister of Australia.

With the return of Robert Gordon Menzies to the prime ministership Australia may be said to have entered the postwar period. His return represented the most remarkable personal political triumph in Commonwealth history, but while his partisans tried to establish that it was a "new" Menzies who had come back, his critics found that the newness was superficial and that the smell of brimstone still hovered around. Menzies was now fifty-five years old. He had been born in the Victorian wheat country at Japarit in 1894, the son of a storekeeper. His educational record had been studded with scholarships, honors, and prizes and capped by a University of Melbourne degree with First Class Final Honors in Law. He had had a brilliant career at the Victorian and Federal bars and in 1929 had "taken silk." Identified with the conservative interests of Melbourne, he had entered state politics in 1928 and had quickly risen in the ministerial hierarchy to the deputy premiership. He had entered the Federal House in 1934, taking the seat just vacated by Sir John Latham. His fortune at the federal level has been recounted. His return to the prime ministership had been supported by a swing to the right in Australia paralleling one in New Zealand at the same time and preceding swings in the United Kingdom and the United States.

In 1949, however, it was by no means clear that the Australian conservatives were in office for the longest run in Commonwealth history. Menzies' apparent political ideal was to administer affairs lightly and sparingly, but he had to deal with a changing nation in a rapidly changing world and to undertake more positive government than it was his personal disposition to favor. If his grip on office proved strong, his government's career was nevertheless stormy. He was still in office in 1963.

While his government was always known as "the Menzies government" and he was always in charge of it, it was in fact a Liberal-Country party coalition in the tradition established by the Bruce-Page government in 1923. The influence of the Country party on policy was therefore constantly debatable. The government's personnel emphasized the continuity with the liberal-conservative past. In the ministry of 1949 were such familiar figures as H. E. Holt, P. C. Spender, and R. G. Casey, while Dame Enid Lyons was surrogate for her late husband, J. A. Lyons. From the Country party were familiars like A. W. Fadden, holding the senior post of treasurer, John McEwen, and Sir Earle Page. While in subsequent ministries Mr. Menzies brought in new faces as old-timers left politics (for example, Sir Arthur Fadden), died (Sir Earle Page), or chose to complete their careers abroad (Sir Percy Spender, Lord Casey), he maintained an unresolved doubt about who would in the end succeed him in leadership, for like so many democratic politicians of autocratic tendencies, he had no fondness for close associates whose prestige might come to rival his own.

Even beyond Australian precedent, the problems of government were problems of economic management. Committed like Labor to growth, full employment, social security, and rising standards of living, the Menzies government sought to guide the economy with looser reins than Labor favored and to rely more explicitly on the free enterprise horses to do the primary pulling. Under the conditions actually encountered, the Menzies government had on occasion to tighten the reins in one fashion or another to impose discipline on a run-away economy. A high rate of growth was in fact achieved, though far from the highest in the world, and the country was consistently prosperous.

A standard of living above that of most of the world but below that of North America was maintained, and there began to be talk that Australia's was indeed an affluent society. While at the federal government level final decisions as to policy were made by the prime minister and cabinet, it was apparent that the senior civil servants were gaining greater influence. If, as has been argued, the Australians have a genius for bureaucracy, the genius was well exercised in the Menzies era. It was commonly supposed that decisions on economic policy were made by the prime minister and cabinet refereeing among proposals of senior public servants brought to cabinet by their ministers. The servants of the Treasury and Commerce and Agriculture were thought to be especially influential. As in other countries of the same general character there now also began, as private enterprise throve and the universities grew and multiplied, that interchange of personnel between the government bureaucracy, private enterprise, and the universities which seems to be characteristic of latter-day democracies.

Since economic growth was the primary desideratum, the question of capital for investment was central. The great bulk of the capital required was supplied by domestic private and business savings, but lacking Labor's inhibitions, the Menzies government turned to overseas borrowing on government account and to the encouragement of a steady inflow of private capital to obtain a rate of growth beyond what was feasible on the basis of domestic savings. The domestic money market steadily strengthened; the stock markets, especially those of Sydney and Melbourne, expanded. Over these years about 35 per cent of capital investment was public, 65 per cent private.

The financial links to the United Kingdom remained overwhelmingly the most important external ties, both on public and private account, but the Menzies government expanded and encouraged the expansion of the tie to the dollar. The government borrowed dollars not only in the New York money market but also from the International Bank for Reconstruction and Development. The distribution of government securities at issue on June 30, 1961, was:

Australia (in £ A.)	3,716,318,213
London (in £ Stg.)	342,030,265
New York (in $)	286,908,714
International Bank (in $)	252,207,000

In addition, the government also borrowed Canadian dollars and Swiss francs. While the Commonwealth's debt was in total far greater than any single state's, the state debts were in total greater than the Commonwealth's. New South Wales had by far the largest outstanding obligations both at home and abroad. In the determination of borrowings and in the management of the debt the Commonwealth's voice was decisive.

As the bulk of the public debt was held in Australia and the sum owed in pounds sterling was far greater than that in dollars, so the overwhelming bulk of the private capital of Australia was Australian, followed by United Kingdom and United States private capital. The American stake was growing faster than the United Kingdom stake, but since the United Kingdom stake was by far the larger and continued to grow, the chances of the balance being tipped in the American favor as in

Canada seemed remote, though the fear was occasionally expressed. British private capital was historically heavily involved in the land industries, especially their servicing institutions, banking, mining, and manufacturing. In this period the bulk of the new capital seems to have gone into manufacturing. American private capital, the history of which was not well understood, also concentrated in general manufacturing but was noticeable in new mining ventures (coal, bauxite, iron ore), in the refining, distribution, and search for oil, petro- and other chemicals, and in heavy construction. Australian economic isolationists criticized this inflow of private capital, alleging it was going to be difficult to service and was in any case fundamentally exploitative, while the American element was attacked as specially tainted with the exploitative poison.

The governing trend of the national income was upward. In the financial year 1948–49, the last full year in which Labor was in office, the national income stood at £A 1,937 million (£A =$2.24). It passed £A 2,000 million in 1949–50 during which the conservatives took office and £A 3,000 million in 1950–51, the sudden great rise being attributable to an inflationary increase in the price of wool (from £A 80 per bale in 1949–50 to £A 180 in 1950–51) under the impact of the Korean War boom, reached £A 4,000 million in 1954–55 and £A 5,000 million in 1958–59, standing at £A 5,825 million in 1960–61.

The 1950's saw three booms which culminated in 1951–52, 1955–56, and 1960–61, and which were followed by three recessions. The troubles arose, in varying combinations, from internally and externally generated inflation, shortages, and bottlenecks arising from uneven development, a persistent shortage of skilled labor not successfully overcome by apprenticeship, technical training, or immigration, the absence of basic facilities, fluctuations downward in export prices, and deficits in the balance of payments. Inflation was at its worst in the first boom when prices rose 60 per cent in four years, but it persisted through the decade. In 1951–52 it was dealt with by budgeting for a large surplus in the government's accounts. The third boom was particularly marked by speculation, especially in city land and buildings and on the stock markets. The recession caused by checking this boom was met by budgeting for a large deficit in government accounts. The Menzies government was commonly criticized for taking corrective action too late. Timing was of course of the essence and difficult successfully to determine.

A consequence of the 1951–52 crisis was the imposition of government-administered restrictions on imports. The restrictions were retained until early 1960. The balance of payments problem was, therefore, one of the most persistent. However, there was more popular concern about and hence more "political" meaning in the unemployment that accompanied the recessions. It was made painfully clear that the Australian public interpreted full employment to mean steady over-full employment and that an unemployment rate of as little as 2 per cent of the work force was deplorable and anything over that figure a calamity. Unemployment immediately brought the immigration program to critical notice and it was made clear that Labor, while the initiator of the postwar program, still clung to its historic position that immigration was only tolerable so long as the resident work force was fully employed. But with all the excursions and alarums, the Menzies government successfully weathered every crisis.

The government's durability was attributable partly to political circumstances favorable to it, but even more to the fact that with all the turmoil the country was undeniably prosperous and employment was normally quite "full." The focal growing point was factory industry. When Labor left office there were 40,000 factories. By 1959–60 the number was 56,600. By category, the greatest growth was in engineering. Steel production was steadily expanding toward 3,800,000 tons a year, and the per capita consumption of steel was rising. The net value of production in the secondary industries, which stood at £A 490,000,000 in 1948, rose to £A 2,174,882,000 in 1960.

While these figures reflect the growth, they do not tell anything about the all-over structure of factory industry. In 1961 a distinguished business leader declared, "Australian secondary industry is now set up on a fairly broad base and has reached quite a high level of diversification. Not all manufactures are represented here yet, of course, but the Australian secondary industry pattern is recognizably the same as that in a number of so-called 'industrial' countries. Scale of production is notably smaller in many cases." Australia at the beginning of the 1960's still had a distance to go before achieving the maximum diversification possible to it. At that time there was a lengthy list of factory products it was still importing to an annual value of £A 1 million or better.

In reaching this position the Australians had made factory industry a principal supplier of jobs. About 28 per cent of the work force was now employed in factories, a proportion greater than that obtaining in the United States. The meaning of the figure, usually taken to indicate that Australian industrialization had become very intensive, was actually far from clear. It possibly meant that efficiency of production by machine was not what it should be, causing an excessive reliance on manpower. It may have meant that Australia had reached and would soon pass the peak of employment in factories and a strong drift to the tertiary or service employments was likely soon to set in.

Because fundamental responsibility for development rested with the states—the Commonwealth cooperating but concentrating on the creation of a favorable climate—there was a good deal of competition for new industries, especially overseas. Each state was clamorous for its own development, and every state wanted more factories not only because this was fashionable but because factories appeared to offer the only support for an enlarged population. While every state made progress in factory industry, the concentration of factories in New South Wales and Victoria was not diminished. The multiplication of factories transformed the domestic character of Australia, but in the world's eyes the country continued to be seen as a producer of foodstuffs and raw materials.

A rethinking of the position of the land industries began about 1952, and their problems were active items on the agenda of government thereafter. The discussion was initiated by the federal Department of Commerce and Agriculture working through the Agricultural Council (est. 1934) which brought together the state and federal officials responsible for governmental decisions with regard to crop agriculture and grazing. Though in 1952 there was a good deal that could be done to help the land industries to overcome war-created handicaps to enable them to increase production over prewar levels, it was not long before it was painfully clear that production at a profit was the basic problem. The long downward slide of prices for primary products that began after the Korean War boom was markedly disadvantageous to Australia as an exporter. The disadvantage was accentuated by the fact that returns from primary product exports were basic to her economic health.

The area under crops fluctuated from 20,000,000 to 30,000,000 acres, 40 per cent of which was normally devoted to wheat. Over a million acres were in pasture, the greater proportion not utilizable in any other fashion because of low rainfall. There was an interchange between wheat and wool, largely on the basis of price, in those areas where the alternative use of land between crop and pasture was possible. The proportion of the work force engaged in primary industry steadily declined until in 1960 it was about half what it had been in the 1920's, when the impossibility of relying on the land industries for the support of an increased population was first perceived. In 1960 the percentage figure was 13.4. Production gains were best in crop agriculture, poorest in dairying, and were on the average about 50 per cent over the prewar levels. In crop agriculture they were chiefly supported by increased use of machines—the number of tractors, for example, increased three times —and increased use of chemical fertilizers—consumption was double that of 1938–39. In grazing, progress was related to the extension of the area of "improved pastures" where this was climatically feasible and to a spectacularly successful attack on the old rabbit pest by the planned spread of the virus disease, myxomatosis.

Within the industries there was a trend toward increased capital investment in the units of production. The profit rate was, however, low, especially as compared to what could be expected from other kinds of capital investment. The sheep population had risen by 1960 to an all-time high of 155,174,000 with New South Wales still the leading state with 71,000,000 sheep. This enlarged sheep population was concentrated on the best watered pastures as in the past. Wool production in the late 1950's was running at 1,500,000,000 pounds annually, of which about 95 per cent was exported. The production of mutton and lamb steadily rose, but domestic consumption also rose, with the result that the percentage of production exported fell from 28 per cent to 17 per cent. On the other hand, beef production rose faster than domestic consumption, and the percentage exported rose from 25 to 40 per cent. In dairying the number of cows remained quite constant, but milk production fluctuated and so did the percentage of production exported, normally standing at around one-third. The wheat crop usually occupied about 12,000,000 acres, and in the best years production reached toward 200,000,000 bushels, of which around three-fifths had to be exported. Sugar cane occupied about 300,000 acres, production ran around a million and a quarter tons, and over half of it had to be sold overseas.

The same considerable dependence on exports characterized the other segments of crop agriculture, including the irrigated production of fruits for drying and canning. However, only the main products of the pastoral industry were sold for what they would bring in the world market without special support from the government. Wheat benefited from an annual bounty paid by the federal government. So also did dairy produce. Sugar was bolstered by a prohibition of competitive imports and a home consumption price. Except for wool, most of the products of the land industries were marketed by boards rather than by the producers in a free market, and in the early 1960's the federal government strongly favored international commodity agreements to guarantee outlets at stable and remunerative prices.

Although the governments were criticized for not spending enough in support of growth and for not spending money wisely, the fact is that the federal and state governments put a good deal of capital into such allegedly neglected areas as transport and power. The internal transport problem was, of course, a hardy perennial. Expenditure on roads not only in the heartland but also in the tributary country greatly increased. A considerable automotive road transport industry developed in relation to the great cities and in the farthest outback. The railway line from the New South Wales border to Melbourne was standardized with federal assistance, thus creating a standard gauge track which was continuous from Brisbane through Sydney to Melbourne. An agreement was reached for the standardization of the Western Australia line from Kalgoorlie to the Indian Ocean—a long step toward a truly transcontinental standard gauge line from the Pacific to the Indian Ocean. The government-owned airlines were strongly supported (and were profit earners), and much assistance was given to the private competition on the interstate lines. The federal government's own contribution in the field of power continued to be its support of the Snowy River scheme on which great progress was made, while Victoria carried forward the development of its brown coal resources and South Australia, having taken electricity generation and supply into state ownership, steadily expanded both. New South Wales added to its coal-fired generating plants. There was a good deal of activity in water-conservation in an effort to make the most of one of Australia's scarcest natural resources.

The federal and state governments and private enterprise collaborated in an intensified search for economic minerals to support and allow the extension of industrialization. The mining industry was thus enabled not only to expand the production of the standard minerals but also to add new kinds. In the new developments established companies such as the Zinc Corporation of Broken Hill played a large role. Mt. Isa Mines in Queensland diversified as well as increased production, and in the early 1960's the modernization of the railway from Mt. Isa to the coast at Townsville, where smelters were built, was put in hand. New companies entered the field, independently or in collaboration with established firms, notably American investors and the famous British Rio Tinto mining interest. Rich deposits of bauxite were found and exploitation was begun. New deposits of iron ore were located. After decades in the doldrums the export trade in coal had a spectacular revival and not only were old fields used but new fields were opened up, notably in central Queensland. The search for oil on the continent, intermittent for sixty years, was progressively intensified, engaging Australian, British, American, and French capital, and, after false alarms, what appeared to be a commercially viable field was found in southern Queensland, but the objective of production equivalent to Australian consumption still eluded. The new Australian refineries continued to be fed from Borneo, Indonesia, and the Persian Gulf. Australia became a uranium producer of world importance.

While not all of the new mineral discoveries were made in the North, many of them were, for example, bauxite and uranium, and their exploitation gave a fillip to the development of that frustrating region. A principal bauxite deposit was found and developed at Weipa on the Gulf of Carpentaria shores of Cape York, Queensland, and a major uranium deposit at Rum Jungle, just south of Darwin in Northern Territory. The federal government gave more attention to and spent more money on its Northern Territory, and it gave special financial assistance to Western Australia to help it develop the state's northwest. While the CSIRO intensively studied some aspects of agricultural production in the Northern Territory and private enterprise attempted commercial production, for example, of rice, it was the conclusion of a special committee of experts that no more than 66,000 square miles of the Territory's 524,000 square miles had an agricultural potential. The future of the North generally was believed to be where its past had mostly been: in cattle raising, supported by local fattening paddocks and locally grown feedstuffs. The health of the export beef trade supported this view. However, the most favored immediate support of the cattle industry was the provision of all-weather roads on which the cattle could be brought out for fattening in more favored areas, in the eastern portion of the North, those of coastal Queensland. At any rate those romanticists who envisioned a development of the North as intensive as that of the economic heartland were still frustrated. The North appeared to be indeed a permanent frontier.

Since growth was concentrated in the Australian economic heartland, including the West Australian "island," the established tendency toward a high degree of urbanization was confirmed. What with a substantial natural increase—the birthrate rose to about 23 per 1000 from the lows of the Great Depression—and a steady inflow of immigrants, the population increased by 2,500,000 between the end of the war and the end of the 1950's, passing 10,000,000 in 1959. Of these people no less than 54 per cent lived in the six capital cities, 25 per cent in provincial urban centers, and 21 per cent in the rural areas. The populations of the states and Northern Territory and their capital cities were estimated in 1960 to be as follows:

New South Wales	3,828,315	Sydney	2,098,490
Victoria	2,891,748	Melbourne	1,831,100
Queensland	1,462,245	Brisbane	578,000
South Australia	945,247	Adelaide	577,000
Western Australia	730,581	Perth	395,000
Tasmania	347,438	Hobart	111,250
Northern Territory	21,800	Darwin	9000

Industrialization gave a new dimension to the foundations of most of these urban complexes, all the more so since new industries showed a strong tendency to locate in or close to the established cities. While in New South Wales, for example, the concentration of factory industry was along the coast from Newcastle to the north of Sydney to Wollongong-Port Kembla to the south, the point of greatest concentration was Sydney and its immediate vicinity. In Victoria the concentration was in Melbourne and the surrounding area. Thus from being service and commercial centers for the rural industries, with factory industry of peripheral significance, the Australian cities, while remaining service and commercial centers, were primarily growing as the result of the expansion of their factory industry bases, even their commercial and service growth being a function of it. Long accustomed to spread their suburbs farther and farther afield, the great cities continued their outward movement. This was encouraged by the firm Australian preference for a single-story, single-family house in a garden. Only in the innermost suburbs did apartment houses appear in significant numbers. Almost inevitably the question was raised whether in fact the suburb was not the characteristic Australian environment.

In spite of the efforts of the planners to get control, the cities were obviously becoming preposterously sprawled, but only in South Australia was an effort made to deal with the problem by building a satellite city to a plan. Road and rail traffic problems were created, and the money and time consumed in traveling to and from work became a matter of concern to economists. Retailing, while maintained in the central cities, was also dispersed to incredibly numerous small, sign-beplastered shops strung in a ribbon development along arterial highways and to American-style suburban shopping centers. Not only were the staples of Australian life thus vended but also the actualities and symbols of success in an affluent society, supported by a hire-purchase system now enormously expanded. Advertising in encouragement and support flourished as never before.

In the central cities rebuilding was the order of the day, and taller and taller "office blocks" usually symbolizing some particular new or old firm's economic success, hotels at last designed to cater to the hitherto scorned sybaritism of foreign tourists, and all the other impedimenta of contemporary urbanity, mostly in one or another architectural version of the "international style," thrust themselves up among the relics of the building splurge of the Victorian 1880's and the less ornate reminders of the 1920's. With the Australian cities turning faces to the world which were ever increasingly Euro-American in character it was difficult to believe that any Australians had ever imagined that they could prevent "Europe" from building its "fatal nest" in their remote continent.

While there was political stability during the 1950's in the sense that the conservatives were continuously in office at the Commonwealth level and did well in most of the states, it was nevertheless the case that the political situation was unsatisfactory because the internal troubles of the Labor party weakened its effectiveness as an opposition. When the Liberal-Country party government took office it was in a minority in the Senate. Two strongly divisive issues immediately arose: the government's proposal for handling the banking question and its proposal to proscribe the Communist party. In effect Labor lost the argument over banking but won the argument over how the communists should be treated. Its victory did it no political good, and in the struggle over banking the Menzies government achieved a double dissolution of Parliament and in the ensuing election won majorities in both the House and Senate, which it maintained.

What the Menzies government sought with regard to banking was to put the Commonwealth Bank under the control of a Board of which the chief administrator, the governor (Dr. H. C. Coombs), was chairman. At the same time relations between the Commonwealth Bank and the private trading banks were liberalized, and the relation of the Bank and the government of the day was made looser without increasing the likelihood of a conflict between them over policy. The Bank was to continue to carry out central banking functions and to carry on its trading functions (general banking, mortgage banking, industrial finance, rural credits, and housing finance) competitively, to varying degrees, with the private banks. Labor took up a position of stubborn opposition to any change whatever from its 1945 legislation, digging in its heels hardest on any revival of a Bank Board. It identified a Board with the Bruce-Page Board and that Board with its role in the Great Depression.

Having managed the double dissolution in 1951, the Menzies government was then able to pass its banking legislation. However, it did not achieve finality with regard to banking, for in 1953 it returned to the matter and legislated to incorporate the general banking division as the Commonwealth Trading Bank and to define more precisely the relation of the Bank as a central bank to the private trading banks. In 1959 it legislated to separate the central bank functions from the existing complex of banking undertakings and institutions and constitute them the Reserve Bank of Australia, changing still again the relation to the private trading banks, to redistribute some of the divisions including the incorporated Trading Bank between the new Reserve Bank and a Commonwealth Banking Corporation, and to assign others to a Commonwealth Development Bank. This left the Commonwealth's banking institutions dominant in the field. The trading banks, however, strengthened themselves by establishing savings banks and acquiring interests in the rapidly growing consumer credit institutions.

The struggle over how to deal with the communists was rather more spectacular. That Mr. Menzies should attempt proscription at all was interpreted as a triumph for the Country party whose policy it was. A Communist Party Dissolution Bill was introduced into Parliament in April 1950. It confronted Labor with a difficult decision. Fundamentally involved was Labor's distaste for proscription of minority opinion—on which Ben Chifley had taken his stand when the anticommunist agitation had first become a political issue—and a civil libertarianism of which Dr. Evatt was the leading exponent. Both positions enjoyed important support from academics and clergymen. But the Labor party was nevertheless anticommunist. Its tactic in the immediate situation was to propose amendments to Menzies' bill—to remove from it those features which most obviously menaced civil liberties—but not frontally to challenge the purpose of the bill or its rationale. This was a strong tactical position, for that the bill was destructive of civil liberties was recognized both in Australia and overseas by persons and newspapers not to be suspected of any sympathy with communism. However, the government would not accept all of Labor's amendments of its bill, and it was assumed that Menzies proposed to use it to set up a double dissolution. Labor did not want to fight an election on the communist issue. Outside Parliament there was considerable division of opinion in Labor ranks about the bill. The communist-dominated unions were adamantly opposed to it in any form; other unions supported the parliamentarians in their effort to amend to protect civil liberties; while still other sections of Labor, anticommunist and fearful of being made to appear procommunist, believed that the bill should be allowed to pass even without Labor's amendments, on the understanding that Labor would amend it on its return to office. Roman Catholics were conspicuous members of this latter group. The holders of this opinion triumphed when the Federal Executive of the Labor party in effect instructed the parliamentarians to let the bill pass without Labor's amendments. Though an affront to the leadership of Chifley and Evatt the instruction was accepted. The bill passed as it then stood.

It was promptly challenged in the High Court by a group of leftist unions and the Communist party. Dr. Evatt appeared before the High Court as counsel for the communist-led Waterside Workers' Federation. In 1951 the High Court announced a six to one verdict against the constitutionality of the act. Debarred from legislating to proscribe the communists, the Menzies government turned to a constitutional amendment. Instead of presenting the voters with a simple proposition, however, it presented a highly technical and complex one. As leader of the Labor party, Dr. Evatt led the opposition in the ensuing referendum. He not only found Fascism in the course the Menzies government was taking, he seized the opportunity demagogically to attack the government for the Korean War inflation, its deflationary budget plans, its acceptance of the peace treaty with Japan (see below), and much else designed to create confusion and put not the proposed constitutional amendment but the government on trial. In the voting the "No" forces won a narrow victory, accounting for 50.48 per cent of the votes cast. Proscription was thus made impossible but other weapons against communism still remained or could be legally forged and a good deal depended on how and how well they were used. Proscription might be dead but anti-communism was not, and the communist question could not be waived aside as an irrelevance.

The Labor party's and Dr. Evatt's conspicuous roles in defeating the Menzies government's proposals to proscribe the communists made both vulnerable to the charge that they were in fact procommunist. Whether fair or unfair, the charge could be, and was, uttered. It could only be conclusively rebutted if in dealing with the communists in their chosen way they were resolute to oppose and defeat them. What actually ensued was as tangled a situation as any in which Australian Labor had ever become involved and productive as it was of intense emotions and bitter disputation, it is impossible even to outline its elements with any assurance that exact justice to all parties has been rendered. Not least of the difficulties is to arrive at a proper statement of the role of the Roman Catholics. Although never alleged to be the sole opponents of the communists in the unions and the party, they were certainly very conspicuous opponents and for obvious reasons of their own, the most militant. Their leader was B. A. Santamaria, child of Italian immigrants, educated at the University of Melbourne, a persuasive Roman Catholic ideologist, publicist, and organizer whose relations as a Catholic lay leader with the Church hierarchy, while indisputably existent, were nevertheless hard to define and in any case were mutable over time and as between the bishops and archbishops of the several states. Santamaria's base of operations was Victoria, the state in which he had greatest influence and in which the Church's hierarchy most openly supported him and most actively attacked his opponents, including in due time, Dr. Evatt and the Labor party.

Santamaria's relation to the emerging situation in the Labor party was complicated by the fact that he found it impossible to conceive of opposition to communism as his sole business in the unions and politics; he was also concerned to advance Catholic social policies in the party even though it was obvious that to accept them the party would have to abandon established positions. The Labor party was by tradition a secular party which had established its policy positions without reference to the views of any church or, indeed, any outside body whatever. In going beyond straight-forward anticommunism Santamaria and his following inevitably raised the vexed question of the proper role of his Church in the secular politics of a free society. What was acceptable to the Labor leadership as anticommunism became unacceptable as an "outside influence" on party policy. Santamaria's activity could be interpreted as an effort by a large and important segment of the party's established constituency to take over the party, suspectedly with the encouragement of and perhaps at the direction of "the Church."

The disastrous upshot was that Dr. Evatt, as leader of the Labor party, attacked the Santamaria following as an unacceptable "outside influence." This badly split the party, especially in Victoria, though with important repercussions elsewhere, notably in Queensland, where the party split and was driven from office. The dissidents and the expelled formed a splinter party, styled the Democratic Labor party, whose fundamental strength was in Victoria. In the situation as it existed, Dr. Evatt's action not only raised the dangerous specter of "sectarianism" but also was a body blow for anticommunism. Up to the time of the attack the anticommunists in the unions had been going from success to success. With the Santamaria militants under attack, their position was severely compromised and in the ensuing intraparty fights the anticommunists, Catholic and non-Catholic alike, suffered a reverse. The effect was to strengthen the position of "the left" both in the unions and the party. With a singular lack of realism, Dr. Evatt and his associates did nothing directly to repair the damage done to anticommunism and nothing clearly to indicate that it was still anticommunist in the manner Chifley had established. The effect was to make the relation of the Labor party to communism more ambiguous than ever, to the profit of its enemies.

Politically, the effect was that the Democratic Labor party, while never able to become a national party or to elect a significant number of candidates to the federal Parliament, was able by setting up three-cornered fights in the constituencies to split the labor vote and give the Liberal and Country party candidates a useful edge. The political beneficiary of the Labor party's internal disruption was the Menzies government. Yet such was the extraordinary durability of the Labor party and the great attraction of its mystique that not only did it survive the turmoil but it retained straight through the piece the loyalty of many of its Roman Catholic supporters, one of whom was deputy to Dr. Evatt. Only in 1961, after a decade hopelessly in the wilderness, was Labor able seriously to threaten Mr. Menzies' hold on office. A few months before this election Dr. Evatt had retired from party leadership and Parliament to the chief justiceship of New South Wales and had been succeeded by Arthur Calwell of Victoria, a Roman Catholic stalwart who, as Chifley's minister for Immigration, had been architect of the postwar immigration program. Benefiting enormously from the heavy protest vote against the economic difficulties of the time for which the Menzies government was held responsible, Labor gained fifteen seats in the House for a total of sixty, cutting the government's majority down to two. Mr. Menzies nevertheless continued as prime minister.

After the war, the dominant cultural expectation was that a break-through was imminent, if not next year, then in the next decade. The decisive shift from dubiety about prospects to confidence was believed to have occurred sometime in the 1930's and, not eroded by the war, the full effect was now to be experienced. The consequences were believed to be imminent in every cultural field and they would have the same meaning. The blessed if slippery and undefinable word "maturity" began to be bandied about.

However, in Australia as in comparable democracies the diversion of an adequate proportion of the national income to the support of cultural workers and institutions, especially those at the blue end of the spectrum, proved easier to advocate and satisfyingly justify than achieve. There was little expectation of any great help from private benefactions, though some were made, and rather less that the audience could fully support the expected expansion, though the marketplace for the arts was in a lively phase, so the disposition was to look to the governments, more especially the Commonwealth government, for the saving subventions. In one way or another more money was made available, but never quite enough. The literary people, dissatisfied, started an agitation for the adoption by Australia of a scheme such as the Canadians had evolved for the encouragement of Canadian culture. The basic difficulty was that while the governments were prepared to channel more money than for-merly to the support of "culture" they were too deeply involved in spending for basic economic growth to spend lavishly on the "tertiary" developments. Even for education they continued to spend a smaller pro-portion of the national income than was characteristic of comparable countries overseas—where the cry was also for more.

In spite of the marked improvement of circumstances, the complaints about the terms and conditions of the cultural life remained essentially the same as earlier. What distinguished the postwar era was the higher level of accomplishment of the participants in cultural enterprises, their greater sophistication, their greater interest in the international "languages" of their arts, and their greater willingness to carry on in Australia instead of fleeing overseas. To be sure expatriation, temporary or permanent, was still a solution which some ardently or reluctantly embraced, but the attraction of Australian pastures was growing and overseas pastures did not look so wonderfully green. A subtle redefinition of the meaning of overseas experience was taking place. It was now viewed as an admirable and perhaps indispensable way of maturing and sophisticating Australian talent for ultimate service at home. The cultural cynosure was still the United Kingdom, but more of those who were drawn to it aimed to make an impact and win recognition as Australians and no longer to achieve acceptance as British-plated colonials.

As in any country in which the population was rapidly increasing, the problem of education from the lowest levels to the highest was in the first instance a matter of "more" in terms of instructional staff and buildings. There could then be faced the problem of what to teach and to whom to teach it and with the aim of satisfying national needs and parental expectations. Below the university level the responsibilities rested wholly on the states. The state schools struggled for the finances to build more schools and to recruit on one inducement or another, including subsidization of preparation for a teaching career, additional teachers. The debate over what and how to teach engaged not only the attention of the professional educators but also to an exceptional degree the general public. A distinctive change in the public attitude toward education was the greater willingness of parents to encourage their children to go on climbing the educational ladder after they had reached school-leaving age. The direction of the upward movement was definitely toward the first degree university level. The pressure of numbers was felt in full force by the "public" schools and the Roman Catholic parochial schools. The Catholics agitated for support of their school system from tax funds. A distinctive advance in educational facilities was the enlargement of the public library systems. Adult education was revitalized, with the most radical experimentation in Victoria.

The upward climb of students reached the universities almost immediately after the war. By tradition and constitutional provision, responsibility for the support of the universities rested with the states. A distinctive development of the postwar period was the acceptance of financial responsibility by the Commonwealth government. This was progressively expanded and in the late 1950's, after the university situation had been studied by a Commonwealth-appointed committee, it was formalized and the amount of money available increased. Not only did the established universities expand, but new universities were set up.

The Labor government led the way by establishing at Canberra an Australian National University which was to be a mixture of a graduate school (to the Ph.D. level) and an institute for advanced studies, the emphasis on the physical, biological, and social sciences but the humanities grossly underemphasized. The older universities also now started Ph.D. programs for the first time. In the states, New South Wales began the expansion by establishing a University of Technology, an obvious response to a lesson learned during the war, which was soon transformed into a conventional university, named the University of New South Wales. It also upgraded the New England University College to university status as the University of New England. Rather later, Victoria added a new university which it named for Sir John Monash. Aside from the housekeeping problems raised by the steady expansion of the university populations, an expansion that was faster than the statisticians at first estimated, the most recalcitrant problems were staffing and the building of libraries for the students and researchers.

The universities most affected by the rising undergraduate flood faced the prospect of a disproportion between the teaching staff and the numbers taught. While there was still an inflow of instructional personnel from overseas, predominantly from Britain but also from New Zealand and Canada, a consequence of the staffing problem was a steady recruitment of Australian personnel until the staffs were at last Australian-dominated, though strategically placed imported professors were noticeable. At all levels the staffs were well supplied with men of accomplishment and distinction, but, as in other countries, the staffs included a good many intellectuals manqué. Predominantly, the higher degrees possessed by the staffs had been obtained in the United Kingdom, and while the Ph.D. was now obtainable in Australia, aspirants to a university career still considered a United Kingdom higher degree definitely the first choice. There were a few American degrees, but in spite of the greater inflow of American intellectual influences and visits of American professors, the Americans were still exotics at the university level.

The universities were much more interested in and involved in the affairs of the general community than formerly, in further development of a trend which appears to have originated in the 1920's, this to be illustrated by the greater university concern with and productiveness in the fields of Australian geography, history, economics, politics, and literature, as well as by the greater frequency with which university people contributed to the periodical press. Indeed, it appeared that the majority of the Australian intelligentsia were university-employed. An astute Australian observer remarked, "There is virtually no free-floating intelligentsia here—our intellectuals are institutionalized."

An important phase of university expansion was the elaboration of the work in the sciences, noted already as a characteristic of the new National University but also true of the other universities. At the same time there has also been a considerable expansion of the work in the Commonwealth's primary scientific institution, now known as the Council for Scientific and Industrial Research Organization. The CSIRO, while continuing its work in the applied sciences relating to the land and factory industries, has also in some areas undertaken pure science, illustratively in radio astronomy. The federal government set up an Atomic Energy Commission with research facilities and its defense-related scientific research was greatly expanded after the war, not least in connection with the Woomera installation—working in collaboration with the United Kingdom, certain continental countries, and the United States. Its considerable Antarctic research is noted elsewhere (Chapter XIV). In 1952 a Royal Australian Academy of Science was founded by eleven members of the Royal Society of London then resident in Australia. Its membership steadily increased. Headquarters was a distinctively modern circular building in Canberra. Australia entered the lists of Nobel prize winners when in 1960 Sir Macfarlane Burnet of the Walter & Eliza Hall Institute of Medical Research won an award for his work in virology.

A noticeable feature of the postwar literary scene was that the writers who were generally conceded to be the exemplary figures of the time were not self-consciously in the nationalistic tradition, although one could, without too much trouble, find distinct traces of the nationalistic literary ideology in their work. Not to complicate the question unduly by trying to account for such deviant figures as H. H. Richardson, there were discernible by World War II at least three strands of demonstrated durability in the Australian tradition: the nationalistic tradition of Lawson, Furphy, and O'Dowd as continued in the work of Palmer, Prichard, Davison et al.—the tradition perhaps best described as participation in the world's cultural heritage, of which Christopher Brennan was the exemplary figure—and normanlindsayism for which "vitalism" has been suggested as the best descriptive, of which the poets Fitzgerald, Slessor, and Stewart were the distinguished contemporary ornaments. It was to one or another of these strands of the tradition of literary production that writers could relate, or be related by their critics.

For fifty years the nationalistic tradition was dominant and its elements had deeply affected even writers who, so to speak, wrote as they pleased but more or less self-consciously as Australians. After fifty years it was apparent that the nationalistic literary tradition, whatever the continuing merits of a component of it like laboristic leftism in politics, was no longer viable to sustain literary production. Except for O'Dowd, who was rather badly battered by poet-critics of a different persuasion, the great nationalistic figures were conceded to be indisputably great, but only if viewed historically. It was now apparent that no strand, not even this strong strand, of the tradition could properly be set up as an orthodoxy from which one departed at the peril of literary damnation. In assertion of their prerogatives as literary commissars the communists had tried this on the basis of the nationalistic tradition and had failed. Literature insisted on being more complex than any politics. Inevitably, in Australia as in other new countries where literature was "maturing," the emphasis was away from how a writer assayed for nationalistic Australianism and toward his quality qua writer, in itself a distinct advance.

There were at least three other important changes. First, there was a multiplication of enduring literary magazines of the highest quality yet known. Ignoring *Angry Penguins,* of Adelaide, which initiated the change for the better, but which after six years of amusing and exciting life died of financial inanition and victim of a clever hoax exploiting its distinctive qualities, the magazine which successfully pioneered the field was *Meanjin Papers.* It first appeared in Brisbane just before Christmas 1940 as a miniscule outlet for a handful of Queensland poets, rode the rising tide of interest in literature and painting to become *the* Australian forum of the cultural life, cultivated an interest in developments overseas, and, when transferred to Melbourne under the patronage of the university in 1945, went from strength to strength as the years passed. Others came later and none surpassed *Meanjin* in scope or quality, but *Quadrant* (No. 1, 1956) was on the same plane, oriented to the right as *Meanjin* was to the left. For the first time Australia had literary magazines worthy of her literary accomplishments. The second change worthy of note was the emergence of the Catholic lay intellectuals. When in 1946 Paul Grano published an anthology of poetry by Catholics not one of his poets was a major literary figure, whereas a decade later two of the liveliest and best informed writers on the literary scene were Catholics—James McAuley, poet, critic, lecturer on colonial administration, editor of *Quadrant,* latterly a university professor of English, and Vincent Buckley, poet, critic, and university lecturer.

The third change was the interest of the universities in Australian literature and the presence of Australian writers in the universities. Acceptance of Australian literature by the universities was the desired consequence of a long campaign by the writers which began before the war and the first result of which was lectures by representative writers on the literature under university auspices. The postwar extension of this involved the English faculties in increased study and criticism of the literature. This development will reach its apogee when a chair in Australian literature is established, but already it is a great distance from the perigee when Henry Lawson advised the professors to get on with their drivel and croak and cavil and keep out of the tracks he was traveling. The other aspect of this matter has been the appearance of writers on the faculties, partly a consequence of the intensive search for staff, partly of the search by writers for an economic base for writing careers.

Since it is notoriously impossible to make a selection among contemporary writers that is without invidiousness and equally unprofitable to take refuge in an unselective listing of names, neither course will be followed here. Rather, it will be iterated that the exemplary figures at this time were, in poetry, A. D. Hope, and in fiction, Patrick White. What distinguished these men among their numerous compatriots were their exceptional powers of expression, their possession of distinctive visions of life, its risks and possibilities, and their eagerness to explore the human predicament as a trap in which all mankind, not merely the Australian segment, is involved.

While poetry and fiction remained the most highly regarded literary arts in Australia, great satisfaction was taken in this period in the appearance of drama playable not only on the Australian stage but in London and New York. The first and therefore the symbolic success was Ray Lawler's *The Summer of the Seventeenth Doll* in 1956. The theater, still a mixture of professional and amateur, was in a lively phase, and in 1954 there was established The Australian Elizabethan Theater Trust to "provide a theatre of Australians by Australians for Australians," financed by public subscriptions and subventions from governments. The trust was interested in both the drama and the opera. It patronized the musical comedy. If it opened with Judith Anderson, returned from the United States for the occasion, in *Medea,* its first success with domestic drama was Lawler's *Seventeenth Doll.* In radio drama the most satisfying contributions were made by Douglas Stewart. Television which arrived in the 1950's was a new challenge. The movies retained a larger audience than in most countries. The best of the locally made movies were documentaries. There was considerable interest in the movies as an art form, expressed in annual "festivals." The performance of music, supported by the Australian Broadcasting Corporation and private benefactors, was still widely popular. There was a marked interest in records. The great musical triumph of the time was the success of the superlative singer Joan Sutherland in Europe and America. The South Australians successfully established an annual festival of the performing and pictorial arts; Melbourne was provided an architecturally superb "shell" by a private benefactor and began the construction of a new art gallery, designed by the pioneer of modern architecture Roy Grounds, on the banks of the Yarra; Sydney undertook to construct an opera house, designed by the Finnish architect Jacob Utson, on Bennelong Point, Sydney harbour. The architects, in a vigorous phase, were having trouble defining a uniquely Australian style in the face of a multiplicity of foreign influences, American, Japanese, and others. There was more architectural criticism than ever before and more writing about architectural history.

The assimilation of the current "international language" of art, while retaining a distinctively Australian accent, was also the problem of the painters, and they, in their remarkable vigor, got a long way toward a variety of solutions. Never before had so many different artists established individual identity and reputation in so many different fashions. The rush forward was so strong that William Dobell became something of an "old master" in his own time. The most conspicuous names were Sidney Nolan and Russell Drysdale, the first a distinct international success while still unmistakably Australian, the other the painter who beyond all others successfully established a new image of Australia, replacing the image projected by the classic impressionists. In view of the fact that the international language was distinctly urban and was so heard by many artists, it was fascinating evidence of the power of tradition that Drysdale's new image was of outback Australia, not of the urbanized littoral, and that Nolan's ambiguous symbolism was historical and nonurban, notably in his Ned Kelly series. The Australian artists maintained a keen interest in landscape and portraiture, though their handling of both was transformed. The conquest of London, still a compelling ambition, was more or less achieved, notably by the comprehensive Whitechapel Gallery show in 1961 in which examples of the work of over fifty different artists appeared. The British comment, while exhilarating, was not distinguished by much knowledge either of Australia or the historical background of painting in Australia. The conquest of New York was next on the agenda.

A significant by-blow of the total art situation was the increase in attention given to the art of the aborigines in its several media by the artists, at home and overseas, the anthropologists, and the general public. In view of the current orientation of the artists, which favored the assimilation of aboriginal influences, it was odd that the few aboriginal artists who mastered European techniques, of whom the most important was Albert Namatjira, worked in the impressionist tradition that the Europeans were abandoning. However, it was remarkable that any aboriginal contribution could be made to the cultural life of the dominant whites, for by and large the position of the aborigines remained about what it had been discovered to be in the 1930's, though the public conscience about them was much quicker.

There was more writing about art in the periodicals. The university participation, paralleling that in literature, was most obvious with regard to the University of Melbourne. Conspicuous patrons of the modernists were John Reed of Melbourne and Kym Bonython of Adelaide.

As international traders the Australians were deeply interested in a general expansion of the world's trade and particularly in the expansion of the markets for the commodities they had for sale. During the 1950's they began a virtual scouring of the entire trading world for outlets, acting in West and East Europe, North America, Africa, Central and South America, Asia, New Zealand, and the Pacific islands. They were involved in the General Agreement on Tariffs and Trade (GATT). They negotiated bilaterally with various countries. They were parties to international commodity agreements. A distinguishing characteristic of their trade was the steady dispersion of their outlets. As the dispersion increased, the proportionate importance of their exports to and imports from the United Kingdom declined, though without altering the United Kingdom's position as the principal trading partner. A feature of the situation was that for certain commodities the dependence for outlets on the United Kingdom remained very high: 90 per cent of canned fruits, 70 per cent of dried fruit, 75 per cent of butter, 50 per cent of sugar. With regard to these commodities especially, Australia feared she would be badly pinched if the United Kingdom entered the Common Market in the early 1960's. Alternative markets for "luxury" temperate agricultural products were the hardest to find. In the search for markets, probably the acutest disappointment was the failure of the market for Australian goods in North America to increase fast enough to increase significantly its proportionate share of total exports.

There was a significant success in the markets of Asia, above all the Japanese. By 1961–62 the Asian markets were taking one-third of Australia's exports. This swing toward Asia in trading fitted in well with the widely entertained belief that the nation's future was bound to be heavily conditioned by developments in Asia. Particularly, Australia's economic stake in Japan's success was constantly increasing. The other Asian markets were far more problematical, and while this did not diminish the Australian interest in them, their expectations with regard to them were more modest.

In the 1950's and early 1960's the export trade still fundamentally involved foodstuffs and raw materials, for the growth of the export trade in manufactures was slow and, though much action to increase it had been taken by both government and businessmen, it accounted for but 10 per cent of total exports. The concentration of the interest of the manufacturers was still, as traditionally, on the domestic market and to some extent they were barred from exploring the export trade by agreements with their principals overseas. Anything like a breakthrough for manufactured exports was a thing of the future. In spite of all the energy put into the export trade, the persistent balance of payments trouble was clear indication that exports were not increasing in value as fast as the rising domestic demand for imports required. This promised to be the case into the visible future. Temporarily, the heavy inflow of capital helped fill the gap, but this was probably a precarious solution, for the inflow might slacken before Australia's need for it was terminated. The only final answer was more exports, and since the growth of manufactured exports was unlikely to assist more than marginally, the answer would have to be supplied in largest measure by foodstuffs and raw materials. The Australians were certain to be agitated by any development, such as the Common Market of Europe, which promised in any way to impede their free flow and interested in any proposals for stabilizing prices at remunerative levels, above all in any schemes for increasing their flow. Australia was a country that had to trade successfully or stagnate and then inevitably decline.

When the Menzies government took office P. C. Spender was appointed minister for External Affairs. He held the office for a little over a year before going to Washington as ambassador. He was succeeded by R. G. Casey, of all Australians the most experienced in diplomacy, who continued in office until 1960 when, after an interlude during which Mr. Menzies was his own External Affairs minister, he was succeeded by Sir Garfield Barwick. Although in theory foreign policy was determined by the cabinet with regard for the support it would command from Parliament and the electorate, it was probable that Mr. Menzies as prime minister was consistently a key figure in policy determinations. While on election results it would seem that the policies of the Menzies government were approved, foreign policy figured only marginally in elections—which were characteristically decided on domestic issues. The relation between the Menzies government's foreign policy and public opinion was therefore highly equivocal, for foreign policy was an elite, not a popular, preoccupation, and a high proportion of the articulate elite was oriented to the left of the government.

Mr. Menzies' general approach to foreign policy was well known, but how his government would handle the questions in detail was uncertain. In a carefully considered speech he delivered in 1944 Mr. Menzies had made it clear that any agreement between himself and Labor with regard to foreign policy was an accidental conjunction of minds operating on different premises. The basic problem was still how best to support the security of a geographically large country with a small population which did not possess the ability to defend itself—standing alone and distant from allies of power. Planted at the center of Mr. Menzies' thinking was the assumption that this country was firmly resolved to preserve its Euro-American character. Placing his emphasis on power rather than the constructions of "high-minded coots," Mr. Menzies emphasized that it was imperative that Australia correctly assess its own power potential and then plan to relate itself wisely to supporting power overseas. In line with tradition, it should seek as of primary importance a close relation with the United Kingdom as the power center of the Commonwealth in terms of foreign policy and defense planning. With regard to foreign policy the emphasis should fall on acceptance of common imperial policy, not upon calculated Australian deviations. The relation to the Empire correctly defined, the next most important relation was that with the United States. Mr. Menzies assumed that a friendly collaboration between the British Empire and the United States was the key to world peace. Together they would have the requisite power, and he believed they would use it creatively in the service of justice. He recognized that the posture of the U.S.S.R. would be of the highest importance. He forecast a world organization in which Australia should participate. But his vision fundamentally involved the Australian relation first to the United Kingdom and then to the United States. He assumed that Australia could enter into a close relation with the United States without diminishing the intimacy of its relation to the Empire. The speech was not prophetic, but rather an occasion to reiterate first principles. Mr. Menzies did not speculate on the probable position of the United Kingdom in the postwar world power constellation, nor did he forecast the impact on Australia of changes in Asia.

By the time a government headed by Mr. Menzies confronted the problems of foreign relations, it was apparent that the British Commonwealth was in a phase of rapid change and that not all the changes were to the advantage of Australia. Like Labor, though with greater rhetorical warmth, Mr. Menzies' disposition was to deny that the changes had any deep effect on Australia's relation to the United Kingdom. Rather, the effect was to elevate the relation of Australia (and New Zealand) to that of membership in the innermost circle of Commonwealth associates. It was not only that it remained monarchical while the new members often chose to be republics, it was that its loyalty to the Crown was qualitatively of the highest intensity. In a peculiarly intimate sense Queen Elizabeth II was Australia's Queen as was demonstrated by the warmth of the reception of the Queen and the Duke of Edinburgh when they visited Australia in 1954. Mr. Menzies' insistence on the primacy of Commonwealth relations in the scheme of Australia's external relations was thus not a tactical move but rather followed from a conception of Australia's system of loyalties. Its relation to the Commonwealth was organic, not functional. What this could mean was illustrated by Australia's role in the Suez Canal affair of 1956. Australia was one of two Commonwealth associates—the other was New Zealand—that consistently supported the United Kingdom government of Sir Anthony Eden. Mr. Menzies played a conspicuous role. It was not merely that he agreed with Sir Anthony's policy with regard to Suez, it was not merely that he believed that the policy served Australia's considerable interest in the Canal as an international waterway, it was that "loyalty" required Australia to support the United Kingdom government. Canada and India might not feel this, but Australia and New Zealand did. This was to them a special glory.

But as the Menzies government's foreign policy evolved it was to a greater extent than could easily have been forecast a policy oriented toward serving Australia's national interests, directly and unmistakably. This was because the shape the postwar world was taking threw greater and greater responsibility on Australia to sustain its own position in the world. The changes continuing in process, the dominant consequence was to force Australia to look after herself. This was particularly true with regard to relations with the United States and Asia.

The Menzies government came to office determined to establish intimate relations with the United States. It regarded an American engagement in the support of Australia's security as indispensable. As Labor had been frustrated by events and circumstances beyond its control from defining a special relation to the United States, so the Menzies government had to wait upon events to open up opportunities to do so. The first opportunity arose in close association with the negotiations over a peace treaty with Japan. The Menzies government had considerable sympathy with Labor's view of Japan but a better appreciation of the need to accommodate to the views of a stronger power. It was particularly in agreement with Labor on the point that Japan should never again be allowed to develop the power to menace Australia's security. When, therefore, John Foster Dulles, acting for the Truman government, proposed a liberal treaty with Japan which placed no stated limitations on Japanese rearmament, he found the Menzies government reluctant to endorse it. The Menzies government was willing enough to accept the necessity of allowing the Japanese full scope for attaining economic viability—already it was apparent that Australia would profit through trade from a Japanese economic revival—and it also accepted that in the face of the communist menace, now clearly recognized as primarily the Red Chinese menace, Japan could not remain a power vacuum. The Australians therefore attempted to solve their difficulty by trying to have the Japanese forbidden by treaty to build or buy long-range sea and air weapons with which they might menace Australia, but to allow them to provide for the defense of the territory over which they would have sovereignty. But even in this they were frustrated. Not only were the Americans opposed to the imposition of specific limitations on rearmament by treaty but so were others, including the British.

Within the treaty the Australians had to take what satisfaction they could from the imposition on Japan of a special obligation to behave in international relations in accordance with the Charter of the United Nations. They also gained points with regard to reparations and the renunciation by the Japanese of all rights they might have in Antarctica. But the Menzies government found the final text of the treaty little to its liking. It was simply the best that could be obtained under the circumstances. It accepted it with reasonable grace with a recognition that it was powerless to obtain anything better by other means, such as bilateral negotiations with the Japanese. Labor, on the other hand, dug in its heels in opposition to the treaty and when it came up for ratification in Parliament voted solidly against it. Dr. Evatt tried to establish that by departing from the Potsdam declaration and other early policy statements the treaty represented a repudiation of solemn international engagements. Simultaneously with the negotiations over the Japanese treaty there was negotiated a defense treaty involving the United States, Australia, and New Zealand (ANZUS). This represented a long first step toward that intimate relation with the United States to which the Menzies government aspired. In accepting this treaty Australia (and New Zealand) was acting on its own. The United Kingdom was not a signatory. It gave access to the highest level of defense planning in the Pacific. Labor voted for ANZUS alleging that after all it merely represented the fulfillment of its policy with regard to Australian-American relations. The American view was that it put into formal language a relationship that had existed implicitly since World War II.

Since the Menzies government put the emphasis on power relations,

it removed the United Nations from the central position in foreign relations which Dr. Evatt had assigned it. The Menzies government took a
far less independent line and became more a reliable supporter of its
powerful friends. But since the role of the U.N. in world affairs was
obviously important and could be crucial, the government participated
in the work of the organization in more elaborate detail than ever before.

The definition of a sound relation to the Asian states proved the
most troublesome problem of foreign policy. The Menzies government
saw clearly the need for friendly and constructive relations with the
emergent new nations of Asia, whether they were within or outside the
Commonwealth, but until the question of independence was settled, it
wished also to be friendly toward the imperialist powers, for example,
the Dutch in New Guinea (see Chapter X) and the French in Indochina. In 1950 the Menzies government demonstrated its general intent
with regard to Asia by sponsoring the so-called Colombo Plan, designed
to help in liquidating Asian poverty, but with an anticommunist overtone.
It was, in its early stages, a Commonwealth plan, but it was Australia's
hope from the beginning that the participation of the United States
could be gained, as it eventually was. The general direction of its thinking was also indicated by its adoption of the American policy of non-
recognition of Red China instead of the British and Indian policy of
recognition. It was the first nation to join the United States in resisting
the North Korean invasion of South Korea. In the midst of the Korean
War inflation it markedly stepped up its defense program.

But the Menzies government's prime Asian policy was a defense pact
to which as many Asian nations as possible would be parties, with Australia and New Zealand, and which would have the direct support of the
United States. An opportunity to arrange such a pact did not arise until
after the collapse of French power in Indochina. Out of an effort to
strengthen the positions of the new nations that emerged in French Indochina came the Southeast Asia Treaty Organization, SEATO. The new
treaty was distinct from ANZUS, but from Australia's point of view
complementary to it. It brought Australia once again into close relations
with the United States. It ostensibly closed a dangerous gap in the defenses of Southeast Asia. It was not, however, as comprehensive in
Asian membership as Australia would have liked. The Asian signatories
were the Philippines, Thailand, and Pakistan, while the protection the
treaty afforded was supposed to extend to Laos, Cambodia, and South
Vietnam. It was pleasing to Australia that the United Kingdom and
France were signatories. But the treaty on the one hand ran into the
hostility of the neutralist powers of Asia to pacts of the kind and on
the other their hostility to the bringing into Asian affairs of an outside

power such as the United States. It was therefore an embarrassment that as time passed the power of France and the United Kingdom in the general area diminished rapidly, and it became a legitimate expectation that it might fade away altogether, for this meant that it was primarily American power that sustained SEATO and that American definitions of situations would have to be accepted and American ends sought and served. While this did not disturb the Menzies government, for it accepted that the primary American ends, national independence for the nations of the treaty area, political stability, and economic progress, were also ends that served Australian purposes and interests, the obviously non-Asian character of SEATO precluded the acceptance of membership by neutralist Asia.

The situation stimulated a great deal of criticism of SEATO in Australia by those who doubted American competence in Asian affairs, those who feared that Australia's conspicuous membership in an organization the Asian neutralists condemned would damage Australia's reputation in Asia, and by those who leaned toward a neutralist policy for Australia itself. Oddly, however, it was not participation in SEATO which inspired the strongest Labor party dissent from Menzies' Asian policy; it was the Menzies government's decision to send Australian military personnel and equipment to Malaya for use against the communist rebels there, essentially a gesture of intra-Commonwealth solidarity. Labor, then allegedly most responsive to leftist influences, protested this move, alleging that it would alienate the Malayans. It did not. On becoming an independent nation within the Commonwealth, Malaya declared that it felt a special friendship for the Australians and New Zealanders. But only a radical change in the outlook of the neutralists, probably to be a consequence of unhappy experience with the Chinese communists, would enable the Australians to engineer the extension of SEATO, or some improved equivalent, to all of Southeast and South Asia in conformance to their original hope.

NEW ZEALAND

CHAPTER VI

Britain's Outlying Farm

While Sir Joseph Ward inherited the prime ministership from Richard Seddon in 1906 and held it until 1912, he did not inherit Seddon's political magic. The divisive tendencies within the Liberal synthesis rather quickly got out of his control. His own bias was in favor of the urban business interests; he was himself keenly interested and involved in merchandising and finance. Ward was unable to control the farmers and his grip on the workers relaxed. The farmers were the first to slip from his grasp. He held the allegiance of the workers longer, but firmly only that section of them who gave their allegiance to the arbitration courts, notably the skilled tradesmen. Another great section of the working class—the coal miners, the waterside workers, and the general laborers—turned to the left, rejected the arbitration court, and experimented with direct (or strike) action before returning to politics and then not to the Liberal party but to a Labour party, mildly sympathetic to the Liberals but fundamentally bent on achieving office and power in its own right. Over the long run the Liberals were squeezed to death between the rightist farmers and left-liberal labor. It took about twenty years after 1912 for this process to work itself out. During the two decades the farmers mostly held office, the Labour party slowly built its strength, and Liberalism waned.

It was prosperity as much as anything that alienated the farmers from Liberalism. Like most farmers who work in a fundamentally commercial agricultural system, New Zealand farmers have shown themselves liberal or radical only in adversity and even then their heterodoxy has tended to be highly "sectional" and self-regarding—a kind of "producers' syndicalism." From 1895, when prices began to rise after the long slump, quite steadily until the price collapses after World War I, the New Zealand farmers did very well. A drop in productivity after 1910 was largely concealed from them by the rising volume of total production. It was a prosperity based on rewarding prices for increasing quantities of primary products in the United Kingdom market, further stimulated by the borrowing of money in London for development. The latter policy, about which Seddon was cautious but toward which he had drifted, was definitely favored by Ward the financier and was pursued steadily by his vanquisher, Massey. In Ward's time perhaps the most consequential single accomplishment under the policy was the completion of the Auckland-Wellington trunk line railway in 1908, this making possible the completion of the opening up of the North Island by the dairy farmers. As the butter, meat, and wool of New Zealand found welcome outlets in the United Kingdom market, the country became in effect a remote farm of Britain, holding a dependent economic relation to its urban-industrial partner.

New Zealand grew and changed and the contextual world in which it had its being changed even more radically. From 700,000 in 1895, the population grew to 1,200,000 in 1921. More people were employed in primary production at the end of the period than at the beginning, but the *proportion* so engaged declined from 39 to 27 per cent. The urbanization of the country proceeded apace, but towns grew more as service than as manufacturing centers. While the processing of farm commodities naturally increased, employment in manufacturing remained steady at about 25 per cent. Butter and cheese factories and meat freezing works were more characteristic than boot and shoe or clothing factories. As in the somewhat differently organized Australian economy, the New Zealand situation seemed to encourage the proliferation of service activities, mostly closely related to the primary industries, their *raison d'être*. Whereas in 1896 commerce, transport, public administration, and the professions provided 26 per cent of the jobs, by 1926 the percentage had risen to 39. However, through all the changes the land industries remained fundamental.

The farmers found their political leader in William Ferguson Massey. Massey, an Ulsterman, was born in Ireland in 1856 and joined his father in New Zealand in 1870. Farm trained, he took up farming in the North Island and was first elected to Parliament in 1894 after he had made himself known by wide participation in the farmers' organizations of his district. In 1896 he won the seat in the House which he held continuously until his death in 1925. Massey began his political career as a member of that group of frustrates who were the Seddonian opposition. In 1900 their position was so hopeless that their leader, Captain William Russell, renounced his position. Not until September 1903 was Massey elected leader. Nine more years were spent in the wilderness before he became prime minister. He dubbed his following the Reform party.

Massey rose to power as spokesman of the small farmers, particularly the dairy farmers, of the North Island. It is significant that in 1902 the seventy-six electorates were evenly divided between the two islands, whereas in 1908 there were for the first time more electorates in the North Island than the South and the differential continued steadily to increase. The liberalism Massey displaced was fundamentally a South Island phenomenon. Massey initiated North Island predominance in politics. In addition to the small farmers Massey had on his side the surviving sympathizers with the pre-Seddonian conservative political orientation of the landed gentry and segments of the urban business class. Within the Massey circle the most conspicuous representative of the gentry was Sir Francis Dillon Bell who in effect was Massey's brain trust, in which capacity he was genuinely distinguished. Massey, however, attended to the politics of the operation. What Massey lacked during the whole of his term as prime minister—he was in office from 1912 to 1925 —was the united support of the urban business interests. Labour was a tiny minority in Parliament of more political use to the Liberals than to Massey, but fundamentally bent on serving its own ends.

During Massey's time there were thus three parties in the field, but politically only two really counted, Reform and Liberal. They proved to be fairly evenly balanced and if Labour took strength away from either it was from the Liberals, especially since the Labour strength and growth potential were in the urban areas where liberalism also had its most reliable strength. Massey's Reform party proved very early in its history not to be able to differentiate itself ideologically very sharply from the Liberals. Both Reform and Liberal parties, as Labour got on its political feet, became more and more obviously non-Labour, with Reform somewhat more sharply anti-Labour, particularly in its early days, and the logic of coalescence against Labour became more and more compelling as time passed. What chiefly prevented this was Sir Joseph Ward's continuing political ambition. Massey therefore maintained himself in office by exceptional political agility.

He came to power by exploiting an issue of strong appeal to a section of the farmers whom the Liberals had placed on the land and brought to strength as producers. The Liberal bias in the land question was against the large landholders and, since these people fortified their power by freehold title, against freehold and in favor of leasehold. It was early perceived by astute observers that once the leasehold farmers were firmly established on their properties they would want full possession of them— freehold—not only because of the relation of sentiment between a man and the land he has nursed from bush to productive farm but in order that he might freely share in the rise in value, realizable only by sale.

Like commercial farmers in other countries, New Zealand farmers found trading in land values a most attractive proposition. Massey exploited the situation vigorously and successfully, even though it was really meaningful only to a minority of the farming community, and when the way was opened for leaseholders to convert to freehold, not all of them did so. Large tracts of land in New Zealand are of such a character that leasehold is the most economic title to them and to this day they are held on that basis. Further to justify the party title of Reform, Massey also had a good deal to say about dealing severely with alleged Liberal corruption. This chiefly came to mean the reform of the public service through the use of competitive examinations for entry into it, thus eliminating the "spoils" type of appointments practiced so astutely by Seddon.

Massey came to power as the consequences of labor's drift to the left had become manifest. This afforded him a chance to prove how wide was the gulf that had opened between the farmers and labor. The necessary transiency of a farmer-labor political alliance under capitalist conditions, such as the Liberals had engineered, was once more demonstrated.

As the law was evolved under the hand of William Pember Reeves, the emphasis as between conciliation and arbitration of industrial disputes was supposed to fall on conciliation. In practice, however, the emphasis was reversed and compulsory arbitration became the rule rather than the intended exception. However, Reeves's system nevertheless accomplished the objective of promoting the organization of the workers into trade unions to strengthen their position against employers. The immediate result was the multiplication of numerous small unions, especially in the trades. From 37 in 1893, they increased to 274 in 1906, with an average membership in the latter year of 124. These unions were decidedly dependent upon the arbitration system for their existence. As long as the decisions of the court appeared to favor unions, particularly with regard to wages, all was well, but after 1903 when the court ceased to favor wage increases—real wages began to decline and money wages were in effect frozen by the court in 1907—doubts crept in. The workers were provoked to question whether they were after all going to share in proper measure in the prosperity which the farmers appeared to continue to enjoy. The alternative was to conclude that they could do better for themselves acting independently, invoking the threat of the strike to enforce their demands. This required a conviction that the workers in a given situation were tightly and comprehensively enough organized to pursue this course on one hand and could develop an ideology to rationalize the course when decided upon on the other. Given the situation in New Zealand it is not surprising that not all the unions felt sufficiently independent of the court to abandon it and hence not all were susceptible to the wiles of a radical ideology. But a sufficient number were convinced on both counts to create chaos in labor relations, roughly from 1906 to 1914.

The radicalization of a significant section of New Zealand labor was in part attributable to a deduction from experience, in part to the fading of Seddon's political magic, in part to the injection into labor affairs of radical ideas from Australia, the United States, and Britain. Symbolic of the first factor was the course of Edward Tregear. Tregear, English-born, arrived in New Zealand in 1863 and participated in the Maori wars. He entered the public service and rose to be secretary of the Labour Department from 1898 to 1911, when he retired. In his leisure he took a keen interest in the Maoris, wrote intelligently about them, and published some passable poetry. He had been closely associated with Pember Reeves and was at first convinced of the rightness of the Reeves approach but, influenced by English socialist ideas, was progressively disillusioned until after retirement he associated himself with the anticourt unions. Marxist and semi-Marxist socialist ideas began to percolate into New Zealand, chiefly from England, in the late 1890's and on the Marxist side they were fortified by the importation into New Zealand of the publications of Charles H. Kerr & Company of Chicago. A socialist party was founded in 1901. As in Australia simon-pure Marxism seems never to have been particularly influential in New Zealand, even on the left, and it is therefore hardly surprising that immigrant Australian-style "socialists" played a most conspicuous role in leftist labor in New Zealand and that, at least at the level of verbalization, the most influential "socialism" from the United States was the syndicalism of the Industrial Workers of the World. It was the mainly dilute socialism of Robert Blatchford that reached New Zealand from England. Exemplary figures among the leftist immigrants from Australia were Robert Semple, P. C. Webb, Michael J. Savage, and Henry Holland, while from Scotland came Peter Fraser. The I.W.W. influence, in the air in both New Zealand and Australia about this time, was carried into New Zealand, not by an American, but by the only New Zealander conspicuous among the leftist leaders, P. H. Hickey. Hickey had been a member of the I.W.W. while working in the mines of the American West. After his incursion into New Zealand affairs he ended his career in Australia. Most of the other leaders, including Semple, Webb, Savage, Holland, and Fraser continued in New Zealand and eventually became partisans of the arbitration court and parliamentarianism.

While the leftist deviation from the amorphous New Zealand liberal orthodoxy developed its greatest strength in Auckland and Wellington in the North Island, its first clear expression in action came in the coal mining districts of Westland in the South Island to which Semple, Webb, and Hickey had gravitated. In 1904 Semple and his associates organized a union among the miners of Runanga which was definitely "socialist" in orientation. Three years later P. H. Hickey and P. C. Webb began to organize branches of a New Zealand Socialist party in the district around Runanga to which they preached the doctrine of the class war, the idea that the wage system was iniquitous, and the idea that the strike weapon should be used politically to force along a social revolution. By 1908 they were able to engineer a strike at the Blackball mine to obtain half-an-hour for the midday meal instead of fifteen minutes. From their success in enforcing by a strike this small reform, though at great cost in disorder and legal maneuvers, they drew the large deduction that after first organizing all the miners in New Zealand into a single union, it would be possible to draw all the workers of the country into a comprehensive federation of leftist orientation. This vision was especially attractive to Robert Semple.

The workers most susceptible to the kind of radicalization Semple and his fellows were aiming to promote were the coal and gold miners, the waterside workers, the railway men, the employees of freezing works, and general laborers, all men it was possible to organize industrially. The world around, many of these groups have proved highly susceptible to radicalization because they pursue trades notoriously rough and tough, often characterized by irregularity of employment, and frequently pursued under conditions which either physically or psychologically, or both, separate them from the general community. It should be noted that most of these men were concerned with the handling of agricultural products on their way from the farms and stations to market. This is true even of the coal miners, for coal was chiefly used by the railways and to generate power in freezing works. Strikes in the industries to which these people were attached could not fail to arouse the hostility of the farmers, particularly as they interfered with the movement of farm products overseas. On the other hand, many of the unionized workers of New Zealand were not susceptible to the radical appeal because they were in small craft organizations, keenly conscious that they existed in such strength as they had by virtue of their positions in the arbitration system. These unions were loosely gathered together in Trades and Labour Councils under a weak national executive. The arbitration court thus became the rock on which the labor movement split. The question that confronted Semple and his people was whether or not he could so conclusively demonstrate the superiority of direct action in gaining the workers' ends that the arbitration court unionists would abandon their allegiance and join his organization.

The first move by Semple and his associates was made in 1908 when they formed the New Zealand Federation of Miners, not registered with the arbitration court. The next step was taken in 1909 when the name was changed to the Federation of Labour. Simultaneously the Trades and Labour Council group wrestled with the idea of a comprehensive and tighter federal organization and started to compete with the Semple group. The latter was soon popularly known as the Red Fed. Competition between the two federations for union and worker support was the order of the day, but equally important was the effort to bring about unity in the labor field. A conspicuous figure in the unity efforts was an itinerant American named W. T. Mills, allegedly a Milwaukee municipal socialist. The first focus of unity was a United Labour party, launched in 1912. However, this did not diminish the redness of the Red Fed which as a matter of fact was more interested in absorbing its rival than joining it on the basis of any compromise, and at that stage was not interested in politics at all. The Red Fed's constitution of 1912 had as its opening line the I.W.W. slogan, "The working class and the employing class have nothing in common."

By the logic of its ideological position and by the intent of its founders, the testing of the Red Fed had to be the strike. It was heartening, therefore, when in 1911 the Auckland General Labourer's Union, the president of which, Peter Fraser, was also secretary of the Auckland district of the Red Fed, won a strike. But when in 1912 the gold miners of Waihi in Auckland province fought and won a strike and then fought and lost a more important one, it was disheartening. Oddly, however, it was after Waihi that the Red Fed group achieved its greatest strength, though only as a preliminary to a final defeat. At a great unity congress held in July 1913 the Red Fed joined the T.L.C. unions in forming a United Federation of Labour. Mills played a role in bringing this about by orating in favor of the Red Fed proposals. While the new organization rejected the Red Fed's I.W.W. slogan, it accepted the socialist objective—the socialization of the means of production, distribution, and exchange—and went on to elect an executive on which the Red Fed was strongly represented. This looked like a Red Fed victory, but there were doubts about how far the old T.L.C. rank and file would follow the congress delegates. It took another and by far the greatest Red Fed strike to find this out.

In October 1913 a strike developed on the Wellington waterfront which was taken up by the U.F.L. Under its direction the strike was extended to the waterfronts of Auckland, Lyttelton, and Dunedin and the miners, carpenters, hotel and restaurant workers, bricklayers, carters, general laborers, and other unionists were called out, leading in the end to a call for general strikes in Wellington, Auckland, Christchurch, and Dunedin. But not all the unionists responded to the strike call and in the end the U.F.L. had to acknowledge defeat. This was a signal for the initiation of a trek back to the arbitration court and the ballot box.

Massey came to political power after the Waihi strike had started and soon demonstrated that he and his farmer supporters agreed with the verdict of the employers that the Red Fed group was dangerous. The Waihi miners, under Red Fed influence, had canceled their registration with the arbitration court. They had won a strike for higher wages. It was discovered, however, that while deregistration was entirely legal, the law could be used to put a deregistered union at a crippling disadvantage. At the behest of the employers a group of Waihi workers formed a new union, registered it with the court, and applied for and were granted an award which, under the law, applied to all the workers in the industry. The Red Fed miners were thus debarred from any role in determining wages and conditions at the Waihi mine. This precipitated a new strike aimed at forcing the "scab" union to disband. The employers fought back and the Massey government supported them, sending police to Waihi to protect the right of the court unionists and strikebreakers to work. In street fighting a Red Fed unionist was killed and several were arrested. The strike collapsed. This showed that while theoretically a radical union could exist outside the court system, it could not, if anybody chose to fight it through the court, successfully function.

The point was underscored by what happened during the waterside strike of 1913. Originating in what the workers interpreted as a lock-out, and fought not only by the workers directly concerned but also by use of the sympathetic strike, it was broken by the use of the "scab union" technique, strikebreakers, and special mounted constables dubbed "Massey's Cossacks." The farmers played a direct role. They acted as strikebreakers and special constables, especially at Wellington, their antilabor feelings stimulated by the fact that the strike prevented the movement of their produce overseas. They therefore undertook to load it themselves and to fight those who sought to interfere. Defeat on this occasion reduced the Red Fed to impotence and demonstrated that direct action under New Zealand conditions was fruitless. Unions could only function successfully if they submitted with grace to that "apparatus of state control," the arbitration court. As enfranchised citizens, however, the workers could also turn to the ballot box. Neither of these courses would eliminate labor's left wingers. They were permanent fixtures. After the 1913 defeat, the unions eventually split into two groups, the old Trades and Labour Councils on the one hand, procourt and predominantly craft unions, and an Alliance of Labour which accepted the court perforce

and was based on the industrial unions which harbored most of the leftists. The split was not healed for over twenty years.

The New Zealand workers first entered politics as Liberal party candidates and supporters thereof. Not until 1904 did the Trades and Labour
Councils sponsor independent action, and not until 1908 was the first
electoral success achieved. In the 1911 general election, four candidates
were elected and in the 1914 election, five. These political efforts, discontinuous organizationally and with organization not well coordinated
when improvised for electioneering purposes, were activities of the
moderate laborites. The Red Fed people, under syndicalist influence,
affected to despise politics. Nevertheless, in the great unity effort of 1913
provision was made for a labor party and when the Red Fed group had
drawn the lesson from the 1913 defeat that politics provided a road to
social power, the time had finally come to found a carefully organized
party. This occurred in 1916. Whereas the earlier labor parliamentarians
were political moderates—their first elected parliamentary leader was an
ex-Liberal—the coming of the Red Fed into politics was signalized by
the adoption of a straight-out socialist objective. The first elected parliamentary leader of Red Fed background and outlook was Harry Holland who entered Parliament in 1918 and succeeded to the leadership in
1919. Holland, an Australian by birth, had been associated with the
English socialist agitator Tom Mann and leftist Australian unions. He
arrived in New Zealand in 1912 and took over the editorship of *The
Maoriland Worker*. A skilled journalist and pamphleteer, with the Australian weakness for writing bad verse, he was a socialist whose thinking
was an amalgam of Marx, Henry George, Bellamy—and the Salvation
Army. He led the parliamentary party for fourteen years in the course
of which its radical rigidity was slowly but considerably relaxed as
achievement of office loomed ever more clearly as a possibility.

As the European New Zealanders sorted themselves out in a new
fashion, politically and economically, though within established forms,
the Maoris touched bottom as a people and, paradoxically, about this
time showed signs of revival. By 1896 they numbered no more than
40,000, including a presumably high and increasing but actually unknown
percentage who had greater or lesser infusions of European blood. As
their numbers had declined, so had their culture tended to disintegrate,
but they had not, except in uncommon instances, become Europeanized,
the ideal fate envisioned for them by most concerned persons since Sir
George Gray. As their response to the Maori wars had differed tribe by
tribe, so their response to the situation in which they had found themselves after the wars differed also. Speaking generally, the Maoris of the

East Coast of the North Island responded most vigorously to the challenge of life in a pakeha-dominated society, while the Maoris north of Auckland suffered a benumbing poverty, and the West Coast tribes, both those of Taranaki who were influenced by Te Whiti, and those of the Waikato who adhered to the king movement, followed a policy of non-cooperation with the pakeha which denied them progress. As Maori numbers had diminished, so also had their lands. They passed from their possession either by state or individual purchase or confiscation. Indeed, diminishing numbers became a reason for permitting the absorption of more and more Maori land into European use or ownership, an implicit admission that no Maori revival was foreseen. An essentially rural people to whom land was life, they were not, by pakeha suggestion or assistance, encouraged to make the fullest economic use of the land remaining to them and they showed, except on the East Coast, no capacity to do so on their own initiative. In their rejection of pakeha culture, including its economy, they were unable to preserve their own culture in healthily viable condition. They showed a strong tendency to drift into rural slum living, basically a Maori-style slum with a thin European veneer (e.g., as to clothing.) Worst of all, many of them accepted fatalistically their decrease in numbers, their economic deprivation, and their cultural disintegration; they accepted their own eventual extinction. "As the pakeha rat drove out the Maori rat, as the introduced grasses drove out the Maori fern, so will the Maori die out before the white man."

While no fundamental attack on the Maori malaise could be made without a shift in pakeha attitudes and governmental policies, a shift in the pakeha approach unaccompanied by a decisive change in Maori attitudes could not possibly succeed. The initiative was really, therefore, in the hands of the Maoris. This was all the more decidedly the case because a fundamental factor in the situation was Maori traditionalism, emotionally based, and only leaders able to reason with the Maoris in the Maori language in Maori terms and in Maori places could possibly make headway against it. At the same time only leaders with a firm grip on the pakeha culture could see what needed doing, how to do it, and formulate a satisfying end to be served by doing it. The leaders had to be in some sense and degree men of two worlds, capable of functioning at a fairly high level in both, but with a powerful bias in favor of the Maori people and culture. Therefore the leaders had either to be Maoris themselves or, if of mixed blood, Maoris by personal choice, and in any case possessed of a pakeha education. It turned out that the best and most decisively useful service the pakehas had rendered to the Maoris was access to pakeha-style education. The leaders whose names have ordinarily been cited in connection with the Maori revival of the 1890's and its continuance down the years have been both pakeha and Maori and sometimes they have had two names, pakeha and Maori. But the names of many who labored to good effect will be recorded only when some scholar writes the much-needed history of the Maori people in pakeha New Zealand.

The precursor of the movement for a Maori revival was James Carroll, a man of mixed Irish and Maori origin, who was a good example of a Europeanized half-caste. As a young man Carroll had served with "friendly" Maoris and the pakehas against Te Kooti. He entered government service as an interpreter in the Native Department and went on to become an interpreter in Parliament. In 1887 he won the East Coast Maori seat in the House but comparatively early in his political career shifted to a European seat, thus illustrating the ambiguity in his position. When in 1892 the Ballance government included a Maori as "representative of the native race" in the executive council, Carroll was chosen for the position. He continued in this post under Seddon and Ward. In 1899 he became the first nonpakeha minister for Native Affairs. He was knighted in 1911. He finally lost his seat in the House in 1919 and ended his political career in the Legislative Council to which he was appointed by Massey in 1921. He died in 1926.

The significance of Sir James Carroll's career is threefold: He contributed, as a man acceptable to both Maoris and pakehas, to breaking down the barriers between them; he rendered creative services to the Maoris; and he extended encouragement to those Maoris who were more intimately involved in the Maori revival. Carroll began his parliamentary career with a speech asking full legal equality for the Maoris, but experience taught him that there was much to be done, particularly with regard to Maori attitudes, to make this a feasible policy. And he found that the changes could not be made in a hurry; the Maoris refused to be rushed. He therefore became identified with a policy called in Maori *taihoa,* interpreted by hostile pakeha critics as "marking time, putting off, bye and bye," but in reality a recognition of the difficulties of persuading the Maoris to any lines of action not assessed by them to be justified under their traditions. Thus while Carroll saw what needed to be done, he did very little himself. He saw in 1891 that the government should "induce the natives to become thoroughly useful settlers in the true sense of the world," but it was reserved for a later Maori leader to act decisively on this perception. On the other hand, Carroll was responsible as Native minister in 1900 for the Maori Councils Act under which the Maoris were encouraged to take responsibility for their own district government and under this act work in health and public sanitation among the Maoris was facilitated. This was basic to strengthening them as a people. And by 1920 Carroll had moved so far from the old idea that Europeanization was the ideal Maori fate that he advised the Maoris, "Hold fast to your Maorihood," thus signifying that in his view the answer was a marriage of cultures, not the substitution of one for the other.

By the proper logic of the situation, it was Maoris and part-Maoris who were profiting from pakeha education who started and largely carried forward the Maori revival. The most famous names in this connection were Sir Maui Pomare, Sir Peter Buck, also known as Te Rangihiroa, Bishop Bennett, the first Maori bishop of the Church of England, and above all Sir Apirana Ngata, the first Maori graduate of the University of New Zealand (B.A. 1893, M.A. 1894, LL B. 1896, Hon. D. Litt. 1948), but many men of lesser fame played a role, like Reweti Kohere, Dr. Tutere Wirepa, and Hone Heke (grandnephew of the original of that name). The movement began at Te Aute, a Church of England secondary school for Maoris in the Hawkes Bay area of the East Coast when in 1891 some twenty "old boys" formed the grandiloquently named Association for the Amelioration of the Maori Race. They were encouraged in this by the pakeha headmaster but, as one of the group subsequently wrote, they were then ignorant of the Maori mind and condition. They had to learn how to influence and guide their fellow Maoris by enduring the harsh and hurting experience of ridicule and rejection at Maori councils, especially those held on the *marae,* the open-air social center in front of the tribal meetinghouse. It was against Maori tradition for the young to instruct the old, for any but hereditary chiefs to lead. The original movement therefore had almost expired of frustration when in 1897 the principal leaders held a conference on the Maori problem as they had come to understand it from which, after candid discussion of the situation and prospects, a Young Maori party emerged. In this form the movement came indeed to permeate Maori life, both by the direct approach and through Parliament and the apparatus of government. Ngata entered Parliament in 1905, Buck in 1908, both as Liberals, and Pomare in 1912 as an Independent, though soon identified with the Reform party. Ngata and Pomare achieved ministerial office, Buck left politics and New Zealand in 1927 to become in time professor of anthropology at Yale and director of the Bishop Museum, Honolulu. Pomare and Buck were especially identified with health and sanitation reform among the Maoris, the preoccupations of this period, while Ngata, for many years the secretary of the Young Maori party, became preoccupied with land reform and use, the focus of interest in the next period. As Buck came to specialize in Polynesian ethnology, so Ngata became a great exponent of Maori language and culture. Education, health and sanitation, land reform and use, and the cultural emphasis were the avenues along which the Maori revival was to move. While all these men had tribal identifications and emphasized the importance of tribe in Maori thinking, they sought to advance the Maoris as a people—to create a national oneness (Kotahitanga), though without purposefully obliterating tribal differences.

The Maori reformers began by attacking with health propaganda what Ngata characterized as the dirtiness, idleness, drunkenness, and immorality of the people. Their original weapon was a pamphlet entitled, "Health for the Maori (Te Ora mo te Maori)," written by James H. Pope (later revised by Pomare). Pope was the first inspector of Maori schools, appointed in 1880. This seemingly innocuous activity caused a crisis in leadership in the Maori world. The traditional leadership was that of the chiefs, usually middle-aged or elderly men. Age was a constituent of their *mana*. The reformers were young, they were not chiefs, though sometimes of high rank, and their apparent assumption of a leadership position was interpreted as a challenge to (and implicit criticism of), the chiefs. The difficulty was solved by a division of labor. Ceremonial leadership was left to the chiefs, while leadership in matters of health, public sanitation, economic enterprise, cultural revival and so on passed to the reformers. It was while attempting to exert this leadership, which involved the reformers in detailed arguments on the many *marae,* that the young men expended that "mental sweat" to which Te Rangihiroa later feelingly referred. In later years he recalled as especially difficult a protracted argument, replete with historical references to ancient Maori practices, over the construction and use of privies. Essentially what the reformers had undertaken was an enterprise in enculturation, but not to Europeanize the Maori, rather to incorporate into their culture pakeha knowledge and ideas and practices which would support their Maoritanga and move them toward that equality with the whites Sir James Carroll had found to be impossible of immediate achievement.

Pomare, in this period, achieved the fullest career, perhaps because he was the elder of Ngata who, in the end, became far more distinguished, perhaps because his field was medicine. Born in 1876, Pomare was the son of a chief of a West Coast tribe, the Ngati Awa. Through his mother, he had some white blood, an inheritance from miscegenation in the whaling days. Educated at Te Aute school, in 1893 he went to the United States under the patronage of the Seventh Day Adventist missionaries to study medicine. After attending a school at Battle Creek, Michigan, for four years, he took his M.D. at the American Medical Missionary College, Chicago, in 1899. On his return to New Zealand he became a medical officer under the Maori Councils Act, this associating him with

James Carroll. A little later Te Rangihiroa (Peter Buck) became an assistant officer in the same service. This was a great step forward from distributing "Te Ora mo te Maori." Pomare directed special attention to the improvement of Maori housing, the deterioration of which had begun so many decades before, the care and feeding of babies to cut down infant mortality, then many times the New Zealand average, and the suppression of the *tohungas,* or Maori witch doctors and associated European faith-healers and other quacks, finally achieved in law in 1907, and campaigned for a law requiring the registration of Maori births and deaths (the latter to outlaw secret burial), achieved in 1912. Results of this activity appeared early; the census of 1906 showed a rise in the Maori population for the first time in many decades. In 1912 Pomare entered Parliament as an Independent representing the West Coast Maoris (the Taranaki and Waikato tribes who had not emerged from their sulks provoked by the wars), but that same year he became the Maori member of the Executive Council in Massey's Reform government. He was given the task of administering the Cook Islands, where he had earlier introduced health and sanitation measures, the first Maori to be concerned as minister with Polynesians outside the country. Pomare did an outstanding job, and in 1923 Massey made him Minister of Health and although there was a public outcry about placing a Maori over Europeans, he made a success of his new portfolio also. In 1925 he was knighted. He continued to administer the Cook Islands and Health portfolios until 1928, when his party lost office. His health was now precarious and seeking to regain it he took a sea voyage, but died at Los Angeles, California, in 1930.

It is the verdict of many students of New Zealand history that World War I had a muffled impact on the country while it was in progress—the fighting was far away on the other side of the world—but that a delayed impact of great intensity, chiefly to be described in economic terms, came in the 1920's and 1930's. While undoubtedly in essence correct, this summing up obscures not only the story of New Zealand's participation in the war but also any account of the country's response to the war as expressed in its conception of its status in the British Empire and the world. New Zealand participated in the war "out of all proportion even to filial duty" to Great Britain; it responded to it by a reaffirmation of filial duty to Great Britain more pious than that of any other member of the British community, save possibly Australia, a point sharpened when the attitudes of Canada, South Africa and Ireland are called to mind. The war intensified rather than relaxed New Zealand's filial piety and made her an obvious exception to any generalization about the relations of the self-governing dominions to Great Britain. Her "mother complex" which New Zealand writers see emerging around 1885 after fifteen years of self-assertiveness, reached fullest, openest and most carefully rationalized expression in the years 1914–35. The New Zealanders sought before the war to get closer to Great Britain, as in the proposals of Seddon and Ward noted earlier, and during the war decided that they had achieved such a position. They thought their idea of a centralized management of imperial affairs, including foreign policy and defense, had been translated into a satisfactory institutional form. They supported the centralizing forces at work in wartime. But they reckoned without the centrifugal forces, chiefly nationalistic in character, at work in Canada and South Africa which began to find active expression on the imperial scene after 1921.

In 1909, when Ward was prime minister, New Zealand adopted compulsory military training for home defense; in 1910 it had the benefit of Kitchener's advice on military policy; and in 1913 it discussed with London the problems of organizing in any future war an expeditionary force for service with the British overseas. However, it conceived of the Royal Navy as its defensive bulwark. In 1887 it began to contribute funds to the British Admiralty for the costs of the British ships on the Australian station. Unlike the Australians, the New Zealanders never really questioned this policy of "tribute"; there was in New Zealand no such movement for the building of a national navy as there was in Australia. The New Zealanders looked askance at the Australian campaign, regarding it as not only a defiance of Admiralty policy of one navy centrally controlled but as a dangerously nationalistic enterprise. Although geographically very similarly situated, they rejected the Australian rationalization of the national navy policy and not because they lacked the resources to carry out a scheme of proportionate magnitude and cost. On the contrary, at the time of the naval scare of 1909 the New Zealanders felt able to guarantee the cost of a battleship to be attached to the China squadron of the Imperial Navy. Only in 1913 did New Zealand order a cruiser to be stationed in New Zealand, but it was to be *automatically* at the disposal of the Admiralty at the outbreak of war. New Zealand's aspiration was to be regarded as organically a part of the Empire, an outlier of Britain, not an associated nation. Its defense would be closely integrated with imperial defense with no disturbing nationalistic divisiveness. Even at that time, when the divisiveness of Australian policy was far more theoretical than real, as British acceptance of it showed, the New Zealanders were against it.

When Britain declared war on Germany in 1914, New Zealand was automatically at war also. There was no room for debate about this in any dominion and the New Zealanders certainly had no disposition to try to find room. Nor did they propose to debate the question Sir Wilfred Laurier of Canada had suggested was debatable: what contribution to the war should now be made by a dominion. To them the question was what Britain wanted of their resources. They were the first to offer an expeditionary force (perhaps because they had partially preplanned one); they were the first of the dominions actually to begin preparations for sending men overseas; and by an accident of circumstances they were the first to take possession of enemy territory—they took Samoa from Germany (see Chapter IX). Before the war had ended, 112,223 New Zealanders had been dispatched overseas or were undergoing training, 19.35 per cent of the white male population, a larger proportion than Australia or Canada, a proportion only exceeded by Britain's 22.11 per cent. It committed over 40 per cent of all males 20 to 45 years of age to war. New Zealand's casualties were high: 16,317 dead, 41,262 wounded, 356 prisoners of war, 84 missing, to a total of 58,019. This was the terrible hurt of war to the home-staying people of the time. In addition to the Europeans, New Zealand also sent some Maoris and Cook Islanders overseas and undertook the training of Fijians. An overwhelming proportion of the New Zealanders who went overseas did so as volunteers, not conscripts.

The New Zealanders entered the war in close association with the Australians, contributing their men to the Australian-New Zealand Army Corps (ANZAC), as tentatively arranged in 1912. Like the Australians, the New Zealanders were partly foot soldiers, partly mounted men (technically mounted infantrymen). Unlike the Australians, but appropriately in view of the New Zealand outlook, they were led by a British officer, Major General A. J. Godley. The first New Zealand convoy joined the Australian ships at Albany, Western Australia, after a curiously sharp dispute with the British Admiralty about the risks of sending ships unprotected across the Tasman and along the southern Australian coast. In the end it was arranged that a Japanese warship assist in protecting them from any stray German raiders. When the completed convoy sailed from Albany, there were ten ships carrying New Zealanders and with the ships carrying Australians, they were accompanied by British, Australian and Japanese warships. Diverted from Great Britain, the original objective, to Egypt, the New Zealanders helped fight off a Turkish attempt on the Suez Canal, participated in the ill-fated Gallipoli campaign and, when Gallipoli was evacuated, the infantrymen were sent to France and the horsemen to Sinai and Palestine. The New Zealanders thus fought on three fronts including the terrible principal front of the war in France, and participated in some of the most memorable operations of the war to the enormous satisfaction of the nation. From New Zealand looking overseas, it was not only a creditable effort, it was a tremendous effort for so small a nation, but reversing the telescope it appeared as but a tiny contribution to the total imperial effort. In any comprehensive summary of World War I, New Zealand is mentioned only very occasionally and usually very incidentally and this is, quite understandably, gall at the bottom of the cup. However, perception of this at the time did not provoke the New Zealanders to a strident assertiveness about their significance but, rather, it persuaded them to a protective rationalization which turned their position into a virtue.

Politically the situation in New Zealand was difficult but not unmanageable during the war. An election in December, 1914 returned Massey to office with a majority of only two over Ward and his phalanx of Liberals and Labour's contingent of five. Massey organized the war effort, particularly relying upon his minister of Defence, Australian-born Sir James Allen, and his minister of Internal Affairs, Sir Francis Dillon Bell. But even with the Liberals committed to the support of the war, Massey's position was precarious and, moreover, the situation reflected a division of the country that appeared to dictate coalition government. The coalition came in August 1915 when a National Government was formed with Massey as prime minister and Ward as minister of Finance. Allen continued as minister of Defence and Bell was made attorney general. This removed the Massey-Ward rivalry from Parliament to the cabinet room, for Ward contended for equality with Massey and unwillingly accepted any subordination to him. It was a coalition government with party rivalry unquieted. Nevertheless, the National Government perforce held together until August 1919 when it was demonstrated that Massey, not Ward, had profited politically from the war. An incidental effect of coalition was temporarily to turn the Labour five into the Official Opposition.

The leftist Red Fed group was politically critical of the war, becoming more so as it wore on. It carried over into wartime its radical attitudes of peacetime. It interpreted the war as a war of the capitalist classes, argued for conscription of wealth, complained about the inefficiency of the economic controls, especially of prices (the upward movement of which lowered real wages), raised the cry for a statement of peace aims, and when it came in 1916, opposed conscription of manpower. Unlike the Australian government, the New Zealand government introduced conscription by parliamentary action without referring the question to the people. It did not even argue that voluntary recruitment was failing to fill the ranks; it simply asserted that conscription was a more democratic way of handling the situation as the pool of manpower got smaller. Labour opposed, as Australian Labor opposed, but it did so after open opposition to conscription had been made sedition under the law and as a result a number of subsequently famous Labour leaders—Peter Fraser, for example—were sent to jail for seditious utterances on the question.

Because of the difficulties and shortages of ocean transport, there was no production boom, but on the other hand there was no disorganization of production from lack of a market. As in Australia there was an *organized* market in which money prices steadily rose as currency inflation took hold. This was provided by the bulk purchase of all surplus production of New Zealand's staple products—cheese, butter, meat, and wool—and most minor ones, also, on behalf of the imperial government. This did not stimulate an expansion of total production, but it did stabilize the farm situation by creating the illusion that the marketing problem had been solved. For this reason farming came to look like a very good thing indeed and in 1915 when the system was instituted, farm land prices began to rise. They rose further at a later stage when ex-soldiers, with government money in hand or available to them, came into the market looking for farms upon which to settle and "repatriate" themselves. Things looked very well indeed until bulk purchasing was dropped—for most commodities in 1920, butter in 1921—and a return was made to the free market, a change unluckily marked by a sharp fall in prices. The farmers then, as we shall see in the next chapter, looked back nostalgically to the controlled marketing system of wartime and attempted by organizing producer-dominated "boards" to regain control and prosperity. Of lesser but not entirely insignificant importance were the relatively elementary experiments in retail price control, both by "direct" control and by subsidy, as the domestic retail price of butter was subsidized by a levy on the butter exported. A unique twist was given these experiments when government butcher shops were opened in Auckland in an effort to bring prices down in the regular shops, a curious use of the "yardstick" approach, hardly to be expected of an anti-Labour government. Both lines of state endeavor—purchasing surpluses on account of the imperial government and experimenting with economic controls on the domestic scene—contributed to a temporary aggregation of power in the government's hands and forecast things to come.

In imperial affairs Massey was a thoroughgoing "colonial," but more by instinct than by rationalized choice. When in 1907 it was proposed that the self-governing colonies henceforth be called "dominions" the better to mark their status, his reaction to this disturbance of the status quo was highly critical. On the other hand his outlook led him, like Seddon and Ward, to favor any development that would bring New

Zealand closer to Britain and allow her influence over imperial policy decisions on foreign affairs, defense, and trade. He therefore responded favorably to Lloyd George's Imperial War Cabinet of 1917. He faithfully supported it through the Peace Conference, where it was known as the British Empire Delegation, and was still an adherent at the meeting of 1921, though now disturbed by and distrustful of the emerging opinions on imperial relations of the Canadians and South Africans. Under the great influence of Sir Robert Borden of Canada, the Imperial Cabinet had been the vehicle which had carried the dominions into such innovations as their separate representation at the Peace Conference—New Zealand, however, had but one representative as against two for Australia, Canada, South Africa, and India; to the separate dominion signatures of the Treaty; and to independent membership in the League of Nations and the International Labour Organization. (At the Peace Conference, Massey stood close to Hughes of Australia on the issues relating to their part of the world. He took a special interest in the disposition of German Samoa, as Hughes did in the fate of German New Guinea. Both favored the solution of annexation to their respective countries, but both had to be satisfied with C-class mandates.) Since the gist of the Imperial Cabinet was centralization of the governance of the Empire with dominion participation, it suited Massey, but he missed the implication of the developments which had occurred under its cover. The Imperial Cabinet was in effect what New Zealand had been looking for since the days of Seddon without the flaws inevitably to be found in any version of imperial federation. In the debate on the Peace Treaty in the New Zealand Parliament, W. Downie Stewart, a man who warmly sympathized with Massey's instinctive position but who had much greater intellectual sophistication, made the point that in signing the Treaty New Zealand seemed to have performed the act of a sovereign state. Where did this leave New Zealand? Where was this leading? Massey hardly understood the point or the questions; he did not perceive that implication in his act; he certainly had no interest in exploiting this—to him— rather hair-splitting as well as hair-raising position. (Neither had Downie Stewart, for that matter, but others might.) Massey replied to Stewart, "We signed it [the Treaty] as representatives of self-governing nations within the Empire—partners, with everything that name implies." The institutional form of the partnership was the Imperial Cabinet.

Massey did not think much of the League of Nations—in which respect at least he differed from his attorney general, Bell. He thought nothing of the I.L.O. He had his doubts about the propriety of New Zealand holding a mandate for Samoa *directly*. He really only believed in the British Empire partnership and the Royal Navy as its shield. He was upset by the currents of opinion he detected running at the ambiguous meeting of the dominion leaders at London in 1921—was it a meeting of the Imperial Cabinet, or what was it? Massey's position was taken up and given a highly sophisticated legalistic expression by Sir John W. Salmond. Salmond, English-born but taken to New Zealand at the age of fourteen, was educated in New Zealand and London, became professor of law at the University of Adelaide, South Australia, and later at Victoria College, University of New Zealand, at Wellington. He was associated as solicitor general with Sir Francis Dillon Bell and helped draw up New Zealand's war legislation. In 1920 he became a judge of New Zealand's Supreme Court and attended the Washington Conference of 1921–22 on disarmament and Pacific affairs as representative of his country on the British Delegation. In his report to his government he addressed himself to the "Questions of interest and importance" as to "the constitutional and international significance of the overseas Dominions at the Washington Conference."

Suggestions have been made in certain quarters that by permitting the presence of the self-governing dependencies of the Crown at international conventions such as those of Versailles and Washington those Dominions have in some manner acquired a new international status—that they are now recognized for international purposes as independent States, although in their constitutional relations they remain portions of the British Empire. It is not easy to attach any definite meaning to this suggestion. . . . The true significance of the presence of representatives of the Dominions at that Conference is not that those Dominions have acquired for either international or constitutional purposes any form of independent status, but that they have now been given a voice in the management of the international relations of the British Empire as a single, undivided unity—relations which were formerly within the exclusive control of the Government of Great Britain.

There the New Zealanders stood, and continued to stand, as the great debate on the implications of dominion autonomy rolled through the councils of Empire.

CHAPTER VII

Insecurity and Experiment

If the state of the world between 1919 and 1939 can be characterized by the words "insecurity" and "experiment," then certainly the state of New Zealand can accurately be so characterized. In New Zealand at one and the same time an effort was made to continue to make progress, largely in terms of increasing the production of the land industries, especially dairying, along both historically established and new lines, while at first dealing with the manifest insecurities by pragmatic moves designed to bolster the position of the producer interest and later by more radical adventures in social reconstruction under a Labour party leadership that invoked the tradition of Seddon.

The uneasy wartime coalition government of Massey and Ward—of the Reform party and the Liberals—quickly broke up when the fighting ceased and in 1919 the era of three-party politics that continued for just over a decade was initiated. The three parties were Reform, Liberal, and Labour, with both the Reform and Liberal parties representing a barely distinguishable New Zealand-type conservatism and Labour espousing a laboristic radicalism. Whereas in Australia in a context more comparable to New Zealand's than any other that comes readily to mind, the Labor party was able by exploiting the divisions of opinion in the electorate to drive its rivals into a "fusion" by 1908, in New Zealand Labour, though intent upon it from the early 1920's, was unable to achieve this until 1936. While the three-way division of the electorate lasted, the political struggle was essentially between Reform and the Liberals, with Reform having the edge until 1928. Reform's strength was in the countryside, especially in the North Island among the dairy farmers, while the Liberals found such strength as they had in the urban areas and the South Island, their traditional strongholds. The Labour party was building its strength in the urban areas, largely at the expense of the Liberals; its political problem was to invade the Reform preserves in rural areas. The effect of the three-way division of the electorate, when combined with the effect of the votes given independent candidates and small, transient parties, was to insure that the victorious party in the elections consistently received a minority of the total votes cast. Reform was victorious in the general elections of 1919, 1922, and 1925. The victory of 1925, achieved under the leadership of J. G. Coates after Massey's death, the greatest victory ever achieved by Reform, was based on 47 per cent of the vote. To an extent this victory was accounted for by one of Reform's rare successes in taking businessmen's votes away from the Liberals, using the American-style bait "More business in government and less government in business." On this occasion the Liberal vote dropped to 20 per cent. Three years later, however, the Liberals, now labeled the United party and led again, after experimentation in other directions, by Sir Joseph Ward, had a resurgence, for businessmen abandoned Coates, and with 30 per cent of the vote Ward took office with Labour support. For Ward this was an after-clap success comparable to Sir Julius Vogel's in the 1880's, and as unsatisfactory. It was recognized as early as 1922 by W. Downie Stewart, that rare example of a conservative intellectual in politics, that the amalgamation of the two conservative parties was logical, desirable, and inevitable, but it was nevertheless not accomplished even nominally until 1931. By that time Sir Joseph Ward was dead and G. W. Forbes, an undistinguished South Island farmer whose parliamentary career had begun in 1908, had succeeded by seniority to the United party leadership. By 1931 Labour was really menacing—it had been advancing in vote-getting power very obviously since 1922; it became the Official Opposition after the election of 1925; it was clearly the dominant vote-getter in the cities —and so the United and Reform parties made an electoral compact to fight it at the polls. Experienced conservative politicians rather expected a Labour victory in the 1931 campaign chiefly because the farmers were plainly unsettled by the Great Depression and Labour was learning how to talk persuasively to them. However, the coalition won the election, possibly because the full impact of the Great Depression was not yet felt, possibly because many farmer protest votes were frittered away on independent candidates preaching fringe panaceas, but the political tide was clearly enough running in Labour's favor. From 1931–35 a coalition ministry led by G. W. Forbes, prime minister, with J. G. Coates and W. Downie Stewart as the strongest members, governed the country and met the full force of the Great Depression. The significant political figure of the time proved to be J. G. Coates. Labour came to office in 1935 with a minority of the vote, but with its radical urban following undiminished and with support from radicalized dairy farmers. The coalition which it had defeated became a permanent political grouping under the name of the National party in 1936. Thereafter New Zealand reverted to what was essentially a two-party system, though transient special-interest parties, independent candidates, and the party affiliations within the four-member Maori parliamentary representation all had significant relation to the fortunes of the major parties.

The central political problem of the time was to forward all-over development, advance producers' interests, and maintain internal prosperity in a world of fluctuating prices for exports. The focus of political interest was upon the condition of the butter, cheese, and meat producers. In all cases "the market" meant primarily the United Kingdom market, for no other had more than marginal significance in relation to total exports; and not only was the United Kingdom market found to be subject to price fluctuations, but it was eventually also found not to be "bottomless." New Zealanders had all along proceeded on the unconscious assumption that their job was to produce and that what they produced that was exported would be absorbed in Britain at remunerative prices. The Great Depression led to the sharp questioning of this assumption.

General development and expansion of production in the land industries appeared to be fairly straightforward undertakings. In the former area the emphasis of public investment (supported by heavy overseas borrowing in the Vogel tradition) fell on road building and electricity supply. Arterial roads became a national responsibility in 1922 and a Ministry of Transport was established in 1929. At this time the railways ceased to expand their mileage—only 323 miles were newly opened to traffic 1920–29—but during the 1920's and 1930's there was investment in linking up separated units of the system, as by driving a major tunnel, the easing of steep grades and sharp curves, the straightening of lines by "deviations," and the electrification of selected stretches. The system's efficiency was increased, though not to any great extent. It remained almost wholly single-track. Road building was closely related to the intensification of the impact of the automobile on the country; New Zealand became one of the top countries in the world in the number of motor vehicles per head of population. In 1931 the impact on the railways of road improvements and motor vehicles led to the passing of a Transport Licensing Act which provided for close regulation of road motor transport, both passenger and freight, with a view to planned coordination of transport—that is, to protect the state-owned railways from too intensive competition. At this stage the probable impact of the airplane on the transport system was not apparent. Domestic commercial air transport only began to take hold in the middle 1930's. (Shortly after exploratory work on overseas air routes—to Australia, United Kingdom, and United States—was begun.) What looked like and was progress in transport was also movement toward vexing problems of definition of the most economic means. State activity in the generation of hydroelectricity, in the resources for which the country was rich, began in 1911 with a scheme, based on Lake Coleridge, for supplying power to Christchurch and the Canterbury district. This project came into operation in 1915. The first major state-built generating station in the North Island, at Mangahao, was commenced in 1922 and brought into operation in 1925. On these foundations, by building additional stations and taking over existing private stations, grids, planned for in 1922, were brought into existence in both islands in the ensuing years. The policy of the central government was to "supply power in bulk," leaving the reticulation and retail supply in the hands of the local authorities—cities, towns, boroughs, and counties, supplemented by coordinated distributing systems run by specially constituted power boards. The first great impact of hydroelectricity on the economic life of New Zealand thus came in the 1920's and 1930's.

The most important single development in the private sector of the economy was the continued expansion of dairying. In terms of employment, for example, this was the most important industry in New Zealand. While the expansion resulted in the scattering of dairying through both islands, the great centers were in the North Island, preeminently the Taranaki and Waikato districts, the former tending to emphasize cheese, the latter butter. The Waikato district developed rapidly in the interwar period; the Taranaki district was more a prewar development. The continuing development was based on three interrelated factors: at first on an increase in the number of dairy cows—from 783,000 cows in milk in 1920 to an interwar peak of 1,807,377 in 1936; and increasingly as time passed on improvements in pasture (grassland) management and the breeding of more productive cows (the index number for butterfat per cow rose to 145.3 in 1936). Jerseys were the favored breed in the 1930's and there was a strong trend in their favor. Expansion of production in dairying was facilitated by changes in the transport of cream from the farms to butter factories and of milk to the cheese factories on the improved roads by motorized vehicles. The better roads and vehicles made for more economic siting of factories. The factories were mostly cooperatives of dairy farmers, but some were private companies: the giant among the cooperatives was the New Zealand Cooperative Dairy Company Ltd., operating in the Waikato. Improved transport also facilitated the movement of supplies from distributing points to the farms, and this in turn influenced the location and growth of towns. On the farms the "separator"—the machine for separating out the cream in the raw milk —was basic equipment; during the 1920's and 1930's there was a rapid and steady increase in the number of milking machines in use, until in the mid-1930's well over a million cows were being machine-milked. The farmers also acquired the machines needed for grassland farming: fertilizer distributors, harrows, mowers, hay collectors, and hoists for building the favored stacks for silage. In the fields, the ampler use of better fertilizer—superphosphate based on rock from Nauru—was the significant change. In the milking-sheds the use of electric power was increasing and in the paddocks so was the tractor. The mechanization of dairying proceeded apace.

There was at the same time an upward movement in the production and export of foodstuffs other than butter and cheese, e.g., meat, apples and pears, and honey. The most important product of the meat trade was lamb, with mutton next. Although New Zealand dairy farmers did not keep pigs in proportionately as large numbers as was customary in others of the world's dairying complexes, there was a rise between the wars in the production of pork, bacon, and ham. On the other hand, New Zealand did not develop a strong beef trade. Not only was a far higher proportion of the beef produced consumed locally than was the case with the other meats, but this trade had to meet severe Argentine competition and also the competition of *chilled* beef as against frozen. The quantity of wool produced and exported rose over these years.

Although some foodstuffs, including notably wheat, were produced in quantities only sufficient to meet domestic needs and in some years not even that, New Zealand was in the broad view one of the leading food producers and exporters of the world. It was, however, chiefly to be identified as a major supplier of certain foodstuffs to the United Kingdom. About nine-tenths of all exports were in the category "pastoral" (that is, foodstuffs derived from the sheep and the cow, and wool)— 91.1 per cent in 1920, 93.9 per cent in 1938. There was through the interwar period a tendency to increase the concentration of exports on the United Kingdom. Whereas in 1929, 74 per cent of exports went to the United Kingdom, by 1938 the proportion had risen to 84 per cent. At no time in this period did the country achieve a useful dispersion of her export outlets. Similarly her imports were drawn chiefly from the United Kingdom—around half of the total in these years, with Australia and the United States the only other important suppliers. From both she bought far more than she sold to them. She felt, however, the attraction of the markets of the Far East, though she did not make much progress in them, but in 1928 she negotiated what then looked like a highly important trade treaty with Japan. New Zealand was a firmly integrated unit of the imperial trading system. This was the material basis —the cash nexus—of her politico-cultural "loyalty."

About 1925 it was quite obvious that increasing the acreage of land in use would in future be of declining importance in adding to the number of animals depastured and to increasing production. It was apparent that future progress in these respects would depend upon improving the pastures then in use by fertilizing them with artificial manures and by the general use of the fruits of grassland research, especially by search for the best strains of native grasses and clovers, breeding of new strains, and the importation of adaptable strains from overseas. To be sure, the making of artificial (or sown) pastures was an old New Zealand activity, but the linking up of pasture-building with science was new. Even as early as 1861 there were over 150,000 acres of sown pastures in the country; by 1925 there were 16,500,000. The perception of the peculiar economic importance of scientific pasture development and improvement in New Zealand is attributed to the Scottish agriculturalist Robert Wallace who visited New Zealand in the 1890's. Up to that point the work of pasture-building had been largely without the taint of science, even of a knowledge of botany, but the Department of Agriculture (founded 1892) gave some attention to research into pasture grasses from 1896. However, the task of making grasslands research and the application of scientific knowledge of pasture building of central economic importance fell into the hands of a botanist, A. H. Cockayne, in 1909. Cockayne began to write about the pasture question in the Agriculture Department's *Journal;* he proved to be not only a great botanist, but, also, a skilled propagandist. Beginning about 1920, his pioneering work was extended by his associate Bruce Levy who emerged as the best of the agrostologists in New Zealand. Levy took up also the task of showing the farmers how to utilize the fruits of grassland science. By 1927, following an important visit from R. G. Stapleton, professor of agricultural botany at the University College of Wales and an ardent exponent of grasslands research, the New Zealand government embarked upon fundamental research at a new station at Palmerston North. Cockayne was in charge. In 1929 a seed certification scheme was sponsored by this station. Within a decade the emphasis of research was shifted from grasslands as such to the scientific aspects of the utilization of the grasses by the economic animals.

The 1920's also saw a very important step forward in the field of forestry, a matter which had, it will be recalled, greatly interested Sir Julius Vogel. Sir Francis Dillon Bell took a particular interest in both forest conservation and afforestation, and established new and advanced policies. He had a bias in favor of the indigenous economically useful timber trees in both respects, but his views were comprehensive and he was not afraid to buck those with a vested interest in the exploitation of the forests. He wished to conserve the remaining indigenous forest even if this involved opposing the absorption of forested land into pastures, the traditional procedure in New Zealand. He also favored planting indigenous trees, as well as exotics. He promoted a policy of selective cutting to insure continuous yield. His view was that the objective of policy should be to guarantee the meeting of future domestic demand for timber from local supplies; he therefore sought to regulate exports which, he thought, encouraged destructive exploitation and raised domestic prices. He believed the forests should be so located as to protect the watersheds. Although contrary to Bell's personal bias, the indigenous forests continued to decline and afforestation with exotic trees became the dominant practice. Of twenty-two exotic forests in existence at the end of the 1930's, eight were established in the 1920's—including some of the largest. Commercial afforestation—with exotics—established itself in New Zealand in the 1920's also. These developments took on far more importance in the future than they appeared to have at the time Bell made his great contribution.

After an abortive attempt to form a Council of Scientific and Industrial Research on the then popular British pattern during World War I, a Department of Scientific and Industrial Research was set up within the government in 1926. While the department's activities were wide ranging—chemistry, geology, astronomy, seismology, magnetism, botany, bacteriology, entomology, meteorology, etc.—the organization reasonably complex, and the influence of the department pervasive through a committee system and through wielding the power of the purse in grants, a complete, rigid coordination of scientific activities was neither aimed at nor achieved. The emphasis was, however, on applied science and the relevance of the sciences to problems for one reason or another of peculiar interest to New Zealand, such as seismology—New Zealand is in the Pacific Basin earthquake belt. (The most destructive earthquake since settlement occurred in the Hawke's Bay district in 1931.) The research stations and laboratories were scattered throughout the dominion and an observatory inherited from the Germans at Apia, Samoa, was utilized in the central Pacific. Laboratories and other research facilities were provided for dairy research (especially into the chemical and bacteriological sides of manufacturing dairy products), plant research (plant diseases, grasslands, field crops, and economic entomology), and special establishments for dealing with soils, wheat, leather, fruit, and flax. Aspects of a broad field were parceled out by plan to several establishments, in the process scattering research not only to specialist institutions but also to private enterprises, such as the Cawthorne Institute of Nelson (established 1920 by private benefaction) and the laboratory of the New Zealand Cooperative Dairy Company at Hamilton, as well as to the two agricultural colleges, Massey (North Island) and Canterbury (South Island), and the relevant schools of the other University of New Zealand colleges. Agricultural education also received assistance at this time. The irony that as research and education intensified their creative impact on the land industries, the economic problem became more and more intractable was not peculiar to New Zealand.

While the pakeha continued his conquest of the land, so the Maori, led by Apirana Ngata, made his most carefully calculated effort to bring his lands into production to wrest from them a pakeha-level income. Although the Maoris had continued to increase in numbers, it could hardly be said that their condition as a people had satisfactorily improved. Judged by their elite, of which Ngata was an especially distinguished representative, they were a people of great potential and accomplishment, but judged by the majority they were still a "problem people" on the periphery of New Zealand society. The reiteration of the dogma of their equality with the pakeha tended to obscure from common knowledge the facts about their position. Even the assertion that they suffered not at all from color prejudice, a veritably sacred item of the popular credo, was covertly denied by specialist observers. Even the great efforts that had been made in the field of health had left an enormous budget of work to be done, not only directly in curative and preventive medicine, but in housing, domestic sanitation, and diet. The old Maori diet was mostly gone, an adequate modern diet had not been evolved; housing was poor in construction and often overcrowded; domestic sanitation was inadequate or nonexistent; and with regard to medicine the Maoris still hovered between two worlds, that of Maori tradition and that of the modern doctors and nurses. Their access to education tended to be confined to the primary level; there was but limited access to secondary and vocational education, and even more limited access to higher education. Until 1931 the Maoris were chiefly served with a version of pakeha academic primary education; in that year an effort was begun to introduce some elements of the Maori cultural heritage; and while the academic approach insured a general mastery of English, it did not prevent Maori from being spoken in most homes and it had small impact on Maori habits of life and labor. The Maoris tended to be rural, unskilled, casual workers, usually but not always combining paid work with some low-level subsistence farming, this producing low incomes. Very few Maoris were skilled tradesmen or white collar workers of any grade. If there was Maori progress to be made on the land, there was obviously not by this time enough land in Maori hands under any kind of title to provide for all the people. Putting Maoris on viable farms to be operated entrepreneurially within the pakeha system meant taking care of perhaps 20,000 people, leaving 60,000 to be taken care of otherwise. This could only mean that the breadwinners among them should be able to find places in the pakeha economic system which would provide adequate annual incomes, and it had to be assumed that this group would grow as the total Maori population increased. The preference of the Maori leadership of this generation was strongly in favor of rural employment for their people. But already the resources of rural employment had proved inadequate, for there was in existence a drift to the town and this was, as pressures built up in the rural areas, or the attractive power of the town and the city increased, sure to speed up, forecasting a development in Maori-pakeha relations of a hitherto largely unprecedented kind.

The idea that the Maoris, or a significant proportion of them, could improve and consolidate their economic position and conserve their culture by working their land by modern means to pakeha economic ends had found expression as far back as the 1890's. Aside from the general apathy of the Maoris, there were two prime obstacles to the development of the land the Maoris still possessed—the fragmentation of holdings by the operation of the Maori laws of landholding and inheritance, as they had been interpreted by the Native Land Courts, and the shortage of capital for investment by Maoris on Maori land. Ngata had been one of the pioneers in circumventing these obstacles. Among his own people of the East Coast, where the earliest successes in establishing Maori families in entrepreneurial farming had been made, he got around the fragmentation problem by the incorporation of the owners of considerable tracts; elsewhere the same objective was achieved by vesting title in trustees, usually pakehas, who managed the land for the benefit of the Maoris. Use was made under both arrangements of the principle of consolidation under which, by a complicated process of swapping, living areas adequate for the support of families were assembled. The normal procedure in land development by pakeha farmers was to borrow the necessary money, usually from a government agency. Pakeha trustees of Maori lands could borrow on the security of the lands they held before Maoris were able to borrow. Maori borrowing was at first permitted, with exacting safeguards, only from private lenders. It was not until 1920 that Maoris were enabled to borrow from their own Native Trust Office, a government agency established in that year to control Maori funds which had been accumulating since 1914. A few years later the Maori Land Boards—that is, Boards holding Maori lands on behalf of Maoris—were also enabled to lend money to Maoris for land development. This was a variety of self-help, but the funds were limited and exhaustible and if there was not to be a crippling lack of funds for Maori land development, the access to state funds that the pakeha farmers had through the State Advances Corporation was necessary. If the Maoris were to become "useful settlers" in any considerable numbers, the financial resources of the state had to be tapped. This was achieved in 1929 by the Native Land Settlement Act. The law and the plan of operations it embodied were the culmination of the campaign begun thirty-eight years before by Sir James Carroll. The act was in large measure a personal triumph for Sir Apirana Ngata.

Under Ngata's direction as native minister in the Forbes government, the land development campaign, state-directed and financed, was not only an economic and technological enterprise designed to set up Maoris in dairying or wool-growing, but also an adventure in applied anthropology. What Ngata aimed to do was to strengthen the position of the Maoris as Maoris, using pakeha means and working in economic terms to pakeha ends, but taking full account of the "historical, traditional, cultural and psychological" factors peculiar to the Maoris as a people. Ngata, indeed, had a deep interest in the preservation of Maori culture, including social customs, arts, crafts, and literature. Within ten years 250,000 acres had been developed under the program and 1700 settlers maintaining 16,000 dependents had been established. The program also influenced the handling of Maori land and settlement outside the scheme, as by the trustees. Ngata's work and interests were complementary to the cultural and economic activities of such leaders as the great Waikato Maori "Princess," Te Puea Herangi, but he was not so sympathetic with the activities of the faith-healing, sect-creating reformer Tahupotiki Wiremu Ratana (1870–1939). Politically the Ratana followers were identified with Labour. As the years passed, Ngata's Maori land development scheme became involved with the provision of work relief for Maoris. In 1932 and again in 1933 the auditor-general reported that the accounts of the land settlement scheme and Maori unemployment relief showed irregularities. This was seized upon by the Labour opposition to the coalition government led by Forbes and early in 1934 Ngata was forced to resign his ministerial post. The portfolio was taken over by the prime minister. The affair was undoubtedly a political maneuver designed to embarrass the government, for it was apparent that Ngata's land development scheme was well conceived and intelligently executed; his personal integrity was clear; he was caught out on details of financial management which, of course, he should have been watching narrowly but for which subordinates were directly responsible. In spite of the success of the political attack upon him, Ngata's position as the greatest of the Maori leaders not only survived, it waxed in the ensuing years. But for pakeha political advantage damage was done to the Maori people who only saw that pakeha politicians had somehow dislodged their leader from his high government post at a time when he was of maximum usefulness to them; this distressed them and made them feel insecure. However, the land development scheme went forward, with Ngata's sympathetic aid, under pakeha control.

During the 1920's prices for New Zealand exports were unstable with a downward trend. They moved erratically from 1921 through 1924, ending at a lower level than in 1920, moved upward to above the 1920 level in 1925, fell off sharply in 1926 and 1927, "recovered" a bit in 1928, began a downward trend in 1929 which carried them to their lowest levels in 1931, 1932, and 1933, while in 1934 a recovery began. Until 1930 the farmers tried to convince themselves that the situation was abnormal but that normality was around the corner. Their answer to low prices was increased production—hence the significance of technologic, agrostologic, and other changes in farm practices which increased productivity in this unencouraging period. Occupiers of marginal land were, under the pressures existing, forced out of farming; the increased production was best achieved on the best land. And it was an adjustment achieved with fewer workers than formerly. In New Zealand as throughout the world where farm productivity was rising, there was a drift of rural people to the urban areas. In 1926 the census showed for the first time more urban dwellers than rural (52 per cent as against 48). The economic logic of the situation was to expand employment in the factories and services—in secondary and tertiary employments—and to an extent this happened, though not so much by conscious policy as by a reflex to the general drift of affairs. New Zealand's heart stayed with the land industries; the country was, in the conception of its leaders, still a great "farm." It was characteristic that a conference on the economic situation held in 1928 suggested that the government "shape the education system in the direction of encouraging as many boys as possible *to take up farming* rather than professional or commercial vocations." Factory industry did expand in the 1920's; the growth was by further multiplication of small units. Butter and cheese factories and meat freezing works were as characteristic as the establishments which assembled imported components (as of motor vehicles or radios), or processed to a slightly higher form imported semi-manufactures. There was little manufacturing in depth and less heavy industry. It is perhaps significant that the one phase of factory industry the conservatives thought it necessary to regulate by licensing to prevent overcapacity was the processing of primary products. While factory industry received some encouragement by tariff protection, the ruling politicians did not really believe in this—they spread the tariff to new items rather than increased the rates, and the rates remained low—and an emphasis on factory industry to "balance" the economy awaited the coming to office of Labour, though it was discussed earlier. Factory industry did not expand enough in the 1920's to affect the increasing slack in employment; it absorbed more people but a declining proportion of the work force. On the other hand, except for domestic service, the service occupations absorbed rising proportions of the employed population. They supported the urbanization rather than factory industry. Unemployment was reckoned a serious problem by 1926, though the explanation was thought to be the moral inadequacy of the victims, not a fault of the economy. Public works employment did not solve, or disguise, the situation. Immigration decreased; the demographers talked of the probability of a stationary pakeha population. The ghosts of the 1880's walked.

Insofar as they had a policy of attack on the situation, the conservative policitians were anxious to do what they felt they could to restore and sustain the profitability of the land industries. It was early recognized that in relation to prices for exports, farms were overcapitalized, usually with borrowed money, and costs were too high. New Zealand farmers started off the postwar period with a boom in land prices, based on inflated expectations about probable prices for exports, stimulated by government land purchases for soldier settlement. The farmers had, moreover, the habit of capitalizing every advantage they perceived or received from the government. The major step taken by the government to deal by plan with the economic side of the farm situation during the 1920's was to give statutory support to producers' marketing organizations. The farmers blamed fluctuating-and-declining prices on the middlemen— those who dealt in New Zealand export produce in New Zealand and London, plus the shipping companies who transported the produce overseas—and believed that if they combined to influence the market and marketing charges in their favor, their problem could be solved. In short, the farmers lost faith in the free market (though not in the "bottomless" character of the United Kingdom market) and turned to schemes to control and administer the market in their interest as producers. Before World War I they had been satisfied with the free competitive market and its agents and after the wartime experience with government acquisition and negotiated pricing, they had turned back confidently to the prewar system in the expectation of finding themselves in *status quo ante bellum,* including the remembered tradition of rising prices. The bad price breaks in the early 1920's, about the time of the abandonment of government controls, disillusioned them with the free market—it was far from what they had expected—and so they turned back to the idea of the controlled market, especially with the idea that they could thus gain remunerative prices, but not this time with the government in charge but themselves as producers. They devised a kind of producers' syndicalism. The meat producers led the way. On February 11, 1922, the government gave a statutory basis to a board of control for meat producers; the preamble of the act gave the rationale of the development:

Whereas the economic welfare of New Zealand has lately been adversely affected by reason of a reduction in the net returns receivable by persons engaged in the business of the production of meat for export, such reduction being due in part to falling prices and in part to the charges payable in respect of freight and other services; and whereas conferences have lately been held of representatives of the Government and of persons whose business is the production of meat for export, and it has been resolved that the public economic welfare will be promoted by the establishment of a Board of Control, with power to act as the agent of the producers in respect of the preparation, storage, and shipment of meat, and in respect of the disposal of such meat beyond New Zealand; and whereas it is desired to give effect to the resolutions aforesaid and to provide by law accordingly . . .

A dairy control board was established in 1923, boards for fruit and honey in 1924. These boards marked New Zealand's abandonment of the free market for export produce. It is worth emphasizing that this occurred at the behest of entrepreneurial capitalist farmers under a conservative political regime.

The establishment of producer-controlled marketing boards was the most radical innovation the conservative politicians undertook prior to the onset of the Great Depression. Though they had thought of unemployment insurance in 1914, they were not persuaded in the 1920's to do much more than tinker with the social security legislation, as by adjusting benefits upward to conform to the changed price scale, rewriting eligibility provisions, extending coverage to a few new categories of persons or to closely associated disabilities, or improving or strengthening existing activities such as public health, child welfare, and school medical and dental services. An attempt was made to improve the Factory Act in 1922, but it failed to bring good conditions into being and in the same year workers' compensation was strengthened. The only really important innovation (under Labour pressure) was the introduction of family allowances—small, noncontributory, weekly payments to low-income families for the benefit of each child beginning with the third—legislated for in 1926. In sum the conservative politicians neither diagnosed the country's economic situation as anything but an unhappy deviation from a normality which would, they expected, return in its own good time, nor did they acknowledge that any pressure was building up in the country, in spite of the difficulties experienced, in favor of extensive new experiments in welfare. And enough voters to sustain them in office obviously agreed with them. It is significant that, unlike their Australian opposite numbers, they were not discredited immediately at the onset of the Great Depression but remained in office to 1935.

When Sir Joseph Ward led the Liberals (styled the United party) to office with Labour support in 1928, the electoral bait he employed was an adventure in neo-Vogelism designed to cure the country's ills as the Liberals persisted in seeing them. His plan involved the immediate borrowing and spending of £70,000,000. The classic story about the vast figure is that Sir Joseph misread his manuscript: that the figure given there was £7,000,000. But however that may be, in essence Sir Joseph was strictly in the well-established New Zealand tradition of sustaining the national income and encouraging development and progress by external borrowing, though it was unfortunate that he proposed acting on the principle at this time. The economists by 1932 considered the prime policy error of the 1920's, of which both Reform and the Liberals were amply guilty, to be, in their language, the overcapitalization of public works. In practice Sir Joseph's spending was more modest, though hardly less traditional, than his professions on the hustings. It involved the making of government-borrowed money more freely available as advances to established farmers, the financing of land settlement, and railway construction (with some modification of priorities in favor of the South Island). This implied no revisionist thinking about the nature of the New Zealand problem. He also sought to deal with road-rail competition by coordination under government control—thus acting to protect the status quo from progress, seeking thus an escape from the insecurities of progress. And he sought to deal with the exasperating unemployment by constituting a board, provided with a special tax income, and a subsidy from general revenue which would first seek to direct the workers into rural productive industries—for example, pig and poultry raising and any new ones that might be turned up, again an unimpeachably "proper" emphasis. (Ward was as good a physiocrat as the rest of them.) Failing success at this, resort could be had to "relief works" not to be confused with *public* works but to be identified with boondoggling, and, as a final resort, subsistence payments. (New Zealand had at this time, of course, no unemployment insurance.) But there must be no "dole"— this was assessed as a corrupter of the British character. In short, Ward's program was strictly within the bounds of ideological probity. But like

Vogel, he had hold of no magic formulae that would either restore the old New Zealand or save the country from the consequences of the depression that was imminent.

Ward, who was ill and tired when he had been returned to the prime ministership, died in July 1930 at the age of seventy-four. Already in the previous May he had passed the office to G. W. Forbes. It was his unpleasant first assignment to announce that the Great Depression had arrived in New Zealand via the United Kingdom in the form of low export prices. His immediate evidence was a large deficit in the public accounts. The visitation was viewed primarily as an externally induced disaster, its origination imputed to the United States, but in common with most countries of the capitalist world, New Zealand's internal maladjustments were extensive, vexing, and proved to require unprecedented steps for their correction or moderation. Depression politics in New Zealand was to be a struggle to sustain orthodoxy against unorthodox proposals. Orthodoxy lost. The difficulties were at their most acute in the land industries, especially dairying, but in one expression or another they ramified throughout the economy. Their most conspicuous expressions, as far as wayfaring New Zealanders were concerned, were as reduced income and increased unemployment, the latter particularly concentrated in the urban areas where it had been chronic for several years. The prime victims were the farmers, caught in a squeeze between a drop of income of around 40 per cent and a decline of out-of-pocket costs of only 10 per cent, and the unemployed, who suffered a rapid pauperization under the Unemployment Board which eventually provoked them to rioting and looting in the principal business streets of Auckland and Wellington. At the worst, it was estimated that at least half the dairy farmers were insolvent and 100,000 persons were unemployed. The bottom was reached in 1932.

Having announced the budget deficit, Prime Minister Forbes proposed to deal with the situation by economies in public expenditures and increases in taxes, thus intensifying the deflation. Borrowing ceased; some debt repayment was accomplished. Public service salaries were cut; through the arbitration courts workers' wages were cut; pensions and other benefits were cut; public health services were cut. The state school budget was cut, the school entry age was raised, the leaving age was lowered, and teacher training facilities were halved. The objective was to balance the budget; it eventually was. On the other hand, every effort was made to increase the volume of exports to compensate for the great price decline. Public money was spent on grants and subsidies and remissions were made to assist the farmers to carry on at increasing production. Production, especially of butter and cheese, *did* continue to rise.

With reduced earnings in London, imports declined as they became more expensive in terms of New Zealand export commodities and demand in New Zealand shrank. An especially difficult aspect of external financial relations was managing the payment of interest on the London-held New Zealand debt (50 per cent of the total). The economists figured that "Owing to the fall in export prices, about 80 per cent more exports must be sent abroad [that is, in 1932] to pay this interest than were required in 1928." The heavy borrowing of years past—including the 1920's—thus came home to roost. Prime Minister Forbes censured Coates and the Reform party for this, even in the face of Ward's seventy million pound program. There was increasingly raucous talk in the country about the "tyranny of debt," the bondholders were regarded as pariahs, currency and credit crankiness flourished, and a suspicion arose that it was all a matter of manipulation, everything turning on who manipulated what and whom in which interest for what end. If orthodoxy manipulated to its ends, then unorthodoxy could and should manipulate to its. This had a powerful impact on politics.

By late 1930 it was apparent that the United party dared not stand alone against the rising discontent, spearheaded by Labour. To fight the election of 1931 a United-Reform coalition was arranged and the combination won. This brought J. G. Coates and W. Downie Stewart into the government. Coates was to become the exponent of a policy which in the ideological context of the cabinet was more experimental than any hitherto, while Downie Stewart strengthened the orthodox traditionalists. There was thus an orthodox-unorthodox controversy within the government as well as in the country. Downie Stewart resisted experiment as long as he could and then resigned, while Coates went on to become the strong man of the government, overshadowing even his prime minister, Forbes. He gave an amazing exhibition of backseat driving; he turned the Treasury into a Ministry of Economic Affairs, thus engrossing the central issues of politics. He was not by native disposition given to favoring unorthodox ideas, but he had a capacity to learn not only from experience but from experts. He was a remarkable man who deserves a better fate than the faint memory of him that is now all that survives. He was conventional enough to want to try to settle the unemployed on ten-acre subsistence farms to provide cheap labor for the commercial farmers, but he was also daring enough to seek and make use of the advice of economists. His weakness was that he was more of a technician of policy than an astute politician. It was too obvious that he had a strong bias in favor of the entrepreneur and he carelessly underplayed the humanitarian gambit, a very serious lapse in the New Zealand context, especially that of the time. If his experiments brought him the rancorous dislike of the conservatives, his failure to invoke and regard the humanitarian shibboleths and his patent effort to keep his schemes within the bounds of "capitalism" brought him the rancorous dislike of the "victims of the depression" and their political spokesmen, especially those who professed "socialism." Political rancor piled up to mountainous heights in New Zealand in the depression years, even more so than in the United States.

It was hoped that as the New Zealand problem was related in large part to the condition of the external market, the Ottawa conference of 1932 on trade would clarify the situation in a positive fashion. Sticking to its dogma that New Zealand's proper policy was production and more production, what New Zealand chiefly sought was guarantees that no obstacles to the free entry of its exports into the United Kingdom market should be erected. It wanted no part of British tariffs on its exports, no "levies" on them for the benefit of United Kingdom producers, no restrictive quotas. Coates was practically alone in even momentarily seeing any merit in a butter quota. The great discovery of the moment was that the United Kingdom authorities no longer considered their market "bottomless" as the New Zealanders had all along assumed to be the case and wished to continue to assume. They felt that if the new proposition was in any sense true, New Zealand should not suffer for it. If anybody had to suffer, then "out" the foreign supplier—the Argentine, the Dane —and let him suffer. Indeed the New Zealanders even argued for preferential treatment beyond all other dominions because their tariffs against British goods were the lowest of all. The *quid pro quo* would be to improve further the United Kingdom position in her markets. This, indeed, was done under "Ottawa." The New Zealanders had no fear of a "closed Empire" with themselves as primary producers in it. Rather they welcomed the idea. That Britain was involved in a world-wide trading network as well as an imperial trading system they tended to ignore. Ottawa became for the New Zealanders a source of anxiety, not of liberation from cares, and they fought with unprecedented fierceness to resist application to them of all United Kingdom restrictive proposals right up to the outbreak of war, when the questions became temporarily irrelevant. They neither saw, nor attempted to see, Britain's actual position with any accuracy. As Ottawa was the culmination of the long dominions campaign to mold United Kingdom trade policy into a shape advantageous to the dominions, so for New Zealand it became a campaign to keep it in a shape advantageous to her. The net immediate effect of the effort was to mortar New Zealand more firmly than ever before into the Imperial trading system.

The failure of Ottawa to bring a solution of the New Zealand problem within clear sight opened the way to purposeful domestic experimentation of a somewhat nationalistic caste. No clear-cut, comprehensive plan was evolved—though planning was talked—and some moves of the time reflected passion instead of brain. The farmer-politicians, for example, vented their antilabor spleen almost as openly as they had in 1913. They took out their feelings on the compulsory arbitration court. Although the court had cut wages, it was, nevertheless, regarded as an obstacle to reducing them to a low enough level to suit the conservative interests. Moreover, it was regarded as a prop of the hated unions which fought wage reductions. So in 1932 the farmer-politicians substituted a weak conciliation system for compulsory arbitration in the expectation that this would loosen the props holding up the unions and wage rates. Far more creative and astute were the measures of brain with which Coates was particularly identified. He was an early advocate of manipulating the foreign exchange rate to raise returns to farmers (in domestic currency) and to increase protection to manufacturers (by increasing prices for imports in domestic currency). At the time most New Zealanders believed they were on the gold standard as an economic consequence of Mr. Churchill in 1925 and even after the United Kingdom went off gold in 1931; they were and had always been on a *sterling* standard, but this was not recognized legally until 1933. Parity of the New Zealand pound with the sterling pound was the conservative desideratum. Determination of the exchange rate was, however, not in the hands of the government but of the trading banks; there was no central bank; the government played no direct role in monetary policy; the treasurer normally deferred abjectly to the banks. In 1931 the banks had been forced to set a rate of £110 NZ to £100 sterling, but all proper-minded people knew this was by force of circumstances and return to par was desired. Early in 1932 Coates, with the support of most economists, some farmers, and some manufacturers, began a campaign to change the exchange rate to £125 NZ to £100 sterling. At that time Coates held a subordinate position in the cabinet. Downie Stewart, as treasurer and decision-maker on the point, opposed the Coates proposal both because he believed the proper line was to return the exchange to par and because he thought the question should be decided by the banks, not the government. However, after a year of argument he lost the game, resigned office, and Coates became treasurer. The new rate was brought into force.

Coates wanted control of credit and currency policy placed in the hands of a New Zealand board of directors. Up to this time there were six note-issuing banks operating in New Zealand, only one of which was controlled by a New Zealand board. Four of the banks were Australian-controlled institutions and one had its head office in London and did a great deal of business in Australia. The single New Zealand-controlled bank was the old Bank of New Zealand which had been, since the 1890's, partially government-owned and had a majority of government-appointed directors. The banks, including the Bank of New Zealand, tended to stand together against the government. They did not have, however, a conscious credit and currency policy in the modern sense, but rather governed their actions by the movement of their London funds as they were generated by private and public transactions. However, the banks did not know precisely the New Zealand constituent of the London funds because the Australian-controlled banks mixed together their Australian and New Zealand funds. This had the effect of making New Zealand subject in this field to the fluctuations of the Australian economy, by far the larger economy of the two. The trading banks were not in the least prepared to take directions or even suggestions from the government, not even the Bank of New Zealand. Indeed, most of the banks *opposed* government policy: they opposed Coates's adjustment of the exchange rate; they opposed efforts to reduce interest rates; they opposed the idea of a reserve bank. The government-appointed directors of the Bank of New Zealand associated themselves with this opposition, so little did they regard the Bank as a government institution. But in 1933 Coates had a Reserve Bank established. It was designed to facilitate the government's banking business and cheapen it and private borrowing by lower interest rates, to monopolize the note issue, hitherto in the hands of the six trading banks, and to deal with foreign exchange and direct monetary policy.

Coates also saw to it that final steps were taken toward the elimination of overcapitalization of farming by reducing the principle and interest of mortgages, this to be carried out by a statutory body. The interference with contractual rights involved alarmed the conservatives, but it was but the logical conclusion of developments initiated by the private "compositions" used quite freely in Canterbury and elsewhere, beginning in 1931. Coates also established a National Mortgage Corporation which was to lend at the lowered interest rates but on strictly business principles.

The state thus appeared to be taking a great deal of power over the economy, but Coates offset this by arranging that both the new financial institutions have large private stockholdings and that neither be subservient to the government's ideas of policy. Additionally with regard to the Mortgage Corporation he arranged that it borrow the money for lending on its own security—not, as had been the case with the old State Advances Corporation, have access to money borrowed by the government. In this period of Coates's dominance, more authority over their industries was given to the marketing boards; they became more markedly producers' syndicates than ever. An abortive attempt was made to coordinate them under a super-board.

Coates operated in an increasingly favorable economic climate. Prices of wool and meat rose in 1934. Unemployment declined a little. But a rise in the price of butter and cheese—a kind of *sine qua non* for economic health in New Zealand—was delayed until 1936. The delay had political consequences hardly less fateful than Coates's failure to pay enough heed to the fact that the conservative program had been too consistently deflationary. When to this was added the already noted flaw of the neglect of the humanitarian emphasis and the tactical mistake of failing to supply the palaver necessary to salve injured orthodox feelings, the stage was set for Coates and his associates to suffer a political defeat at the polls just when it was clear that recovery had begun. The conservative collapse—and it was a collapse—was a political disaster, not an economic failure.

Labour's victory in the election of December 1935 was the reward for two decades of political skirmishing and a consequence of an adjustment of policy to New Zealand realities. In the face of considerable unpopularity generated by its wartime activities, its bitter criticism of the Versailles Treaty which was equated by the newspapers with disloyalty to Britain, and its firm allegiance to a rather vague but dogmatic socialism, it nevertheless in 1919 was able to win eight seats in the House and in 1922 to increase its representation to seventeen. This was, however, its apogee as an avowedly radical socialist party as it was also the year of its largest party membership and biggest income. In 1925, when Coates and Reform had their great vote-getting success, Labour's representation was reduced to twelve seats. This is commonly taken as the year in which Labour began to shift its ideological stance and to try to square an eclectic left liberalism with the political possibilities. The job was eventually done without official abandonment of the socialist objective—this did not come for many years after—but by adopting the established Australian tactic of placing the propaganda emphasis on the successive electoral programs and the stands taken on specific issues in Parliament. Though this development at first reduced the party membership and income, it eventually paid off politically. In 1928, even with the strong Liberal tide running, Labour won nineteen seats and in 1931, though battling a coalition of conservative parties, it gained twenty-four seats and commanded 34 per cent of the votes cast.

In one aspect this shift of Labour party outlook was a movement from left to right, the process forcing the party leftists either out of the party altogether or to adjust their personal views to the new line. It was a line involving loyalty to the arbitration court system, social reform through parliamentary action, and no disruptive assault on capitalism. The aim was to humanize capitalism by changing the social context and socially redistributing the fruits of the capitalist system of production. In 1921 a Communist party had been formed, its original membership recruited from various Marxist "study clubs" established earlier by the expected mixture of manual and white-collar workers and intellectuals, which then began a career marked, as elsewhere, by a waxing and waning of influence in response to developments in Soviet Russia and in the international and domestic arenas, and the coming and going of personnel as this particular "god" failed them. Although the communists asked several times in the middle 1920's for formal admission to the Labour party, their applications were rejected. The incompatibility of dogmatic Soviet-directed Marxism and Labour's developing liberal heterodoxy was too obvious to be obscured by tactics. Communists, however, found their places in the leftist trade unions, especially as the 1930's wore on, and concealing their party membership, sometimes won places as union delegates to Labour conferences. However, they had no obvious influence on party policy. In addition the Labour party also combatted the communists by forbidding its members to join or associate with communist front organizations. Insofar as the communists gained any significant power, it was in a few—often important—trade unions and as spokesmen for a variety of leftist opinion taken seriously by more intellectuals than ever actually joined the party, especially at the depth of the Great Depression and during World War II. The non-communist left within the Labour party had a thin time of it too because its natural leaders—men like Harry Holland, Michael Savage, and Peter Fraser—were effective agents of the rightward drift, while a man like Walter Nash, an English immigrant of 1909 and a small-business man, influential in the party from 1919, was always of the right, deriving his basic outlook, it has been suggested, perhaps ironically, more from Richard Hooker's sixteenth-century *Ecclesiastical Polity* than from even the most dilute Marxism. The arrival of the party in power, significantly enough, led to the only spectacular and open right-left split in party history, as we shall see. What set going the rightward drift was, very apparently, political ambition. By 1925–28 it was obvious that while Labour had a distance still to go in engrossing the vote of the urban workers, manual and white-collar, even if this were accomplished it would leave the party short of the goal of office and power through electoral victory. It would concentrate Labour voting power in too few electorates. In the New Zealand context it was therefore necessary somehow to win over enough small-town and farmer voters to take some rural seats, especially in the North Island dairy districts, The fundamental problem was to disaffect the farmers from the Reform party, by now obviously Labour's principal opponent. This could be done either by devising attractive policy-bait, or by awaiting adverse economic developments. In the end it was done by a combination of the two. On the policy front the experimentation was fairly cautious as long as Harry Holland was alive and the party parliamentary leader; he himself never really abandoned the socialist objective but signified a kind of resignation to its de-emphasis by concentrating on criticism of the details of conservative policy; but when Holland died in 1933 and Michael Savage was elected parliamentary leader, with Peter Fraser as his deputy, and Walter Nash a conspicuous policy-maker, the pace of change was stepped up. The currents of thought that influenced the party leaders have never been precisely and exactly identified, but among the strong possibilities mentioned are the teachings of W.E.A. lecturers, Roosevelt's New Deal, the British Labour party, the British Fabian Society, the writings of John Maynard Keynes, the various financial heterodoxies that flourished at the time including Douglas Credit, and J. G. Coates insofar as he was regarded as moving in the right direction in certain respects (though not far enough in any). Particularly important was a firm conviction of their ability to use state power to control and direct economic forces; they were ardent partisans of the state-directed economy. But when Michael Savage chose an exemplary figure of New Zealand politics with whom to associate himself and his party, it was Richard Seddon. Draping the capacious mantle of Seddon about himself, Savage made it clear that Labour was the party of the Seddonian "humanities." He thus struck with a great clang precisely the note the conservatives, including the unlucky Coates, had so ill-advisedly neglected.

In 1935 the party objective was "to utilise to the maximum degree the wonderful resources of the Dominion. First: For the purpose of restoring a decent living standard to those who have been deprived of essentials for the past five years. Second: To organize an internal economy that will distribute the production and services in a way that will guarantee to every person able and willing to work an income sufficient to provide him and his dependents with everything necessary to make a 'home' and 'home life' in the best sense of the meaning of those terms." This was a characteristic example of that de-emphasis of hard socialism in favor of warm sentiment that was the particular contribution of Savage to the party's approach to the voters. On the foundation of his own personality he projected an image of party-leader-as-father-of-his-people. However, the party did have a program for restoring internal prosperity largely by the distribution of purchasing power and for "insulating" the internal economy from adverse external influences, of which the elements had an appeal not only to the wage workers but also to the still depressed entrepreneurial dairy farmers, the whole intricately involving the handling of finance—the magic word was "credit"—a great extension of the state's economic powers, and a heavier emphasis on the socialization of the fruits of production than of the *means* of production. The great virtue of the program, insofar as it was apprehended or apprehendable by the electorate, was that there appeared to be something in it for everybody and nobody was going to be hurt, except those who deserved to be hurt. It was a laboristic program, but national as opposed to sectional in its emphasis. To help Labour's cause along at the election a new right-wing party appeared, the Democrat party, built of the resentments Coates had inspired among the conservatives by his experiments, not strong enough to win any seats but yet strong enough to help give Labour an edge in three-way contests. It insured that Labour should win a sweeping victory in terms of seats with a minority (47.3 per cent) of the votes. But Labour's victory was nevertheless its own in the sense that there was a strong voting tide in its favor, strongest precisely where it was needed most. Whereas the Labour vote rose 27 per cent in the cities, it rose 45 per cent in rural electorates and 69 per cent in country towns. Labour took fifty-three of the seventy-six pakeha seats and two of the four Maori seats. It brought to cabinet office a surprising number of men of the old Red Fed, much subdued in emotions and ideas, who had survived the chances and changes of the years: Michael Savage, Peter Fraser, Robert Semple, P. C. Webb, all but Fraser of Australian origin. Prime minister and leader was Michael Savage, "Mick" Savage, a politician who won and held the affection of the electorate. When he died in office in 1940, there was such an outburst of mass grief that any notion that the New Zealanders were a stolid people was destroyed forever. His successor as prime minister was Peter Fraser, a far more austere man, widely admired but not regarded affectionately, in manner a foxygrandpa, a very clever politician and a good fist at true statesmanship. Third member of the top trinity was Walter Nash, treasurer (more accurately minister for Economic Affairs) under Savage and then Fraser, to become after Fraser's death party leader and in the end prime minister in his own right. Highly capable with the manner of a very senior clerk, far less colorful than either Savage or Fraser, a gray eminence but nevertheless "good old Walter," it was his misfortune to become leader when the party entered the ideological doldrums in the 1950's.

The Labour government took office on December 6, 1935, destined for a life of fourteen years, not leaving office until December 12, 1949. It therefore spanned World War II and dealt with both the internal and external adjustments the war made necessary. However, Labour reached the peak of its popularity, as measured at the polls, in 1938 when, although it won no more than the fifty-three seats of 1935, it gathered in 55.9 per cent of the votes. Although it never repeated this astonishing performance, it did gain 51.4 per cent (but only forty-two seats) in 1946, after having been down to 47.4 per cent in 1943. In 1949 it went out of office with thirty-four seats and 47.1 per cent of the votes. It was during the four prewar years that it established its basic program.

Labour proceeded to bring its program into force with such vigor once it was in office that it is difficult to establish a topical sequence, especially since everything it did was intertwined with everything else. Its initial emphasis was on the restoration of purchasing power, the establishment of a "consumption economy." It began by granting a "Christmas bonus" to the unemployed. It then proceeded to restore wage scales to predepression levels, as Coates had timidly begun to do, to step up public works and substitute standard wages for relief scales, and to increase the pensions and other benefits of those suffering from the assorted disabilities then covered by legislation. Apart from a public works program, which involved expenditure on railways, roads, electricity schemes, public buildings, and land clearance, it initiated a separate program of building houses for rent at low rates and lent money at low rates to private builders. A feature of this resumption of works was the free importation and use of modern mechanical aids. The primary and secondary schools and the libraries were given creative attention. Public investment rose sharply. While unemployment declined it had not been eliminated by 1939 and the outbreak of war, but with declining numbers on the rolls, expenditure on their relief steadily mounted. To fortify the position of the workers, Labour restored the powers of the compulsory arbitration court, put into effect a five-day forty-hour week in all occupations where it was at all feasible, established a basic wage, extended coverage of the court to workers in the land industries, and instituted compulsory unionism in all cases where an award of the court applied. Further to strengthen the position of the compulsorily enlarged unions—if compulsory unionism was a strengthening and not an intensification of dependence on the court—a new central organization was formed, a Federation of Labour, taking in about seven out of ten union members. As a sop to the union leftists, the Federation's objectives included socialization of the means of production. To direct this powerful central organization Finian P. Walsh, an ebullient character, master of the raucous threat who in the 1920's had been into and almost immediately out of the Communist party, was chosen. Walsh became, by virtue of his position, a great influence in government counsels, notably during the war when Fraser was prime minister.

To deal with the problems of the primary producers, especially the difficulties of the dairy farmers as currently the most troublesome, Labour instituted a policy of price guarantees and compulsory acquisition and vending of the export produce by the government. As set out in the Primary Products Marketing Act of 1936, the rationale of the policies was: *"Title:* An Act to make better provision for the marketing of dairy-produce and other primary products so as to ensure for producers an adequate remuneration for the services rendered by them to the community." *"Preamble:* Whereas it is considered essential in the public interest that producers of primary products should, as far as possible, be protected from the effects of fluctuations in market prices thereof; and whereas it is thought that the most effective and appropriate way of affording such protection, as far as related to primary products intended for export, is to provide that the Government, on behalf of the Crown, shall acquire ownership of such products at prices to be fixed and promulgated from time to time, and, so far as relates to primary products intended for consumption in New Zealand, is to empower the Government in its discretion either to acquire the ownership thereof at fixed prices or to control the sale and distribution thereof. . . . ." (The next year the government took control of internal marketing.) Specifically with regard to price the Act provided that it should "be such that any efficient producer engaged in the dairy industry under usual conditions should be assured of a sufficient net return from his business to enable him to maintain himself and his family in a reasonable state of comfort." These quoted passages contain significant statements of Labour ideology of the time, notably the propositions that capitalist enterprisers of a defined worthiness—that is, those who render a service to the community— should command support and assistance from the government; that it was the government's duty to protect the worthy producers qua producers from the adverse effects of the trade cycle; and that in doing so the government should guarantee them a rather vaguely defined but presumably high standard of living—all this a long way from socializing the means of production. But there was a price for the producers to pay. The marketing function which the farmers in their flight from the free market had passed to boards of their own constitution was passed by Labour to a cabinet minister. Distinguishing features of the Labour government were its willingness to take on onerous responsibilities on the one hand and its conviction that cabinet ministers were the proper people to "run" the nation's affairs on the other. This transfer of administrative functions into the hands of ministers applied not only in such a case as marketing butter and cheese, but to the running of the railways, the direction of broadcasting, the control of policy in secondary industry, the determination of monetary policy. It was *étatism* far beyond the wildest dreams of the Seddonian Liberals.

While Labour was deeply concerned to make primary production re-munerative, it recognized more clearly than its predecessors that manu-facturing had to be further developed if the increasing population was to be fully employed—all the more so if there was ever to be a revival of immigration—and self-sufficiency promoted. At its worst the de-pression had reduced employment in industry and had led to the collapse of a good many enterprises, but manufacturing showed itself resilient in the face of improving opportunities, probably at a higher level of effi-ciency and with some diversification of product. However, the basic structure changed little prior to the outbreak of war; the most notable small change was a slightly increased emphasis on metal-working and engineering. The conservatives had considered legislation with regard to industry and the manufacturers had put suggestions before the govern-ment. When Labour came to legislate on the matter, its shibboleth was "efficiency," but its methods were coordination and rationalization, either by legislatively ratified private schemes or schemes imposed by a min-ister. To control overcapacity, or the threat of it, Labour resorted to licensing to prevent establishment of new, potentially redundant plants. In Labour's hands the licensing technique was that principally used until the outbreak of war and it applied it not only to industry but to retail distribution. It made it possible for manufacturers to borrow from the State Advances Corporation to finance expansion—e.g., to purchase machinery in *Britain.*

Just before the election of 1938 Labour introduced its social security system and established New Zealand's claim to leadership in what be-came a world-wide movement toward the welfare state. This involved not only the confirmation of Labour's policy of liberalization of "benefits," as cash and other allowances now became known, the filling up of gaps in areas already partially covered and the liberalizing of the accessibility of benefits, but a frontal invasion of new fields such as the medical, pharmaceutical, and hospital. The heads of the 1938 legislation gave a conspectus of the proposed coverage: superannuation, age, widowhood, orphanhood, family, invalid, miners', temporary incapacity (sickness, accident), unemployment, Maori War, emergency, medical, pharmaceu-tical, hospital, maternity, and "supplementary." To finance the scheme, provision was made for putting it on a contributory basis by levying a

Social Security Contribution (or tax) of 5 per cent on all salaries, wages, and other income, together with registration fees of five shillings annually for juniors and women and £ 1 for males over twenty-one, but the funds accumulated were to be regularly added to by grants from the Consolidated Fund (or general revenue fund), this being required because while contributions were on the basis of *means* the benefits received were to be on the basis of *needs*—hence the impossibility of achieving self-support. A new department of government was set up to administer the scheme, the Department of Social Security. The Act came into operation on April 1, 1939. In 1940 the system was absorbing for cash and other benefits 5.8 per cent of the national income while a decade later it was absorbing 11.2 per cent; in 1940 the scheme accounted for 20.1 per cent of all governmental expenditures and in 1949 it was 27.3 per cent. The basic approach was, in harmony with Labour's outlook, paternalistic, with an emphasis on sustaining consumption, encouraging reliance upon the state, and weakening the vital impulse to self-reliance, an aspect eventually criticized by such an ardent exponent of the welfare state as Sir William Beveridge, but the program was, as Prime Minister Savage was well aware, of great appeal to the electorate. The result of the election of 1938 ratified his insight into the mind of the wayfaring New Zealander, always more accessible to humanitarian sentiment than to sociological or economic appeals. The only curb to exploitation of the system was a "means test," reluctantly and unevenly applied—and progressively to be removed.

The social security scheme was legislated and the ensuing general election was fought as a financial crisis unfolded. Labour's changes in the financial structure of the country were essentially designed to eliminate the influence of private capitalists on basic policy and to transfer direction to the government. Finance, in a sense, was to be a substitute for socialization of the means of production. The private stockholders in Coates's Reserve Bank were bought out at market prices, insuring them a tidy profit by the appreciation of share values, making the institution wholly government owned. In two steps policy-making was passed from the Bank's officials to the minister of Finance (Mr. Nash). (On the other hand, Labour did not disturb the status of the semigovernmental trading bank, the Bank of New Zealand.) One purpose of this change in the status of the Reserve Bank was to make it a ready source of credit for government operations such as guaranteed prices, housing and public works, loan money for the use of state lending agencies, and other government activities. At the same time Coates's Mortgage Corporation was also taken entirely into government ownership, its name changed back to State Advances Corporation, its loan money to be derived from the Reserve Bank, with basic policy-making in the hands of the minister of Finance.

This was putting enormous power into the hands of the finance minister, but in the eyes of Labour's left-wing, personified by John A. Lee, parliamentary undersecretary for Housing in the Ministry of Finance, the minister of Finance was far too cautious an innovator in policy to be tolerable, particularly as to the use of credit. Mr. Nash feared inflation, Mr. Lee did not. Out of this difference came a left-right conflict within the Labour party and government. Lee was a veteran of World War I in which he had lost an arm. He was a fluent and prolific journalist, a pamphleteer and novelist, a man with an active, agile mind. He had been in Parliament since 1931. Self-designated a socialist, his definition of socialism was rather elastic; he was really utopian—he once expounded how New Zealand could be renovated on the basis of electricity and plastics—and an anticapitalist credit crank. Lee finally got into trouble by an oblique attack on Savage for retaining his power while ill and then refusing to accept censorship of his utterances by the party hierarchy. In 1940 he was expelled from the party, reverted to political journalism, tried to establish a party of his own, failed at the polls, and lapsed into silence, earning his living as a bookseller. In spite of this triumph of Labour "responsibility" over leftist "irresponsibility," troubles multiplied. Although when Labour arrived in office at the end of 1935 it had found that Coates had accumulated a very substantial sterling balance in London, and although prices for exports were good in 1936 and 1937, insuring a satisfactory income, the expansionist spending policies of Labour stimulated imports both on government and private account. This decreased the sterling balance precipitately, especially when prices fell in 1938 and 1939. At the same time the country experienced a "flight of capital" as money held in New Zealand was transferred to London (and Australia) when it became apparent that Labour was not going to redeem its campaign promise to return the pound to par. (At the same time there was a run on the Post Office savings bank, but that is a different matter, though illustrating a panic atmosphere in the country; the situation was saved by putting Reserve Bank credit behind the savings bank.) Finally there was the unlucky fact, all the more calamitous in the then existing circumstances, that a little over £17,000,000 sterling of London loans would be due on January 1, 1940. This very difficult situation was not only exploited politically by the conservatives during the 1938 campaign, but they also carried on a vigorous antigovernment campaign in London in an effort to have the minister of Finance renounce his heresies as the price of London's assistance in solving his difficulties. Whether because of this campaign, or because of London's then regnant political and financial conservatism, the minister had to accept a rather hard solution. He obtained a loan almost covering the £17,000,000, but had to promise to pay it back in installments over five years; he was allowed to institute exchange control and import selection only after promising the United Kingdom government that he would not use either to promote domestic industry to the permanent compromising of the interests of British exporters to New Zealand.

Thus by the outbreak of war New Zealand Labour had voluntarily or perforce adopted all the elements of what was eventually considered to be its policy of insulation and economic stability: compensatory domestic expenditures to counter drops in income caused by external price declines, guaranteed prices, exchange and import control and the promotion of economic balance and self-sufficiency by industrial expansion. Whether the policies were in all respects compatible with productive efficiency and economic growth was not then asked, for Labour was trying to accommodate to what Paul Valéry called a "finished world."

Whereas the Australians, beginning in the 1880's and 1890's, were able to hack away at the colonial crust and let in local air for some expression of the nationalistic impulse in painting and writing—though they were subsequently to coast a dangerously long time on the "tradition" then established—the New Zealanders were slower to find a national expression in either field. Indeed, they have regarded themselves as at their weakest in the visual arts—more so in architecture than in painting—especially since the best artists tended to expatriate themselves, long after they have felt able to take an aggressive stance with regard to their literature. However, as late as 1947 it was the verdict of a New Zealand writer in an astringent essay that "The amount of significant work [in the arts] by New Zealanders is small indeed, and its influence on the life of a Philistine community has been slight." Like their Australian opposite numbers, to whose company New Zealanders have nevertheless from time to time expatriated themselves, New Zealand producers of aesthetic products have consistently regarded themselves as odd men out whose audience was miniscule. The truly popular heroes have been sportsmen. Mountaineers could hope to gain general esteem; mountaineers of the spirit could not count on doing so.

The period 1890–1930 has been expertly assessed as particularly arid in the sense that little fructifying water welled up from native springs. It was as though the oppressive weight of what was symbolized by Home had lowered the spiritual water-table in New Zealand. The country was, of course, copiously irrigated by *English* books (and English editions of non-British books). New Zealand supported a very lively book trade and per capita consumption of imported books was remarkably high even as the expected sale of a domestically produced book—by Whitcombe & Tombs or Reed—was 500 copies for a prose work, fewer copies still of poetry. The great majority of the books of New Zealand origin and relevance were published in England.

It was characteristic that in 1921 there appeared *in Scotland* the first edition—there were two subsequently, both with expanded texts—of what was to be hailed as a New Zealand classic, *Tutira: The Story of a New Zealand Sheep Station* by H. Guthrie-Smith. In its final form it was to become a vast book of 444 large pages, a remarkably meticulous, faithfully studied, observed, and recorded account of the evolution of a station, including its geological foundations and geomorphological changes, from the arrival of the Maoris on the site through its successive fortunes in the hands of European occupants, told in terms of the land, the vegetation, the native and economic animals, the birds, the impact of economic and political forces—everything integrated around the history of this particular plot of New Zealand earth. But was it the summing up of "Europe" in New Zealand, or did it record the beginnings of New Zealand? Was it the analogue of Gilbert White's *The Natural History and Antiquities of Selborne,* with which in their passion for identification with the source, New Zealanders compared it, or was it something *sui generis* to New Zealand? Preferably the latter, perhaps unluckily the former. The ambiguity of the evaluation was fundamental.

Before World War I an immigrant Englishman named William Satchell (1860–1942) had tried manfully to domesticate the novel in New Zealand. He produced five between 1902, by which time he had spent sixteen years in the country, and 1914 when he lapsed into silence. While there is dispute about which is the best, two by virtue of revival at a later and literarily more alert time are commonly cited, *The Land of the Lost* (orig. pub. 1902, reprinted 1938) and even more frequently, *The Greenstone Door* (orig. pub. 1914, reprinted 1935), the former a Hardy-esque study in "circumstances," the latter the most popular of the novels of historic Maori life, its only competitor being F. O. V. Acheson's *Plume of the Arawas* (1930). As Satchell wrote several novels to achieve belated recognition for two, after the war Jane Mander (1871–1949) wrote four, best remembered of which is her first, *The Story of a New Zealand River* (1920). In the short story, the pattern of excellence was, of course, set by Katherine Mansfield in expatriation, but a domestic product—artless, homespun—was produced by B[lanche] E. Baugham (1870–1958) in *Brown Bread from a Colonial Oven* (1912) and by Alice Webb (1876—) in *Miss Peter's Special* (1926). The eyes of these writers were mostly on New Zealand, or a small segment of it, and this, rather than literary skill, was often seen as their merit. They carried over from the reportage of earlier times a keen concern with the Maoris with whom New Zealand artists—both literary and pictorial—have consistently been concerned to make their peace. Indeed, fiction writers have reputations based largely upon their relative success in depicting Maoris as, for example, Alfred A. Grace (1867–1942), author of *Tales of a Dying Race* (1901), and William Baucke (1848–1931), author of *Where the White Man Treads* (1905). There was, too, a theme which recurred with frequency: the contrary pulls of Home and New Zealand; it was dealt with by Satchell, by Mander, by short story writers, and by a didactic novelist of an earlier day, Edith Grossmann (1863–1931), who can properly be placed here since her last novel, *The Heart of the Bush* (1910), was devoted to it. In 1927 the journalist and general writer Alan Mulgan summed up the pull of Home in a book called, simply and precisely, *Home*. He neither sought to nor succeeded in exorcising this compelling place.

And then, by one of those conjunctions of circumstances so difficult to explain, New Zealand writers found their feet in the depression years of the 1930's. Why in a time when "economics" was regnant the poets— for it was the poets who were dominant—should have been stimulated to expression is impossible to say, even taking account of the fact that one of their motivations was to protest the destructive vagaries of capitalist economics. However, it was not social protest, either Marxist or non-Marxist, that gave the work literary significance, however it influenced its earlier substance. Rather, it appears to have been, at least at first, the effort to see the New Zealand earth plain, to reconcile New Zealand landscape and man alone in this remote place, to find a humanizing frame of reference for this landscape, and to derive poetry from the New Zealand "reality" conceived largely in geographical terms—"a response to the land rather than to the people," though not in traditional "nature poetry." A more subjective poetry rooted in personal psychology came later. It was an anti-Romantic, anti-Victorian, anti-Georgian poetry, but the prestige of Home was not so much diminished and displaced as put into a different perspective, and for the rejected models Eliot, Pound, Yeats, and Auden were substituted, not to be nostalgically echoed but to be set to work on the New Zealand problem. One of the poets identified with this time, R. A. K. Mason (1905—), began in the 1920's, uncertain of his way—the *characteristic* poet of the 1920's was Eileen Duggan—and with him were associated A. R. D. Fairburn (1904–57), Allen Curnow (1911—), and Denis Glover (1912—). The centers of literary activity were Auckland and Christchurch, with Christchurch the home of a wonderfully creative publishing house, Caxton Press, headed by Glover. Probably the most significant books of the time were Fairburn's *Dominion* (1938), in which a social protest with many echoes of the "debt slavery" sort of thing was dominant, and Curnow's *Not in Narrow Seas* (1939) in which "the land" was the integrating concern: "In your atlas two islands not in narrow seas/ Like a child's kite anchored in the indifferent blue,/ Two islands pointing from the Pole, upward/ From the Ross Sea and the tall havenless ice . . ."

Looking back for New Zealand ancestors these poets reappraised the poetry of their predecessors and, while finding a poem here and there —as in the verse of Pember Reeves or B. E. Baugham—found most to please them in the poetry of Mary Ursula Bethell (1874–1945), with its concern with the Canterbury earth and reconciliation to it. They adopted the prickly eccentric expatriate D'Arcy Cresswell (1896–1960), partisan of an impossible ideal in a drab and real world. And they inevitably attempted not only to assimilate Maori poetry as such to their tradition but also to reassess for adequacy earlier attempts to borrow Maori imagery and themes, paralleling the tendency of the younger historians to begin the New Zealand story with the arrival of the Maoris in the islands.

While the poets dominated the scene, the fiction writers were not wholly idle. None—indeed no writer—achieved greater prestige than Frank Sargeson (1903—), who, in *A Man and His Wife* (1940), established himself as the most important storyteller in the country. In the novel none surpassed John Mulgan (1911–45), author of *Man Alone* (1939), the very title of which became a "symbol" in New Zealand writing. And fiction-as-propaganda had its exponent in John A. Lee, perhaps best represented by his *Children of the Poor* (1934), an angry study of the lower depths. Sargeson learned a great deal from Sherwood Anderson, Mulgan from Ernest Hemingway, John A. Lee from Upton Sinclair, but why America should have had so strong a literary influence in New Zealand at this time is obscure. A. D. R. Fairburn once used Huck Finn to beat the long-favored image of Tom Brown. Writing at this time, too, was Robin Hyde (1906–39), who is perhaps best represented by a fictionalized biography of Baron de Thierry, *Check to Your King* (1936), which exhibits a kind of fussy, feminine insight into the character of a male eccentric.

And a rationalization of the effort to bring New Zealand to literary expression was provided by M. H. Holcroft in *The Deepening Stream* (1940), a ruminative essay, sometimes turgid, sometimes pretentious, very often brilliant in its insights, subtitled "Cultural Influences in New Zealand."

CHAPTER VIII

A Small Nation in the Pacific

The Massey view of imperial relations, rationalized by Sir John Salmon in 1922, effectively ruled the New Zealand politicians as long as the conservatives were in office. On the one hand this came to mean that New Zealand was passive during the intra-imperial discussions of the questions of dominion status that were finally epitomized in the Balfour formula and given legal shape in the Statute of Westminster 1931 and, on the other hand, that New Zealand did not assert itself on foreign policy. The failure of the London authorities to work out any completely satisfactory machinery for consultation on foreign policy troubled the New Zealand conservatives only a little; and they were not upset at all when confronted with *faits accomplis* such as Chanak. In the early 1920's they excused their quiescence on the grounds of lack of knowledge and experience in the foreign political field; or, as a Labour parliamentarian put it, they gloried in their insufficiency. In 1926, however, J. G. Coates felt it wise to form a small staff in the prime minister's Department to study and advise on the issues that came up, with particular attention to Pacific Basin questions. This illustrated both the percipience of Coates and his firmer conviction that New Zealand should form her own opinions, especially in matters involving her "interests." And in the 1930's Prime Minister Forbes was sharply rebuked by the press for an unusually inept statement of quiescence in imperial foreign political actions. In general, though, as the tenor of Forbes's indiscretion illustrated, the conservatives of both parties maintained a strong faith in the discernment of those assigned in the United Kingdom to deal with foreign affairs. This was especially true when the conservatives were in power. What was good for the United Kingdom, they believed, was good for New Zealand. They were less comfortable when Labour took office in Britain. However, they showed little spirit about arguing foreign policy with Labour—they saved their complaints for the conservative opposition.

What the New Zealand conservatives were prepared to argue with *any* United Kingdom administration were defense (e.g., Singapore) and intra-imperial economic policy (e.g., the questions that arose at Ottawa). There was little disposition in any connection to let the general public in on disagreements or disquiets. Little or no effort was made to take a hand in the formation of public opinion in New Zealand or openly to take account of any critical discussion of foreign affairs by editorializing newspapermen or interested intellectuals, academic or lay, which constituted about all the public opinion there was.

When Labour came to power in 1935 it began to change all that, but not obviously in response to public demand. Labour won office on its proposals for domestic reform, not on its foreign policy ideas. It had, however, contacts with the informed intellectuals; its most conspicuous liaison man was Walter Nash; notably with the intellectuals associated with the New Zealand Institute of International Affairs, founded in 1934, and the New Zealand branch of the Institute of Pacific Relations, founded in the 1920's. It was, however, slow to make "machinery" changes. In accordance with New Zealand's conception of its constitutional position, communication with the United Kingdom government was via the governor-general; no United Kingdom high commissioner was received until 1939. Labour, however, did not like having a flow of information passed off as consultation. It had ideas about foreign policy and the will to give them *public* extra-imperial expression, even when they clashed with imperial policy as expressed by London. Their chosen forum was the League of Nations, but Prime Minister Savage put a strong case for the positions at the Imperial Conference of 1937. Sophisticated Britons found them naive; to one Mr. Savage suggested a character by colonial socialism out of Rousseau. It is interesting that New Zealand Labour's willingness to express forthrightly its own particular views in the international forum to which it had access by right was unaccompanied by any interest in the question of status. Mr. Savage was as uninterested in this as Mr. Massey. At the League, New Zealand's principal spokesman was W. J. Jordan who was also her high commissioner at London where, earlier in life, he had been a newspaperman. Jordan's statement of the New Zealand Labour viewpoint brought him the wondering attention of the whole world and advertised as rarely before the contribution to international discussion that could be made by a small country. Labour's "line" involved two stances which in its view reciprocally sustained each other: ardent support for what it took to be the fundamental positive ideas of the League, notably collective security; and assertion that the best way to eliminate war from the world was to extend to every nation and people the laboristic welfare emphasis (or the "socialist" emphasis) in public policy as undercutting the unrest and aggressiveness believed to arise from material poverty and insecurity. These two ideas, variously represented, were the fundamentals of New Zealand Labour policy not only in the prewar years but through the ensuing war and into the postwar period. However, as the relations of the powers deteriorated in 1938–39 and the impossibility of expecting any longer that conversions could be made to the New Zealand outlook became manifest, the Labour government without signifiying its acceptance of the Chamberlain policy of appeasement, or any specific settlement like Munich, acquiesced in the patent fact that New Zealand would have to go where the United Kingdom led. It became discreetly silent. And when war came it was as securely there as if the conservatives had ruled all along. Prime Minister Savage declared: "Both with gratitude for the past and with confidence in the future, we range ourselves without fear beside Britain. Where she goes, we go, where she stands, we stand. We are only a small and young nation, but we are one and all a band of brothers, and we march forward with a union of hearts and wills to a common destiny." An ineluctable necessity was thus made to appear a free choice.

An integral part of Massey's view of imperial relations was his conviction that the Royal Navy was the bulwark of the Empire and hence of New Zealand. He put the Royal Navy before the League of Nations or any treaty that might be worked out. Although he looked approvingly on the Washington treaties of 1922—after all, Britain had accepted them—he seems not to have pondered what they implicitly admitted with regard to the relative decline of the Royal Navy and particularly as a force in the Pacific Basin where it counted for most to New Zealand. Or if he did he was soon able to compensate for his perception by giving strong support to the building of a great base at Singapore. He was still prime minister when in 1924 the New Zealand Parliament approved the Singapore project, proposed at the Imperial Conference of the previous year; and Parliament was acting in his spirit when in 1927, under his successor J. G. Coates, it voted to contribute £1,000,000 to the cost of the base. The money, paid over ten years, was one of the few expenditures not pruned or postponed by the conservatives during the Great Depression.

New Zealand's defense problem, when it began to be considered seriously in the middle 1930's, was considerably complicated by uncertainty about what it was to prepare to defend itself against. It accepted as basic the imperial position that it was its duty to provide for its domestic defense. It was also axiomatic that since it relied heavily on benefitting from imperial defense it should contribute to imperial defense. It was just possible, as some argued, that its close imperial association, political and in trade, the latter giving a strong interest in the protection of the trade routes New Zealand-United Kingdom, intensified rather than moderated the domestic risks it ran as a small, isolated island in the Pacific of low self-defense potential. With regard to both aspects of defense—domestic and imperial—how should it order its relations with its neighbor Australia? But in any case, who was New Zealand's "enemy" against whom defense should be provided; what kind of war, involving the British countries, was likely to occur in the predictable future, and what shape was New Zealand's participation in it likely to take?

Since New Zealand saw Europe through British eyes and kicked little against the pricks this involved, speculation about a future war focused on the possibility of war arising out of the European situation, in which the United Kingdom would be a primary participant. What role should New Zealand expect to play in such a war: one patterned on its role in the 1914–18 war, or something different? There was a possible complication which would condition defense in both its aspects, domestic and imperial—the role of Japan, in World War I a friendly ally. The reactions of the New Zealanders to the alarums raised by the actions of the Japanese were much milder than the reactions of the Australians, but were parallel to them. The New Zealanders' sense of being detached, not implicated, observers of the world drama operated here even more than with regard to Europe. Labour, of course, applied its collective security, antiaggressor, policy to the Japanese, differing from the Australians in this regard. The New Zealanders appeared to feel that if Japan had imperial ambitions southward—far better than they expend their energies on continental Asia—then in the Southwest Pacific Australia was the primary and New Zealand a secondary target. As the world moved toward World War II, however, the possible or probable role of Japan— friendly, neutral but unfriendly, actively hostile?—was the factor in the situation it was impossible precisely to define but opinions about the way Japan would probably go had influence on defense policy decisions. This continued to be the case even after World War II actually broke out. With regard to domestic defense, it was concluded that New Zealand should strengthen its capacity to resist raids on its coasts, while with regard to the exact nature of its contribution to imperial defense, beyond aiming to continue to supply food, it would be necessary to wait upon events. The major question in the latter connection was whether or not an expeditionary force should be sent overseas. Closely related to speculation about Japan's probable course was, of course, the speculation about the probable course of the United States, not only with regard to war in Europe but in the Pacific also. It was generally assumed, though without any real grounds for certainty, that the American course in the Pacific would be favorable to New Zealand's interests.

The New Zealand army was built around a Regular Army of volunteers, consisting of 500-600 officers and men and a Territorial Force of a strength ordinarily around 7000 but authorized to 30,000, also dependent on volunteers, liable to mobilization in any emergency. From 1909 to 1930 compulsory military training was enforced; it was suspended in 1930 as a depression economy and had not been resumed up to the outbreak of World War II. The trainees provided a body of prospective recruits for the Regular Army and the Territorial Forces. The tradition of World War I was that an imperial force would be specially recruited for overseas service in wartime, at first on a volunteer basis, later by conscription, built around the officer corps of the Regular Army and the Territorial Force and manned by the compulsorily trained and others. At the outbreak of World War II, however, New Zealand did not have a very useful number of men trained for immediate participation in modern warfare but rather a considerable body of men well prepared to undergo quick, intensive training for such service, possessed of a tradition of soldiering of a high order and a vigorous morale.

Under an act of 1913 provision for a New Zealand Division of the Royal Navy was made, but World War I made it impossible to carry out the scheme. Not until 1920 was the Division constituted. The proposal was for New Zealand to provide for the maintenance of such ships as were supplied to her by the British Admiralty, to recruit and train a portion of the manpower required for their operation, to subsidize a dockyard at Auckland, and to build up a naval reserve to be a source of recruits for United Kingdom ships in wartime. The scheme was administered by a Naval Board of which the minister of Defence was chairman. At the outbreak of World War II the New Zealand Division consisted of two light cruisers and a minesweeping trawler which had been in New Zealand waters since 1936. Thus up to the outbreak of World War II the New Zealand naval force was a part of the Royal Navy, not as in the Australian case a national navy with a close association with the Royal Navy. The New Zealand force did not become the Royal New Zealand Navy until 1941.

The effective establishment of an air force occurred in 1923, but it remained a branch of the army until 1937 when it became a separate arm of the defense forces. At the outbreak of war the emphasis was on the training of air personnel to be fed into the Royal Air Force in time of war. A fighting New Zealand air force was yet to come.

The Labour party, of course, had a strong antimilitarist tradition flowing from its political position during World War I. Unlike the conservatives who resisted all British proposals to stop or slow down the construction of the Singapore base, Labour consistently opposed Singapore, a position based on the thesis that the base was a "provocation" to Japan. Labour hardly found it regrettable when the conservatives pared down defense expenditures as an economy measure in the Great Depression. Rearmament began in New Zealand in 1934 and Labour thus came to office while it was in its early stages. Up to that point it would be correct to say that the armed forces were neglected well beyond the dominion average; after that date an effort was made to get control of the problems involved. Labour did not retard rearmament but accelerated it, though lethargically, even in the face of its differently oriented effort to prevent the deterioration of the international situation. In 1937 it directed a reorganization of the defense establishment; it abolished the old Department of Defence (which by tradition was the army department) and set up separate departments for Army, Navy, and Air, coordinated by a Chiefs-of-Staff Committee and a Council of Defence. Within the prime minister's Department an Organization for National Security was established to explore the defense problem in all its multifarious aspects and in depth. Though the defense chiefs in New Zealand did their own thinking decisive influence came from the Committee of Imperial Defence in London. The service chiefs had regular contacts with their opposite numbers in Australia, but at the cabinet-to-cabinet level contact with Australia was underdeveloped. An effort by New Zealand to improve the latter situation received little encouragement from Canberra.

In April 1939 a conference of defense experts from Britain, Australia, and New Zealand was held at Wellington on the initiative of New Zealand, following up a proposal made at the Imperial Conference of 1937. Essentially what New Zealand was looking for was guidance in defense policy on the implicit assumption that Japan would go to war while war was on in Europe and that in that case New Zealand would be menaced. It proved impossible to evaluate the political questions involved, but out of the discussions the New Zealanders drew two conclusions: that they should continue to strengthen their army to improve its capacity to repel raids and to have a force ready to dispatch overseas if that course became wise and feasible (as it was not then clear it would be); and that their defense activities vis à vis Japan in the islands should be focused on Fiji (see Chapter X). New Zealand was encouraged to build up her military stores, but she was definitely not encouraged to suppose she would find it easy to draw upon either Britain or Australia to equip her forces for active campaigning, especially once war had broken out. Singapore, of which Labour had signified its "acceptance" at the Imperial Conference of 1937, was treated as a deterrent to Japan which New Zealand should help to strengthen. It remained, that is, the ambiguous symbol of Britain's power in the East. It was apparent that a different appreciation of Far Eastern developments between Wellington and London was likely, but London's views continued pro tem to rule.

Labour took quick and decisive steps to bring New Zealand not only into World War II at Britain's side but, also, at the identical moment that Britain declared war. Parliament willingly ratified the *fait accompli:* Labour or conservative, all were equally dedicated to the defense of the British world and the destruction of Hitlerism by force of arms. The question then urgently arose as to what New Zealand should do to assist the imperial cause. The general form of New Zealand's collaboration was surprisingly similar to that of World War I, though in specific substance there were important differences. She rather quickly committed herself to sending an expeditionary force overseas, outpacing Australia in this respect, basing the decision on the British appreciation of the probable development of the war not only in Europe but also the Pacific. The "phony" war of the months from September 1939 looked surprisingly (if not too utterly convincingly) like World War I. Even the rapid and catastrophic Hitler-directed developments in Europe in the middle of 1940, which gave clear notice that history was not, even in the broadest outlines, repeating itself, left it even more desirable that New Zealand contribute its overseas army to the British forces in North Africa (integrally of Europe since Roman times) to fight, as part of a British army, the Italians, then the Germans and Italians, in defense of Suez and Middle Eastern oil, contribute from North Africa forces for the disastrous actions in Greece and Crete against the Germans, and to the forestalling of the Germans in Syria, and contribute (even after the outbreak of war in the Pacific) to the drive across North Africa to join up with the Americans and then up the boot of Italy to Rome and beyond.

While the army was so employed, the New Zealand naval Division was at the disposal of the British Admiralty, New Zealand recruits for naval service went to British ships, and the air recruits largely also to the British service via the Empire Air Training scheme based in Canada.

This way of deploying New Zealand's fighting men was justified by the old thesis that New Zealand's defense was best conducted far away from New Zealand on the basis of a British appreciation of the requirements of the defense of the "heart of the Empire" in Europe. The assumption was that as long as the United Kingdom stood in Europe, and only so long, could the associated nations, wherever located geographically, expect to be secure. British strategy was, with impeccable logic, Europe-oriented and it was traditional that the associated nations, no matter where their homelands were, should fall in with this orientation, expecting then by way of direct assault nothing worse than hit-and-run raids. If, as was the case in World War II, the United Kingdom, even when fully backed by its associates, could not expect to defeat a major enemy—a point the British recognized in 1940—then it was the responsibility of the United Kingdom (not the associates) to find an ally who could add the decisive measure of strength. It was, in short, the United Kingdom's job to deal with the United States and in the early stages of the war only the Canadians were bold enough to strengthen their homeland security by initiating direct dealings with an extra-imperial country—the United States. But what if the war was spread by Britain's enemies to the Pacific or, alternatively in interpretation, a new war against Britain, her associated countries, and her colonies was launched in the Pacific while the European war was still undecided? What if Japan moved southward—how then New Zealand?

Unlike the United Kingdom, but like all the other dominions, New Zealand fought the war with a single-party government. Although there was a great deal of talk about the need for a coalition, or "national," government, and some persuasive pressure to that end, the Labour government never finally conceded the point. This pressure came, of course, from the right. Such pressure as was exerted on Labour from the left was, once John A. Lee was disposed of, chiefly from the leftist trade unions in the form of strikes, and at certain stages of the war, from the Soviet-oriented communists. Between Labour and the political right there was, during the whole war, a large measure of common interest in effectively prosecuting the war and it was in recognition of this that Labour tried to devise ways and means of associating its political opponents with the war effort as such. In this it was only indifferently successful. In part this was because the opposition was not happy within itself. When the Forbes ministry fell and Labour took office, leadership of the opposition passed to Adam Hamilton who had been a member of Forbes's cabinet (not to J. G. Coates—he was regarded as "discredited"—the ablest member of the party). Hamilton and Coates, however, were in general agreement that while the opposition should certainly continue to oppose, it should also co-operate with the government in the advancement of the war effort, and they acted on their position. There were, nevertheless, conspicuous members of the opposition who felt that the duty to oppose transcended any patriotic duty to cooperate with Labour in prosecuting the war. Pressures to this effect were exerted upon the parliamentarians from outside Parliament. Hamilton was unable to contain the unrest in his own party and in 1940 was deposed from leadership and replaced by Sidney G. Holland.

Holland had been a member of Parliament since 1935. His father had been a member before him. He was a successful businessman of Christchurch and had lately bought a farm, thus establishing a footing in the second and perhaps more important of the two conspicuous "interests" underlying New Zealand conservatism. While Holland proved to be the man who would lead the conservatives to office again, he was unable—perhaps unwilling—in the immediate situation to establish a stable balance between political opposition to Labour and co-operation in the war effort. Hamilton and Coates stayed with a so-called War Cabinet (an all-party body responsible for decisions relating to war matters) continuously from 1940. For a few months in 1942 the War Cabinet was complemented by another all-party construction known as the War Administration, in which they also participated. Holland as leader of the opposition was admitted to both these bodies but stayed only briefly with either. In fact, he destroyed the War Administration by his departure on the occasion of a disagreement over the handling of a strike of coal miners and weakened the all-party character of the War Cabinet. Coates, who died in May 1947, sacrificed party to the war effort and at his death was an "independent." Hamilton, who served in the War Cabinet until its dissolution in 1945, was still in his party at the end but was a spent political force. Holland was master of his party, but Labour was in a position to deny him office for another four years. Thus the hypertrophied politics characteristic of New Zealand at that time, a heritage of the depression, in effect continued throughout the war. Labour confirmed its position by its success in the wartime general election of 1943.

The war was thus in effect Labour's war and there was irony in the fact that Labour was vigorously to direct a war, recollecting its view of the earlier phase of the cycle of violence in which the world was involved and especially the experiences earlier of Peter Fraser, the party leader in charge from March 1940, when "Mick" Savage died. But, as noted, Labor's suspicions about World War I were *political* rather than *pacifist* and it had recognized the possibility that this other fateful means of international politics would have in the end to be used for political ends in which, this time, it believed, when in 1935 it accepted and advanced rearmament. The war now actually afoot was made more than merely palatable by the imperial patriotism of the immigrant New Zealand Laborites like Fraser and Nash and by the fact that it was an antifascist war, success in which could be viewed as the indispensable prelude to a world-wide advance for the social-political views held, a point made especially clear when policies for the future were formulated. The war carried Fraser to the point that he was widely regarded as an elder imperial statesman, comparable to South Africa's Jan Smuts; it also brought him onto the international stage as a "socialist" reformer.

New Zealand, however, like its associates in the Empire, acted in the war as an autonomous nation, an ally of the closest kind of the United Kingdom, but not a part of the United Kingdom. The point of autonomy was made in the declaration of war when an effort was made to differentiate it as peculiarly New Zealand's, this not obscured by the interestingly tortuous constitutional ambiguity involved. If New Zealand's declaration was less decisively its own than that of Canada, it was more its own than Australia's. New Zealand also underlined its position by the way in which it defined the position of its army in relation to the imperial forces. Like the other dominions, it was concerned to make it clear that the New Zealand forces were those of an allied nation, not integrally a part of the British army (conceived of as the army of the United Kingdom). It was, therefore, important that the New Zealand forces be handled as an identifiable unit and not broken up and distributed around in an effectively anonymous disunity. By the same token, the use made of the forces was at the decision of the New Zealand government and the field commander, not the United Kingdom government and its field commanders under whom the New Zealand forces might be serving in actual operations. That this was the New Zealand government's firm decision on the point was as hard for the British field commanders and the British government, especially as embodied in Winston Churchill, to learn as in the cases of the other closely allied Empire forces, though they had far less trouble with the New Zealanders than with the Australians. Unlike the Australians who brought forward from their own forces their own top field commander, the New Zealanders had no one in their army to take the parallel position. Instead they turned to a New Zealander making a career in the British army (the British armed forces generally were well supplied with New Zealanders). This was Major-General Bernard Freyberg, a veteran of the New Zealand forces of World War I. Freyberg was as interested in guarding the final decision on the use of the New Zealand forces and their integrity as a force as the New Zealand government. In fact, he himself drafted the original formulation of the position. The most distinguished New Zealand soldier matured during the war was Major-General Sir Howard Kippenberger who came out of the Territorials.

New Zealand's problem was how to make a maximum contribution, defined differently at the various stages of the war, on the basis of an economy strong on the side of the land industries but weak on the side of factory industry, to a war in which a decisive factor was industrial capacity founded directly on heavy industry which New Zealand did not have. Her weak war potential did not diminish her determination to do her utmost. The stages through which the effort passed were, first, from the outbreak of war in Europe to the outbreak of war in the Pacific with a signal for intensification in 1940 with the Nazi successes in Europe, second, from Pearl Harbor to 1943 when New Zealand ceased to be directly menaced by Japan, and third, from 1943 to the end of the war. Labour insisted that no matter how intensive the exploitation of the economy (including the manpower), the welfare emphasis should not be lost from sight. All erosion of workingmen's privileges was regarded as temporary, subject to immediate restoration on the return of peace. The social security system continued to expand during the war. Not only did the numbers eligible for age benefits steadily increase, but the medical and hospital provisions of the 1938 law became operative only after war had broken out.

The country entered the war at a time when an upswing in industrial development had started. Such capacity as existed was brought under the government's close control and fully exploited. By coordination of small units, improvisation, and some difficultly wrought extension, it was expanded in some respects, contracted in others. Production for civilian use was severely restricted. There was a rise in factory employment of about 12 per cent from 1938–39 to 1942–43 and while the labor was available, employment reached even greater peaks. More was wrested from New Zealand's industries for war purposes than could certainly have been forecast, in spite of their total dependence on overseas heavy industry. The most considerable contribution was made by the clothing and the boot and shoe industries, particularly the former, which were diverted to military clothing and footwear, but the engineering shops including the very smallest units, geared in peacetime largely to maintenance, repair, or assembly operations, were coordinated to produce, often piece by piece in widely scattered shops, a considerable range of small fighting equipment as well as a wide variety of miscellaneous supplies. Not only did the factories contribute to the equiping of the country's own armed forces, but they produced goods for the Eastern Group Supply Council and, at a later stage, for the United States forces.

But the fact remained that New Zealand's central economic contribution as a belligerent was in terms of foodstuffs and wool, the produce of its land industries. Throughout the war the United Kingdom was the prime beneficiary. New Zealand supplied about three-fifths of Britain's butter during the war and almost half its cheese. It also supplied its own civilians and its armed forces and in due course supplied foodstuffs to the American forces in the Pacific, even extending production for their benefit, notably with regard to fresh vegetables. To make her basic contribution, the commodities had to be transported across the seas to the United Kingdom, one of the world's longest hauls, beset in wartime by the risk of hostile enemy action against the ships, shortages of refrigerated capacity, and by the United Kingdom's understandable preference for drawing equivalent supplies from sources nearer by. To meet the inadequacies and uncertainties of shipping, the New Zealanders had rapidly to extend the local storage capacity (including cold stores), they had to be prepared to make changes in commodities produced (as when they shifted the emphasis from butter to cheese and back again), and to change the preparation of commodities for export, as by deboning and dehydrating meat and canning meat, milk, fruit, and vegetables. (This is why there was a rise in employment in the "primary processing" industries.) However, the over-all increase in production was small, especially as compared to overseas countries, and there was a shift away from dairy products in favor of meat and wool.

Production of commodities within New Zealand was not without its difficulties. Not forgetting the drainage of manpower from the farms that mobilizations caused, and the inadequacy of efforts to replace it by women workers, mention may be made of shortages of metal and rubber spare parts for the equipment of the dairy industry, shortages of fencing wire for the sheep stations, and the dropping off of the supply of superphosphate when Nauru was bombed. Pest and weed control lost ground. On the other hand, every effort was made to step up the mechanization of the land industries during the war years. One of the important contributions of American Lend-Lease was to supply farm machinery (and food-processing equipment). The development was spurred by the establishment of the practice of having outside contractors carry out machine operations on the farms for a fixed fee.

The perennially vexing problem of marketing was considerably eased. Not only was distribution within New Zealand already in the hands of the government, but the control was intensified by rationing. The wartime arrangements with Britain put exportable commodities into the government's hands also, in extension of the marketing approach used up to the time only with regard to butter. As the United Kingdom offered to buy the exportable surpluses of butter, cheese, meat, and wool in bulk, so the New Zealand government became the agent for their acquisition. Prices, renegotiated annually, were determined in relation to the costs of production in New Zealand, not by the world market. For the United Kingdom, one of the benefits of this was supply at lower cost than the open market afforded. For New Zealand its advantages were certainty of sale and adequate return. However, it was not for New Zealand an unalloyed boon, for while prices were satisfactory in the light of the New Zealand factors involved, prices of the imports brought in in return reflected the conditions of another economy and rose more steeply, steadily worsening New Zealand's terms of trade. However, this was disguised in wartime because imports were then brought to a minimum by shortages in the supplying country and rigorously administered New Zealand controls.

In directing the economy, full use was made of price, wage, and rent controls. Price control was very elaborately developed. Controlled prices were very often as a last resort underpinned by subsidies, a practice which gained a firm hold on the New Zealand political imagination. Taxes rose; almost half of all revenue for war expenses was obtained from taxes; income tax rates rose, the sales tax was quadrupled, and a special war levy was placed on incomes. Most of the other half of the funds to support the war came from loans. With market supplies constricted and wages buoyant, savings inevitably rose. A feature of the borrowing for war was that it was done internally. Some London-held long-term debt was repaid and British credits for war purposes were repaid promptly. Thus while public debt held internally rose, externally held debt declined. The burden of external debt also eased as the national income rose and the proportionate significance of interest payments receded. Much of the internal debt came to rest in the accounts of the government departments. The net effect was to increase New Zealand's financial self-dependence. When Lend-Lease was added up, New Zealand "owed" the United States $30,000,000, but this was not a burden. In financial terms, the war cost about £600,000,000 (ignoring rehabilitation costs), of which almost £500,000,000 was spent on the armed services. Since New Zealand suffered very little direct destruction—chiefly loss of commodities at sea—a prime economic cost was the erosion of capital equipment.

It was manpower and the problem of its proper distribution between the armed forces and industry that caused a crisis of the war effort, with important domestic, intra-Commonwealth, and international political repercussions. For the first two years of the war, no intractable difficulties were experienced. The intensification of the war effort after the disasters in Europe in mid-1940 was accomplished with reasonable ease, though under strong political pressure. Forces for overseas service, home defense, and service in the islands were recruited without causing any difficulties that could not be solved administratively. Those unemployed at the outbreak of war were absorbed, hours of labor were lengthened, women hitherto not employed were drawn into active work, those who came of working age were promptly employed, and a redistribution between occupations directed. The outbreak of war in the Pacific precipitated the crisis. There was an immediate intensification of mobilization for home and island service and an effort, probably overconscientious, was made to provide a force to fight alongside the Americans in the Pacific. The latter effort was made particularly difficult by the decision not to recall the troops in the Middle East—they were not reinforced for months, however. A force for island service was supplied, but the emphasis fell, not on the army, but on air and sea collaboration and on supply. Once the Japanese pressure south of the equator ended in 1943, the New Zealanders began to redistribute their manpower in favor of the factory and the land industries. In 1942 there was a correspondence with the British potentially as explosive as the Australian about the best use of the troops in the Middle East, the conservative parliamentary opposition severely criticized the handling of the manpower, and Peter Fraser came to wonder if he had not diminished his political influence in Pacific affairs by not pouring out more "blood"—there was less question about "treasure"—in the fighting. Throughout the war years the manpower controls were administered with sensitivity in a rapidly changing scene. The armed forces were conscripted from 1940; the controls over all manpower, including civilians, reached a peak of intensity in 1942. From the end of the war in 1945 they were progressively removed, occupation by occupation, but they did not finally disappear until June 1946.

That the New Zealanders made their commitment to the war on the assumption that Japan was hardly likely to attack southward in the predictable future and thereby menace New Zealand's security did not mean that the Japanese question was put out of their minds. Rather, the question nagged constantly, but as the New Zealanders were no more knowledgeable or percipient about Japanese intentions or capabilities than their fellows, they continued to acquiesce in British views and policies even when they did not particularly like them. The fundamental proposition of relevance was that New Zealand was incapable of unassisted self-defense against an enemy of power. The corollary was that she was dependent upon outside defense, traditionally read to mean imperial defense. Having "accepted" Singapore in 1937, Labour perforce accepted the thesis that Britain would unfailingly reinforce the base if the situation in the western Pacific deteriorated and New Zealand's security was weakened.

When, therefore, the British government in June 1940 notified the New Zealanders that in view of the worsened situation in Europe it "was most improbable that we could send reinforcements to the Far East" if Japan should attempt to alter the status quo, the effect on the New Zealanders was "apocalyptic." As Prime Minister Fraser noted in replying to the June dispatch, the announcement deviated

from the understanding, reinforced by repeated and most explicit assurances, that a strong British fleet would be available to and would proceed to Singapore should the circumstances require even if this involved the abandonment of British interests in the Mediterranean.

This "understanding" was nothing less than the "basis of the whole of New Zealand's defence preparations." Though Fraser went on to express the hope that the understanding would be reaffirmed if circumstances again changed—Churchill did indeed renew it in October, though in a form less comforting than hitherto—Fraser's real concern was to raise the question of what New Zealand was now to do to get her security underwritten. His answer was that the New Zealanders should follow the Australians, whose predicament was so similar, and turn to the Americans. In November 1939 the New Zealanders had been told, on the basis of an assessment by Lord Lothian, the British ambassador in Washington, that while New Zealand was hardly vivid in the American mind, it would unquestionably profit from American moves in the Pacific, and should rest content with that probability. Fraser now asked if this Micawberish position was sufficient. Would it not be best for New Zealand to make a case in Washington? After some discussion, it was decided that New Zealand should establish diplomatic relations with the United States with the purpose of reinsuring her security. The decision made in December 1940 was followed by eleven months of delay before choice of a New Zealander for the position of Minister to Washington was announced. It was difficult to find a New Zealander sufficiently prestigious who could be spared. In the end Walter Nash was chosen. He, however, did not reach Washington until February, 1942. New Zealand was not, therefore, represented diplomatically in Washington when Pearl Harbor occurred. The choice of Nash, second in New Zealand affairs only to Prime Minister Fraser, emphasized the importance the New Zealanders attached to the mission.

New Zealand moved toward war in the Pacific under the cover of British views—particularly, Winston Churchill's views—of what was happening and was likely to happen. In gist those views discounted the possibility that Japan would go to war and if it foolishly went to war, it would be stopped long before New Zealand's security was jeopardized. Pearl Harbor, the Philippines, Singapore, and the immediately sequential events were therefore quite frightening to the New Zealanders, though their reaction was milder than that of the Australians and, oddly, milder and less political than the reaction to the European crisis of 1940. There was, however, a fairly acute fear of actual invasion and this influenced governmental policy in the first instance. Naturally enough the fear was intensified by the patent lack of any particular power to resist an invasion. New Zealand was practically without the equipment and short of the manpower to plan to repel a direct attack of any magnitude. It had, for example, no antiaircraft guns at all. The tendency was to overdramatize the prospect of invasion and its probable scale and therefore to maximize the quantities of matériel asked for to meet the crisis. Fear intensified the effort to break out from behind the British arras, so vigorously guarded by Churchill, and make direct contact with the Americans to find out what was really going on as well as to gain access to military assistance. In February 1942 the New Zealanders agreed with the Australians—the predicaments of the two countries were now thought of as identical—that they would accept an American commander in chief. The expectation was that the two countries would be embraced in a common defense area. They were also just as little satisfied as the Australians to follow Churchill's proposal that the Pacific war be run with the advice of a War Council in London; they joined in the Australian campaign for a Pacific War Council in Washington. They were, moreover, as critical as the Australians of the "Hitler First" strategy. With this feeling of identity of interest with the Australians running so strong, it was entirely natural that they should have reacted critically and with a sense of disappointment to the American action of placing them in one defense area and Australia in another. The New Zealanders were placed in the South Pacific Area which embraced their islands, Fiji, New Caledonia, part of the Solomon chain, and other islands south of the equator and east of the Southwest Pacific Area in which Australia found itself. The South Pacific Area was a naval responsibility; the first commander in chief was Vice-Admiral R. L. Ghormley who set up headquarters in Auckland on May 21, 1942; he was succeeded by the more famous "Bull" Halsey in October. By that time, the idea that New Zealand was in danger of invasion was dead; it had been slain by events after having been sharply discounted earlier in the assessments of both the British and American defense planners. New Zealand therefore came to contribute to the Pacific war as a base for offensive operations in the islands —a base at which American marines were trained for combat and which was a major source of supply for American and New Zealand forces. The American forces were not there to defend New Zealand itself, but the better to get at the common enemy—the Japanese—in the islands to the north. As always, New Zealand was best defended away from New Zealand. (For the war in the islands, see Chapter XI). The vast difference to the New Zealanders was that their dependence for security was now on the Americans, not the British, as by tradition it should have been. Yet they had not swerved as far away from their tradition as the Australians, as is symbolized by their acquiescence in Churchill's wish that they leave their forces in the Middle East. They regarded the United States as a surrogate for Britain, not as a new and probably permanent ally for security purposes. They came uneasily and late to the melancholy conclusion that the surrogate had come to stay, and many of them long continued to find the fact one to which it was exceedingly difficult to accommodate their minds and emotions.

When the preoccupation with strategy and logistics began to lessen in 1943, international political questions insistently raised their heads again. It was in 1943 that the New Zealand Parliament passed an External Affairs Act which provided a legislative basis for the full development of a foreign affairs department on the foundations rather casually laid in the prime minister's Department back in 1926. The ideas and policies to be given firmer expression were a heritage from prewar days when Labour first revealed its hand in this field, given a sharper edge by a sense that New Zealand must speak up in a more decisively autonomous fashion than ever before, and by a strong feeling that the Americans, though pleasantly friendly, tended to discount the importance of the views of small nations and—equally annoying—to put forward such an inextricable mixture of idealistic and sympathetic and tough and repellent policies that vigorously voiced selectivity was of the essence of New Zealand's need. The New Zealanders were drawn to Australia in the expectation that jointly they could make a more powerful impact in international affairs than if they spoke individually. The initiative came from the Australians, specifically from the Australian minister for External Affairs, Dr. Herbert Vere Evatt. The basis of agreement between New Zealand, with Peter Fraser as spokesman, and Australia with Evatt as spokesman, was wide, though not absolutely comprehensive, not least because both were Labour men, though temperamentally very different. If Evatt was, as a New Zealand historian has concluded, the "natural spearhead" of the joint diplomatic effort, he never became the whole show. Fraser carefully preserved the separate character of New Zealand and himself. (For these developments from the Australian angle, see Chapter III.)

Evatt began to feel out the New Zealanders in October 1943. It was historically apt that the first question he sought to explore was "the islands," which lay at the root of both the burgeoning foreign policies. The discussions were almost immediately given urgency and increased range by the common critical reaction of the two countries to the decisions the big powers were announcing with regard to policy at conferences —Moscow, Cairo, Teheran—to which Australia and New Zealand were not invited, on matters affecting them as nations, especially as nations in the Pacific where, they now considered it axiomatic, their primary interests lay. These affronts to their dignity, as they were regarded, of which both Churchill and Roosevelt were equally guilty, hastened them on to a comprehensive joint policy declaration known as the Australian-New Zealand Agreement, drawn up at Canberra, January 1944. While this was a peculiarly Evattian adventure in foreign policy, Peter Fraser found himself 75 per cent in immediate agreement with the policies enunciated. The greater part of the time of the conference was used up in dealing with the remaining 25 per cent. Yet it took but six days to reduce the repertory (see Chapter III) to an agreed form. The New Zealanders especially contributed a great deal to moderating the language employed and to eliminating from the documents certain specific illustrations of general policy which were especially controversial between the two countries as well as between the two countries and the United States and the United Kingdom. They were successful in inserting a phrase giving their common membership in the Commonwealth conspicuous notice. Of the many points covered, New Zealand took a special positive interest in "trusteeship" and international aviation. But if they "moderated" the document, they did not succeed in completely disguising its "edginess" and some of their moderating contributions helped make the declarations ambiguous rather than clear. Above all, the New Zealanders were later embarrassed to find themselves responsible for a decidedly "regional" declaration when their policy was decisively international. However, the document, with all of its positive and negative merits and demerits, was, nevertheless, an authentic statement of New Zealand policy as of 1944. That is how it was read "officially" in the United States and Britain, though in America especially particular individuals, groups, and newspapers took a hostile view of some of the points made.

Using the machinery set up at the Canberra conference to facilitate their consultations, the New Zealanders and the Australians held discussions at Wellington in November 1944 to formulate their views on the proposed new international organization. Here again Australian formulations were the bases of discussion and there was again a wide area of easy agreement. With regard to international organization, the New Zealanders were still of much the same mind as in 1936: they still believed that the foundation ideas of the League of Nations were sound. They felt that if the League covenant were lightly and sparingly blue-penciled, it would be the best possible basis of discussion. They favored a "rule of law" approach, an organization with teeth it was disposed to use, with emphasis on the collective approach to security. They accepted the necessity for a Council with the Big Powers as permanent members, but they were hostile to the veto; they favored a General Assembly with wide powers and comprehensive authority; they wanted the role of the Economic and Social Council to be central, for in it their social reformist views would find freest expression. In short, they took a "small power" view of the questions involved but a small power strongly committed to international law, order, and welfare. New Zealand strongly supported a radical view of "trusteeship," proposing to extend United Nations supervision to all colonial possessions, a view far more flagrantly objectionable to the United Kingdom than the United States. Although at San Francisco Peter Fraser made New Zealand's views on all the contentious questions abundantly clear, he was definitely in the shadow as spokesman for the small nation point of view of his Australian colleague, H. V. Evatt. Fraser impressed himself most definitely on the conference as chairman of the Committee on the Trusteeship Chapters of the Charter. At San Francisco he reached the apogee of his career as an international statesman and political leader of New Zealand. He committed New Zealand as decisively to the United Nations as Labour had been committed to the League of Nations.

New Zealand came out of World War II with its Labour government infirmly in the saddle, promptly to be badgered from both left and right, the leadership tired and more than a little irritable, and its thinking somewhat confused after ten years continuously in office, half of them wartime years. In the 1946 election the government retained office only by virtue of the fact that the four Maori seats were all held by Labour members; on the pakeha side there was an even division. Three years later it went down before the conservatives by a margin of four seats. A year later Peter Fraser died (December 12, 1950) and was succeeded in the party leadership by the veteran Walter Nash. Labour was again defeated in 1951 in a "snap" election occasioned by a sharp collision between the conservative government and the restless left of the trade union movement, and in 1954 it was still again defeated, though less decisively. In 1957 it regained office by the narrow margin of one seat after eight years in the wilderness. Just before that election Holland retired because of ill health—he died in 1961—and was succeeded as conservative leader by his deputy, Keith J. Holyoake. Labour was turned out of office by Holyoake in 1960. Thus out of six elections held from 1946 to 1960 Labour won but two, neither by any impressive margin.

While this clearly showed that Labour's mystique, which sustained it in office for fourteen years after 1935, had become sadly bedraggled, the fact that its defeats were only a little more pronounced in terms of seats than its victories showed that a very substantial proportion of the electorate was prepared to stay with it through thick and thin. Recognizing that a Social Credit political party, established in 1953, drained away a protest vote never big enough to elect a single member of the House, which otherwise might have gone to Labour, it can be said that the electorate of New Zealand after the war was almost evenly divided between Labour and the conservative Nationalists, with the conservatives holding the edge.

Ideology was not the principal constituent of the "edge." When Labour lost in 1949 it was not obviously and decisively a defeat for "socialism" or a victory for free enterprise (or any other procapitalist position) and when Labour came back in 1957 it was not because the electorate had reverted to "socialism" but, rather sadly, because Labour had not scrupled to outbid its opponents in promising material benefits (tax remissions, increased social security benefits, more liberal loans for housing, etc.) to the wayfaring elector. Rather, in postwar New Zealand, the political battle, whatever the allegations of the politicians, was over the manner in which an elaborately controlled economy could best be administered for the welfare of the people (welfare constituents being continuous full employment, high material standards of living, social security), economic "stability" assumed but not fetishized, and growth (in what shape, in what direction, under which auspices, private or governmental) to be provided for. This was to be done on a national basis within an economy heavily influenced by the movements of prices of certain luxury primary products on the international market. The political split was over the emphasis of policy within a context that did not in fact permit either contender for power to break away decisively from an administered capitalism that had its genesis far back in New Zealand history. Labour had not had in the postwar period either the will or the ideas which would have allowed it to break away to the left toward socialism, while the conservatives were persistently trapped by general circumstances, domestic and international, into continuing the status quo as they had inherited it, perforce administering it with an emphasis that was not decisively transforming, however their intentions were verbalized in election campaigns.

Labour apparently did not conceive of the country's general economic position as likely to be fundamentally different postwar from what it had been prewar, however different it might appear on the surface. Conspicuous surface differences were the highly regarded over-full employment, inflation, and "prosperity," but underneath things were thought to be much the same. Labour's fundamental interests continued to be in insulated stability and the directed distribution and redistribution of the national product. Its policies kept taxes high and the general economic situation justified high taxes. Labour settled for the detailed administration of a controlled capitalism, though it wearily resigned ministerial control of vexatious matters, even if this put stability in jeopardy. Its compromising and compromised position comported oddly with the anti-capitalist sentiments it had cultivated in the past and which still flourished on the trade union left. Labour's new, unrationalized orthodoxy lacked the purpose of transforming society and regenerating the New Zealand fraction of mankind (now 2,000,000 persons). It was difficult to see what vision Labour had of the New Zealand future; it certainly was not following any beckoning star easy to identify. Hardly was the war over than the "bankruptcy" of Labour began to be talked about and the talk was still current in the 1960's. Labour was in the ideological doldrums but not, as a party, completely moribund.

In 1944 Mr. Nash, still the chief architect of Labour's economic policy, said in his report on the Bretton Woods conference from which the International Bank and Monetary Fund emerged: "It was consistently stressed by the Chairman of the New Zealand Delegation that the New Zealand Government did not propose, and would not, under existing world conditions agree, to alter in any way its right to select imports, and whilst taking every step that would foster the general policy of expansion of world trade, it would on all occasions so order its total imports as to insure that the necessary exchange for current transactions would at all times be available. This would entail control of the purposes for which, and the extent to which, overseas commitments as a whole could be entered into." This by implication was a reiteration of all related policies and in effect was an affirmation that Labour stood on its policies of 1938 and earlier. It stayed out of the Bank and Fund.

If Labour's avoidance of the Bank and Fund, in spite of Lord Keynes's association with them, was in part supported by a reiteration of prewar policy, it was also, to a degree unknown, sustained by the hostility to those institutions of the banking and monetary heretics, including the Social Credit people, who had been part of Labour's constituency from the 1930's. They saw behind the proposed institutions the schemers of America's Wall Street, allegedly seeking to gain control of the world's financial system. The New Zealand experimentalists were afraid of this; they wanted no part of it. They were, as a matter of fact, distrustful of any internationally oriented financial institutions, being convinced that salvation by credit policy within New Zealand was not only possible but only thus possible; they were economic nationalists. Nor was the influence of these people wholly negative. They played a part in forcing the government at last to nationalize the Bank of New Zealand in 1945. This gave the government the largest trading bank—which it did not really want—as well as the Reserve Bank, which it regarded as sufficient for its purposes. Total nationalization of banking was on these people's minds, as it is still today. But that the financial nexus with London was still cherished was illustrated by the decision in 1948 to *appreciate* the New Zealand pound to par with the pound sterling, at the cost of a 20 per cent cut in returns from exports in New Zealand currency. When the pound sterling was devalued by 30 per cent in 1949, the New Zealand pound was also. New Zealand was, of course, integrally of the Sterling Bloc. It was a "dollar short" country.

Aside from general pressure to relax the more exasperating controls introduced in wartime, e.g., those over labor, which Labour was well disposed to do as rapidly as seemed wise, Labour was chiefly under pressure from the farmers for increased returns from their production and from the workers for higher wages. Both of these were inflationary demands in an inflationary context.

All during Labour's continuance in office to 1949 and for a number of years after, exports continued to be handled on a "bulk purchase" basis, this entailing their sale to Britain at less than world market prices. This was regarded as a contribution to helping Britain in her postwar difficulties. However, the negotiated prices rose over wartime levels and not only gave profitable returns to producers but allowed the building up of "reserves" in the government's hands against a fall in prices, when the reserves could be paid out to sustain the producers' position. The government, however, was under constant pressure to maximize current returns and to an extent it acceded. Price was a political question. Labour negotiated a renewal of the bulk purchase contracts in 1948.

Imports began to rise from their very low wartime volume in 1946. They rose steeply and in spite of controls outpaced the returns from exports. The net result of this powerful propensity to import operating in a context of less than world prices for exports and very high prices for imports was that in only one year in Labour's term of office was there a favorable balance of trade. In every other year the country had a deficit in its international accounts. Nevertheless, in 1946–47 the government repaid London loans totaling 67.4 millions. The conservatives also repaid loans under similar conditions in their time.

The pressure on the Labour government for increases in the wage rates was, in 1945, turned to the arbitration court, thus giving that institution a central role in the determination of economic policy. The court responded by stepping up the increases in wages. Between 1939 and 1950 money wages rose 63 per cent, mostly in the postwar years, while real wages rose 14 per cent. Leadership in the campaign for higher wages was taken by the Federation of Labour. The government took a "permissive" attitude toward this effort to break down a barrier to inflation, and, as a result, there was no alienation between the Federation and political Labour as long as Peter Fraser was alive.

The government's exhibition of tenderness to the "sectional" interest of trade union labor did not gain it any particular credit with the left of the Labour movement (any more than higher prices reconciled the farmers to the government politically). The left of the trade union movement—the coal miners, the waterside workers, the railway workers, the freezing works workers—had been restless throughout the war. Prime Minister Fraser, acutely sensitive to the fact that he had begun life on the left himself, had been disposed to appease the left when it struck, even at the risk of the inevitable censure of his conservative parliamentary opposition and disruption of relations with it. But as his personal identification with the war was intense, he was driven on occasion to use severe measures to break strikes and prevent chaos on the home front, even if he contrived to minimize the impact of the measures on persons once the men went back to work. Important to the understanding of the situation is recognition of the fact that the leftists and the politicians were moving ideologically in opposite directions. Political Labour was moving away from socialism and in 1951 removed the socialization plank from its platform. The leftist unionists, on the other hand, were voicing a muddle of syndicalism (worker control of industry) and nationalization, both historically established constituents of leftist thinking in New Zealand, and the weapon they proposed to wield to whatever their ultimate end might be was "direct action" against the employers for immediate gains, a throwback, in historical terms, to the period before World War I. Communists, naturally enough, played a role in the exploitation of the explosive situations thus generated; and Fraser and his associates became more and more violently anticommunist. In effect what the trade union leftists were doing was challenging political Labour's new orthodoxy of tightly administered consumption-slanted capitalism by invoking "revolutionary" slogans which affronted the politicians all the more as they raised the now highly unwelcome ghosts of the old Red Fed days. Increasingly after the war Fraser was disposed to meet the challenge of the leftist dissidents with angry oratory, charging that they were out to "wreck" the labor movement. He sought to contain the dissidents of the waterfront, where the agitation was causing the most troublesome unrest, by attempting to govern labor relations there through specially legislated institutions of control. The situation finally exploded after Labour had gone out of office.

The postwar labor force was larger than the prewar force by about 65,000. The proportion of the force employed in farming was down, the proportion in manufacturing was up, while in the services it was up except in domestic and personal service. Over all, labor was in short supply. While the natural increase of population was at a very favorable rate, New Zealand Labour did not take as optimistic a view of possibilities as Australian Labor and did not redefine its immigration policy as radically as the Australians. Immigration policy was, indeed, still being argued in New Zealand in the 1960's. Productivity was rising at the slow rate of a little over 1 per cent per worker per annum, but the implications of this were not clear in the heady atmosphere of overfull employment.

As a complement to raising the return to producers and increasing the wages of workers, Labour bolstered the position of the wayfaring New Zealander by constantly tinkering with the social security system, increasing benefits and abolishing the legal obstacles to ready access to them of all hands. It also carried over from wartime the policy of keeping down the costs of living and production by fixing and subsidizing the prices of a wide range of goods and services beyond the considerable list normally administered by the government in operating the railways, electricity supply, etc. The subsidy system came to crisis in 1947 because of the constant upward movement of the total cost and the intensifying complications of administration. From 1942–43, when they began to be paid, to 1947–48 subsidies rose from £3.3 million to £13.6 million. In 1947 subsidies reckoned to cost £12 million a year were eliminated, chiefly in agriculture, where they were compensated by increased payments to farmers. It proved harder to deal with consumer goods and services. In the result the subsidies actually declined only a small fraction of the theoretical £12 million and within a year their net cost had risen to a peak of £14.6 million. At this point the conservatives took in hand the task of trying to get rid of them.

The catching up of the arrears of investment accumulated in wartime had really just begun when Labour went out of office. By 1949 gross investment as a percentage of Gross National Product was at 18 (10 per cent private, 8 per cent government), after having been down to 5 per cent in 1943. Government investment in greatest volume went into housing and electricity supply, in neither field matching needs, but covered also a wide miscellany of pressing necessities from railways and roads to school buildings. It was becoming obvious that in a consumption economy like New Zealand's saving and investment were to be chronic problems, but favorable conditions of economic progress were nevertheless usually present. The problem was to define (and then carry out) a creative program, both in its directional and other aspects, including scale (that is, how big could New Zealand be?). Capital issues continued to be closely controlled; there was no developed capital market. The final governance of economic expansion was in the hands of the government. Rather from necessity than from any socialist proclivities, the government after the war became the residuary legatee of large investment undertakings. It put considerable amounts into aviation (in part in association with the Australian government) and, in collaboration with overseas private investors possessed of technical expertise, into a pulp and paper industry, this bringing into prominence a forest industry based on the exotic plantings of years past, a promising economic growing-point, not least because a high proportion of the product was to be exported. Labour also began to canvass the possibility of an iron and steel industry based on local resources, but this was still only on the agenda at the beginning of the 1960's. However, private enterprise stepped into the picture by establishing a plant to make steel from scrap. It was common knowledge that the climate was considered inimical to enterprise by both domestic and foreign investors, but Labour was long indisposed to make any radical changes of policy. An unhappy by-product of tight control of investment and close direction of the expansion of production facilities was the accentuation of the strong monopoly tendencies in the economy. It was not until toward the end of Labour's 1957–60 term of office that Labour really came around to the conclusion that something should be done to stimulate private enterprise. By that time Mr. Nash was prepared to say (italics added):

Now we stand at the beginning of the 1960's and it is time to shift the emphasis from security and stability—we shall take these broad aims for granted—and to direct our efforts toward growth; *time to shape our policy less in terms of the past and look to the future.* And unless New Zealand develops at a faster rate we cannot be assured of security, nor can we be assured of the higher living standards that it has been the purpose of stabilization to preserve.

In spite of this, Mr. Nash lost the ensuing election.

Led by Sidney George Holland, the conservatives gained office in mid-December 1949 with a majority of four in the House. After fourteen years out of office they were a power-hungry lot, inexperienced in ministerial work, to an extent negative minded, more bent on destroying than creating, but insecure about what were the viable alternatives to the operative devices. Committed by political necessity to full employment and the welfare system, they nevertheless wanted to do away with as many controls as possible, run the government economically, stop the steady erosion of the purchasing power of the pound, end inflation, and release the fettered energies of the private entrepreneurs. There was a distinctly raucous note in the conservative voice, slogans were preferred to carefully articulated ideas, but an embarrassing gap was soon to develop between word and deed. It was found that there was no easy or certain escape from the toils of a tightly managed economy.

It fell to Holland's lot to deal with the trade union leftists who had troubled Labour's last years in office. Whether history was repeating itself as tragedy or farce—both verdicts have been rendered—the affair was strangely reminiscent, in superficialities, of Massey's collision with the unionists of the Red Fed in 1913. This was, in general, Holland's assessment of the situation. One of the superficialities was that on both occasions the focus of disagreement was the waterfront. The questions at issue were both bread-and-butter and political, confused beyond easy statement, as it was also difficult to make out whether the watersiders had struck against or had been locked out by their employers. In its political aspects—in retrospect the more important—the collision was not merely between the conservative government and the radical, adventurist waterfront unionists but also between the watersiders and their sympathizers —the seamen, the freezing-works employees, the railway workers, the coal miners—on the one side, and the unionists of the Federation of Labour led by F. P. Walsh and the Labour politicians led by Walter Nash on the other. Walsh carried the burden of labor opposition to the rebels; Mr. Nash for impenetrable reasons professed a bored, feeble-sounding, neutrality with regard to the economic demands of the watersiders. The affair was a violent boiling up of the ideological muddle in which the New Zealand labor movement was involved. In 1950 the leftists had tried to put over their political program—abolition of the arbitration system in favor of direct action, repeal of compulsory unionism as dampening to militancy, syndicalist control of industries (e.g., the waterfront, the coal mines, the railways) plus extended public ownership—on the Federation of Labour and, on being rebuffed, and in the case of the watersiders expelled, had formed a Trade Union Congress with 75,000 members as against the Federation of Labour's remaining membership of 150,000. The T.U.C.—and the watersiders especially—had communist assistance and support; they contributed to the "revolutionary" political overtones, even a rancorous anti-American note, by asserting that Holland was collaborating in the alleged American drive for war. (At this time the New Zealand communists were, by Moscow's direction, strongly under the influence of the Stalinist Australian party.) In the strike, or lockout, of 1951 the watersiders raised basic political as well

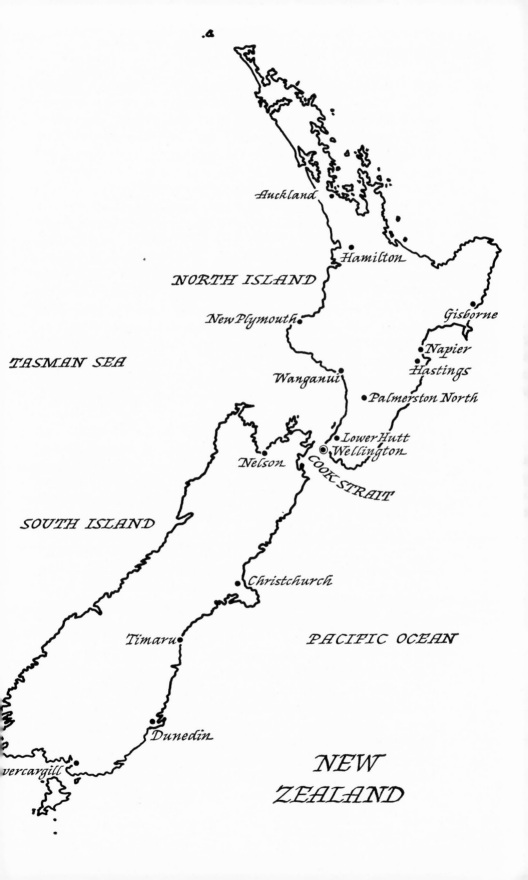

as bread-and-butter questions. It was a struggle for power: who was to run New Zealand labor—perhaps New Zealand? Thunder and lightning were added by a clash of antithetical personalities expressing antithetical purposes. When, therefore, Holland defeated the watersiders he won not only a personal victory but, also, a victory for his political opponents, the moderate trade unionists and the parliamentary Labourites. Holland, however, had the bad judgment—his authoritarian temperament did him in—to employ against the watersiders, in addition to the established weapon of union deregistration (i.e., union destruction), newly legislated weapons, allegedly aimed at communists, that badly compromised everybody's civil liberties. Mr. Nash, with astuteness, concentrated his fire on these errors and he was joined by alarmed academic intellectuals and liberal-minded citizens generally. Holland's reaction to criticism was to call a "snap" election—the first in New Zealand in the twentieth century —as a kind of referendum on his conduct. He won. But what had the electorate approved? Probably the defeat of the leftists, but not necessarily all the weapons used to accomplish it and certainly not Holland's general conduct in office since 1949.

The Holland government found that while it could change the emphasis of policy, or shift from one means to another, it could not radically transform the situation—illustratively, price control and subsidies. In an inflationary situation an adjustment of prices upward was inevitable and one way of letting prices find their level was to discontinue fixing them and withdraw any subsidy. Labour had begun the process in 1948, item by item. Seeking freedom, the conservatives on attaining office speeded up the process of decontrol. By 1951, however, they had found that in the New Zealand situation some prices, notably essential components of the cost of living, had for political reasons to be fixed and subsidized, like it or not. The list might be flexible, but conspicuously permanent were butter, milk, bread, and flour. It could even be found good strategy to *reduce* some prices by increasing the subsidy! Subsidy might rise to 50 per cent of price to the consumer.

By the late 1950's, subsidies were running at £12 million annually. It was obvious, too, that prices of items freed from control would, in inflationary times, rise sharply and this would support wage increases by the arbitration court, require increases in social security benefits, etc. In short, disturb one set of prices and you upset *all* administered prices, and in New Zealand the range of these was very wide. During the 1950's prices and wages rose steeply, faster as to prices than in the larger Western countries, a poor advertisement for conservatives allegedly bent on putting value back into the pound.

The controls could, however, be administered differently. As Labour had shown before its defeat a disposition to reduce ministerial responsibility for marketing (e.g., of butter), so the conservatives pushed this further and aimed to get back to the producers' syndicates, with the eyes of the ministers on them, of the 1920's and 1930's. Further, they also freed the Reserve Bank from direct ministerial direction, transfering ultimate decision to Parliament, but leaving the Bank quite free as long as it kept within the ambit of general government policy. And, too, they could and did shift the emphasis of housing policy from the provision of rentals to the sale of the houses built or building; they could abolish controls over building. But if they could dismantle the elaborate system of imports control Labour had built up, they had, when hard pushed in a balance of payments crisis, to achieve the same end by exchange control and Labour could and did restore its control system. And so in one way or another the alleged wide gap between Labour and the conservatives was eroded away. New Zealand was inexorably committed to an elaborately managed economy. If the conservative politicians felt trapped, they were in a trap forged over a thirty-year period and they had made large contributions to the forging.

The general trend of production during the 1950's was upward with shifts between commodities from time to time in the land industries as demand fluctuated and profitability varied. As an exporting economy the dependence was still, as traditionally, on a narrow range of land industry products sold in very large proportion in London: in order of value, wool, meat, dairy produce. Marketing not production was the plaguing problem. The labor force was increasing in size, more from natural increase of the population than from immigration. By 1960 there were 2,370,000 New Zealanders. While the numbers employed on the farms declined, efficiency of production gave a larger output. Mechanization continued apace—more tractors, etc., technological innovations were introduced, managerial skills improved. The supplying of missing trace elements in pastures became common practice, certain plaguing diseases of stock were brought under better control, the practice of utilizing productive but expensive machines by hiring outside contractors to do the work on farms (top-dressing, transport, ditch cleaning, sheep dipping, harvesting, etc.) became more common and, especially significant to marginal holdings, aerial top-dressing boomed. There was a marked increase in the numbers employed in manufacturing, though not in the proportion of workers so employed. The fastest growing factory industries were pulp and paper, rubber products, automobile components, agricultural machinery, and electrical goods. New Zealand industries remained heavily dependent on imported capital goods, raw materials, and components; they had to be developed on the basis of a small population and without a foundation of heavy industry. However, the most marked increase in employment was in the services. Urbanization intensified and not only did the established cities increase in size, but several towns grew to the dimensions of small cities, illustratively Hamilton and Palmerston North. But the shifts and changes in the way in which the work force was deployed was not accompanied by a general increase in productivity per head, whatever the situation in particular occupations. A study showed that increase of "output per head of the labour force [in the 1950's] has been only about half of that of the United States, Sweden, Belgium and Norway, about a third of that of France, and less than a quarter of that of West Germany and Japan."

Capital investment, the key to economic growth, failed to achieve a level sufficiently high, or to be sustained steadily at the highest annual levels achieved, to be entirely satisfactory. Under the conservatives it rose by 5 per cent to a peak of 23 per cent in 1953 and 1955, but this peak was a low rate as compared to the needs of New Zealand, estimated to be 30 per cent. Within the gross percentage figure the private investment figure achieved a plateau of about 12 per cent of GNP, with a peak of 14 in 1955, the time of greatest conservative economic successes, while the government component reached a peak of 10 per cent but was ordinarily below that level, less than prewar. Of the private investment, building was consistently the largest single element. Of "other" private investment spending on industrial plant achieved a peak in the middle 1950's and then receded, but began to rise again in 1958. Much of the capital actually invested in manufacturing came from Britain and Australia. Investment in the land industries was consistently about adequate to pressing needs. Government investment was distributed to support the standard of living and the better to service and supply the economy. While maintaining government investment in housing as a major item, the conservatives let it decrease a bit, compensating by encouraging private building, and made electricity supply the largest single item. They also increased spending on railways, telephones, roads, land conservation and development, and educational facilities. There was thus a concentration on transport (upgrading roads rather than extending them, improving railway rolling stock rather than extending mileage, improving ports to handle more goods outward and inward, building airfields for the expanding air services), essentially a justifiable contemporary version of a well-established preoccupation. The figures do not show that the Labour government of 1957–60 essentially modified the conservative pattern, even though they reflect to a slight degree Labour's bias in favor of public housing. From the record it is apparent that in spite of encouragement from the conservatives, private investors did not take the lead in building a new New Zealand, although at various times in the 1950's it appeared they might be going to do so. They sighted no open road forward, as their Australian opposite numbers did, or if they did they were unable to begin work on it. In spite of logic, argumentation, and exhortation emphasizing the necessity to expand factory industry, local private investors did not find this a steadily attractive field of activity, or could not find the money in the constricted local capital market. There was no proper "development bank" to assist. As it happened both Labour and Holland's government took a hand in developing the most strikingly creative investment in this field, the pulp and paper industry, and as its 1957–60 administration drew toward its end, Labour announced that the government would collaborate with Australian-based private enterprise in the building of an aluminum works in the South Island, using raw material from Australia's rich resources of bauxite and local hydroelectric power. What all this meant with regard to the future of private enterprise in New Zealand was difficult to say. The 1960's promise to be the testing time; they might well show that any large undertakings were impossible without heavy investment support from the government.

If the internal economic situation was manageable after a fashion not too upsetting to the average fully employed and protected wayfaring New Zealander, however the contending politicians and the intelligentsia might react, the external forces operating on New Zealand periodically assumed a shape considered menacing by everyone. Bulk purchasing came to an end in 1954 when butter ceased to be so handled, this removing a prop from the external market. An agreement made in 1957 assured New Zealand free entry for certain basic exports into the United Kingdom market for ten years. But the foreigners pressed the New Zealanders hard in that market. While the percentage of total New Zealand exports going to the United Kingdom, and of imports from the United Kingdom into New Zealand, was declining—in 1958, exports to United Kingdom 56 per cent, imports 53 per cent—showing a declining dependence on that market, this did not apply to some of the more important of the New Zealand exports; for these the dependence was from heavy to close to absolute. A satisfactory dispersion of export outlets had not been achieved, though a beginning had been made. The economy continued to show a very strong propensity to import, stimulated by internal inflation, and on occasion there developed "storms" of importing not related to favorable developments in the means of payment. The balance of payments was at best precarious. Import controls in some form were required both by Labour and the conservatives, to the chagrin of the latter. What New Zealand needed was a market of steadily remunerative prices capable of steadily absorbing its export commodities. Instead, it had a basic market characterized by price instability and subject since the 1930's to the threat of crippling limitations on its absorptive capacity. Thus in 1958, under Labour by the fortunes of political warfare, a decline of butter prices in London, at work since 1956, now aggravated by a "storm" of imports, brought a severe crisis only surmounted by borrowing in Australia, London, and New York to replenish external financial resources, and in 1961, under the conservatives, the New Zealanders were violently upset by the excursions and alarums incident to the United Kingdom's effort to enter the European Common Market. The 1958 experience brought the conservatives around to joining the International Bank and Monetary Fund (August 31, 1961) after their return to office in 1960. The Common Market proposal, menacing their United Kingdom outlet by threatening both free entry and preference, raised for the New Zealanders the problem of economic survival, phrased in the General Assembly of the United Nations: "If this equality of nations under the Charter does not mean that a country which efficiently produces goods needed by mankind should be able to live and prosper without being squeezed out of existence by monster continental organizations, it is hard to see how the Charter's concern for nations large and small has any reality."

Before Labour went out of office in 1949, it took several legislative steps of a political nature concerned with the status of New Zealand in the Commonwealth and domestic political arrangements. After protracted discussions and hesitations, Parliament adopted in 1947 the vital sections of the Statute of Westminster 1931, the last of the old dominions to do so, thus bringing status and legislative capacity into line with the functions that had been assumed just before and during the war. A major step away from the cherished colonial status—at least a major step symbolically, it left New Zealand still a monarchical member of the Commonwealth, still fervently "loyal" in the traditional manner, ready and willing to acknowledge Britain's Queen as its Queen when the time came to legislate to this effect, still as close to Britain as could be managed. Ironically, however, the step was taken so belatedly that within two years New Zealand found itself again among the traditionalists in general attitude and constitutionally; it found itself associated in the Commonwealth with republican members, products of the anticolonialism of which Labour so strongly approved, who excluded the monarch from their systems of government and only acknowledged him (or her) as a symbol signifying the unity of a loosely woven Commonwealth community. To complete the transition to which it had submitted, New Zealand, also in 1947, arranged that the protective provision of the

Statute of Westminster that prevented the legislature from altering the New Zealand constitution by its own action, be repealed by the imperial Parliament and the power lodged in the New Zealand Parliament. In the immediate sequel this did not lead to any radical action by Labour but rather, interestingly enough, by the conservatives. The action was the abolition of the New Zealand upper house, making the legislature unicameral. Although discussion of this measure had begun while Labour was still in office, it was pushed through under Sidney Holland's leadership after the Nationalists had come to power. The argument for the step was that the upper house had been *de facto* powerless to perform its ostensible functions ever since the Ballance government had established the Australian principle of control by swamping in the 1890's, and that all efforts since to give it a reasonable status and viable function had failed. Abolition was argued to be a desirable economy and the Nationalists were avid for economy. From February 1951 New Zealand had a unicameral legislature. Earlier Labour had upset another political device of some antiquity. In 1945 it had abolished the "country quota," or the practice of arbitrarily adding 28 per cent to the actual population in delimiting rural constituencies, followed since 1889. All that was retained was a statistical "tolerance" of 5 per cent in favor of rural constituencies, not a prescriptive addition to their populations. Otherwise town and country were on a par. It made no discernible political difference.

Like Australian Labor, New Zealand Labour went out of office before it was possible to undertake that redefinition of foreign political relations which the postwar power situation ever more urgently required. The redefinition was therefore a charge upon the Nationalists. The intellectuals were not altogether happy about this, discerning in the conservatives a lack of knowledge and sophistication about foreign affairs that disturbed them. However, the Nationalists in fact showed no disposition to develop any strong particularistic line of their own, either obtusely traditional or experimentally bizarre. Strong support of the United Nations proved to be axiomatic; the United Nations action in Korea was actively supported with ships and troops; it was a Nationalist appointee, Sir Leslie Munroe, who rose to the presidency of the General Assembly. And like their Labour predecessors they associated themselves with their Australian opposite numbers, the Liberals, who had come to office about the same time. The range of possibilities open to the New Zealanders was essentially the same as it was for the Australians, the varieties of dissent from the arrangements finally made essentially the same in both countries, with nostalgic "Empire" loyalty stronger in New Zealand. The likelihood of escape from the eventually devised resolution of the "Anzac dilemma"—

the expression of a New Zealander, Professor F. L. W. Wood—was even less probable, barring a staggering revolution in public opinion, for the New Zealanders standing alone than for the Australians standing alone. The first indicative act of the Nationalists was to support the Australians at Ceylon in their proposal to aid the new nations of Asia through the so-called Colombo Plan, anticommunist in resonance but antipoverty by deliberate focus. In 1947 New Zealand Labour had associated itself with Australian Labor in seeking a "hard" peace treaty with Japan, but now the Nationalists followed the Australian Liberals in accepting the "soft" treaty devised and proposed by the Americans—the effective agent was the Republican John Foster Dulles acting for a Democratic administration—not liking it in all particulars but accepting it, especially when presented in conjunction with the ANZUS (Australia-New Zealand-United States) defense treaty worked out parallel in time. And they again went along with their Australian confreres into the SEATO organization, another of Dulles'—now a Republican secretary of State—arrangements, designed to deal with the uneasy situation in Southeast Asia. As New Zealand Labour had accepted the proposition that the country's primary foreign political responsibilities were in the Pacific, so in 1955 the Nationalists signified an important meaning of this by announcing that in future defense forces would be sent to Southeast Asia rather than the Middle East, hence the stationing of New Zealand troops in Malaya. Thus the Nationalists accommodated the country to the apparent necessities of its new position, accepting, if without enthusiasm, the fact that the United States, wartime surrogate for Britain, was now indeed New Zealand's ultimate external reliance for security. Although the details of the arrangements were likely to change in time, the solution of the Anzac dilemma the Nationalists worked out with their Australian colleagues was unlikely to be disturbed as long as it was majority New Zealand opinion that outside support of the country's security was inescapably required. But that that was the traditional conclusion about national security had not made the shift of reliance from Britain to the United States an exactly popular development. Hard and vastly regrettable necessity alone made it acceptable; it did not make it palatable; and the somewhat frantic canvassing of alternatives illustrated how unpalatable, both to old-fashioned imperialists and extreme and sentimental leftists, it really was. New Zealand's strong support of Britain in the Suez affair of 1956 clearly illustrated how far from vestigial her ancient loyalties were. But the new scheme for underwriting security was unimpeachably realistic.

The two most significant developments among the Maoris from the middle 1920's into the postwar period were their rapid increase in numbers and the intensification of their urbanization. Although they still remained predominantly a rural people, it was no longer possible even for their own leaders or their best pakeha friends to envision their future exclusively as a rural people. There was important work to be done in developing the land still in their possession and improving their techniques as farmers, but more clearly than ever there was not enough land to support them all.

From 1926 when the Maori population was 64,000, the total rose rapidly to 137,000 in 1956. The birthrate doubled in that time, reaching a decidedly higher level than the pakeha rate, and the death rate declined, even though the health problem was still far from mastered. Assuming no marked increase of the pakeha population by immigration, the proportion of Maoris in the total population was forecast to rise from 6 per cent in 1952 to a projected 8.6 per cent in 1972. Whereas in 1926 only 5 per cent of the Maoris were to be found in urban areas, by 1956 the figure was 17 per cent, a far sharper rise than was characteristic of the pakeha population. About 75 per cent of the Maori urban residents were to be found in the North Island cities and towns. In Auckland between 1939 and 1956 the Maori population increased six times. World War II was an effective agent of urbanization. (In addition Cook islanders, Tongans, and Samoans have also been attracted to Auckland in recent years.)

Maori incomes, rural and urban, ran about 25 per cent below pakeha incomes. Reflecting their residence, those following rural occupations were naturally a proportionately larger group than in the case of the pakeha. More indicative of their general economic position, however, was the fact that whereas only about 10 pakeha in 100 were classified as manual workers, 30 out of every 100 Maori workers were; and whereas 25 out of every 100 pakehas were white collar workers, only 4 Maori workers were. The disproportion was greater, therefore, as education became the decisive factor. In 1958 only 21 Maori boys and 33 Maori girls out of 1000 of each about to leave the secondary schools expressed the intention of entering the teaching profession, seeking other professional training or going to a university.

The Maori handicaps, twelve decades after Waitangi, were expertly assessed to be "educational . . . , poor housing, low incomes, a low rate of capital formation, high incidence of some diseases, and behaviour problems arising out of social change." The official approach to the Maoris remained a muddle of assimilation, for historical reasons savoring of Europeanization, and integration, or the design of bringing the Maori to equality without wholly destroying his cultural heritage. The Maori was reckoned to have legal and political equality and most Maori contacts with the government were practically the same as the pakeha contacts and the benefits were identical; the government's ancient Department of Maori Affairs (so renamed from Native Affairs in 1947) had a diminishing range of particularistic responsibilities to the Maori people. There remained, however, the subtle and vexing problem of psychological distance between the Maoris and their best friends, government servants and others, and the alarming question as to whether or not the Maoris suffered the disability of social prejudice and whether this was at its most intense in the urban environments. The popular and official disposition was to deny that social prejudice existed, but the allegation that it did could not be silenced. In short, the Maoris remained an issue of conscience to the pakeha, as well as a difficult problem of sociological economics, and making one's peace with the Maoris was a conspicuous item on both the moral and intellectual agendas of the New Zealand people, with "Waitangi" the reconciling shibboleth-symbol.

Although to give politics a decidedly economic tinge by emphasizing who gets how much and how continuously in terms of a standard of living has long been characteristic of New Zealand, this has been far from the whole of the New Zealand story. There has been wide agreement among critics of an aesthetic or religious turn of mind that the average New Zealander has been a simple, unreflective materialist, but as a complete and unalloyed materialist is a rather rare specimen of the human species, so an entirely materialist nation is unknown to history. All have their learning and their arts, however derivative and though consigned to the care of marginal people. Whether from congenital folly or from an inextinguishable impulse to assert their dignity as men in terms other than butter and wool, some New Zealanders, like some members of all human communities, have constantly been preoccupied in other directions: climbing Mount Everest in the far Himalayas—such as Sir Edmund Hillary; adventuring in Antarctica (see Chapter XV); setting the Samoans free (see Chapter XI); teaching and learning; making music; writing poems, short stories, and novels; painting pictures.

It has been characteristic of New Zealand, as of all other modern democracies, to conceive of cultural and intellectual enterprises as fundamentally private undertakings, but activities which somehow should command patronage since, other than in rare and exceptional circumstances, they are unlikely to be self-sustaining economically. In New Zealand because of the prevailing patterns of property and income distribution the logical patron has been the government. By tradition the cultural activity most comprehensively dependent upon government patronage has been education, from primary school through the university. In postwar New Zealand the most conspicuous innovation has been the exploration of ways and means for bringing government money to the support of the arts of the adult population, especially for the direct benefit of practitioners, actual and potential, with the expectation that thus the audience will be benefitted if only by the easier accessibility of more expert performance. Credit for initiating this innovation goes to Prime Minister Peter Fraser; the year of initiation was 1947. On the Whitmanian principle, great artists require great audiences, but artists are, with all their foibles, easier to assist than audiences. The problem of audiences abides.

In its earliest phases public education was primary education. During the last quarter of the nineteenth century an examining university, the examiners resident in Britain, teaching colleges affiliated with it, was developed. This left a gap between the primary schools and the university colleges which was in the beginning mostly filled by private enterprise, but from 1900 on the government began to move toward dominant participation, developing technical and liberal arts high schools, slowly asserting its authority over the private liberal arts schools. This development was only completed as lately as 1950, leaving the surviving private schools far less conspicuous on the educational scene than, say, in Australia. New Zealand became a state-educated community. At the same time there was by plan a steady erosion of local authority and responsibility for education and an equally steady building up of *central* authority and responsibility. To fit its needs, as the leadership conceived it, with the substance and rather distorted shadow of the British example resting heavily, it had developed a government-supported, centrally administered system, periodically swept by waves of reform or rejuvenation, either under the influence of the professional head, for example, George Hogben (1853–1920), whose impact was felt in the time of Seddonian Liberalism, or by virtue of a keen interest in education of a minister, for example, Peter Fraser in the early years of Labour's rule. Argument over education, since the Greeks of the essence of the educational enterprise, has indeed been a hardy perennial in New Zealand and still is. It was in part given an institutional form by the Carnegie Corporation of New York which, in 1933, established a Council for Educational Research; in 1945 it passed to financial dependence upon the government. Since the end of the war the substantial expansion of the physical plant for education has been a conspicuous activity. In the late 1950's expenditure on education was about 3.7 per cent of the national income.

Most of the money was being spent on the state schools, for the social obligation to them was most widely recognized and the clientele was largest. The university colleges were caught in a tradition of struggle for funds and the struggle had not eased as their students had increased in numbers and variety of demands. Whereas in 1938 there were 5700 students in the various affiliated colleges, in 1958 there were 12,900. By then the typical university college had come to consist of a group of professional schools—medicine, dentistry, law, architecture, engineering, commerce—clustered around the original core of the liberal arts course, each college specializing in one or another of several varieties of professional training. An analysis of the distribution of the students (including candidates for diplomas) as of 1958 showed that 40 out of 100 were doing arts, 16 out of 100 commerce, and 12 out of 100 science, while the rest were doing agriculture, architecture, dentistry, medicine, law, divinity, and so on. As in other democracies, training encroached upon education, degree hunting upon cultivation, heavy teaching loads upon research, the utilitarian end upon the cultural purpose. Constantly without adequate means, the colleges nevertheless constantly turned out graduates who won distinction at home and overseas, as if to demonstrate the truth of the story about Mark Hopkins and the log. In 1960 no university college had a library of as many as 200,000 volumes. Moreover, the university colleges have been beset by fierce struggles to establish professorial autonomy and dignity, to gain control over examinations from the external examiners in England, and to gain academic authority over management from the predominantly nonacademic controlling body of the university. For the higher reaches of their specializations students were drawn overseas, chiefly to Britain; seeing no straight path to a career in New Zealand, they often remained overseas as expatriates, even though only in Australia.

After World War II the great pressure upon the university colleges was that of numbers, a pressure not to be evaded in view of the obvious need for a better and more diversely educated citizenry in an increasingly complex world. The only reasonable response was the wise spending of more money. The university problem was expertly reviewed by a specially appointed committee in 1959. Since more money meant more government money, this raised in the New Zealand context a question which plagues every Western-style democracy: how best to allocate tax income —this involving a sharp conflict of opinion among those seeking to achieve discrepant goals. A significant structural change, completed in 1961, was the abolition of the old University of New Zealand and the constitution of the university colleges as independent universities, without implying that each should develop a full panoply of "schools."

An expert assessment of the libraries in New Zealand, released in 1960, was rather depressing, especially to those of scholarly proclivities: ".... about one work out of fifty is available locally, there being an estimated 600,000 individual titles in the country out of a total of more than thirty million which have been issued since the invention of printing ... the number of libraries ... is only 286. They contain 5,462,487 volumes, or less than the New York Public Library alone does. There is no large library in the country ... collecting in depth is not prevalent ... the predominant part consists of books and periodicals issued in Great Britain and New Zealand." But the wayfaring citizen is perhaps better served than this dark picture indicates—that is one of the dangers in the situation! Just before and just after the war important innovations in library administration were undertaken to increase the number of libraries and to facilitate access to the book resources at hand, directed toward both school and public libraries. Here again the need was for more government money. Private benefactions are certain to be as marginal here as in education proper, even though the country's richest collection of New Zealandiana and Pacificana, of English literature, and of rare editions of "great" books in the Alexander Turnbull Library at Wellington was a private benefaction of 1918, subsequently supplemented by other private benefactions, but supported as a functioning library by the government.

When it came to the relation of the government to the cultural interests of the adult citizenry, the key figures were the ministers and permanent heads for the time being of the departments of Internal Affairs and Education and of Broadcasting and the National Library Service. Together with chosen representative private citizens, among whom were normally a number of academics and commonly a representative of the Maoris, these people constituted "councils"—e.g., the National Council of Adult Education (founded 1947), the Arts Advisory Council (founded 1960) —whose primary duty was to spend wisely the government money made available for legislatively specified purposes. The key department with regard to the arts was the Department of Internal Affairs, but not all money available to support cultural affairs came through it. The National Orchestra was attached to the Broadcasting Service. The government printer, who produced an exceptionally wide variety of books and pamphlets of literary, historical, and scientific importance might be acting for almost any division of the government. In the Department of Interior, however, were found the Literary Fund, a matter of prime interest to the writers, established in 1947, to systematize the grants already being made to individuals and book and magazine publishers as well as the larger Cultural Fund established in 1960 to deal with the problems of patronage for musicians, actors, dancers, and those Cinderellas of the arts, the painters. However, artists of any kind are normally restless people, if not physically, then mentally and spiritually, and while this impressive structure of state patronage has been pleasing, they still have found it possible to complain of its adequacy in money terms, that the councils were over-loaded with public servants, that the beneficiaries were ill-chosen, that the work done by them was often of questionable worth, or that the public was still, in its philistine beastliness, disposed to argue that the money could be better spent in other directions.

There was, however, no reason to suppose that the systematizing of government patronage stood in determinable cause and effect relationship to the postwar upsurge of cultural activities. To be sure there would be no National Orchestra if Peter Fraser had not taken the initiative in estab-lishing one, but in most other directions the government assisted in-dividuals and organizations already at work in their special fields. Poets and novelists are by definition self-starters. The government could assist the admirable quarterly *Landfall* (founded 1947), but it could not con-jure into existence the "copy" from which the editor expertly selected the contents of the successive issues. It could subsidize the publication of a book of poems if somebody had the energy to get the poems written, a historical work if someone had chosen to do the research and writing, or the ballet if someone had promoted a company; it could sustain but it could not evoke.

Although to select uninvidiously from a host is impossible, mention may be made from among the poets of Allen Curnow, still a powerful figure both creatively and critically, of James K. Baxter, Kendrick Smithyman, Alistair Campbell, M. K. Joseph, and Keith Sinclair. And from among the novelists, with similar hesitation and with the notation that Frank Sargeson still remains the exemplary figure for the writers of fiction, one may distinguish Don Davin, James Courage, Guthrie Wil-son, David Ballantyne, Ian Cross, Sylvia Ashton-Warner, Janet Frame, M. K. Joseph, some thus far one-book novelists, but any one possibly the creator of an impressive array of works. Nor had the short story writers relinquished their activity. There were, for example, Maurice Shadbolt, Roderick Finlayson, and A. P. Gaskell. The New Zealand scene and its denizens were being worked over ever more intensively to the great profit of both writers and readers. Both the sense of the uniqueness of New Zealand as a place and the "personal voice" were finding fuller expres-sion, the sense of special identity intensifying.

New Zealand, then, stood in the early 1960's a small nation in the Pacific, contemplating with uneasiness a world it had only assisted peripherally in making, hesitant about how now best to deploy its energies to achieve a defined objective because no realizable objective could easily be defined, but destined, it would seem, to be as distinctive a success as a small nation in the Southwest Pacific as Switzerland, Denmark, or Sweden were in Europe, probably in ever closer regional association with Australia, in any case (to paraphrase Robin Hyde's much-quoted remark) finding "for ever England" still evocative, but "New Zealand" more evocative yet.

THE ISLANDS

CHAPTER IX

Land, Europeans, and Natives

The state of the islands at the turn of the century has been described by Dr. J. C. Beaglehole as "more or less exploited, more or less missionized, less rather than more administered." Their history from about 1900 to the outbreak of World War II, in terms of the Western impact on them (which is our primary concern), consists in largest measure of an effort by the responsible political authorities to strike a defensible balance between promoting the exploitation of the land resources by white entrepreneurs and safeguarding native interests. Tensions were due chiefly to differing opinions of what a proper balance between the two great interests really was. The differences of opinion varied in character and intensity between the island groups, but in no case at this stage were they ever absolutely polarizing at the policy-making level because neither the resident government officials nor their home governments were entirely clear about what was or should be the ultimate fate of the indigenes nor were they disposed to deny that the demands of the intruding entrepreneurs were as legitimate in the prevailing circumstances as any conception of a "future" for the natives. A more or less unique combination of "circumstances" determined the situation in each island group, as will be made clear below.

Ordinarily the incoming whites, whether as individuals or employees of companies, were most interested in land and the labor supply or in the trade arising from the successful conjunction of the two. With land available on satisfactory terms, labor was, in their conception, to be supplied by local recruitment, interisland movement, or from outside the islands altogether—from India, China, Japan, Indochina, or Java. Save in New Caledonia, where mining was the predominant activity, the land and labor were wanted for plantation agriculture, mostly for tree-culture, with labor for mining subordinate. It was the assumption that it was the responsibility of the European enterprisers to carry out productive activities on their own initiative and to market the products, but policy and service assistance from the governments was normally expected and sometimes raucously demanded. The consequent export-import activities were not only the most often observed indicators of significant economic activity and its growth but also a principal source of government income. The governments were normally heavily dependent on taxes laid on goods entering and leaving the colonies. Since it was the prevailing idea that colonies should be self-supporting in the sense that government spending should be limited to the income that could be derived locally, and European enterprises were the principal generators of taxable income, this tended to throw an emphasis on their promotion if only to improve a government's finances. The limitations on local government income tended to confine governmental activities to a narrow range of "essentials," and if a metropolitan government granted a subsidy it was designed to support a conception of the "essentials," not to underwrite any elaboration of, say, a welfare program for the natives. In this situation, little was normally available for education, medical or public health services, or public investment to support or stimulate economic growth. Taking the islands as a whole—a perspective rarely entertained—there was an irregular expansion of white enterprise during the forty years under review in this and most of the next chapter.

The attitude of the resident whites serving economic interests was frankly exploitative, though not necessarily involving any openly expressed animus against the natives; they were in the islands for what they could make out of them and the natives were regarded as labor supply. After the heavy task of establishing and maintaining production, the preoccupation of the Europeans was on its sale. As in only a few and minor cases were the vendible commodities unique in the world market, the normal situation was that the island commodities were but a marginal fraction of the world market supply. The markets within the area were small and quickly oversupplied, or access to them was impeded, as the Australians eventually impeded the movement of island bananas and sugar onto their market in favor of supplies from tropical Queensland. The dependence of the island producers was therefore on the world market. It was very distant, overseas in Europe, North America and, as time passed, Japan. There was always, therefore, a gap between the return to the island producers and the prices ruling overseas, which was at least partly accounted for by the cost of transporting the goods overseas to the consumption-markets. In the islands the local traders, whether independent operators or agents of large concerns and the operators of island shipping services, sometimes combined in a single organization, were the mediators between the European producers and the world market. Within the area, Sydney in Australia was the leading focal point of the enterprises engaged in trading and shipping in the islands. Auckland, New Zealand, was a secondary focal point. Any direct shipping to Europe was competitive with the Sydney and Auckland services. The remoteness of the islands from their consumption-markets could be a depressant to the establishment or expansion of production, and adverse price movements in the overseas markets could not only embarrass the island producers but on occasion could cause the cessation or abandonment of production in the islands, for example, rubber. Other depressants, aside from pests such as the rhinoceros beetle, rats, etc., were the appearance of artificial substitutes for the island products, such as artificial vanilla, and competition in the world market between commodities of parallel uses, for example, the competition between coconut oil, cottonseed oil, whale oil, and soybean oil.

It was usually an idea of the island administrations that native production for market should be established and encouraged to expand in order to give the natives the cash income they needed to put a gloss on a standard of living which still rested fundamentally on a subsistence agriculture. Native production for market normally involved far lower capital investment than European, had lower operating costs, and resulted in the marketing of goods of lower grade than the Europeans offered. The proportion of exportable commodities supplied by the native producers on the one hand and the European producers on the other varied from group to group and commodity to commodity. The native contribution was normally greatest with respect to copra. It was, however, part of the general idea that the native contribution should not only steadily increase but become diversified by the invasion of areas of production pioneered by the Europeans, such as cocoa and coffee. This seemingly purely economic activity was mixed with a conception of the future of the natives as peoples.

Aside from the whites with direct economic interests, the resident Europeans were mostly government servants and missionaries. On the government servants, no matter how "technical" their ostensible preoccupations, beat the variant ideas about the future of the islands and the island indigenes. The activities of the missionaries not only directly impinged upon native belief and custom but also influenced the outlook of the governments. In addition to their preoccupation with religious issues, the missionaries were also concerned with education, medicine and public health, and sometimes production for market. In the context of the prevailing ideas about what the governments could properly spend money on, the missionary contribution to education was usually fundamental and to medicine and public health extremely important. With regard to questions involving the present condition and future prospects of the natives, the missionaries were normally philo-native and therefore critical of the views of the more forthright European entrepreneurs, whose horizon was "labor supply," and governments careless of the native interest.

The number of resident whites usually remained quite small. They were normally concentrated in the principal trading ports, especially if the port was also the seat of government. They were also scattered widely through the colony on plantations or at mines or at government or mission stations. While in certain groups "old island hands" were fairly common and families established in the islands for several generations were not unknown, the Europeans in the islands were mostly people who had arrived as adults and considered themselves transients, even though the transciency might involve the greater part of a working life. While the Europeans became wedded to island life and presumably "liked" it, only a minority long entertained notions about its romance, whatever role it may have played in bringing them to the islands. They were kept in the islands by the exacting pursuit of economic gain, the pursuit of careers in a public service, or by religiously motivated devotion to the native peoples. The few who were drawn to the islands south of the equator by the persisting rumor of an idyllic, romantic life there were mostly attracted to Tahiti and associated French islands and in almost all cases to some island in Polynesia. Remarkably few of these spent a lifetime in the islands.

In these forty years no Polynesian group south of the equator, except New Zealand, was anywhere near as exhaustively "westernized" as Hawaii north of it. In Melanesia, Fiji and New Caledonia were most strongly effected by the Western impact. The frontiers of westernization were chiefly found in Melanesia, notably in New Guinea and the Solomons. The model pattern of westernization for its partisans south of the equator was, therefore, Hawaii.

With regard to the native interest, no government was as consistently straightforward in advancing it as the whites were in advancing theirs. This was not because of ill-will toward the natives but because of a genuine insecurity about the end to be sought and the compromises with regard to means forced on the administrators by the need to accommodate to some degree to the necessities of the European entrepreneurs. If any common end can be generalized it was somehow to *adjust* the indigenes usefully to themselves and the intruders to the conditions being created by the westernizing forces at work. There was, of course, variation in the approved pattern of adjustment as between island groups, arising out of the stage of development of the natives themselves, the ways in which the westernizing forces operated locally, and the nature of the inheritance of governmental policy. In no group were the natives by policy exhaustively sheltered from the westernizing forces, but there were continuing efforts to soften the impact in Fiji, Samoa, and Papua, to cite variant examples. The natives, of course, had been adjusting in one fashion or another ever since the whites first came among them. There was, however, an increasing self-consciousness about the business supported by ideas circulating in the British colonial service. What successful adjustment was, was nevertheless very hard to say, but certainly physical survival was an element of it and the working out of some creative relation to the "western" economy was another. The physical survival element was largely the concern of the administrations, with assistance from the missionaries and private philanthropy, but the relation to the "western" economy had to be worked out in a context of conflict between the administrations and the European entrepreneurs. In this respect there was a difference of opinion between those who believed that labor service on plantations and in mines should be a principal means of "adjusting" the natives to the new conditions and those who, while accepting such labor service as necessary in the prevailing circumstances, wished also to place heavy emphasis on developing both the native subsistence agricultural economy to improve the native food supply and the native commercial production. This, however, is to focus on the economic element in a conflict of views over how the natives should be dealt with that ramified into other vital areas. And it seems to be the case that more trouble was caused by the failure to define a widely accepted end for the natives than by the disagreements over means that claimed so much attention.

However, it was the common assumption that the natives were, as a matter of fact, fading away and this was complacently regarded as a historical inevitability. Even the specialist literature of an anthropological-medical character was long dominated by the idea of depopulation. Although the numbers of indigenes present in the various groups of islands at the times of original discovery were uncertain, it was generally supposed that practically everywhere they were greater than they were in the first decades of the twentieth century. Although some inquirers suspected that a decline had begun even before the Europeans arrived, it was widely accepted that the arrival of the whites speeded up the decline in ways already reviewed. About 1920 the English anthropologist W. H. R. Rivers, considering specifically the case of the Melanesians, made much of the old notion of *tedium vitae* as an important contributor to decline, or the idea that population decline was rooted in the decay of native culture and its incentives and the failure of satisfying new life-values to appear. However, Rivers' refurbishment had but a short run, for before World War I, while depopulation was obviously continuing in Melanesia, elsewhere in specific situations, particularly in Polynesia, the populations had begun to increase and before World War II came around, overpopulation in relation to land resources began to be identifiable. If not causally related to the spread of medical care and public health service, the upturn was certainly supported by them and in any case it became apparent that given "the tools" the natives could not only survive as a diminishing remnant but also actually increase in numbers toward and even beyond their historically reported maximums. If this were to happen, everything in the island world would change.

About the same time native expectations of life also began to rise and since the expectations were ordinarily defined in terms of goods and services of "civilization" as they were learned of in contacts with the whites, ready access to them became a progressively more pressing issue. During World War II these expectations were to be greatly inflated in islands that knew metropolitan and foreign armed services men. The rising native expectations were not necessarily accompanied either on the part of the natives or the administrations by any clear understanding of how the coveted things and services might be obtained by the natives. Or an obviously desired and desirable service, such as native education, might be hamstrung by inadequate finance. Lacking any understanding of how to obtain the coveted goods and services by their own efforts, or despairing of ever getting into such a position while caught in the traps that presently ensnared them, the natives occasionally showed a highly significant restlessness supporting cultist activities, strikes, and political agitation, all in their various ways forecasting things to come to a more marked extent after the vast disturbances of World War II. A shift in attitudes, policies, and actions with regard to colonial welfare and development began about 1924 or 1929 but came to really significant expression only after World War II.

Beginning about 1900 anthropologists progressively improved understanding of the aboriginal cultures of the islands and as time passed began to explore the "adjusted" cultures the natives were evolving, ranging from the adjustments made after minimal contact with Europeans to those of the most radically transformed natives living on the outskirts of the larger island towns. The multiplication of anthropological studies does not seem to have been the cause of any fundamental revolution in policy in any of the island administrations. Rather, more and more men, including policy-makers, were provided with a firmer basis for more or less philo-native policies on which they had already determined for quite other reasons. In time the anthropologists became another "interest" in the array of interests having a stake in the island colonial situations and since their orientation was interpretable as hostile to that of the more extreme exponents of European exploitation, they provoked an astonishingly rancorous "know-nothing" reaction.

Before sketching the histories of the islands under British, Australian, New Zealand, French, Dutch, and American control, the story of Germany's adventure as a colonial power south of the equator in the Pacific can properly be told. Linking back to the account of the arrival and progress of the Germans given in Chapter XXIII of *The Southwest Pacific to 1900,* it will be necessary to indicate the relation of their activities in New Guinea and Samoa to their activities in Micronesia *north* of the equator.

The establishment of the Germans in the islands north of the equator is a fairly intricate story, reeking of imperialism. They began their activities north of the equator in the 1860's as a phase of a search from Samoa for new sources of copra. While the Germans traded in the islands north and west of Samoa, including the Gilbert and Ellice groups, they apparently considered them a British preserve and appear never to have tried to gain possession of them. But when they extended operations to the north and west into the Marshalls and beyond, they eventually did seek possession. At the time the various groups to the west were ostensibly under Spanish sovereignty or were derelict. Insofar as they were Spanish they were associated with the Philippines. Actually the Spanish took little interest in them, aside from Guam in the northern Marianas. They made no pretense to governing the numerous other islands. The German venture into the Marshalls was pursued simultaneously by the Godeffroys from Samoa, and private German traders whose base was in Honolulu, and the Hernsheim people operating from bases in the Carolines. British copra traders out of Australia and American traders out of San Francisco were also active in the Marshalls at the time.

The Spanish took no notice of the activity in the Marshalls but when the Germans and the British became quite active in the Carolines, closer to the Philippines, the Spanish began to stir. In 1875 the governor of the Philippines attempted to enforce licensing and taxation on all foreign traders in the Carolines. The Germans and the British protested and two years later the Spanish government conceded absolute freedom of trade and indicated that the home government did not claim the sovereignty the governor of the Philippines had implied. In the following year, 1878, the Germans began to tighten their hold on the Marshalls. They concluded a treaty with the chiefs of Jaluit Atoll, chiefly involving the Ralik Chain, which gave them special trading rights and the right to establish a naval station. Jaluit Atoll thus became a seat of German trade and administration. Spain made no protest. But in 1884 the Spanish asserted that after all they did have sovereign rights in the Carolines. The Germans challenged. The argument was focused on the island of Yap in the West Carolines where German trading companies had branches, but to spread their claim, the Germans also raised their flag at Palau, Ponape, Truk, and elsewhere. The Spanish referred the issue to Pope Leo XIII, since their rights in the Pacific derived from a Papal determination of 1494, and in December 1885 the Pope ruled in favor of Spain as far as sovereignty and responsibility for government were concerned, but required it to grant complete freedom to German traders, planters, and fishermen and even to allow coaling stations for German naval vessels. In January 1886 the British obtained from the Spanish equality of rights with the Germans in the Carolines and in April of the same year in defining their respective spheres of interest and influence in the Pacific islands (see Chapter XXIII, *The Southwest Pacific to 1900*), the British and the Germans exchanged assurances of "reciprocal freedom of trade and commerce in their possessions and protectorates." The previous year the Germans had taken *all* the Marshalls under the imperial wing as a protectorate.

The Germans found the opportunity for clearing up their status in the Carolines and also in the Marianas (aside from Guam) by buying them from the Spanish after the Spanish-American War of 1898. When the war ended the Americans were not certain that they wanted any part of Spain's Pacific possessions. They indulged in a good deal of shilly-shallying before they even decided that they would take all of the Philippines, plus Guam. In the course of the discussions with the Spanish the Americans at one stage proposed to take some of the Carolines, but not all of them. The Spanish were not under obligation to accede to American wishes with regard to the Carolines, as they were with regard to the Philippines and Guam, and they refused to discuss the matter. Their reason was not that they proposed to retain them as a Spanish territory but that they had secretly made a deal with the Germans involving them. Immediately after the Spanish-American armistice the Germans had committed the Spanish to sell "certain" islands in the Carolines and to "grant Germany favorable consideration in any future disposal of Spanish insular possessions," subject to the treaty with the United States. A few months later the Germans arranged to purchase all of the Carolines, including the associated Palau group, and all of the Marianas except Guam, paying Spain $4,200,000. The Germans disclosed their deal to United States Secretary of State John Hay and obtained his promise of noninterference. Although Hay "reproached" the Germans he accepted the *fait accompli*. The Germans thus became neighbors of the Americans in this part of the Pacific at about the same time that they became neighbors in Samoa. It was also at this time that the Americans finally took possession of Hawaii.

For administrative purposes the Germans in 1899 attached their Micronesian islands except the Marshalls to the government of New Guinea, with branch administrative posts at Ponape, Yap, and Saipan. The Marshalls, with which they had associated the island of Nauru south of the equator—it had come to them under the Anglo-German agreement of 1886 and formal possession had been taken in 1888—were under the commercial and administrative control of the private Jaluit Company. In 1906, under circumstances to be discussed below, the Jaluit Company was relieved of its administrative responsibilities and the Marshalls were placed under the Ponape office of the New Guinea government.

A phase of this shuffling around of the Micronesian islands was the progressive reduction of the scope allowed the American Protestant missionaries who had been active in Micronesia since the late 1850's. When the Spanish asserted their rights in the islands they were insistent about ousting the American Protestants in favor of Spanish Catholics, while the Germans when they took over replaced the Spanish Catholics by German Catholics. As a result, by the turn of the century the Americans were left with but two mission stations in German Micronesia, one at Kusaie in the Eastern Carolines near the Marshalls and the other at Jaluit in the Marshalls. At that time the principal American economic interest in the Carolines was that of the trader Captain D. D. O'Keefe, originally from Savannah, Georgia. He operated between Yap and Hong Kong and invested his profits in Hong Kong real estate. He disappeared in a typhoon in 1901 leaving behind a lively legend and a half-caste family.

Since in the scramble for concessions in China that came in the wake of the Chinese defeat in the Japanese-Chinese war of 1894–95, the Germans had in 1897–98, as a phase of the Kaiser's struggle for a place in the Pacific sun, successfully established that Shantung was their "sphere of influence," they now had possessions slantwise across the Western Pacific from China to New Guinea and Samoa. In the atmosphere of the time it was inevitable that these fruits of imperialism should be assessed in terms of naval strategy as often as in economic terms. The Australians and New Zealanders thought that the Germans now held a naval position in the Pacific potentially inimical to their security. Although the Americans, on British cue, were suspicious of

German purposes, they apparently made nothing in particular at this time of the fact that German possessions cut across their line of approach to the Philippines. Some naval men felt that the Carolines should have come into American possession to secure the approach to the Philippines but the greatest of all the naval theorists, Mahan, "saw no sufficient reason for our opposition" to their transfer to Germany. Only belatedly did anything like unanimity about their strategic value emerge. Nevertheless, two decades later, the Americans had to acquiesce in their transfer from Germany to Japan, under circumstances far more exasperating to the United States government than the alleged bungle of 1898.

It will be recalled that in 1884 a sizable portion of the island of New Guinea (c. 70,000 square miles) and an assortment of associated islands totaling in all 600 (containing 22,000 square miles) had come into German possession. The following year the Neuguinea Kompagnie, which had taken the initiative in New Guinea, was assigned comprehensive but not exclusive economic rights and also responsibility for government in the possession. Although within five years it was apparent that the Kompagnie was making heavy weather of its task, it continued in control for another decade. On April 1, 1899, the imperial authorities assumed the government and paid the Kompagnie compensation in money and land grants. At the same time the government of German Micronesia except the Marshalls was attached to the New Guinea administration. Seven years later the Marshalls, including Nauru, came under its jurisdiction. Thus by 1906 the Germans had all their island possessions in the Western Pacific under a single government. Samoa to the east in the Central Pacific was separately governed.

In taking possession of New Guinea the Germans had raised the flag at Matupi in New Britain, Mioke in the Duke of York group, where their trading operations had been initiated in the 1870's, and at two points on the New Guinea mainland. In a fit of vanity they renamed the principal portions of their territory: New Britain became Neu Pomern, New Ireland Neu Mecklenburg, and the Duke of York group Neu Lauenburg. The islands comprehensively were named the Bismarck Archipelago. The territory on New Guinea was dubbed Kaiser Wilhelm's Land. But in the long run only the term Bismarck Archipelago and a scattering of detailed terminology survived.

The Neuguinea Kompagnie made a strong effort to establish an administrative capital in Kaiser Wilhelm's Land, presumably the heartland of the possession. In succession they built towns—they proved very good at planning and building tropical towns—at Finschafen on Huon Peninsula, at Stephansort on Astrolabe Bay, and finally at what is now known as Madang still farther west. The prevalence of malaria caused this shifting about. Madang became a principal settlement but did not remain the capital. Furthermore the Kompagnie began the practice of establishing outstations of varying grades. It set up posts at Morobe on Huon Gulf near the British boundary and at Aitape to the west near the mouth of the Sepik River. Before the end of the German regime posts had also been established at Kavieng in the north and Namatanai in the south of New Ireland, at Kieta on Bougainville and Larengau on Manus Island in the Admiralty group, and plans had been made for still other stations. When the imperial authorities took charge they abandoned the attempt to establish the capital in Kaiser Wilhelm's Land and in recognition of the facts of economic development turned to New Britain, and established government headquarters first at Herbertshohe (now Kokopo) and then in 1910 at Rabaul on Simpson Harbor, Blanche Bay. Here on the Gazelle Peninsula was the most intensive plantation development of the possession and Simpson Harbor was, moreover, one of the pivotal strategic harbors in this part of the Pacific.

The assumption of control by the imperial government appears to have involved a recognition of the fact that economic development, the principal end the Germans sought, was impeded as long as the Neuguinea Kompagnie had to carry the expense of administration. On the facts it appears that the economy definitely and progressively strengthened after 1899, though never to the point that the colony was economically viable even within the narrow idea of obligatory expenditure then ruling. The Neuguinea Kompagnie achieved prosperity as a private enterprise and remained the leading company in the possession, but other companies, notably the Deutsche Handels und Plantagen Gesellschaft (successors of Godeffroy), the Hernsheim A.G., and Hamburgische Sudsee A.G., also throve. The last named was the successor of the Forsayth Company which had been established by "Queen" Emma, one of the half-caste daughters of Jonas Coe, an American consul at Samoa, whose career was one of the romances of the South Seas before World War I. Moreover, the practice of the big companies of financing individual planters, many former employees, gave them effective control of that expanding element of the economy. The administration definitely favored the companies over individual enterprisers. However, in spite of the growth of production and an effort of the imperial authorities to increase colonial revenue by increasing the tariffs on imports, levying an export tax on copra, and laying a head tax on the natives within reach, the imperial government had heavily to subsidize the administration. By 1914 the subsidy had reached 1.7 million marks.

The Germans never escaped dependence on copra. Progress was in

large measure a matter of establishing more and more coconut plantations and expanding their planted acreage. By 1914 there was a considerable planted acreage that had not come into production, indicating
that the future was with copra. The imperial authorities tried to relieve
the almost total dependence of the enterprisers on copra by promoting research in tropical agriculture, conducting experiments with sisal,
kapok, cotton, tobacco, and pepper and making an extensive survey
of the possibility of obtaining rubber from native plants in Kaiser
Wilhelm's Land. The companies, especially the Neuguinea Kompagnie,
also experimented with new crops, notably tobacco, coffee, cocoa, and
rice, the latter for local consumption by the native workers on the
plantations. But by 1914 little progress had been made in diversification.

The imperial authorities laid great emphasis on transport and communications, but it is difficult to disentangle the purely economic motive
from the strategic. Once Rabaul was founded it became the focal point
within the possession. Special emphasis was laid upon enabling the producers to ship their goods directly to Europe. The Neuguinea Kompagnie
had made an agreement with the Nord-Deutscher-Lloyd line to establish
a branch of its Far Eastern service from Singapore via the Netherlands
East Indies, while the imperial authorities were in a position to make the
subsidy of the German Far Eastern and Australian services dependent
on the provision of a regular service to Rabaul. Great care was taken
to maintain easy connections with Singapore, Hong Kong, and Sydney.
Burns Philp was active in the New Guinea service from its base in
Sydney. Internally the small boat services seem to have been in the hands
of the big companies. The administration gave much attention to the
improvement of harbors and the provision of wharves. Whether or not
the Germans sought a shipping (and trading) monopoly within the New
Guinea portion of their area, it is clear that they made a try at it in
Micronesia, and particularly in the Marshalls. Pressure was put on foreign
traders and shipping companies to drive them out. The Japanese
traders in the Carolines felt this pressure, though they weathered it.
The Australians not only felt it but fought back. The Jaluit Company in
the Marshalls made a particularly strong effort to achieve monopoly,
colliding with Burns Philp. Taking a stand on the German-British reci-
procity agreement of 1886, Burns Philp resisted, engaged the support
of the British government, and eventually established its point. A consequence of this success was that the Jaluit Company was deprived of its
administrative responsibilities, allegedly because it had abused them for
purposes of economic warfare. Actually the Australians were in a fairly
strong position, particularly as suppliers of European-style foodstuffs
without which Europeans could not live in the tropics. By 1913 both

imports into New Guinea and exports from it in payment were moving in favor of the Australians. With regard to communications, the Germans made Yap an important cable center, building lines from there to Menado in the Dutch Celebes, to Guam, and to Shanghai. At Guam a junction was made with lines to the United States and Japan. Toward the end of their regime they were building a network of wireless stations to link Apia in Samoa, Nauru, Rabaul in New Britain, and Yap in the Carolines with their naval base at Tsingtao on Shantung Peninsula in China and Berlin in Europe. Naval coaling stations had been established at Yap, Jaluit, Rabaul, and Apia, but no defense works had been built in the islands. The coal needed was obtained in Australia and New Zealand.

The Germans were quite free with land grants but there was a wide gap between land thus made available for exploitation and land actually in use. A feature of the German procedure was the liberal use of freehold title. By 1912 they had adopted the common policy of allowing purchase of land from the natives only by the government. Some idea of the size of the gap between land held and land developed can be gained from such figures as those for the Neuguinea Kompagnie which held 368,118 acres but had but 21,962 acres under cultivation and the Hamburg company holding of 62,271 acres of which only 9985 acres were planted, but it must be kept in mind that other companies and individuals with smaller holdings had planted a larger proportion of their acres. The 120 German small planters came much closer than the big companies to planting all of their acreages. However, the point that the small planters were controlled by the big companies through loans and trading agreements should be kept in mind. Practically all the land actually brought into use was along or close to the coasts or on small islands just off coasts. Coconuts do not normally flourish more than twenty miles from the sea.

While the Germans scattered their plantations widely through the possession they did not develop any compelling economic motive for looking for usable land in the interiors of any of the considerable land masses. Only one exploring expedition crossed New Britain in German times. An attempt was made to cross the main island of New Guinea but the Europeans either died or were killed en route and only a few natives finally emerged on the Papuan coast. Only New Ireland among the large islands was at all adequately explored. Bougainville in the Solomons was not deeply penetrated, though Buka was. Like their predecessors in Kaiser Wilhelm's Land, the Germans entertained the notion that good country for European occupation (and also gold-bearing country) was to be found inland. A tactic of attempting to gain knowledge of the interior by following the rivers was initiated about 1890. The first such effort was an expedition up the Gogol River, so named by Miklouho-Maclay perhaps with an oblique reference to the dead souls thereabouts, from its mouth in Astrolabe Bay near Madang. Although much troubled by malaria and hostile natives, the expedition reported some useful country, but nobody attempted its exploitation. A good deal of attention was subsequently given to the Ramu and Markham rivers and their valleys but perhaps the most remarkable of all river explorations were those on the Sepik River, the greatest of the rivers of New Guinea. The existence of this river had been suspected since early in the seventeenth century but it had not actually been discovered until Otto Finsch, making his preliminary survey of New Guinea for the Kompagnie and the imperial government, entered its mouth in 1885. From then on a succession of expeditions probed the Sepik and one of the last explorations made by the Germans was directed to it. However, the Sepik valley proved one of the most fecal in New Guinea, so its economic significance was dubious. With regard to the interior mountains, quite as spectacular a feature as the rivers, the Germans discovered many ranges, but their actual work in the mountains was mostly confined to defining exactly the borders with British and Dutch New Guinea. While all the inland exploration had great geographical significance and on occasion resulted in important increments in anthropological knowledge, its economic significance was marginal. It revealed an interior in terms of great rivers and interesting valleys and mountains, some of the latter surprisingly high, although the highest New Guinea mountains were subsequently to be discovered in Dutch New Guinea. It also made it clear that there were probably more natives in Kaiser Wilhelm's Land than could be deduced from the contacts actually made. But it was also made clear that the interior was not easily amenable to "development" western-style. With their usual diligence and enterprise, the Germans built up an enormous "literature" on their possessions. When it came to pioneering the interior, the German Lutheran missionaries led the way and their knowledge of the geography and the resources was probably superior to that of any commercial enterprisers.

It was a disappointment to the Germans that there was no significant gold discovery in Kaiser Wilhelm's Land in their time. Traces of gold were found in the Ramu River and it was suspected that Australian prospectors had found payable gold on the German side of the boundary, but nothing significant came of either the discovery or the suspicion. The really important mineral discovery was of phosphate rock, the rock which as the basis of so-called super-phosphate fertilizer became so important in the agricultural and pastoral life of Australia and New Zealand.

The phosphate rock trade was an outgrowth of the guano trade which in its day had brought to many otherwise insignificant islands near the equator a transient importance. Of the two principal discoveries in the German-held islands, one was exploited by a German company whose market was in Europe, while the other was exploited by a British company whose market was in Australia and New Zealand. The German company worked the deposit found in 1903 on Angaur, the southernmost island of the Palau group in the Western Carolines. Exploitation began in 1909 and by 1912 the company was paying dividends. The labor force was Micronesian natives. The other deposit was found on Nauru Island south of the equator, administratively part of the Marshalls, up to 1906 a preserve of the Jaluit Company. That Nauru contained phosphate was accidentally discovered by a New Zealander, A. F. Ellis (subsequently Sir Albert Ellis), who had begun his island career in the guano trade. At the time, Ellis was working in the Sydney office of the Pacific Islands Company Ltd., of London. The Pacific Islands Company was successor of the John. T. Arundel Company, also British, which had been the principal operator from Australia in the guano trade and which as it faded had transferred its investment to the copra trade. Mr. Ellis uncovered the fact that Nauru had phosphate rock when he analyzed a long unregarded lump of rock that had been lying around the Sydney office. That his determination was correct and important was proved by investigations at Nauru in 1900. At about the same time it was also ascertained that Ocean Island, not far away from Nauru, then more or less derelict but to be associated with the British Gilbert Islands, was also rich in phosphate rock. The Ocean Island deposits were exploited before the development of the Nauru deposits began. The German authorities granted rights of exploitation of the Nauru deposits to a German company but the Germans chose to make a deal with the Pacific Phosphate Company which the Pacific Islands Company formed. They agreed that the British company should work the deposits and pay the Germans a royalty. Incidental to this arrangement, the Pacific Islands Company sold its coconut plantations and trading stations on German-held islands to the Germans and the Germans were permitted to acquire shares in Pacific Phosphate. Actual exploitation began in 1906. The local management was mixed British and German and the working force was mixed Pacific islanders, Chinese, and Japanese. The white population numbered about 100.

Since the Germans emphasized economic exploitation the natives figured in their calculations as labor supply and little else. What contributions they made to native "advancement" were incidental to making the natives more easily manageable, as in subsidizing the missionaries to teach them German—"pidgin" was, however, the *lingua franca*—attempting to upgrade the skills of some natives to provide an alternative to Chinese tradesmen, and encouraging native participation in the copra trade, as by levying a head tax. That natives could ever be anything more than laborers or strictly marginal commercial producers was not in the German conception. The Neuguinea Kompagnie had forbidden the sale of liquor, opium, and firearms to the natives but had done little about regulating recruiting practices and had allowed a "hard" but not hopelessly unjust discipline to be practiced on the plantations and in government service. The most questionable practice was that of allowing the plantation owners themselves to decide upon and administer floggings to their native workers without reference to any government supervisor of labor conditions. However, in 1907 an Australian Methodist missionary wrote that "on the whole, the native policy is a just one" and when it became useful to the Australian government to allege that the system involved atrocities, it could not get even its own officials in New Guinea to supply any solid evidential support. Nevertheless, the natives certainly had no wish to work for the Europeans. The fundamental cause of their reluctance was, of course, their utter unfamiliarity with the employment offered and their lack of need to accept employment, but their alienation was undoubtedly intensified by their resentment of the way in which the Germans made free of their land, their resentment of corporal punishments, and perhaps most violently by the German practice of drafting them for forced labor on government projects, such as roads. As time passed many natives found it possible to earn what cash they needed, as to pay the head tax, without taking work with the planters. The Germans were steadily throughout their time short of labor even though the natives in employment steadily rose to 17,500 in 1914. Unable to recruit enough labor in their own possession, they sought to exercise their right to recruit in the British Solomons. To outsiders the shortage appeared inexplicable because the German possession was considered populous. The reason seems to have been that on the one hand a large part of the suspected population was not under "control" and on the other the native population which could be alleged to be under control was not readily to be recruited. Nor was the labor supply as large as optimists supposed. Seeking to solve their labor problem the Germans tried Chinese coolies under contract but found them too expensive for profitable employment in agriculture and abandoned the experiment in 1901. Chinese, however, continued to arrive in the possession but found employment as traders on their own account, trading agents for German concerns, skilled workers in ship-repair and building, and even as plantation operators in New Ireland. These people, rather than the coolies, became the ancestors of the permanent Chinese community of New Guinea. There also grew up a smaller Japanese community in German New Guinea. The Chinese were given a status somewhere between Europeans and natives, while the Japanese were counted as "Europeans." The Germans never solved their labor problem.

They never had more than a very imperfect control of the natives resident outside the immediate vicinities of the plantations and government stations, the very areas that had to be tapped if an adequate labor supply was to be developed. From the late 1890's they tried, in areas where they had some influence, to improve control by taking a close interest in the election of village headmen, or *luluais,* and their assistants, or *tultuls,* and attempting to devolve upon these native officers responsibility for carrying out the administration's wishes, aiming to transform them into agents of the administration. Native perception of this purpose sometimes damaged the positions of the *luluais* and *tultuls* in the eyes of the natives. The imperial administration also developed the native police force which the Neuguinea Kompagnie had started. Many of the administration's candidates for *luluai* or *tultul* were ex-police-boys who understood "pidgin" or perhaps even German and were thus open to communications from the administration. The Germans also introduced medical *tultuls,* or in "pidgin" *dokta boi,* in an effort to do something about native health problems. However, relations with the natives were precarious throughout the possession and the record of native violence against whites continued unbroken year after year, not only against whites adventuring in the interiors but also against those living on isolated plantations on the coasts and islands. As time passed the Germans concluded that meeting native violence with police violence, which had long been their policy, was not the answer. It simply compounded the trouble. The final German governor before the colony was lost was noted for his conciliatory native policy. It is perhaps significant that he was particularly concerned to insure that the natives were more justly treated than hitherto when land was in question. A true rebellion of the natives of Ponape in the Carolines was only finally put down in 1911; there was significant native "cultist" unrest on Buka Island in the Solomons in 1913 and around Madang on New Guinea Island which flared into rebellion in 1904 and 1912.

Missionaries played a conspicuous role in German New Guinea, often serving as agents of the government which was consistently understaffed in relation to responsibilities. They were, as remarked, the most adventurous of pioneers into the wild country; they had considerable commercial interests in that they often developed plantations of their own; and they carried on almost all the educational activity.

The Australian Methodists who had pioneered mission work in the territory continued their work throughout the German period, but German Lutherans and German-speaking Catholics became far more numerous and were closer to the administration, and even the Australian Methodists used more and more Germans in their work. While the administration's pressure on the religious organizations in favor of German personnel and of teaching German in their schools had an obvious "political" motivation, it is not clear that the German or the Germanized missions had any political character. Their objective was the conversion of the natives to Christianity and their secular improvement. Unlike the British and the Australians in their part of New Guinea, the Germans insisted that the native women cover their breasts.

At the outbreak of World War I the European population of the colony, including the Micronesian portion, was about 1500, of whom two-thirds were Germans and the rest British, Australians, and Japanese (counted as "Europeans"). Additionally there were a few hundred Chinese, some Malays, and a scattering of wanderers from other island groups. Among the adult males, missionaries, mostly German nationals, were the largest single European occupational group (232), followed by planters among whom the Australians were mostly numbered (172), and government officials (109). Approximately half of the Europeans were resident in the Bismarck Archipelago, mostly on New Britain in or near Rabaul, while of the balance about one-third were scattered over the Micronesian islands, with noticeable concentrations in the Carolines and on Nauru, while only a fifth were living in Kaiser Wilhelm's Land. The native population was currently estimated to be around 450,000, of which 40 per cent was believed to be living in the Bismarck Archipelago, but actual numbers were but a rough approximation. It is practically certain that there were far more natives in Kaiser Wilhelm's Land than the Germans supposed.

Before looking at the fortunes of the Australians and the Dutch in their portions of New Guinea an account of the German administration in Samoa may properly be given. The resident Germans learned that Samoa was an imperial possession as an item of cable news brought to Apia by a New Zealand ship from Auckland. To govern the new colony the imperial authorities designated Dr. Wilhelm Solf (1862–1936), a Berliner who was at the moment consul at Apia and currently president of the municipality. He received official notification of his elevation to the governorship in February and on March 1, 1900, raised the German flag at ceremonies on the historic Mulin'u Peninsula. Solf continued in office until 1910 when he was succeeded by his chief justice, Dr. Erich Schultz-Ewarth. Solf then returned to Germany and the following year became head of the imperial colonial office, a post he retained until the Kaiser's government collapsed at the end of World War I. He then became foreign secretary in the government of Prince Max of Baden and from 1920 to 1928 he served as the Weimar Republic's ambassador to Japan. He was by far the most distinguished German colonial governor to serve in the Pacific colonies.

When Solf took charge in Western Samoa the Germans had already been in the group for over forty years and therefore had a clear idea of its character and potential. Solf sought to found German rule on the prestige derived not so much from legal paramountcy as from demonstrable power. His first purpose was the pacification and stabilization of the possession after the long period of divided responsibility and attendant misgovernment. While vis à vis the natives, about whose political capacity he suffered no illusions, he took the position that "The natives are our protégés and the German Government must for their sakes assume the obligation of making the interests of the natives its own. For we do not wish to exterminate the natives but to preserve them. This is the moral duty which we assumed when we hoisted the German flag." How far he was influenced in taking this position by his firsthand observations of British government in Fiji is impossible to say. His conduct showed, however, that he entertained not the slightest doubt that Europeans ruled natives by right, whatever the moral element might be, nor about the correctness of maintaining that right by force. His native policy, while conciliatory, steadily resulted in the subordination of the natives to the government's authority, obviously in recognition of the fact that much of the trouble in Samoa in times past had arisen from the native assertion of the right to govern. But this did not mean that he slanted policy to the exclusive advantage of the European entrepreneurs in an effort to give his regime a strong economic base. He, unlike some island governors, understood that in his territory the resources available for exploitation by Europeans were limited and even if exhaustively exploited in disregard of the native interest, would make but a trivial contribution to the German economy, let alone the world market. He therefore encouraged the entrepreneurs but refused to make their interests paramount. One of his aims was economic viability within the ruling definition of a government's financial obligations to all concerned. He achieved it. German Samoa was subsidized by the imperial government from 1900 to 1907 to help it get on its feet. The subsidy never exceeded $65,000 in any one year. But after 1907 there was a surplus in the government accounts which from 1910 was paid into the imperial treasury as Samoa's contribution to the central administration of the imperial colonies. Having the German interest in building suitable tropical towns, Solf set out to provide Apia with appropriate government offices, something hitherto unthought of. To help this along, a wealthy German banker, retired to Samoa after years at Vladivostok in Russia, purchased Robert Louis Stevenson's old home and gave it to the colony for conversion into a residence for the governor. Much attention was given to road building, a standard item in German colonial practice. On the other hand, while in the colonial British interpretation of naval strategy the Germans had sought possession of Samoa to menace New Zealand, the Germans built no fortifications. Samoa was indeed the southern terminus of a chain of naval "fulcra" anchored at Kiaochow in China, but all the links in the chain were to prove to be surprisingly weak.

In the German time there were never to be more than 600 Europeans resident in Western Samoa. At that stage there were 35,000 natives. By inheritance from the past, the Europeans were a mixture of Germans, British, colonial British, and a few Americans. The impact of the western-style economy of which these people were the exponents was far less important in Samoa than contemporaneously in, say, Fiji. Dr. Solf, like the New Guinea administrators, favored development by companies rather than individual enterprisers, apparently in his case because individuals attracted by unofficial publicity in the early years rarely had what he could regard as sufficient capital. He did not propose to "bail out" distressed private enterprisers. By 1914 European production was in the hands of forty-one individuals and companies operating fifty different holdings. Copra was the principal commodity produced but as a result of a program of diversification begun at the time of take-over, cocoa had become the second most valuable crop and some rubber, coffee, vanilla, and pineapples were marketed. In 1914 half the exports were going to Germany in German shipping, two-fifths to Australia and New Zealand, and one-twentieth to the United States, while Australia and New Zealand were supplying no less than 60 per cent of the imports including the indispensable temperate-climate foodstuffs, the United States 9 per cent from San Francisco, and Germany only 15 per cent.

The natives were involved in the European economy only through their participation in copra production. They did not serve as laborers on the European plantations. The great bulk of the land remained in their hands and the Germans showed no disposition to disturb them in their possession. They mostly lived within a subsistence economy. Since the Samoans were not available as "labor" it was the tradition that Melanesians were imported as plantation laborers. When the Germans took over New Guinea they ruled that recruiting should be for service only within that colony, since they suffered a labor shortage, and the British

Solomons also ceased to supply labor to the Samoan planters. In 1903, therefore, the Samoan government agreed to the bringing in of Chinese indentured laborers from Hong Kong. To handle this traffic, a special department of government was set up. By 1909 the Chinese were sufficiently numerous for the Chinese government to send a consul to Apia. In 1912 he obtained the right for them to purchase land and engage in trade. By 1914 there were 2200 Chinese in Western Samoa, or almost four times as many as Europeans.

If Dr. Solf had any interest in indirect rule of natives as practiced in Fiji, he showed himself in practice to be more interested in the shadow than the substance. He freely modified native institutions, allowed them to fall into desuetude, and introduced new ones of his own devising. The office of "King" had been abolished just before the Germans took over. To discourage any Samoan effort to revive it, the office was assigned to Kaiser Wilhelm who was styled *der Tupi sili von Samoa.* The highest office a Samoan could occupy was Paramount Chief, or *Ali'i Sili.* Mata'afa held this post until 1912 when he died. It was then abolished and as a substitute *two* Samoans were chosen as High Advisers to the governor, called *Fautua.* The traditional native representative body, the *Fono a Faipule* or, so to speak, chamber of deputies, was reduced first to an advisory status and then allowed to fade away into innocuousness. The Germans, in short, took all national power into their own hands. Ostensibly they left village administration in Samoan hands, but even this the Germans closely supervised and really controlled. Since it cannot be assumed that the Samoans lost their aptitude for politics when the Germans took over, it is something of a tribute to German astuteness that they deprived the Samoans of effective political power without stirring up an implacable opposition. On only one occasion during the German period did important opposition emerge. Significantly the oppositionists had as their objective the restoration of the Samoan kingship and its prerogatives of government. In 1908–9 a "talking chief" or "orator" of the island of Savaii named Lauati led a movement with this purpose which was called *Mau a Pule.* Dr. Solf easily faced down this challenge without actually using violence to make his point, though he insured himself of an ace by sending for warships for use if needed. Lauati and his principal associates were exiled to Saipan in the northern Marianas.

If the Germans took away all effective power from the Samoans, they allowed little to the Europeans either. A Governor's Advisory Council of six was set up, but it was indeed only advisory. In the early years it had two British members, but in later days it was all German. The Europeans complained about their lack of substantive political rights and about allegedly arbitrary over-government and overspending by government, but it was nevertheless apparent that the central issue between the Europeans and the government was the issue that divided the two in every island group: the Europeans in Samoa alleged that the government was too solicitous of native welfare and did not properly look after the European interest, the unexpressed premise being that the European interest should be paramount. The government, however, enforced its version of a proper balance until its end.

While the Germans were installing themselves in Western Samoa the Americans were doing likewise in Eastern Samoa, but whereas the Germans acted purposefully to establish a *colony,* the Americans acted to establish a naval station and while so acting became entangled in a miniscule colonial problem. As a matter of fact, the Americans had committed themselves to a naval station before the deal dividing the Samoan group had been consummated and when the deal occurred they did not, in their inexperience, see that a shift of gears was necessary.

The notion that the time had come to do more with the wonderful harbor at Pago Pago than maintain a coal pile there on a site rented for $10 a month appears to have originated with Admiral Kimberly as a reflex of his experience in the hurricane at Apia in 1889. At any rate, immediately subsequent to that disaster the Admiral visited Pago Pago and selected a site for a naval station which was purchased for $5241.59. It took five years to complete the purchase, such were the complications of Samoan land law, and another four years passed before the Navy let a contract for the necessary earth-moving and construction to a San Francisco firm. To take charge as senior officer at Pago Pago the Navy early in 1899 assigned Commander B. F. Tilley. Tilley proceeded to his new post in the auxiliary freighter "Abarenda" which was loaded with coal to augment the celebrated pile, and structural steel. Traveling from Norfolk, Virginia, via Cape Horn, Tilley arrived at Pago Pago in August. He found the San Francisco contractor in trouble with his men. In December Tilley, still at Pago Pago but preparing to go to Auckland, New Zealand, for a cargo of construction materials, heard of the division of the islands with Germany, but what this portended for him he did not know. He eventually learned, however, that President William McKinley in February 1900 had loosely assimilated the project of a naval station to whatever political and administrative responsibilities had devolved upon the United States by the partition, directing that "The island of Tutuila of the Samoan Group and all other islands of that group east of longitude 171 West of Greenwich, are hereby placed under the control of the Department of the Navy for a naval station. The Secretary of the

Navy shall take such steps as may be necessary to establish the authority of the United States, and to give the islands the necessary protection." Following up the President's rather unilluminating directive, the secretary of the Navy issued a General Order stating that the islands specified "are hereby established into a naval station to be known as the Naval Station, Tutuila, to be under the command of a commandant." Tilley was appointed the first commandant. In instructing him the assistant secretary remarked that "While your position as commandant will invest you with authority over the islands embraced within the limits of the station, you will at all times exercise care to conciliate and cultivate friendly relations with the natives [who then numbered 5679]. A simple, straightforward method of administration, such as to win and hold the confidence of the people, is expected of you." Tilley thus became commandant of the Naval Station, Tutuila, but his job was not wholly naval in character for he was also expected somehow to administer civilian affairs within the area of the Station, not least to deal with Polynesian natives about whom he knew nothing, not only those living on Tutuila but also those living in the outlying Manu'a group as well.

To confirm the authority of the United States Tilley negotiated with the chiefs of Tutuila for a Deed of Cession. By a document dated April 2, 1900, the natives of Tutuila "gave" the island to the United States. When Tilley attempted to bring Manu'a into line by asking the Tui also to sign, he ran into difficulties. The Tui Manu'a considered that his islands had no political connection with Tutuila and he wanted none. He and his people had had no role in the politics that had led to the partitioning of the Samoan group. The Manu'ans were an independent people and the great powers had no right at all to dispose of them and their land. Although professing to be favorably disposed toward the Americans, even prepared to acknowledge United States sovereignty, the Tui refused to sign the Deed. When the American flag was formally raised at Pago Pago on April 17, the Manu'ans were present only as "observers." (The only foreign dignitary present was Governor Wilhelm Solf of German Samoa.) Following the flag raising at Pago Pago, a similar ceremony was held at Manu'a with the Tui's consent and also at the third section of the new possession, uninhabited Rose Island, or Muliava, to the southeast of the Manu'a group. The Deed of Cession was acknowledged by President Theodore Roosevelt but only after he had been prompted to do so by Dr. David Starr Jordan who had been visiting Samoa to study marine life. A letter from the President was read to the chiefs at Pago Pago on January 16, 1904, at which time each signer of the Deed was presented with a medal and a silver watch. The Tui Manu'a did not agree to sign the Deed until later in 1904 and, because bad weather kept those in charge of the document away from Manu'a on their first try, did not actually sign it until 1905. Roosevelt's letter, of course, was not a formal acceptance of the "gift" by the United States, for it was the responsibility of Congress to accept new territory, but rather was merely a polite gesture to the Samoans. Congress did not act for twenty-five years.

In running Samoa the best the successive commandants could do—under the naval system of "tours of duty" there was a new commandant every eighteen months—was to attach to the normal machinery of an American Naval Station some kind of machinery for governing native affairs. This inevitably caused a good deal of ingenious improvisation, especially since Washington proved uncooperative about providing funds and whatever was done that involved expense had to be paid for out of available local revenue. In effect the only subsidy allowed Samoa was what could be diverted from Naval funds by local administrative direction, chiefly free services. In 1907 it was explicitly ruled in Washington that the Navy Department had no duty whatever "to make improvements in the islands outside the Naval Station." Since Congress gave no indication of its understanding of the situation, the legal status of Samoa and its native inhabitants was left indeterminate. The Samoans were, however, decided to be American "nationals" but not citizens and therefore they could not claim, and nobody could claim for them, the rights and privileges that might inure to them had they been citizens. Everything therefore turned on the intelligence and good will of the commandants and their senior associates and fortunately most of the commandants took their responsibilities to the Samoans seriously, legally vague though they were. Commandant Tilley had had the idea that so far as possible Samoan law and custom, or fa'a Samoa, should be preserved and he therefore decided on what was really "indirect rule." "The government I propose to establish," he wrote, "is a government of the chiefs who are to receive additional appointments by the commandant." The laws of the United States were to be enforced, but all Samoan laws and customs not in conflict with them were to be preserved. To advise on Samoan law and customs more or less in a judicial capacity, Tilley appointed a New Zealander named E. W. Gurr who had fled Apia when the Germans took over. In practice the commandants went beyond the high chiefs in using traditional Samoan officers in government, notably in the villages where they really had no choice but to deal with the matai, or heads of extended families. They also early instituted a Fono of American Samoa which advised the administration on policy, major and minor, within the range of its interest and competence. Thus while the final executive responsibility remained with the commandants, the Samoans from the beginning had some say in the management of their affairs. It was soon apparent that the governance of the Samoans and the few resident outlanders, Europeans and Pacific Islanders, was a very important part of the duty of the commandant and that their legal position, the machinery of government, and the laws should be validated by United States Congressional legislation. None could be obtained, not least because the Navy Department, remote from Samoa, could not be persuaded that it was a matter of any urgency. However, the title of commandant was changed to governor in 1905 and the designation Naval Station, Tutuila, to American Samoa in 1911.

Whatever the intent of the commandants the fact remained that two highly disparate cultures were in intimate contact, and consequences to fa'a Samoa inevitably ensued. The resolution of conflicts between United States law and Samoan law and custom in favor of American law insured that fa'a Samoa would suffer erosion and some kind of adaptation would be required of the Samoans. Not all the erosions were bad or even unwelcome to the Samoans. The effects were felt first on Tutuila. The islands of Manu'a retained their Samoan character far longer. Up to World War I the erosions and adaptations caused little disquiet either for the commandants or the natives, but ex post facto it became apparent that factors then injected into the situation eventually generated disquiet and disorder.

Basic to an understanding of what happened is the fact that American Samoa was a possession without a substantial economic hinterland. With the suppression of native war and the extension to the natives of medical and health services, the population began to increase. In the first twenty years of American rule the population rose from just short of 6000 to over 8000 and a sharply upward trend was established. Medical and health services were achieved by making available to the natives services in any case supplied to the naval personnel. A native hospital was built after a clinic for natives had been improvised and some Samoan women were trained as nurses. On the other hand, the commandants did not succeed in establishing a public school system they could regard as adequate because Washington refused funds. The best they could do was to win the cooperation of the Protestant and Roman Catholic missionaries. Thus a factor which could help in a major way in insuring the welfare of the enlarged native population was in important measure missing. The presence of the Naval Station was of economic significance to the natives insofar as it was a source of income to them, but it could not supply sufficient income to support the entire expanding community (had that been at all desirable), least of all at rising standards of living, even though under the Samoan "extended family" system the income percolated to far more people than would have been the case in the United States. Not only were natives employed as laborers on the Station and as houseworkers in the homes of naval personnel, but a few were trained and employed as nurses, a few were employed as school teachers, and some men were recruited as a native guard, called the Fita Fita, comparable in status to marines but not employable outside the possession. (The Fita Fita was thought of as a leadership training enterprise in addition to its primary utility but quite without intent it generated a new kind of elite which was abrasive of the authority of the traditional native elite, the *matai* and the high chiefs.)

Thus with all the income supplements taken into account the natives were still heavily, and in the majority of cases wholly, dependent on the native economy. The commandants had seen to it that title to the land remained in the hands of the Samoans; it could not be alienated to outsiders. It was obvious very early that there was no room on Tutuila or in the Manu'an islands for European plantations. By the time of World War I, however, it was beginning to be obvious that the native economy of Tutuila—the Manu'an situation was easier—was under pressure. The Tutuila native economy was a subsistence economy with copra as its cash crop, the natives being dependent on the returns from the cash crop for access to such European commodities as had become indispensable to them. To maximize the returns from copra the commandants monopolized the marketing of production, cutting out the trader-middlemen and, incidentally, gaining a position to make a deduction from the gross return for the benefit of the government's exchequer. Fortunately both the quantity of copra produced and the market price moved irregularly upward through World War I. The government's share of the returns from copra, plus customs returns, supported the welfare and economic activities that benefited the natives, but there was never enough money. In 1914 to meet the needs of the government and the local merchants and perchance to teach thrift to natives whose way of life was inimical to it, a Bank of American Samoa was established with a capital of $5000 supplied by the administration. This was not only the first American bank south of the equator but also the first bank in any of the islands that was not a branch of a metropolitan institution. By this time Pago Pago was developing in a tentative way some of the characteristics of an island port town that was also the seat of government.

The partitioning of New Guinea in the middle 1880's left the British with 90,500 square miles of little-known country, mostly on the main island (87,800 square miles) but also including off-shore islands and groups of islands, of which the best-known were the D'Entrecasteaux, the Woodlark, the Louisiade, and the Trobriand groups, all off the eastern tip of the main island. However, none of the lesser islands of British New Guinea proved as important a center of European development as New Britain was in German New Guinea. Whereas the Germans could in a sense find compensation for their frustrations on the main island in their progress on New Britain, the British had to get on with the job on the main island or hardly at all.

The British first organized their territory as a protectorate but in 1888 formally annexed it to the Empire. From the beginning of British rule until 1906, however, control and responsibility were not single but dual as a consequence of the curious political history of the area. Because the London government regarded the British presence in New Guinea more the result of Australian pressure than of its own wishes, it was assumed that the neighboring colonies, including Fiji and New Zealand, would contribute to the costs of government. While the colonies were more willing than they had proved earlier in the case of Fiji, in regard to which the imperial authorities had made the same assumption, not all of them were prepared to contribute much or for long, and the burden, such as it was, soon fell on Queensland, New South Wales, and Victoria. The sum at issue was £15,000 (c. $75,000) prorated among the colonies on the basis of their populations. The senior colony was Queensland, the initiator of the New Guinea adventure, whose governor was made the superior of the person, appointed by the Colonial Office in London, in charge in New Guinea. It was an issue in the financial relations that the London government appeared to want to make but a minimum contribution to the costs, while the colonies thought their contributions should be but supplements to, or importantly supported by, an imperial contribution. The financial problem, which was murky straight through the piece, did not begin to clarify until 1902 when the new Australian Commonwealth took over responsibility.

Since the Australian colonies helped with finance they felt they should have some influence on policy and in one way or another they did, Queensland naturally wielding the most obvious influence. The Australians had originally based their public case for taking New Guinea on defense considerations, thus making a specific application of the old dogma that the islands were a defensive screen against hostile powers and should therefore be in British possession. In the circumstances of the time, simple possession was sufficient. It was not thought necessary to build defense works in the territory. However, never far behind was the conviction that something should be made out of the possession by trading, gathering, mining, labor recruiting, and the development of plantations. Therefore, the central policy issue soon became the familiar one of striking an acceptable balance between conservation of the native interest and the promotion of the interest of the incoming white entrepreneurs. Theoretically the definition of a balance suitable to the conditions obtaining in New Guinea was the task of the British Colonial Office but it does not appear that the Colonial Office was much interested in New Guinea and there is considerable evidence that the actual definition was made by the imperial servants in charge or, after the Australians took over, the Commonwealth appointee. However, this meant that the definition was of a description definitely within the ambit of the evolving British tradition of concern for native welfare. In this situation the characters and outlooks of the appointees were of great importance. It can be generalized that all had a more or less intelligent concern about the natives, while none, with one possible exception, was hostile to the white entrepreneurs. What balance was defined from time to time was an improvised compromise. Not the least important theory influencing the compromise was the widely entertained idea that employment in white enterprises was good for the natives—that the modifications imposed on native societies by the direct involvement of natives as laborers in white enterprises and their attachment otherwise to the Western economic system were creative changes definitely contributing to the advancement of the natives. This idea had been entertained even by the proponents of the old, notorious "labor trade." Any idea that there was, on balance, any conflict between native welfare and white enterprise was denied or repressed. In the New Guinea situation this was relatively easy for many years because for a variety of reasons white enterprise remained marginal to the total situation. However, pressure in favor of the entrepreneurial interest was a conspicuous element of the Australian contribution to policy formation. Because there was little knowledge of or interest in New Guinea in Australia, there was little public opinion and such opinion as did find influential expression was, on the one hand, that generated and supported by the business people, especially Burns Philp, and on the other, the opinion of the missionary interest. From the metropolitan government's point of view, only as white enterprise expanded could viability in the sense of support of the possession's government in all its phases from colonial revenues be achieved. As a matter of fact the government of British New Guinea and of Papua, as the possession became known to the Australians, did not at any stage achieve such viability. On the contrary, the metropolitan subsidy tended steadily to increase. Yet even with the subsidy, the colony's income was never "enough" and this constricted its activities, not least any specifically intended to benefit the natives.

Seven persons were in charge during the British period. The first was

Sir Peter Scratchley, a British military engineer, veteran of the Crimean War, who a little earlier had surveyed the forts defending the Australian cities. He was, as head of a protectorate government, designated High Commissioner. His power actually to govern under the commission he held was very narrowly interpreted by Samuel Griffith of Queensland. After unedifying negotiations with the Australian colonies over finance, Scratchley arrived in New Guinea in August 1885. He died of malaria the following December while being rushed back to Sydney for treatment. He therefore had little time to make an impact. However, he decided that Port Moresby should be the administrative capital and designated Samarai on what was then called Dinner Island off the eastern tip of the main island the first administrative outpost. He scrutinized very severely such land claims as came to his notice but made no definitive awards. There were, as a matter of fact, very few whites living in New Guinea at that time—a small mixture of missionaries, traders, and explorers—and he limited any possible influx by requiring all to obtain special permission to come. The major problem was how to protect them from the violence of the many natives. It was Scratchley's impression that the future of New Guinea rested with the natives, at minimum as the only available labor supply. He was therefore anxious somehow to "protect" them, a position which foreshadowed the native policy developed by his successors. But what Scratchley might eventually have done with his difficult assignment is impossible to know.

Scratchley's immediate successor was his deputy commissioner, H. H. Romilly, but Romilly held the post only until February 1886 when he was displaced by the Honorable John Douglas. Douglas was an English-born colonial politician who had been premier of Queensland 1877–79. It casts a curious light on the status of former premiers in those days in Queensland that in 1885 he accepted appointment as Queensland's resident at Thursday Island. In December of the same year, however, he was also appointed special commissioner for British New Guinea. Douglas had a strictly limited view of how much of the protectorate he could hope to bring under control: "thirty miles inland and fifty miles east and west of Port Moresby." During Douglas' term of office efforts to suppress native violence continued, exploration by private persons continued, and a formula was devised for defining the inland boundary between British and German New Guinea. But far more important was that at this time Samuel Griffith, now premier of Queensland—he had been Douglas' attorney-general—set about to obtain a more satisfactory status for British New Guinea and a more reasonable definition of the powers of the person in charge. Griffith set out to *annex* British New Guinea, McIlwraith's old ambition. Essentially what Griffith sought was a constitution for British New Guinea which would put it under an administrator appointed by "the Crown" who was to report to and consult with the governor of Queensland (in effect the *government* of Queensland for the time being) on all important questions, the administrator to have the support of an Executive Council consisting of the senior officers of his establishment and a Legislative Council with the same membership plus some appointees, both officers and in due course private citizens. The laws of Queensland, subject to modification to meet New Guinea circumstances, would apply in the colony. At the Colonial Conference in London in 1887 Premier Griffith secured the adoption of his scheme of government by trading the *sine qua non* of annexation of the protectorate to the Crown for an acceptance by Queensland of responsibility for the annual subsidy, part of which it could recoup from New South Wales and Victoria if possible. (Victoria, when it fell into a doldrums, gave Queensland the most trouble in this regard.) The imperial government was to supply and maintain a steam vessel for the use of the administrator, a necessity in a colony in which communication was wholly by water. The annexation agreed to, Dr. William MacGregor was appointed the first administrator under the new system.

Dr. William MacGregor (1846–1919) was the most remarkable of the appointees to the top post in British New Guinea and held the post longest—1888–98. In his time the designation of the senior post was changed to lieutenant-governor. Born in Scotland, MacGregor won his M.D. at Aberdeen in 1874. For reasons of health he had already migrated to the tropics and had entered the colonial service as a medical man. His first tour of duty was in the Seychelles and he then served in Mauritius. He came to the notice of Sir Arthur Gordon. Gordon took MacGregor with him to Fiji as his chief medical officer but, cultivating his obvious talent, employed him in a variety of ways, even as acting governor. From Fiji MacGregor was appointed to British New Guinea. After his New Guinea service, he was in turn governor of Lagos (Nigeria) 1899–1904, Newfoundland 1904–9, and Queensland 1909–14. He was knighted in 1889.

When MacGregor entered New Guinea it was in effect as wild an island frontier as it had been in 1884. Only to a limited degree could it be said to have been explored and to an even lesser degree had it been pacified. What resources of interest to European enterprisers actually existed was unclear, though expectations ran very high. MacGregor expended enormous energy on what was essentially exploration and was continually involved in pacification both as a by-blow of his explorations and as punitive expeditions against natives who had committed violence against Europeans. As an explorer MacGregor is chiefly remembered for having been the first to ascend Mount Victoria in the Owen Stanley Range (which T. H. Huxley had so named), the highest mountain in the colony. MacGregor climbed the peak not simply because it was there but in the hope that so signal an accomplishment would put an end to private exploring expeditions in the colony, so often ill-found and unwisely led. He was seeking to make exploration a government prerogative and, by making pacification an integral part of the activity, he was providing the precedent for the "patrols" both into known but imperfectly pacified country and into wild country that became a feature of successor administrations.

While MacGregor's service in Fiji had made him familiar with Sir Arthur Gordon's ideas about how to deal with natives, conditions in New Guinea were so different that about the only obvious carry-over was a frame of mind. That frame of mind made it quite certain that MacGregor would emphasize the conservation of the native interest and indeed it was he who established firmly, for Scratchley had adumbrated it, the philo-native bias in British New Guinea policy. In New Guinea there were no chiefs controlling numerous tribesmen and considerable territory, let alone any who could be elevated with European support to the status of "kings," but rather a highly fragmented society from which any political "structuring" useful to a European administration was largely absent. New Guinea was a land of loosely controlled villages and the fragmentation was further accentuated by a multiplicity of varying customs and languages.

MacGregor sought to pacify the New Guinea natives by demonstrating to them that the government was possessed of force superior to any they could command. While he himself tried to avoid killing natives, except when they had been proved guilty of killing Europeans, some of his subordinates were not so scrupulous, or so skillful in avoiding the ultimate discipline, and even MacGregor was so convinced of the necessity of over-awing the natives that he was not above allowing the killing of a few to impress the many. MacGregor sought to use force to punish violence already or at the moment being committed in the hope of promoting pacification over the longer term. In 1890 in this connection he organized a native constabulary, staffed at first by Fijians and Solomon Islanders, but intended to be staffed by local natives, as it soon was. This organization served the interests of the government over the whole colony. To reach into the villages and provide a permanent representative of government in the primary units of native society, he shortly after instituted the office of village constable. MacGregor was immensely proud of these devices for pacification. It was his boast that he never had a collision with the natives that he could not handle out of his own resources.

Just how far MacGregor got in exploring and pacifying his domain would be difficult to convey even if the areas covered in one or the other fashion, or both, could be exactly delimited on a map. While he extended both the area known and the area pacified—and British New Guinea was better known and safer in 1898 than in 1888—it is illuminating that for over sixty years after exploration and pacification were continuously on the government's agenda. To the ports of entry, Port Moresby and Samarai, which MacGregor had inherited, only Daru, located on a small island to the west of the mouth of the great Fly River, the largest in British New Guinea, was added (1893) as a service port for the Torres Strait pearl-shell and *bêche-de-mer* trades which New Guinea natives then served as labor. Daru, however, long remained a poor third to the other two. MacGregor also elaborated the practice of stationing government officers in the field. He had a post set up at Mabadauan on the coast west of Daru, at Mekko inland in the center of the colony, and at Papangi to the east of Port Moresby.

Although MacGregor was disposed to favor the interests of the natives over those of the incoming Europeans, he was by no means hostile to the white entrepreneurs, though they chose to allege he was. He was simply insistent that the colony be "ready" for the Europeans before they be allowed freely to pursue their purposes. "Readiness" meant pacification and pacification was a protracted business. Evidence in the entrepreneurial case against MacGregor was the land ordinance of 1890 which, as MacGregor once defensively pointed out, was critically reviewed and approved by Samuel Griffith before it was promulgated. Essentially what MacGregor (and Griffith) sought to do was to protect the native title to the land, to give the government the sole right to purchase land from the natives, and to make the price of land sold or leased to Europeans turn upon the use to which it was to be put and to insure that it was in fact so used or returned. A consequence of this approach was to insure that the great bulk of the land remain in the possession of the natives, though without any guarantee about quality, of which, indeed, very little was known at that time. This land ordinance did not frustrate the European enterprisers, for the government did not allow itself to be short of land for sale to them. The Europeans, to be sure, grumbled about the fact that under the ordinance they could occupy neither native or Crown land without specific permission, but where their "right" to be squatters resided was rather obscure. They could obtain freehold title to agricultural land for any unspecified crop at ten shillings an acre or if they proposed to introduce a new crop, for two shillings six pence an acre, or they could lease agricultural land for twenty-five years at one shilling per acre per year. Land specified to be for a coconut plantation could be had for five shillings an acre. If land was wanted for a fishing or trading station, the price was £5 an acre. Improvement conditions were attached in all cases and if not met caused the reversion of possession to the government. Aside from the fact that the native interest in the land was protected and speculative acquisition by Europeans was made difficult to engineer, it was not apparent that the MacGregor-Griffith ordinance was obstructive of European enterprise.

It was true that MacGregor rather favored the small man whose land needs were modest over companies that wanted thousands of acres, but in this he was conforming to an established Australian prejudice, amply illustrated elsewhere in this history, and even on the point he was less rigid than the Australian colonial governments. The hostility of the latter wrecked a British company proposal involving broad acres which Mac-Gregor definitely favored. However, the net of it was that to the end of MacGregor's time only 6574 acres had been alienated of which 2645 acres represented validated claims to land purchased from the natives before the protectorate had been proclaimed. Under the 1890 ordinance only 2600 acres were alienated for agricultural purposes and only a fraction of these were brought into use. At the time much was made of an alleged Australian reluctance to invest in a colony not wholly under Australian control, but this seems an unlikely explanation for Australian money was being invested in other island groups Australia had no expectation of ever controlling, for example in German New Guinea (notably as to plantations on Bougainville) and Samoa. The reason seems rather to have been that by the time MacGregor was ready to take a permissive attitude toward the entrepreneurs, capital for island ventures was scarce in depressed Australia, and New Guinea, still largely an unknown quantity, was not regarded as an attractive place for the scarce money to be sent. At any rate, economic development in MacGregor's time was minimal.

Since the agricultural development which was regarded as basic advanced only a little, the returns from gold mining assumed greater importance than their intrinsic significance perhaps warranted. The search for gold in New Guinea was at once an acknowledgment of the old idea first formulated by the Portuguese long ago that New Guinea would prove a gold-rich country and a logical extension to the possession of that fascination with prospecting that had flourished in Australia since 1851. Indications of gold in the British territory had been reported by explorers from time to time since 1852 and "professional" prospectors were intermittently active on the main island from 1878, but no payable field was actually found until 1888 when a rather patchy alluvial field was located on Sud Est Island in the Louisiade Archipelago. A little later another patchy alluvial field was found on Misima Island in the same group. In the classical fashion of gold fields, these island fields attracted more miners than they could support. On the main island no field of importance was found until after MacGregor had left the colony.

The only agricultural product that was won in increasing quantities in his time was copra. At this time nuts were brought in by natives to traders, independents or representatives of firms of which Burn Philp was the most important, who processed them into copra. However, the Europeans, especially Burns Philp, were interested in establishing plantations, but made very little headway. The government sought to induce the natives to plant coconut trees in a systematic fashion to increase the flow of nuts to market. Insofar as an economic ideal for the natives could be formulated at this time, it appears to have been to continue them as subsistence agriculturalists—in New Guinea, gardeners—while inducing them to regard coconuts as their "cash crop." To show the natives the way, the government established plantations on its own account and this led on to governmental experimental plots of other crops. The only indication that diversification beyond copra was likely was the appearance of a small quantity of rubber among the exports in the middle 1890's. For the rest the exports were the old island staples, pearl-shell, *bêche-de-mer,* and sandalwood, the typical commodities of the gathering stage of island economics.

Since MacGregor was deeply concerned with pacification he naturally warmly appreciated the help he got from the missionaries, whose interest in suppressing native violence of all kinds was as keen as his own. It was MacGregor's considered conclusion that "The two finest and best institutions I left in New Guinea were the constabulary and village police, and the missions." Pacification, whatever the means, necessarily involved interference with and suppression of native beliefs and customs and while MacGregor was certainly philo-native, he seems to have been indifferent to the consequences of such interference and suppression to native society. His view, in short, was untinctured by anthropological thinking. Later administrators were to take a slightly different view. When MacGregor had arrived in New Guinea the L.M.S. mission was, of course, well established. A Roman Catholic Sacred Heart Mission, staffed by French priests, had been on Yule Island for two years. Two other missions were established in his time, one by the Church of England and one by the Methodists. MacGregor followed the practice of "dividing the field" instituted by the British years earlier in Polynesia, and while the Protestants conformed willingly, the Roman Catholics, as traditionally, did not. The Catholics were strongly bent on penetrating the main island.

When MacGregor left the colony in 1898 to go to Nigeria it was already commonly assumed that control of British New Guinea would probably pass to the Australian federation when it was established. It was not, however, foreseen that it would take eight years to shift the responsibility wholly to the Commonwealth. A period of marking time and drift set in shortly after MacGregor's departure. All the elements of change in the situation as he left it remained active, but no very inspiriting developments occurred, least of all any satisfying to the vocal few who saw in the rapid expansion of economic exploitation the real justification for the European presence.

MacGregor's immediate successor was George R. Le Hunte (1852–1925), a Cambridge-educated barrister, whose career in the colonial service before appointment to New Guinea included periods in Fiji, the West Indies, and Mauritius. From New Guinea he went to the governorship of South Australia and from there back to the West Indies as governor of Trinidad. Le Hunte did not take MacGregor's delight in journeys of exploration; he was as interested in pacification but mostly left the work to the men posted in the field, while he chiefly concerned himself with administration at Port Moresby where he could work with and through his associates on the Executive Council. He was present in New Guinea for only about half of his term; the rest of the time he was in Australia or on leave in England. A significant first step was taken toward a medical and public health service.

In Le Hunte's time the Yodda gold field, inland from Buna Bay, was developed. Those who flocked to the field usually brought little capital to their adventure and had little knowledge of the tropics. The gold won—and it was considerable—was paid for in the decimation or worse of the miners who succumbed to disease, exposure, exhaustion, starvation, and death at the hands of natives. To cope with the problems of law and order on the field, the outstation at Papangi was moved to Kokoda. About the same time, a field was developed on Woodlark Island.

These fields in the east of the colony turned Samarai into the principal port of entry for a time. Its trade was temporarily several times as large as Port Moresby's. But while trade and colonial revenue thus showed an upward trend, uncertainty about the future of the country inhibited the making of large plans for development. Rubber production temporarily ceased to expand, but coffee and tobacco now appeared among the exports. Discounting the gold boom as likely to be short-lived, British New Guinea was still a copra colony.

In retrospect, the event of most fateful consequence to the administration in Le Hunte's time was the murder of the Reverend James Chalmers by the natives of Goaribari Island, westward of Daru, in April 1901. Because of Chalmers' enormous prestige as a pioneer missionary—he had been in New Guinea since 1877—the murder was far more than a routine act of native violence against a European; it could be viewed as a very serious challenge to the administration's authority; and how it was to be dealt with raised fundamental questions about the techniques of pacification. Le Hunte recognized that it was of major import and himself went to Goaribari where, after consultations with his field people, he decided not, as customarily, to burn down all the villages implicated but only the *dubus* (buildings occupied only by the fighting men). Under the circumstances this was a moderate punishment. Early in 1902 Le Hunte returned to the island to make peace with the natives but also to take some hostages. Thinking better of it, he left without hostages saying he would return to get Chalmers' actual murderers and his bones. This, however, he was unable to do before his departure to the governorship of South Australia.

The completion of the Goaribari affair therefore fell to C. S. Robinson, a Queensland lawyer, Le Hunte's chief judicial officer and candidate for the lieutenant governorship. Robinson went to Goaribari and attempted to take the murderers by inducing the natives to board the government boat to trade. When he ordered the alleged murderers in the crowd to be seized, a scuffle naturally ensued and the natives in the canoes about the ship sent up a shower of arrows. Robinson and his men replied with rifle fire. This was reckoned worse than a blunder; it was assessed a crime against the natives. The episode roused a storm of public indignation in Australia, stirred originally by statements of the Reverend C. S. Abel, a L.M.S. missionary whose information was, as it happened, secondhand. The government resolved to appoint a commission of inquiry and to appoint not Robinson but Captain F. R. Barton, head of Le Hunte's native constabulary and his private secretary, to the lieutenant governorship. Barton was Le Hunte's own choice for successor. When Barton arrived in New Guinea from Australia Robinson was informed of developments. He swore in Barton as lieutenant governor and then committed suicide. The commission of investigation eventually returned a verdict of excess of zeal, not evil intent, but the real issue was methods of control and pacification. The role of violence in achieving these ends was not clarified by the commission's finding.

Meanwhile, moves had been made to transfer British New Guinea from dual control, with title held by the United Kingdom, to exclusive control and possession by the Commonwealth of Australia. In 1901 the Commonwealth Parliament indicated its willingness to take over the colony and, to demonstrate its serious purpose, increased the annual subsidy to £20,000. The next year the colony was formally transferred to the Commonwealth by Royal Letters Patent. There then ensued a long delay, enlivened by a protracted debate, before the Commonwealth actually assumed responsibility for government. There was a striking disproportion between the prolixity of the debate and the knowledge and understanding of New Guinea it revealed. The strategical argument for being in New Guinea was not particularly emphasized, although it was to be revived by W. M. Hughes in World War I, and the emphasis was thrown on the problems involved in realizing on the allegedly lush economic prospects. In this general context a great many specific questions were raised, ranging from whether or not alcoholic beverages should be absolutely prohibited to whether or not Englishmen were as fit as Australians to carry out Australian purposes. This latter discussion was in part suggested by the alleged disarray of Captain Barton's administration and in part reflected the aggressive nationalism of the Labor party. Along the way a good deal of attention was given to the central policy issue of what was the proper balance between regard for the interests of the natives and regard for those of the European entrepreneurs. It became apparent that while the Australians certainly intended no harm to the natives they felt that purposeful attention should be given to facilitating Australian exploitation of those lush resources. The notion that New Guinea was a kind of warehouse from which all the tropical products of which Australia had need could be drawn—a notion that was to survive the chances and changes of the next half-century—was born. There were, of course, disagreements about how this should be done, reflecting the positions of the conservative and Labor politicians, but there was no significant disagreement about the need to do it. The government servant most knowledgeable about New Guinea, Atlee Hunt of the Department of External Affairs, favored it. The Burns Philp people favored it. The royal commissioners who investigated Barton's administration in 1906 favored it. They assessed prospects good for copra, rubber, sugar, coffee, tea, tobacco, cocoa, and kapok. As to the labor required, it was *assumed* that the native supply was ample and that it would be "good for" the natives to be put to work. At any rate the White Australia policy absolutely precluded any possibility that Asiatic labor could be brought in. As to land, it was *guessed* that there would be plenty if all that the natives did not obviously require for their support was taken over by the government. A certain favor for the small enterpriser was suggested, but large companies were not excluded.

An approach to the problem of the colony having been hammered out and the Commonwealth Parliament having passed a machinery of government act in 1905 (proclaimed at Port Moresby on September 1, 1906), there remained the question of who was to direct affairs in Papua. It was impossible that Captain Barton be continued in office for not only was he an Englishman but also the Royal Commission had adjudged him a weak and uncertain administrator, unclear both about the role of the natives and of the European entrepreneurs. He was given a year's leave of absence with the understanding that he would not return to office. The British government took care of him by appointing him financial adviser to the Sultan of Zanzibar.

The Commonwealth finally turned to J. H. P. Murray who had first been in Papua, as the Australians now called the colony, as a member of the Commission that looked into Robinson's handling of the Chalmers affair and who had been appointed chief judicial officer of the colony under Barton. Murray was a far more fateful choice than anybody could have imagined at the time. J. H. P. Murray was the elder brother of Gilbert Murray who about this same time became Regius Professor of Greek at Oxford. The Murray family had been settled in Australia since 1828 when a father and son—the father had been in the country earlier as a military man—took up pastoral properties on the future site of Canberra. The son, who became the father of J. H. P. and Gilbert, built a house called Yarralumla which in time became the governor-general's residence. J. H. P. Murray was born in Sydney in 1861 and was educated in Australia and at Oxford where he took a double first in *literae humaniores* and distinguished himself in sport. Trained in the law, he returned to Sydney to practice as a barrister but not doing very well he became a parliamentary draftsman, a Crown prosecutor, and an acting circuit court judge. He served with distinction in the Boer War. At the inquiry into Barton's administration the gravamen of Murray's testimony supported the thesis that Barton was weak and unsure. Because he was on leave in Australia while Prime Minister Alfred Deakin was trying to make up his mind about what to do in Papua, he had been frequently asked for information and judgments. That Murray had ideas about colonial administration was obvious, but how his ideas would stand up in the actual situation in Papua and how his mind would move were, of course, unpredictable. He was a humane man, a hard worker, a constant reader, not least of the literature of colonial administration. He made a point of the fact that he was an Irishman and he was a Roman Catholic by deliberate personal choice. He came to feel more political sympathy with Labor than with the conservatives. He was appointed acting administrator for the period of Barton's leave and in 1908 was appointed lieutenant-governor by Andrew Fisher's Labor government. Subsequently W. M. Hughes took credit for the appointment, which is ironic in view of Hughes's views and actions with regard to New Guinea.

Murray retained his post from 1908 to 1940 when he died still in

harness while on an official visit to Samarai. In the course of his unusually protracted term as a colonial governor he became identified with
Papua and Papua with him. He became a legendary figure and his policy
totemic even to himself. Yet he never ceased to be an amateur of colonial
administration. Though he had his troubles with staff, he derived much
strength from the strong belief in his policy which many of his staff developed. The policy appears not to have sprung full-blown from Murray's
mind in 1908, but his mind began to move almost as soon as he took
office and continued actively to move at least until he gave his ideas
classic expression in the 1920's. Although Murray never turned away
from the entrepreneurs, though for years they accused him of having
done so, he certainly developed a philo-native tendency in the tradition
of MacGregor. He himself explicitly recognized MacGregor as an intellectual ancestor and knew that this put him in a vital British colonial
tradition. There was but little more of an anthropological constituent in
his thinking than in MacGregor's and he was clearer about the general direction in which he thought the natives should be induced to move than
about any ultimate end for them. He saw the natives as normally
sentient people who had somehow to be moved from their "stone age"
position into the modern world and he had the idea that they should be
encouraged to bring some of their inherited baggage with them—but
what? However, he never became so philo-native that he was unprepared
to make at least a qualified defense of the Papuan system of indentured
native labor without which, he agreed, the European entrepreneurs could
hardly hope to survive in the colony. Murray's policy was therefore
clearly in the nature of a compromise—a wise and good compromise,
mayhap—but definitely the child of its time, place, and maker. Almost
before it was understood and appreciated by the general public, including
some of the resident entrepreneurs, it was outmoded in view of the ideas
being developed by the professionals of colonial administration, notably
in Africa. In spite of the enormous prestige he built up, Murray never
felt secure in his office. He was always acutely aware that some of his
superiors in the Australian government, the more aggressive business
interests, and some of the politicians, were highly critical of him not
only, he thought, because they were hostile to his colonial policy but even
at times because he was Irish and Roman Catholic. He was aware that,
while the world thought of his policy as *the* Australian colonial policy,
there was also a quite different and tougher policy that had powerful
partisans in the country. He was knighted in 1925 and became Sir
Hubert Murray. Since the Murray legend was just taking its characteristic shape as World War I broke out, an account of Murray's Papua

may properly be postponed until the story of Papua is resumed in Chapter X.

Between the turn of the century and the time of World War I Dutch New Guinea almost but not quite stood still. Trading along the coasts continued. The first effort to find oil was made in 1905 by the Royal Dutch Oil Company but it was unsuccessful and when in 1915 the Company tried again, it again failed. What was known of the country was, in terms of economic development, discouraging. The interior was pictured as a place of lofty, steep-rising mountains and swampy malarious valleys, the soils badly leached by the heavy rainfall and thickly covered by a forest growth it would be costly to remove for agriculture, and the native population, reckoned to be about 400,000, thinly spread and very unpromising as a labor supply. New Guinea was therefore viewed by the Dutch as a "reserve" area of the Indies to be considered for economic use only when nothing else remained, or the international political situation dictated action. However, between 1907 and 1914 an important effort to acquire exact knowledge of the interior was made. The topographers of the Indies service carried out a series of explorations and in 1919 produced the best map yet. As they were ordinarily accompanied by geologists, botanists, and ethnologists a considerable body of data was accumulated, but in relation to the unknown it was but a fractional contribution. The Indies government also continued to add to its stations, the most memorable of this period being Hollandia on the north coast near the German border in 1910. In 1905 after fifty years of effort the Protestant missionaries had five stations but only 260 Christian converts. However, they felt they were on the verge of a breakthrough and they indeed steadily added to their stations and converts in the ensuing years. By 1918 they were in a position to establish a school at their principal station, Mansinam, for the teaching not only of native missionaries and school teachers but also tradesmen, particularly carpenters and dressmakers. Since doctoring was an integral element of the missionaries' work, they also made progress in meeting the staggering health needs of the natives. On the other hand, the Catholics working from Merauke suffered a sharp reverse. After establishing two new stations away from Merauke in 1909 and 1910, they found themselves unable to penetrate the sense of superiority of the natives they were working with and by 1914 the mission had shrunk to one stubborn priest at Merauke. As if to demonstrate that native "cults" which occasioned bothersome unrest were peculiarly apt to arise on the fringes of European-native contact, the pioneer Dutch Protestant missionaries had first observed the so-called Mansren-myth native cult as early as 1857. As time passed, the Mansren cults picked up elements of Christianity, "cargo" (by 1886), and eventually acquired political overtones.

By 1900 it was apparent that Fiji was to be a principal center of European economic activity in the islands south of the equator—*the* principal center of *British* activity. Its only rival within the area was French New Caledonia where the pattern of development, centering on minerals, was quite different. Fiji's development in its European phases was agricultural, involving field and tree crops, and while in the years after 1900 there were recurrent efforts to diversify production, or to recover a diversification that had existed briefly earlier, the export dependence *circa* 1900–1920 was primarily on sugar, copra, and bananas. All three steadily increased in export volume. The sugar industry was controlled and directed by Europeans employing an Indian labor force; the copra industry was partly in the hands of Europeans employing a Fijian and Pacific islander labor force and partly in the hands of self-employed Fijians for whom copra was the cash crop of their communally operated subsistence agricultural economy; while banana production was dominated by Fijians, though the marketing was in the hands of Europeans. The sugar industry was concentrated on Viti Levu with a subsidiary offshoot on Vanua Levu; copra was produced on both these main islands, on Taveuni where European plantation owners were especially strong, and on the small islands of the Lau group where the Fijian producers were dominant. Bananas were produced chiefly on that part of Viti Levu of which Suva was the natural port.

In the economy of Fiji a small number of strategically placed Europeans made the important decisions. Not only was this true in agriculture, but in wholesale and retail trade, in the export-import trade, and in banking. In banking the field was divided among branches of strong banks whose headquarters were in New Zealand, Australia, or London. A minor phase of the economic story from 1900 to World War I was an effort by the Indians to establish a self-directing foothold in agriculture and retail trade. In this way they had but limited success and as a people they lived enmeshed in the European sugar economy or on its periphery. The Fijian economy was fundamentally an "independent" subsistence agricultural economy, but it was linked in a peripheral fashion to the European economy by its "cash crops." In government the Europeans were also paramount, but the Fijians held a special relation to the government, fortified exegetically by reference to the Deed of Cession and Sir Arthur Gordon's policy. The Fijian special position in this period came under pressure—pressure focused on their possession of so much of the land. The Indians also were wards of the government, but this relation was not as profitable to them as in the case of the Fijians. In economic rewards the system was three-tiered in that the Europeans received the largest returns, in part because they were Europeans, in part because of their relation to capital investment, with the Indians a bad second, and the Fijians bringing up the rear.

By 1900 it was obvious that sugar was to be the basic European-controlled industry and the signs pointed to a boom in the industry. While sugar, after its establishment in the 1880's—in 1882 exports exceeded all other exports in value and totaled 1731 tons—had shown a steady rise in export quantities, reaching an average of just short of 30,000 tons, worth $2,000,000, in the quinquenium 1895–1900, the industry had had a difficult time. Fiji, in common with other tropical cane producers, had been adversely affected by the bounty system devised in the middle 1880's by governments seeking to promote temperate climate beet-sugar production. Not until 1898 at an international conference at Brussels, Belgium, was a *modus vivendi* between temperate beet and tropical cane arranged and not until 1903 were the effects fully felt. The Fiji industry had also been depressed to an extent by the economic troubles in Australia, then its principal market, in the 1890's. In the course of the years 1882–1900 the per ton price of Fijian sugar had dropped from £34 in 1882 to a low of £9 in 1895 and stood at but £12 in 1900, a level which was, however, not to be exceeded until after the outbreak of World War I. In the years 1885–1900 many of the smaller-scale European cane growers had been driven out of the industry.

It was significant of the time of troubles that he who controlled the milling of the cane was, barring the government's intervention, in a position to wield great influence over the industry in all its phases. Difficult times tended to drive the smaller mills serving single plantations or limited cane-growing areas into bankruptcy and out of production. This brought about a concentration of milling facilities in sizable units serving large areas, the concentration receiving technical support by the development of narrow-gauge (two-foot) cane-carrying railways to bring cane from the remoter areas to the mill. In Fiji, however, there was small likelihood of the concentration of milling at any single geographical point, even on the island of Viti Levu. The geography of cane growing dictated several mills on Viti Levu and at least one on Vanua Levu. By 1900 it was apparent that the Colonial Sugar Refining Company of Australia was in a fair way to dominate the industry through its control of most of the mills, not to mention its extensive holdings of cane land, freehold and leased. It had not, however, achieved a monopoly of milling and did not do so for another quarter century and never sought to engross the lands on which cane could be grown. That Colonial Sugar could make progress during difficult times was attributed ex post factor to the overlapping into Fiji of factors which supported its success contemporaneously in Australia. Its great strengths were possession of ample capital—its Fijian investment doubled between 1882 and 1900—direction by an extremely able management, and its wise policy of employing its own cane and milling scientists and using their findings. After its original mill at Nausori in the Rewa Valley near Suva, which had begun crushing in 1882, the C.S.R. built a mill called the Rarawai on the Mba River, Viti Levu, a much superior cane-growing area, which began to crush in 1886. Originally controlled by the subsidiary New Zealand Sugar Company, the mill passed to direct C.S.R. operation in 1888 when New Zealand Sugar was absorbed into the parent company. In 1894, when the depression was still on in Australia, C.S.R. brought into operation a mill called the Labasa on the Qawa River in Vanua Levu. And in 1899 it began to build a mill at Lautoka Point, Viti Levu, which was to grow into the biggest sugar mill in Fiji, while around it was to grow a very important port town. This mill first came into operation in 1903. At this stage the only mills of importance the C.S.R. did not control were the Penang Mill at Raki Raki, Viti Levu, owned by Melbourne, Australia, interests and the Amanua Mill on the Navua River, Viti Levu, a mill serving a single plantation which was to be bought and expanded by Vancouver, Canada, interests in 1905. This remained the situation until the middle 1920's when new difficulties in the industry led on to a C.S.R. monopoly of milling.

After 1900 and well into World War I Fiji sugar experienced a boom. The expansion can most conveniently be measured in terms of exports, since domestic consumption was trivial. Whereas in 1900 actual exports were 29,969 tons, ten years later they had doubled to 58,771 tons and by 1917, under the stimulus of wartime demand, they had reached 98,382 tons, though this figure was a peak not to be exceeded for seventeen years thereafter. Over the same years the price per ton slowly rose from £12 in 1900 to £15 in 1917. However, the highest price was not reached until 1920 when £29 per ton was obtained. By this time, as remarked, the industry was immersed in a new sea of troubles.

Around 1900 the C.S.R. grew the bulk of the cane it milled on land it owned or leased, operating on an extensive plantation basis with Indian field workers. C.S.R. thus accounted for around four-fifths of the cane produced in any given season. Additionally, it bought cane from surviving independent European plantation operators within the ambit of its cane-carrying system and about 1906, as though trying to restore the position existing before 1885, began to emphasize the leasing of plantations to former senior employees to increase the number of independent European growers. In the years between 1900 and 1920 also, "free" (that is, nonindentured) Indians began to appear in numbers, as explained below, and while some dispersed into other occupations, agricultural and non-agricultural, most of them struck out for themselves as cane growers on land either leased from C.S.R. or the Fijians. Most of their cane went to the C.S.R. mills but until the 1920's some of the independent cane growers could sell to the mills the C.S.R. did not own or control. Only the cane farms of the Indian leasees were small. The other farms of whatever control or ownership were true plantations of extensive acreage, dependent on Indian labor. Since the sugar industry was in a dynamic phase, the demand for land was strong and this brought pressure on the land resources. Since the bulk of the unused land was in the hands of the Fijians, this in effect meant that the pressure was on the Fijians, with consequences that became dramatic around 1905.

In this general context and particularly with regard to the sugar industry, the labor supply for European enterprise was of crucial importance, as it was in all the island groups. Any faltering in the flow of recruits into the labor market and any fundamental change in the terms and conditions of their employment would force adjustments difficult enough to constitute a crisis. The organization of an industry might have to be fundamentally changed. Although until 1912 Solomon Island natives were recruited for service in Fiji, labor supply in sugar meant Indians. It was after 1900 as the sugar industry expanded that the Indian indenture system in Fiji achieved classic expression and absorbed most recruits most rapidly year after year, but by 1910 the system began to come under attack on social and moral grounds, rather than economic, and after a decade of skirmishing around the questions, the system came to an end. This left the Indians still the indispensable labor force of the sugar industry but as "free" labor and also and very importantly as a permanent, rapidly growing constituent of the population of the Fiji Islands, in ever-increasing proportion Fiji-born.

The condition of the Indians under indenture in Fiji was in large part determined by the way in which their employers regarded them, while actual conditions in particular situations were more or less determined by the overseers, in large proportion young Australians, directly in charge. In essence the Indians were seen as coolies from whom a maximum return in labor of minimum cost was to be wrung before they were repatriated. In some measure this view of the Indians was supported by the facts about their status in India. With some warrant they were regarded as *déracinés,* off-scourings of the Indian villages who were in any case fleeing unimaginable poverty and probably in high proportion with the police at their heels. Even the Australian Methodist missionaries who began to work among the Indians in Fiji in the late 1890's emphasized the large criminal element among them, though in actual fact it seems to have been no more than 10 per cent. Grinding poverty, not criminality, was the prime mover in indentured emigration. In recruiting and in transporting recruits to Fiji, caste was ignored by those in charge and in the result it was downgraded by the Indians themselves. The castes actually present were those normally found in villages. Religion as a factor of dissidence was treated similarly; most of the migrants were Hindus. No great effort was made to keep the sexes in balance and the emigrants were overwhelmingly males. Traditional factors in personal and social control were thus weakened. On the Fiji plantations the Indians were badly housed in "lines," or roughly constructed barracks consisting of a double row of small rooms. Sanitation, including water-supply, was poor. Diseases brought with them became rife: hookworm, dysentery, and syphilis. Both men and women were worked hard in the fields, usually on a "task" rather than a time basis. Wages were low, the food supply inadequate. Although the traditional Indian controls were eroded, nothing was done in Fiji either to rehabilitate them or supply new ones. The result was a sharp decline in personal and social discipline. For example, sexual conduct was described as "promiscuous polyandry." The crime of assault was commonplace, murder almost equally so. Mortality was heavy, including the self-induced mortality of suicide. Yet it was considered, on balance, that these people were better off economically in Fiji than in India.

Efforts to improve the condition of the Indians began around 1900 as voluntary acts of employers, around 1908 by legislative action with regard to housing and sanitation, including water supply. These were attempts to ameliorate a bad system which was nevertheless to be retained. But as so often happens in situations of this kind, the admission that ameliorative changes were needed seems to have induced fundamental criticism of the system. This first found thoroughgoing expression in 1910 when Dr. J. W. Burton, an Australian Methodist missionary, published a book in which he expounded the thesis that the indenture system was socially and morally an evil thing and should be abolished. In the same year, however, the system was formally defended as having saved Fiji from economic stagnation to which lack of a labor supply would have condemned it and as having brought great economic benefits to the Indians involved. However, about this time, the question of the supply of indentured labor from India began to be agitated in India as a major political question. The Indian politicians alleged that the system was a species of slavery which branded the Indian nation with the stigma of helotry and thus degraded India in the eyes of the whole world. While the agitation against indenture in India was necessarily directed against the British Raj—hence its great political use and significance—and as such the agitation was participated in by men like Motilal Nehru (father of Jawaharlal) and Mohandas K. Gandhi, the conditions complained of were overseas. Fiji was at the time the chief receiver of indentured labor. Firsthand investigation of the situation in Fiji fell to Gandhi's long-time associate, the Englishman Charles Freer Andrews. However, Andrews was preceded in Fiji by a British-Indian commission which concluded, once again, that the system was justified by the patent economic benefits enjoyed by Indians in Fiji as compared to the poverty they suffered in India. Andrews shifted the attack to the social and moral consequences, as Burton had done, but moved in two steps toward an all-out indictment, reaching his most radical position only in 1917 when he passionately advocated abolition. By that time the authorities in India had more or less accepted the position of the Indian politicians. In 1915 the government of India notified the India Office in London that the agitation could not safely be ignored. In 1917 the government of India, utilizing powers of the Defence of India Act, prohibited recruiting for the duration of the war and two years after. Andrews agitated for abolition in Australia, aiming his fire at the Fiji government and C.S.R. The women's organizations of Australia were especially impressed by his case but in 1919 financed a new study. In essence it supported Andrews' indictment, though in more moderate terms. The women demanded cancellation of indentures. The employer interests attempted a defense of the system but promised fundamental reforms, much in terms earlier employed by Governor Sir Bickham Sweet-Escott in replying to Andrews. In the face of mounting pressure, however, the Fiji government, now headed by Sir Cecil Rodwell, capitulated and after fixing the date of cancellation as August 1, 1920, moved it up to January 1, 1920.

In theory the employment of indentured Indian labor did not require the establishment of a permanent Indian population in Fiji. As in the Pacific island-labor trade, repatriation was an integral element of the system. The Indians exercised their repatriation right during the indenture period and after and the right was not finally canceled until 1958. It has been estimated that 40 per cent of the indentured immigrants went back to India sooner or later but as a proportion of the repatriates returned to Fiji as free immigrants, how this reduced the group in Fiji is uncertain. However, repatriation was never required and very soon the Fiji government began to encourage the Indians to settle down. Settling down was, of course, in line with Indian conduct in the American, African, and Asian countries to which they had also been taken. For a while the employers expected those who proposed to stay on to renew their indentures, but this seems to have been to make labor discipline easier to enforce, not an implied objection to the development of a permanent free Indian population. The idea that such a population would serve Fiji well seems to have developed in the 1880's. An acting governor phrased it thus: "It is in the multiplication indefinitely of these industrious people . . . that the bright future for the Colony lies." Just when free Indians began to be an important element is not clear but in 1886 Indian hawkers to the number of a hundred, presumably free men, were reported. It was the multiplication of this element that insured that Fiji would indeed have a permanent Indian population. By 1904 the free Indians in Fiji numbered 10,000, or nearly half of all in Fiji. Save for off-spring born in Fiji, these were ex-indentured people plus a small group of free immigrants who had arrived from Indian overseas settlements such as British Guiana and Mauritius. The ex-indentured became artisans and storekeepers in the towns and country districts but most of them became farmers and most of the farmers specialized in cane growing. The free immigrants were artisans, jewelers, grocers, drapers, laundrymen, bakers, and bootmakers as well as farmers. The farmers who were not in cane growing grew rice, maize, pineapples, tobacco, and vegetables and kept cows. While a few Indians acquired land in freehold title, most of them could only lease land, from either Europeans or Fijians. The net of all this was that in 1921, after all indentures had been canceled, Fiji had a permanent Indian population of 60,000 of which the ex-indentured were already a minority and the Fiji-born the majority.

In thus establishing an Indian population in Fiji the Europeans in government and agriculture were following their economic noses toward a labor supply without giving careful thought to the "consequences" whether in terms of the requirements of a rapidly multiplying, prevailingly agricultural, introduced people for land, their role in politics and government, or of the effects of their establishment upon the position of the "protected" indigenous Fijians. Some of the consequential problems had emerged into the open before 1920 but they became far more difficult at a later stage as the Indian population grew toward equality with the Fijian. The arbiters and mediators in Indian-Fijian relations were the Europeans, particularly those in government, with the British-appointed governor at their head, but the resident European entrepreneurs, in large proportion Australians, also played a role (which, however, it is difficult to define). The Europeans were consistently a small minority vis à vis both the Indians and the Fijians at all stages and did not increase in numbers at as rapid a rate as the other peoples. They numbered 2459 in 1901 and 3878 in 1921. However, the Europeans had a significance out of all proportion to their numbers, especially because it became the prime Fijian policy to pressure the Europeans to perform their arbitral and mediatory function in the light of their "protective" relation to the Fijians allegedly provided for in the Deed of Cession. Efforts by the Europeans to escape or reduce the constrictions on which the Fijians insisted brought nobody any glory. Rather, in the long run the effort to loosen up the context of decision to allow more free play for those making the decisions in a multi-racial and multi-economy society only provoked the emergence of a Fijian leader whose great point was to refurbish the machinery of government protective of the Fijian people. From the record it is plain that the Fijians consistently sought to evade the competition, peaceful or otherwise, that was a basic factor in the complex society in which the Europeans had so absent-mindedly inextricably entangled them.

The Europeans and the Indians were not the only "foreign" elements in the resident population. There were small groups from several of the Pacific islands of whom the Rotumans, a people of very mixed background, were migrants from an island administratively part of Fiji. Others were Melanesians from the Solomons who had been brought in by the labor traders and Melanesians from the New Hebrides of the same origin. Also relicts of the labor trade were some Ellice islanders. By 1921 these groups numbered all told around 2500 persons. There were also some Chinese, whose history was obscure. Chinese were in Fiji by 1900 but they did not appear in the census records until 1911 and by 1921 still numbered less than one thousand. And there were the "Part-Europeans," as the census described them, mostly European-Fijian half-castes. These people had first appeared in the very earliest days of the European presence in Fiji and were recorded as totaling 1516 in 1901 and 2781 in 1921. These were small groups indeed as compared to the Indians and even, at this stage, the Europeans, but they also could pose problems.

Around 1900 and for twenty years after it was the prevailing idea that the Fijian population was in decline and while something was being done about it, it was not yet certain that the downward trend, which indeed appeared to be accelerating, could be reversed. It was generally believed that at cession there had been between 130,000 and 150,000 Fijians; in 1901 there were but 94,397. The counterattack had been begun in 1884 when Dr. William MacGregor's scheme for training selected young Fijians in the treatment of the commoner diseases had been adopted and it had been stepped up after the investigation of the problem by a Commission in 1893 when Sir John Thurston was capping his astonishing career with a term as governor (1888–97). The Commission made no fewer than thirty-six suggestions for counteraction which could be roughly grouped under such heads as food production and diet, child welfare, medical care, and public sanitation (including housing and water supply), all programs to be focused in the villages in which most of the Fijians dwelt. At the time, the implementation of the proposals was much impeded by lack of funds and some of them were not instituted until years later, but in 1899, when Sir George O'Brien was governor, and public revenues were increasing, steps were taken to improve the medical services by building provincial hospitals and the better to police the sanitary regulations. The epidemic diseases such as measles and dysentery still exacted a toll, the incidence of pulmonary diseases was high, and yaws and hookworm were disastrously common, but much progress in disease control was made between 1904 and 1910. A new attack on the problem of yaws began in 1912 and about the same time hookworm was given special attention. Whether consequentially or not, the period 1905–11 was subsequently determined to be the period when the downward trend of the population was stopped, stability was achieved, and the population began to increase. However, the Fijians suffered heavy losses in the influenza epidemic of 1918 and their actual numbers were at an all-time low in 1921—84,475. Thus it was that the Fijians were just achieving a position where their numbers might be expected to increase, barring unique disasters like that of 1918, when the Indians were rapidly multiplying, chiefly by immigration but also by natural increase. In 1901 the Fijians constituted 80 per cent of the population of the islands; in 1911 the proportion had fallen to 60 per cent; and in 1921 it stood at 54 per cent. At that stage the Indian proportion was 39 per cent. There then ensued a kind of race between the Indians and the Fijians to see which would be the majority population of the islands, leading on to the Indian victory about a quarter-century later.

It was in the context of the boom in the European-directed sugar industry and the increase in the number of land-utilizing Indians that contention over land policy developed. The pressure for access to more land —the land held by the Fijians—was at this stage stronger from the Europeans than the Indians, but later on, the position was reversed. Since the Fijians were declining in numbers, it was assumed they possessed more land than they had need for, a common assumption about the land (see the New Zealand situation, for example) when an island people was declining. It was overlooked that such calculations could be sadly awry if the indigenes began to increase, but this was not expected. Moreover, the Fijians were reckoned to be very inefficient users of land, as compared to European or even Indian users, and since Western-style criteria ruled at the time, this was a weighty point. The Fijians used land communally in a subsistence economy and the Europeans (and Indians) individually in a commercial agricultural economy, so the contrast was indeed striking. But whatever the ins and outs of the question, the fact remained that the Europeans wanted more land and the Fijians held it.

It fell to the government as arbiter and mediator to try to deal with the demand for more land and, miscalculating the strength of the Fijian position, it proposed a program which decidedly compromised that position. This was probably "inevitable" in the circumstances of a time when island governments were strongly disposed to assist the European entrepreneurial interest in any ostensibly leigtimate way, on the ground that a strong Western-style economy was a principal contribution to native welfare. The "need" to open the way to Europeans was first perceived by Governor George O'Brien, in office 1897–1902, but the actual moves to modify the land ordinances were made by Governor Sir Everard F. im Thurn, in office from 1904 to 1911. Although over the previous twenty years a good deal of energy and time had been put into validating the Fijian communal titles to the land, in 1905 the local judgment was that certain parcels of land known as "waste lands," or lands not actually occupied but nevertheless hitherto assumed to be owned by the Fijians, were in fact available to the Crown, that is, the government of Fiji as surrogate, for disposal on 99-year leases or as freehold. Between 1905 and 1909 some 20,184 acres of this land were sold, bringing the total freehold in the hands of non-Fijians up to 434,799 acres. The position that freehold titles could properly be given was then challenged in the House of Lords in London by Lord Stanmore (formerly Sir Arthur Gordon), invoking not only his idea of the facts but also the agreement of Queen Victoria with him in conversations about Fiji. The matter was referred to the secretary of State for the Colonies, who concluded that the "wastelands of Fiji must continue to be regarded as the property of the natives as much as the occupied lands." In 1909, therefore, the 1905 legislation with regard to freehold title to "waste lands" was suspended. The leasing of waste land for 99 years continued for a time but in 1911 this too was stopped when it was suspected that speculation rather than use motivated some who were seeking leases. In 1912 it was again laid down that Fijian lands could be sold only to the Crown. However, the problem of handling leases of Fijian land remained and only by leasing could net additions be made to the land accessible to European—and Indian—enterprisers. The Fijians had normally been quite free about granting leases but capricious about *renewing* them. In 1915 and 1916 there was a retreat from the 99-year practice which, in any case, seems never to have appealed to the Fijians, and the 21-year term of earlier days became the maximum again. Attention was given to the formalities of leasing which had been rather catch-as-catch-can, with the purpose of giving leasees more security of tenure and placing on the Fijian owners responsibility for paying compensation for unexhausted improvements on land for which they were refusing to renew the lease. This was regarded as a deterrent to capriciousness. Provision was also made for the passing of final decision about renewal to the government in certain circumstances. If no decision was made before the expiry of a lease, the tenant could stay on a year-to-year basis. Leasing land turned the Fijians into landlords, and while annual payments became in total quite sizable under the Fijian system of landowning, it was difficult for any individual Fijian to achieve affluence from such income. These events made it fairly clear that the land problem was to be a continuing problem and the demographic history of the Indians was to lead to their deep implication in it.

Not only were the Fijians under pressure at this time to make their lands more freely available to other peoples but they were simultaneously under pressure to change their own system of landholding and use. The Fijians had traditionally held and used their land communally, the basic unit of organization being the *mataqali,* consisting of village families of common ancestry. The *mataqali* was, of course, but one of the Fijian institutions involving both benefits and obligations which knit the Fijian individual firmly into his village and Fijian society at large. The Fijians were wedded to their system of holding, using and sharing the fruits of use of land, and, indeed, to the other systems of benefits and obligation which were the fabric of their life. However, this way of life contrasted sharply with the European and Indian ways. It was obvious that if one were to adjust the Fijians to the Western-style economy, a way of escape from the *mataqali* and the associated systems and the concomitant material obligations was required. The refuge of the escapees, if any, would be the Western individualistic system of landholding, use, and disposal of production. In 1880 Sir Arthur Gordon had provided by ordinance for an escape, involving a cash composition of the obligations to the village. This had not resulted in any significant loosening of the established system, and some Fijians who had attempted to escape into the Western system had suffered defeat and had returned to their villages. The escapees had little encouragement from their fellow-Fijians and indeed with their exceptional holdings of goods and other material things they might well suffer a species of victimization because of Fijian customs which involved sharing the wealth. Fijian society, like most island societies, made little allowance for the accumulation of wealth on an individual basis, least of all by commoners. Moreover, Fijian society did not allow the development of personalities that could easily deal with the competition that was integral to Western society. As a result the pressure to loosen up the *mataqali* system came mostly from Europeans seeking to adjust the Fijians to the Western-style society. These people were often extremely dogmatic about the necessity of it. The traditionalist Fijians could only regard them as anti-Fijian even when it was obvious that they simply entertained a different idea about what was good for the Fijians. By Governor im Thurn's time, three decades after Gordon's, a common European view was that the Fijian institutions controlling landholding and use were an impediment to Fijian welfare and were probably in an advanced state of decay in any case. To these people a movement toward individualistic landholding should not only be provided for; it should be strongly encouraged, if not insisted upon. Only if the change was made could the Fijians survive in the economic context then rapidly developing in Fiji. Governor im Thurn tried to speed up the individualization of landholding and land use by Fijians by making it easier for individual Fijians to acquire land in freehold and leasehold. In this he had the support of his colonial secretary, Joseph Chamberlain. However, the Fijians did not respond in numbers. No more than with regard to the release of land to non-Fijians were the Fijians at all avid about changing their customs ruling landholding and land use.

The pressure of the Europeans on Fijian institutions extended also to the system of government that had been provided for the Fijians by Sir Arthur Gordon. Although attached to the machinery of the crown colony government, and although Europeans worked in it at various levels, Fijian government was to a high degree separate from the crown colony government and was deliberately designed to serve the needs and interests of the Fijians as distinguished from those of any intruders. Although Gordon had certainly recognized that the Fijians, like all island peoples, would somehow have to adjust to the situation created by the Western forces operating in Fiji and thus to some undefinable extent accept Europeanization, it was his idea that this should be done by the Fijians themselves within the framework he was providing. While European officials helped to work the Fijian government, it was staffed in largest part by Fijians in all its aspects. In close correspondence to the way in which Fiji had been organized before cession, Fiji was divided into provinces and the provinces into districts, under which were the villages. A Fijian *Roko* headed each province, a *Mbuli* each district, while each village was headed by a *Tauraga ni koro*. (*koro*, Fijian for village.) The *Roko* were almost invariably high chiefs, the *Mbuli* prevailingly chiefs of lesser rank, the *Tauraga ni koro* commoners. From the *Roko*, executive authority ran upward to the Native Regulation Board whose task was formally to sanction Fijian custom and formulate new regulations as required. Beyond the Board, authority ran to the governor. There was a Native Affairs Department to supervise the system. To cap the councils which were associated with the *Roko* and the *Mbuli,* and to preserve an institution believed to date from about 1850, a Council of Chiefs was kept on. It was given an advisory relation to both the Fijian administration and the crown colony government, specifically, in the latter case, the governor. Beginning in 1904 two Fijian members were added to the Legislative Council, further attaching Fijians to the crown colony government. These members were chosen by the governor from a slate submitted to him by the Council of Chiefs. Fijian government was to a high degree government by a native elite, the hereditary chiefs constituting the elite, and their role can profitably be compared and contrasted with the roles in government of the native elites of Tonga, the Samoas, and New Zealand.

After thirty years it was a common European judgment that the Fijian government was unsatisfactory in that it was not producing acceptable results from the European point of view. Under the influence of the chiefs, it was alleged, it was being used less to facilitate the adjustment of the Fijians to the West than to protect them from the Westernizing forces. The chiefs, it seemed, aimed to preserve the status quo. But what was the status quo? The chiefs could not allege that they were aiming to preserve a pristine Fijian society, for already that society had been considerably adjusted to changed circumstances. Change had been constant since the early 1800's and the best anthropological study of the Fijians at this time was significantly subtitled a study in the *decay* of custom. But to the chiefs it was a legitimate question how far the adjustment should be allowed to go in a European direction, while their European critics obviously had in view total Europeanization, particularly at the level of economic organization. The Europeans also strongly felt—this in the general context of population decline—that the quality of the Fijians was declining, more particularly the quality of the chiefs, so vital to good government. The chiefs were undereducated, they were sloppy administrators, their probity in financial matters was questionable—when Fijian custom tangled with probity as Westerners defined it, Fijian custom ruled, to the disaster of public finance. On the other hand, the authority of the chiefs had been weakened by European administrative action, beginning in Gordon's time, as the Europeans had demanded of the Fijians acceptance of policies which set up conflicts between the Fijian administrators and the Fijian people. The commoners alleged that policies such as those which demanded close conformance to public health ordinances and required labor on roads were in essence European notions, not Fijian, and in resisting them the commoners resisted their chiefs in their guise as administrators under European influence. The dissatisfaction of the Fijian people under the pressures they felt found expression in the remoter areas in pseudo-religious cults of an anti-European complexion, beginning as early as 1885 and continuing sporadically down the years. The first was a so-called Tuka movement which Europeans believed had some connection with the Hauhau cult in New Zealand.

The British crown colony government showed its own general agreement with the European indictment of the Fijian government by steadily increasing the role of European officials in Fijian government at all levels. In 1913 the Colonial Office proposed that the Native Affairs Department be abolished and its tasks be handed over to European administrative and judicial officers working in the field. In 1916, over the protests of the *Roko*, the Native Affairs Department was deprived of its independent status and became a branch of the Colonial Secretary's Department, and in 1921 the secretaryship of Native Affairs was abolished and its duties were assigned to the colonial secretary. Thus by 1921 the role of Europeans in Fijian government had been greatly expanded and insofar as it had an effective head, that official could not be presumed to have any specialized knowledge of Fijian custom and affairs. From Gordon's "indirect rule," the Fijians had been moved a considerable distance toward direct rule, not because they had achieved an effective adjustment to the westernizing conditions—even that they had made a physical adjustment was not then recognized—but because they had been adjudged by the Europeans to have failed to manage indirect rule to their own and Fiji's profit. The burden of the indictment fell on the chiefs. The unlovely consequences of their failure fell on the Fijian commoners.

As the Fijians lost to the Europeans some of the initiative in their government of themselves, the Indians for the first time were granted a voice of limited range in the general government of the colony. Until 1904 the Legislative Council had consisted of ten members of whom six were officers of the colonial government and four were resident Europeans nominated by the governor and approved by the colonial secretary in London. In 1904, after the resident Europeans had campaigned for changes in the Council favorable to themselves, a by-blow of which had been their flirtation with Seddon's proposal that Fiji and New Zealand federate, the Council was expanded to a membership of eighteen. Ten of these were to be officials, six "unofficial" European members who were to be *elected* (two to represent Suva, one Levuka, two to represent general agriculture, one to represent sugar), while two Fijians were to be chosen from a slate nominated by the Council of Chiefs. In 1916 the Council was again expanded, this time to a membership of twenty-one, with the governor as president additional. Seven members, all Europeans, were to be elected to represent defined constituencies, two from Suva but none from Levuka, this illustrating the decline of that place. The two

Fijians retained their places and the method of their selection remained unchanged. Eleven of the twelve *nominated* members were to be officers of the government, while the twelfth nominated member—chosen by the governor—was to be an Indian. This continued to be the political position until 1929.

As the political problems arising from the partitioning of the islands died down, the high commissioner of the Western Pacific—at this stage still also the governor of Fiji—was left with a variously defined special relationship to Tonga, the Solomon Islands, the Gilbert and Ellice islands, the New Hebrides, and Pitcairn Island.

One of the British compensations for acquiescing in the division of Samoa between the Germans and the Americans was the abandonment by the Germans of their claim of 1875, supported by a treaty, to a naval-commercial fulcrum in Tonga. The elimination of the German interest opened the way for the British to define a special relation with Tonga which was designed to place it within the British orbit but to allow it to remain an independent Polynesia island kingdom, the last surviving example of this species of government. The British defined the new relationship in two steps in 1900. In May they established a protectorate and in December they concluded a Treaty of Friendship with the government under which the high commissioner at Suva was to be continuously represented in Tonga by a British agent and consul. This official was to have jurisdiction over the British residents, most but not all of whom were New Zealanders and Australians, but was not to interfere in Tongan internal affairs. Under the protectorate, Britain had control of Tongan foreign relations and provided naval protection.

The survival of native government in Tonga, as contrasted with its eventual eclipse in Tahiti, Fiji, Samoa, and Hawaii—and survive it has to the present day—appears to have been the consequence of a unique mixture of plus and minus factors in the Tongan situation and the resolution of the British to be satisfied with a protectorate rather than to go on to taking sovereignty. To begin with, while the two hundred Tongan islands were scattered over a considerable expanse of ocean, not all of them were inhabitable and the minority that were did not provide any considerable acreage for agricultural exploitation and no other resource existed. The agricultural resources were not sufficient to arouse any very hearty expectations in the breasts of European entrepreneurs. With little difficulty, therefore, Europeans were prevented from acquiring any freehold and the area they acquired on leasehold remained small, chiefly involving sites for trading enterprises. Technically, title to all the land was retained in the hands of the monarch—even the holdings of the nobility were subordinate to the monarch's policies—and an ingenious scheme was devised to give the commoners certain access to land (use-rights, subject to a moderate money-tax, to eight and three-quarters acres of cropland, and a village homesite) as they came of age. The ruling Tongans, who were in effect an elite of hereditary nobility, were astute enough to give the commoners a sense of participation in government and also astute enough to employ the assistance of Europeans in government without allowing control to slip entirely from their hands. More-over, it would appear that the Tongans were also assisted in maintaining their independence by the fact that their islands, which were so early discovered and had once seen considerable ocean-going traffic as the point of entry to Fiji, progressively fell outside the lines of heavy commercial traffic by sea (and much later by air). The considerable measure of isolation proved valuable. And their independence was sustained to an extent difficult to measure by their relative success in adjusting their Polynesian inheritance to the Western forces working on them. Their Methodist religion, which had caused such unseemly uproars in times past, became progressively more benign, though not a less pervasive factor in Tongan life, and as an influence toward Western-style education, a decidedly creative factor, not least in that the Tongan elite early pioneered obtaining high school and later university education in New Zealand and Australia. While subsistence agriculture was retained as the basis of the economy, steps were taken to insure everybody's participation in copra production by prescribing the planting of coconut trees on a fixed proportion of the land assigned to them, thus giving the people access to the Western goods they had come to "need" and the government much of the revenue required to pay for the Western goods and services it decided the country must have. By 1918 exports stood at £169,757 and imports at £177,151, and both were increasing. At this stage, the export-import trade and the retail trade within Tonga remained in the hands of Europeans. As in all the island situations, there was noticeable a qualitative difference in the impact of Westernization between the principal port and center of government, Nukualofa on Tongatabu Island, the outlying settlements of the Tongatabu group, and the settlements in the less important Ha'apai and Vavau groups.

The real test of the Tongan experiment, if indeed anybody ever saw it as an experiment, did not come for many years. Between 1900 and 1918 it was a question of carrying on under a mixed Tongan and European leadership in a social situation which appeared to be no more stable or instable than that of any other of the island groups. The major question at issue was what the balance should be at the governmental level between the Tongans and the Europeans. In the general climate of the times it was probably inevitable that the Europeans should not only be fairly numerous in the small Tongan governmental hierarchy but also powerfully situated and that the prevailing pressure should favor their position. One of the hardest tasks of native island peoples was to accept and understand the Western money economy. Not unexpectedly in 1904 Tongan finances were found to be in chaos. High Commissioner Sir Everard im Thurn intervened in person and showed his bias in favor of the European participation in government. He ordered the deportation to Fiji of the Tongans who were then premier and treasurer; he insisted that the British agent and consul should be given supervision over the kingdom's finances, even though under the treaty he was prohibited from interfering in internal affairs. The agent-consul's new relation had to be legalized by a revision of the treaty in 1905. The customs schedule and service were reformed. It was provided that the budget had to be approved by the British agent and he was given a right of veto over items of expenditure he disapproved. Furthermore, the agent's consent to appointment of Europeans to the Tongan service was required. The im Thurn reforms thus brought European influence in Tongan affairs to its highest pitch. However, the premiership was retained by a Tongan. In 1914 the Tongan parliament was reduced in numbers to seven members representing the nobility and seven representing the commoners, plus the cabinet, including the Europeans. In 1918 King George Tubou II died. He was succeeded by his eldest daughter by his first marriage, born in 1900. She came to the throne as Queen Salote. Her husband, Prince Uliame Tungi, who had been educated to the preparatory school level in Australia and who had already been a cabinet officer, became premier in 1922.

The distribution of the Solomon Islands between Britain and Germany had finally been completed by 1900. In 1893 Britain had assumed a protectorate over the so-called Southern Solomons of which Guadalcanal, Savo, Malaita, San Cristobal, and the New Georgia group were the principal components, while in 1899 it had added the Santa Cruz group, rich in historical associations, and in 1900 as a phase of the Samoa deal, had taken over from Germany the Shortland Islands, Santa Isabel, Choiseul, and the outlying Ontong Java group. When with these were included all small islands and groups of small islands in their vicinities, the British had possession of all the islands considered to be in the Solomons except Bougainville, its much smaller associate Buka, and their immediate outliers. The latter Germany retained as part of its New Guinea possession. As the place-names indicate, neither the British nor the Germans had had conspicuous roles in the discovery of the Solomons. Rather, the honor was chiefly the property of the Spanish and the French, and in the case of Ontong Java, the Dutch (Tasman in 1643). However, the British had been associated with the Solomons since Carteret's time and the Shortland group was the discovery of the British Captain John Shortland while en route from Port Jackson to Batavia in 1788. The British had first been induced to take responsibility in the Solomons in the 1880's on law-and-order considerations, not least because so many of the Europeans transiently or permanently present were British subjects. At that time they began sending warships on visits to the islands. In 1893 they wanted to improve their position in that respect beyond what was feasible as long as the Solomons were technically derelict. The disorder they were seeking to quell, insofar as it was not indigenous to the native societies, was the creation of itinerant and resident traders and labor recruiters, tempered to a slight degree by the missionaries, then the workers of the Melanesian Mission. Between 1893 and the early 1920's the British authorities moved little from their law-and-order stance, although the Europeans moved forward to the plantation stage, from the European point of view both a consequence of and a major contributor to the progressive pacification. The Solomons nevertheless remained a quite wild island frontier, even as law and order improved.

The British official in charge was called the resident commissioner; he was a subordinate of the high commissioner in Suva. His headquarters was established on Tulagi, a small island closely associated with another called Florida, lying between Guadalcanal and Malaita. At it reached the resident commissioner at Tulagi, British law in the Solomons consisted of regulations and Orders in Council issued in Suva and was additionally supported in its civil and judicial aspects by the Pacific Order in Council of 1893, issued in London. The first preoccupation of the resident commissioner was the suppression of native violence in the New Georgia group and on Malaita.

The indigenes of the Solomons were predominantly Melanesians and had a racial affinity to the Melanesians in New Guinea and the New Hebrides, but there were tiny enclaves of Polynesians, or proto-Polynesians, as on Ontong Java, Rennell Island, and Tikopia Island. The social organization of the Melanesians was as highly fragmented as in New Guinea, and it was as weak in "political" expressions of use to Europeans attempting to rule. Direct rule was called for in the first stages; indirect rule could be attempted only at a later time. As indicated, the contacts between Europeans and the indigenes had been of the familiar kind and had resulted, it goes without saying, in the introduction of European diseases among them, including sexual diseases, which were added to malaria and yaws. In the context of native violence and European depredations—headhunting was the most spectacular and macabre kind of native violence—this meant that the population was assumed to be declining. The population in any case was very unevenly distributed over the islands with a heavy concentration—often mentioned to be 40 per cent of the total—on Malaita. This made Malaita a center of attention for labor recruiters. What the total population was *circa* 1900–20 cannot be stated with any confidence, particularly since the contacts with the natives were, at this time, wholly confined to the coasts of the islands and what number of natives resided in the interiors of the larger islands was utterly unknown. An estimate was 100,000.

The Solomon Islanders by 1900 had been involved in the labor trade for at least twenty years and they had been taken in numbers to such important reception places as Samoa, Fiji, and Queensland. The coming of the British in the middle 1890's had resulted in some improvement in the tactics of the labor recruiters but not in the cessation of the trade. The Solomon Islanders were thought to be good workers and were in constant demand. Movement to Queensland did not cease until after 1900. The German planters in Samoa had their Solomon Island supply cut off about the same time and had turned to Chinese labor. The Germans in New Guinea were frustrated from drawing labor from the British Solomons in spite of their rights under the Anglo-German agreement of 1886. The supply of laborers to Fiji ceased in 1912. In sum, the Solomon Islanders were before World War I recruited for service only within the British Solomons, although apparently British Solomon Islanders were allowed to go to the Australian plantations on Bougainville, but they were otherwise kept at home. This did not mean that the demand lessened, for the local plantations were expanding, nor that the workers served on their islands of residence, for the distribution of the population precluded that and the distribution of the European plantations confirmed it. Plantations were normally established on leasehold—no land could be bought as freehold from the natives—at coastal locations where suitable land was abundant and natives relatively few. The recruits were brought from islands where population was abundant—e.g., Malaita—to these locations. In any case it was not considered wise practice in the Solomons, any more than in other island groups where local recruiting continued, to have the recruits serve too near their homes. If taken well away from home, it was thought, they were less apt to attempt desertion.

In this period the European entrepreneurs were wholly preoccupied with the development of the copra trade of which pro tem the establishment of coconut plantations was the most significant phase. The pioneer traders had initiated the copra trade, getting their coconuts from native suppliers. The pioneer planters were in effect seeking to supplement, or perhaps supplant, the native suppliers. The pioneers had been "small" men. After 1900, however, there was a marked shift of emphasis from the small man as the characteristic enterpriser to the "big company," of which the most conspicuous were Lever Pacific Plantations, Ltd., and Burns Philp. In the long run the big operators were to squeeze out a high proportion of the small operators. The Lever company had originally been a copra crushing concern in Sydney which around the turn of the century had entered the plantation business by buying out the remaining properties of the Pacific Islands Company, Ltd., which was then moving into the mining of phosphate rock at Ocean and Nauru islands. Lever entered the Solomons in 1904 and began building up what became the biggest single plantation operation in the group. Its headquarters was at Tulagi. The Burns Philp operations in the Solomons, which were initiated in 1908, also had a headquarters at Tulagi. These companies became the chief employers of Solomon Islands natives, maintaining a ratio of about a thousand natives to about four Europeans controlling and directing them.

A significant phase of this opening up of the Solomons was the multiplication of missions, mission stations, and workers. The Melanesian Mission (Church of England) remained, as historically, the best established and oldest and largest of the missionary enterprises. It was active mostly in the islands in the south of the chain, with its headquarters by 1919 on Florida Island. This headquarters station was the third in a series; the others had been at Auckland in New Zealand and on Norfolk Island. The Roman Catholics—Marists—had returned in 1898 after an absence of over fifty years—the Catholic pioneers had been ignominiously expelled by the natives in the 1840's—and established themselves in the Shortland group. The Methodists came in 1902, allegedly at the suggestion of Solomon Islanders who had encountered them in Fiji, although it is known that George Brown, of sacred memory, had had his eye on the Solomons for years. They began their work in the New Georgia group. In 1904 the Solomon Islanders who in that year were repatriated from the Queensland sugar fields by the White Australia legislation—those who did not elect to go to Fiji—were accompanied by a woman missionary who had begun her work on her brother's plantation. This enterprise developed into the South Sea Evangelical Mission. In this period it was the missions that did whatever was done for the natives by way of education and medical care, but their principal preoccupations were nevertheless the suppression of the more horrendous native customs and the propagation among the natives of their alternatives to pagan religious beliefs. By this time all the missionaries had lost the desire to dress the natives in Western-style clothes and make them live in Western-style houses. Their work habits were in the hands of the plantation makers.

Although the Gilbert and Ellice islands had experienced to the full the impact of "the West" in its several phases and forms, beginning with the Spanish explorers in the sixteenth century, they were not brought formally under European control until 1892 when the British proclaimed a protectorate, first over the Gilberts and immediately after over the Ellice Islands. The native inhabitants of the Gilberts were Micronesians, and Micronesians had also once inhabited the Ellice Islands, but several centuries back had been displaced by Polynesians, believed to have come as invaders from Samoa. These people lived in a world of atolls. Their atolls had but severely limited agricultural possibilities and it was difficult to wrest a satisfactory food supply from them, harder in the Gilberts than the Ellice. Naturally enough, then, the natives placed a high value on land and constantly fought over it. A native war over land was going on when the British arrived to arrange a protectorate. Warfare had tended to generate mutually hostile petty chiefdoms, or "kingdoms." The first permanent European residents to drift in were the classic mixture of runaway convicts from Australia, deserters from whalers and other merchant vessels, and a few individuals of better antecedents and intentions. Whalers were active among these islands from *circa* 1820 to 1870. The earliest European residents were noticed in the 1830's and appear to have been satisfied to be beachcombers, but they graduated in time to being factotums to island chiefs and especially to the status of petty traders, complete with native wives and half-caste children, sometimes with significant power over the nearby native community. About 1850 the labor trade began to hit these islands hard, particularly the Ellice group, where in the ensuing quarter-century the population declined by 17,000 to 3000. Trade had begun with the exchange of native curios for the standard items of European "trade goods," graduated to coconut oil, and, when copra had been "invented," became based on it. The trade was carried on by locally resident traders with their more or less intimate ties with the natives and by ship-based itinerants out of Sydney, San Francisco, Honolulu, Apia, and Auckland. Australians, Britons, Germans, Americans, and strays of other nationalities such as Frenchmen and Austrians were involved. It was at this stage that the resident European population probably reached its maximum.

Missionary work had begun in the northern Gilberts in 1857 when the American, the Reverend Dr. Hiram Bingham, representing the American Board of Foreign Missions, arrived from Honolulu. Bingham did all the work of reducing Gilbertese to writing, compiling a dictionary and a grammar, and translating the Bible. He was active in the Gilberts, with a long interval elsewhere in Micronesia, until 1875. He and his associates spread Christianity not only south in the Gilberts but north and west through the rest of Micronesia. By 1900 their mission headquarters was at Kusaie in the Carolines. In 1865 L.M.S. missionaries led by A. W. Murray, who was later to go to New Guinea, arrived in the southern Ellice from Samoa and gradually spread their influence north. A Roman Catholic mission began work in 1888 and eventually made converts throughout the protectorate, but the Protestants continued to be far more numerous and in some of the Ellice islands were monopolists. However, paganism had its partisans into the twentieth century. In 1917 the American mission withdrew in favor of the L.M.S. An L.M.S. missionary is said to have decreed, "Gilbertese women must wear drawers," while a Catholic worker is quoted as saying, "Il faut être toujours réaliste." While Gilbertese women acquired no inhibitions about bare-breastedness, they retained a horror of being seen wholly naked. Natives have their folkways too.

Before they assumed the protectorate the British had for some years been regulating the relations of British subjects and the natives by the occasional action of commanders of touring naval vessels and after 1877, when the high commissionership had been instituted, had fortified the authority of the naval commanders by making them deputy commissioners. By the protectorate the British acquired jurisdiction over not only the natives but all the resident Europeans as well. Associating the two island groups for convenience, the British established an administrative headquarters at Tarawa Atoll in the Gilberts. The administration was under the jurisdiction of the high commissioner in Suva, the principal local representative was a resident commissioner, while subordinates called district magistrates were posted in the other principal islands. An economical system of indirect rule was instituted. Building on precedents established by the missionaries and incorporating British laws adjudged relevant, a law code was devised. To administer it in both its judicial and executive phases, the traditional native councils were constituted courts, called *Kabowi,* of which the village headmen, or *kaubure,* were members, presided over by a native magistrate. The *Kabowi* even had considerable financial autonomy for some years. The British functionaries stood to the courts in the relation of advisers and supervisors.

The Gilbert Islands straddled the equator. To the north and northwest were the Marshalls which had become a German protectorate a few years before. The Ellice lay south of the Gilberts spreading east in the direction of Samoa. To the east of both groups over a very considerable expanse of ocean lay islands in groups, chains, and isolation which historically had had particular significance and value to Europeans and might have it again, especially either to the British or the Americans or both. Many were at this time, however, uninhabited though some could perhaps support inhabitants under special conditions. In the years before 1892 the British had formally declared their concern for many but not all of these islands and had with regard to some indicated their belief that they had rights over them by such acts as leasing them to Europeans, mostly Australians or New Zealanders, who proposed to make use of their resources, agricultural and mineral, by establishing coconut plantations or mining guano. A scattering of the islands were technically derelict. Who had discovered these islands was sometimes not established. That the British had had a conspicuous role was clear, but Spaniards, Frenchmen, Russians, and Americans had also been involved; some of the islands had had several names in the course of time, or were known by alternative names currently; and some were named differently on maps of different national origin. The American association with these islands, which was in time to be important again, dated back to the whaling days; Charles Wilkes's men had surveyed some of them in the 1840's; Americans from San Francisco had for years traded for copra among them; and Americans working from continental United States or Honolulu had exercised proprietary rights, with the federal government's backing, when the guano trade had been active. To the northeast of the Ellice was the Phoenix group, currently uninhabited, over most of which the British had declared a protectorate in 1889, perhaps on cue from John T. Arundel who had been getting guano from them since the early 1880's. This protectorate at first included Canton, Enderbury, Birnie, Hull, Phoenix, and Sydney islands. Gardner Island was added in 1891. South of the Phoenix group was the Tokelau group, inhabited; it was also declared a British protectorate in 1889. A distance to the northwest, almost due south of Hawaii, was a wide-spaced chain of islands of which three—Washington, Fanning, and Christmas—were *annexed* by the British in 1889. A fourth, Palmyra, was also annexed at that time, but in 1898 the United States Congress by legislation included it in the Hawaiian Islands and the claim was maintained, largely by private persons in Honolulu interested in the copra trade.

The Gilbert and Ellice protectorate thus appeared to be the last of a series of British actions during the 1880's and early 1890's which were designed to clarify the British relation to the numerous islands along or just below the equator. The clarification proved in the long run not to be wholly successful, its validity not universally acknowledged. Only to a very limited degree was the motive of clarification economic, for these islands, even when inhabited, had but a low agricultural potential or had (or had had) only "wasting" mineral resources, or were barren in all respects. In staking claims to them the British appear to have been engaged in tidying-up a disorderly situation which might cause trouble if left alone, seeking perhaps to support law and order, with perhaps some vague reference to naval strategy. Between 1892, when definition of status ceased for a time to concern the British, and the end of World War I, the economic significance of these islands was measurable only in terms of coconut growing, save Fanning which not only had plantations but also from 1902 was the site of a relay station on the All Red transpacific cable. Companies such as the Pacific Islands Company, its successor Lever Pacific Plantations, Ltd., and the Samoan Shipping and Trading Company of Apia operated plantations, directed by Europeans with a labor force of islanders, on various of these islands.

When in 1900 it was ascertained that Ocean Island, a small somewhat isolated island geographically related to the Gilberts which had a complicated history of European contacts, mostly involving beachcombers, dating back to around 1840—it had been discovered in 1801 by an American—was rich in phosphate rock and when shortly after the working of this resource began, Ocean Island was *annexed* by the United Kingdom and placed under the administrative authority of the resident commissioner of the Gilbert and Ellice Protectorate. Ocean Island shortly became the principal source of public revenue for the protectorate, making nearly nine-tenths of the total, while the future of the island natives—called Banabans—was provided for by a royalty on rock mined. The development of mining opened up employment opportunities for the Gilbertese and the Ellice Islanders who were used in the operations along with Japanese. The recruiting of native labor was done by the administration with the help of the *kaubure*. Ocean Island soon became the island of the protectorate best served by shipping as well as the island best supplied with what the British call "amenities." In 1907 the administration shifted its headquarters from Tarawa Atoll to Ocean Island. In 1915 the British annexed the protectorate and in January 1916 it became the Gilbert and Ellice Islands Colony. In 1916 also Ocean Island was formally added to the new Colony as were the Fanning and Washington islands. Later in the same year the Tokelaus were added. In 1919 Christmas Island was added. In this fashion the British consolidated their position.

The improvement of government revenues seems to have had but a limited effect on the services that the British were prepared to provide the natives. The expansion of local employment possibilities seems to have been their chief benefit. To be sure, the native police force was enlarged, but this was chiefly to meet the increased law-and-order responsibilities on Ocean Island. The missions continued to do all that was done by way of education, and while a European doctor was employed by the administration, he had constantly to travel the islands, was normally overworked, and was rarely available anywhere in a sudden emergency. At Tarawa Atoll the most highly regarded "doctor" was a Fijian native medical practitioner, trained at Suva hospital, and stationed at Tarawa for many years. The native law code was revised in 1917 and the authority of the *Kabowi* was by and large confirmed, but such financial autonomy as they had was taken away and the revenues centralized. Although the administration was aware that the natives had a land problem, and that disputes about land were endemic, no positive step was taken to deal with the situation until 1919. A major interference with native custom, of which an articulate member of the administration disapproved, was engineered through the Colonial Office by the missionized natives: an attempt was made to enforce Western-style monogamy. The native economy remained basically subsistence and was attached to the Western economy by copra and was in neither aspect satisfactory. Communications were haphazard, except at Ocean Island: a trading vessel, usually a Burns Philp ship, from Australia once in six months or so, L.M.S. or American missionary ships occasionally. Yet it appears that in general this period was a golden age for the islanders. The native population achieved stability and about 1915 began to increase—forecasting an acute population pressure on extremely limited resources. Just before World War I broke out it was believed that about 25,000 natives were living in the Gilberts and 3300 in the Ellice group.

The New Hebrides, strung along a northeast-southwest axis between the Santa Cruz group of the Solomons, well beyond the Barrier Reef off the coast of Queensland, and the Loyalty Islands dependency of New Caledonia remained as much a problem group as they had been for many years past. From the Western point of view the essence of the difficulty was the impossibility of deciding who was to possess the islands, the British or the French. While the French were unquestionably dominant in terms of resident nationals, land ownership (or claims), and plantation development, the British—or more precisely, the Australians—refused to leave or be pushed out. From the French angle the New Hebrides were unquestionably geographical as well as economic satellites of New Caledonia, but they had not been taken under French sovereignty in 1853. The British position was more complicated, for the British and the Australians did not take quite the same view. As a problem in international politics and diplomacy the New Hebrides tied in, for the British, to their relations with France in Europe. It was because of the developing entente with France that the British preferred to compromise the New Hebrides question. In terms of an economic stake, missionary involvement, and status in international law, the New Hebrides were a primary concern to the Australians. The Australians took an attitude almost as aggressive as the British attitude was conciliatory and pressured London to *act,* not temporize. The British resident population, holding land and developing plantations, was mostly Australian and because of the activity of the Burns Philp people, external trade flowed in considerable proportion to and from Sydney. At this time the principal export commodity was copra, with coffee, cocoa, and cotton of much lesser importance. For the French, Nouméa in New Caledonia was the first external point of reference, as Sydney was for the Australians. However, even after 1900 there was some sentiment among the British planters favoring annexation by France.

While the Europeans were enormously discontented with the situation in which they found themselves and did not hesitate to express their discontent, the prime victims of the unlucky position were the natives. The natives, Melanesians closely similar in character to the Melanesians of the Solomons, had, it will be recalled, suffered severely from the labor trade and while they were no longer being recruited for service outside their islands they were still being recruited for service within them. They were a people obviously in decline, and little or nothing was being done to arrest the decline—it was even accelerated, particularly by the French who were notoriously careless of native welfare in recruitment, employment, and in facilitating access to hard liquor. The natives, as we shall see, existed legally in a kind of limbo. Apparently the only people who had an active concern for them were the missionaries. The established missions were the Presbyterian from Australia, the Melanesian Mission of the Church of England, whose emphasis was now shifting to the Solomons, and the Roman Catholic Marists whose peculiar concern was the Melanesians. As though attracted by the very badness of the native situation, the Australian Church of Christ established a mission in 1905, the Salvation Army a mission in 1908, and about the same time Seventh Day Adventists began work.

As in other island groups, the Western impact on the New Hebrides was uneven. There were perceptible differences in the impact between the southern islands of the group and the northern islands. In the northern islands the natives were "wilder," though no better off really. Around 1900 it was apparent that Vila on Efate Island was going to be the principal European town and presumably the center of government when government came to rest. Such government as there then was, was literally "floating" and peripatetic, for under the Anglo-French Convention of 1887 the New Hebrides were in charge of "A joint Naval Commission ... composed of British and French naval officers on the Pacific Station." These officers had the duty of "maintaining order and of protecting the

lives and property of British subjects and French citizens. . . ." The natives were ignored except as they might be menaces to life and property.
In effect this scheme was a version of old "gunboat" government. In the
British view, however, the New Hebrides also came under the authority
of the high commissioner for the Western Pacific in Suva, Fiji. In 1902,
therefore, the high commissioner dispatched a resident commissioner to
the New Hebrides and directed that he establish himself at Vila on Efate.
In 1900 the French had adopted the high commissioner idea for their
possessions in the Pacific, designating the *Gouverneur* of New Caledonia
also *Commissaire Général de la République dans l'Océan Pacifique*.
After the British had acted in 1902, the French high commissioner
promptly sent a *délégué* to Vila also. Thus was instituted the first land-
based government the group knew. When in 1904 the British and the
French agreed on their so-called *Entente Cordiale* Declaration, reference
was made in it to situations in Siam, Madagascar, *and the New Hebrides*.
With regard to the New Hebrides a commission to deal with land claims
was called for; in the same context, it was proposed that jurisdiction be
taken over the natives without, however, in either case necessitating any
"modification of the political status quo." The *Entente Cordiale* Declaration was the product of the wisdom of Lord Lansdowne and M. Paul
Cambon. The implementation of the New Hebrides proposals was the
work of M. Paul Cambon and Sir Edward Grey. It was one of Grey's
less fortunate essays in "fixing things up."

The implementation, known as the Convention of 1906, provided a
Franco-British condominium for the New Hebrides. It came into operation in December 1907. The basic idea was that the New Hebrides "shall
form a region of joint influence in which the subjects and citizens of the
two Signatory Powers shall enjoy equal rights of residence, personal
protection and trade, each of the two Powers retaining jurisdiction over
its subjects or citizens and neither exercising a separate control over the
group." Persons of neither French nor British nationality in the islands
were to be required formally to opt under which of the two legal systems
they proposed to live. Neither power was to build fortifications, and to
smother an old Australian complaint, neither was to maintain any penal
establishment. The scheme of having the two Pacific high commissioners
represented at Vila by resident commissioners was continued. (In 1907
the French created the special office of *Haut-Commissaire de France
dans l'Archipel des Nouvelles-Hebrides* and assigned the title to the
governor of New Caledonia.) Each resident was provided with a police
force, the forces to be exactly equal in size. The police headquarters were
to be at Vila, stations maintained on Tanna Island to the south and on
Santo Island (Quiros' Austrialia del Espirito Santo) to the north. More-

over, the naval vessels of the powers might be called on to assist either's police and the commandants might in "urgent" situations act independently. A Joint Court was provided for; it was to have a British and a French judge; it was to deal with the land claims; its proceedings could be in either language, with translation from one to the other; and all records were to be kept in *both* languages. Labor recruiters were to be licensed by the resident commissioners according to the nationality of the recruiters and an elaborate code of conduct for employers of native labor was laid down, this helping to plug up a big hole in the old system. It was provided, for example, that "Employers must treat their employees with kindness" which was certainly a very goody-goody injunction to the rowdies of the New Hebrides. However, the natives were prohibited from becoming subjects or citizens of either party. In greeting the new regime at Vila in December 1907, British High Commissioner Sir Everard im Thurn, ignoring a good deal of very significant history, adverted to the native question thus: ". . . for the first time in history the natives of these islands will be brought under civilized rule . . . it should be clearly realized that this rule over the natives will be as much to their own interests as in the interests of the white men who have settled among them . . . and this, to my mind, is a matter of supreme importance . . . they will be protected against each other and from exterminating each other." At this time there were 401 French citizens resident in the group and 228 British. How many natives there were was unknown; they had never been counted; but certainly there were far fewer than, say, in 1850. The leading French company operating in the islands, now called *La Société Française des Nouvelles-Hébrides,* controlled almost three-quarters of all the land claimed by Europeans. The largest British single landowner, or claimant, was Burns Philp. There was a very wide chasm between land claimed and land in use, but the prevailing ideas about the New Hebridean potential were still quite roseate, and the British—that is, the Australians—were still grimly determined to hang on. They were, however, as displeased with the condominium as they had been with the still looser form of control that had preceded it. In 1914, therefore, Sir Edward Grey negotiated the supersession of the Convention by a Protocol, but as World War I delayed the ratification of this until 1922, what it signified will be examined in Chapter X. Briefly, however, it did not bring good government to the New Hebrides, did not release the British and the French from stalemate, nor did it convert either side to the ways of the other.

The island of New Caledonia, 248 miles long and 31 miles wide, known to the French as La Grande Terre, second in size in the Pacific only to

New Guinea, was by 1900 not only the principal French possession in the Southwest Pacific, though Tahiti was far better known, but was also after Fiji the principal seat in the islands of European-style economic development. The emphasis economically was on mining with agricultural and pastoral development definitely secondary. Of the total area about half was a jumble of hills and mountains (which rose to 5000 feet) that was uncultivable but the locale of the considerable and remarkably various mineral wealth. A feature of the island was the wide variation in average annual rainfall which explained why large areas were savannah-like country and only about 6 per cent was at all heavily forested and a source of commercial timber. About one-fifth of the total area was potentially useful as pasture but as the native grasses were not highly nutritious, intensive use of this resource by dairying was not feasible except on pastures carrying sown introduced grasses. Another fifth was reckoned agricultural land and some of this was quite rich. The largest segment of the alienated land was in the hands of the government which at all times had plenty available for disposal to settlers; the Roman Catholic mission had extensive holdings acquired from its earliest days in the colony; and there were the European holdings in mining leases and agricultural and pastoral properties. The natives, a declining group of Melanesians, were assigned to reserves which were considered adequate to their needs but which were a very tiny proportion of the useful land which, of course, had once been entirely in their possession. Of New Caledonia's dependencies, only the Loyalty Islands to the east had any considerable area (800 square miles) but as they carried a heavy and increasing native population they were "reserved" to it and contributed to the European economy only a quantity of copra. The other dependencies were not only small but only a few of them carried a permanent native or European population, though all supplied copra to market. Hence it was that New Caledonia's most important ancillary economy was that of the New Hebrides, attached to Nouméa, the colonial capital, in a trade relation. The New Caledonian economy was to a very marked degree a dependent economy not only because it was the French economic policy to attach colonies to the metropolitan economy as far as possible, as by the manipulation of export and import duties, but because of the vagaries of the overseas markets for New Caledonian minerals. External trading relations within its geographical area were predominantly with Australia, secondarily with New Zealand.

In New Caledonia, assuming remunerative export of production, the problem of labor supply was as crucial as in any of the island groups. By 1900 the economy had taken such a shape that the resident European population had developed a marked bias in favor of managerial and clerical work. The local indigenes had never been a labor resource of much significance, least of all in the mines where they had consistently refused to work underground, and now they were declining rather rapidly. Whereas in 1887 they numbered 42,000, by 1914 they were down to 28,000. Only about half of them resided on La Grande Terre. They were a disgruntled people and in 1917 there was a native revolt which, while less serious than the uprising of 1878, was nevertheless an alarming portent. The French had of course obtained other islanders as labor through the "labor trade," but after 1900 this supply quickly dwindled to a few Loyalty Islanders and fewer New Hebrideans who drifted to New Caledonia as free workers. In the convict era a white unskilled labor force had been available for use on the land and in the mines but this resource was not replenished after 1896 and though it took a long time to fade away was decidedly a diminishing resource and had apparently never been "sufficient." Since agricultural and pastoral development was lethargic the labor problem was to a peculiar degree associated with mining. The mine managements early turned to Asiatic indentured labor. The mining people had first turned to Asiatics in 1892 when the *Société le Nickel* had brought in Japanese indentured labor from Nagasaki. When the Japanese had completed their indentures, however, they had chosen to settle down in and around Nouméa in New Caledonia and, abandoning mining, had set themselves up as artisans, small businessmen, market-gardeners, and so on. Since they had brought few of their women with them and the French had refused to tolerate the "picture bride" system, the Japanese had married or cohabited with the Melanesian women and French white women and produced a cross-bred population which might have fascinated a student of Mendelian principles but which displeased the French. When about 1900 the mining people again felt it necessary to look to Asia for labor they turned to Indochina (specifically to Tonkin, taken by France from China in 1885, later to be known as North Vietnam) and to Java in the Dutch Indies. From these two sources the French had drawn 1620 workers by 1911 and 3130 by 1921 in a proportion at the latter date of two to one in favor of the Javanese. These people were obtained on five-year contracts on completion of which they could reengage, exercise their repatriation rights, or could apply for permission to settle down. Profiting from the Japanese contretemps the sexes were kept in reasonable balance and the women were worked along with the men, though only above ground at the mines. Only in carefully selected cases could these people obtain permission to stay on in New Caledonia. For this reason New Caledonia did not at any stage approach the condition of Fiji. In the spectrum of races on La Grande Terre the Europeans were definitely the largest single resident group, the only island in the Southwest Pacific where this was so. In overwhelming proportion the Europeans were French but there was a steady minority of New Zealanders, Australians, and even a few Americans, most of whom were, however, transients associated with mining as prospectors, engineers, and managers. Since immigration from France had slowed down to a trickle by 1900 with the failure of Governor Feillet's agricultural policy, the French New Caledonians became in ever larger proportion native born, a fact that eventually had political consequences. But since the French who had arrived before 1900 had included a very considerable number of convicts, only a minority of whom, if they stayed permanently in the country at all, had been able to marry, and because there was a trickle of emigrants to Australia and back to France, there arose the paradox that the white population was at its maximum *circa* 1901 when it stood at 23,500 and thereafter slowly declined for twenty years toward a low of 16,800 in 1921. By 1911 it had become apparent, moreover, that Nouméa was growing faster than what was loosely called "the interior." Not only were the Europeans strongly affected by the drift to the town but also, as already noted, the Japanese. When they were free to locate where they chose, the Tonkinese and Javanese followed suit. Even a few natives congregated at Nouméa to become the earliest *assimilés*. Nouméa acquired a Franco-cosmopolitan flavor unique in the islands.

The extraordinary range of minerals discovered to be present in La Grande Terre opened up a wide range of possibilities for commercial mining but not all were consistently realizable in fact. This was not so much because of the "wasting" of resources through exploitation as because of the vagaries of market prices, the distance from markets and the cost of carrying the minerals to them, and the rise of competitive suppliers geographically nearer the major markets. Among the minerals available in commercial quantities were nickel, chrome, iron, coal, manganese, cobalt, antimony, mercury, cinnabar, copper, lead, zinc, and gold. Gold was chiefly won alluvially during the decade 1870–80 and thereafter was unimportant. In the years between 1900 and World War I cobalt, manganese, chrome, nickel, lead, and zinc were being sent to market overseas. However, in this period New Caledonia lost its world monopoly position with regard to cobalt when rich mines were opened up in Canada and the Congo province of Katanga and its dominance in nickel as the Canadian mines at Sudbury, Ontario, came into production. By value the most important minerals in New Caledonia were chrome and nickel. At this stage New Caledonia accounted for over 90 per cent of the nickel produced outside Canada. Nickel production was dominated by the *Société le Nickel,* not only because it conducted the largest mining operations but because it owned a smelter at Nouméa at which it prepared the nickel for export as matte. Once this works, which was started in the 1880's, had been built up in capacity most of the nickel went away as matte and only small quantities as ore. Therefore, except as they could sell their ore for export the small producers were beholden to *Société le Nickle* to purchase it for smelting into matte. *Société le Nickle,* ostensibly a French company, was really an international cartel in which German and Belgian capital was represented, while its principal competitor, *Société Minière Calédonienne,* had a tie with the Canadian nickel interests. The German money in *Société le Nickel* was supposed to be Krupp's. There was also Australian and American money invested in mining. The strategically important nickel smelter at Nouméa, established in 1883, was dependent on Australia for its coal.

The leading agricultural export in this period was coffee; the leading pastoral export was canned beef. In terms of money these were much more important than the old island staples of copra and pearl shell. The Marist missionaries had introduced coffee as far back as 1856 and by 1865 they had had it at the plantation stage. It was taken up by Governor Feillet's free settlers and was, aside from commodities disposable on the local market, the economic reliance of the European farmers. In 1911 it suffered badly from disease, but this disaster was weathered and in 1914 it was assisted by a premium on all exported to metropolitan France. Cotton was at this time declining to unimportance. The beef canning industry was in the hands of Australian capitalists.

The key political figure was the governor who ruled under forms established in 1885. After him the principal functionary was the *sécretaire général,* who along with the heads of departments staffed a Privy Council. The secretary general presided over an administrative body called the *Conseil du Contentieux* which was composed of the Privy Council membership without the governor. The local population had representation only in a *Conseil Général.* All these councils were consultative vis à vis the governor, without legislative or executive authority. Because the governor was appointed in Paris, as were the secretary general and the heads of departments, and the French colonial service was characterized by short stays in a series of colonies, the officials posted to New Caledonia were naturally more familiar with standard administrative procedures than with the local scene and its unique problems. The inevitable result was a growing sense of difference between the local permanent population and the official element which in time was to have considerable political significance.

As *Commissaire-général de la République dans l'Océan Pacifique* the governor of New Caledonia was chiefly responsible for the Wallis and

Futuna islands, especially after 1907 when his relation to the New Hebrides was provided for separately. However, the French relation to these two closely associated small island groups was in a state of flux into World War I. Futuna, consisting of two small islands, was in effect a satellite of the Wallis group consisting of nine islands lying closely together. The groups together had a native population of around 5000, four-fifths on Wallis; they were Polynesians and perhaps were migrants from Tonga. Located northwest of New Caledonia between Fiji and Samoa, Futuna was a discovery of the Dutchmen Schouten and Le Maire, and the Wallis group of the Englishman Samuel Wallis, who had also discovered Tahiti. French Roman Catholic missionaries had established themselves in these islands in the 1830's and in the 1840's the French naval people at work in the islands had negotiated a protectorate which, however, was repudiated by Paris as likely to offend the British. It was not until 1887 that the French finally proclaimed a protectorate over the Wallis group; they added the Futuna islands the following year. Between 1910 and 1917 there were discussions about annexation between the French and the native sovereigns and in the latter year the two groups, joined for administrative convenience, were constituted a French colony. However, the French continued to recognize the native sovereigns, in contrast to their policy in Tahiti and New Caledonia, and technically the relations of the *Commissaire-général* were with them. The capital was Matautu in the Wallis group and the French resident and associated officials were posted there. Copra was the economic link with the Western economy.

Before proceeding to the French possessions in eastern Polynesia, a glance at New Zealand's Cook Islands is required. The Cooks were all the New Zealanders had won of South Sea Islands after sixty years of campaigning. Like the Australians in Papua, they were in the Cooks from a mixture of purposes and motives, ranging from a conception of defense strategy in which the islands figured as a defensive screen for the North and South islands, to notions about a proper "dominion over palm," to hope of economic profit, and confidence that they had a special competence to govern Polynesians developed during their sixty years of dealing with the Maoris. The Cooks differed in legal status from all other island groups in that they had been made an integral part of New Zealand by inclusion within the country's boundaries. However, the New Zealanders did not proceed to administer them as if they were indeed simply an addition to their country, but more or less "colonially." This ambiguity was to persist. A special department of government for the Cooks was established, with a minister in charge. Under the minister, a senior representative in the islands called a resident commissioner was posted at

Rarotonga and under him were agents stationed on the other islands. While an effort was made to govern in some part through native councils in which the *ariki,* or native chiefs, were conspicuously influential, and even to establish a senior native council at Rarotonga to head the local councils, in a relatively short time decisive executive power had passed to Europeans.

Geographically the Cooks fell into three divisions. The southern islands, to which alone the name of Captain Cook had originally been applied, were mostly volcanic, quite fertile, and the most populous. All told they contained 53,000 acres. In this group were Rarotonga, Aitutaki, Mangaia, Atiu, Mauke, Mitiaro, Manuae, and Takutea. The northern group was made up of coral atolls which inclusively contained 9650 acres: Palmerston, Suwarrow, Pukapuka, Nassau, Manihiki, Rakahanga, and Penrhyn (or Tongareva). Associated with these was the island of Niue, Cook's Savage Island, which had been annexed by Britain once it was freed of its entanglement with Germany by the agreement over Samoa. It contained 64,228 acres and thus was bigger than all its fellows put together.

All of these islands were inhabited by Polynesians. When the New Zealanders took charge the populations were still declining as they had been for some years past, though at a slower rate than formerly. Shortly they were to stabilize and soon would begin to increase. However, the position in the early 1900's was uncertain and it then appeared that the labor supply needed supplementation if the resources were to be fully exploited. The British representative in the islands had recommended bringing in Japanese; the New Zealand representative expressed the hope that British settlers could be induced to come. Fortunately neither happened. At the time, the relatively few resident Europeans were mostly traders and missionaries. The traders were New Zealanders associated commercially with Auckland, Germans representing the German trading company based at Papeete, and Americans whose provenance was also Papeete and more remotely San Francisco. There were also a few Chinese.

These islands, had, of course, experienced the impact of the West in all its phases from Spanish times except the establishment of a significant European plantation economy. By 1900 they had achieved a fairly stable accommodation between the missionary vision and native custom and the European trading interest and native production. Among the natives, the key figures in the maintenance of this accommodation were the *ariki.* However, the authority of an *ariki* ordinarily had but a limited territorial range, not embracing even a single island. Within its range it was quite authoritarian. With the coming of the New Zealanders and the idea of a comprehensive administration for the whole group there was bound to be a collision between the European authority and the authority of the *ariki*. The New Zealanders judged the authority of the *ariki* "harsh, dictatorial and undemocratic"; they sought to install a European-led regime that was paternalistic and focused on social welfare. Until World War I the impact of the New Zealanders may be summarized as involving a systematic undermining of the authority of the *ariki,* particularly with regard to the use of land and the direction of labor in its use. This effectively debilitated the Cook Islands economy and left the natives a good bit worse off economically at the end of the period than they had been at the beginning. At this stage the principal exports were copra, fruit, and coffee, all but copra exclusively from the southern group and all but copra chiefly finding a market at Auckland.

The complex of associated French possessions in eastern Polynesia was known to the world by the name of one of them as Tahiti but to the French as *Établissements Français de l'Océanie*. The complex had been rather laboriously assembled from the 1840's to the 1880's (see Chapters XII, XXII, XXIII, *The Southwest Pacific to 1900*). The five archipelagos which comprised the *Établissements* were the Society Islands of which Tahiti was one, the Marquesas, the Tuamotus, the Gambiers, the Australes, and the isolated island of Clipperton, north of the equator off southern Mexico. (Clipperton had first been claimed by France in 1858 in the guano-gathering times, but the claim was at this stage still not firmly established. In 1897 the United States had made a counterclaim which the French had successfully repelled. The Mexicans were about to set up a firmer claim, which also was repelled.)

Although in theory and in administrative practice these islands gave the French dominance in eastern Polynesia, this had little actual significance either in power-strategic or economic terms. There was no power-base here and the French stationed little power in the area; economic development was weak. France's position as a Pacific power was not founded here at all but in Indochina and as far as the Southwest Pacific was concerned, in New Caledonia. While the opening of the American Panama Canal in 1914 changed the communications route to and from France, it did not, as the French had long anticipated, enhance either the strategic or the economic significance of the *Établissements*.

A French expert on colonies once remarked that such colonies as this had, in default of any significant economic value, "un intérèt politique incontestable," which may possibly be so, but the real value of the *Établissements* by 1900 appears to have resided almost wholly in the almost tangible and in any case highly negotiable romantic appeal of

"Tahiti," both in terms of scenery and *la douceur de vivre,* in a tradition established by Bougainville long ago and so assiduously propagated by a long line of others since. However, there was a less agreeable side even to this, for beginning with Captain Cook there had been those who regretted that this "paradise" ever had had to suffer the European impact because it had had such a disastrous effect upon the natives and their society. These islands were almost classic locales of the dismal drama of population decline and of the equally depressing drama of cultural ruination, neither of which to this time the French had been able to terminate. France's assimilationist policy, which was working here as it was not in New Caledonia, was not in any case calculated to stay the decline of the native culture, but if the medical and public health services could be improved, the population might stabilize and even begin to increase. However it was already established that the surviving people, pure Polynesians (probably a minority) and part-Polynesians, would have as a culture a Franco-Polynesian compromise and they would be French nationals.

The French by 1900 had been able to establish their franc as the medium of exchange over the Spanish "dollars" from Valparaiso, thus putting an end to the Spanish influence in this part of the Pacific (except for the continuing Chilean control of Easter Island). They had also established the indigenes and part-indigenes as the owning and operating manpower of a basically subsistence agricultural economy, of which copra and vanilla were the cash crops. Land titles, however, were in confusion. By 1904 steps had been taken to underpin the pearl shell foundations of the Tuamotu economy by a law designed to insure that the beds were protected to guarantee permanent yield. By 1908 the *Compagnie Française des Phosphates de l'Océanie* began to mine the rock of Makatea Island in the Tuamotus, this instituting an enterprise which was to contribute strategically to exports for over half a century into the future. Although in 1892 the metropolitan government had begun to try to attach the *Établissements'* export-import trade to France, trade remained to a large extent still obstinately with San Francisco in the United States and Auckland in New Zealand.

By 1914 there were about 1000 Frenchmen resident in the *Établissements* and 400 British and Americans who, if they were not rooted there, would certainly stay a good while. There was also still a small group of Germans. The French were variously engaged, but the British, the Americans, and the Germans were mostly at this time associated with trade and shipping. A Chinese population, which even then had a history running back forty years, was growing toward numerical parity with the Europeans and establishing a strong position in the retail and importing trades, miscellaneous store-based services, and market-gardening. Although the Europeans and the Chinese were scattered through the islands where, for instance, the Chinese store was becoming an indispensable fixture, the concentration of foreigners was in Papeete, while the indigenes and part-indigenes dominated elsewhere.

The government had been given its general form in 1885 and closely resembled that of New Caledonia, and the Tahitian bureaucracy was as highly peripatetic. However, in 1899 representation of the outer islands in the *Conseil Général* had been abolished and in 1903 the *Conseil Général* was discontinued altogether, not to be revived for thirty years. Thus by 1903 the governor's power was unalloyed except as it might be tempered by the consultative Privy Council and the consultative *Conseil des Contentieux.*

The Germans were driven from all their island possessions south and north of the equator and from Shantung in China early in World War I. This was carried out by the New Zealanders and the Australians acting on British cue but supported by their own strong wishes with regard to Samoa and New Guinea and by the Japanese with reluctant British acquiescence. Superficially these were "spoils of war" operations but in reality they were moves at the highest levels of European and Western Pacific international politics.

The original British intent appears to have been that the German possessions in the Pacific would be taken away by British action and held under British authority pending final disposition at the end of the war. Obviously this would also involve the elimination of German naval power in the Pacific either by its destruction in battle or by forcing it to flee. British naval power in the Pacific consisted of a squadron based on Weihaiwei and Hong Kong, while German naval power consisted of a squadron based primarily at Tsingtao on Shantung Peninsula. The most powerful German warships were the "Gneisenau" and the "Scharnhorst." Weighted one against the other the German squadron was the stronger, as both the Germans and the British knew, but the advantage would shift to the British if they could draw assistance from the ancillary Australian squadron. The Australian battle cruiser "Australia" was more powerful than any single ship the Germans had. While the Australians regarded destruction of the German squadron as their first duty, they had a responsibility also to prevent raids by the Germans on Australian ports, but they were by agreement subject to British direction. The British predicament in the Pacific could also be eased if they could use certain elements of the Japanese fleet, the only battle fleet in the Western Pacific. Japan was Britain's ally. The British certainly wanted Japanese assistance, particularly for operations north of Hong Kong, but they did not want Japan to declare war on Germany and participate as a principal in gathering up German spoils. They feared that if Japan operated on full war footing she would take advantage of the situation and upset the precarious balance of forces in the Western Pacific. In this ticklish situation the British maneuvered to take over the German spoils before the German squadron had been disposed of, proposing to deal with Shantung themselves and to have the Australians and New Zealanders take New Guinea and Samoa.

However, the British plan was frustrated. Against British wishes the Japanese declared war on Germany and participated as a principal in dealing with the German possessions. The Japanese took Shantung and also German Micronesia. The Australians took New Guinea and the New Zealanders Samoa.

The Germans avoided an all-out battle in the Western Pacific and eventually sought to escape into the Atlantic via Cape Horn. In carrying out their escape the chief problem, aside from dealing with any opposition they might encounter, was to acquire coal and food.

The German withdrawal from the Pacific really began on August 13 at Pagan Island in the northern Marianas, but the final decision to flee was not made until the squadron commander, Count Maximilian von Spee, received confirmation that Japan had declared war. He then assembled his ships at Eniwetok Atoll in the Marshalls to take on coal—some of the coal was obtained at Honolulu—and completed the operation at Majuro Atoll to the southwest, also in the Marshalls. Accompanied by the colliers the Germans then headed for a rendezvous at Christmas Island where it would be decided what to do about Samoa. En route to Christmas ships were detached to destroy the British cable relay station on Fanning Island. At Christmas Island von Spee learned that the New Zealanders were in possession of Samoa but he decided to visit it nevertheless. He appeared off Apia on September 14. This gave the British and the Australians their first "hard" knowledge of the whereabouts of the Germans. Finding Apia without naval protection, von Spee chose not to shell it. The Australians now concluded that the Germans were heading for some South American port where they could anticipate a welcome. The British, however, figured that they meant to shell Suva in Fiji or perhaps some New Zealand port. The Australian ships were therefore ordered to patrol duty in Fijian waters. Actually, the Germans headed for Tahiti, visiting Bora Bora en route, and when they found signs of resistance at Papeete on their arrival on September 22, they threw some shells into the town. From Papeete they proceeded to a rendezvous at

Nukuhiva in the Marquesas and from there they went to Easter Island. At Easter it was learned that a British squadron had come around the Horn into the Pacific. This formation the Germans met and defeated at Caronel off the Chilean coast on November 1. Proceeding then around the Horn they were in their turn met and defeated by a British squadron based on the Falkland Islands. Von Spee went down with his ship.

On leaving the Pacific von Spee had left behind a number of small armed ships and the light cruiser "Emden." All along the British had feared that the Germans would use their squadron to depredate commercial shipping moving to and past Singapore and in the Indian Ocean. The "Emden" gave reality to that fear. In a short career it did a great deal of damage, capturing, sinking, and looting merchant shipping, especially on the trade routes of the Indian Ocean. She was finally cornered and destroyed at the Cocos Islands by the Australian light cruiser "Sydney," detached from her duty as escort of a troop convoy proceeding from Australia to Ceylon en route to the Middle East.

The earliest suggestion that the Australians should act against the Germans in New Guinea and the New Zealanders against the Germans in Samoa reached Melbourne and Wellington from London on August 6, 1914. The British government which constitutionally had sole initiative in such affairs was at first concerned only with the destruction of the German wireless stations, but it soon shifted to the occupation of the German territories.

The New Zealanders were ready to act first. A New Zealand expedition left on August 15 and proceeded to Nouméa, New Caledonia, escorted by three tiny British cruisers. At Nouméa the Australian battle cruiser "Australia" joined the light cruiser "Melbourne," and the French contributed the cruiser "Montcalm," by chance in the islands en route home from a South American visit. From Nouméa the expedition went to Suva in Fiji where a token contingent of Fijian troops was taken aboard together with fifteen refugee Samoans who were to disperse to their villages and explain the New Zealand action. The small armada arrived off Apia on the thirtieth. The Germans offered no resistance but would not formally surrender, insisting that was the Kaiser's prerogative. The next day the New Zealanders landed troops and raised the British flag. The ships then dispersed, one visiting Pago Pago to explain the position to the Americans, another visiting Tonga to explain it there, and a third carrying captured German officials, including the governor, to internment in a camp on an island in Auckland Harbor. Thus the New Zealanders installed themselves in Samoa, realizing a dream first dreamed by Sir Julius Vogel.

Preliminary to launching their expedition against the Germans in New Guinea the Australians moved ships and troops north to Palm Island (off Townsville), Thursday Island, and Port Moresby in Papua, but the final rendezvous was off the Louisiade Archipelago on September 9. The protective naval force was led by the "Australia" and consisted of seven other fighting ships, including Australia's two submarines, one of which was lost while on patrol outside Blanche Bay. The invasion fleet arrived at Blanche Bay in New Britain on September 11. Landing parties were put ashore to push inland to find the wireless station. These parties encountered the only opposition and suffered the only casualties. The Australians lost two officers and four men, the Germans one officer and thirty native troops. Rabaul and Herbertshohe were easily occupied but Governor Haber, like his counterpart in Samoa, declared he could not surrender the possessions under his jurisdiction. However, the Australians were in occupation and after discussions, Governor Haber signed a capitulation on September 17. On the twenty-fourth the Australians occupied Madang in Kaiser Wilhelm's Land. It was understood by the Australians that they were now in possession of all the territory the Germans had ruled from Rabaul, including the Micronesian islands.

The Japanese occupation of Shantung led to the famous Twenty-one Demands on China of January 1915 and to the sequential politics of the Western Pacific of the ensuing fifty years. The Americans, who at this stage of the war were neutral, saw in the Japanese move at Shantung a challenge to the territorial integrity of China. They therefore not only resented Japan's role in the affair but also Britain's role as well, even though they could understand that Japan had forced Britain's hand. It was now apparent that as Britain's campaign in the Pacific was closely related to her campaign against Germany in Europe, her inability to deal alone with Germany in the Pacific had caused the entangling of the ousting of the Germans in Japan's imperial ambitions. The Japanese decision to take German Micronesia followed as obviously from those ambitions as the Shantung adventure because the islands could very well serve as a defensive screen against easy access to Japan's proposed sphere of paramountcy from the east. For the Americans the Japanese presence in Micronesia emphasized that the Philippines, the American territorial stake within the Japanese sphere, were indeed the Achilles heel in the Pacific President Theodore Roosevelt had said they were.

Whatever the British had had in mind with regard to the final disposal of the German possessions, it soon became apparent that the Japanese, the Australians, and the New Zealanders wanted to keep what they held. In fact, the Australians had less than they had wanted and less than at one time they had thought they had. Their only compensation for the loss of German Micronesia was that they had Nauru—and that island simply because it happened to be south of the equator. That the equator figured as a dividing line was the idea of the Japanese.

It was the British from the China station who had first invaded Micronesia. They were concerned to put the communications at Yap in the Carolines out of commission. The Japanese also looked in at Yap for the same purpose. Both assumed that the Australians were to take over the islands in due course. However, the Australian action was delayed and the Japanese came under pressure at home to take over the islands. The Australians first learned that the Japanese would take Micronesia on November 24 and the information was confirmed on December 3. The news came from London and while they did not like it, they were in no position to challenge London's acquiescence. When in 1917 the British asked the Japanese for naval assistance in the Mediterranean—hitherto the Japanese had been active only east of Suez—the Japanese *quid pro quo* was support of their claim to permanent possession of the Micronesian islands. The British accepted, countering by committing the Japanese to supporting British, Australian, and New Zealand claims to permanent possession of the German territories south of the equator. This understanding was embodied in a treaty which was later adhered to by the French and the Russians. While the negotiations were secret, the Australians were informed but could do nothing except to insist that their right to annex the territories they held be protected. The affair did not become a matter of general knowledge until 1918 when the Bolsheviks opened the imperial Russian archives and published the secret treaties they found there. What happened with regard to the ex-German islands at the Peace Conference has been told in Chapter II. As Prime Minister Hughes of Australia had to settle for a C-class mandate for New Guinea, so also did the New Zealanders for Samoa and the Japanese for Micronesia. Nauru was mandated to the United Kingdom, Australia, and New Zealand jointly.

CHAPTER X

Toward Native Paramountcy (1)

In the islands in the 1920's the situation was as unsatisfying for the European enterprisers as it was in most of their home countries, largely because of the difficulties in finding markets for all the kinds of commodities that could be produced. Without implying that island agronomy was without its deficiencies and problems, it was obvious that the islands could produce more and a greater variety of commodities than it was possible to market profitably. The state of the world markets for island produce was the main explanation, but it was also true that politicians endeavoring to bolster their own domestic economies, impeded the flow of island produce. And if agriculture had marketing difficulties, so also did base metal mining. Only gold mining seemed to be a reliable support of European economic progress. The successful phosphate mining was too special and too limited in impact to influence the general economic situation in the islands. Oil was sought but not found. While in the 1920's agricultural commodities other than copra were particularly difficult to market successfully and therefore unattractive, the depression of the 1930's plunged even the copra industry into the doldrums—the major oil and fats importing nations concentrating on whale oil, which could be made more readily available in increasing quantities. In the 1930's even more than in the 1920's, gold seemed the "reliable" sustainer of European enterprise in spite of its increasingly peculiar position in world economy—hence the great satisfaction taken in the successful gold mining in the Territory of New Guinea and Fiji at that time and the effort to get gold mining started in the Solomon Islands. In the late 1930's there was a renewed interest in agriculture as prices improved.

The great trading-shipping-plantation firms carried on vigorously during these years. Burns Philp in one or another guise was active in practically every place of any consequence throughout the islands; Morris Hedstrom was active in Fiji, Samoa, and Tonga; and a new firm, W. R.

Carpenter & Company, Ltd. (established in Sydney in 1914), began in the Territory of New Guinea after the war and made a rapid growth in planting, trading, shipping, and aviation, spreading from New Guinea into the Solomon Islands, the Gilbert and Ellice colony, and Fiji.

In spite of the troubles of the 1920s the demand for native labor increased as it did for Asiatic labor. During the Great Depression, this demand lessened and native ex-workers (and many native producers for the market) were forced back within the native subsistence economy, while the Asiatics were repatriated. While the demand was steady all European enterprisers and most administrators felt that employment in European enterprises was a solidly creative educative experience for natives. Whatever doubts were expressed concerned the percentage of the employable males that could be taken from the native villages without dangerously damaging native life, not whether it was right or wrong to take them at all. Even where pronative tradition was strong, as in Papua, employment in European enterprises was, if only by default, the principal educational experience available, for it was not in those islands where native labor was used that most progress was made in bringing formal education to the natives or in medical care and public health.

In no island group did the European masters envision a future which included the establishment or reestablishment of native sovereignty. Any ideas of the paramountcy of the native interest were bounded by the idea that the natives obviously required tutelage—including the tutelage of wage labor under Europeans—for many years to come; it seemed fantastically improbable that native sovereignty in the twentieth century could be sustained any more successfully than in the nineteenth century. If the natives were to be better educated, made healthier, to have a greater role in the lower levels of government, to increase and diversify their contribution to local and export markets, there was no expectation that these developments, singly or collectively, would lead to political independence. It was almost universally assumed that the islands were destined by their very nature to be permanent colonies. While the balance between the native interest and the European entrepreneurial interest might change within specific situations, there would nevertheless be no departure from the colonial condition.

One of the notable characteristics of the situation in the islands between the wars was that new ideas about colonial rule and the future of colonies then being generated in Africa, England, and elsewhere made little impression—that they made some impression on certain members of the intelligentsia and certain of the politicians of Australia and New Zealand did become apparent after World War II. This is true even though men of ideas were as numerous in the islands then as at any time in history: the younger members of the British colonial service, the exponents of the "Murray policy," the people on the Mandates Commission of the League of Nations, the policy-minded anthropologists, and the newcomers among the missionaries. All of these except the Murrayites were aware of the currents of thought running overseas, and the Murray partisans can be included because while they were no longer advanced in their thinking, they were not on the side of the tougher-minded traditionalists. What these men possessed was not a comprehensive new ideology, but a miscellaneous set of ideas fairly certain to be included in any new view of colonialism (or anticolonialism). It was remarkable how strongly these people were criticized and opposed by the entrepreneurs and their journalistic spokesmen, many administrators, and even their own older associates. Although the metropolitan British came to date their changed point of view with regard to colonies from 1924, when they ceased to employ amateurs in the colonial service, or alternatively from 1929 when Parliament made its first tentative move toward the development and welfare approach, in the islands any general awakening to the thought that a fundamental change in outlook even impended came only after World War II.

From 1914 to 1921, when the Australian military was in charge in German New Guinea, they intended to maintain the status quo as far as possible pending the final disposition of the possession at a peace conference. The Australians on duty found themselves in general sympathy with the ideas of the Germans, though differing in particulars, and in the end there was a considerable carry-over of German positions into the succeeding Australian administration. However, it was not possible, even in wartime, to make New Guinea stand still. The German planters left in charge of their properties, unable to remit earnings to Germany, invested their money in improvements and extensions of their plantations to increase their stake and claim for compensation if in the end they lost their property through confiscation. This forecast an increase in production within a few years. The Australians, short of manpower, allowed direct contacts with the natives through patrols to decrease and roads and port facilities to fall into disrepair.

In 1921 the administration was transferred from the military to civilians under the C-class Mandate. Although Murray of Papua—through membership on a royal commission on what should be done with the new responsibility—wished to amalgamate New Guinea with Papua and apply the "Murray policy" to it, the Hughes government (see Chapter II), supported by the majority of the commissioners, launched the Territory of New Guinea, its new official name, on a different course. This course tended to accentuate the differences between the Territory and Papua, and although for various reasons amalgamation was considered again in 1934 and 1939, it did not prove feasible to carry it through until after World War II.

At the time of take-over the Australians had essentially, a "copra colony." A C-class mandate gave them a practically free hand in running it. The Mandates Commission of the League of Nations could question and criticize—on the basis of what the Australians chose to put, or not to put, into their annual reports to Geneva—but it had no power to investigate any situation firsthand and had no means beyond moral suasion to compel conformance to its recommendations, major or minor. The Australian administration was, in fact, exposed to steady criticism by the Commission, with a great deal of attention to its native labor and native welfare policies. Observing their White Australia policy the Australians prevented Asiatics from coming into the Territory, but while they expelled all but about fifty of the Japanese inherited from the Germans, they had to accommodate the far more numerous and economically more important Chinese. And while they proceeded to expropriate and deport the German planters, a good many Germans, especially missionaries, stayed on and added to their numbers from time to time. In the late 1930's two-thirds of the missionaries working in the Territory were of German nationality. Nevertheless, in time, the largest single nationality group among the Europeans was the Australian.

Hughes had supported the Australian claim to the Territory by reference to the defense argument, but under the mandate it was forbidden to build defense works and this was reinforced by the provisions with regard to defense works in the Pacific islands in the Washington treaties of 1922. Australian interest in defense works outside the continent became centered on Singapore. Nevertheless, the idea that possession of New Guinea was vital to Australian continental defense continued to be important, and while the much resented criticism of the Australian administration of the Territory was chiefly directed against quite other phases, it was alleged by a larrikin minority proposing to end the "nonsense" by annexing the Territory in defiance of League and overseas public opinion that this was necessary to insure Australia's security. The Australians had a specific enemy in mind—the Japanese and their presence in Micronesia just to the north of the Territory was viewed with suspicion. However, most of the actual "incidents" involving the Japanese and the Australian authorities in these years took place—not in the New Guinea area but in the waters off the continental coast and along this coast from Thursday Island around to Broome—in consequence of questionable conduct of Japanese participating in the pearl shelling that flourished there. As the temperature of international politics rose in the Pacific, it was commonly believed that some of the Japanese "fishermen" were really naval officers making hydrographic and geographic surveys. Although in theory the mandate should have been so administered as to move it toward political independence, this idea seems to have had but a limited reality to the administration, to the European residents of the Territory, or to the general public of the Commonwealth. Indeed, in an official report to the Commonwealth government, published in 1939, one commissioner expressed the opinion that a statement to the effect that the Territory should be prepared for independence would come as a surprise to most Australians. The Australians, as a matter of fact, were intellectually uncertain about the status of the mandate in international law—where did sovereignty reside, what exactly was the mandate's constitutional position in regard to the Commonwealth? They even argued over from which provision of their constitution their power to rule the mandate was derived.

It was not the Australian idea that the Territory should continue to be a "copra colony." Rather, it was hoped that agricultural production could progressively be diversified. Early and late the administration put a good deal of effort into advising and assisting both European and native producers to that end. However, for various complicated reasons little success attended these efforts. Although by 1930 there were in the Territory 2527 acres under cocoa, 1490 under coffee, 2611 under rubber, 658 under kapok, and 101 under tobacco, it could hardly be said that diversification was booming or had ever boomed. As development under the Germans had shown a geographical imbalance in favor of the islands of the Bismarck Archipelago and against the mainland of New Guinea, so too Australian development was identically unbalanced and largely for the same reasons. At least three-quarters of the diversified production was in the Archipelago.

The same distribution was also characteristic of the coconut plantations. The most important agricultural product remained copra. In 1913 the Germans had produced 14,266 tons. During the war years production fluctuated, but by 1920 it was up to 22,708 tons. It was with the plantations that Hughes and his advisers were greatly concerned, and indeed it turned out that, until the plantations had passed from German to Australian hands, the management and transfer of the expropriated plantations and other commercial properties dominated the Territory's administration. This would seem to imply that the interest of the Hughes government in New Guinea was fundamentally entrepreneurial, and indeed it was. The royal commission appointed on ex-German New Guinea was packed with men strongly in favor of the entrepreneurial interest, specifically Atlee Hunt and W. H. Lucas—these two effectively offsetting J. H. P. Murray and his view. Hunt was a public servant long identified with island affairs and well known to be critical of the "Murray policy," while Lucas was a director of Burns Philp whose island experience had been obtained in their service in the Solomon Islands.

Hunt and Lucas successfully prevented Murray from introducing his policy into the Territory, and Lucas, resigning from the Burns Philp service, undertook the management of the expropriated German plantations and their eventual sale to Australians. In his opinion Australia could make a "good thing" out of the Territory of New Guinea if enterpreneurial types were given their heads. The prevailing Australian idea that a proper reward for an ex-soldier was establishment on the land—hence that the plantations should go to ex-soldiers—was applied, as was the continental policy of "closer settlement." While some of the purchasers were able to capitalize their holdings at a reasonable figure, others were not so fortunate and started out heavily in debt. All had everything to learn about tropical agriculture. Although the administration was supposed to favor the small man, the door was left open for the big companies.

Profiting by the fruit of the wartime German plantings (and eventually the bearing of Australian plantings), copra production steadily rose, reaching a peak of 63,800 tons in 1930, at which time the price, having passed a peak of £A 22/3/6 in 1926, was in a slow decline— soon to become precipitate—reaching a low of £A 4/11/0 in 1934. The price then began to rise again, standing at £A 16/2/4 in 1937, the best year prior to the outbreak of war. As is the case with most agricultural commodities, production kept up better than price, the smallest production after 1930 being 59,040 tons, and it reached a new peak of 76,409 tons in 1937. The big companies, of which Burns Philp was the most conspicuous, appear to have first intruded into the situation by offering to finance the purchase of plantations from Lucas' organization, thus raising prices and causing overcapitalization. During the depression many of the overcapitalized plantations were in acute difficulties, and just before World War II it was revealed that the big companies owned or effectively controlled no less than 30 per cent—by value—of the old expropriated properties. It was also made public that the purchasers of expropriated properties had never been able to pay off more than onethird of their capital debt. At the time the number of coconut plantations in the Territory was 464, and they occupied all but 10,000 acres of the land devoted to agricultural production. Of the acreage under coconuts, 80 per cent was in the islands of the Archipelago. The Territory had become the greatest producer of copra in the Southwest Pacific, but the

Southwest Pacific accounted for only one-eighth of the copra of the world.

More or less simultaneously with the dealings in the expropriated properties the authorities took steps to bring the land laws into reasonable conformance with Australian practice. This chiefly involved making leasehold the required tenure for future acquisitions. However, the freehold tenure inherited from German times was kept, making the situation between the Territory and Papua permanently different. While it was alleged that the new land ordinance made acquisition of land difficult for prospective planters, economic and agronomic obstacles were of greater significance in impeding European progress. It should also be noted that quite fantastic ideas about how much of the usable land could safely be taken by Europeans without endangering the native position were current. It was also true that in 1938 the Europeans were actually using only about half the land to which they held title. At no time was nearly as much land held in leasehold title as in freehold.

It is plain that if the Territory had remained dependent for revenue on the imports and exports of the agricultural economy it would have been about as impecunious as Papua. What saved it from this fate was the discovery of payable gold. (The only other mineral actively sought was oil—beginning in 1921, when a geological team sent by the Anglo-Persian Oil Company made a survey. In 1930 small speculators were drilling in the Sepik district, and in 1936 a detailed survey of the Territory was begun. No oil was found.) The richest goldfields were in the inland mountains of the main island—a part of the Territory where agriculture had made least progress. Because the years of mounting gold production were the years of the Great Depression, the economic significance of the discoveries was enhanced, not only because they created a small boom but because the devaluation of the Australian currency made it feasible to win gold at relatively high cost, since the selling price of gold was good in Australian money. As the deposits were found inland from the coast in a roadless area served only by fantastically difficult tracks, the cost of mining was exceptionally high, even when the gold was alluvial. It remained high when considerable capitalization became necessary to finance dredges, stamping machines, electric generators, etc.

Since it was not feasible to supply the operations, once they attained any magnitude, over the abominable tracks and when a plan to build a road for trucks came to nothing, dependence was on airplanes. This gave the Australians invaluable pioneering experience in air transport over the roughest imaginable terrain and under the most tricky air conditions, not only of passengers and supplies of moderate bulk and weight but also of heavy, awkwardly shaped machinery as well. Everything required had to be brought by ship to a coastal point and then moved inland by air. The discovery in the interior mountains thus not only stimulated a demand for goods from Australia and overseas, but it immediately stimulated the growth of coastal towns in New Guinea, the growth of air services, and the building of towns in the mountains. The capital came mostly from Australia, but an important contribution came from Canada. The excitement generated was tremendous, and the only point about the dramatic development that was obscured at the time was that the gold, after its well-known fashion, might peter out leaving a disconcerting wreckage behind. In the end this was in large part avoided by switching investment into a new channel at the mountain site.

The center of the gold-mining activity in the Territory was in the mountains back of Huon Gulf in the Morobe district, with Salamaua at first the principal point of entry. The first discovery of consequence in the gold-bearing area was made by a British-Australian professional prospector named William ("Sharkeye") Park, who had worked for years in Papua and had moved across the inland border. His discovery of fairly rewarding alluvial deposits was made in 1922 in Koranga Creek, a tributary of the Bulolo River. The news of his discovery brought about twenty miners to Koranga within twelve months. Prospecting farther afield in the vicinity followed, and in 1926 a team of three prospectors— W. G. Royal, A. Chisholm and R. M. Glasson—discovered exceptionally rich alluvial deposits in the upper reaches of Edie Creek, another tributary of the Bulolo. This discovery induced a rush which not only affected the Territory and Papuan communities but also lured men from Australia. The great Territorial gold boom was subsequently dated from 1926. Later discoveries, whether of alluvial, reef gold, or gold recoverable by dredging were concentrated along the Bulolo and Watut rivers and their tributaries, and in smaller quantities at various points in the Morobe district. The principal inland goldfields town became Wau at the eastern end of the major field, with Bulolo to the west as a secondary town. As the fields developed and the inadequacies of Salamaua as a center of air traffic (though not as a port) became apparent, the air terminal was shifted to Lae, twenty miles to the west, where the harbor was poor. The idea of connecting Salamaua and Lae by road was being canvassed in 1939. After a disastrous volcanic eruption at Rabaul in 1937 it was decided to make Lae the Territory's capital, but the shift had not been completed at the outbreak of war.

The history of the companies formed after about 1930 to exploit the gold discoveries was, as is usually true of such ventures, enormously complex, but two of especial importance emerged, Guinea Gold N.L. and Placer Development Ltd. Guinea Gold was the promotion of C. J.

Levien, who went into gold from his position as District Officer at Morobe. He was also associated with the pioneering of the air service. In collaboration, the two famous companies formed Bulolo Gold Dredging Ltd., which came to dominate this method of gold mining. Production in the Territory rose steadily in both quantity and value, reaching a peak of 263,113 fine ounces worth £A 2,808,835 in 1941. All fields in the Territory other than the Bulolo-Watut were of trivial importance; they were in the Sepik district, on Bougainville, and on New Britain.

The great "success" of the Territory's administration was that it was able by sharing in the gold prosperity to pay its way without a subsidy from the Commonwealth. In no year before 1930 did it receive a true subsidy of over £10,000, and after 1930 it was on its own. By 1938 it was supporting a budget of £500,000 a year. It was, however, a budgetary position achieved by keeping within a fairly narrow and wholly traditional definition of defensible expenditure. There was no experimentation whatever. Like most island governments it was dependent for revenue on imposts on the export-import trades, both dominated by Australia. After 1930 gold constituted four-fifths of the exports.

The natives were used almost exclusively as labor supply. Those who saw them in any other guise, such as the missionaries, the anthropologists, the League of Nations people, and some Australian intellectuals, were far from the prevailing view. The Germans had never found it possible to employ more than 17,500 natives and had had difficulty in recruiting that number, but after a small decline during the Great Depression, the Australians had 41,675 under indentures in 1939. Once firmly established in the Territory the Australians began systematically to extend "control," and as a consequence more natives were within reach of the recruiters. Since on the outer frontiers "control" was decidedly qualified, many areas were designated officially as only under government "influence" or "partial influence" or simply as "penetrated by patrols," which appears to have meant that the area had been traversed by exploratory patrols.

The Territory was divided into seven administrative districts, with a district officer in charge of each: New Britain, New Ireland, Manus, and the Kieta District (the heart of which was Bougainville) in the islands and Morobe, Madang, and Sepik on the mainland—all districts including associated islands. The areas under "complete government control" were the coastal regions of all the several divisions except for a stretch of coast on Bougainville, and in most instances a significant distance inland. However, the only sizable island reckoned to be under "complete" control was New Ireland, though many of the minor islands were. In New Britain, in spite of the concentration of European activity, there were considerable entirely unknown areas in the interior and other areas that were simply under "influence" or "partial influence." On the mainland only the Morobe district was in major proportion under "complete" control and it contained a small still unknown area. All the other mainland districts had large areas either completely unknown or penetrated only to a minimum degree, but, except in the west of the Madang district, such areas were well back from the coast in the mountains along the border with Papua.

What might be found in that mountainous region was long a matter of speculation, and such bits of evidence as came to hand between 1914 and 1930 did not resemble the actuality. The Germans had first reached the general area when probing the upper reaches of the Sepik in 1914, and in that year Captain Hermann Detzner, who had left Madang as the Australians approached intending to escape into neutral Dutch New Guinea by some interior route, saw more of it. In 1928 the Papuan patrol officers Karius and Champion, in making their famous crossing of the island from the Fly to the Spik, also had a glimpse of it. But none of the glimpses began to add up. The amazing reality was not known until after 1930–33, when gold prospector Michael Leahy and his companions, working from the Bulolo country, penetrated into the area from the east and on the first try emerged from it down the Purari River into Papua, all the while intending to return to the Territory coast. After this it was rapidly revealed by Leahy and other prospectors and administration patrol officers, but it was not fully explored when war came to New Guinea. The area contained a vast elevated plateau, extending to the Dutch border, which carried a very large native population of as high a level of development as any ever found in New Guinea. Working from the Papuan side, J. G. Hides entered a similar kind of plateau country in 1935. By 1939 none of this new highland country had been brought to a higher level of control than "under partial government influence." It was the opinion of Assistant District Officer J. L. Taylor, who made an important journey into it in 1938–39, that "we should adopt the policy of the Government of Kenya and reserve the highlands of New Guinea for Europeans . . . The existence of these highland areas makes New Guinea, normally a land of moist tropical conditions, something between a second Java and a second New Zealand." The administration seems to have been favorably impressed by this proposal to give European settlement priority in all useful parts of New Guinea, but before any program could be officially formulated, let alone executed, war came to New Guinea, and after the war the perspective had changed.

Of the 41,675 natives under indenture in 1939 not less than 20,657 were employed on plantations, 7162 in mining, 7107 in "shipping, commerce and industry," 4498 in domestic service, 2190 by the administration, and 61 were working at miscellaneous jobs. The principal districts of indentured employment were Morobe (12,972) and New Britain (11,-374), which accounted for almost three-fifths of all the indentured workers. Other major centers of employment were the New Ireland and the Madang districts. There was some employment available in all districts, and many workers were employed within their districts of birth, though usually away from their normal places of residence. The leading source of workers was the Sepik district, which had the largest "enumerated population"—though by a margin of only 10,000 over the Morobe district. The reason it supplied so many workers elsewhere was that employment opportunities within the district were very limited. Native migration to employment opportunities was thus characteristic of the Territory, but just how many natives were affected by indentured employment over the years is unclear, though it is worth noting that the turnover of native labor appears to have run at about 50 per cent a year. The "enumerated" native populations of the districts in 1939 were as follows: Sepik 151,086; Morobe 141,233; Madang 117,044; New Britain 104,-593; Kieta 49,379; New Ireland 42,813; and Manus 15,104. By adding natives enumerated but unclassified by district, there were over 600,000 natives in the Territory, of whom about two-thirds were in the three mainland districts. The Australians thus appear to have counted 200,000 more natives than the Germans had supposed were in the Territory and to have shifted the locale of concentration from the Bismarck Archipelago to the mainland. In addition it was then estimated that the native population of the newly found highlands was about a third of a million. At that time the European population was about 4400 and the Asiatic, mostly Chinese, about 2000. The largest concentrations of Europeans were at Rabaul, the capital, and on the Morobe goldfields; the largest Chinese concentration was at Rabaul. Practically all of the European population was transient, though it was hoped that the highlands might provide a place of permanent residence for Europeans. The Chinese could not go to Papua, let alone Australia.

While the administration was not averse to a slow shift from indentured to free labor, the employers of native indentured labor showed themselves little interested in any change. The administration considered employment a valuable civilizing experience for a native. Its headtax, first levied in 1921, was a prod to seek employment. Such pressure as there was within the Territory in favor of a free labor system seems to have come from the missionaries, who publicly declared in favor of it in 1927, while from outside there was the pressure from the Mandates Commission. The administration laid down rules to govern free labor in 1922, and in 1927 it was prepared to amend and liberalize the rules, but as the majority of the employers did not favor that system, nothing was done. Free—or casual—labor only became of any significance around Rabaul and in part of New Ireland. At no stage were there more than 2500 free native workers in the Territory. This appeared to indicate that a free labor system could only be generally adopted when the natives had achieved a sophistication about employment that did not exist in the Territory between the wars and when the employers became certain that their labor needs would be met under the system. A general shift to a free labor system would thus represent progress in the adjustment of the natives to their new situation, but since it could not be achieved between the wars, such improvements as were made in the position of the natives as labor took place within the indenture system.

Under criticism from the Mandates Commission, some pressure from within the Territory from missionaries, and some from Australia the practices of the recruiters were improved: the minimum age for recruitment was raised, regard for physical condition was insured, the rules governing the recruitment of females (never more than a tiny fraction of the total) were more closely defined, the feeding, housing, and clothing of the recruits were improved, a strong effort was made (by instituting prosecutions) to suppress physical violence on workers by employers convinced that only by "bashing" the "coons" could you get anything out of them, increasing attention was required to public health measures on plantations and to personal medical care, and earnings had to be paid in money, not "truck," and only one-half paid during the course of the contract to insure that the workers had something to show for their labor at the end of the indenture. However the basic wage paid to agricultural labor in the Territory was the lowest in the Melanesian islands, half the Papuan rate, and for mine labor one-sixth less than the Papuan rate. If the Territory's indenture system was much improved in terms of the welfare of the workers at the end of the period over what it had been at the beginning, it was far from satisfactory and the criticism of it seemed to intensify as improvements were made.

It was also believed by the critics that the limit of the number of indentured laborers that could safely be recruited in any given year was closely in sight. It began to seem likely that native labor would be in short supply long before the land available for European use was exhausted. A little leeway might be won by making improvements in native labor productivity, as by better job training, more by improving agricultural technology, and perhaps some by drawing on Papua's reserves—if in fact they existed. But sooner rather than later the Territory's employers were going to be caught short if European development continued to expand at its current rate, in one measure by 6000 acres a year. In this situation, an administrative shift from indentured labor to a free labor system could precipitate a crisis. A crisis always occurred in the islands when a change in the labor system took place.

The emergent situation was apparently an unwonted end result of giving the entrepreneurs their head with regard to labor policy. Recruitment under indenture bore heavily upon the natives and surprisingly quickly became over-recruitment with unhappy consequences in the villages. Recruitment and indenture combined to be the most powerful of all influences for change in the native society. Pacification was treated in the Territory largely as the indispensable preliminary to recruitment. It was ordinarily allowed at the earliest possible moment after a new stretch of country had been opened. Labor was regarded as the most desirable moral equivalent for the violence that pacification had suppressed. Both the administration and the missionaries saw the work in that light, and many missions in the Territory, Catholic and Protestant, developed plantations around their stations, in part at least to provide the therapeutic work. But by the late 1930's it could hardly be alleged with success that the consequences to the native societies had been altogether happy. That they had been changed under the impact was entirely clear, but that the change was invariably for the better was difficult to establish. Quite evidently there was nothing to be gained by a planned reversal either of the European penetration or of native social evolution, but it was equally evident that more decisive steps had to be taken to strengthen the native position. What had been done was woefully insufficient.

Probably the most significant failure was with regard to native education, expenditure on which had actually declined after 1927–28. At maximum the Territorial authorities supported six government schools enrolling 500 students at a cost of about £A 8000 a year. Because so many of the missionaries were Germans, no government money was granted to support mission schools, and hence the government had no say about their quality or what they taught. In the absence of influence over education, the administration could not implement its program of making English the *lingua franca* of the multi-languaged Territory and had to settle for "pidgin English."

After the Mandates Commission pointed a critical finger at the situation in the late 1930's, the administration reviewed its policy, but up to the outbreak of war nothing had been done to correct the deficiencies. It did not do appreciably better with regard to encouraging native agricultural production for market. But it did far better with "public health," expenditure for which steadily increased from 1921—fortunately, for disease was a major native handicap. The administration was something of a pioneer in requiring newly recruited officers to take training in anthropology at Sydney University—using its crypto-anthropologists "to record outstanding customs, particularly those of newly-discovered people and those coming under the influence of ordered government." While understanding the pristine native customs was unquestionably required, this might better have been left to professionals and the talents of the administration's employees directed to the problems of the natives involved in the "clash of cultures" and in the struggle to "adjust" to the new situation that was rapidly developing. This the government's professional anthropologist recognized, but the administration seems not to have profited from the insight. One difficulty was that the European impact was very uneven, taking the Territory as a whole, ranging from a fairly intensive impact around Rabaul of which the Tolai people were the beneficiaries or victims, to hardly any impact at all on certain of the people of the highlands, with all sorts of variations in between.

As a rule the natives were passive, with sporadic indications of restlessness ranging from semi-European "strikes" among the "advanced" natives at Rabaul in 1929 and 1937 to cultist reactions of the "cargo" and anti-European variety in the Sepik, Madang, New Britain (away from Rabaul), and Kieta districts in the 1920's and early 1930's, and in the Morobe district a little later. Although the genesis and significance of these "disturbances" among the natives caused extensive discussion which varied widely in its sophistication, they can be "read" to relate to native dissatisfaction with their situation as a result of the European penetration. However unsophisticated as explanations of the native predicament and however foolish from the European point of view in their programs for improving the native position, they were warnings that the native mind was on the move, seeking economic betterment, if by magical means, and perhaps the way to something that would have to be called nationalism.

No phase of the redistribution of responsibility for the islands as a consequence of the German expulsion was more productive of controversy, acridly flavored with rancorous suspicions, than the installation of the Japanese in the ex-German Micronesian islands. Although the Japanese certainly hoped to profit through economic development, more important in explaining their course were political and strategic considerations. As a Japanese writer put it in 1940: "Important as is the economic value of the islands to Japan, it was not this which inspired Japan's occupation of the islands so much as the political and military importance of the Micronesian Islands in the international politics of the Pacific." The Japanese had supposed that they had secured possession by the deal with the British in 1917, but this turned out not to be the case, for the Americans perceived the political and military importance of the islands in Western Pacific affairs and disliked the idea that the Japanese should hold them. The controversy pursued its course through the peace conference at Paris and the Washington conference on Pacific affairs of 1921–22 and only died when the Japanese were finally dislodged from Micronesia after World War II. The American interest was almost wholly strategic and political.

The controversy is only intelligible if it is understood that the Micronesian islands were inextricably mixed up with a conception of high naval strategy in the Pacific (influenced of course by the redistribution of naval power in the world as a consequence of World War I, a shift which was reduced to a formula at the Washington conference) and with political-diplomatic policy in the Far East (or Western Pacific), especially American policy. While the Australians and New Zealanders, whose suspicions about the Japanese were equally as strong as the American, came to see the Micronesian islands as the spearhead of the much-feared Japanese "southward" drive in their direction, the Americans saw them as likely to become a formidable obstacle to the naval strategy of proceeding from Pearl Harbor through the islands north of the equator to the Philippines and Western Pacific waters generally. In this view Japan's possession of the Micronesian islands strengthened her position as the predominant naval power in the Western Pacific precisely by reducing the possibility that a hostile naval force could readily reach Western Pacific waters from the east. However the force of this opinion was tempered, or appeared to be tempered, by the settlement finally reached, for under the mandate the Japanese could not fortify any of the islands and the prohibition was reinforced by a Washington treaty. Only after Japan freed herself of these inhibitions by unilateral action in the middle 1930's were these fears and hopes revived. However, the American naval authorities did not modify their basic strategical ideas until after the outbreak of war in the Pacific in 1941 and then only under compulsion and with the intension of reasserting the strategy at the earliest possible moment.

The Australians and New Zealanders were in effect under the direction of the British, and the British seem not to have taken a dim view of the Japanese in Micronesia at any stage. After toying with Admiral Jellicoe's proposal that the Pacific dominions collaborate with Britain in building a stronger Far Eastern fleet than had existed pre-war, they finally decided on the Singapore base, far distant from Micronesia. The politico-diplomatic phases of the situation involved China, especially the American opposition to Japanese actions and intentions in China, specifi-

cally at first with regard to Shantung, and peripherally even such a seem-
ingly remote affair as the unwantedly strong and unassessably purposeful
Japanese participation in the Siberian adventure against the Bolshevik
Russians by the United States and Japan.

William Morris Hughes of Australia, at the Paris peace conference,
fought the battle for the right to annex the ex-German Pacific islands,
and in doing so he was also, ironically, a proxy for the Japanese who had
an identical objective. When the Hughes effort failed, the Japanese had,
like the Australians, to settle for a C-class mandate which they, no more
than the Australians, wanted. However, the Americans unsettled even
this settlement—after they had failed to join the League of Nations—
when they tried to establish the point that while under the League's
charter the Mandates Commission assigned the mandates, the United
States as an associate power of the victors in the war retained a say-so
over "spoils of war"—which the German Pacific islands certainly were.
This unsettled the positions of the Australians in ex-German New Guinea
and the New Zealanders in ex-German Samoa as well as the Japanese
in ex-German Micronesia, but the Americans seem to have had chiefly
in mind to unsettle only the Japanese position. And the American interest came to settle exclusively on the single island of Yap.

The significance of Yap was that it was a communications center,
originally built up by the Germans, at which cables to China, the Netherlands Indies, and Guam (and from Guam to the United States and
Japan) could be controlled, and by extension a center of radio also, if
Yap became a strategic relay point in international radio communications. The Americans believed that if Yap passed unrestrictedly to the
Japanese they would be in a position to censor and otherwise control
communications to and from China and the outside world, including the
United States. It was taken as axiomatic that the Japanese would so act
to strengthen their position in regard to China. From their point of view,
the authorities in the Netherlands East Indies took a comparable view
of the situation. The British did not. To them the American effort to
keep the cables at Yap free was simply an episode in a struggle over the
control of international electrical communications in which the British
and the Americans were normally principals. (Interestingly enough,
when the first American minister arrived in Australia in 1940, high on
his agenda was the loosening in favor of the United States of the British
monopoly of electrical communications with Australia.) After pursuing
its way through the negotiations at the Washington conference, the Yap
issue was finally settled by direct negotiations between the Americans
and the Japanese. The Americans gained free access to deal with cables
and radio on a footing of equality with the Japanese.

After this the controversy over the Japanese position in Micronesia simmered rather than boiled for about a decade and this was largely because the Japanese discouraged visits to the islands by foreigners, turning the islands into something like a "closed" area. Although the Japanese made annual reports to the Mandates Commission, little was known about the islands from first-hand observation. In 1933 the Japanese announced that they were withdrawing from the League, which they actually did in 1935, but their right to retain control of the islands was not challenged at Geneva on the basis of the covenant nor at Washington on the "spoils of war" argument. Thereafter, as the situation in the Western Pacific deteriorated, suspicion was rife about what the Japanese had done or were doing in Micronesia, especially to increase the value of the islands for purposes of defensive or offensive warfare. While the most positive allegations were made, it was impossible to be certain in the absence of an opportunity for first-hand observation. At minimum, it was believed, the Japanese had developed port facilities and airfields far beyond any commercial necessity. After World War II, however, it was the opinion of the American Admiral Nimitz that "Japan's maritime investment during the 20 years of her mandate had gone into her fleet and not, as many had supposed, into building up an oceanic Maginot Line."

Since no completely independent study of the situation in Japanese Micronesia, least of all any exhaustive study by a foreign expert, has ever been made, it is still impossible to write a circumstantial history of a hectic episode that lasted about twenty years. A few supportable generalizations can, however, be advanced. Although the islands were not rich in natural resources, the Japanese were diligent beyond any precedent in comparable islands in exploiting the available resources. This fairly intensive exploitation was not achieved by using the native economy as the basis of development and diversification but by imposing a Japanese economy in conformance with the classic pattern of island exploitation by Europeans and by bringing in the labor from metropolitan sources to man the undertakings. This meant that the foreign population of the islands was enormously increased, to numbers fantastic in relation to all other island groups (except Hawaii). Whereas before the Japanese arrived, the foreign population was never more than a few hundred, under their regime the foreign (Japanese, Korean, Okinawan) population rose from 3671 in 1920 to 51,861 in 1935 and undoubtedly continued to increase after that. At the same time the native population increased over-all by but 5 per cent, though not uniformly either as between the two divisions the Japanese made—the Chamorro and the Kanaka (or Micronesian)—or between the islands. A Japanese writer observed that while the native populations of Saipan (Chamorro) and Ponape (Kanaka) "definitely" increased and most of the other islands showed a "slight" increase, Yap (Kanaka) showed a "startling" decrease.

The native economy was allowed to continue in its own path outside the Japanese pattern of exploitation though it was, it seems, considerably commercialized if only by the efforts of the natives to get into Japanese markets and gain access to Japanese manufactured goods. The natives were not systematically recruited for work in the Japanese enterprises, since the work was mostly reserved for the foreign immigrants, though they continued to be recruited for the phosphate mines of Angaur (which supplied about 10 per cent of Japanese requirements). The natives as "free" workers could usually find jobs with the Japanese if they wanted to, but the employment was of a menial kind with few opportunities open for advancement. In fact the most pointed native criticism of the Japanese regime was precisely that it provided but limited opportunity for the natives to make progress either individually or collectively. They were, for instance, given access to education but only to the fifth year level, whereas Japanese could go on much farther. However the Japanese took pride in the fact that the administration "protected" the natives and did not permit their destruction. When the Japanese were expelled and a turn was taken toward making native advancement the premier policy, the natives had much to learn about every problem of self-direction and self-advancement in the constricted environment of their own economy.

Nauru was occupied by an Australian army force from Rabaul in November 1914. As the island was south of the equator, it fell to the British under the tacit agreement that the equator should be the dividing line with regard to the German "spoils." During the course of the war administration was in the hands of an official of the British colonial office, but when in December 1920 the island was mandated to His Majesty the King, an agreement about administration was made by Lloyd George, W. M. Hughes, and William Massey under which the Australian government appointed an administrator and directed the administration through the governor-general. The interest of the three British governments was in the island's phosphate. Fully six-sevenths of the twelve square miles of the island was believed to be phosphate-bearing, with reserves of upward of 50,000,000 tons. Production had reached 350,000 tons annually before the war. The three governments purchased the Pacific Phosphate Company's interest for £3,500,000 in the proportions of 42 British, 42 Australian and 16 New Zealand. The price also included the Company's rights and works at Ocean Island in the Gilbert and Ellice Islands Colony but not its interests elsewhere in the Pacific. Management of actual production was passed to a board of commissioners on which each government was represented. It was hoped to raise production quickly to 500,000 tons annually and to distribute it in proportion to each country's investment (i.e., 42. 42. 16). Actually, in the late 1930's after recovery from the depression decline, production was running over 800,000 tons annually and distribution was 67 per cent to Australia, 23 per cent to New Zealand, while 10 per cent was sold on the world market, including consignments to Japan. The distribution reflected the intensified use of "super-phosphate" in the agricultural and pastoral industries of Australia and New Zealand.

The native Nauruans, a Micronesian people, numbered about 1200 in 1920 and were believed to be increasing. In 1936 there were 1647. They continued to live on a strip of fertile land between the beaches and the coral cliffs which marked the edge of the phosphate-bearing interior plateau, where there were few places that native food plants would grow, but all the plateau was nevertheless in native ownership. When the phosphate commissioners leased the plateau land they paid a bonus, and beginning in 1921 they paid the native owners a royalty of a few pence a ton on the phosphate extracted. From 1927 a little over half the royalty was paid periodically directly to the natives, a small portion was set aside by the administration to create a fund to support native welfare projects, while about a quarter was banked at interest for twenty years when the annual interest would be paid out to the natives. To encourage native industries, the administration gave annual prizes for meritorious productions. It also assisted a native-managed cooperative store by auditing the accounts. Up to 1923 native education was in the hands of the two missions—the LMS and the Roman Catholic—but in that year the administration assumed responsibility and established a system of schools more or less on the Australian pattern. The school-leaving age was set at sixteen. The final year of schooling was devoted to technical training. A health service was provided which included the isolation and treatment of lepers.

Up to the war the basic labor force in phosphate mining had been Micronesians recruited in the Caroline Islands, with some natives from German New Guinea. And a turn toward using Chinese coolie labor had been made. After the war the use of Micronesian labor was not resumed, the New Guinea natives were found unsuitable because of the deleterious effects on their health, and their employment was ended in 1924; reliance was placed on Chinese coolies obtained from southern China through Hong Kong (an arrangement which, from the Chinese government's point of view, involved illegalities). The indenture of Nauruans for labor in the mines was prohibited, though occasionally a few were employed as "free" laborers for short periods. In the late 1930's the Chinese working on the island numbered over 1200. They were kept in compounds and isolated from the Nauruans. Directing operations were a few less than 200 Europeans.

In effect Nauru was an illustration of what could happen when a "wasting" island resource was systematically exploited by Europeans. Almost literally, the island was being dug up and carted away.

Although Papuan affairs between the world wars were usually seen through the special ambience that surrounded the "Murray policy," it cannot be said the situation at any stage was entirely happy. The Murray partisans—and Murray himself on occasion—insisted that the "policy" was in closer harmony with the Mandates Commission's ideas than was that of the Territory, implying that it was superior. This was particularly true of native policy, including the native labor aspects of it. The basic characteristic of the "Murray policy" was, however, a circumspect humanitarianism, not programmatic boldness.

Economic circumstances in Papua were rather more exiguous than in the Territory. It was not only that Papua was, so to speak, an economic operation of only about half the magnitude of the Territory but that it did not in these decades profit from any economic stimulant, such as the Territory's gold, though its gold production increased in the 1930's. Its dependence was almost wholly on agriculture, and an uncertain reliance it proved to be, not least because of adverse external circumstances. Papua never achieved budgetary viability on the basis of internally derived revenue, as the Territory did, even with an expenditure policy quite as circumscribed as the Territory's, and over the two decades its subsidy from the Commonwealth had slowly to be increased. However, the subsidy was at no stage designed to allow the administration to pursue a liberal spending policy in any direction but simply to maintain its established position. Seen comparatively, the gist of the matter was that while the policy differences between Papua and the Territory were fairly easy to discriminate, and, on balance, Papua's policy was usually more liberal and philo-native, the constricted way in which the colony had to operate prevented it from reaping what should have been its reward. The result was that at the end of the period the two situations, while in detail different, with the advantage to Papua, were, in the large, rather similar. All through the interwar period the differences, however evaluated, were enough to make amalgamation seem not only unwise but impossible, quite apart from any doubts about the legality of amalgamating a colony with a mandate. But when after World War II the two were amalgamated, the differences between them seemed less important than the marked difference between the prewar policy of either and the post-war policy for both.

When Murray took charge in Papua in 1908 the general context in which he had to think and work had already been defined. Essentially, his task as he saw it was to watch out for the interests of the natives while paying constant heed to the interests of the European entrepreneurs. Murray's view and the Commonwealth's view was that the primary task of the entrepreneurs was to develop the natural resources of the colony in default of which native progress was unlikely. As Murray saw it, the unique feature of this formulation of the colonial task was the heavy emphasis placed upon conserving and advancing the interests of the natives. While he recognized that care for the native interests was a well-established element in British colonial policy, he nevertheless felt that this was, about 1908, a position which in actual practice was peculiar to Papua and therefore enormously creditable to the Australians. He believed that the commoner colonial policy was to emphasize the development of production of tropical produce for sale in the metropolitan and world markets regardless of the consequences to the natives. However, he was aware of the ambiguities that lurked in the two-winged policy he had embraced. Looking back in 1920 he wrote: "Having assumed responsibility for the territory, the Commonwealth found it had to face the double problem which nowadays confronts the Administrators of tropical countries under British rule, namely, the problem that arises from the duty of developing the natural resources of the country, and the problem that arises from duty to the native population." Since he saw that there were two problems he was aware that any administrative handling of them simultaneously would inevitably involve him in compromises. The "Murray policy" was, therefore, a compromise like any other, subject to redefinition as Papuan circumstances changed, not a rigid formulation devised outside the circumstances and thereafter rigorously imposed.

This was all the more the case since Murray saw Papua and its natives in the following terms: "Papua, then, was a large territory, not very fertile, but still capable of considerable agricultural development, and of almost untouched and unknown mineral resources—a territory consisting largely of impenetrable swamp and almost inaccessible mountains, and very scantily inhabited, principally by head-hunters and cannibals, or at least by semi-barbarians, separated from utter savagery by only a short generation of very superficial civilization." He thus saw the resources as more limited and problematical than most of those who spoke up for the entrepreneurial interest, and he saw the natives as extremely "backward" and "primitive"—but men nevertheless—whom it would take a very long time to civilize to any standard that would make self-rule worth talking about. Pro-tem the administration must stand in the relation of a tutor to the natives, but a tutor who was much clearer about what the natives should *not* do and be than about what they should do and be. The operative idea was that they should be "adjusted" to a world they were not going to make but in which they found themselves as a result of the European intrusion. As Murray put it, the task was "to show how the civilization of the twentieth century can be introduced among a people in the stone age, not only without injury to them but to their lasting benefit and their permanent advance upon the road to civilization."

It is a commentary on both Murray's frame of mind and the state of anthropology—it was then just ceasing to be wholly preoccupied with native cultures in their pristine state—that Murray only slowly saw that it had any value at all for the administrator who was self-conscious about his task of tutelage in "adjustment," even though he saw that what was involved was to hasten the decay of bad old customs and to inculcate presumably good new ones. Murray's best opinion of anthropology was that it might possibly be of some help in carrying out a native policy based on quite other considerations. He never got to the point of adopting the Territory's policy of requiring staff recruits to take instruction in anthropology at Sydney; indeed, he did not require any university training but remained an unrepentant amateur who preferred to train his amateur associates himself. Finally, Murray held firmly to the traditional conception that a colony should strive for self-support. Although Papua was consistently subsidized, he kept the ideal before him, and one of his more remarkable variations on the theme was his scheme for having the natives provide the funds to support their own education (and an anthropologist to study their more bizarre activities).

Between 1908 and 1910 the entrepreneurs were decidedly optimistic about the prospects of rapid progress along the lines then laid down. In 1908 the Commonwealth's new land ordinance had provided that only the Crown could acquire land from the natives and that Europeans could only acquire leasehold title to the Crown's land. Rentals for leased land were moderate; requirements as to "improvement" were eminently sensible. The way appeared open for rapid expansion of tropical agriculture, and there was a considerable forward movement which did not exhaust its impetus until 1920. From 2089 acres of land leased in 1906, there was a rise to 364,088 acres in 1911. However, about 1910 doubts seem to have seized those whose interest was primarily speculative, for the 1911 acreage proved to be the all-time maximum up to World War II. After 1910 as the term for meeting improvement requirements began to expire, thousands of acres reverted unused to the Crown every year. The number of acres held under lease declined until it stabilized at about

200,000 acres in 1915, where it remained for the ensuing quarter century. That this movement did to an extent unknown represent the departure of the speculative element is indicated not only by administrative action in 1909 to make it more difficult to take out leases on "spec," but even more clearly by the course of the figures for land under cultivation. In 1907 it was reported that 1467 acres were under cultivation. This area steadily increased until 1920, when the figure was 62,264 acres, which proved to be a maximum up to World War II.

After 1920 the acreage under cultivation hovered around 60,000. Thus, while only about 30 per cent of the acreage under lease was normally under cultivation, it was fairly clear, taking into account the prevailing economic conditions, that the leaseholders were serious and persistent agriculturalists. This is also indicated by the fact that while the acres under cultivation stayed steady for years on end, the number of plantations in existence increased. In 1908, 76 were reported; in 1930—as the Great Depression settled down—331 were reported. This would seem to indicate that Papuan European tropical agriculture steadily drifted into the hands of serious small enterprisers. Consistently, the bulk of the crop acreage was under coconuts. The initial burst of coconut plantings ended in 1915, after which the coconut acreage only slowly increased until it stood at 44,000 acres, or about two-thirds of the acreage in crops, in 1940. By 1940 there were 18,000 acres under rubber. In the late 1930's there were 700 acres of hemp, 190 acres of coffee, and 92 of kapok. By that time tobacco growing had been entirely abandoned, and a scheme for growing sugarcane—New Guinea was a source of wild sugarcane stock the Australians had been using for years—had been mooted and abandoned without a start being made. This was the harsh reality of diversification. About five-sixths of the acreage under crop was in the Central and Eastern divisions of the colony. From 1907 when it was 690, the European population rose to 1186 in 1914. There was little increase in the 1920's and 1930's.

If tropical agriculture tended, in terms of acreage used in relation to acreage theoretically available for use, to stabilize at a low level and with a derisory amount of diversification, neither did Papua make out well with regard to minerals, the other facet of Murray's original economic hope. Perversely enough, leadership in gold production, in which Papua had shown the way, passed to the Territory in the middle 1920's. Although gold discoveries had continued to be made in Papua after 1908—there was a famous rush to Lakekamu in 1910 and the field continued to produce until 1917—after 1916 gold ceased to be the colony's single most valuable export. By 1930, when the Territory's gold production was bounding upward, Papuan production was down to 3634 fine ounces worth only £10,000. Thereafter, however, there was a marked rise, and, in 1940, 42,239 fine ounces worth £136,000 (a mere patch on the Territory's figure) were exported. Gold was then being won on such a historic field as Misima Island, at Yodda on the mainland, and at other places in the Eastern Division.

If gold could be expected to make something of a comeback, copper, the only other mineral ever seriously exploited in Papua, showed no resilience. The Astrolabe copper field in the mountains back of Port Moresby had been announced in 1906. In spite of severe transport handicaps the field was developed, and in 1914 there was talk of stabilizing it by building a railway in from Port Moresby. This was not done, but truck and tramway transport was provided, and in 1924 the situation looked good enough for a smelter to be built at the field. Copper mining and smelting then provided work for 1000 natives and 100 Europeans, and this was the largest single enterprise in the colony. Within two years the enterprise had collapsed under the weight of "technical" troubles, and it was never straightened out and revived. The only other alluring possibility was oil. Although traces of oil were detected in the valley of the Vailala River in 1911 and search for commercially worthwhile deposits was prosecuted either by the Commonwealth government, the Anglo-Persian Oil Company acting for the government, or independents, until 1930, no oil of any consequence was found. The search was resumed in 1936. The road to prosperity through mineral production appeared to be excessively rough and not easy to follow. Yet the idea that the Melanesian islands, including New Guinea, were mineral-rich persisted.

Since it was not supposed that there was any shortage of rich land for European purposes during most of these years, nor until very late in the period that a labor shortage serious enough to impede European expansion was likely, nor that any utterly baffling agronomic trouble existed, it would appear that the explanation of the stagnation—Murray's word—that beset Papua over so many of these years must be sought in external circumstances. That Papuan development was slowed down during World War I, when European manpower was drained away from both the plantations and the administration, that it did not get going again during the postwar depression, and that it was not actively prosecuted during the Great Depression, hardly requires detailed demonstration. Rather what needs notice, is the bungling by the Commonwealth authorities of external transport policy, 1921–25, and the persistent failure to recognize in just what way Papuan development was dependent upon markets, not least the markets the Commonwealth itself might provide.

The 1921–25 episode with regard to transport involved the thoughtless application of the Commonwealth's Navigation Act to Papua. The Act was designed to improve the condition of Australian labor at sea and to exclude foreign shipping of lower standards from the Australian coastal service. It was one of W. M. Hughes's notable contributions to the welfare of workers on the sea and the waterside. By making the Act applicable to Papua the effect was to make it impossible for foreign shipping to bring imports to Papuan ports or to lift Papuan exports consigned overseas. This forced the carrying of the imports past Papua to Sydney and their transshipment there for Papua and the carrying of the exports to Sydney for transshipment to their overseas markets. This raised the cost of Papuan imports and the cost of production in Papua and increased the shipping costs on Papuan exports, lowering the returns to Papuan producers. Moreover, the effective exclusion of foreign shipping from the Papuan ports gave an effective monopoly of transport to and from Sydney to one Australian company, Burns Philp. Monopoly not sufficing, the Burns Philp people demanded and were granted a subsidy for their service by the Commonwealth. If all the necessary imports into Papua had been obtainable in Australia at competitive prices and if all Papuan exports had been finally marketable there, the situation would not have been too bad. But the fact was that vital Papuan imports had to be obtained overseas and Papuan exports, especially the fundamentally important copra, had to be finally marketed overseas. Thus, what may have been good for Australia—even this was debatable—was not good for Papua. Murray mounted a protracted campaign against the application of the Navigation Act to Papua. Probably nothing he ever did convinced more entrepreneurs that his heart was in the right place. After a Commonwealth royal commission had investigated the situation, Papua was exempted from the Act. This did not cause any upsurge of development in Papua, though it helped the established producers.

The matter of encouraging production in Papua by facilitating the marketing of the produce in Australia—involving tariff concessions and bounties—raised a policy question that was to prove enduring. While Sydney continued to be the principal center of the islands trade in the area, at no historical stage was it a market that could absorb unlimited quantities of island produce. When production in the islands rose above the capacity of the Sydney market to absorb it, the excess had to be sold overseas. The classic example of this was copra. There were at the same time commodities which could be produced in quantity in the islands which also could be produced in the Commonwealth. When this was the case the Australians showed a strong preference for encouraging the production on their continent and excluding the islands production. The classic case of this was sugar. In the 1920's bananas became another. And there were tropical commodities for which a market existed in Australia, sometimes one of size, which had traditionally been supplied from outside the Southwest Pacific. If production of any of these could be achieved in the islands, the produce had to be marketed in Australia in competition with the established foreign suppliers. In the case of Papua, therefore, the use of tariff concessions and bounties would be to encourage production by improving its competitive position in the Sydney market vis à vis the established foreign suppliers. If successful, production would rise in Papua, and Australia's dependence upon foreign suppliers would be reduced. The economic integration of the Commonwealth and its colony would be promoted.

After some skirmishing around the questions, the Commonwealth took positive action as of January 1, 1927. Bounties were provided for a period of ten years for a long list of tropical products including cocoa, hemp, kapok, vanilla, bamboos and rattans, and a range of spices (but not sugar). At the same time entry into Australia duty free was allowed to whole and prepared coconuts and specified fruits (not including bananas). However, this stimulated neither the production of the commodities already being cultivated nor did it lead to the cultivation of any new products.

It was demonstrated that the decisive external "control" on production in Papua was the state of the world market, particularly as to price. An illustration of this was the course of rubber production in Papua. The producers throve when the world market price was good; they were depressed when it was poor; and the price was never good enough long enough to boost production to a level which made Papua more than a marginal supplier to the Australian market. Rubber had eventually to be "saved" by Commonwealth tariff concessions. Very obviously there was nothing in the Papuan situation that gave producers any special advantage in relation to the world market.

Murray's expectations in 1908 about European economic activity and his strongly felt obligation to support it, required him to define a policy with regard to native labor. Since he saw his obligation to the natives in terms of their welfare, he was at once confronted with the possibility that unless he struck a carefully formulated balance between the position of the employers with regard to the natives and his obligations to the natives, his labor policy might lead to serious difficulties. Since the White Australia policy made it impossible to ease the pressure on the natives to take work by importing Asiatic labor and no justification existed for bringing in native workers from outside, there was nothing to do but to arrange for the employment of Papuans. Murray seems to have held a common opinion that one of the undesirable consequences of pacification was that by suppressing native violence it left the males with too little to do. It was apparently necessary to redirect their energies by teaching them the uses of systematic work and how better could this be done than by placing them under European employers? Native labor might thus become a primary underpinning of native welfare, especially if the habit of labor could be brought to the support of native production for market.

Murray, therefore, confirmed in 1908 the system of indenturing natives for labor in European enterprises which had been MacGregor's policy earlier. In accordance with his preoccupation with native welfare, he gave careful attention to permissible methods of recruitment, conditions of work, including food, clothing, shelter, medical care, remuneration (eventually the Papuan basic native wage was double that of the Territory), term of service, permissibility of reindenture, and repatriation. Indenture applied mostly to males, females could be indentured only for household service, and the taking of families to places of work was not allowed because it was feared that it would lead to the creation of a landless native proletariat. Indentured labor was obtained primarily from the Eastern Division of the colony, secondarily from the Central and Western Divisions, the other divisions supplying only a few workers or none at all.

It became the common opinion that Papua's indenture system was as good as an indenture system could be, and while Murray had a sharp struggle with employers of an exploitative turn of mind, in the long run it won employer acceptance and, indeed, passionate defense. However Murray himself was never wholly satisfied with it, although for years he could see no true alternative to it if European enterprise was to survive in Papua. "The indenture system may be defended on the plea of necessity," he wrote in 1928, "but it is really rather like slavery in many of its incidents and it is not an institution which anyone would care to perpetuate." (The notion that nobody would seek to perpetuate it turned out to be wrong!) The available alternative was so-called casual free labor, but while Murray encouraged its development, as by liberalizing the rules governing it in the late 1920's, it did not become predominant, though it did become proportionately more important in Papua than in the Territory.

Murray saw clearly enough that whatever effect, educative and quite otherwise, indentured labor might have on the natives involved, and however "good" the condition of the indentured might be made by government regulation and employer initiative, the impact to be watched was that on the native villages and the subsistence economy which supported them. The villages were the heart of native life. What transpired in them would deeply influence the native future. While indenture provided a method of taking underemployed natives out of them and placing them in a situation where they would learn to work systematically and purposefully it was nevertheless the case that their absence from their villages tended to disorganize family and village life, throwing heavy burdens on those left behind. If a stage of overrecruitment was ever reached (and how was that to be defined as a percentage of employable males?) the effect on the villages might be disastrous. This was especially likely if in the ideal future the natives were to be peasant proprietors with a concern for some production for the commercial market; in order to work such a system would require the presence of the natives on their own land most of the time.

In Murray's time there were never more than 10,000 out of an estimated 300,000 natives in Papua who were laborers in any given year, but the suspicion arose that the permissible limit of recruitment was being approached—a suspicion identical with that which arose in the Territory. Since European employment provided for 10,000 natives, it followed that the other 290,000 were either largely or wholly dependent on the native economy. The administration could not afford to let the native economy weaken but had always to try to strengthen it. The favored way of strengthening it, after assuring that it met the food needs of the people, was to encourage production for market. It was one of Murray's misfortunes that he had so little luck with his schemes for encouraging native participation in the market economy. In the late 1920's he had most hope for native ventures in coconuts for copra, coffee and cocoa. It was established that a fundamental criterion of native advancement was the extent and degree of success of their participation in the European market economy.

The European impact was as uneven in Papua as it ordinarily was elsewhere in the islands. It was at its most intense in the native village of Hanuabada adjacent to Port Moresby, more intense to the north and east of the capital—where most of the white enterprisers were to be found and most of the indentured workers were employed—than to the west, and least intense in the newly penetrated outlying areas. Constantly throughout the Murray regime new areas were brought under the government's influence and then gradually under full control. By 1938 the Papuan administration was taking the final steps toward full control throughout the entire colony. The patrol was the chosen instrument for this work in its successive phases, and the patrol officers engaged Murray's especial admiration, not least when a patrol was in the nature of exploration into new territory. Murray's particular contribution to patrol work was his emphatic insistence that violence against the natives be kept to an absolute minimum and that all officers be held accountable when it was employed. In introducing a patrol officer's book in the 1930's Murray interwove with a statement of what followed for the natives from being brought under control a succinct definition of his attitude toward the natives and their customs:

... generally speaking, I may say that our policy has been to endeavour, as I once put it many years ago, "to transform the tribe of disappointed warriors into a race of more or less industrious workmen."

We compel the natives who have been brought under Government control to attend to the sanitation and cleanliness of their villages, to improve their gardens and the village paths, and to carry for the Government when a patrol passes their way. And we encourage them to cultivate new food plants and, mindful of the old adage, we encourage them, where possible, to play such games as cricket and football.

The great thing is to enable them to preserve their self-respect, to give them opportunities for learning a trade, and to afford them facilities to work, either for themselves, or for a white man at a reasonable wage. Above all, we do not wish them to become a tenth-rate type of European; and for this reason we are careful to do what we can to preserve native custom in all cases where it is not actually and definitely bad. I must confess that, to me, many of these customs seem unutterably foolish, just as even the best of native art appears to me crude and entirely lacking in inspiration; but probably if I were less ignorant I should be more appreciative. And, in any case, if a custom or an art does not harm and gives pleasure to anyone, it would be an administrative crime to endeavour to suppress it or to ridicule it out of existence, merely on the ground that, to Europeans, it seems absurd.

The undertone of melancholy that sounds from beneath this and the revealing reference to not wanting the natives to become inferior types of Europeans, clearly indicates that Murray had his reservations about what was inexorably being done. Beyond forcing the natives to drop their more horrendous customs, clean up their villages, improve their food supply, and strike up some relation to the European economy, Murray was not clear about what it was best to do with the natives. Nevertheless, he favored denaturing the native culture and relating the people somehow to the European culture (in its Papuan expression). He was thus supporting a program which left the natives sensibly deracinated from the one culture but not rooted in the other, a predicament not to be contemplated without the question arising of how long the natives could be kept in this state of cultural disequilibrium. And if not for long, in which direction should the natives be guided, or pushed? Obviously, toward the European side of the balance, with their native cultural baggage increasingly disheveled, for their "progress" was certain to be defined in European terms, not native.

While Murray often insisted that a native was a *man,* not a childlike creature or a commodity called labor, he seems to have had a pessimistic idea of the time it would take to fit these men to direct themselves and their affairs into the quasi-European circumstances that obtained in a tropical colony. That seems to be why his ruminations on the vital question, "What are we, then, to do with the Papuans," were in the nature of troubled brooding and hardly at all programmatic. He hoped that the natives would progressively "improve," and he favored keeping the roads of advancement open to them, but in government, for example, he could not clearly see how they were going to get beyond a larger participation in running their villages and service in the lower levels of the central government, while in economic affairs, he felt, they would be lucky to become marginal producers for the market. Nevertheless, he made special provision for facilitating their progress in these directions, though none to force the pace.

Although Murray's sincerity in insisting that the administration's prime concern was with native welfare could not be questioned, it was hard to deduce this from what the administration was able to do between 1908 and 1940 with regard to medical care (including public health measures) and native education. Medical care had to be made extensively available if the natives were ever to be rescued from the bog of poor health in which they were mired. What needed to be done was reasonably clear, but there was never enough money available to do it. There was never enough money for education either, but here what was required and how to do it was not utterly clear. The record actually made in both fields would have been less impressive if it had not been for the work of the religious missions.

Murray's view of the missions and missionaries was of a piece with that of MacGregor, though perhaps not as warmly expressed. To the old established missions, the LMS, the Methodist, and the Roman Catholic, there were added in his time the so-called Kwato Industrial Mission, an off-shoot of the LMS, which was established independently in 1911 with headquarters on an island off Samarai, the Seventh Day Adventists, who scattered small missions over the colony, and the Unevangelized Fields Mission which worked in the Fly River country. The LMS continued to work along the south coast, the Methodist mission in the east of the colony's mainland and on nearby islands, while the Roman Catholics established themselves in the interior mountains from their original base on Yule Island. All in all, the Roman Catholic missionaries were perhaps the most sophisticated in their view of the natives, though not at all less determined to root out horrendous native customs, while the Seventh Day Adventists were least sophisticated, most traditional in their views, and most radical in the changes they made in native custom.

The Papuan administration had begun to spend money on **native** medical care in 1903, when it provided a subsidy of £100 each to the native hospitals at Port Moresby and Samarai. From this beginning, partly under the stimulus of severe epidemics of introduced diseases among the natives, more native hospitals were provided—some of them temporary to meet emergencies. The subsidy was considerably increased. The hospitals proved to be of most use to native indentured labor and native government employees and hardly touched the village natives at all. In 1912 a traveling medical service was established to reach the villages, serviced at first by Europeans trained as ambulance attendants, but progressively by natives trained to the level of "orderlies." In 1922 natives of the grade of Native Medical Assistant began to appear, and in 1933 an abortive effort was made to improve their training by sending a few natives to the University of Sydney's medical school. To the administration's medical service the missions added theirs. The LMS, the Anglicans, and the Methodists maintained hospitals and did some outpatient work in the villages, and most missionaries were prepared to offer simple medical treatment. There were never more than four European doctors in the administration's service. The inadequacy of all this in relation to the medical needs of 200,000 to 300,000 natives was obvious.

While Murray recognized that native education was an administration responsibility and had proposed a government school system in 1908, no money was forthcoming and the scheme never went into effect. From 1908 to 1919 such native education as was available was provided by the missions in close relation to their religious purposes and supported exclusively from their own funds. After 1919 the administration provided small subsidies for the mission schools, but did not attempt to establish a system of its own. An effort was made to define a standard curriculum and to measure achievement by standard examinations. Queensland "inspectors" were employed, but the scatter of the schools made it impossible for comprehensive tours to be made. By 1939 there were forty-five school "centers" and more so-called "out-stations" where mission-schooled natives taught natives. Technical education was being encouraged, and of course the Kwato Mission specialized in it. The administration sought to encourage the teaching of English, and teaching in English, in an effort to make English the *lingua franca* of multi-language Papua. (Currently, however, the nearest thing to a *lingua franca* remained "police Motu," the Port Moresby dialect. Murray despised "pidgin.") A fundamental difficulty was that so little was known in Papua about how best to teach natives, and there was a great deal of uncertainty about what it was best to teach them. Study of these problems began in the late 1930's. Until they were solved, the best that could be hoped for was that some natives would become literate in English. It was doubted that even the literate natives had any great capacity to think in English, even those employed as teachers, and what contribution was being made to broadening native cultural horizons was undeterminable.

Since neither the colony's local income nor the subsidy received from the Commonwealth ever allowed the administration to support any of these schemes at all adequately, least of all support their fuller development, from 1919 Murray tried to provide additional money by levying a tax on the natives, the proceeds from which were earmarked for welfare. The tax, however, never produced any considerable sums, and what little was forthcoming was spread thinly over a variety of projects. It was from this fund that mission education was subsidized, hence the minimal character of the subsidy. Some money was allotted to the traveling medical service as the service reaching most natives. A little was invested in native plantations, the profits from which helped augment the fund. And the administration's anthropologist was supported from the fund instead of as earlier from the medical care allotment. The gap between need and supply remained vast.

It will be recalled that Murray entered the Papuan service as chief judicial officer. He retained that post in combination with the lieutenant governorship during his entire term. His interest in rendering European justice to natives was unflagging, and some of his best writing was devoted to discussions of this challenge. Murray acquired enormous prestige with the natives, not least because of the justice he rendered, and, unlike Governor Grey and the Maoris, he never lost it and, indeed, it survived him as was illustrated by the native-style "funeral" he was given at Port Moresby in 1940. Most of the cases with which Murray dealt represented conflicts between the European and the native codes of conduct, not least with regard to the taking of human life, the survival of native practices like sorcery, which illustrated very imperfect enculturation, and straight-out evil doing that could occur in any human situation. Even comprehensively they did not represent anything that could be called significant native unrest.

Papua did, however, experience native unrest in Murray's time. The earliest manifestations of it had occurred before his time as evidenced by the activities of the Milne Bay prophet, Tokeriu, around 1893 and the native troubles on the Yodda goldfield a couple of years later. The most impressive cultist outbreaks occurred after World War I. A so-called "Taro Cult" flourished intermittently around Buna Bay and inland from around 1913 to the early 1930's; and a so-called "Vailala Madness," first reported in the Vailala River country in 1919, was still spreading in spite of administration efforts to stamp it out in 1923. It did not finally die out until the early 1930's. Although it was noticed that these cults had anti-European and economic (i.e., "cargo") aspects, the fact that the most important of them was called a "madness" indicates that their true significance was missed.

Between the world wars Dutch New Guinea was attended to a little more closely by the Indies authorities than earlier, but it cannot be said that their efforts incorporated it any more firmly into the Indies governmental system and economy. The vast majority of the indigenous population, estimated at 200,000 to 300,000 and mostly not under the control of European authorities, was still involved in a subsistence economy, and such of the coastal natives as had dealings with the Western market economy dealt in copra and other tropical produce. The Dutch approach was variously motivated, but in its economic aspects was necessarily hesitant, for in 1911 an expert assessed New Guinean economic prospects as very poor. After almost two decades of effort in the 1920's and 1930's Dr. Hubertus van Mook surveyed the situation and arrived at the same opinion. The emphasis of the Dutch approach in the 1920's was on tightening political control, with economic activities secondary; in the 1930's the emphasis was in effect reversed, with the Dutch anxious to counter what they took to be Japanese ambitions in New Guinea. Like the Australians and New Zealanders the Dutch worried about the Japanese "southward" drive, even as a matter of trade and investments in raw material production, and were concerned by any indications that it might turn into an effort to obtain territory for settlement and exploitation.

World War I had signalized a shift in the economic orientation of the Indies away from Europe and toward the Pacific. The Japanese interest was one phase of this. Between 1923 and 1940 the number of Japanese resident in the Indies doubled, trade with Japan steadily increased, and during the Great Depression the Japanese intensified their search for trade outlets in the Indies and for opportunities to invest in the production of raw materials. In Dutch eyes a compensation, or balance, for this was an increase in trade with the United States and an increase in American investment, especially in oil production. In this same context the Australian and New Zealand interest in the Indies increased, chiefly in terms of trade.

The Australians were familiar with the idea that the Indies constituted for geographers, anthropologists, zoologists, botanists, etc., a kind of bridge between the Asian and Australian worlds—famous efforts to define the place of transition from one world to the other being those of the naturalists Wallace and Weber. The anthropologists, for example, were well aware that in remote times the peoples now considered indigenous to the islands and the continent—the Australian aborigines, the Melanesians, the Polynesians and the Micronesians—had migrated out of Asia into the Indies and eventually on into the Pacific countries and islands. They knew that the human stocks represented in New Guinea were also to be found in islands to the west, notably the Moluccas. However, these theories and the facts supporting them had never given the Europeans in Australia any acute sense of being somehow involved in Asia. Between the world wars the Australian interest in the Indies was chiefly in tea and oil, and late in the period, when there arose the question of the possible role of the Indies in Australian defense, this question was argued in connection with the British base at Singapore and the Dutch bases at Ambon Island and at Surabaya in northeastern Java. As with regard to trade, the Australian strategic focus on the Indies was to the west, away from New Guinea. Dutch New Guinea was, as a matter of fact, hardly at all oriented toward the Pacific islands; it was oriented west to the rest of the Indies. The consequence was that while the Australians had firm ideas about the role of New Guinea in their security, they did not include Dutch New Guinea in their definition of New Guinea. Since their eyes were on Singapore, it is unlikely that it ever entered their calculations that the easternmost islands of the Indies could serve as stepping stones to and from the Philippines, with Dutch New Guinea one of the steps. Rather, in this vicinity, their eyes were on the islands of Japanese Micronesia. When in 1940 a distinguished Australian diplomat offered as a revelatory opinion that the Dutch Indies hung "above" Australia like a protective umbrella, he not only did not hint that he knew how leaky the umbrella was, but he also did not imply that he was including Dutch New Guinea in his image. Rather his thinking was focused on Java. Thus even in strategy Dutch New Guinea was an unregarded backwater.

The Dutch political attention in the 1920's was chiefly addressed to the Vogelkop Peninsula, west of Geelvink and Bituni bays. Attention to the eastern portion of the territory was much less active. The chief economic effort was to establish Dutch Europeans and Eurasians on plantations. The effort was a failure, chiefly because of the difficulty experienced in finding suitable soils. A theory was evolved that the basic natural difficulty with regard to soils was that there had apparently been no volcanic activity in New Guinea in recent geological times. The north coast generally and that of the Vogelkop Peninsula in particular, together with the Schouten Islands just outside the wide mouth of Geelvink Bay, had traditionally been the parts of the territory most visited by foreign peoples. Here that kind of Malay variously known as "basic," "bazaar," and "pidgin" was the *lingua franca* that made communications with the natives possible, here trade was an established activity, and here the Dutch Protestant missionaries had been working for seven decades. While most of the activity, political and economic, was coastal, explorations were made inland, but no heartening resources for European exploitation were uncovered.

From 1919 to 1923 Dutch New Guinea was a separate administrative unit of the kind the Dutch called a residency, but in 1923 the New Guinea Residency was abolished, and the territory was placed under the Ambon Residency and thus reverted to a kind of governmental anonymity. A few years later New Guinea was transferred to the Tidore Region under the government of the Moluccas, a part of the Great East Province. Service at the government posts in New Guinea was treated as a kind of punishment for fractious civil servants from the more attractive posts elsewhere in the Indies. Manokwari was the capital.

In the late 1920's, when the Dutch were having a good deal of trouble with leftist Indonesian politicians, particularly in Java, they began to use New Guinea as a place of punitive exile. Exile from Java was an established punishment, and exile to New Guinea signified that it figured in the official mind as the wildest and least desirable part of the realm. There had been nationalistic political activity among the natives of Java from around 1908, but after World War I, with the rule of the Bolsheviks in Russia and the establishment of the Third International, an attempt was made by Indonesians who called themselves communists—and were in touch with the Third International—to push the proto-nationalists to the left. The road to the left in Java had been opened earlier by Dutch socialists, but it was traveled farther by Indonesian converts. The Third International at this stage was keenly interested in the radicalization of the Asian proletariats, though in its perspective the Indies was a sideshow as compared to China. The communists caused considerable commotion among the nationalists, but in the middle 1920's were pushed out of the organizations. They seem not to have gained leadership of any considerable number of people who could accurately be called communist converts. Rather in the end they were driven by frustration into an adventurist course and engineered uprisings in western Java and on the west coast of Sumatra by exploiting the traditional resentments of the native peoples. These uprisings in the established tradition of agrarian revolt were put down mercilessly by the Dutch without difficulty. However, instead of executing the identifiable communists they captured, the Dutch exiled 1300 of them to New Guinea. They were sent to a special settlement called Boven Digul far up the Digul River in the swampy country of the southeast, from which escape was so unlikely that no formal guard was necessary. A political consequence of the communist disturbances was to tighten the grip of the conservatives on the Indies government and to weaken the influence of the liberals. The Dutch began sending dissident nationalist (but noncommunist) Indonesian politicians to New Guinea in the 1930's also, and there grew up several settlements of exiles along the Digul River, one of which in 1934 had as residents two men subsequently prominent in the affairs of the revolutionary Indonesian Republic of Java—Soetan Sjahrir and Mohammed Hatta. In New Guinea itself such political agitation as occurred among the indigenous people was of the cultist variety, not the "advanced" political kind of Java. The authorities were troubled by a series of more or less complicated cults, the root of which was the Mansren myth, but having both "cargo" and political elements. These appeared mostly along the north coast and among the peoples of the Schouten Islands. All were broken up, chiefly by arresting and detaining the leaders.

About 1935 the Dutch developed the conviction that they must develop New Guinea or lose it to the Japanese. The Japanese had entered New Guinea as traders operating in competition with the established Dutch, Chinese, and Malay merchants, but in the early 1930's they took over land from a German company and proposed to grow cotton. This enterprise was in the charge of Nanyo Kohatsu Kaisha, a subsidiary of the so-called Oriental Development Company which was expanding into New Guinea from Palau in the "mandate." A proposal in 1935 to bring in 1000 Japanese laborers to provide the work force for this enterprise was rejected by the Dutch. They were afraid that it was a forerunner of a Japanese claim to a comprehensive concession in the obviously underdeveloped territory, involving unlimited rights of settlement and exploitation. It was still not certain that New Guinea was wholly lacking in worthwhile resources. Exploration was still going forward.

Perhaps the most spectacular discovery in the interior in this decade was of 60,000 highly skilled native agriculturists living in the isolated valley of the Balim River inland from Hollandia in the Snow Mountains. This was not a Dutch discovery, although Dutch personnel were with the expedition, but was to the credit of an American, Richard Archbold, the leader of a collecting enterprise for the American Museum of Natural History. This was the climactic expedition of three into New Guinea which Archbold had led, working gradually west from Port Moresby to the Fly River country of Papua and into Dutch New Guinea.

For the Dutch the most heartening result of exploration economically was the finding of oil. At the time it was popularly supposed that the Indies floated on a sea of oil, but none of commercial significance had been found any place in New Guinea, Dutch or Australian. In the early 1930's the Nederlandsche Nieuw Guinea Petroleum Maatschappij was granted a "survey" area of 25,000,000 acres near Humboldt Bay east of Hollandia from which it was to select 2,500,000 acres for intensive exploitation. The company was a joint venture of the Royal Dutch Shell (40 per cent), Standard Vacuum of New York (40 per cent) and Standard Oil of California (20 per cent). Oil was found, but the field had not come into production when war broke out in the Pacific. Considerable money and energy were also put at this time into prospecting for metals, including gold, but the results were negative. At no stage in these decades were there more than 400 Europeans resident in Dutch New Guinea, although Indonesians were more numerous. When the Archbold expedition was at Hollandia in 1938 it found that the permanently resident European population was four.

When the dust of the controversy over the future of Germany's Pacific possessions had settled, the New Zealanders were with regard to Western Samoa as much frustrated annexationists as the Australians were with regard to New Guinea or the Japanese with regard to Micronesia. Prime Minister W. F. Massey had stood with W. M. Hughes in the battle to establish the right to annex, although he had his doubts about New Zealand as the annexing power, inclining toward Britain. When it became a question of settling for a mandate, it was arranged that Western Samoa be mandated to His Majesty the King, with New Zealand assuming the task of actual administration. The New Zealanders were more dubious than the Australians about their constitutional power to undertake extra-territorial jurisdiction. Massey had been motivated in seeking control of Western Samoa by the strategic and defensive considerations which had taken New Zealand into the Cooks earlier, but the wish to possess was reinforced in different terms by a vocal minority of New Zealanders interested in planting and trading. To these people Western Samoa was a "warehouse" from which tropical products useful to New Zealand could be abstracted, the Samoans doing the indispensable work—which would undoubtedly improve them.

A countervailing idea established itself, however, quite early in the minds of government people. This was that whatever might be done in Samoa, the native interest should be paramount. Confidence that New Zealanders had a special gift for dealing with Polynesians was derived from the alleged success they had had in dealing with the Maori. (With the Samoans under their care, the New Zealanders would be ruling over half of all Polynesians—Samoans, 22 per cent; Maoris, 27 per cent; Cook Islanders, 5 per cent.) In any early official statement the New Zealand government had not mentioned the idea of "mission" in any terms, but had frankly referred to Western Samoa as "New Zealand's share of the fruits of victory," and in 1924 Sir Francis Bell quashed the idea that New Zealand was preparing the Samoans for independence with the assertion that "nothing but the defeat of the British Empire in war can ever sever [the Samoans] from the Crown of England." The Labour party opposed annexation—Harry Holland wrote an impassioned pamphlet against the proposal—and when, about two decades later, Labour was in office and had to deal directly with Western Samoa, it tried to act with intelligent good will under the guidance of League of Nations sentiments. Apirana Ngata had asked sardonically earlier, "Why do you not leave them alone and let them enjoy themselves in their own way? Is yours the only way in which a human being can enjoy himself?"

What the New Zealanders had taken from the Germans was, even by islands standards, a relatively small agricultural colony in which production was much more diversified than was commonly the case, though copra was still the premier export commodity. Cocoa was the second most important export. As commonly in the islands, the prime indicator of economic success would be the health or sickness of the export-import trades. The government's basic local income would be derived chiefly from imposts on these trades. As it was not likely that mining, timber, or any other alternative to agriculture would ever contribute significantly to exports, agricultural development had to be taken as the way to economic progress. Fortunately, the economic upswing that had begun in German times continued under the New Zealanders until about 1930, when the Great Depression had its effects, though there was a break in the continuity during and just after the war. However it did not prove possible to continue all the kinds of production for export the Germans had established—for example, low prices for rubber intermittently caused cessations of rubber production—but at least one new export was developed, bananas from 1928. Production for internal consumption was considerably diversified by the New Zealanders.

A feature of the agricultural situation between the wars was that while the total acreage under cultivation appears to have increased very little, there was important change as between commodities—coconuts, cocoa, and "other"—in favor of cocoa and "other" and as between the European cultivators and the Samoans in favor of the Samoans. This indicates that the New Zealand administration was having greater success than most other island administrations in inducing the natives to produce for the commercial market. This conclusion is especially clearly supported by the increasing acreage the Samoans had under cocoa and the rise of banana production for export, exclusively a Samoan enterprise. Moreover, the Samoans began to engage in commerce, mostly at this stage in retail trading in the villages. In 1927–28 the land under cultivation was divided between the Samoans, the private planters, the New Zealand Reparations Estates, and the missions, the latter three controlling the European agricultural economy. The figures available are not reliable in detail, but the proportionate relations of these groups can be taken as reasonably accurate. About 75 per cent of the land under cultivation was in the hands of the Samoans, of the remainder about 16 per cent was in the hands of Reparations Estates, 8 per cent in the hands of the private planters, and with the missions cultivating only a fraction of 1 per cent. Insofar as any trend could be discerned it was in favor of the Samoans. Both the private planters and the Estates administration were reducing their cultivated acreage, and in some unknown proportion were transferring land to the Samoans. The Reparations Estates were the ex-German plantations which had been taken over by the New Zealand government as reparations when the owners were expelled. They were operated commercially as a unit on the government's account.

Samoan production was not, of course, organized on a plantation basis, at least not as Europeans understood it, but was organized as "village agriculture." The Samoan villages were the centers of Samoan life, supported by a subsistence agricultural system (supplemented by fishing), with production for market annexed. The units of Samoan commercial production may have been small as compared to the European, but in the aggregate they probably accounted for more acreage and hence for more production. In 1927–28 the Samoans held four-fifths of the total acreage under coconuts, but at that time had no acreage at all under cocoa. Copra was, of course, the original native market crop. As the acreage under coconuts declined in the ensuing years, the proportionate decline was less in the case of the Samoan than of the European cultivators. This production had a strong hold over the Samoans. But what indicates the strength of their wish to participate in the "Western" market is the rise after 1927–28 of the acreage devoted to cocoa and the rise of the commercial production of bananas. However, during these decades Samoan political agitation and the Great Depression rather obscured what was going on, and the development mentioned did not, as a matter of fact, become fully meaningful until after World War II.

While the merchant and planter interests in New Zealand had conveyed to the public a rather exaggerated idea of the Samoan potential for European exploitation, the administration's view was very similar to that of Dr. Solf. It saw an opportunity for the expansion of European-directed agriculture, but while it supported it with regard to labor it was not disposed to facilitate the acquisition of land in freehold. Such new land as the European enterprisers acquired between the wars was mostly leased from Samoans. The administration took the position that Samoan rights in the land were paramount and not only accepted the fact that 80 per cent of the land was in their hands currently but over the years transferred to them some of the land alienated earlier. It also leased some of the government's lands, either land held directly or by the Estates, back to the Samoans. It exercised its sole right to buy land from the Samoans only to acquire sites for public works. The net effect was to strengthen the Samoan position slightly.

Viewed from one angle, the handling of the land question reflected the policy of placing the native interest first, but from another it can be seen as a response to the rapid increase of the native population. In 1911 the Samoans numbered 38,084. Under the devastating impact of the influenza epidemic of 1918 the figure dropped to 37,157 in 1921. Thereafter, however, the increase was steady as medical care and public sanitation improved, the figure for 1936 being 55,946 and the rate of increase was accelerating. This in itself—and quite apart from the policy of native paramountcy—required that the emphasis of any program of progress in agriculture fall upon the land of the Samoans. Between the wars it became more and more obvious that the economic strength of the Europeans and part-Samoans was in trade, not agriculture, the leading firms being Burns Philp of Australia, Morris Hedstrom Ltd., of Fiji, and O. F. Nelson, the most forceful part-Samoan of his time. The headquarters town of the trading concerns was Apia, but they usually had shops scattered throughout Upolu. Many of the Samoans who kept stores in the villages were in effect agents of the large companies in Apia as these establishments were so commonly branches of great overseas companies.

Since it was the Samoan tradition not to take employment in European enterprises at all freely, the New Zealand administration from its beginnings had a labor problem. Under the military government which held office until the mandate came into effect, an effort was made to eliminate foreign labor—Chinese and Melanesian—by compulsory repatriation, even though this was extremely costly. The considerable Chinese work force was reduced by over 60 per cent to 832, the less numerous Melanesian force by almost 80 per cent to 201. This operation was carried out at the direction of the New Zealand government, which acted under pressure from London. In 1916 the British government disallowed the use of indentured Chinese in British territory, and it promptly pressured all British governments to conform. In Western Samoa this sudden reduction in the labor supply was disastrous. The planters protested angrily. Because the British and Australian governments steadfastly refused to allow recruitment for Samoa in the Solomons and New Guinea, no relief from these traditional sources was at hand. There was nothing for it, then, but for the New Zealand government to exert counter-pressure on the British government to obtain permission to bring in indentured Chinese once again. The first of the new lot of indentured Chinese arrived in Apia from Hong Kong in August 1920, just as the civilians were about to take over government from the military.

Reversion to indentured Chinese labor was strongly criticized in New Zealand, particularly by the Labour party, and in 1923 the Samoan administration, seeking to satisfy its critics, announced that while the Chinese would be retained, their status would be changed from indentured to something more like free labor. This stopped the criticism in New Zealand (and also in Geneva), but when Labour came to office a dozen years later and examined the situation in Samoa, one of the decisions it made was to repatriate the surviving Chinese. The theory was that they could be replaced by Samoan workers. The planters, particularly the cocoa planters, vehemently denied that the Samoans would or could fill the Chinese places, but the government was unmoved. The management of the Reparations Estates undertook to train Samoans to work in cocoa. To ease the labor situation, some laborers were brought in from Niue. From about 1936 the numbers of Chinese slowly declined until after World War II they were less than 200, not counting Chinese-Samoan half-castes. The converse of this was the speeding up of the induction of Samoans into the ranks of free labor. This was, in a way, a phase of "Samoa for the Samoans," and the means employed were not only training for plantation work but familiarization with wage labor by employment on public works.

Visible exports and imports followed a very irregular course between 1920 and 1940 but the all-over trend in both by quantity and value was upward. There were export surpluses in all the twenty years except 1920, 1921, and 1926. Exports were of highest value in 1928, of lowest in 1934. In 1940 the position was, exports £ 222,000, imports £ 165,000. What the situation was with regard to the invisibles of trade was not exactly known. All banking transactions were with the branch of the Bank of New Zealand at Apia. In these years there were marked changes in the direction of trade. In 1917, 77 per cent of the exports went to the United States, but this was a wartime situation, and by 1929 the United States was taking but 26 per cent, and in 1938 the American percentage had dropped to 10. New Zealand, which had taken but 8 per cent in 1917, was taking 10 per cent in 1929, while 63 per cent went to Europe, but by 1938 the New Zealand percentage had risen to 34 and the United Kingdom was also taking 34 per cent. Australia, which had taken 15 per cent in 1917, dropped out altogether during the ensuing two decades. Thus, under what passed for normal conditions between the wars, Western Samoa was chiefly dependent for outlets for its produce on New Zealand, its metropolitan country, and the United Kingdom, New Zealand's most important trading partner. As an exporter, Samoa was well within the British trading system.

On the import side the situation was rather different. That the United States percentage of imports should decline was only to be expected once the constrictions of wartime had been loosened, and that New Zealand should quite consistently supply about a third of the imports was also quite expected. But by 1938 the dispersion of sources of imports was rather remarkable. The United Kingdom was supplying 15 per cent, Australia, more important as a supplier than as a market for produce, was supplying 14 per cent; Canada 8 per cent, mostly timber, Japan having been driving for island trade for two decades, 7 per cent, and the Netherlands Indies 3 per cent (oil).

Although when the New Zealanders took over from the Germans Western Samoa had been running budgetary surpluses for a number of years, for the first thirteen years under the mandate there were deficits in the public accounts. This was partly because production and trade were disordered through most of these years for one reason or another, but more because the New Zealanders carried on a more liberal public spending program than the Germans had. From 1919 to 1932 the mandate government was subsidized by the metropolitan government to a total of £244,000. During these same years the government financed its public works by loans from New Zealand, and by 1932 the public debt of the mandate stood at £165,200. However, after 1932 to the end of the interwar period the government ran surpluses in the public accounts, even during the depression years, partly by cutting down expenditure, and used the surpluses to pay off the public debt, a process completed by 1944. The New Zealanders achieved budgetary viability at a higher level of expenditure than the Germans had ever contemplated; this was allowed in largest measure by the increased production of export commodities.

Beginning its work under the influence of the idea that New Zealanders had special knowledge of how to deal with Polynesians, the mandate government emphasized public works in great part closely related to economic development, welfare with particular attention to medical care, public health and education, and greater participation of Samoans in government than the Germans had allowed. At this early stage, as far as can be ascertained, the Samoans appear to have recognized that full autonomy was temporarily impossible, though they nevertheless expressed the wish for more autonomy than was conceded and within a few years mounted a campaign for more and as a tactic of complaint indicated that they would prefer the United Kingdom to administer the mandate rather than New Zealand.

The New Zealanders instituted a government in which an administrator (called in Samoan a Kovanna) appointed by the government of New Zealand was advised and assisted by an executive council consisting of (a) the New Zealand civil servants heading up the government departments and (b) the two high Samoan advisers, the Fautua (whose office the Germans had instituted). They also set up a Fono, or legislative assembly in which the Samoan members were heavily predominant. The powers of this were increased as early as 1923. Eventually, elected European members were admitted. The Samoan members were drawn from the *matai* group, strategically important in Samoan native government. The New Zealanders aimed at establishing a chain of authority beginning at the village level and moving upward through the districts which were in charge of district executives and judicial officers to the Fono and up to the administrator and his Executive Council. In the Samoan view, however, while the government might profess that the native interest was paramount, its system allowed the Samoans far too little autonomy and it was weighted at every level and especially at the top in favor of the authority and decision-making of Europeans.

Within five years of the commencement of civilian government, to the great surprise of the administrator, who had overlooked Sir Joseph Ward's warning that the Samoans were exceedingly able politicians and hard to rule, and to the scandal and often horror of foreign observers, the Samoans launched a campaign of nonco-operation with the government. The Samoan discontents were cultivated at first by Europeans and part-Samoans who had economico-political grievances against the administration. The most conspicuous and forceful of the anti-government spokesmen was the part-Samoan businessman, O. F. Nelson. (He had been born in Samoa in 1883, had lived under the so-called condominium and the German government, and had built a trading business inherited from his father into a major concern; he died in Apia in 1944.) The anti-government movement became known by the Samoan name of Mau, or "opinion" movement, and while the Europeans and part-Samoans continued to promote their causes through it, the Samoan leadership quickly gave the emphasis to the struggle for autonomy ("Samoa for the Samoans") and the restoration or preservation of native Samoan customs.

By 1926 nonco-operation was the Samoan's principal tactic. Thus challenged, the government pursued a policy of "sustained repression." It exiled O. F. Nelson and other European and part-European members of the Mau to Auckland. Nelson was in Auckland from 1928 to 1933, when he went back to Apia only to be immediately banished again, this time for ten years. However, he challenged in the New Zealand courts and in 1936 the Labour government permitted him to return to Apia. He was elected to the Legislative Council in 1938. Meanwhile, in Samoa, the Samoan Mau partisans set up a shadow government at the village of Vaimoso outside Apia. In December 1929 the Samoans held a demonstration in Apia during which a bloody clash with the European police occurred and a much-admired Samoan leader was killed. The Mau leaders then dispersed into the bush, but three months later after a truce parley with the government, they were permitted to return to their homes. They did not, however, renounce nonco-operation, and in fact the Samoan women became its most forward exponents.

A distinguished anthropologist saw the Mau as a characteristic native cult movement, even suggesting that it was related to the Hauhau movement in New Zealand, but while it undoubtedly included cult-like elements—notably the rejection of such European practices as medical care, public sanitation, production for export market, co-operation in government—it was nevertheless decidedly a political movement. Quite obviously it linked to Samoan politics as practiced in the old days when Samoans had sought to establish a king in office to maintain their autonomy against the intruding Germans, British, and Americans, and time was to make it clear that by the emphasis on autonomy it linked forward to the more Europeanized politics of campaigning for self-government after World War II.

When the Labour government turned to deal with the tangled Samoan situation in 1936, it induced the Mau leaders to resume their places in conventional political life. Many of the offices dealing with native affairs were made elective, and the Mau leaders were able to stand for and win them. They were thus absorbed to an extent into the administration. Nonco-operation ceased, tension was reduced, but that the Samoans had abandoned their wish for autonomy was improbable.

The history of American Samoa between the wars—while in essence "more of the same," continuing to deal with a miniscule colonial situation as a kind of side issue of the primary task of running a naval station—was enlivened by a very curious multiple-act drama that illustrated Samoan discontents and showed that very considerable problems could develop within small colonial areas as well as large. An addition to the possession in this period really added nothing to its resources. Swain's Island—200 miles north of Tutuila in the Tokelaus and fully populated and exploited for copra—was in 1925 transferred from American family ownership to American national ownership and attached administratively

FIJI, SAMOA, AND TONGA ISLANDS

Rotuma

Wallis

Futuna

VANUA LEVU
Lambasa
Lautoka
Yasawas
Mba
Nandi
VITI LEVU
FIJI
Taveuni
Koro
Ovalau
Nausori
Suva
Leuuni
Kandavu

LAU GROUP
Lakemba

Ono-i-Lau

Ninatoputapu

WESTERN SAMOA
Savaii
Apia
Upolu
AMERICAN SAMOA
Pago Pago
Tutuila
Manua
Rose

Late

Vava'u

Tofua

Haʻapai
TONGA
Nukuʻalofa
Tongatapu
Eua

Ata

to the Naval Station, Tutuila, not American Samoa, still an entity unknown to the law. The complicated intra-family legal battles which inspired this move were not concluded until 1939. It was the contemporary judgment that life in American Samoa was placid as compared to that in the New Zealand mandate, even though American Samoa also had a Mau movement which flourished from 1920 to 1935 and thus began earlier and lasted as long as the Western Samoan. Hurricanes—there were bad ones in 1921, 1926, 1931, and 1936—were reckoned far more disruptive than any of the disturbances contrived by mortal men.

The income of the Samoan population, apart from that derived from work in the homes of the senior naval personnel and in the public services outside the naval establishment, such as the medical and educational services, was largely dependent on subsistence agriculture and its commercial extension, the copra trade. The trade remained a government monopoly, and the returns, after deduction of the administration's levy, constituted the principal money income of the Samoans. Exports—exclusively to the San Francisco market—fluctuated from a maximum of 1750 tons in 1924 to less than a thousand tons in hurricane years and to none at all on the monopoly's account in the depression years 1933 and 1934. Price per ton fell from $108 in 1926 to $30 in 1932. In 1933 the governor set up a board to examine the problems of the native industries, and while little was accomplished with regard to agriculture, success was achieved by encouraging the more systematic production of "native artifacts"—floor and table mats, tapa cloth, carvings in wood, etc.—this incidentally stimulating the planting of pandamus trees. Production was chiefly disposed of at Pago Pago to passengers on the American ships that stopped en route from San Francisco and Los Angeles to New Zealand and Australia and back. While in terms of return per hour of labor required to produce the articles, the rewards to the natives were pitifully small, in the aggregate the returns in the late 1930's amounted to around a third of what had been obtained for copra in most good years and more than the copra returns under depression conditions.

The single most important social pressure at work in American Samoa was population pressure. The native Samoan population rose from 8056 in 1920 to 12,908 in 1940, and the pace of increase was quickening. The population was overwhelmingly pure Polynesian, but there was a steady rise of mixed-bloods, mostly European-Samoan crosses—fitting them into the socio-legal structure of Samoan life caused some trouble, though the Samoans had no prejudice against them. The white population remained at not more than 300, of whom the naval establishment ordinarily accounted for two-thirds, all transients. There was an almost invisible minority of Chinese, Japanese, and American Negroes. The only vents for Samoan emigration were Hawaii, to which remarkably few went in this period, and, more particularly for the half-castes, continental United States, to which even fewer went.

The governors and their colleagues were more concerned with the implications of the population increase than were the Samoans—particularly in relation to the implications for agriculture. To improve native agricultural practices and thus returns in terms of foodstuffs and exportable commodities, a scheme of agricultural education had been advocated for years. However, none was worked out in these decades, for Washington refused the money and the natives had no visible interest. An observer sardonically remarked that as far as he could see the natives had not changed their techniques in the 200 years of contact with Europeans. In 1932 the governor set up an experimental farm at Taputimu, but it was not of much effect, since it was run by amateurs and the Samoans ignored it. The only success the authorities had in agricultural affairs was in inducing the Samoans systematically to pursue and destroy the rhinoceros beetle—a menace to coconut trees which had reached American Samoa from Western Samoa in 1917. No expert study of native agricultural methods was actually made until 1939, when a specialist from Hawaii examined the situation, though there had been an unofficial study of land use in 1937. The Hawaiian expert's advice was rejected by the Samoans on the ground that it was not compatible with *Fa'a Samoa*.

Samoan agriculture, effectively under the direction of the *matai* and carried on close to the villages, was traditionally a small-scale operation, the units of production were fractions of an acre and a mixture of tree crops and field crops, the latter involving shifting cultivation. The prevailing topography in the populated areas was normally so rough that an American farmer would have declared the land uncultivable. The soils were mostly thin and poor, though in their wild state they carried a heavy vegetation. While during these decades the pressure on the land resources was obviously increasing, an expert assessment was that by native standards there was still considerable land in reserve, though some of it was awkwardly situated in relation to the existing villages and some of it was theoretical rather than actual in that it would have to be created by shifting tree culture to the steeper slopes, releasing more level ground for field crops. However, this was not an argument against improving productivity on the existing cultivated area. The Samoans, like most island people, were less interested in systematically increasing the supply of indigenous food than in gaining access to exotic imported foods, such as New Zealand canned corned beef and canned fish from North America.

The administration continued to maintain free medical care and public health services to the Samoans by means of the naval establishment. A Department of Health had been in existence since 1914. American Samoa had a reputation for enforcing public health regulations more rigorously than customary in the islands. The principal extension of the services in these decades involved the building and staffing of new clinics in outlying parts of Tutuila and in Manu'a. The Samoan proneness to disease remained comparable to that of the natives of other islands. Conspicuously problems were diseases of the eyes and ears, filariasis, the preliminary to elephantiasis, and tuberculosis. Yaws was under control. Infant mortality, though declining, still stood at 75.05 per 1000 in 1940.

Although the governors understood that only through education could the Samoans be adjusted to their new and rapidly evolving situation, they were not able to set up a satisfactory system of public education because of lack of funds. It was possible to send a few Samoan boys to Hawaii for secondary school education beginning in 1914, and the first Samoan students reached the University of Hawaii in these decades. This was made possible by the mission schools, which not only dominated the field but were decisively better. In dealing with the Mau in its earliest manifestation a governor tried to set up a public school system—the villages to supply the buildings—but this was not a success, and by 1928 a voice advocating the abolition of the schools was heard in the Fono. Not only were funds exceedingly limited, but, in spite of the provision of a "teacher's institute" in 1922, the native teachers were woefully undereducated, little more advanced than their pupils.

In the 1930's private philanthropy injected a new and highly creative element into the educational situation. The parents of Frederic DuClos Barstow of Hawaii set up a foundation, capitalized at $200,000, to assist in native education in Samoa. Young Barstow had visited Samoa about 1930 and had become interested in the Samoans. On his death shortly after his return to Hawaii, his parents set up the Memorial Foundation to support a leadership training program based on education valid in terms of both Samoan and American ways of life. Half the annual income was to be spent on education in Samoa, half abroad where educational opportunities were richer. In practice the latter expenditures provided scholarships for Samoan teachers in Hawaii and candidate medical practitioners in Fiji, while in Samoa the foundation paid the salaries of the teachers at the Feleti (i.e., Frederic in Samoan) School established in 1935 at Taputimu. The school buildings were provided by the *matai,* other costs were met by the naval administration. Although theoretically open to all Samoan youths, including half-castes, in practice the school became an avenue of advancement for Samoan elite from the *matai* upward. At the same time the public school system continued in a precarious condition, though it lived on.

The natives remained devoted to *fa'a Samoa*. Basic in their lives was the *aiga* or "extended family," headed by a *matai* above whom were the high chiefs. This system was integrally related to the organization of all work, the participation of the Samoans in government, and in anti-government politics. It was the chosen Samoan instrument for controlling the people—including the distribution of income and the resistance to unwelcome foreign enculturation. With regard to income the control was so effective that it was reckoned that only about half of the income derived from government employment remained with the worker's biological family, for the other half was percolated through his "extended family." With regard to politics in these days, the *matai* and the high chiefs acted with or reacted against the Mau.

The organizations known collectively in the history of American Samoa as the Mau first appeared in 1920, were fairly virulent until 1927, and by 1935 a governor felt able to pronounce the Mau dead. As in Western Samoa, the discontents in American Samoa that the Mau expressed were cultivated and kept alive by Europeans and part-Samoans seeking to promote their own purposes in the islands. However, unlike their fellows in Western Samoa the non-Samoans promoting the Mau of American Samoa were not residents but outlanders living in Hawaii and, more particularly, California who either had connections with Samoa by blood or by a claim to land by family inheritance or both. They conducted a propaganda campaign, both in the press and in Washington, designed to establish that the Navy's government was illegal and tyrannical. To the Navy people in Samoa, the outlanders became known, ironically, as the "California Mau." What these people were seeking to gain was possession of land—on which they proposed to set up plantations—to which they allegedly held title by inheritance from the Samoan side of their family line. As Samoan land could not be alienated to Europeans and was inheritable only in accordance with Samoan custom, what these people sought was to upset the law, and they pursued their line to the point of questioning the legality of the American presence in Samoa, even arguing that the Mau was the legitimate government of the country.

When the Mau first showed its hand the then governor was in difficulties largely arising from conflicts of opinion over the enforcement of the Navy's regulations, disagreements between the governor and the Samoans over a ruling on the sex relations of a Navy man and a Samoan woman, on the qualifications of Navy nurses versus missionary nurses, and over the administration's right to tax. It was into this situation that the Mau injected itself. The Mau professed to be upset about a variety of matters, including whether or not the governor's ruling on sex relations between naval personnel and Samoan women constituted an "insult" to the Samoans, whether or not the Samoans had, as they alleged, been kept in ignorance of the administration-made laws under which they were living, whether or not the secretary for Native Affairs was fit to hold that office, whether full information on public finance was being communicated to the Samoans, the poor condition of the roads outside Pago Pago, the low quality and limited availability of public school education, whether the administration's justice was truly tempered with mercy, and whether or not the navy hospital's drugstore was charging extortionate prices. If these were, indeed, the Mau's complaints, it was remarkable how many of them referred to deficiencies and problems adverted to by governors in times past. Since this was true, the governor might have taken action to correct the situations complained of in all instances in which he felt the complaints justified. However, he failed to act decisively. Worse still he was double-crossed by subordinates who associated themselves with the Mau. And at this trying time the outlanders, now directly represented in Samoa, sought to tangle their demands and complaints with the Mau's. The situation continued to worsen and the governor shifted from indecisiveness to despair and committed suicide just when a naval court of inquiry was proceeding to Pago Pago to investigate the situation. The court's findings did not tell against the dead governor but against his disloyal subordinates and the outlanders and their agents.

The president of the court succeeded to the governorship, and he eased the situation by attempting to launch a public school system, directing the improvement of the roads, and ordering the compilation, translation into Samoan, and publication in a single volume of the code of Samoan laws —up to this point difficult of access after their original promulgation (in English and Samoan). In 1921 he called a meeting of the high chiefs, knowing that many were mixed up in the Mau, and bluntly asked them to put into writing whatever complaints they still had. Instead, they decided to declare that in their opinion the situation in Samoa was satisfactory.

The troubles were not over, however, for a local agent of the outlanders induced a considerable number of disaffected *matai* to turn against the high chiefs, reactivate the Mau, and put the assassination of certain of the chiefs on the agenda. Seventeen of the *matai* conspirators were chased into the bush and caught, arrested, tried, and sentenced to prison terms and the loss of their titles. When a principal outlander arrived in Pago Pago at this time, he was denied permission to land. A new governor then entered directly into discussions with the leaders of the Mau and ascertained that their remaining complaints were either trivial or unfounded, such as their dislike of the closing of a government-operated ice-cream parlor. By 1924 things had quieted down so much that the jailed *matai* were offered release from prison if they would swear allegiance and renounce their claims to their titles; they agreed the next year.

The next burst of Mau activity was inspired by a part-Samoan who sought to use the organization as a weapon in his quarrel with the governor. He had sought to assume the title Tui Manu'a, dormant since 1909, and had been denied permission on the ground that it was incompatible with American republicanism for any of its nationals to assume a royal title. At his urging, the Mau addressed a letter to the governor demanding "civil government" and stating that the Mau members would not pay taxes until the demand was met, nor would they any longer participate in the copra pool. (This seems to have been the first occasion on which the Mau articulated what was later alleged to be one of its two chief objectives—civil government and the ousting of the Navy, the other being American citizenship in place of the prevailing "nationality.") To deal most effectively with this challenge the governor went to a formal meeting of the Mau and pointed out that frank discussion of complaints and proposals was the best way of dealing with public questions. Without conceding anything he deflated the Mau with such skill that it was never quite the same thereafter. Its last public act of any significance was to present its case to a presidential commission on American Samoa at hearings at Pago Pago in September 1930.

Although a senator had attempted unsuccessfully in 1926 to clear up the legal ambiguities of American Samoa's status, it was not until 1929 that any really significant moves were made, and even these ended eight years later in frustration. Along the way something was accomplished for Samoa, but in the end the work was cut short by congressional indifference. Certain citizens of Hawaii had been actively interested in American Samoa, not exclusively because of the Mau and its outlander partisans. There was a Hawaiian tradition of interest in the Polynesian peoples, centered at the Bernice P. Bishop Museum in Honolulu, with which some of American Samoa's friends were associated. These were all "Europeans" except Dr. Peter Buck, who was part-Maori. These Hawaiians captured the interest of United States Senator Hiram Bingham of Connecticut, scion of the Bingham missionary family which had done such notable work in the early days in Hawaii and Micronesia, in his own right a historian of Spanish South America and specialist in diplomatic practice. He successfully introduced a "public resolution" (No.

89 of the 70th Congress) into the Senate which accepted—after twenty-five years—the cession of Tutuila as of 1900 and Manu'a as of 1904 and provided that President Herbert Hoover should appoint a commission to study the situation in American Samoa. The Commission consisted of Senators Bingham and Joseph E. Robinson of Arkansas, Representatives Beedy of Maine and Williams of Texas, and three Samoan high chiefs, who sat only in Pago Pago, one representing Tutuila, one Manu'a, and one the Mau. Hearing but astutely avoiding entanglement with the "California Mau"—its remarks were now much moderated—the commission heard in Honolulu and Pago Pago a wide range of witnesses from whom it learned that conspicuously on their minds were such matters as what the status of Samoa should be in the American system: traditional territorial, the status eventually given Puerto Rico, or an adaptation of Tonga's position in the British system; whether or not the administration should continue to be naval or become civilian; whether or not American citizenship should be accorded the Samoans; various views on how to handle the half-castes with regard to the holding of Samoan land and Samoan titles; and that a cardinal point of policy must continue to be the protection of *fa'a Samoa,* while a calculated policy of inducting the Samoans into the twentieth century must be pursued. The Mau demanded territorial status, the end of naval administration, and a grant of $1,000,000 to set the new government going.

From a mish-mash of distinctively "American" opinions, traditional and experimental views about how to deal with a Pacific island and its people, and a variety of Samoan imprecisions, the commissioners drew some intelligent conclusions. They proposed that Congress give American Samoa an organic act; that the Samoans be granted a dual citizenship, American and Samoan, the qualifications for the latter to be laid down by the Fono, thus turning over to the Fono the final determination of the status of the half-castes; that only bona-fide Samoan citizens hold title to Samoan land, implying that half-castes could hold land and Samoan titles if they had been accepted as Samoan citizens; that the governor be either a Navy man or a civilian at the discretion of the President; that the governor's veto could be overridden by a two-thirds vote of the Fono, whereupon the question at issue would be referred to the President for final judgment; that appeals should be allowed from the Samoan High Court to the United States District Court in Hawaii; and that the status of Swain's Island remain as it was, since it was of little value to Samoa.

This looked very much like solid progress, but it proved impossible to get an organic act through Congress—it failed in the House in 1933 and was rejected by the Senate in 1937. The foundation of government in American Samoa therefore remained President McKinley's executive order of 1900. Any reforms undertaken had to be made within the framework of that order. A bill of rights which it had been proposed to include in the organic act was inserted into the law code of American Samoa. The positions of judge and secretary of native affairs were separated, the judge having his judicial duties only, leaving native affairs and an extraordinary miscellany of other concerns—passports, prisons, the management of the copra monopoly—to a new officer, the attorney general. Essentially, the situation in American Samoa was "more of the same." As recently as 1927 a governor had concluded after study that a governor's duty still was "to govern the people of American Samoa in such a manner as to facilitate the maintenance of the naval station." The only significant recent change on the station had been a shift from coal to oil in 1922. It was the changes in Samoan life that were pregnant with significance, but what was news out of Samoa to Washington?

In Fiji between the world wars the surgar industry—the hard core of the European-style economy—went through difficulties both with regard to the circumstances under which it operated and with regard to its relation to the world sugar market. In the former respect the great change was the shift of Indian labor from partly indentured to wholly "free," though largely working as peasant farmers within the ambit of the Colonial Sugar Refining Company or just outside it but still concerned with sugar-cane. In the latter respect difficulties were chiefly experienced from the fluctuations of prices in the market but also with regard to insuring certain outlets for the sugar. In these years cane sugar as a proportion of all sugar marketed—the competition was beet sugar— declined from 71 per cent in 1920 to 62 per cent in 1940. Fiji cane had to be marketed in competition with great tropical cane producers such as Java and Cuba and such lesser producers as Mauritius and Formosa. Viewed against its competitors Fiji was a minor supplier of the market. Within its geographical area, Australia became self-sufficient in sugar about 1924 and thereafter absorbed only small quantities of Fiji sugar and molasses each year. New Zealand remained the only nearby market of any significance. The prime Fijian markets became Canada and the United Kingdom. In the latter market Fiji enjoyed "preference." The price per ton for Fiji's sugar fluctuated from a maximum of £29 in 1920 to £9 in 1930, 1931, and 1936 and stood at only half the 1920 price in 1940. Production exported—72,985 tons in 1920—fell to a low of 44,109 in 1923 and then rose to a high of 140,864 in 1936. By quinquennial averages the movement was from 83,641 in 1920 to 123,415 in 1940, a gain of roughly 50,000 tons in twenty years, but since the price went down, the "sugar cheque" decreased by over £800,000 between

1920 and 1940 in spite of the considerable increase in exports. Fiji sugar gained some security in its British Commonwealth outlets under the Ottawa trade agreements of 1932, and in 1937 Fiji was a participant in the International Sugar Agreement, an attempt to control sugar production and distribution.

Changes in sugar production in Fiji had been going on for some years when the abolition of indentures precipitated a crisis. The changes had chiefly involved an attempt to re-establish Europeans in cane production as managers of plantations and to establish free Indians in cane growing. The abolition of indentures—with a "strike" of the Indian sugar workers in 1920–21 which deprived the Europeans of field labor—and the fall in price caused many of the European planters to abandon the industry. In 1923 Colonial Sugar Refining production fell off by two-thirds. The company difficulties were most immediately related to the fact that the Indians disliked working leased small acreages within larger European-controlled areas of which managerially they were an integral part. The Indians had also found it hard to find labor for large plantations. To meet the situation the Colonial Sugar Refining Company proposed to redesign the lease system into what became known as the "tenant farming" system. This dated from 1924. Insofar as this involved the production of cane on relatively small acreages, it was suggested by Queensland experience. In practice it led to leasing the Indians blocks of lands of eight to fifteen acres assumed to be operable as cane farms by the farmer and his family —a "family farm" scheme. It led to a four-way division of cane farming which was increasingly weighted in favor of the Indians as the cultivators.

In 1925, when the total acreage under cultivation for cane was 64,963 the distribution of the acreage by mode of control was: (1) Colonial Sugar Refining Company plantations directly operated 52 per cent; (2) European-managed plantations 7 per cent; (3) Indian and Fijian tenants 10 per cent; (4) Indian and Fijian "contractors" (i.e., cultivators not on land leased from the company) 21 per cent. The Indians were the predominant labor force; while the naming of Fijians as tenants and contractors was quite correct, actually this signified only small numbers. Once convinced that the new system was a success, the company persistently promoted it, and by 1940 the situation on the 91,624 acres then under cane was: (1) Company operated plantations 3 per cent; (2) European-managed plantations less than 1 per cent (206 acres); (3) Indian and Fijian tenants 52 per cent; and (4) Indian and Fijian contractors 45 per cent. The Fijians were still a tiny minority of the cultivators, and cane-growing was accurately described as an Indian industry. The Europeans now directly concerned with cane production were experimental scientists, technical advisers to the farmers, and managers of services. Sugar milling, from 1926 a company monopoly, was not only owned but managed and at the higher levels staffed by Europeans, mostly Australians. At the lower levels the mill staffs were a mixture of part-Europeans, Indians, and Fijians.

Although the structural change in cane production had reduced the European role to apparent insignificance, the reduction in terms of managerial influence was far from being so drastic. The Colonial Sugar Refining Company continued its responsibility for the state of cane-growing and the welfare of the growers, more particularly for those working land leased from it. In the middle 1930's no less than 60 per cent of Fiji's commercial farmers were dependent in one way or another on the company, which, acting as a prudent landlord, undertook to assist the cane growers in a variety of ways, some of which in a more complex society would have been a responsibility of government. Its primary interest was to insure the production of sufficient cane annually and of as high a sugar content as could be managed—payment was by sugar content, not bulk—and, with regard to the growers, to maintain the social peace.

The company continued its practice of supporting field experiments with new varieties of cane and dispersing good varieties to the growers, of maintaining the cane-carrying railway, and of exercising direct influence over the recruiting and employment of the cane-cutting teams—these became a field for Indian "politics." It set up and manned with Europeans an "extension service" to the tenant cane-growers which provided them with expert agronomic advice. The productivity of company tenants ran 10 per cent above that of the "contractors." It closely supervised the use of the cane lands under a system of rotation and kept the Indians from drifting into subsistence farming by attempting to grow their own food—from some points of view, the least wise company policy. It supplied fertilizer at cost. It advanced money against the grower's annual return from cane to finance the crop, for a capital investment or for an improvement in family living arrangements. From 1937 in an effort to increase Fijian participation in the industry it maintained a special cane-growing school at Drasa. But wisely prudential as these and the other services the company undertook might be, they did not in the long run forestall a diverging of the interests of the cane growers and of the company as miller and vendor of the sugar in a difficult market.

After sugar the most important agricultural exports of these decades were copra and bananas. There were, of course, other exports than these, even including such old island specialities as bêche-de-mer and shell, but none returned much money. Copra production continued to be a mixed European-Fijian industry, the Europeans mostly to be found in these decades on the island of Tavenui and the coast of Vanua Levu opposite, while the Fijians, responsible for three fifths of the production, were widely scattered through the islands and predominant in the Lau group. Most of the Fijian production was as a "cash crop" of the subsistence communal farmers, while the European producers were wholly dependent upon Fijian labor. Copra thus provided the Fijians with one of their most important connections with the European economy. As in the case of sugar, the price of copra rose during World War I, fell during the post-war depression, and rose and fell thereafter, again being low at the outbreak of World War II. The unremunerative levels of the copra price naturally had greater significance to the European producers than the Fijian, but it was observed in the Lau islands during the Great Depression that the Fijian producers were forced to forego the use of certain European commodities to which they had become accustomed and to revive some native crafts to produce the local alternatives. The banana industry which had achieved an all-time peak of production with 1,800,000 bunches in 1914, received a "hard knock" in 1921 when Australia laid a protective tariff on imported bananas to reserve the market for the Queensland growers after forty years of competition. This made the Fijian producers dependent upon the smaller New Zealand market, with the western Canadian market the only market open for exploration. What potential the Canadian market had was not certain when war cut it off. When the depression hit New Zealand its banana market was flooded with fruit, for it received supplies not only from Fiji but also from the Cook Islands, Tonga, and Samoa. In 1932 the New Zealanders imposed a quota system on the suppliers. This assured remunerative prices for the reduced quantities that could be consigned. The Fiji industry stabilized at about 300,000 bunches.

Diversification proved not only a knotty problem in itself, but it was clearly shown that success or failure turned not on feasibility of production so much as on the state of the world market for the product. Cotton growing, revived in 1923, struggled along in a small way until the late 1930's when it expired once again. Rubber production—the trees were already there—rose from a trivial amount in 1922 to a peak in 1926 and then reverted to triviality in 1929. "Secondary" industries proved more rewarding: it was in these decades that biscuit making and the making of soap from coconut oil from local copra became established industries and even acquired export markets in neighboring islands.

The most protracted struggle for diversification involved pineapples for canning. Here the elements of success seemed all to be present, and Hawaii offered a pattern of what success could mean. Nevertheless, the only reward for heroic effort was frustration. In the 1920's the conviction arose that Fiji had advantages of soils, price of land, labor, etc., that might allow it to become a producer of canned pineapples competitive with all the British producers and the Hawaiian. The pineapple had been established in Fiji so long that it could almost be taken as indigenous, but it was produced commercially only for local consumption, with a few exported fresh to New Zealand. In 1926 the government in collaboration with Canadian interests carried out experiments which forecast success. In 1928 a commercial venture at Wainaloka on Ovalau Island started bravely but failed within four years. In 1928 also Hawaiian interests began experiments at a site on Vanua Levu, but abandoned them after five years, apparently thinking of the huge stocks held in Hawaii. In 1930 a company began canning at Nandi on Viti Levu, but suspended in 1933. Finally at the request of the government, the Colonial Sugar Refining Company built a cannery near Lautoka in 1936. Idle during the war, it reopened in 1945 only finally to close down in 1955, ironically, when diversification was as needed in Fiji as at any time in its history.

There was some "internal" diversification in the 1920's and 1930's, for example beef cattle were raised both on coconut plantations (to keep down undergrowth) and on grazing properties, dairying was undertaken (and small quantities of butter exported), and the Indian farmers raised cows, rice—an Indian staple of diet—and a variety of European and even Fijian foodstuffs.

There was a great success, however, in diversification, but not in agriculture—in gold mining. That there was gold in Fiji had been certain since 1868, but until the late 1920's no deposit of much consequence had ever been found, certainly none that would justify the cost of a mine and treatment plant. In 1922 an attempt was made to establish a mine on the basis of a gold deposit first located in 1885. This deposit was near the Yanawai River, which flows into Savusavu Bay, Vanua Levu. The venture was a failure, but in 1929 J. L. Stark discovered a promising deposit on the opposite side of the river from the failed mine on the flank of Mount Vatukaisia. In 1932 Mount Kasi Mining Company began operations at Stark's discovery and continued them for eleven profitable years, only closing down because of supply troubles during the war. However, the richest of all the Fijian gold fields was on Viti Levu. The discovery was made in 1932 near Tavua, six miles inland from the north coast of the island, by a veteran prospector of Australia and New Zealand named Bill Borthwick, "grubstaked" for his Fiji venture by a Suva "pub" keeper named P. Costello. Borthwick uncovered what proved to be one of the richest finds of the twentieth century, but a deposit of great geological and chemical complexity, expensive to work. After a short promoters' boom in syndicates and companies, the field came under the

control of three responsible companies. Costello disposed of his extensive
option over the field to a syndicate headed by E. G. Theodore of Australia (who had been treasurer in Scullin's Labor government, "Red" Ted
of Queensland politics). Production rose steadily from 1935. In the first
decade production was 607,385 fine ounces worth £5,556,558, with
some silver additional (while in the second decade production was over
twice as great.) Thus from 1932, when returns from agricultural exports
were down, Fiji's export returns were notably and increasingly improved
by gold. On the Viti Levu field rose the town of Vatukoula ("Gold
Rock"), which was to become the largest urban center outside Suva in
Fiji, the mines the largest single employer of Fijian wage laborers in the
colony. Fijians constituted about three-quarters of the work force. During its lifetime the mine on Vanua Levu also employed Fijian workers.
Since it was not the Fijian habit to stay on a job for an extended time,
the mines actually employed more Fijians than the roster of jobs would
imply.

As a trader Fiji had traditionally kept within the British trading system. Between the wars it consolidated its ties directly to the United Kingdom. By the 1930's both exports and imports to and from the United
Kingdom had not only increased in value over earlier decades but had
also become proportionately more important in the Fijian trade than
those of any other country. Within the geographical area, Australia continued to be the most important supplier of imports (though of a value
less than those coming from Britain), but Australia absorbed only a
small proportion of Fijian exports. New Zealand, on the other hand, at
considerably lower levels of value, bought more from Fiji (chiefly sugar
and fresh fruit) than she supplied. Canada, because of its sugar purchases, was the second most important export outlet, but it supplied a
much smaller proportion of the imports—mostly timber—than the United
Kingdom, Australia, or even India. India figured as a fairly important
supplier because of the Fiji Indian demand for Mother India's goods, but
India purchased very little from Fiji. Japan built up a considerable trade
in piece goods, while the United States, whose trade with Fiji had become very small, supplied machinery and automobiles and split the trade
in oil with the Netherlands East Indies. Almost three-fifths of the colonial
government's income was derived from customs in the middle 1930's,
with another quarter derived from excise taxes, licenses, and fees. Little
was derived from direct taxing of the Fijians. Small sums were received
from the United Kingdom's Colonial Development Fund of 1929.

Between the census years 1921 and 1936 the Indian population increased from 60,634 to 85,002 and although there was some Indian im-

migration into Fiji in the 1920's, it was far less important as an addition than for its social composition—considerable numbers of merchants arrived—and its economic impact on the resident population. Natural increase largely accounted for the increase and this insured a steady rise in the proportion of the Fiji-born population. Although the Indians were increasing faster than the Fijians and the handwriting on the wall was plainer and plainer, they did not in these decades overtake and surpass the Fijians, though they cut the Fijian advantage from 24,000 to 12,000. As a people the Indians were in 1920 confronted with very difficult problems, internally with regard to general social progress, externally with regard to their relations with the Fijians and the Europeans, in and out of government. The hard and distressful fact about the Indians of 1920 was that, by and large, there was no Indian community but a collection of atomistic individuals, mostly poor and mostly illiterate. This disadvantaged mass had yet to demonstrate that it could produce the leaders to find the answers to its problems with regard to land, political rights, education, general improvement of social condition, and relations with the Fijians and Europeans. During the ensuing twenty years the Indians did make some progress on all these fronts but less through cooperative action with the Fijians and the Europeans than by their own efforts. They have rarely been given the credit they deserve.

The Indians continued to be concentrated in the countryside; they were predominantly rural, but unlike their former position in India, in Fiji they did not collect in agricultural villages, but were dispersed on their farms, a dispersion imposed upon them by the conditions of cane culture, not by their own choice. Geographically, they were not spread evenly over either Viti Levu or Vanua Levu—they were few in any other of the Fijian islands—but were concentrated in the cane-growing areas or in places contiguous to them. The majority of the Indian farms were either devoted exclusively to sugarcane or grew cane in a mixed farming context, while only a minority were mixed farms without cane. Annual net incomes were very low. The farming areas were loosely related to market towns were not only Indian storekeepers (the economic aristocrats of the people) had establishments but also the Australian firm of Burns Philp and the Fiji-based company of Morris Hedstrom. Farther afield was the metropolis of the country, Suva, close to only one of the cane-growing areas. The country market towns were dreary places indeed. In the countryside, stores operated by Indians were scattered about; they sold but a limited range of merchandise. There was some tendency for service establishments such as barber and tailor shops to gather near them. Many of the storekeepers were also moneylenders, ordinarily on a petty scale, but in Fiji, as in India, the indebtedness of the Indian farmers was an oppressive phase of their lives about which remarkably little was known.

Careful study of the Indian areas of settlement at a later time established that either the collapse of Indian customs had been less exhaustive during the indenture period than was supposed or the Indians succeeded in rebuilding the structure of customs rather quickly once they had attained freedom, for while it was true that Fiji Indian customs were somewhat modified from the Indian models, nevertheless, the continuities were impressive and highly explanatory of the new patterns. There was no very lively image of Mother India in the minds of the Fiji-born Indians and little wish to visit her. It was in keeping up old customs that the Indian farmers often fell into debt. There was divisiveness within the Indian population arising not only from the very nature of the society in which they lived—involving as it did a sharp struggle to survive economically—but also from differences arising from province of origin in India (i.e., north versus south particularly), language, and religion, though the divisiveness was markedly less in Fiji than in India. Religious differences were surprisingly modulated, but all Indians tended to retain their religious beliefs and practices and to resist attempts to convert them to Christianity. In religion the Hindus were greatly predominant over the Muslims, and while minority languages were spoken (usually by small groups of people), Hindi and Hindustani were clearly predominant, and Hindi was considered the *lingua franca* of the Fiji Indians. The most important minority language was the Urdu of the Muslims. The Indians showed no unwillingness to learn English or to dress European-style. As to leadership, during the indenture period the most revered leader had been Totaram Sanadhya, who had arrived indentured but had won acceptance as a pandit. Of lesser prestige was Moganlal Manilal, who had arrived free from Mauritius, spoke English, and pioneered Indian journalism in Fiji. There was a tradition of listening to immigrant leaders, but after the abolition of indentures contention arose between the Fiji-born aspirants to leadership and the immigrant aspirants. The Indian leaders were usually more interested in political than socio-economic objectives.

The Indian "psychological distance" from the Fijians and the Fijian distance from the Indians continued to be unbridged. It was vastly more important than the relative lack of physical contacts between the two races. The Indian relation to the Europeans in government and outside continued to be less a matter of cooperation to achieve defined ends on which both agreed, than pressure by the Indians on the Europeans, often implemented by propaganda and even dissident conduct, to win concessions or assistance. The Indians appear to have felt that they were in Fiji but not of Fiji; residentially and administratively they were indeed apart from the Fijians and the Europeans. As no image of Fiji was ever devised that appeared to include them, they developed no warm loyalty either to Fijian Fiji or Crown colony Fiji, a fact much complained of during World War II. The word *Fijian* applied only to indigenous natives, never to Fiji Indians or even Europeans.

Between the wars the condition of the Fijian people was far from satisfactory. Insofar as they were conscious of their situation they were more aware of being buffeted about by the cross-currents running in Fiji than of having any common objective they could pursue with all deliberate speed. It was out of this situation, however, that the most forceful Fijian leader since Cession appeared, and his objective became the rehabilitation of the special machinery of government that Gordon had designed to protect the Fijian people. He argued his case in the terms of Lugard's "indirect rule." This leader was Ratu [i.e., hereditary chief] J. L. V. Sukuna, who was born into the aristocracy of Bau—King Cakobau's island—giving him automatically a distinguished place in the Fijian chiefly elite. His position was fortified by an education at the expense of the Fijian public. Prepared at Wanganui in New Zealand he graduated B.A. from Oxford and became a barrister of the English bar. In World War I, after service in the French Foreign Legion during which he was wounded and decorated, he returned to Fiji and joined the Fijian labor corps for further service in France. His eventual army rank was colonel. After the war he exercised his hereditary right to interest and action in Fijian affairs and in the 1920's was serving as district commissioner of Lau (the only Fijian district commissioner in the service). A man of natural force and more completely the man-of-two-cultures than any other islander of his time except certain New Zealand Maoris, he rose rapidly to a position of power and exceptional prestige in the Fijian Administration, the Council of Chiefs, and the Crown colony government, working closely with the British governors both as counselor and ceremonial associate in relations with the Fijians and the British. Genuinely distinguished, he was temperamentally and by reasoned conviction a conservative, especially in Fijian affairs, and therefore disposed to compromise the issue of Europeanization well over on the Fijian side, he was still able to see the need and wisdom of assimilating certain elements of Europeanization the better to fortify the Fijian position. Fully competent in the dialectic of discussion and a writer of excellent English, he disguised the ambivalences he must have felt and put the Fijian case with force and clarity. It was, however, a case, not an indisputable revelation, and inevitably Sukuna became to later students of the Fijian predicament not simply a great Fijian conservative but a reactionary.

That the Fijians were under heavy pressure from the Europeans to get on with their Europeanization has been made clear earlier. In the European view the Fijians could not expect to be exempted from the consequences of the total situation in Fiji, and they were therefore willing to help the Fijians adapt—one illustration of this was the Colonial Sugar Refining Company's agricultural school at Drasa. However, the Fijian elite gave very little leadership in adaptation, and the Fijian majority stayed immersed in its traditional communal society centered in the thousand-odd villages scattered through the islands, dependent upon a gardening-type, shifting, subsistence agriculture. The villages had become in effect fortresses against any thoroughgoing westernization of the Fijian people and were the refuges of those who had tried to break away and had failed. The Fijians remained in overwhelming proportion traditional Fijians, in largest measure because they clung to their villages and their culture. It was village life that molded the Fijian personality and "set" the Fijian value-system. Unluckily, it produced a personality and incorporated a value-system that was anything but helpful in adaptation to the new situation in Fiji. What the Fijians were was entirely sympathetic to all but the narrowest and toughest of the Europeans, but it was of no help in what the Europeans regarded as the great task confronting the Fijian people. Most of the Fijian resistence to Europeanization was entirely passive, if not apathetic, but there was evidence that the most nativistic kind of resistance to or evasion of adaptive change could still appeal in Fiji. This was illustrated by the bizarre career of the anti-European, anti-Indian agitator Apolosi Nawai, called by one governor the Rasputin of Fiji. This charismatic man supported his violent xenophobia with mythological references highly sympathetic to the Fijian mind, pseudo-religious mystical declarations, a political pretension to being "king" (i.e., Tui Viti) of Fiji, and used his leadership position freely to exercise his superpotent sexual appetites on his female followers. First active in 1914, he was still active in 1940, not at all cooled off by extended periods of government-enforced exile in Rotuma.

Such Fijian acceptances of the new conditions as could be instanced were all marginal, not central in any sense, and even in total could not be argued to reflect any Fijian purpose to make a holus-bolus change. The Fijians somewhat changed their dietary by adopting certain European foodstuffs, they found a compromise between Fijian and European dress (not the least admirable that of Sukuna), they incorporated European elements into their housing, but all this without really compromising the Fijian character of their food, clothing, shelter regimen, and with least effect in proportion to the distance of the villages from the European towns. Over the years, too, they had built a kind of annex or ell to their subsistence agriculture by undertaking the growing of coconuts for copra for the European market. They had also annexed the production of bananas for market. They had become active on the margin of the European-Indian system of sugarcane production, not least with the encouragement of the Colonial Sugar Refining Company. They had taken up "individual" farming European-style, not least under encouragement from the government. They had drifted from the villages into certain wage-paying occupations such as plantation, mine, and wharf labor. They had gone into government service at clerical and administrative levels, into trading as shop assistants (but never as enterprisers), they had acquired and successfully used quasi-professional qualifications for school teaching and doctoring and, more rarely, had acquired European-style higher education and professional qualifications. Yet if all the individuals involved in Western-style activities had been added together they would at any time be found to represent but a small fraction of the total Fijian population. Even the fairly numerous Fijians who produced copra for market, or worked on European coconut plantations, were still so entangled in the subsistence economy that their significance in relation to what the Europeans meant by "adjustment" was minimal.

That the Fijian elite was biased toward the *status quo* was less culpable—since conservatism is a defensible position—than their failure to fortify their position by seeing to it that life in the villages was maintained at the traditional level of quality and, indeed, improved. While the situation in the villages in these decades appears not to have been expertly studied, such fragmentary evidence as has come to hand indicates that it was not at all good. Thus, while the Fijians were making a poor fist of their Europeanization the villages were losing their effectiveness as the fortresses of Fijianism they were assumed to be. Discouraged by the aridness, tediousness, and unrewarding laboriousness of life in the fortress villages, individual Fijians were leaving them less from any purposefulness than from boredom and desperation. Having failed to develop any collective will to adjust, the Fijians had also failed to develop the only visible counterpurpose, the maintenance of the vitality of village life. The villages were becoming stultified, and the escapees were evidence that the stultification was causing them to ravel at the edges.

At the level of government the swing of the pendulum away from the governance of the Fijians by Fijians as a separate and special fraction of the population of Fiji toward their governance by Europeans reached its maximum in 1921. This had left the structure of Fijian government essentially unchanged, but its manning at the strategically important levels was mostly in the hands of Europeans, many of whom did not read, write, or speak Fijian and had no specialized knowledge of the Fijian people or their affairs. In 1923 the pendulum appeared to be about to begin to swing back, for in that year on the motion of the chiefs, the office of secretary of Native Affairs was reestablished, and in the next few years the Fijian administration was reorganized, though largely to reduce the number of units of government rather than to give the administration a pro-Fijian emphasis. At any rate this did not lead on to the diminution of the European role or to any increase of Fijian influence either. Rather the position seems to have been that the Europeans, with whom fundamental decisions rested, waited more or less fatalistically to see what was going to happen.

As the years passed it was increasingly obvious that the Fijians were not adjusting successfully, least of all purposefully, and the choice became either to force the pace of Europeanization, if means could be discovered and the economic climate turned right, or to turn once again to the Gordon policy of allowing the Fijians to govern their own affairs and contrive such adjustment as they thought proper. The provocation of such a turn would be a judgment that such Europeanization as had taken place was a "failure," and while there was apparently nothing that could be done to erase it from the Fijian scene or even to stop its further disorderly elaboration, it might be possible to switch the emphasis of policy to the revivification of Fijian village life, so consistently the vital center of Fijian life and perhaps the key to its indefinite preservation. This would probably involve some changes in the organization and management of the villages, particularly the economic activities, but the changes could perhaps be made with scrupulous regard for the Fijian tradition.

The judgment that the effort to Europeanize the Fijians by a slack permissiveness had failed was made by Governor Sir Philip Mitchell, an old African hand, familiar with classical "indirect rule," in office in Fiji from 1942 to 1945. He made his judgment in 1943, mostly on the basis of what he saw of the life of the "individual" Fijian farmers. The rehabilitation and refurbishing of the Fijian administration into a pattern of "indirect rule" took place in 1944 and 1945. The man chosen to run the refurbished administration was for the first—and probably last—time a Fijian, Ratu J. L. V. Sukuna. What nobody in Fiji perceived was that "indirect rule" was returning in Fiji just as the winds of change were about to sweep it out of its home and bring in political freedom in its place.

To the Fijians the Indians were a challenge, largely in economic terms, secondarily in political terms. The two peoples were culturally quite incompatible, and any sense of superiority was commoner among the

Indians than among the Fijians. The Fijians were acutely aware that these people were intruders into their land, and they well remembered that the British were responsible for their presence. Contemplating the Indians the Fijians could only marvel at, without wishing to imitate, their general economic purposefulness, their acute money and property sense, (of which the Fijians had too little for their own good), their sustained diligence (whereas the Fijians were sporadic workers), their apparently endless occupational mobility. Where they collided was over the land. The Fijians held the bulk of the land, and if the Indians were to increase their share they would have to lease it from the Fijians. By the second half of the 1920's the Indians had begun to think that they had leased about as much land from the Fijians as they were ever likely to get under existing conditions, and they were further frustrated by the fact that, in spite of government supervision of leasing, the conduct of the Fijian leasors was still exasperatingly and destructively capricious. The Indians felt that they could not get enough land and that their tenure in what they had was dangerously insecure. (Partly as a reflex of their insecurity they were guilty of much deliberate "soil mining" and where they subleased to fellow Indians, they practiced exploitation of the tenant in excelsis.) The earlier to-do over the land had taught the British in government that Fijian rights in the land were paramount and that it was dangerous to tamper with them.

When Indian leaders began to pressure the government to do something to get more land released to Indian cultivators, the government in effect tried to turn the pressure onto the Fijians. This brought the issue before the Council of Chiefs. The chiefs recognized that the Indians had a problem of two faces, the need for access to more land and greater security of tenure under the leases. The Fijians were aware that they should not, merely to appease the Indians, give up to them land which they genuinely intended to cultivate themselves, nor throw open land to Indian occupation that should be held in reserve against future Fijian needs. Since when the land question was under discussion the government was in a phase of encouraging the Fijians to take up "individual" farming, the land needs this involved had also to be kept in mind. The argument in all its complexity was joined in 1933 in the Legislative Council, when K. B. Singh presented the Indian case and Ratu Sukuna the Fijian. The obvious solution was to determine Fijian needs for land, current and prospective, and to make whatever land was then left over available to the Indians. The Council of Chiefs approved a resolution to that effect in 1936 and further suggested that the management of the leasing of Fijian land be turned over to the government. This resolution formed the basis of the Native Trust Ordinance of 1940. The Indians got access to more land than formerly and also greater security in their leases generally, while the Fijians were relieved of the headaches and the temptations so long associated with land leasing. But the Indians had to accept that as far into the future as could be seen they would be living and working on leased land, the property of Fijian landlords. They would permanently be tenants, not landowners. Such freehold as the Indians had ever acquired—and it was little—had been purchased at exorbitant prices from Europeans and was in effect hopelessly overcapitalized in terms of possible production at Indian levels of productivity. Moreover, with the Indian population growing fast and certain soon to surpass the Fijian, the Indian need for land was bound to increase faster than the Fijian. There was thus no assurance whatever that the 1940 settlement was a final settlement, least of all if the Indians ever found a way to upset the political balance in Fiji.

In the maneuvering for a more secure position with regard to the land, the Fijians were not unaware of the wisdom of drawing the British closer to them. The Fijians understood that while possession of the land gave them an economic leverage of great strength, it could be weakened by political means. It was wisdom to engage an ally in defense of the Fijian position and the logical (and only possible) ally was the British. In fact the more ways in which the Fijians could involve the British in their affairs, the stronger their political position with regard to the Indians. Paradoxically, perhaps, a further move of this character was the recommitting of the British to "indirect rule" in 1945, for this could only be worked while the British were in Fiji to protect it. In short, seven decades after Cession the Fijians were in essentially the same political position with regard to the British as Cakobau had occupied in 1875. Then the British appeared to be masters in Fiji. Now they were being maneuvered into the position of captives of the Fijians. This is not to discount the genuineness of the Fijian devotion to the Crown; they were indisputably a "loyal" people; it is merely to point out that loyalty in Fiji as in most overseas British countries had an "interest" component of great potency. The Fijians felt they had to have the British to survive. It was an oddity that the Fijians were trying to involve the British deeper in their affairs just when other colonial peoples were trying to push them out of their affairs. The reason was the presence of the Indians in Fiji.

During the years between the wars there was a realization in Fiji that an attitude rather less casual should be taken toward the social services, even though it was still believed that all expenditure on them should be kept within the limits of local revenues. The services to which the Fiji government, like most island governments, gave special attention were education, medical care, and public health. More progress was made with regard to the latter because private philanthropy took a much larger hand in it.

As far as the Fijians were concerned, education had its roots deep in the native society, but on the European pattern and primarily involving literacy, in the teaching efforts of the missionaries, especially the Methodists. (Probably seven out of ten Fijians were Methodists, two out of ten Roman Catholics, the rest belonging to a variety of churches including the Church of England, the Seventh Day Adventist and the Mormon.) The Methodists began their teaching very early, but first in the light of "professional" understanding in 1852, desiring to make as many natives literate as could be managed the better to convey religious instruction to them. The Catholics, who had arrived in 1844, began their schools in 1868. Whereas the Methodists favored vernacular schools in the villages and then set about to build a structure of secondary schools upon them, the Catholics, perhaps because of their smaller numbers, from 1888 began to concentrate their efforts on secondary boarding schools in which intensive teaching was feasible. These were open to boys and girls, Fijians, Indians, and Europeans. The Methodists built up a structure of secondary boarding schools for theological, teacher, and technical training, beginning in the 1860's, and in 1908 established their principal station for advanced education at Davuilevu. They concentrated attention on Fijians with incidental work with the Indians when they began to come in. About 1900 they began to give special attention to Fijian girls, hitherto rather neglected and considered definitely backward compared to the boys.

The first public—government—school was that at Levuka in 1879. One was opened in Suva in 1883. Meanwhile, in 1881 the government opened its first technical school. The government schools and those which came later were patterned on the Australian model and were "inspected" by schoolmen from Victoria. They were supported partly from local taxes and partly from central government grants. However, the government did not push the development of its schools into a system of comprehensive coverage. The Fijian villagers established some vernacular schools on their own.

In 1906 the Council of Chiefs provided most of the necessary endowment for the Queen Victoria School at Nasinu; it was especially designed to provide secondary schooling for their sons. Members of the Fijian elite were also on occasion able to go abroad for secondary schooling and even before 1914, as the case of Sukuna illustrates, to go on to a university.

It is indicative of the especially difficult position of the Indians at the ending of indentures that the only schooling available to them at that time was what was offered by the Christian missions, whose religious teaching they normally resisted. The government offered them nothing. Nor were the Indians at this stage much interested in schooling. Within the Indian community the original impulse to establish schools came from the Hindu and Muslim religious organizations, mostly to sophisticate religious knowledge, but soon groups of Indians living in places where a sense of locality had developed began to establish schools with a more secular emphasis, supported by voluntary assessments on parents. Indian parents, however, showed far more interest in education for boys than for girls—the government eventually had to take special action to encourage education for Indian girls—and in so-called "white-collar" education than technical, but in any case no real fervor for education developed until very late in the 1920's. At that time the Fiji Indians had yet to produce a single professionally trained teacher, nurse, doctor (or "native medical practitioner"), or lawyer, and none of them was employed as a clerk or otherwise in any Fiji government department. However, in the next decade a predominant ideal of young Indians became to find white-collar jobs in the towns, including Suva.

The only secular philanthropist (so-called to distinguish it from the religious missions) that offered help to the schools was the Colonial Sugar Refining Company, which provided small subsidies for schools serving their employees—Fijian, Indian, or part-European. The children of Europeans usually got their schooling beyond the elementary level in Australia or New Zealand. The steamship companies established special low fares to bring the boys and girls to Fiji for their holidays.

The government first showed an awareness that the educational "system" was chaotic and of low standard in 1909. A few years earlier it had upset the Methodists, whose schools were the most numerous by far, by demanding that all schools teach English and offering a subsidy as an inducement to do so. This demand, which was aimed at the Fijians, seems to have originated from the government's difficulties in recruiting Fijians proficient in English for government service at both the clerical and administrative levels and thus was tied to the effort—then running strong—to Europeanize Fijians. This was the time when Governor im Thurn was in office. The missionaries, supported by the Fijian chiefs, did not at all favor the teaching of English to the Fijian commoners, both for much the same reasons: that mastery of English would not be "good" for commoners, but would unsettle them, and English should be taught only to the Fijian elite. (It was, it may be noted, selected as the medium of instruction for the Queen Victoria School.) The Methodists also thought that to require instruction in English would be a crippling burden on their vernacular schools and contribute to establishing an undesirable emphasis on European-style academic education as against technical education.

In 1909 the government set up a commission to study the school "system," and while it rendered a report that *inter alia* declared that the schools should be free, compulsory, and secular, nothing much followed until 1916, when a Board of Education—manned entirely by government servants—a Department of Education, and a Superintendency of Schools were established. This in effect gave the government authority over all schools—mission, private, government, Fijian, Indian, European—and some coordination resulted, but standards remained low and teacher qualifications poor. To improve matters an arrangement was made in 1924 whereby New Zealand teachers could be recruited for service in Fiji. After another commission study of the situation in 1926 a further tightening of government control occurred, with especial attention to the enforcement of standards for the instructional staff, the curriculum, and pupil achievement. The end in view was chiefly to be achieved administratively by requiring the registration of all schools, old and to be established, acceptance for registration turning upon the meeting of the prescribed standards, and refusing any government money to substandard schools. At this time the Indian schools were given attention. An inspector of Indian schools was appointed, and the language problem was compromised by making Hindi the language of instruction, but providing that the other languages could be taught at specially appointed times and places. The Fiji system was progressively tied more closely to New Zealand's, notably with regard to staff and standards, especially with regard to the latter as determined by examinations.

A consequence of all this was retreat of the missions from elementary education and the ever-increasing assumption of responsibility for it by the government. This shift continued during the depression. The change was about completed by 1936. The system as it then stood was about as sound as could be achieved within the prevailing ideological assumptions about colonies. When the new ideology of "development and welfare" began to percolate into Fiji, as it did about 1943, a reorientation of education was soon required.

As compared to other Pacific colonies, the government of Fiji had a decent record in medical care and public health. Above all, it had pioneered the training of native medical practitioners—forty years earlier. Yet in the 1920's the health of the Fijian and Indian populations was still not good. The prevalent diseases were thought to be tuberculosis, filariasis, yaws, ulcers, leprosy, measles, and a variety of skin diseases. (For sufferers from leprosy there was a hospital at Makongai which served not only Fiji but also all the British and New Zealand territories in the area and was considered a model of its kind.) When the Rockefeller Foundation set out to eradicate hookworm in the Southwest Pacific after World War I it found that 98 per cent of the Fijians and Indians were infected, the fundamental reason being the contamination of their shallow wells by the latrines. The elimination of hookworm was a major step forward for Fiji. The Rockefeller Foundation workers had arrived in the Southwest Pacific in 1919, when they did their first work in northern Queensland. They then moved into Papua, where Lieutenant-Governor Murray eyed them with unaccountable skepticism, and went via the British Solomons to Fiji. Dr. S. M. Lambert, the chief Rockefeller official on the spot, thereafter made his headquarters in Fiji until he retired because of failing eyesight in 1939. Lambert in time visited, and sometimes revisited, practically every island group. His politics and economics were conventional, but his public health ideas were progressive. He was capable of condemning the Mau in Western Samoa simply because as a phase of its nonco-operation it had deliberately neglected all the public health practices that had been taught.

It was Lambert's perception that most could be accomplished in public health if there was interisland co-ordination, and after much pressuring of the political authorities and some wire-pulling, he got a considerable measure of coordination of the activities in the High Commission territories. But somehow his most remarkable accomplishment was the improvement he brought about in the training of native medical practitioners at Suva. Although practitioners under Sir William MacGregor's scheme had first been graduated in 1888, there were no school buildings until the late 1920's. When a much improved hospital—the Colonial War Memorial Hospital—was opened in 1923 it called attention to the improved prospects for teaching. At Lambert's urging of both the authorities and the Rockefeller Foundation, the opportunity was taken to provide the school with proper buildings and to upgrade the educational standards.

The Foundation contributed generously to the cost of the project, and in 1928 the buildings of what was now called the Central Medical School were opened at Suva. The school was "central" because it drew its students not only from Fiji—and not only Fijians but also Indians—but also the High Commission territories, the New Zealand territories, and American Samoa. The Australian territories kept apart until 1947, largely because the administrations felt their natives were educationally unprepared to benefit from the School's training, while the French territories stayed outside because of the language bar. This linking of the islands across the political boundaries was to be a valuable precedent for action in other technical fields after World War II. (However, it should be recalled that interisland cooperation was rooted historically in missionary activities, especially in the employment of natives of one group in the missionizing of the natives of another.)

The gist of politics between the wars was the effort of the Indians to improve their position by exerting pressure upon the Crown Colony government. In 1924 an Indian Reform League was formed which was not political by intent but sought to encourage a sense of solidarity among the Indians—something this atomistic people peculiarly needed—by promoting outdoor and indoor games and what can only be called adult education. However, the Indian politicians proved to be not so much interested in such things as in acquiring the vote and increasing Indian representation in the Legislative Council (which had been one nominee since 1916). In 1927 in a move to get closer to the Indians and perhaps offer them some guidance, the government set up an Indian Department headed by a European secretary, who had had experience in India and spoke Hindi. But as to the vote and greater representation in the Council, the Indians had a protracted wait.

Although the colonial secretary of Fiji first attempted to gain this for the Indians in 1923, it was not achieved until 1929, when three communally elected Indian members were added. The elected members immediately asked that a common role of electors be introduced in Fiji, the obvious objective being to increase the number of Indian elected members at the expense of the Europeans—since the Indian population was so much larger than the European, by the most recent census 60,034 as against 3,878. Since all Fijian members of the Council were nominated by the Council of Chiefs and the governor, they were not directly involved in this argument. By their own choice, or the choice of the chiefs, the Fijians did not have voting rights, but it was nevertheless obvious that if they ever accepted the vote and a common roll and arithmetic as the determinant of voting results, sooner or later they would be confronted with Indian predominance also. Refused the common roll the Indians resigned and stayed away about a year. Their places, however, were kept open. On their eventual return they renewed their demand and the question was referred to London. When the colonial secretary in London returned a negative answer in 1933, the Indians once more resigned. However, they soon returned and showed what was on their minds— equality—by such demands as trial by jury (and for the Fijians also, since they did not have it either), equal number of scholarships for Indians and Fijians for study abroad, and appointment of Indian clerks to the Fiji post office. All these things were refused.

In 1934 K. B. Singh (see the discussion of the land question above) again complained that the so-called communal roll was unjust and he equated it to racism. He denounced the special privileges given to European settlers, which, he said, could not be supported by anything in the Deed of Cession. Finally, in 1937 a "solution" of the representation tangle that lasted a decade was adopted. Representation in the Legislative Council became: official members—all Europeans, 16; nonofficial Europeans: elected 3, nominated 2; Indians: elected 3, nominated 2; Fijians: nominated 5. The official members constituted a majority of 1, but more indicative of probable future trouble was that the five Europeans represented (1936 census) 4,028 persons, the five Indians 85,002 persons, and the five Fijians 97,651 persons. This was hardly "equality" by anybody's standard.

CHAPTER XI

Toward Native Paramountcy (2)

In an era in the Pacific when native progress toward self-government, let alone political independence, was commonly regarded as a fantasy of disordered idealists, the Tongans continued not only to govern themselves but to maintain their independence within the framework of the protectorate which gave them a link to Britain through the high commissioner of the Western Pacific. By the middle 1930's there were 30,500 Tongans, 475 half-castes, and 378 Europeans, the latter government servants and traders, for there were no European planters in the kingdom. The government, headed by a Privy Council, was firmly in the hands of the Tongan elite led by the increasingly prestigious Queen Salote. Executive authority was in the hands of the Queen's consort, Prince Tungi, serving as premier and having, in addition to general responsibility for executing the Privy Council's decisions, special responsibility for education, the health services, agriculture, wireless, telegraph, and telephone services, and the government's interisland shipping service. In running the more important services the premier (and of course the other ministers) relied heavily on the senior civil servant of the department, usually a European. At the Privy Council level after 1928, however, there were only two Europeans, the minister of Finance and the chief justice. (In 1928 also the jurisdiction of Tongan courts over Europeans was a little extended.) As the years passed it was observed that the Tonganization of the public service could safely go several steps further. The Tongan legislature was completely dominated by the executive. Most obviously affected were the seven commoner representatives, in any case a minority in the legislature, but any distress they may have felt was probably tempered by the moderately good condition of the Tongan commoners. But since the seven commoners represented 30,000 people, it was, on democratic principles, a striking underrepresentation.

Tonga was not, however, without problems. Economically there was the low efficiency of the subsistence agriculture on which the people were dependent, as well as such problems as prices for export commodities, security of markets, and diversification. Since subsistence and export agriculture were related, there was little call for wage labor in Tonga and the few available workers were mostly immigrant Fijians and Solomon Islanders. The government was somewhat bothered by a tendency of the people to drift from the land into the villages and towns and in 1927 brought in a new land law designed to curb the drift. But not until the late 1930's was a comprehensive reform program for agriculture evolved by the European in the senior post, and it had not been implemented by the outbreak of war. It was proposed, however, to improve the efficiency of subsistence agriculture by a comprehensive program of agricultural education, rooted in the schools, and to diversify export production, initially by encouraging the growing of peanuts. It was also hoped to make use of the Tongan traditional skill in crafts by building up an export trade in *tapa*. However, during the 1920's and 1930's the Tongans as exporters were dependent on copra, of which they were normally selling about 10,000 tons a year, mostly in the markets of Europe. Their secondary export was bananas, and there were a few other items, none of which brought in much money. The banana trade, which had collapsed during World War I from lack of shipping, was not revived until the end of 1931, and in 1932 the Tongans were put under a quota by the New Zealanders, the sole purchasers, which effectively limited expansion. Hence the experiment with peanuts, also for the New Zealand market (since the Australians produced their own peanuts). Since the overwhelming bulk of Tongan copra was sold in Europe and New Zealand took all the bananas, there was little left for sale in other outlets. In the middle 1930's the chief suppliers of imports were, in order of value, New Zealand, the United Kingdom, and Australia, with Japan pushing Australia hard. All of Tonga's suppliers sold more to her than they bought from her. The imports were in large proportion temperate climate foodstuffs (meats, flour, and "biscuits") and textiles (into which trade the Japanese were making inroads).

The export-import trade was largely in the hands of Europeans, more particularly the island traders Burns Philp of Sydney and Morris Hedstrom of Suva. As a move to increase the profitability of the export trade to the Tongan producers legislation was passed in 1940 to put it in the hands of the government. The internal retail trade was far less centralized, for there were many small shopkeepers scattered throughout the islands, though their numbers had decreased during the depression. Like most island governments, the Tongan government was heavily dependent on customs for its revenue (44 per cent), but unlike some it derived as much as 20 per cent from taxes on its own people. In the 1930's revenue was running slightly over £A 60,000 annually. There was but one bank in the country, a Government Savings Bank, founded 1926. But what really distinguished Tonga financially from the other island countries was that it had large accumulated assets abroad, around £A 250,000. This money, not offset by any government debt, was invested abroad. The question arose as to whether it should not be repatriated for use in "development and welfare," for example, the proposed agricultural reforms.

There was a health problem in Tonga which was peculiarly the government's problem because all medical and health services were free to the people. In the 1920's a good deal of hard work was done on insuring a sanitary water supply, something not easy to guarantee in a country where running streams were not common, the soil was exceptionally porous, and the dependence was on shallow wells and rainwater. Tonga benefited from the Rockefeller campaign against hookworm, and Queen Salote herself decided that Tonga should participate in the Central Medical School at Suva. She made this decision at a critical moment in Lambert's campaign to commit as many governments as possible to the school. As to education, in 1927 the government made it compulsory for all children from six to fourteen. The elementary schools were partly government and partly mission, and until 1930 the government school buildings were a charge on the villages, but after that on the central government. While secondary schools had long been established in Tonga, they were not further developed in these years, though they undertook the training of elementary school teachers. A bias in favor of vocational education was developing. Tongans of rank traditionally went to New Zealand and Australia for secondary and higher education, thus giving those countries a strong cultural influence in Tonga. In 1923 Queen Salote attempted to end the old split in the ranks of the predominant Methodists by engineering the union of the Wesleyan and Free Wesleyan churches under the name of the Free Wesleyan Church of Tonga with herself as its head. While this was by and large successful, a splinter group called the Free Church of Tonga continued to function under a European clerical leader.

Between the wars there was change in the British Solomon Islands but not necessarily progress. What sustained faith in the group was the knowledge that it was one of the largest in the Southwest Pacific and the last in which development had been begun. At least among people who had the promoter's psychology, belief in the group's potential remained active. The entrepreneurs in the islands, however, experienced the insecurities

SOLOMONS, NEW HEBRIDES
AND NEW CALEDONIA

consequent on a very heavy dependence on copra and its vagarious price in the world market; the missionaries were advised that even the best of the natives were only in a superficial sense converted; while the administration was for most of these years trapped within the boundaries of the "old colonial" idea that nothing should be done that couldn't be paid for from local revenues, for only very late in the day were the consequences of a changing outlook felt even faintly.

Entangled in the unfolding story were about 95,000 natives, about 500 Europeans, and 300 to 400 Chinese. The natives were unevenly distributed over the dozen islands and groups of islands, 43 per cent on Malaita, 15 per cent on Guadalcanal (although it was a larger island than Malaita), 7 per cent on Gizo, and the remaining third scattered widely. The Europeans were divided in an unknown proportion among the missions, plantation work, trade, and shipping, and government employment. There were a few old island hands who had married native women and were raising families. The scattered residences of the Europeans made them seem fewer than they actually were. The Chinese who had begun to come in right after World War I were small traders—their competition had a deadly effect on the European small traders—or skilled workmen, such as boat repairers and builders. Tulagi, the government's center and the headquarters of the big plantation and trading companies, was the only semblance of a town. Its population was a mixture of Europeans, Chinese, and natives.

The entrepreneurs did very well during the 1920's while copra prices remained remunerative, and by the beginning of 1937 about four-fifths of the acreage the Europeans had under coconuts was to be found on the three islands of Santa Isabel, Gizo, and Guadalcanal and their close outliers, but they also had substantial acreage elsewhere, as on Malaita and in the Shortland group. There were small acreages under rubber on Guadalcanal and Santa Isabel, ivory nuts in the Shortlands, and cocoa on Guadalcanal. There was really nothing else to justify even a tentative reference to diversification in agriculture. The most substantial "diversification" was timber getting, the cutting of kauri on the island of Vanikoro in the Santa Cruz group, carried on by the Kauri Timber Company Pty., Ltd. There was also some production and export of *bêche-de-mer* and trochus and turtle shell, but these items brought in very little money.

The big disappointment of the 1930's was the failure to discover technical and financial ways and means to take out the gold known to be on Guadalcanal. Not even E. G. Theodore from Fiji could solve the problem, and the Solomons missed the stimulation that gold brought to Fiji and the Territory of New Guinea. The two big companies that had be-

come active before World War I—Burns Philp and Lever Pacific Plantations—and the new and aggressive W. R. Carpenter & Co., Ltd., continued to be very active, but the fall of copra prices in the depression
undermined the position of the small operators who had survived, and
many sold out or were foreclosed by the big companies. The big companies, of course, did a great deal of business outside the Solomons as
well and had always attracted a good deal of antagonism, but during the
depression the Lever company was nominated ogre number one of the
copra producers and was bitterly attacked as somehow responsible for
the disastrous fall in prices. The export trade, which had reached a peak
of £451,994 in 1926–27 and then had slowly receded to £111,669
in 1933–34, had recovered to a little over £300,000 in 1936–37. After
the expansion of the 1920's, copra production ran from 20,000 to 25,000
tons. Australia dominated the export-import trade. While much of the
copra went directly to Europe, large quantities went to Australia for
transshipment or processing. The imports were drawn (in order of value)
from Australia, the United Kingdom, Burma, the United States, India,
Japan, and China. (The presence of Burma and India was accounted
for by substantial imports of rice, a constituent of the diet of the plantation workers.) The administration was largely dependent for revenue on
export and import taxes and never had enough income to much more
than pay the salaries of its European staff. It spent nothing on education
and only a minimum on medical care and public health.

Although the natives were chiefly thought of as labor supply, ex post
facto it is entirely clear that what was happening to them was of almost
determining importance to the future of the Solomon Islands. The three
important influences working on them were that of the entrepreneurs,
that of the missionaries, and that of the government. Although it was
believed in 1914 that the natives were all under government control, the
withdrawal of personnel during the war made it possible for some of
the natives to revert to their earlier condition and it was not until 1941
that it was once again believed that they were completely under control.
Choiseul was the last island on which the natives had unobstructed freedom.

By the late 1920's the entrepreneurs were employing a little over 6000
natives and although the work force fell below 4000 during the depression, by the late 1930's it had stabilized at just short of 6000. Since it
was not the same natives who worked year after year, the number who
gained some work experience between the wars was far more than 6000,
but how many more is not clear. The men were recruited and indentured
wholly within the Solomon Islands, most numerously on Malaita. Pay in
the earlier years was £1 a month and keep, but during the depression

the money wage was cut in half. The diet was prescribed by the administration—it was probably vitamin deficient—and the employers were also expected to provide adequate housing, clothing, bedclothes, soap, and tobacco. The work week was fifty hours with Saturday afternoons and Sundays off. Most of the native laborers worked on the coconut plantations but some were employed on interisland shipping, as household servants, and in the government's service as policemen, etc. To sign up for work became fashionable among the natives and they developed a distinction between the men who had been away to work and the "bush natives" who had not. Their motivation was to earn money and thus gain access to European goods, though the original stimulus was to gain the money to pay the government's head tax, and to inspect the European culture as it manifested itself in the islands. That the natives sought money did not mean that they understood a "money economy" or even that they would be wise spenders of the money they might acquire. Probably their most important purchases were steel tools of one kind or another, European-style clothes were of doubtful value to them, especially in relation to their health, while buying European gewgaws instead of acquiring the productions of native craftsmen was culturally disastrous. What detailed effects the artifacts and experience these people acquired had on the native societies was at the time a matter of consuming interest only to anthropologists.

The missionaries had by this time greatly moderated their demands and expectations with regard to dress, housing, labor, and so on and had come to pay most attention to the inculcation of Christian beliefs, with due regard for sectarian variations. How thoroughly even their most ardent constituents had been converted was a vexing but fascinating question. The missionaries were the sole suppliers of education to the natives, but for them it was a handmaiden of religion, not a means of adaptation to a new secular world. In the earlier years they taught in the native languages—Mota became something of a *lingua franca*—but under prodding from the administration they reluctantly undertook the teaching of English. In any case the teaching was very often at a subelementary level, especially when native teachers taught other natives. Some ambitious natives aspired to gain an education without accepting the missionary *quid pro quo,* but this was not possible. None was to be had, with one exception. The administration dispatched a few Solomon Islanders to the Central Medical School at Suva. That the young men did well was a great tribute to their innate capacity, for obviously their educational preparation was inadequate. Only very late in the 1930's did it even appear that the administration was going to take a hand in education, but no action had been taken when war broke out. The missionaries also made an important contribution to medical care and public health by maintaining hospitals and doing some doctoring in the field, but here the government did take a (somewhat feeble) hand. The single most important stimulus in this field came during the 1920's and 1930's from the Rockefeller Foundation people. It was they who discovered that tuberculosis was a major problem in the Solomons and strengthened the hands of the no-clothes-for-natives people. From his special point of view, Dr. Lambert divided the missionaries into "good, bad and confused."

The administration's particular preoccupation was "law and order" which, of course, implied as much or even more interference with native custom than missionary work or indenture for plantation work. The administration divided its domain into eight districts with an officer in charge of each. While for most of these years it was a question of direct rule or none, some progress was made toward a kind of "indirect" rule in the later years. The first move in that direction was the appointment of village "headmen," usually natives who had had substantial contacts with Europeans, with a preference for those who had served in the police. Later in the day some of the more adventurous district officers were experimenting with native councils for the management of village affairs and even the performance of judicial functions. Although the new situation of the natives was the consequence of the full variety of influences at work, it was the government that attracted the displeasure of the natives. In 1927 there were two quite separate murders of government officers, one on Guadalcanal, one on Malaita. The first was clearly motivated by resentment of administration interference with native sex customs, the other by resentment of the head tax. Neither had any obvious political or, really, economic overtones. In 1934, however, there were disturbances among the natives on Gizo, Santa Isabel, and Savo islands which did have both economic and political overtones. The trouble began as a protest, led by an indentured worker from Malaita, against the head tax. It was asserted that the natives were not getting anything worthwhile in return for it. This protest grew into a demand for higher wages—they had just been reduced—and a native voice in the Advisory Council of the administration on which the 95,000 natives were then unrepresented. The administration discerned no useful message to it in these demands and complaints and met the situation with repression.

By 1920 the Gilbert and Ellice Islands Colony was a strange miscellany of islands. Moreover, more islands were to be added to the colony, while some were about to be subtracted.

GILBERT, ELLICE, AND ASSOCIATED ISLANDS

Washington •
Fanning •

Christmas ◊

Jarvis •

LINE ISLANDS

Malden •

Starbuck •

Tongareva ⁞
Rakahanga •

Pukapuka ⁞
Nassau •

Canton • Enderbury •

McKean • Birnie • Phoenix •
Gardner • Sydney •

PHOENIX ISLANDS

Atafu •
Nukunono • Fakaofo •

TOKELAU ISLANDS

Swains •

Makin Meang
Makin • GILBERT ISLANDS
Tarawa •
Maiana • Abemama •
Aranuka ⁞ Nonouti
Ocean • ⁞
Onotoa • Arorae •

Nanumea •
Nanumanga • Nui • Vaitupu •

ELLICE ISLANDS ⁞ Funafuti
Nukulaelae •

Nurakita •

Economically the colony represented an artificial linking of two distinct parts. Ocean Island which was married to the colony for convenience had a rich economy based on phosphate mining, while the economy of the other islands was based on a poor copra production. The copra islands had no hope of ever being anything much more, though they were unlikely ever to be less, while it was easily imaginable that Ocean Island's phosphate might one day be mined out and the island derelict once more. However, in the 1920's this seemed a rather remote possibility and by 1930 the facilities for stepping production up to 400,000 tons a year had been installed, though in the economic circumstances of the 1930's, 230,000 tons was the annual average. Even so, it was phosphate mining that made the colony's finances "easy." In 1936–37, no less than 35.4 per cent of the revenue of a budget of £A 68,443 was stated to come from "Consolidated contribution from the British Phosphate Commissioners" (who ran the operation at Ocean as well as that at Nauru). The item overshadowed the usual standby of colonial revenue, export and import taxes (23.9 per cent).

The Phosphate Commissioners were the colony's leading employers of labor, in the 1930's giving jobs to over 800 islanders along with about 70 Europeans and from 350 to 700 Chinese, depending on the demand for phosphate. The Chinese were, like those employed on Nauru, ostensibly from Hong Kong though really from Canton, and there was, at least in the eyes of the Chinese government, a taint of illegality of about their service overseas as indentured laborers. The islanders and the Chinese did not get along and in the middle 1920's there was a spectacular riot on Ocean which, if it did not frighten the participants, certainly frightened the administration. Beyond going to Ocean to work for the Phosphate Commissioners, all the islanders could hope for was to go from their homes, where their work was subsistence farming and copra cutting for cash, to other islands—the Phoenix group, Washington, and Fanning (but not Christmas, for it got its labor from Tahiti)—to cut copra. Copra production ran about 6500 tons a year. It was sold to native cooperative societies—cooperation took hold early in these islands—Burns Philp, W. R. Carpenter & Company, or the Chinese-Australian firm of On Chong & Company. Burns Philp had a large establishment at Betio Island, Tarawa Atoll. The companies maintained small ships that gathered copra from every copra-producing island in the colony. The only "ports" ever visited by ocean-going ships to pick up copra or drop imports were, other than Ocean, Tarawa and Butaritari in the Gilberts and Funafuti in the Ellice. Traffic with the outside world was mostly with Australia. About three-fifths of Ocean's phosphate went to Australia, one-fifth to New Zealand, the rest to Japan. Over a third of the copra went to Australia; the rest was split among Mexico, the United States, Germany, Spain, and Japan. Australia was the principal supplier of imports, with the United Kingdom ranking second, followed at a long distance by the United States, the Netherlands East Indies (oil), and Burma and India (rice). After 1934 the United Kingdom enjoyed a substantial tariff preference. There was no commercial bank in the colony. There was no public debt. In the 1930's the colony had surplus funds of over £100,000 on deposit in Australia and England.

In 1925 the imperial authorities, for reasons never made clear, removed the protectorate of the Tokelau Islands from the charge of the Gilbert and Ellice administration and put it under the jurisdiction of the governor-general of New Zealand to be administered by the New Zealanders at Apia in Samoa. There was little administering to do for the Tokelau islanders were largely self-governing. In 1937 the protectorate over the uninhabited Phoenix Islands was canceled and the islands annexed to the Gilbert and Ellice Colony. At the same time an old American interest in certain islands in the Phoenix group and in other islands in their general vicinity revived as over-ocean aviation was pioneered.

Between the wars the Gilbert and Ellice Colony had a population problem. According to the census of 1931 there were 26,518 persons living in the sixteen Gilberts and 4074 in the nine Ellice islands. Ocean Island had a population of 2609, while there were 467 persons on Fanning and Washington and around 30 transient copra-cutters in the Phoenix group. The pressure of population on resources for subsistence was felt mostly in the Gilberts; it was supposed that the Ellice could take care of some of the Gilberts' surplus of people. The Gilberts were, as compared to the Ellice, poor agriculturally, normally had less rainfall and, moreover, were subject to droughts. Athough the 1931 population of the Gilberts was only about half of an estimate of 1841, it nevertheless appeared that at the standard of living now obtaining, pressure on resources was acute. Several proposals for relieving the situation were considered but finally it was decided to colonize certain islands of the Phoenix group. The project was in the charge of Harry Maude who had been working as Native Lands Commissioner, proving native land titles (a task not finally completed until after World War II). The year of decision was 1937. Maude made a close survey of the Phoenix group in that year, officers of the Gilbert and Ellice Colony were posted to Canton and Hull islands, and the group was annexed to the Gilbert and Ellice Colony. (It had been a protectorate under the high commissioner's jurisdiction since 1889). The next year the Gilbertese settlers began to arrive. Gardner Island was chosen as the headquarters of the settlers, while Hull and Sydney were also occupied. The significance of posting an officer to Canton Island appears when the American activities are recounted.

When the Americans began to take an interest in the islands of this part of the Pacific world air routes westward across the Pacific had already been pioneered. It was now proposed to pioneer them southward from Hawaii to either Samoa or Fiji and from there to New Zealand and to Australia via New Caledonia. (For a report on the Australian view of transpacific aviation, see Chapter IV.) It was the need for landing places between Hawaii and Samoa or Fiji that drew attention to the islands just south of the equator; they could be extremely useful when airplanes in commercial service had a relatively short flying range.

The possible utility of the small and largely forgotten islands to transpacific flyers seems first to have come to notice in 1928 when the Australian, Kingsford-Smith and his American companions flew from California to Australia via Hawaii and Fiji. Kingsford-Smith learned in Honolulu that he could land on either Canton or Enderbury. Actually, he flew nonstop from Hawaii to Fiji. By 1935 the possibilities of commercial flights southward were under active exploration. On the assumption that land rather than seaplanes were going to be used, parties of young men, recruited in Hawaii, were sent to Baker, Howland, and Jarvis islands to make meteorological observations. Since the question of the national ownership of the islands might be raised, the men were often dubbed "colonists," settlement being vital to the maintenance of sovereignty in international law. The three islands and others which became involved in this business had either been discovered by American whaling captains, or had been exploited by American guano gatherers, or both, but British subjects had discovered others and had gathered guano from islands the Americans had exploited. There was therefore considerable confusion about which islands belonged to whom. The earliest American "settlers" were in the employ of the Army and were serviced by the Coast Guard, but in 1936 President Roosevelt transferred the whole problem of the islands to the Department of the Interior, the normal custodian of territories and insular possessions.

Attention was focused on Canton Island in the Phoenix group in 1937. In that year, as noted before, the British posted an officer of the Gilbert and Ellice Colony there, since it was proposed to annex the Phoenix group. In 1937, also, United States and New Zealand scientists visited the island to observe an eclipse of the sun. While there both made gestures intended to support British or American sovereignty. The next year parties of American meteorological "colonists" were established on Canton and also on nearby Enderbury. Canton was an utterly barren island, described by Sir Harry Luke as "a nudist among atolls." It was, however, a conspicuous candidate for use as a stopover point on flights southward from Hawaii and it could serve both land and seaplanes, the former by an airfield to be built on the coral, the latter by the lagoon. However, Pan-Am did not use Canton on its pioneering flights south in 1937 but rather Kingman Reef. But it proved to be Canton the Americans wanted. The British insisted it was a part of the Gilbert and Ellice Colony. The question of sovereignty was set to one side in an agreement made in April 1939 which provided for joint occupation by the Americans and the British for a period of 50 years, during which the island would be governed like a condominium. In 1940 Pan-Am built facilities for seaplanes and a hotel at Canton, thus giving it a character like that of Midway and Wake on the route westward across the Pacific. Enderbury was included in the Anglo-American agreement but was not much used and quickly dropped from sight. Canton became an important way station on the route Hawaii-Fiji-New Zealand and Fiji-New Caledonia. The expectation at the time was that the British would establish a service Australia-Canada also using Canton as a stopover. This they did not do until after World War II.

In addition to Canton and Enderbury the United States had claims to no fewer than twenty-three other islands in this part of the great ocean. These included six more islands of the Phoenix group, all of the Tokelau group, four of the Cooks (Tongareva, Manihiki, Rakahanga, Pukapuka), the so-called Line Islands (Vostok, Malden, Starbuck, and Caroline), and Christmas Island. The British maintained that they were sovereign in the Phoenix group and Christmas Island, and they claimed the Line Islands as part of the jurisdiction of the high commissioner. New Zealand claimed the Tokelaus and the Cooks. In the very loosest sense the American claims have been maintained or at least never formally abandoned. Only if one or another of the islands became of vital importance to the United States was it likely that a claim would be pushed to a showdown.

When the Protocol of 1914 with regard to the government of the condominium of the New Hebrides was finally ratified and brought into force in 1922, the feeling was that in spite of the careful elaborations— e.g., of the machinery for validating land claims—no fundamental change had been made. The islands were still to have a three-part government: a French administration for Frenchmen, persons enjoying French "protection," and foreigners who had chosen to live under French law; a British administration mostly concerned with Australian planters and traders and foreigners who had chosen to live under British law; and a condominium administration which was a kind of "natural child" of the other two. The natives were still left largely free, though they were impinged on at some points. They could not, however, be regarded as either British or French. The French metropolitan government supported its New Hebridean administration, the United Kingdom government its administration, while the condominium government was supposed to be supported from local tax revenues (four-fifths from customs). It was solvent until the depression when it developed deficits which had to be covered by the French and British.

Among the many things that went on at the Paris peace conference with reference to the islands was a French effort to get sole possession of the New Hebrides. It of course failed, not so much because of any United Kingdom opposition but rather because the Australians had not lost their ambition to gain sole control. Yet the Australians were then at an economic disadvantage vis à vis the French, and continued to be, especially during the depression. In spite of this the Australians—those at home, those trying to earn a living in the islands, and even on occasion the Commonwealth government officially—felt that they should not only stay in the New Hebrides but should by right take them over completely. (The Australian covetousness of islands was strong. There was private sentiment in Australia favoring taking over the Solomons from the British, but the government seems not to have responded warmly to this proposition.)

The French preponderance was believed to be due in largest measure to French policy but in some measure also to bad Australian and British policies, or lack of policy. There were more Frenchmen in the islands than Australians, they had more land and more plantations, were better organized economically, had a better labor supply, produced more exportable goods in greater variety, and had a superiority in marketing facilities. They did, however, have their troubles. Even in as prosperous a year as 1924 the *Société Française des Nouvelles-Hebrides* went bankrupt. Since it was the largest landholder and the vital center of French economic strength in the islands—the French preferred "grande colonization" over "petite colonization"—the Australians tried to strengthen their position and weaken the French by offering to buy the *Société's* land. This brought the French to the rescue with metropolitan and New Caledonian capital, and the *Société* was effectively reorganized and renamed the *Compagnie Française Immobilière des Nouvelles-Hebrides*. During the depression, some of the smaller companies and some of the *petite* colonists either had to affiliate with the *Compagnie* to survive or had to accept absorption into it. This was what was meant by superior French organization.

The French felt that the New Hebrides were a "colonie d'exploitation," not at all a "colonie de peuplement" for Europeans, if only because of the execrable climate: hot, humid, "enervating and on the whole unhealthy." The relatively small number of settlers was not the point; the point was the proportion of one nationality to the other. In 1923 there were 745 French and 303 British; in 1928, 842 French and 228 British; in 1930, 950 French and 232 British; in 1935, 731 French and 178 British; in 1939, 687 French and 218 British. With regard to land, with title confirmed or simply claimed, the French had an even greater preponderance. When the courts confirmed 282 out of the thousand claims outstanding, mostly on the island of Efate, it was the French who profited most. (The Commonwealth government had a direct stake in the Australian land claims, for when Sir James Burns of Burns Philp died in 1923 it was found that he had left his claims on Efate, Epi, Aneitum, and Eromanga to the government.) The French were also responsible for most of the production and for such diversification as there was. When copra production was running from 10,000 to 12,000 tons a year they produced three-quarters of it. When cocoa was extensively planted by the French companies after World War I, notably on Espíritu Santo, the Australians did not follow suit but stayed with copra. New Hebrides became the leading cocoa producer in the Southwest Pacific between the wars. It was the French who introduced coffee just after World War I, and in 1931 received very important encouragement from the French government. The Australians did not follow suit. As long as the cotton boom of World War I lasted, it was the French *petite* colonists who profited, not the Australians. The French grew all the maize. They produced the tobacco so necessary in dealings with the natives.

The rather difficult labor situation was argued to favor the French in spite of their greater needs. The British recruitment and employment regulations were rigid and exacting, while the French regulations were much looser and, moreover, the French were tolerant of illegal practices such as selling hard liquor to the natives. (The French small traders were blamed by the British for selling liquor; the French came to blame the Chinese.) Moreover, the French labor problem was greatly eased when in 1921 they could import indentured Asian labor, on which from 1925 they became wholly dependent. The British were forbidden to employ Asians, allegedly because of the critical representations of the Commonwealth government. In 1923 the French were using 3500 natives and 882 Asians, while the Australians employed 804 natives. Thereafter, the French turned wholly to Asians and in 1928 had an Asian labor force of 5540. The depression forced them to repatriate most of their Asians and to work once again with a mixed labor force. In 1934 the Asians were down to 822, but the number of natives employed had risen from none at all to 900. By 1938 the French were employing 2023 Asians and 697 natives. In that year the Australians were down to 75 natives, one-third indentured, two-thirds casual free workers. The French Asian workers were almost all Tonkinese recruited from what was to become North Vietnam, but there was a tiny minority of Javanese. In the 1920's the French also brought in some indentured Chinese and Japanese artisans. When their indentures ran out, these people became not only free artisans but market-gardeners and petty storekeepers. It was not the intent to let the Vietnamese settle down but rigorously to repatriate them. The war made this impossible.

No census of the natives was undertaken between the wars but it was estimated that they numbered between 40,000 and 60,000, of whom perhaps half were living on five islands: Malekula, Espíritu Santo, Pentecost, Tanna, and Aoba. It was still commonly believed that they were declining in numbers, but there was evidence that they were increasing on Tanna. However, health conditions were not good and during these years they suffered epidemics of measles and dysentery. With help from the Rockefeller Foundation the condominium government made some progress in health services to the natives. Graduate native medical practitioners from the Suva school were employed and some New Hebrideans were sent to Suva for training. Scattered through the islands were some quite good hospitals run either by missionaries or the French and British governments. Native education, however, was still in the hands of the missionaries; there was only one government school and it was for Europeans, not natives. The most effective mission was the Presbyterian, with the Church of England Melanesian Mission and the Roman Catholic missions the runners-up. The degree to which the natives were affected by European contact depended on their place of residence. The natives of the interiors of the islands were reckoned to be "wilder" than the coastal natives anywhere and the wildest were believed to be in the interior of Malekula. It was thought that their subsistence economy amply fed the natives in normal times and that they were able to satisfy their acquired needs for European goods—for example, tobacco—by production for market. That is why they didn't have to work for Europeans. Native market production was mostly a matter of copra of which they were reckoned to supply one-sixth, but they were also the suppliers of shell, *bêche-de-mer,* and sandalwood. While the natives were little involved in the European economy it was important to them and if they were going to progress the New Hebrideans, like the other island peoples, would presumably have to get into the market more and more. In view of the gyrations of prices during the depression this was a rather disconcerting conclusion. That the New Hebridean natives were restless throughout these years was shown by their active interest in "cargo cults."

An anti-European, procargo movement known as the Naked Cult sprang up on Espíritu Santo in the late 1920's and, although supposed to have been suppressed by the shelling of the bush by an Australian cruiser, arrests, and jailings, it again rose up in 1937. In 1940 the John Frum cult, something of a classic example of the anti-European cargo cult, came to notice on Tanna. It continued to trouble the waters, native and European, into the postwar period.

The export-import trades, which were of course closely to be associated with shipping and storekeeping, provided an arena for French-British rivalry. In overseas shipping the principal French company was *Messageries Maritimes* which maintained a service from France via the Panama Canal to the Pacific colonies, with Nouméa in New Caledonia the terminal point (as it was also the commercial focus of the French in the New Hebrides); it also maintained a service from Papeete via Nouméa and the New Hebrides to French Indochina. The Australian rival was Burns Philp which, however, could not offer a direct service to Europe but only to Sydney where goods, passengers, and mail had to be transshipped. Burns Philp, however, did more than *Messageries Maritimes* with regard to interisland service. Its French rival here was the Ballande company of New Caledonia, also the chief French trader in the islands. Burns Philp was, of course, a trader as well as shipping firm, but comparatively little New Hebridean produce went to Sydney. The commercial strength of the Australians was as suppliers of imports, notably temperate-climate foodstuffs. During the depression the Japanese cut deeply into the import trade, particularly the textile and miscellaneous aspects. The natural disposition of the French producers to send their goods to a French market was encouraged by the fact that their colonial produce was given preference when imported into France and by such special inducements as the premium on coffee. But the natural disposition of the Australians to send their goods to the British market was inhibited by the United Kingdom refusal to give preference to goods originating in the condominium. Therefore, since it was French practice to regard New Hebrides produce consigned to France by French merchants in French ships as qualifying for French preference, a good deal of Australian-origin produce found its way to France. The port of entry for the New Hebrides was Vila on Efate, also the seat of the governments, the leading trading center, the place of residence of some six hundred-odd Europeans, French and British, the largest concentration of Chinese and Japanese—and eventually Vietnamese—and the place from which radiated the strongest European influence on the natives. As a port, however, it was curiously underdeveloped, lacking even a wharf able to accommodate ocean-going vessels.

The truth of the New Caledonian axiom, *Quand la mine va, tout va,* was conclusively demonstrated between the wars. After World War I during which the great handicap of distance had practically canceled out the active demand in the world markets for New Caledonia's minerals, and after the short depression of the early 1920's when demand in the world markets was slack, the mines went well until 1930 when the Great Depression began. By 1935, however, there was a revival of demand caused in largest part by the competition for minerals necessary for war. On the fall of France in June 1940 there was an economic and political crisis which, with some assistance from Australia, the New Caledonians resolved in favor of De Gaulle.

It is an allegation of French writers on colonial questions that, while between the wars the French had a great plenty of colonial territory, they were short of creative ideas about what to do with the colonies. In the middle 1920's it was the verdict of one student that the Pacific island colonies were the most "sterile" of all. It was odd, therefore, that one of the two or three French leaders who did something about colonial affairs chose to address himself to the situation in the Pacific colonies. This was Albert Sarraut, at various times governor-general of French Indochina, minister of Colonies, and premier, who in 1923 published *La Mise en valeur des colonies française* in which he advocated shifting the emphasis from the ancient concept of assimilation to a new concept, association. While he was governor-general of Indochina, Sarraut proposed a policy of bringing the resources of Indochina to the service of the somewhat lethargic Pacific island colonies. The relation, he thought, could be cemented securely by capital investment and trade. Although from about 1923 this was tried, it did not work out satisfactorily. The Banque de l'Indochine continued to be the only bank operating in the Pacific island colonies, but it did not bring much capital to bear upon their production. As a matter of fact, the agriculturalists and the commercial people found "credit" a constant problem in spite of the presence of the Banque, while the New Caledonian mines, which absorbed a good deal of capital in the good years, either drew it from their overseas French connections or obtained it from British, Australian, Japanese, or German sources. The government-subsidized steamship company *Messageries Maritimes* established a service from Papeete via Nouméa and Vila to Saigon, but the bulk of the trade continued to go via the Panama Canal to France. The most significant contribution of Indochina to the French islands continued to be the provision of indentured Tonkinese laborers, though perhaps something can be made of the fact that wireless communication between Papeete, Nouméa, and Paris was routed via Saigon.

The production of the premier New Caledonian mineral, nickel, continued at about the level already achieved in 1912 until 1930—that is, 5000 to 7000 tons per annum. In 1930 it faltered under the impact of the depression, and in 1931 the interests of *Société le Nickel* and the *Société Calédonienne Minière* (founded 1902) were amalgamated. In 1935 the Germans and the Japanese entered the nickel market and put some capital into mines. Their interest was not in the matte which the French produced—they had begun the electrification of their smelter at Nouméa in 1928 when hydroelectricity became available from Yaté. The Germans and Japanese were interested in buying and exporting low grade ore which the French were not technologically able to use, for the Germans had invented a technique which permitted the economical recovery of the nickel from such ore and the Japanese had the use of it on license. The expansion of nickel exports was therefore a matter of the expansion of the exports of ore. The French were complacent about their technological backwardness and did nothing to modernize their technique at this time.

Second in importance to nickel was chrome, for which the United States was the chief market. As New Caledonia had lost its world leadership in nickel production to Canada early in the century, so in 1921 it lost its preeminence in chrome production to Southern Rhodesia. Chrome mining was dominated by two French companies, *Tiebaghi* and *Société Chimique du Chrome,* the former having a close relation with the world chrome cartel which had its headquarters in London. There was some British money directly in New Caledonian chrome and in the late 1930's some Australian mining money was invested in it. The Japanese were not much interested in New Caledonian chrome, for they drew supplies from the Philippines, but the Germans bought some in the late 1930's. The Japanese were, however, interested in New Caledonia's iron ore. In the late 1930's they provided the capital for a company with a "front" of French directors to develop iron ore mines in the south of the colony, complete with a modern port and ore-loading facilities for the Japanese ships that would take the ore to Japan. However, as production did not commence until 1939, the Japanese got little benefit from this undertaking. After the depression, these three were the only minerals under exploitation immediately before war broke out.

During the 1920's and 1930's the French realized that whatever might be the future of minerals, the future of agriculture was problematical. It was tending to become concentrated on copra and coffee. Cotton, which had enjoyed a boom during the war and which in 1926 had obtained a subsidy from the taxes levied on foreign cottons entering France, gradually come to nothing in the 1930's. The depression practically destroyed the export market for canned beef. The pastoralists became dependent on the domestic fresh beef trade and what canned beef could be sold in the New Hebrides. Copra production had long been more of a native than a European undertaking, and the situation between the wars confirmed it. From about 1930 the authorities began to encourage the natives to grow coffee, and in the late 1930's the European coffee growers began to rent out their plantations to natives or, alternatively, to Asiatic farmers. This turned the "colons" into landlords of sharecroppers. The usual arrangement with natives was for a 50-50 sharing of the crop, but with Asiatics the Europeans arranged a one-third, two-thirds division. However, the Europeans continued to dominate coffee production and to control the export trade in it. Europeans dependent on anything but coffee found it exceedingly difficult to make a living and had to supplement farming with wage labor.

While metropolitan France continued as largest taker of exports and supplier of imports, its position had to be supported by "preference" for colonial goods at French ports, a premium on New Caledonian coffee, and the manipulation of the New Caledonian tariff to favor French over foreign suppliers, as well as the payment of a subsidy to *Messageries Maritimes* from 1923 to carry the goods to and from the Pacific colonies. While the theoreticians argued that this system was good for both France and the colonies, and in truth many colonial producers only survived by virtue of favors received, the New Caledonians were not entirely convinced. They therefore strove for autonomy with regard to decisions about the New Caledonian tariff, thinking particularly of their trade relations within their geographical area, especially with Australia. In 1928 they gained a measure of autonomy, but New Caledonian decisions remained subject to a Paris veto. Trade with the Australians was important because they were the favored suppliers of temperate-climate foodstuffs and coal, second only to metropolitan France. However, the Australian relation to New Caledonia was like its relation to so many of the island groups: more imports were supplied than exports were taken away. The French alleged that the quantities bought were much lower than they should be because the Australian tariff operated to impede imports from New Caledonia. A feature of the New Caledonian trade situation in the late 1930's was the rapid rise of imports from Japan.

During these years the European population remained practically static. It was 16,794 in 1921 and about 17,000 in 1940. The most significant change was in the internal distribution of the Europeans. More Europeans choose to reside at Nouméa, and in 1936 it was found for the first time that there were more Europeans there than in the bush. This tendency increased until in 1940 of the 17,000 in the colony, 10,000 were living in Nouméa. The natives were believed by 1921 to have stabilized, but did not increase perceptibly up to the war. However, the number of native *assimilés* increased considerably during the 1920's and 1930's. There is no record of native unrest in these years, but assimilation was sure to prelude changes in the native's political situation. The number of Asiatics under indenture or free settlers—chiefly Tonkinese (Vietnamese) and Javanese (Indonesians)—fluctuated with the state of mining. The Japanese group was practically static, as also was the small Indian group. During the depression large numbers of indentured laborers were repatriated and not replaced. In 1921 there were 2098 Javanese and 1032 Tonkinese in the country; in 1929, 7602 Javanese and 6933 Tonkinese, while in 1937 there were 4510 Javanese and 2356 Tonkinese. It was these latter who were caught in the country by the war.

Except for the money Governor Guyon spent on them to fight the depression, education and public health changed little between the wars. Guyon spent more money on roads and port works. The government system of elementary education for Europeans and natives was maintained, but no attempt was made to take over the missionary schools. Nouméa continued to have the only secondary school in the French Pacific colonies, the Collège La Pérouse. New Caledonia was one of the few Pacific colonies in which the Rockefeller influence in health affairs was not felt at all. The structure of government was static and in effect had been since 1885. The permanent residents had but a small voice in it. This concealed from the French that the ideas of the local people and those of the metropolitan bureaucrats sent to rule over them were diverging more and more. Granting that the circumstances were entirely exceptional, it is nevertheless correct to say that this was dramatically demonstrated in 1940.

The Wallis and Futuna islands continued to be a curiously anomalous French colony in that it was ruled by its own elite. The most important change that occurred there was that Burns Philp sold its trading interest in copra and shell to a French concern. Burns Philp had attached the colony to Fiji commercially; the French successors returned it to New Caledonia. Population pressure was building up but it had not yet caused any extensive emigration in search of employment. When it came after the war, the movement was to the New Hebrides and New Caledonia.

It was the official view that the situation in New Zealand's Cook Islands was satisfactory during the 1920's and 1930's, but ex post facto it became apparent that difficulties began to develop which by 1945 were to be the causes of economic and political unrest. The Cook Islands were, it will be recalled, an integral part of New Zealand, though administered like a colony. They were not homogeneous in character but an artificial politi-

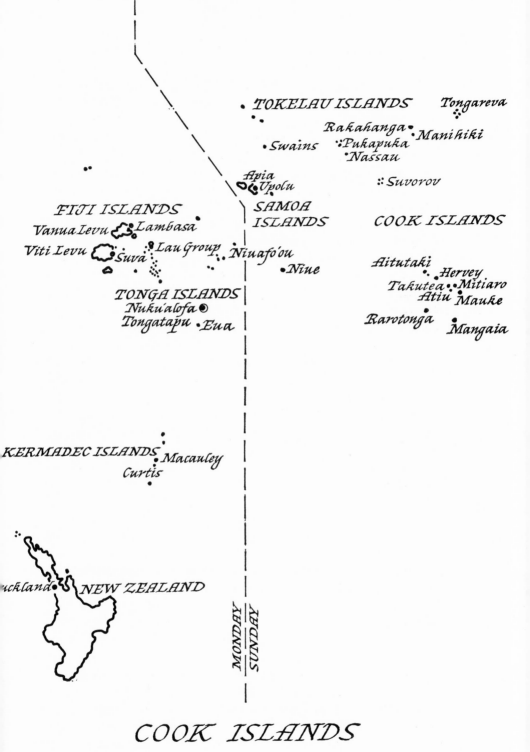

COOK ISLANDS

cal creation. The volcanic southern islands had the most people and resources, the northern coral islands had few people and very limited resources, while Niue, the largest single island, was kept a little apart from the rest. From 1915 the Cooks were governed under the provisions of the Cook Islands Act of that year, for the act of 1901 had fallen into desuetude by the time of World War I. The 1915 Act put ultimate authority in the hands of a New Zealand cabinet minister who was represented in Rarotonga by a resident commissioner and on the other islands, save Niue, by resident agents. The local councils of residents were carried over from earlier times—they were of native origin, manned by nominated Europeans and native *ariki;* but the 1915 Act allowed them only limited powers. Niue was within this scheme but had a special resident commissioner of its own. In 1932, however, it was transferred from the care of the minister in charge of the Cooks to the minister for External Affairs, though it is not clear why. The Cook Islands administrators believed that New Zealanders had a special aptitude for dealing with Polynesians. They combined tutelage—for what was not entirely clear: independence or New Zealand citizenship?—with the tactic of marking time, known to the Maoris as *taihoa.* A New Zealand anthropologist characterized the policy as "insulating the islanders from social change by metaphorically wrapping them in cotton wool and supporting them on a mattress of pumped-in subsidies." For a time in the 1920's the Cooks were actually under a Maori minister, Sir Maui Pomare, and there were normally Maori doctors in the health service (e.g., Pomare himself at an earlier time and Te Rangi Hiroa). (See Chapter VI.) Theoretically, the administration was dependent on customs for its revenue, like most island administrations, but it was never sufficient to support the administration and its services, so the New Zealand government had to supply subsidies. The Cooks, unlike Western Samoa, failed ever to achieve viability from local revenues, and a considerable disconnection developed between the actual cost of the services and the capacity of the island economy to support them. The Cooks in effect got "welfare" without commensurate economic development.

The services were thought to be quite good, especially the health service. Education, a mixed government and missionary enterprise, was in most of the islands of the lower elementary kind, but bright boys and girls could climb a bit higher at Rarotonga, and it was possible for the best of them to go on from there to a Maori secondary school in New Zealand. Dr. Lambert examined the health situation in the 1920's at Pomare's request and pronounced it good but understaffed, though he commented on the prevalence of gonorrhea introduced, he thought, from Tahiti. While services were good, implicit difficulties were slowly arising from the growth of the population and the failure of agricultural productivity to show a general improvement as the population increased.

The population of the Cooks grew fastest from 1926 to 1936, but at the end of this burst there were indications of a fairly high rate of growth for the future. Between 1936 and 1945 the population grew by 12.18 per cent (5 per cent less than 1926–36), giving the islands 14,000 people, 12,000 in the southern islands, 96 per cent being pure Polynesians, the rest Europeans (c. 180), Chinese-native mixes (c. 135), and European-Polynesian mixes. Cook Islands agriculture was dependent on the New Zealand market, except for copra, the staple and economic dependence of the northern coral islands and very important to Niue, which had to be sold on the world market. The southern islands sent to the New Zealand market, which is to say Auckland, oranges, bananas, tomatoes, orange juice, and fresh coconuts (in descending order of value). Only the productivity of the tomato growers was satisfactory. Niue, the social services of which were comparable to those of the rest of the islands except that missionaries played a larger role in education, exported bananas, kumara (a native sweet potato), and hats and fancy baskets made from pandamus palm to Auckland; and as noted earlier in connection with Western Samoa, the Niueans left their island to work for Europeans. Although it was perfectly obvious that the population increase forecast pressure on resources for subsistence and export production, no crisis occurred during the interwar decades. In 1945, however, there was trouble because of the unionization of the casual workers and a demand by them for higher pay, while a political demand for more native participation in government was raised at the same time.

The discordance between the economic and political reality of the French Établissements and the romantic legend of "Tahiti" continued to be great. If the Établissements were, in Western terms, economically weak and politically elementary, the Tahitian legend was inexhaustibly spellbinding and in every generation drew people in search of romance. Not the least potent factor in the spell was still that figment of the eighteenth century imagination, "the natural man," or, more accurately in the Tahitian circumstances, "the natural woman." But the "natural woman" was not now the Tahitian woman, for she was indeed much as Gauguin had depicted her, but the mixed-blood woman who so often conformed in satisfyingly abundant measure to the Western ideal of face and figure. Another part of the spell was the idea that in Tahiti if anywhere life was better in that it was lived in a leisurely fashion, more insouciantly, and with more regard for the aesthetic and the pleasurable in nature and woman than for the severely practical and the inhibitingly moral, more in the feelings than the brain. By some whim of the gods many of those attracted were brain-exploiting writers who insisted on inflicting their stories on the Western reading public in selectively composed, enticingly illustrated books that contributed a very great deal to keeping the old legend virile.

Although later 1910 was selected as the approximate date on which the Polynesian—or Océanien—population ceased to decline after many decades and began to increase, because of the vagaries of census classifications it was not possible to be sure whether it was the pure Polynesians or the mixed bloods who accounted for the increase. In the Marquesas the decline of population continued until around 1930, when it began to increase. In 1926 the total population of the Établissements was 35,862; in 1931 it was 39,226. The 1931 population could be broken down as follows: Océaniens, French citizens, 21,378; Océaniens, French subjects, 11,326; Océaniens, foreign nationality, 777; Chinese, 4056; Indochinese, 319; European French citizens, 900; British (including A. and N.Z.), 301; United States citizens, 169. Most of the Europeans and Chinese lived in Papeete, while the Indochinese were concentrated on the island of Makatéa as workers in the phosphate mines. The Chinese were also to be found scattered throughout the islands as shopkeepers and some Europeans also found reasons to reject, or were compelled by economic reasons to forego, the sophistications of Papeete. The permanent population of Papeete in the 1930's was around 7000, or a little less than half the people then living on the island of Tahiti, who in turn made up about four-tenths of the inhabitants of the Établissements.

The Établissements had never been considered a "colonie de peuplement," but neither were they now a success as a "colonie d'exploitation," though they had had their moments. The Océaniens were, of course, mostly subsistence agriculturalists, but they also produced most of the copra and vanilla that was exported. The copra they traded to the Chinese shopkeepers in lots of one hundred pounds for money and commodities and it was forwarded to Papeete by the Chinese for shipment overseas. As in the other copra-producing islands, production was irregular. In 1922, 15,000 tons were exported; in 1929, 11,000, in 1933, 17,920 tons, so even at best the Établissements were not a major producer even among the Pacific islands. The export quantities of vanilla varied also, ranging from 172 tons in 1922 to 80 tons in 1929 and 529 in 1933. The Chinese had an important role in the vanilla trade also. The gathering of shell, which was in the hands of the Océaniens of the Tuamotu Archipelago, varied a good deal also, from 1333 tons in 1924 to 219 tons in 1933. Other exports of appreciable value included coffee, rum made from locally produced sugar (although the islands were not self-sufficient in sugar), and, of course, phosphates. By order of value the exports were going in the 1930's to France, the United States, Japan, Australia, and New Zealand, while the imports were supplied by the United States, France, Australia, New Zealand, and China. The exports to France were three times as valuable as those to the United States, but the United States surpassed France as a supplier by very little.

The large American role in the trade justified the judgment that Tahiti was of more economic interest to the United States than any other island group of the Southwest Pacific. San Francisco was the center of this trade. The Americans took most of the vanilla, not for flavoring extract but for use in perfumes, and some copra and shell. Japan ranked high as a customer because she bought quantities of phosphate, while China sold considerable quantities of goods, presumably to the Chinese importers, but bought very little indeed. Both Australia and especially New Zealand sold more than they bought. The New Zealanders also had the only regular steamship service between Papeete and North America. The Établissements, like New Caledonia, were kept within the French economic orbit by tariff preferences at the French ports and by the carrying of the goods to and from France via the Panama Canal in the subsidized ships of *Messageries Maritimes*. The Tahitians also sought tariff autonomy and in 1928 obtained it, subject to a Paris veto. The administration derived most of its revenue from levies on the export-import trade. When the budget showed deficits during the depression, they were covered by the metropolitan government which also supplied some extra money for local public works. This money was chiefly spent on the facilities at Papeete harbor. The internal retail trade, along with most of the services such as restaurants, tailor shops, etc., was more and more in the hands of the Chinese who also did a considerable amount of wholesale importing. The Océaniens did not engage in trade and they even relinquished one branch of agriculture to the Chinese, market-gardening to supply Papeete.

Although the Établissements were expected to thrive on the opening of the Panama Canal, they did not do so, and although they were involved in Sarraut's scheme for attaching the Pacific colonies to Indochina, the effects in Tahiti were minimal. Very few Indochinese ever reached the Établissements, as the population figures show, and while Papeete was the terminus of the steamship service to and from Saigon, that seems to have turned little of the trade to the west and if the Banque de l'Indochine was the sole bank in Tahiti this appears to have meant only as little or as much as that wireless messages to Paris went via Saigon.

The government maintained hospitals and a medical service to deal with the prevalent diseases: syphilis and gonorrhea, tuberculosis, typhoid fever, elephantiasis, and leprosy. The Rockefeller influence did not reach the Établissements. The government, the Protestant and Catholic missions, and the Chinese philanthropic societies all maintained schools, but the government schools were the most numerous since they were not only established in Papeete but throughout the islands. (The Océaniens were predominantly Protestant and the native pastor was an important figure in the villages.) Although there was an École Centrale in Papeete which combined an elementary and a secondary school and a teacher-training institute, the Établissements had no school as good as the Collège La Pérouse in Nouméa. All the important powers of government remained in the hands of the governor, but after 1930 experiments were made in coopting local people to give advice on economic and budgetary matters.

As compared to the light impact of World War I in the islands, World War II had an impact like that of a hurricane. The extremely heavy fighting by the Allies against the invading Japanese caused widespread destruction of property, laid heavy burdens of labor on the natives and exposed them to what appeared to be a dazzling technology with consequences not yet resolved, and caused a great loss of life. The war also opened the way to an ideological revolution which profoundly changed the attitudes of both natives and Europeans toward the policies to be pursued in the postwar period. The war in the islands cannot, of course, be properly understood outside the context of World War II in general and the war in the Pacific in particular, so what has been said elsewhere in this book about the war, including the account of how the Americans came to fight in the islands, should be brought to mind (see Chapters IV and VIII). Here, as earlier with regard to the war in Europe and the first phase of the war in the Pacific, no attempt will be made to detail the combat in the islands (see the Suggested Readings) but rather to sketch the general geography of the combat and the related ancillary activities with particular attention to the islands which were directly involved in the one respect or the other.

Although both the Australians and the New Zealanders had long regarded the islands as a protective shield against aggressors and though during the 1930's they discussed at times what should be done to make the shield effective against the Japanese, little of any great consequence was done prior to the outbreak of war in Europe in 1939, and too little after to make any great difference. From 1920 until after the outbreak of war both the Australians and New Zealanders were unable by the terms of their mandates to build fixed defenses in the Territory of New Guinea, Nauru, and Western Samoa, and from 1922 when the Washington treaty governing fixed defenses in the Pacific islands was signed, it was not legally possible to build them in any other of the Southwest Pacific islands either. How and for what short-term and long-term purposes the Japanese sought to gain control of the shield and how they were ejected from such positions as they attained is the gist of the war in the islands. The shield theory survived the war because the Japanese were repulsed in islands which were integrally sections of the shield and Australia suffered only to a limited extent from Japanese attack and New Zealand not at all.

The earliest action to make the shield effective was the extension into the islands of the Australian Navy's coastwatcher service designed to provide a more continuous watch than could be provided by sea and air patrols. The service began in 1919, originally applied only to the continental coasts, but when radio made quick communication with Melbourne possible, the service was extended to Papua, the Territory of New Guinea, and the British Solomon Islands. At the outbreak of war in Europe the coverage in the islands was "thin and spotty," especially in relation to strategic positions, often places where Europeans did not usually live. Between September and December 1939, however, the system was considerably strengthened by recruiting additional watchers, was extended to Nauru and into the New Hebrides, and reporting centers were established at Rabaul, Tulagi, Vila, Port Moresby, and Thursday Island, from whence the "intelligence" was transmitted to Townsville in Queensland (area headquarters of the Australian armed services) and to Melbourne where chiefs of staff were located. New Zealanders had also spread a coastwatcher service through the islands for which they had responsibility to supplement and support the sea and air patrols they had been maintaining—the sea patrols since the end of World War I. Their service was scattered over the islands from the sub-Antarctic Chatham, Campbell, and Auckland islands to the south of the home islands, through the Kermadecs, the Cooks, Fiji, Tonga, Western Samoa, the Tokelaus, the Phoenix group, the Line islands, the Ellice and Gilberts north to the equator, with reporting centers at Suva, Wellington, and Awarua. The coastwatchers suffered severely from the initial Japanese incursions into the islands—they were subjected to summary execution when caught— but the corps went on to perform with amazing resource and heroism in support of Allied combat operations during the war. Their conduct gave a touch of romanticism to an otherwise brutal warfare.

The coastwatcher service in its prewar phases, like the sea and air patrols, was in the nature of an "early warning" service and of no particular significance in actually repelling armed invasion or occupation. It was in providing solid defense against invasion and occupation that the Australians and New Zealanders fell down, not because of any lack of will or failure to calculate possibilities correctly, but because what means they had at their disposal were sent, first, to the war in Europe and then to the defense of Singapore and Java, the latter carried out just when, as later realized, they should have been bolstering their positions in the shield islands. It was not only that the preparations against invasion in the islands were inadequate when the Japanese struck; it was that the defensive resources of the homelands from where the defense personnel and materiél for the islands should have come were at a desperately low ebb when most needed.

The earliest concrete discussion of the defense of the islands appears to have taken place at the British-New Zealand-Australian defense conference at Wellington in mid-April 1939. At that conference it was assumed that the Australians had responsibility for New Guinea and the islands generally on the western side of the ocean, while New Zealand's attention was known to be directed to the central islands and now to Fiji specifically. Fiji's significance had been pointed out by Lord Jellicoe when he analyzed the problem of the Pacific in 1919. He designated it (*not* the Cooks) as New Zealand's "immediate outpost." At the Wellington conference New Zealand was asked to garrison Fiji to supplement the local defense forces and to develop airfields at Nandi and Nandali and seaplane facilities at Nandi also. The New Zealand troops landed at Suva and Lautoka on November 1, 1940. However, the New Zealanders were not able to establish substantial defenses on Fiji or Western Samoa. The Australians were not able to do any better in Papua, the Territory, Nauru, the British Solomons, or New Caledonia, in all of which they posted small contingents of troops, some of which were withdrawn even before the Japanese attacked.

Before the arrival of the Japanese, the principal evidences of the war's impact, aside from developments in local defense forces in some of the groups, the departure of Europeans to enlist, and the diversion of commerce into wartime channels, were the activities of German raiders in Australian waters—in the Pacific they were serviced in the Marshall Islands. The German raids involved a direct assault on only one island, Nauru, where an effort was made to bomb the phosphate works, especially the elaborate ship-loading machinery, indicating that the Germans understood the great importance of phosphate in the agricultural and pastoral industries of Australia and New Zealand. (The Japanese occupied Nauru and Ocean Island for the same reason.) The Germans also laid mines in the shipping lanes and torpedoed vessels. The mines accounted for a number of ships, including the American-flag ship "City of Rayville" off the Victorian coast and the famous old passenger ship

"Niagara" of the New Zealand-owned Australia-North America service, outside Auckland harbor.

The political upsets in the French islands on the fall of France were major political dramas on rather small stages. With pressure from Vichyites in Indochina, the administrations of New Caledonia and the Établissements tried to accommodate to Vichy. In New Caledonia the great majority of the permanent European residents supported De Gaulle and pushed their cause hard. However, the leadership to drive the Vichyites out was simply not there. It came from the New Hebrides where the French *délégué*, Henri Sautot, had early espoused De Gaulle's cause. The pro-Free French line was favored by the Menzies government in Australia, which took a hand in New Caledonian affairs when it acted to relax the economic paralysis that descended upon the colony on the fall of France by arriving at a special arrangement in support of the New Caledonian currency and banking and of the exports and imports. Politically, the Australians favored Sautot, and when he left Vila to challenge the Vichyites at Nouméa (in a Norwegian freighter), successfully as it turned out, an Australian warship stood by in support. After sending the only French warship in the Pacific from Papeete to Nouméa to support the Vichyite cause, the administration of the Établissements was challenged and toppled by the Tahitian population. The New Zealanders were the sympathetic bystanders in support of the Free French cause. This left only the tiny Wallis and Futuna colony in the hands of a Vichyite administration. It was not driven from office until after Pearl Harbor.

The Japanese first struck at the islands of the Southwest Pacific two days after Pearl Harbor when they bombed Ocean Island and from their Marshalls sent raiding parties against Makin and Tarawa atolls in the Gilberts. During the next few months they visited almost every island in the Gilberts, rounding up the few remaining Europeans—coastwatchers, administration people, and LMS missionaries—whom they took to Tarawa and executed. The Japanese stationed troops on some of the Gilberts, and built fortifications on others, notably on Betio Island, Tarawa Atoll. Most of the Europeans and some of the natives fled the Gilberts soon after the Japanese first appeared and the Europeans were evacuated to Fiji, while some of the natives, in the care of missionaries, found refuge as far away as South Australia. The Europeans of Ocean Island mostly went to Australia in February 1942. The refugee administration first set up temporary headquarters in Sydney, but in 1943, when the Americans occupied Funafuti in the Ellice preparatory to a drive through the Gilberts into the Marshalls, the administration followed and later moved to Tarawa, where a new capital for the Gilbert and Ellice Colony was built after the war. Ocean Island became a by-passed island (see below) and was not freed from the Japanese until 1945 when the Australians reoccupied the island. The Japanese moves in the Gilberts were designed to protect their positions in the "mandate" against attack from the east.

The Japanese first bombed and subsequently occupied Rabaul on January 23, 1942. The choice of Rabaul as the first place to occupy south of their mandate indicated that they fully understood its strategic importance. The question immediately arose as to what they intended to do, for from Rabaul they could move west or east in the islands. The Australians felt that the Japanese purpose was to move into New Guinea and take Port Morseby in Papua, there to mount an invasion of the Australian continent down the coast of Queensland to the heartland in the southeast. After the war it was ascertained that the Japanese did propose to invade Australia eventually, but their immediate purpose was chiefly to cut off Australia and New Zealand from the United States on the theory that if they did not do so the United States would use them to mount an offensive against the southern border of the vast area they were about to bring under control. If Australia was indeed successfully isolated it would be left to wither away and only in the ultimate invaded. The Japanese seem not to have thought much about New Zealand's ultimate fate, at least not in terms of invasion. When they arrived at Rabaul the Japanese regarded themselves as definitely "on schedule" with regard to their conquests and prepared to embark on the plan for isolating Australia. Ex post facto, what they did and even more what they tried to do represented an "over-extension" of a fatal character. They proposed to take Port Moresby, from where they could dominate the Queensland coast and push east into the Solomons, and then on to Samoa and Fiji farther east and to the New Hebrides and New Caledonia to the south. The Japanese never got to Port Moresby, however, and they were not able to maintain the position they occupied in the Solomons.

The first task of the Americans vis à vis the islands was to keep open communications between North America and Australia and New Zealand, and thus to prevent the Japanese from executing their plan for gaining mastery of the islands. The next step was not only to stop Japanese progress in the islands, but if possible to begin the lengthy task of pushing them back to their homeland. However, what kind of war could be fought in the islands depended on how, and how rigidly, the strategy of "Hitler First" was to be pursued (see Chapter IV). In the event, General MacArthur and Admiral King were successful in arguing for far more latitude for an aggressive warfare on the Japanese than the

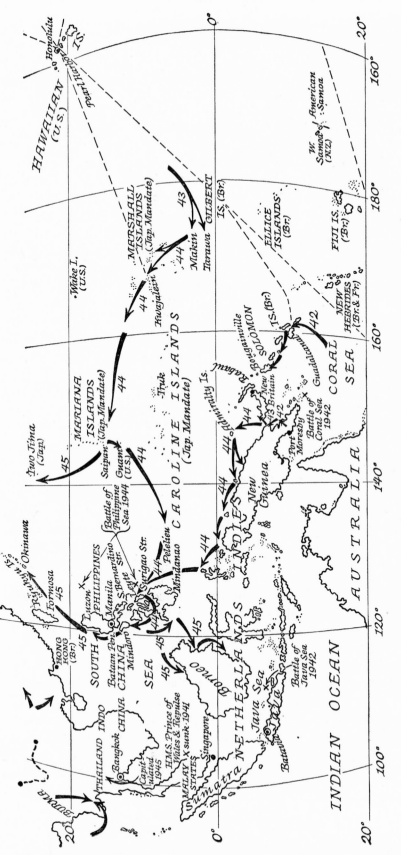

WORLD WAR II IN THE ISLANDS

planners provided for. In the first phase of the fighting in the islands the announced objective of both General MacArthur and the Navy's leaders was the taking of Rabaul. It is one of the ironies of the war that after establishing that the recapture of Rabaul was vital, it was by-passed and other ways north were pursued.

In guaranteeing communications from North America, either from the West Coast direct or via or from Hawaii or from the East Coast via the Panama Canal, numerous islands were occupied and used by the Americans. While a few of the occupied islands were used only for communications, some were used in several ways, such as training grounds for island warfare, assembly places prior to dispatch to the fighting front, rest areas for battle-weary troops, for fueling and servicing ships and planes, and so on. Among the islands occupied for these purposes were Canton, Western Samoa, American Samoa, Tonga, Fiji, several islands in the Cooks, Bora Bora in the Établissements, New Caledonia (a major command post of the Navy), and islands in the New Hebrides as advanced air and naval posts, notably Efate and Espíritu Santo. The actual fighting was done in the British Solomons, in the Territory of New Guinea, in Papua, in Dutch New Guinea, in the Gilberts, and in the Japanese mandated islands.

Although the Japanese had been made aware of the Allied presence earlier, the first significant battle between the Allied forces and the Japanese in the Southwest Pacific was the naval battle of the Coral Sea. This arose from an effort by the Japanese to move an invasion force by ship from Rabaul through the Coral Sea for an assault on Port Moresby. Although in many respects inconclusive, the Battle of the Coral Sea, May 3–8, 1942, not only prevented the Japanese from executing their plan but, in combination with other factors, drove them from the Coral Sea for the rest of the war. It became the symbolic key to Allied victory and as such is commemorated annually by Australians. However, in relation to the war on the Japanese as a whole, it was far less important than the Battle of Midway in early June. The Coral Sea closed to them, the Japanese were forced to try to reach Port Moresby overland via the Kokoda trail across the Owen Stanley Range. This attempt was stopped by the Australians just short of the town in a campaign fantastic in its difficulties in the extraordinarily jumbled mountains. Meanwhile, Admiral King had made the decision to hit the Japanese in the Solomons, knowing that a Japanese success there would open the way to Samoa, Fiji, the New Hebrides, and New Caledonia, while an American success would breach the way to the north via Rabaul. The Japanese provided the decision of just where to strike by taking Tulagi and beginning to build an airfield on Guadalcanal. The Americans therefore aimed to place a ground force on Guadalcanal to take over the airfield. From the American success in doing just that arose a long series of battles on land, sea, and in the air in which the Americans operated from Fiji, New Zealand, New Caledonia, and the New Hebrides and the Japanese from Rabaul. Assisted by Australian and New Zealand ships and planes and small contingents of New Zealand and Fijian troops, the Americans in the end forced the Japanese to evacuate Guadalcanal, signalizing the death of their larger ambitions in the islands. There then began a long climb "up" the Solomons toward, but not quite to, Rabaul. In New Guinea, American and Australian troops, ships, and planes fought a long series of battles from south to north in Papua and then by amphibious leap-frogging westward along the north coast of the island into Dutch New Guinea at Hollandia. Only tentative gestures were made toward an invasion of New Britain aimed at Rabaul, but important sea-air battles were fought to gain dominance of the waters around New Guinea. Rabaul was thus not frontally assaulted by the forces operating in the Solomons or New Guinea, but rather was isolated and by-passed. From New Guinea, MacArthur proposed to go north via the Admiralty Islands, in the course of which operation a great naval base was built at Manus Island. To relieve the Japanese pressure on MacArthur from the east, the American Navy undertook an operation into the Gilberts, of which the most famous single action was the battle for Tarawa, and after feinting toward the Japanese strongholds in the mandate, as they were then believed to be, swerved north to gain possession of islands from which the main Japanese islands could be bombed. While the ultimate objective of all these operations was of course the main Japanese islands, where alone, it was believed, the final decision could be reached, MacArthur had a peculiarly personal interest in the relief of the Philippines—"I shall return." When he left Australian territory, MacArthur left his Australian troops behind to deal with the numerous Japanese left behind in various islands, including an estimated 100,000 at Rabaul. The Australians thus fought numerous dirty battles and were still at their task when the war ended in 1945. While they recognized that what they had to do was indispensable, they would have much preferred the glory that attached itself to the liberation of the Philippines (in which units of the Australian Navy participated). However, the Australian forces eventually did go north to eject the Japanese from Dutch and British Borneo. There was active warfare in the islands for forty-four months.

If fighting, other military activities, and the disruption of normal economic life had been the whole of the story of World War II in the islands, the task in the postwar period would have been to repair the destruction and generally restore the *status quo ante bellum*. There were those who saw the task in essentially these terms, but they reckoned without the fact that war pushed men into new predicaments quite unanticipated by those who direct and fight the war and conjure up a vision of the ends it is allegedly going to achieve. Therefore, repairing the damage and disruption of war in the islands, though an important and often laborious undertaking, was in effect a short-term enterprise. The greater task was to deal creatively with ideas about the future of the natives and of the islands politically, which were deliberately imported into island affairs or forced upon the political masters of the islands by men and events overseas. The ideas not only had a profound effect on the Europeans in charge, but also on the natives, and in the early 1960's it was by no means clear where either was being carried. The response to the ideas was both accommodating and resistive, both welcoming and disdainful, both euphoric and depressive, both wise and irresponsible, especially among the Europeans, some of whom saw in the changes little but the beginning of the end of their traditional roles in island affairs—a fact they deeply resented.

While in relation to specific situations in the islands the new ideas and consequent actions were many and various, most of them could be comprehended under the rubric "native paramountcy." "Native paramountcy" could, it was clear from historical experience, allow a colonial-type accommodation between the Europeans and the natives reasonably satisfactory to both parties, but it could also lead to a revival of the old "native sovereignty" or, in contemporary terms, political independence. Although the pressures in favor of political independence as the necessary ultimate goal began to be exerted in the islands right after the war, both from sources within and outside the region, the vast decolonization that developed in Africa and Asia deflected attention from the Southwest Pacific and so it was generally anticipated that the Southwest Pacific would feel the full strength of the anticolonial pressure only late in the 1960's. It was paradoxical that, as the natives were to be purposefully moved toward freedom to be themselves, it was argued that this absolutely required that their Europeanization be speeded up. By an accident of world circumstances, the Southwest Pacific promised to be the stage on which the last act of the extraordinary drama of decolonization would be played.

Although discussion of the postwar future in the islands that forecast radical change appears to have begun as early as 1942 when the implications of the Atlantic Charter were examined, and a flow of pamphlets began the following year, the first major indication at the level of government that the *status quo ante bellum* was not going to be purposefully restored was the way in which the question of the islands was handled in the Australia-New Zealand agreement of 1944, while the second major indication was the line taken with regard to the Trusteeship Council of the United Nations by the New Zealanders and the Australians in collaboration at the San Francisco meeting to write the Charter the following year. (See Chapters IV and VIII.) The propositions in the Agreement with regard to the islands were of a mixed character, for in addition to a declaration of a decidedly "development and welfare" nature, there were traditionalist declarations with regard to the proposed role of the islands in regional defense and prohibitory declarations with regard to the retention of island bases obviously aimed at the United States.

After San Francisco, however, it was entirely clear that the Labor governments of Australia and New Zealand had committed themselves not only to development and welfare but also to native paramountcy and, as the ultimate objective, political independence. However, this was not to say that future conservative governments of these countries would not take a different line and, indeed, when they came to power in late 1949, they deliberately let a lot of the steam out of their predecessors' ideas. The Labor governments were, of course, far from controlling all of the Southwest Pacific islands and native peoples, though they did control a high percentage of both Melanesians and Polynesians, and their policy declarations with regard to the islands as a whole paid careful heed to the sovereignty of other powers. Essentially what they sought as a way of advancing their ideas was to commit all the powers holding islands in the Southwest Pacific—besides themselves the British, the French, the Americans and the Dutch—to a cooperative program of research and counsel below the level of political and economic decision-making with regard to health and economic and social development. Such a venture was given institutional form at Canberra in 1947 when the South Pacific Commission was agreed on; it began its work the following year with a headquarters in Nouméa. The Australian government committed itself to the largest proportion of the cost (30 per cent), while New Zealand guaranteed 15 per cent, and the other and wealthier members divided up the rest. The policy positions of all the governments involved in the Commission were favorable to the development and welfare emphasis. The British development and welfare approach, derived from the Act of 1940, had reached Fiji by 1943 (ignoring the far less significant impact it had had in the early 1930's from the British act of 1929). But no one wanted to relinquish any power of political and economic decision in their islands, least of all the Australians under Dr. Evatt. The regional precedents for the Commission were not related to political ideas, but such inter-administration cooperative activity as the common use of the

Central Medical School at Suva by the British, the New Zealanders, the Americans, the Tongans, and (about this time) the Australians (but not the French or the Dutch). The extra-regional precedent was probably the Anglo-American Caribbean Commission of 1942, which had become the more comprehensively cooperative Caribbean Commission in 1946. The United States joined the SPC as an original member on the basis of its possession of American Samoa. In 1951 it brought its Trust Territory of the Pacific Islands (the ex-Japanese mandate) within the scope of the Commission, once again affirming the now historic association of these islands north of the equator with the islands to the south of it. It is interesting to note that the Americans, the British, the French, and the Dutch were members of both the SPC and the Caribbean Commission. The SPC became the coordinating body for the work of many international organizations working in the Southwest Pacific islands, for example, the World Health Organization which came to play a role in the islands not unlike that of the Rockefeller Foundation in the 1920's and 1930's. Aside from the fact that the SPC could not deal with its problems other than regionally, it consciously cultivated regional sentiment through conferences of native leaders of the island groups.

The political problem of the islands was something quite else again, whether with regard to reducing the political fragmentation of the islands by federal, pseudo-federal, or cooperative arrangements or by the transfer of sovereignty from one government to another or with regard to granting either local self-government or political independence. Historically, of course, the Australians and New Zealanders had sought to avoid the political fragmentation by advocating that all—or as many as possible—of the groups be brought under British sovereignty, but after the frustration of this rather chauvinistic proposal by irreversible events and British tolerance of foreigners, a turn had been made to the possible uses of federation. Who first thought of reducing political fragmentation by federating some of the islands is unclear, but Prime Minister Richard Seddon of New Zealand gave it serious thought, specifically with regard to joining Fiji and New Zealand, though less to solve the island political problem than to aggrandize New Zealand. Seddon was frustrated, even though he commanded some popular support in Fiji, by the resolute opposition of the British. (See Chapter IX.) After World War II there was a revival of the federation idea, married to the political independence proposal, when it was suggested that New Guinea, possibly both Australian and Dutch New Guinea, be joined with the British Solomon Islands and possibly the New Hebrides to form a Melanesian Federation as an independent state. In the form suggested this was an impossible proposal, but the idea did have some influence on thinking about the islands. The idea of transfer of sovereignty appears to have sprung up in the wake of the changes made in the control of islands as a result of the German expulsion in World War I. The Australians at that time believed that it would be all to the good if, now that the Germans had been eliminated, British-held islands were redistributed between Australia and New Zealand. They were particularly interested in obtaining the Solomon Islands. Also, though the political context was different, the Australians sought sole possession of the New Hebrides. Allegedly, Dr. Evatt sought to incorporate the transfer of sovereignty idea into the Australia-New Zealand Agreement of 1944, again with the objective of having the British islands distributed between Australia and New Zealand.

Far less drastic than either federation or transfer of sovereignty was the idea of inter-administration cooperation to achieve uniformity of practice, or exchange of information, or whatever. This idea was promoted by persons variously interested in the islands after World War I in order to conquer the disabilities of political fragmentation. The most forceful exponent of the approach was R. W. Robson, editor of *Pacific Islands Monthly*. As World War II approached, there was a marked increase in such proposals, either covering one matter of supposed common interest or several, from the circulation of international economic intelligence on the copra trade to quarantine regulations, missionary activities, and an inter-library loan service. However, inter-administration cooperation seems rarely to have gone beyond the exchange of certain information about health matters, except within the high commission territories where an interchange among several nominally separate administrations was relatively easy.

But for all the number of the proposals and the sound logic of some of them, the effect on the islands administrations was very small at the political decision-making level. And although it is difficult to see how many of the problems confronting the islands are ever going to be solved short of dealing with them regionally (and including Australia and New Zealand in the region), at the level of political and economic decision-making, the island administrations have continued to think and decide almost exclusively within the compass of their own island groups, while the home governments have directed their attention in largest part only to their own islands. However, New Zealand has a better record than Australia for working across political boundaries, for example, with regard to health, to defense, civil aviation, and education in Fiji, and education in Tonga. Regional thinking, however, seems largely confined to the big trading concerns, certain heavy investors, and the South Pacific Commission personnel. The political future of each island group is carefully kept in the hands of the several metropolitan powers acting separately, subject to whatever influence the native people can exert and the pressures flowing from the metropolitan publics and from overseas.

It has been made abundantly clear earlier that the island groups differed widely in character and stage of economic development. They had differed greatly in respect to economic viability in terms of the expenditure thought adequate up to World War II, and it was believed that none could generate the revenue needed to support the probable "development and welfare" expenditures. The proportion of the European population to the native population differed as did the proportion of non-European peoples to natives. Even the significance of European economic activity was very different in the different groups. The islands differed in size and in resources available for the support of the people, let alone welfare developments. Wisdom about one group could be folly about another. There were, most relevant here, differences between groups with regard to the strength of the native wish for independence as against local self-government but continued colonial status or similar relation with a metropolitan power. Native opinion, indeed, was an amorphous thing, though often more in the eye of the beholder than in actuality, but it did range from support of the idea of freedom by the fantastical ideological fumblings of "cargo cults" to the sophisticated politics of the Western Samoans and the little less sophisticated politics of rejection of the idea by the Fijians.

Although in European terms native paramountcy and independence were politico-moral conceptions of great potency, it was perfectly obvious that neither could be fully operative if their economic bases were inadequate. Without sound and growing economies the island societies could not be expected adequately to support the new politico-moral positions granted to them or won by them. The economic problem was complicated by the fact that to advance on the politico-moral front, it was adjudged necessary for the home governments to pour subsidies into the colonies in support of economic development and social advancement. Colonies which had not before World War II received regular subsidies were now granted them, and those which had, now received larger subventions. Unless it was possible to achieve a rate of growth and a rise in local revenues that would overtake the increased spending to support the new structure of government the country would be more dependent on external economic support than ever, in spite of the achievement of political independence. In fact, many publicists of the colonial powers questioned whether they could ever be free of the moral obligation to sustain ex-colonies economically. In situations where self-support at an acceptable standard of life seemed impossible even in the long run, it came to be doubted that political decolonization was the answer. However, this view ran head-on into that of the people who had made a fetish of political freedom.

The economic problem was complicated almost in proportion to the extent to which the natives remained involved in their traditional subsistence economies or, conversely, it was eased to the extent to which they engaged in production for market. While in earlier years the extent to which the people had participated in the market economy was a criterion of native advancement, after World War II it became a matter of critical importance. Great efforts had to be made to expand and diversify their production for market. In islands where population pressure was building up, the increase in productivity had to be great enough to surpass the rate of growth of the population, making the task one of great difficulty. When the need was felt for special means for facilitating native participation in the market economy, the choice was normally selling and buying cooperatives which had, as a matter of fact, begun to creep into the islands between the great wars, or as in an advanced situation like Tonga, to pass the task of selling the produce into the hands of the government. Yet painfully little was known about how to induce the natives, particularly natives only lately in contact with Europeans, to enter the market economy, in spite of many years of effort. Where the old subsistence economy was still predominant, therefore, the task became to increase productivity within the subsistence context to raise the general economic level. Normally the reliance for movement into the market was the hope that the native leaders, usually those with the longest and most intimate contacts with the Europeans, would more and more encourage the laggards forward. Absence of understanding of Western economic processes was widespread and truly grotesque misapprehension was at the bottom of the "cargo cults."

However, it was obviously pointless to stimulate native production of any kind unless a market was in fact there and prices were fairly consistently remunerative. Once the supported and stabilized markets represented by British and French bulk purchasing disappeared in the late 1950's the island producers once more inherited the disabilities and insecurities of producers of primary produce for the world market everywhere. Though tropical agriculture was the basic industry in all the islands, except New Caledonia, and progress in it everywhere the basic concern, there was still hope in the Melanesian islands that mining would figure largely in the economic future, that fishing and canning of fish for the export market could be developed, that timber-getting could be expanded, that processing of native export produce could be moved a step or two upward and even that in some of the islands manufacturing could be established or increased in range and volume. While all of these policies and possibilities had historical roots, the change in political ends made it now so urgent to get forward with them that they had the appearance of new problems altogether. And implicit all along the line was that the natives must be further Europeanized.

With regard to the services and native participation in government there was nothing absolutely new either in most island colonies. It had long been understood, even if the understanding had been but imperfectly acted on, that if the natives were, first, to survive the contact with the West, second, to replace and increase their numbers, and, finally, enter the twentieth century, as the phrase was, in full possession of their physical powers, the problem of native health was a challenge that simply had to be met. How the challenge had been taken up was one of our themes above. The record was very uneven between island groups. In the postwar years the health question had a new urgency and therefore a steep rise in expenditures on health services under the rubric welfare occurred. Yet as late as 1958, an administrator of Papua-New Guinea emphasized that the native health problem still underlay all the problems, economic and political alike.

In the postwar predicament, the urgency of vast improvements in education was patent but of the two fundamental services, the past record in education was least impressive. In 1945 the education available to natives was nowhere regarded as adequate, especially in the light of the new ends of administration then about to be pursued. In some of the groups where political independence could be regarded as a possible end, the educational record was very poor indeed. Obviously, education for natives could not be regarded and handled as a simple proposition to be conceived largely as applying the lessons of metropolitan experience in the colonies. The educational needs of the natives were multiple. The vast majority of the populations required, first, literacy, probably in the language of the metropolitan country as well as the native *lingua franca;* second, since economic progress was a *sine qua non,* there was much need for education in economics and vocations; and, third, since self-management and self-government were in view, higher education had to be made available to the future leaders. However, it had also to be recognized that if these people were educated but the opportunities commensurate with their training and understanding failed to appear, a body of disemployed "intellectuals" would constitute a social and political menace. Education could lead to the creation of a somewhat deracinated native elite whose political ambitions could far outrun those of their less well educated compatriots. Thus there had to be some kind of balance between education and opportunity for educated natives, and this balance was not easy either to define or achieve. Meanwhile, the spread of literacy was a heavy task, more especially in the Melanesian islands.

In regard to natives in government, the precedents were entirely clear, though various in character between the colonies, but in the postwar situation it could not remain simply a matter of placing them at the lowest levels. It had to be a matter of advancing them farther and farther up the hierarchy, with accompanying displacement of Europeans, not only into the highest decision-making posts but also in the legislative branch to the point of being a majority of the membership which wielded decision-making powers. This, indeed, was the ultimate nub of the decolonization problem, for as long as decision-making remained the prerogative of alien rulers, there could be no true independence.

Thus the drive for native independence inevitably raised the question of the role of the Europeans in the islands in the future. Pro tem, the role of the Europeans in government was clear. Insofar as it was assumed that the colonies could not, for one reason or another, ever be granted independence, their role continued to be much as it had been all along, though with a shift from the "proconsular" outlook to "development and welfare." But where independence was not merely an eventual possibility but was, in response to outside pressures, an increasingly urgent requirement, the Europeans came to feel that all they were doing was training natives to displace them from their jobs and they became restless about their own futures. Yet experience elsewhere showed that the shift from European to native rule often left the Europeans with considerable roles in all the familiar connections and some new ones. It all depended on the atmosphere when the Europeans and the natives came to the parting of the ways. The feelings of the European entrepreneurs were various. Some felt that the political climate and the intensified emphasis on native production for market were hopelessly inimical to their interests, hostile to further European private capital investment (at a time when capital investment was much needed), and that therefore their days were numbered. Others developed a "hanging-on-to-see-what-will-happen" psychology which made them rather less enterprising than they normally would have been. But still others professed to see the possibility that "foreign investors and investment" would continue to be welcome under native rule, from absolute economic necessity if for no better reason. The future position of the big trading concerns was difficult to forecast, for although there was no question that the export-import trades would continue to be of central importance in island economics, the rise of native selling and buying cooperatives and the enhanced role of native governments in trade indicated a considerable change in the big trader's role. A great deal depended on the capacity of the firms to deal directly with natives rather than through European intermediaries. However, the Australian and New Zealand manufacturers and dealers in commodities in demand in the islands tended to look on the islands as an expanding market.

Dividing the islands very roughly into minor and major situations, it may be said that the minor situations included Tonga, the Solomons, the Gilbert and Ellice Colony, the New Hebrides, Nauru, American Samoa, the United States Trust Territory, the Tokelaus, the Cooks, Wallis and Futuna, and what the French from 1957 called French Polynesia (instead of Établissements Français). On this reckoning the major situations were Fiji, New Caledonia, New Guinea, and Western Samoa.

Tonga's position and problems were little changed by the war. However, the population increased from 32,500 in 1938 to 58,000 in 1957 and continued to rise. Already self-governing before the war and independent under the shelter of the United Kingdom's protection, the United States served as surrogate protector during the war and then returned her to *status quo ante bellum*. The drift in Tonga had long been toward the full Tonganization of the public service within the framework of rule by the hereditary Tongan elite. The problems remained to increase the productivity of agriculture, both in its subsistence and export phases, and the diversification of production, to wrest from the market maximum returns to the producers by government participation in the export trade, and to continue to improve the standards of life for the Tongans by the introduction of Western goods and services with the hope that they would not too radically erode the Polynesian character of the people. Of all the major countries of the region, New Zealand's direct influence was probably greatest through the participation of her teachers in Tonga's educational system. When Tongans emigrated, they went to Auckland.

In the Solomons the situation was a good deal more difficult after the war than before. The scene of exceedingly bitter fighting in World War II—of all the island fighting that which promises to stay longest in the American consciousness—the inpouring of armed services personnel and technology had a tremendous impact on the native mind which triggered off the most spectacular "cargo cults" yet experienced in the Southwest Pacific, their politico-economic implications entirely explicit. The islands had a slow economic recovery, though native production for market was much greater than prewar, and only in the early 1960's was there much optimism about the economic future. A good deal of British development and welfare money poured in. Grants-in-aid reached £434,000 in 1959 and total expenditure was £1,400,000 in that year as compared to £65,500 in 1938–39. The basic export continued to be copra, but there was hope for cocoa as a secondary export. Copra exports were running about 20,000 tons a year in the late 1950's. Private native wage employment was largely on European coconut plantations. Public employment was the only important alternative. The Melanesians numbered about 108,000, the proto-Polynesians about 5000, while there were around 700 Europeans, perhaps 400 Chinese, and a scattering of Indians, Fijians, etc. The political future was obscure. From 1952 the seat of the British high commissioner of the Western Pacific was removed from Suva and the possession of the governor of Fiji to the new capital of the Solomons, Honiara on Guadalcanal. On his retirement from office in 1961 High Commissioner Sir John Gutch suggested that the Solomons should be associated with New Guinea. If that were done and Australian New Guinea attained political independence, the Solomons would automatically attain the status. If it were not done, the future of the Solomons appeared to be self-government under close British tutelage and protection, both continuing indefinitely.

The probable future of the Gilbert and Ellice Colony after the war took shape as self-government within some variant of the British colonial framework. The inherited structure of self-government was strengthened in the native interest, including the restoration of much of the financial autonomy taken away in 1917 and the addition of an all-islands native conference to meet occasionally. The beneficiary of development and welfare spending, the economy was strengthened for the benefit of the native producers by the fuller development of the cooperatives that had first appeared between the wars. However, a fundamental problem remained the pressure of population on resources, especially in the Gilberts. The resources of the Phoenix group proved insufficient for the support of Gilbertese migrants, who moved on in the 1950's to islands in the northwest Solomons; and some Ellice islanders moved to Kioa Island, Fiji. Even so, the pressure in the home islands continued to mount, and if the birthrate did not fall soon, the exploration of supplementary sources of income would have to be intensified. It was suggested that the islands might set out to attract tourists. Another menace to the stability of the colony was the now forecastable exhaustion of the phosphate deposits on Ocean Island. During the war many of the Banabans (i.e., Ocean Island natives) had been exiled to the Marshalls and Carolines by the Japanese. On their return after the war they found their villages destroyed and it did not seem worthwhile to reestablish them. In 1947, therefore, they were resettled on Rabi Island in the Fiji group, which had, indeed, been purchased for them out of phosphate royalties in 1942. When phosphate mining finally ceased on Ocean, the Gilbert and Ellice revenues would be embarrassingly reduced.

The Japanese also exiled many of the natives of Nauru, sending them to Truk. After the war the welfare approach was more fully applied at Nauru. In the early 1960's it was apparent that although the phosphate would last about thirty years, the island was becoming less and less a suitable residence for the people. Therefore, a hunt for an alternative was begun, but none was immediately fixed upon.

With regard to the New Hebrides the temptation was to say that the more things changed, the more they remained the same, though it was not quite as simple as that. The government continued to be split three ways and the French maintained their preponderance in the resident population. In 1958 there were 1350 French and 500 British, while there were 160 Chinese who had chosen to live under British law, and the French had 1950 Vietnamese and 500 Tahitians and Wallisians under their "protection." The natives were now estimated to number just over 60,000. In 1957 there was a new outbreak of the "John Frum" cult, which had received a good deal of stimulation from the presence of armed services personnel (including American Negroes) and technology in the islands during the war. By value copra was by far the most important export, followed at a very considerable distance by frozen fish, then by cocoa, though the New Hebrides had now lost their preeminence in the region as a cocoa producer, with coffee well behind cocoa. The French were taking three-quarters of the exports on the average, while the Australians were taking only 2.5 per cent. However, the Australians provided over half of the imports, while the United Kingdom was now actually supplying more than the French. Factors which either indicated or promised change in the future were the considerable increase in the socio-economic research being done in the group by British and French specialists working under the patronage of their national development authorities, the stimulation of health activity by the World Health Organization, the enlargement of the educational system, the rise of the fishing and fish-freezing industry, the intensive search for minerals in which field the first fruit was the discovery of a commercially exploitable deposit of manganese on Efate, and the building of a port at Espíritu Santo. But the prospect of the New Hebrides ever being other than a colonial dependency seemed poor.

When it was finally realized during World War II that Tutuila was a naval base of rather limited value, the transfer of responsibility for American Samoa as a small colonial problem to American civilian authority became inevitable. After four years of intragovernmental negotiations, initiated in 1947, the transfer from the Navy Department to the Department of the Interior was completed on July 1, 1951. Five years after, in 1956, an official "Statement of Objectives and Policies" was issued in which two themes were stated (and then elaborated): "To provide for the orderly and progressive development of the people toward self-government" and "To assist the people to attain the maximum possible self-support." Finally, in October 1960, a constitution for the territory came into effect, this completing for the time being the assimilation of American Samoa to the traditional position of a "territory" in the American political system. While the declaration of "objectives and policies" stated that an American type of self-government was a prime objective, there was not a hint that independence was even remotely in view. Indeed, even the traditional fate of an American "territory," absorption into the union as a state as Hawaii was absorbed in 1960, seemed an unlikely fate for American Samoa. It was more likely to remain a "territory," because it was far away and above all because it was poor. The careful phraseology of the economic objective of 1956 reflected an understanding of its poverty by the choice of such words as "assist" to hint at means of alleviating the poverty and "maximum possible" to hint at probable results of assisting. The least likely American achievement in Samoa was solution of the economic problem. The single substantial local addition to the subsistence-plus-copra-for-export economy during the 1950's was a fish cannery at Pago Pago, established in 1954, which by 1960 was giving employment to 340 Samoans, but the most important economic relief was the emigration of Samoans to Hawaii and continental United States (San Francisco). Since those who emigrated successfully were apt to be relatively young, among the most vigorous, and those who had profited from the much improved public education civilian rule had brought, it was suggested by an acute observer that American Samoa was exporting her potential leaders. It may be wondered why American Samoa was not rejoined to Western Samoa when the latter became independent. This was perhaps geographical, political and even historical logic, but it was not a feasible proposal, for the Western Samoans would have had to be persuaded to accept an economic liability and the American Samoans to give up the hope of United States subsidies at home and the prospect of escaping into the affluent societies of Hawaii and California abroad. Posterity often has to pay for the land-grabbing errors of its imperialist ancestors.

Having occupied certain of the Japanese mandates during the course of fighting World War II, after V-J day the United States Navy systematically visited the by-passed islands of the group and deported, first the Japanese military and then the Japanese civilian residents, in effect returning the islands to the Micronesians, though with a totally wrecked economy and with some islands in a state of devastation. At this time the American interest in these islands was strategic, and it was decided to hold them. (For the background of this thinking, see Chapters IX and X.) Confirmation of control would require dealings with the United Nations. In 1947, therefore, the islands were created a strategic trust territory—a variation on the usual trust territory—under the United Nations and administrative responsibility was assigned to the United States. President Truman thereupon put them under the care of the secretary of the Navy. However, with the rapid change in weaponry and strategic conceptions from the end of World War II, the significance attached to the islands underwent a rather rapid redefinition after 1947, and while they were still of some strategic importance, by 1951 it seemed pointless to burden the Navy with their administration. Administrative responsibility was therefore transferred from the Navy to the Department of the Interior which set up a civilian administration. However, two years later, in 1953, the Navy resumed administrative responsibility for all the islands in the northern Marianas except Rota, presumably because of the relation of these trust islands to the base on Okinawa. The Navy's administration was on Saipan, while the Interior's was on Guam, not a part of the Trust Territory, though an American possession since 1898.

The Trust Territory was an artificial political construction arbitrarily put together in the first instance by the Germans. It had little natural coherence and little had ever been developed artificially. The islands included in the Territory were scattered in several groups over an area equal in size to the land area of the United States. The groups lacked a common character. Some islands were of volcanic origin, others were coral atolls. However, the natives were uniformly Micronesians and after the expulsion of the Japanese, there were few alien residents. There was no discernible identification with the Territory as a whole, but an intense identification with the island or atoll on which an individual was born. This situation was not at all changed when the islands were sorted, for better management, into administrative districts: Rota, Palau, Yap, Truk, Ponape, and the Marshall Islands.

Economically, the administration's objective was to assist the Micronesians toward self-support; but the Territory's economy was hopelessly deficit, it had to be subsidized by the United States government, and there seemed no likelihood that viability could be attained. Fundamentally the dependence was on a subsistence economy based on agriculture and fishing, with copra as the principal cash crop and export commodity. The Marshall Islands District contributed most copra by quantity and value (and little else, save some shell), while the other districts, except Rota, exported some copra and usually some other specialty, such as Palau's handicrafts. Rota was dependent on the export of vegetables to Guam. About all that could be done to improve the agricultural situation was to direct the replanting of the coconuts on a more rational scheme than came naturally to the natives. To a degree quite exceptional in the islands, trade including the export trade was in the hands of the Micronesians, the administration supplying capital on loan. The administration put much emphasis on education and public health. Self-government was the objective, but there was no hint of ultimate political independence.

New Zealand's 1600 Tokelauans, who had largely governed themselves for years, were neither an economic nor a political problem. As long as the copra market held up and the islanders received assistance in such forms as the blasting of boat passages through the surrounding reefs, building water-storage facilities, and maintaining the hospital, they could get along quite nicely. The Cook Islanders were another story. The population in the Cooks reached 16,573 in 1956. There was a drift of islanders to New Zealand and Tahiti, and the people of Pukapuka, the coral atoll in the northern Cooks, took over nearby Nassau Island both as living room and for its coconut resources. The economic problem was studied by New Zealand economists in 1955, though their recommendations applied to the more populous southern Cooks. It was suggested that a great help would be to facilitate the export of perishables, especially fruits, by the erection of storage and packing facilities on Rarotonga and to provide a larger, better equipped ship for the service to New Zealand. Over the next five years, this was done by the New Zealand government. However, the Cook Island economy seemed doomed to be a deficit economy, for while local revenue rose by £200,000 between 1949 and 1959, the New Zealand government's subsidy rose by almost the same amount. Heaviest spending was on administration, education, health, and public works. Politically there was a considerable move forward toward local self-government in 1957 and another forward move was promised in 1962, but as the Cooks were part of New Zealand—the people were legally New Zealand citizens from 1948—the question of political independence did not arise nor was it feasible in the economic circumstances.

While it may shock the romantics to find French Polynesia described as a "minor situation," in reality it is difficult to see what else it is. On the other hand, nobody would dispute that the Wallis and Futuna situation was minor. A copra colony, its population rose to 8600 by the early 1950's. Largely self-governing under native elite assisted by French

MARQUESAS ISLANDS

Nuku Hiva • Atuna
Ua Pu • ◉ Hiva Oa
Tahuata • • Fatu Hiva

• Flint

• Puka Puka

Matahiva •··· Rangiroa
Tahaa Makatea • ◉ Apataki • Raroia
Raiatéa • • Huahiné • Takaravu
Mopélia Moorea • • Anaa
• ◉ Papeete • Hao • Réao
Tahiti • Pinaki
SOCIETY ISLANDS   TUAMOTU ARCHIPELAGO

Duke of Gloucester ·•··
Tematangi • ··· Actaeon

Iles Gambier
Rimatara • Rurutu • Timoé Oeno
Tubuai • Raivavaé   • Henderson
• Pitcairn   • Ducie
TUBUAI ISLANDS

TROPIC OF CAPRICORN

• Rapa   Easter

FRENCH POLYNESIA AND RELATED ISLANDS

colonial officers, the most significant postwar development was the emigration of the Wallisians as workers to the New Hebrides and New Caledonia. In French Polynesia the population reached 73,201 in the middle 1950's and was rising fast. About half the people lived on the island of Tahiti, 17,250 of them at Papeete. The Marquesans had doubled in numbers since they began to increase around 1930, about 1700 living on Nukuhiva and 1500 on Hiva Oa. Of the total population, 63,700 were Polynesians by census classification but pure Polynesians were presumably a minority and those with admixtures of foreign blood, European and Chinese, the majority. The Chinese numbered 6750, of whom the greater proportion lived in Papeete, and there were 2300 European French, perhaps 250 British, and around 150 Americans. The "Polynesians" were French citizens from 1946. Export production in order of value still consisted of copra, phosphates, vanilla, and shell. France still was the principal export market, followed by Japan (for phosphates), the United States (vanilla), and Australia, while the imports came from France, the United States, Australia, New Zealand, China, and the United Kingdom.

Although there were more people in French Polynesia, the basic economic—and social—situations had not changed. Change was almost wholly political. French Polynesia felt the winds of change that swept through the French Empire during and after World War II. The effect in Tahiti was to stir the fires of nationalism, almost literally and in any case figuratively, but in the end to leave the islands with greater powers of self-government but within the Empire still. When the colony found itself on its own in 1940 with the fall of France, it chose to follow De Gaulle. After the war France was busy with events in Africa, and the Pacific colonies were not particularly on the minds of the constitution-makers. However, in 1945 Tahiti was granted a Representative (later Territorial) Assembly elected under universal suffrage which at least had the right to discuss all local questions and some influence on local policy. Final authority, however, remained firmly in the hands of the governor. When development and welfare funds began to flow in from Paris, the governor directed their use. In 1946, along with the other colonies, Tahiti was granted the right to send representatives to the National Assembly, the Council of the Republic (Senate), and the Assembly of the French Union, all in Paris. This was to tie the colony closely to France. Decentralization of the Empire, the effect of which would be to increase local autonomy, began to be discussed in the early 1950's. In Tahiti the increased autonomy was reflected in the enlarged powers of the Territorial Assembly of 1957 and the creation at the same time of an executive body called the Council of Government to carry out the Assembly's decisions. With the prospect of more power over local affairs, the local residents were vastly stimulated politically.

The most striking development was the revelation that the rural residents particularly and the economically disadvantaged people generally were responsive to demagogy. This situation was exploited by a character called Pouvanna a Oopa, who talked of "Tahiti for the Tahitians," expressing himself in a language laden with Biblical phrases, enormously appealing to the native pastors in the villages, and with cargo cultish overtones. Pouvanna went far toward winning control of the local government. His more moderate opposition stood for maximum local autonomy combined with a continuing close relation with France. The climax came in 1958 when De Gaulle conducted his famous referendum on the future relation of the colonies to France. Pouvanna a Oopa advocated a "No" vote, but French Polynesia went "Yes" by 63.7 per cent. This rebuff, together with others equally disillusioning earlier, turned Pouvanna's thoughts toward violence and soon after the referendum he was arrested on the charge of conspiring to burn down Papeete, tried, convicted, and sent to prison and exile in France. It was the verdict of the Tahitian majority that, while maximum autonomy was desirable, the association with France was, in the Tahitian circumstances, indispensable. Or if not with France, with what country—the United States? French Polynesia could not stand alone. Even to stand it had to develop, on the Hawaiian pattern, its great potential as a tourist attraction.

At the end of World War II the New Guinea situation became divisible into two parts, the Dutch and the Australian. The Dutch part was reserved by history for a special fate, absorption into the Republic of Indonesia, successor to all the rest of the territory of the Netherlands East Indies colony, with only a contingent possibility of ever having the opportunity to elect to be independent. The Australian part of New Guinea, eventually to be called Papua-New Guinea to signify that it was an administrative union, effected in 1949, of the Australian colony of Papua and the Trust Territory of New Guinea, was early committed by its metropolitan government to eventual independence, but on what terms and conditions vis à vis the metropolis and when became contentious matters. New Caledonia was to elect to stay within the French imperial orbit for much the same reasons and on much the same terms as Tahiti, while the Fijians were to resist any suggestion that they accept political independence, largely because they felt unable to cope with the Indian majority without the British, and the Western Samoans alone were not only immediately to embrace the idea of independence but also were to be the first indigenes of the Southwest Pacific to achieve the status (January 1, 1962).

Driven from their Indies empire, except for a portion of southern West New Guinea, by the Japanese, the Dutch were challenged for possession at the war's end by the Indonesian revolutionaries then led by Sukarno and Hatta. The Indonesians issued a declaration of independence on August 17, 1945. Although the strength of the revolutionaries was in Java, their claim was that they were the heirs to the entire territory of the Netherland Indies. The Dutch response to this challenge was a series of maneuvers and actions designed either to defeat the pretensions of the revolutionaries altogether or to limit the territory that would pass to their control. These maneuvers began immediately after the Indonesian declaration of independence and did not finally come to an end, or what then appeared to be the end, until May 1, 1963. From the Indonesian point of view, the resistance to the Dutch was in all its many phases chapters in the completion of the revolution. It was in the course of trying to salvage some part of their Indies empire that the Dutch chose to make a stand on retention of sovereignty in West New Guinea. That West New Guinea was chosen appears to have been an accident of circumstances rather than a careful calculation, for the Dutch started out to retain far more of their old colonial domain and they certainly had no reason to harbor any special illusions about West New Guinea either as a possible settlement colony for refugees from the Indonesian Republic or as a candidate for development toward political independence. However, it is clear that by the end of 1946 the Dutch felt that West New Guinea should be given some kind of special relation to the Netherlands state regardless of what relation other portions of the Indies might elect or be forced by circumstances to accept. At no time did the Dutch deny that West New Guinea had originally been claimed by them because it was an integral part of their heritage from native rulers and therefore part of the Netherlands Indies. It was, after all, an established historical fact that the Dutch had for that reason been the first European power to claim sovereignty over any part of New Guinea, preceding all others by almost six decades. On the other hand, the Indonesian revolutionaries never conceded that West New Guinea could be excepted from their claim to the entire territory of the old Netherlands Indies. However, when the Dutch finally agreed to transfer sovereignty to the Republic under the Round Table or Hague Agreement of 1949, it was provided that a final decision on the status of West New Guinea should be made only after further discussions. The discussions took place in 1950 but no mutually agreeable conclusion was reached. The Dutch were left in effective possession of West New Guinea but the Indonesians had not relinquished their claim to sovereignty.

An effect of the Dutch retention of West New Guinea was the reorientation of the territory away from the Indies toward the Southwest Pacific. This was more a matter of sentiment than a consequence of any new material attachments. That the Dutch anticipated the importance of this orientation is clear from the fact that they were a party to the South Pacific Commission in 1947. However, the Dutch relations with the Australians, which would be most important, were not as warm in 1947 as they might have been, because during the protracted struggle of the Dutch and the Indonesians over the body of the old Indies, Dr. Evatt's diplomats (with American support) had played a role quite favorable to the cause of the Indonesians. However, by 1950 when the Dutch had become effectively the masters of West New Guinea, the Labor party had been voted out of office and the Liberal administration under R. G. Menzies was in charge. The Menzies government was very favorably disposed toward the Dutch and during the ensuing decade supported their position in West New Guinea more consistently than any other government. This pro-Dutch line was first formulated by Percy Spender in 1950, as follows: (a) as part of the island shield, integrally necessary to Australia's security, West New Guinea was safe in Dutch hands; (b) the Indonesians had no case for sovereignty at law; (c) if the Indonesians got into West New Guinea they would infiltrate Australian New Guinea and make trouble; and (d) Australian and Dutch purposes in New Guinea were identical and would admirably complement each other. At later stages the Australians developed such additional arguments as that Indonesia was economically unable to supply the needed aid to West New Guinea; and that it was highly dangerous to have a common frontier with a communist-"rotten" country like Indonesia. The climactic demonstration of Australian-Dutch solidarity came on November 6, 1957, at a time when the Dutch-Indonesian argument was hot. The agreement of 1957 emphasized that Dutch and Australian purposes were parallel and complementary and it was announced that they would collaborate in realizing them. Though not part of the agreement, it was commonly understood that the Dutch rather favored the idea that the long-term political future of West New Guinea lay with Australian New Guinea, perhaps under some form of a politically independent Melanesian Federation. Whatever strategic value West New Guinea may have had, either to the Dutch, the Australians, or others, it was never possible to exploit it, for the Dutch were not included in the only international arrangement involving defense that emerged in the area, SEATO.

The original Dutch intent was to make West New Guinea a home for the Eurasians who chose not to stay in the Indonesian Republic or to go to Holland. But the Eurasians were not in fact attracted to West New Guinea, and by 1952 this rationale was passé. The Dutch therefore emphasized that their purpose was to develop the country by public and private enterprise while preparing the indigenous peoples for political independence. In view of the fact that in 1954, of an indigenous population of perhaps 700,000, only about half were then under administrative "control," this promised to be a protracted business. In general the Dutch policy was "development and welfare." There was thus a heavy emphasis on health and education, but because of the rationale of the Dutch presence, political advancement was high on the agenda. The economy, definitely never very healthy, was consistently deficit throughout the Dutch time. Between 1950 and 1958, while expenditures increased about four times and local revenues a little over three times, the home government's subvention consistently took care of 50 per cent of the budget and constantly swelled in size. About half the exports went to the Netherlands, no other customer except Singapore taking as much as 10 per cent. Singapore bought 12 per cent (1958). The Australians took 5½ per cent. The exports were as encouraging as they were only because of oil which accounted for three-quarters by value. Of the so-called "native exports" which provided the balance, copra, nutmeg, and crocodile skins were steadily produced and sold in increasing quantities, but there was no stability in the other native production. Worse still, by the late 1950's it was clear that oil was not going to last long unless new fields could be found. Private enterprise in other directions was, it was alleged, snarled in bureaucratic red tape, but there was hope that the proved deposits of nickel would shortly be under exploitation, partly with the aid of American investment. But if economic stability and growth, let alone anything approaching viability, eluded, the Dutch nevertheless responded to the pressure to get on with political advancement of the indigenes by instituting a Legislative Council in 1961 which had a Papuan majority, 16 of whom were elected by the 100,000 indigenes it had been found possible to enfranchise. When the Council began its first session there were celebrations in Hollandia attended by representatives of all the South Pacific Commission nations except the United States, which stayed away to emphasize its neutrality between the Dutch and the Indonesians in the dispute over the sovereignty of West New Guinea just then coming to a boil.

From 1952 Indonesian pressure to get the Dutch out of West New Guinea steadily increased. Although both sides took up dogmatic positions, scholars did not find that either side had an impeccable case. The Dutch attempted to establish their legal right to sovereignty while the

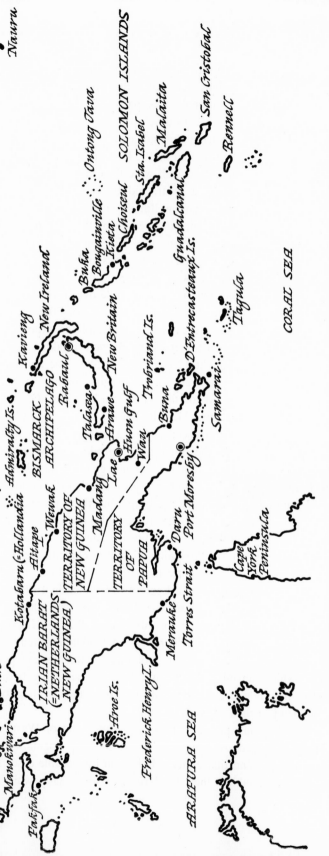

NEW GUINEA AND ASSOCIATED ISLANDS

Indonesians argued that the problem was political and not juridical: whether or not they were going to get the Dutch out of West New Guinea and thus "complete" their revolution by taking sovereignty over all the territory of the old Netherlands Indies. By 1954 the Indonesians had promoted the issue to first place in their increasingly acrimonious dialogue with the Dutch. The Dutch stand on sovereignty was rigid, in large part for domestic political reasons, and they refused to discuss its transfer to Indonesia, while the Indonesians would not discuss it to any other end. In 1954 the Indonesians tried to get the UN to order the Dutch to discuss transfer but failed to get the necessary voting support. The Afro-Asia Conference at Bandung in 1955 resolved in favor of the Indonesian case and in 1956 the Indonesians tried again at the UN and again failed. They then turned to pressuring the Dutch by nationalizing their economic interests in Indonesia and expelling Dutch nationals (to the number of over 33,000 in seven months). When this failed to move the Dutch, the Indonesians severed diplomatic relations in 1960 and the next year asked the British to cease representing the Dutch in Indonesia. The Indonesians began to prepare for war and the Dutch prepared to resist. Some fighting had actually occurred when, early in 1962, the secretary-general of the UN proposed, with United States support, that the Dutch and the Indonesians meet in Washington under an American mediator (Mr. Ellsworth Bunker) to try to work out a solution. A Dutch-Indonesian Agreement was announced on August 16, 1962. Essentially, it provided that West New Guinea pass temporarily into the care of a United Nations Temporary Executive Authority and that the UNTEA hand the territory to the Indonesians on May 1, 1963. To protect the position of the indigenous people, provision was made for a referendum by the end of 1969 on whether or not they would remain with Indonesia or become an independent nation. On the appointed day, West (or Dutch or Netherlands) New Guinea became Irian Barat and Hollandia became Kotabaru. The reintegration of West New Guinea into the Indies began. Shortly, Dutch diplomats were to return to Jakarta.

Throughout these increasingly riotous proceedings Australia was a vitally interested party. Its pro-Dutch position, first clearly enunciated in 1950 by the Menzies government (and in essence supported by Labor), was given its most concrete form in 1957. The position stemmed from the historically established dogma that the integrity of the islands as a defensive shield must be maintained and was supported by the Australian prejudice against a common frontier with any nation, let alone a nation about which grave suspicions were harbored. As the situation with regard to West New Guinea became more and more heated, the Australians, perceiving the direction of the drift, emphasized that while they were strongly opposed to the use of force to obtain a solution, they would abide by any solution achieved by peaceful negotiations, provided that the principle of self-determination of peoples was maintained. The Australians came to recognize that the defensive viability of the island shield did not depend so much on whether West New Guinea was in Dutch or Indonesian hands—after all, the territory had been in foreign hands for over thirteen decades—as on the actual situation in Indonesia as a whole. This was further to underscore the point that Australia's future was to be heavily conditioned by the situation in her Near North and her diplomatic and other relation to it. However, the prospective passing of West New Guinea from the Dutch to the Indonesians unquestionably intensified Australia's sense of isolation from the powerful friends by whose goodwill Mr. Menzies set so much store. It was therefore relevant that at an ANZUS Council meeting in Canberra early in 1962 the secretary of State of the United States should have declared that the mutual assistance obligations under that treaty applied (italics added) "in the event of armed attack *not only on the metropolitan territory* of any of the parties *but also on any island territory under the jurisdiction of any of the three governments in the Pacific.*"

The war had hit Australian New Guinea hard both physically and ideologically. Civil administration ended in February 1942, when it ceased to function at Port Moresby, and was not restored for over three years. In the interim Australian New Guinea was under military government by the Australian New Guinea Administrative Unit of H.Q., New Guinea Force. While one of the tasks of ANGAU was to maintain civil government insofar as possible, its overriding task was to direct New Guinea's native affairs in the light of military necessities. This involved such tasks as maintaining production on those plantations that were not within battle-zones or enemy lines and marshaling the native labor force to meet the army's extensive needs. ANGAU had marked success in keeping up production in general and a particular success with rubber production. It began to return plantations to their European owners as early as 1943. In marshaling the native labor force ANGAU had to over-recruit in available areas and the impact on native society was deleterious. The labor force was at its maximum numbers in 1944. Since Papua was the first to be free of Japanese control, recruitment there reached a total more than double the prewar average, whereas in the Territory, where some of the best recruiting areas stayed in Japanese hands beyond 1944, the maximum was about half the prewar average. But recruitment for work was only part of the impact of the war on the natives. Some 60,000 were displaced by the fighting and many of their houses and gardens were destroyed; the absence of workers from the villagers reduced food production and prevented house maintenance even where fighting did not occur; and they had to assimilate and evaluate as best they could the experience of contact with allied military personnel and technology and the Japanese invaders and their technology. ANGAU made an excellent record in taking care of native health needs in wartime and improving the peacetime service, although malaria and dysentery were introduced into the highlands from which they had hitherto been absent. Native education, however, lapsed altogether.

Consideration of reconstruction began in 1944 (see Chapter IV for the domestic context) and civil government was restored in 1945, first in Papua and the Morobe District of the Territory. In his statement of post-war policy, E. J. Ward, the Labor minister responsible for New Guinea, offered a compound of "native paramountcy," development and welfare, and political advancement. He said, "The Government is not satisfied that sufficient interest had been taken in the territories prior to the Japanese invasion, or that adequate funds had been provided for their development and the advancement of the native inhabitants. Apart from the debt of gratitude that the people of Australia owe to the natives of the territory, the Government regards it as its bounden duty to further to the utmost the advancement of the natives, and considers that that can be achieved only by providing facilities for better health, better education, and for a greater participation by the natives in the wealth of their country and eventually in its government." Since most of the natives were dependent on their subsistence economy, attention would be directed to its improvement to raise standards in the villages where most of them lived. The participation of the native producers in the market economy was to be systematically increased. The role of private enterprise was to be defined in relation to "the welfare of the natives generally." In accordance with the general orientation, it was emphasized that a shift was to be made within a few years from an almost total dependence on indentured labor to a system of 'free labor" under government management.

Although "Ward's policy" was in effect simply a reconsideration of position toward those elements of the New Guinea situation toward which anybody would have to define a position, since they were elements of an historical heritage, the positions taken by Ward were considered radical, partly because of the pace of change it was proposed to achieve, partly because they were Ward's, for he was identified with Jack Lang and demagogic laboristic radicalism. Opposition came from those who were comfortable in the old ruts of policy, particularly the European enterpreneurs. There were angry mutterings about the alleged "departure from the Murray tradition" and, with a rasp of hatred, references to "socialism." (The same people scorned the United Kingdom's postwar colonial policy as "socialism" also.) But from observation of the climate of discussion of reconstruction in Australia, it was obvious that "Ward's policy" for New Guinea had been strongly influenced by intellectuals keenly aware of the ideas about colonial policy that were then circulating overseas and which had influenced United Kingdom policy, especially around 1940. As an informed British observer of the situation remarked, the "Ward" ideas were "progressive," "in the innocuous sense of conformity to practice well established elsewhere"—e.g., in Africa. Ward was, in short, but the vehicle for one of those abrupt updatings of Australian thinking that correct the cultural lag which so many Australians cherish.

The Ward policy had a sharp impact on New Guinea affairs, particularly labor relations and finance, but the times were not propitious, and never became propitious during the next four years Labor was in office, to move forward with the reordering of New Guinea society that Ward had forecast. Not only was far more money made available to the administration than ever before, but considerable cash was put into the hands of the natives through payments for the "war damage" their properties had suffered. The labor situation became chaotic less from any abrupt attempt to end indenture than from an effort to shift quickly from the compulsion of wartime to a liberal "agreement" proper to peacetime. Native wages were substantially improved. There was considerable native unrest, expressed by the more sophisticated by strikes for more pay and better conditions, by those less Europeanized in cargo cults or near relatives of them. The administration was handicapped by shortages of personnel to carry out its purposes, for example, a shortage of men able to attempt to guide natives in market dealings. The "Ward policy" shook up New Guinea and more importantly those whose thinking was hopelessly old-fashioned, but it did not usher New Guinea into the millennium, either by European or cargo-cult definition.

In 1950 New Guinea policy passed into the hands of the Menzies government, with Paul Hasluck as the responsible minister. Hasluck (who was still in office in 1963) was the first cabinet minister to have territories as his sole responsibility. A Western Australian, once a newspaper leader writer and university lecturer in history, author of a book on Western Australian native policy, Hasluck had for a time been a member of Dr. Evatt's diplomatic corps, when he turned up on the opposite side of politics. The New Guinea policy Hasluck came to propound (and implement) eschewed laboristic planning, resisted "target dates," and was largely a matter of selecting means pragmatically to achieve very specific ends that fitted into a pattern of development toward self-government and limited national freedom at some undefined but presumably remote time in the future. Above all, Hasluck's policy was conservative and "prudential." However, what Hasluck did was not so utterly different from what Ward had proposed, as those who abhorred Ward tried to persuade themselves, for "Ward's policy" was an adaptation to an overseas climate of opinion that continued to influence what the Australians did in New Guinea. But because Hasluck was fairly stubborn about not setting "target dates" he assumed a stance of opposition to the U.N. Trusteeship Council, to which "target dates" were of the essence, and this helped establish his position as more conservative than it really was. Moreover, Hasluck's thinking included no cut and dried definition of political freedom for New Guinea, because he believed that to conserve Australia's interest in New Guinea with regard to defense and international policy, it might be necessary to limit New Guinea's independence and at the very least it was absolutely necessary to cultivate in the New Guinea population a sense of identification with Australia which would keep the two countries close together indefinitely. In the early 1960's, therefore, it was debatable whether Australia would be allowed time by the interested overseas parties to carry through its New Guinea program at the Hasluckian pace. The optimists were then of the opinion that Australia would be required to grant New Guinea freedom within ten or fifteen years, while the pessimists, taking notice of the fact that the full pressure of the decolonialization drive was yet to be exerted in the Southwest Pacific, believed that Australia had far less time than that. Hasluck, avoiding any target date, implied that Australia needed thirty to fifty years even to grant New Guinea conditional freedom.

The New Guinea economy was not, of course, viable. Indeed in terms of the postwar expenditures, it was less viable than prewar when Murray had had but a small subsidy and the Territory was self-supporting. There was a tendency after the war to deflate optimistic views of the potential, especially the agricultural potential. It was estimated that only 15 per cent of the area was cultivable. That it was rich in minerals remained a hypothesis, not a proved fact. No oil had been found. Gold mining had declined toward insignificance. The indigenous population of the combined territories, Papua and New Guinea, was 1,800,000, of whom all but perhaps 300,000 were under administrative control. The bulk of the population was in New Guinea. In 1958 the labor force in employment totaled 62,000 persons of whom 13,500 were in government service, while 29,350 were working for private employers under "agreements," and 19,225 were "casuals." Of this force two-thirds were New Guineans and one-third Papuans. There were 8555 "non-indigenes" (mostly Europeans) in Papua in 15,073 in New Guinea. While the dependence of the overwhelming proportion of the indigenes continued to be on subsistence agriculture, and it was questioned that they were all adequately fed, they were also producing copra, rice, cocoa, coffee, and peanuts as cash crops for local or export market. They had advice from an "extension service" and were encouraged to form selling and buying cooperatives. For the European agriculturalists copra was still the leading product, but rubber ranked second (mostly produced in Papua), followed by cocoa and coffee, with small quantities of tea, peanuts, and fibers. By value, exports were rising in the late 1950's, though slowly, exceeding £12 million in 1957–58, £9.6 million being from New Guinea, £2.7 million from Papua. The administration was spending £15.5 million in 1957–58, of which £4.7 million came from internal revenue and £10.8 million was subsidy from the Commonwealth government. Therefore two-thirds of the expenditure was from subsidy. £1.5 million was then being spent on education, including the education of selected natives in Australian schools, while £3.4 million was being spent on public health. Not until 1963 were institutional arrangements being made that would lead to a native majority in the Legislative Council.

As long as the war in the islands was an active concern of the Americans and the New Zealanders, New Caledonia was a prime strategic base in relation to operations via the New Hebrides against the Japanese in the Solomons, as it had been a prime strategic objective of the Japanese in the early stages of the war. The American-New Zealand activities there were on a scale commensurate with the island's exceptional size. While the allied activities had the effect of making the social situation rather chaotic, inducing a considerable inflation of living costs, it was difficult two decades later to discover in what respects the effects were permanent. Hurricanes, like other atmospheric disturbances, are apt to have transient effects. The differences between prewar New Caledonia and postwar New Caledonia were in particulars, not fundamentals.

After the war as before the economy was dominated by mineral production, now nickel and chrome. The production and export of iron ore was in abeyance. Nickel production was still dominated by the *Société le Nickel,* with two private individuals operating in mining on a considerable scale, all parties using subcontracting miners, "petit mineurs." There was a considerable technological advance in the industry, especially on the treatment side, to allow the remunerative recovery of nickel from ores of low nickel content, and the capacity of the hydroelectric installation at Yate was increased. The nickel was chiefly exported to the *Société's* refineries in France and Belgium which were tied into the European Coal and Steel Community. The Japanese reentered the market. In chrome production the most significant change was not in volume of production but in the transfer of control of the great Tiébaghi mine from British to American capitalists. A prime market for New Caledonian chrome was the United States. During the war the minerals were in constant demand in the United States or Australia. A side effect of the coal shortage in Australia after the war (see Chapter V) was the supplying of the smelter from the United States under the Marshall Plan for European rehabilitation. Postwar demand for New Caledonian minerals was stimulated by the so-called Korean War boom, but by the early 1960's it was evident that the insecurities inherent in total dependence on fluctuating overseas markets had not been escaped. While Australia was booming industrially, the demand there for New Caledonian minerals was not great enough to make much difference. The traditional *dépendance extérieur,* complicated by the factor of distance, was unabated.

Agriculture continued to be but a secondary economic reliance and the harsh word "failure" was used to characterize its condition. Of the land available to Europeans, 3 per cent was held by small farmers, 25 per cent by small graziers, and 72 per cent by large graziers, including *Société le Nickel* and *La Maison Ballande.* To survive, the small farmers had to take wage work in the mines or find government jobs. Grazing, chiefly to produce beef, was disadvantaged by the wartime importation of the cattle tick from Queensland and marketing troubles. It supplied the local fresh beef and exported some canned beef to the New Hebrides and France. By the middle 1950's the natives were supplying about half the copra exported—the center of copra production was the Loyalty Islands —and they were also producing about half the coffee on the east and west coasts of La Grande Terre. The agricultural future seemed to be with them. New Caledonian native agriculture was reckoned more productive than African native agriculture.

France continued to be the principal market for exports (except chrome) and the leading supplier of imports by value. The Australians were second to the French as suppliers of imports but took only a small proportion of the exports. From 1945 there was an independent Pacific franc which after the war moved in value in sympathetic relation to the French franc. The single bank, which managed the currency, continued to be the *Banque de l'Indochine.* Internal trade was dominated by large local companies of which the most prepossessing was *La Maison Ballande* whose interests ramified into shipping, insurance, and grazing as well as wholesale trade. There was a considerable proliferation of small retail shops, especially those operated by Asians in Nouméa and the bush, both dealing in merchandise and supplying services.

Beginning in 1947 there was an inflow of metropolitan money from the *Fonds d'Investissement et Développement Economique et Social.*

This money was spent on an *École Pratique d'Agriculture* which was, significantly enough, mostly attended by indigenes, a technical college, and on harbor works, roads, the telephone system, dispensaries, hospitals, and waterworks. There was a considerable expansion of research activities. In 1939 Maurice Leenhard had founded the *Société des Études Mélanésiennes;* in 1946 the French government set up an *Institut Français d'Océanie* for research in entomology, oceanography, geophysics, hydrology, ethnography, etc. The location of the South Pacific Commission headquarters in Nouméa enhanced the town's pretentions to being the center of island intellectual life, but this did not weaken the British conviction that the honor should go to Suva.

The population in the middle 1950's was 64,871, divided into indigenes 34,900, Europeans and assimilés 22,800, and Asians 7171. Of these people, 21,000 of the Europeans, 15,400 of the indigenes, and practically all of the Asians were to be found on La Grande Terre. The prewar drift of population to Nouméa continued and the mixture of the population there continued to be remarkable. No fewer than 15,000 of the Europeans and assimilés were living there at the end of 1955, along with 2600 indigenes, 2340 Indonesians, 2260 Vietnamese, 580 Wallis Islanders, 380 Tahitians, and 60 New Hebrideans. Secondary concentrations of Europeans were developing at Thio and Koumac. Of the Asians, the prewar Japanese population was deported to Australia at the time of Pearl Harbor and from there eventually to Japan. The Vietnamese and Indonesians (as they were to become known) were kept under their indentures until the end of the war and then given their liberty in the expectation that they would soon be repatriated. A proportion promptly went into business. Eventually many were repatriated, the Vietnamese to a homeland that was in the hands of the communists under Ho Chi-minh. Indenture of Vietnamese was not resumed, but some Indonesian labor became available after 1949. However, the labor situation in the mines was difficult. It was in part relieved by the recruitment of Wallisians, the only natives available for service outside their homelands. The immigration of Tahitians into New Caledonia, which began in wartime, was for general work, not employment in mining.

The political objective of the New Caledonian Europeans who dominated the situation was greater local autonomy, but their nationalism, rooted in an emotional attachment to the country by heritage and birth, uncommonly extended to advocacy of independence from France. The New Caledonians were not, therefore, particularly pleased with the first postwar imperial structure which was a highly centralized scheme, although they took advantage of all it offered including membership in the legislative bodies of the metropolis, but they were better pleased with the decentralization that characterized political developments in the 1950's. New Caledonia produced no Pouvanna a Oopa. In De Gaulle's referendum of 1958, 96 per cent of the New Caledonians voted to stay with the French empire. However, the New Caledonians were left short of self-rule, for though they had considerable influence in the Territorial Assembly, including some control of the budget, the governor retained a veto over the Assembly's decisions. (Budget funds were derived from import-export imposts and a government tobacco monopoly.) Political parties expressing local ideas and aspirations were formed. The franchise was granted to certain categories of indigenes. The precarious economic position was a powerful reason for not insisting on political independence, and it did not seem possible to correct this by proposing a policy of integrating New Caledonia with Australia and New Zealand, since neither was in a position to absorb the minerals, on the remunerative sale of which everything depended. There was, indeed, some worry that if the doors were opened too wide to the Australians and New Zealanders they might erode the positions of the New Caledonian merchant houses without the slightest compensating stimulation to the basic economy.

The Fijians were a people with a strong sense that the islands were theirs who rejected the very idea that they should accept political independence either as a goal or a gift. In this respect they stood in contrast to their long-time associates, the Tongans, who had long maintained their freedom, and their near neighbors the Western Samoans, who had embraced the idea right after the war and had achieved the condition by 1962. The reason was the presence of an alien race in Fiji.

A fact of not only great demographic but also of great economic and political significance was that the Indians had won the population race and now outnumbered the Fijians. The census of 1956 showed that there were 345,737 persons in Fiji of whom 169,403 were Indians (49 per cent) and 148,134 were Fijians (43 per cent). Additionally, there were 6042 Europeans, politically and economically of a significance entirely disproportionate to their numbers, of whom three-quarters were Australian, New Zealand, or Fiji-born, 4155 Chinese and part-Chinese, 4422 Rotumans, and 5320 Pacific islanders of various derivation, including the Ocean Islanders settled on Rabi and the Ellice Islanders settled on Kioa since the war. The economic consequence of this increase in population and of the continuing increase it forecast was not so much a pressure on resources as on employment opportunities. The resources for more economic development were believed to be there and studies were undertaken to improve knowledge of them, but how they could best be brought into use was unclear. It was difficult to manage a rate of economic growth commensurate with the population growth.

Both the Indian and the Fijian populations were fundamentally dependent on agriculture—a quite different agriculture, to be sure, subsistence as contrasted to commercial—the Fijians dependent in the proportion of 636 per 1000, the Indians 491 per 1000. Both had dispersed workers into other occupations, but the Indians more successfully than the Fijians, with a significant exception, largely because the Fijians still based their position on the preservation of their traditional society. In factory work the proportions were: Indians 88 per 1000, Fijians 24; in construction, Indians 78, Fijians 51; in commerce, Indians 70, Fijians 25, and so on. Only when it came to "administration and government" and "professional and allied" workers did the Fijians have a superiority, with regard to the former, Fijians 21, Indians 10, with regard to the latter, Fijians 39, Indians 24. The apparent meaning of all this was that while the Indians purposefully sought out occupational opportunities, the Fijians merely drifted into nonagricultural occupations as the villages continued to unravel at the edges and were purposeful only about administrative and clerical occupations (stimulated by easy entry into the structure of their own government) and the prestige occupations classifiable as professional or quasi-professional. This led to an increase in urbanization especially among the Indians. Suva, for example, had in 1956 19,321 Indians and 9758 Fijians.

Sugar remained the basic industry, particularly for the Indians and the Europeans. Over 85 per cent of the cane growers were Indians. Sugar, however, was no longer as dynamic as it had been historically, although total production was still increasing, because Fiji sugar was caught in the international sugar marketing situation. It was estimated that Fiji had the land and certainly the farmers to produce at least 50,000 more tons a year than it was currently producing, but no advantage could be taken of this and the expansion of employment opportunities it represented, for sugar sales had to be made under the constrictive British Commonwealth and international sugar agreements. As a result of this and of the absence of a free development of employment opportunities elsewhere in the economy, there was a good deal of unrest. Among the Indians this began in 1943 and was still exceedingly active in the early 1960's. The Indians concentrated their ire on the most visible target, the sugar-milling CSR, not on the total Fiji predicament or even the sugar industry. To forward their cause, the Indian cane growers formed unions led by educated Indians who were weak in economics but strong in leftist political radicalism. As the situation developed it was more and more obvious that the governance of the sugar industry must somehow be brought under public supervision. A proposal to this effect was made by an outside expert in 1944, but the situation was allowed to drift, as peace succeeded war and war peace, and not until 1961 was an ordinance passed by the government "To provide for independent guidance and in certain circumstances control in the sugar industry in the colony, to constitute a sugar board and a sugar advisory council, to provide for the settlement of disputes and for the control of sugar exports and for matters connected with the aforesaid purposes." In the course of the protracted and often bitter arguments over sugar, the CSR suffered a disadvantage from a too rigid adherence to the common Australian business practice of avoiding full "disclosure" of the state of its internal affairs. It was brought out that CSR in Fiji was run by a Fiji Division located in Sydney. One of CSR's contributions to peace-making was to set up its Fiji operations as a separate corporation governed locally. Through all the argumentation CSR took care to try to maintain its image as a wisely prudential capitalist corporation. This was successful, except among the Indians.

Although it was obvious that the key to a peaceful and rewarding future in Fiji was purposeful "development" to provide expanding employment opportunities for a growing population, little was accomplished in this regard between the end of the war and the early 1960's. Both the program for economic growth announced right after the war and the proposals of a special Commission in 1959 were frustrate, not least because of the intransigency of the Fijians (and the acquiescence of the administration in their position), though it must be recognized that neither the internal situation of Fiji nor the external marketing prospect was encouraging. Diversification, including the development of factory industries, was the obvious emphasis, but the discrepancy between agronomic and technological feasibility and the condition of the market for the products made success elusive. However, that the failure of employment opportunities to expand was adversely affecting not only the Indians but also the Fijians, especially those in the towns, was demonstrated by the Fijian and Indian participation in the nasty riots in Suva in December 1959. Some nervous Europeans heard through these disturbances a bell tolling for them, but they were actually more symptomatic than fundamental.

The Fijian position toward the situation was, while understandable in the light of history, of no help under existing conditions. Instead of facing the situation and recognizing that solutions could be worked out only in an atmosphere of goodwill between the races, the Fijians showed themselves more interested in protecting their traditional position and keeping the British in Fiji to guarantee its protection than in dealing with the problems of a complex multiracial society in a time of crisis. One of Ratu Sukuna's assumptions had been that his fellow Fijian leaders would, once it was clear that heavy emphasis was to be placed on preserving the essential values of the Fijian way of life, be as interested as himself in working out a progressive policy with regard to the context in which the Fijians would have to live. One of his great disappointments was that the Fijian leadership proved to have an emotional fixation on the Fijian way of life and suffered a poverty of ideas about anything else. They were not, as a matter of fact, prepared even to deal directly with the preservation of Fijian values, for when Sukuna retired in 1954—he died in 1958 —he was succeeded in office by a European. The Indians were a King Charles's head to the Fijians, but they showed no capacity to deal with them on equal terms in the economic arena and they were bedeviled by the certainty that they were a minority in their own country and would be even more decidedly at a disadvantage if a democratic arithmetic were ever applied to Fiji politics. These feelings of inadequacy and fear made them seek protection of their status as a special people in Fiji and to cling to the British as their pledged protectors. A paradoxical element of the situation was that their position required the Fijians to glorify the memory of Sir Arthur Gordon, though it was Sir Arthur who had imposed the Indians on them. In the early 1960's the prime political dogma of the Fijians was the preservation of the tie to the British crown and the rationalization of the tie as organic (not functional only) in terms for which there was no historical warrant. The political relevance of this from the Fijian point of view was entirely clear, but its relevance to the working out of the problems of multiracial Fiji was not, unless it was assumed that the British could be expected to perform a miracle in the penultimate phase of their long history as rulers of colonies. The Fijian tactic of evasion promised to serve the Fijians ill in the long run, for the problem of expanding employment opportunities could not be wished away; nor could the Indians be expected to stand around with folded hands while the Fijians wrapped themselves comfortably in an Aubusson blanket of imperial patriotism.

In 1947 the Western Samoans, stimulated by the news that New Zealand was about to enter into a Trusteeship Agreement for their country with the United Nations, petitioned the General Assembly for immediate autonomy and self-government, qualified only by the suggestion that New Zealand should continue as protector and adviser. The petition was signed by forty-six chiefs. Nobody acquainted with Western Samoan history since the arrival of the Europeans, least of all since 1920, was surprised by this action. The Samoans had long since demonstrated that they were astute and aggressive politicians. A reasonable guess at that time was that it would take them a quarter-century to achieve their goal, but in fact they achieved it within fifteen years.

Even before a special commission of the Trusteeship Council had had time to ascertain whether or not the Samoans were "ready" for what they asked, the New Zealand government had decided to take them at their word. The first steps proposed by the government accorded closely with what the Council members eventually suggested. In 1948, therefore, the title of the New Zealand representative in Western Samoa was changed from administrator to high commissioner. A Council of State was constituted consisting of the high commissioner and the high chiefs Tamasese and Melietoa. The old Legislative Council with its "official" majority was replaced by a Legislative Assembly with a Samoan majority, which was accorded full legislative and financial powers. Provision was made to introduce Samoans into the higher levels of the public service, for, while 80 per cent of the staff was Samoan, the higher, decision-making posts were in European hands. A scheme for familiarizing the Samoan legislators with the techniques of running departments was instituted.

By 1953 it was possible for the New Zealand government to issue a White Paper setting out the steps still necessary to achieve autonomy and self-government. The following year a constitutional convention began its work, which ended in the adoption of a finished constitution late in 1960. In 1959 cabinet government (a prime minister and eight other ministers) was instituted. The first prime minister was the former minister of Agriculture, the Hon. Fiame Mata'afa Mulinu'u II. A plebiscite, with voting by universal suffrage, in which the Samoans accepted the constitution and indicated their approval of independence, was held in May 1961. Western Samoa became an independent state on January 1, 1962, the first of the Pacific islands countries to regain "native sovereignty."

Western Samoa's transition from colonial status to independence was made at a time when the population was rapidly increasing: 66,761 in 1945, it passed the 100,000 mark in the late 1950's. Of the 97,300 people reported in the 1956 census, 88,000 were Samoans and 7900 part-Samoans, Europeans numbered 662, and "others," mostly Pacific islanders but including a few Chinese, 800. This was a highly homogeneous population. In the economic phases of preparation for independence, much attention was given to agriculture. The Samoanization of production for export, including the direction of the old Repatriation Estates, proceeded apace. The Samoans were well represented in the export-import trade and the internal retail trade. The leading exports were cocoa, bananas, and copra, and the principal customers were New Zealand and the United Kingdom. New Zealand and the United Kingdom were also the leading suppliers of imports. The government's income was derived in largest part by taxes on imports and exports. A step in the economic preparations for independence was the establishment of a

Bank of Western Samoa in 1959, owned jointly by the Western Samoan government and the New Zealand government-owned Bank of New Zealand. The Western Samoan pound was maintained at par with the New Zealand pound and was attached to it, though legal provision was made to sever the two currencies. Under a Treaty of Friendship, New Zealand had charge of all Western Samoa's foreign relations.

Threaded through the island story has been an account of the islands as a scene of man's quest for knowledge, and note has been taken of the intensification of the quest since 1900, more particularly by the anthropologists. Since World War II the quest has continued in historically established ways, but a new twist has been given to the story by the use of islands as allegedly legitimate places on which to conduct, or from which to launch, atomic tests, first in 1946 at Bikini and in 1948 at Eniwetok in the Marshall Islands of the United States Trust Territory, then in 1962 at Christmas Island, one of the many islands to which both Britain, as part of the Gilbert and Ellice group, and the United States lay claim, and Johnston Island, which the United States inherited with Hawaii, its claimant since 1858. The French have announced that they will test later in the 1960's from some island in French Polynesia. The legitimacy of this use of the islands may be questionable, as indeed the higher propriety of testing at all is questionable, but it is part of the heavy price the islands have had to pay for their involvement in the Western world, an involvement which has provided the substance of this story. The activities of the geophysicists in the islands during the IGY in 1958 were in the more reputable historical tradition. Since the war there has been a noticeable shift of emphasis among the researchers toward investigations, the results of which will presumably be of benefit to the indigenous people. Many of these are snared in the paradox that only through further Europeanization will the islanders find salvation. The continued emphasis on Europeanization is proof that even in the seventh decade of the twentieth century, "Europe" has no intention of retreating from the islands it first entered over four centuries ago, and whatever the islands may become in the future, they will not, if the Europeans have their way, revert to their pristine condition either via political independence or by any other route. History is irreversible.

ANTARCTICA

CHAPTER XII

The Heroic Age

Although the period from 1900 to World War I is commonly known as The Heroic Age of Antarctic exploration, the designation has never been popular with the men who were active in it. They have preferred to call it the renaissance age of Antarctic exploration, or the age of reconnaissance, or simply as the age of steam, as contrasted with the preceding age of sail and the succeeding age of oil. It was labeled "heroic" by outsiders largely because so many of the leaders of expeditions of the time appeared—indeed still appear—larger than life-size, because the technology of exploration was rather primitive compared to what it was to become and the risks involved in Antarctic work therefore still very great. In spite of the fact that the emphasis on scientific projects steadily increased, science had not yet overshadowed adventure, the aspect easiest for everybody and anybody to understand, and the adventurers were patently heroic in stature and deed. The heroic-adventurers, most of whom were adventurer-scientists or scientist-adventurers, and only a few purely one or the other, were of many nationalities: British, German, Swedish, French, Norwegian, Japanese, and Australian, but the age was dominated by Robert Falcon Scott and Ernest Shackleton, British, though the then ultimate sporting prize of first to reach the South Pole was snatched by a Norwegian, Roald Amundsen.

Between 1901 and 1916 there were sixteen expeditions, major and minor, Antarctic whaling got on its feet, and the first political moves were made. Twelve leaders were involved. Of the expeditions, Scott led two; Shackleton, after participating in Scott's first, led two of his own; the Frenchman J. B. Charcot led two; while Amundsen had been to Antarctica with De Gerlache before leading his own expedition; and the Australian Douglas Mawson had been with the second Scott expedition before he became a leader on his own. The other leaders were new to Antarctica, though some had experience in the Arctic. Of the leaders two,

Shackleton and Mawson, worked in the Antarctic in the next period, after World War I.

The first Scott expedition was at once the British response to the high-level agitation for systematic work in Antarctica and an effort to re-establish British leadership in polar exploration which had been lost in the latter half of the nineteenth century. What was wanted was not only a worth-while British accomplishment, but, also, a clear demonstration of superiority of capacity over competitors—foreigners. The work was definitely to be undertaken for the greater prestige and glory of Britain. The patriotic motive was conspicuous both in Scott and his patron, Sir Clements Markham, president of the Royal Geographical Society. Mark-ham had been resolved upon an Antarctic expedition since 1893. Finance was supplied by the Royal Society, the Royal Geographical Society, and private individuals and companies. Scott was appointed leader on June 10, 1900. The expedition was at once experimental and transitional. Scott himself was without polar experience. Born June 6, 1868, he had entered the navy as a cadet at thirteen, and by 1900 had risen to the rank of commander. He was a specialist in torpedoes. Of a gentle family that had fallen into difficult circumstances, he was a Tom Brown-like English-man, resembling in some respects James Clark Ross, though of far more equable temperament. He was as skeptical of the lesser breeds outside the Royal Navy's circle. Scott's second in command had been in the Arctic, but only the Australian physicist-meteorologist Bernacchi had been previ-ously to the Antarctic.

Everything had to be learned, most of all, travel into the continental interior. Scott and his fellows had to deal with the problems of food (quantity per day per man, kind, preparation in the field), clothing, shelter, and method of powering of the sledges. The ways and means of the Norwegian Nansen were closely studied and the methods of the American Peary were considered, but the exemplary British predecessor, much on Scott's mind, was Sir Leopold McClintok who had done his work in the Arctic fifty years earlier. Clothing, portable shelter, and sledges were not particularly troublesome, but Scott never mastered the food question, aside from its preparation in Nansen's field cooker, either as to quantity or kind, in large part because of the prevailing scientific ignorance of nutrition, in part because of Scott's personal prejudice in favor of short rations and punishingly hard work—a kind of moral im-perative with him. His emotions about animals stood in the way of a satisfactory handling of the problem of motive power for the sledges. Scott had an understanding of science without any specialist expertise of his own; he willingly satisfied his scientists with time and opportunity for work; and he was conscientious about facilitating the collection of data along his lines of travel for working up later. Nevertheless, his expedition was weighted on the side of adventure rather than science. He was a successful leader of men; they respected him; but his personal preference was for men who had had the discipline of the Royal Navy and he doubted his capacity to lead others. It was not by his choice that his second in command, Armitage, and his traveling companion, Shackleton, were merchant marine men.

The expedition finally sailed from England in the ship "Discovery" on August 6, 1901, and headed for Lyttleton, New Zealand (port of Christchurch), via the Cape of Good Hope, traveling far enough south of Australia—to within 200 miles of Adélie Land, in fact—to reach ice and to pay a brief call at Macquarie Island. From New Zealand a course was made to Cape Adare through the ice pack; the Cape was reached on January 9, 1902. Scott then coasted along the Ross Ice Shelf, traveling east; he found that the face of the shelf was farther south than reported by Ross; he reached the eastern limit of the shelf and observed land trending northeast which he named King Edward VII Land, thus confirming Ross's suspicion that there was land nearby. Returning west, the party landed on the shelf and a captive balloon was twice sent up to 800 feet for observations. Scott made the first ascent, Shackleton, provided with a camera, the second. The balloon and the camera were the most novel technological innovations of the expedition. A wintering camp was established at Hut Point on Ross Island, McMurdo Sound, by 400 miles the farthest south of any wintering attempted to that time. The island, on which the active volcano Erebus and the extinct volcano Terror, first seen by Ross, were located was first determined by Scott to be an island and named for Ross by him. The ship was deliberately frozen in, a deviation in procedure, and it, rather than the hut on land, was the expedition's headquarters. On the arrival of the relief ship "Morning" the following summer, it proved impossible to free the "Discovery" from the ice in which it was locked, so the expedition was continued through a second winter. The Scott party finally left the Antarctic in the "Discovery" accompanied by the two ships of the second relief—the "Morning" and the "Terra Nova"—on February 18, 1904. The "Terra Nova" was sent by the British Admiralty in a fit of acute anxiety about Scott's fate. On the way to New Zealand, Scott took his ship west toward the Balleny Islands and then made a reconnaissance still farther westward until convinced (incorrectly) that he had disproved some of Charles Wilkes's discoveries: "There is no case for any land eastward of Adélie Land." (The British skepticism of Wilkes was then still strong.) After a stopover at Auckland Island, "Discovery" went on with its relief ships to Lyttleton and sailed from thence via Cape Horn for England. The expedition had spent twenty-six months south of the Antarctic Circle.

The geographical significance of this first Scott expedition was the fact that he and his men began the penetration of the interior of the Antarctic continent. On November 2, 1902, Scott, accompanied by Ernest Shackleton and Dr. Edward A. Wilson, started out with dog teams to get as far south on the Ross Ice Shelf as possible. It was then thought not unlikely that the shelf might reach to the South Pole, though it had been noted visually at the hut that the coastal mountains trended south and might well stand between the southern limit of the shelf and the interior. Scott and his party traveled south for fifty-nine days and reached a point 380 miles from their headquarters at 82° 16′ 13″ South, 163° 30′ East on December 30, 1902. Careful observations of all matters of interest along the way were made—Wilson, in the absence of a camera, made drawings of their surroundings at each camp at the expense of an attack of snow blindness. At the camp farthest out they could clearly see a mountain barrier looming in their southward path, including one peak 15,000 feet high which they named for Markham. These mountains would have to be crossed to reach the interior and the Pole. The party was short of dogs (and underfed them) and from the beginning did much of the hauling themselves; before the journey's end all the dogs had died, confirming Scott's prejudice against them. But worse still, all three men came down with scurvy from malnutrition, Shackleton suffering most severely, to the point that he could no longer help with the pulling of the sledges and for a time had to ride on one. But they all survived, though Shackleton to his mortification was sent home on the relief ship "Morning" which had arrived via New Zealand while the party was absent. The experience gave warning that there was something wrong with the food supply—quantity, variety, or both. Even before scurvy appeared, they had suffered from chronic hunger. The homeward journey took thirty-fours days, making a total of ninety-three days spent on the trail.

Meanwhile, another party, led by Albert B. Armitage, the second in command, had discovered a route into the interior. By climbing Ferrar Glacier (so named later for the expedition's geologist), thirty-five miles long, flowing into McMurdo Sound, they found their way westward onto a vast plateau which became higher the farther they traveled on it. They reached an elevation of 9000 feet. This party was the first to see the interior continental plateau and obtain authentic information about what Antarctica was like beyond the coastal mountains.

The next season Scott himself followed the Ferrar Glacier route to the interior and with two companions—Petty Officer Edgar Evans and Stoker William Lashley—traveled 200 miles westward from the head of the glacier, reaching 77° 59′ South, 146° 33′ East on November 30, 1903. The sledges were man-hauled throughout. Scott judged the country "the most desolate region in the world." On the return journey to the hut, they deviated from the track on Ferrar Glacier and came upon a narrow valley free of ice, the first "oasis" found in Antarctica.

Scientifically the expedition made studies of sea and land ice, meteorology—the observations were made farther south than any compiled earlier—geology, vertebrate and invertebrate zoology, and magnetism; it made seismic, gravity, and auroral observations; and it made a limited contribution to oceanography, chiefly a miscellany of soundings. Dr. Wilson's triumph was the discovery for the first time of emperor penguin rookeries, this making possible rough observation of the great bird's eccentric habit of breeding in the depths of the Antarctic winter. As Scott remarked, the expedition "was not conducted in a spirit of *pure* adventure but . . . strove to add, and succeeded in adding, something to the sum of human knowledge."

On August 11, 1901, five days after Scott left England, a government-financed German expedition under Erich von Drygalski, a professor of geography at the University of Berlin who had earlied worked in Greenland, sailed from Kiel in the ship "Gauss" (named for the great pioneer of terrestrial magnetism). The expedition was the German response to the same forces that had brought Scott's into existence. Drygalski proposed an attack on the Antarctic continent far to the west of Scott whom he knew to be heading for the Ross Sea. Sailing via the Cape of Good Hope, Drygalski went on to Kerguelen Island where an advance party of scientists who had traveled by chartered steamer from Australia was at work. After a month's stay with them, Drygalski took his ship south and then southeast via Heard Island—roughly following 90° East—aiming to explore between Wilkes's westernmost reported land—Knox Coast—and Kemp Coast, reported in 1833 by the "Enderby" captain, Peter Kemp. He sighted land almost on the Antarctic Circle on February 1, 1902, but on the twenty-second the ship was caught in the ice, fortunately at a point where destruction by pressure was very unlikely. It remained imprisoned for a year. Making the most of the opportunities for scientific study on and around the ship—Drygalski had with him a naturalist, a meteorologist, a geologist, and a magnetician, but most of his study was oceanographic—Drygalski also led an expedition over the ice to what he presumed to be the mainland. The journey of about fifty miles took three and one-half days.

He discovered a 1000-foot nunatuk, the cone of an extinct volcano, which he called Gaussberg and, ascending in a balloon to 1500 feet, he photographed a great expanse of ice-covered country which he called

Kaiser Wilhelm II Coast. In the distance he espied high mountains which he thought were on the mainland but which proved, after Mawson's close investigation in 1914, to be on Drygalski Island (so named by Mawson). Not until February 1903 was the "Gauss" able to move. Drygalski then traveled in the ice from 90° East to 80° East where he gave up his quest, made for open water, and sailed for Capetown. Although he wanted to return for another winter, he was ordered home and arrived in Germany on November 24, 1903.

About the same time, again in response to the forces at work in the world of science, but far to the east in the islands around the tip of the Palmer-Graham Peninsula, mostly on the Atlantic Ocean side, an even more exciting drama was being unfolded. On October 16, 1901, a privately financed expedition of ten scientists left Gothenburg, Sweden, in the good ship "Antarctic," the same ship Bull had used for his visit to the Ross Sea. The captain was Carl A. Larsen, mentioned earlier. The purpose was primarily scientific. Director of the expedition was Otto Nordenskjold, professor of geology at Upsala University, nephew of Baron A. E. Nordenskjold, the first man to negotiate the Arctic northeast passage from the Atlantic to the Pacific (1878–79). The expedition had been planned since 1899. Reaching the South Shetland Islands in January 1902, the party surveyed De Gerlache (formerly *Belgica*) Channel and worked its way south to 66° 10′ South, 60° West. Nordenskjold then decided to set up a winter headquarters for a shore party of himself and five others on Snow Hill Island on the eastern side of the peninsula. During the winter, Captain Larsen was to take the ship to Ushaia in Argentine Tierra del Fuego, the Falkland Islands, and South Georgia, where scientific studies were to be made. Before settling down for the winter, the Snow Hill party sledged south down the coast to Richtofen Valley at 65° South. On its return from its winter voyage late in 1902, the ship did some exploration and then while trying to reach Snow Hill Island was beset by the ice. It was a very bad ice season. It was frozen in on January 9, 1903, about twenty-five miles southeast of Paulet Island, and was abandoned on February 13 shortly before it sank. The men reached Paulet Island after a perilous journey over the ice flows with some of their food and gear. A little while before, anticipating that the ice might well make it impossible to reach Snow Hill, a party of three men had been put ashore to make its way overland to the Snow Hill people and assure them they had not been abandoned. This party found itself unable to complete its journey. The expedition was thus broken up into three groups—the party on Snow Hill Island, the overlanding party, and the ship's company—isolated from one another within a distance of fifty miles. All had to winter where they were as best they could, the ship's company and the overlanders with no preplanning for such a contingency whatsoever. Nevertheless, all three parties survived with the loss of but one man, and he died of heart disease.

The next spring (1904) Nordenskjold prospected northeast and miraculously chanced upon the three overlanders moving down toward Snow Hill Island to join him. The parties met at Vega Island, named for the ship in which the Baron had made his famous voyage. When the leader of the long-haired, ragged, filthy overlanders came toward Nordenskjold, he said—not "Mr. Nordenskjold, I presume"—but "How do you do, Otto?" The two parties returned to Snow Hill. On October 13 Captain Larsen and five of his party started from Paulet Island to reach Snow Hill over the ice; they arrived on November 8. By an utterly miraculous coincidence, that same day an Argentine relief expedition in the ship "Uruguay," captained by Julian Irizar, arrived at Snow Hill and picked up the three groups of survivors. The castaways still at Paulet Island were rescued on the tenth. While it was an Argentine ship that carried out the rescue, Sweden, France, and Great Britain initiated plans to do so, or assisted others to act. In the light of a later passage in his life, it was appropriate that Shackleton was the British representative for co-operation with the Argentines. Like Drygalski's, Nordenskjold's people were able, in the midst of turmoil and peril, to continue fruitful scientific work. Nordenskjold's personal passion was the study of fossils. It was Nordenskjold who, in 1903, suggested that the two geologically distinct parts of the Antarctic continent, with the division along a line drawn from the Weddell to the Ross Sea, be called East and West Antarctica by reference to the hemisphere in which they fell. West Antarctica had, Nordenskjold noted, a geologically Andean character, while East Antarctica, twice the size of West, was a great geological shield.

Still another expedition was in the Antarctic at this time—the Scottish National Antarctic Expedition, led by Dr. W. S. Bruce; its locale was the Weddell Sea. An expression of Scottish nationalism, it was privately financed, largely by James and Andrew Coats. Bruce, it will be recalled, had been in the area with the Dundee whalers. His scientific interests had then been frustrated. This time he placed the emphasis firmly on science, especially oceanography and meteorology, but also zoology and botany. Bruce talked with Scott, Drygalski, and Nordenskjold before their departures with the idea of co-ordinating observations, thus increasing the worth of everybody's work. His ship was the "Scotia," a rebuilt Norwegian whaler captained by Thomas Robertson who had commanded the "Active" on the Dundee whaling expedition. Bruce's main objective was to illuminate the nature of the Weddell Sea. He hoped for discovery of coastal lands, but aside from a shore station for wintering, he did not plan land operations and specifically and rather self-righteously disclaimed any interest in the great sporting challenge, the Pole. The "Scotia" sailed from the Clyde on November 2, 1902, and proceeded via the Falkland Islands, the South Orkneys, and the South Sandwich Islands into the Weddell Sea. Soundings to determine the configuration of the ocean bottom were constantly and carefully made. The farthest south reached on the first try was 70° 25′ South, 170° 12′ West on February 22, 1903, when heavy pack ice forced a retreat. (This was short of Weddell's mark.) A wintering station was built on Laurie Island, South Orkneys, where the emphasis was on meteorology, though a general ecological survey of the island was carried out. The ship was frozen in. The next season the "Scotia" put to sea on November 27, 1903, leaving the meteorologists to their work, and visited the Falklands, then went to Buenos Aires where arrangements were made for Argentine co-operation in the weather station at Laurie. (Under Argentine government patronage the station became permanent, the first permanent station south of 60°, eventually with fateful political consequences.) At the Falklands Bruce learned of the troubles of the Scott, Drygalski, and Nordenskjold expeditions, as far as they were known, and at Buenos Aires he met the Frenchman Jean Charcot, outward bound for the west side of the Palmer-Graham Peninsula and the "Uruguay" which rescued Nordenskjold. After landing a party of Argentine meteorologists at Laurie, the "Scotia" went south into the Weddell Sea, sounding as it went, and on March 6, 1904, discovered land runnning northeast-southwest between 20° and 37° West which was named Coats Land (now Coats Coast), the first land discovered at the head of the Weddell Sea. It indicated where the continental coast was in this area—if it was continental coast. Farthest south on this voyage was 74° 1′ South, 22° West, beyond Weddell's maximum. Continuing soundings, the "Scotia" sailed via Gough Island for Capetown and reached the Clyde again on July 31, 1904. The expedition immeasurably increased the knowledge and understanding of the Weddell Sea and established the underwater association of South America and the Palmer-Graham peninsula.

The last of the expeditions of this first group of the twentieth century was that of Dr. Jean Charcot of France. Charcot, who became an exemplary figure in French polar work, was a physician, son of the doctor of the same name who was one of Sigmund Freud's teachers. It was Charcot's wish to participate in the rescue of Nordenskjold that had turned his thoughts to Antarctica, but while he was at Buenos Aires the "Uruguay" returned with the Nordenskjold party. Charcot had been accompanied from France by De Gerlache of the "Belgica." De Gerlache went home from Buenos Aires and Charcot went on to the west coast of the Palmer-Graham Peninsula to continue the "Belgica's" work, cued by De Gerlache as to what needed doing. Charcot arrived at the South Shetlands in his ship "Le Français" on February 1, 1904. After straightening out some geographical confusions in the maze of coastal islands, the party wintered on Booth Island (also known as Wandel) and the next season charted the western coast of the Palmer Archipelago. He mistook Adelaide Island for mainland and named it Loubet Land (after the president of France)—the name Loubet was afterward transferred to a stretch of peninsula coast. Still sailing south, Charcot sighted Alexander I Land (now Island) but was unable to reach it because of ice. Suffering a serious accident to the ship, he turned north, discovered the excellent harbor of Port Lockroy on Wiencke Island, and reached Puerto Madryn, Argentina, March 4, as anxiety for his safety was mounting. The ship was sold to the Argentine government, and Charcot returned to France by liner. He had already determined upon another Antarctic voyage. His burgeoning reputation was for being the most insouciant in the face of danger of all the Antarctic leaders. His scientific work was first-class.

The failure of the Dundee whalers of 1892 to find the kind of whales they knew from their Arctic experience how to handle, and Captain Carl A. Larsen's identical experience at the same time, caused a delay in the initiation of whaling in Antarctica until 1905, when technological changes in the industry made feasible the taking of the whales of far southern waters. Thereafter until the 1920's Antarctic whaling was concentrated around and on either side of the Palmer-Graham Peninsula. The industry boomed, with the 1910–11 season a peak, up to and into World War I, when there was a slump. When the industry revived in the early 1920's, the whalers invaded the Ross Sea, where Bull had explored the whaling possibilities back in 1895.

The pioneer of the industry, its grand old man and first citizen, was Carl A. Larsen. On his return to Argentina with Nordenskjold, he had stayed on in Buenos Aires and with Argentine backing formed the Compañía Argentina de Pesca. The company employed Norwegian whaling ships, equipment, and personnel. The whaling he planned was based on capture of the animals at sea by small vessels which would tow them to a factory on shore for processing. The first factory was built by Argentine workmen at Grytviken, South Georgia, in December 1904. This site had been visited and named by the ship "Scotia," Larsen in command, during the Nordenskjold expedition. The very first year the operation made a substantial profit. In October 1905 the first modern "floating factory" or factory ship, Norwegian owned, came into the area and made its base at Admiralty Bay, King George I Island, in the South Shetlands. A shore factory was set up on Deception Island, South Shetlands, in 1910. Charcot's Port Lockroy was also used as a base for whaling. In the 1913–14 season a floating factory was established by Norwegians in the South Orkneys; a little later a shore factory was built there. By 1912, with the Norwegians dominant in the industry, there were 37 factory ships, 27 shore stations, and 148 small whale catching ships working around the three centers: South Georgia, the South Orkneys, and the South Shetlands. Seven thousand men were employed. About half the world's supply of whale oil was then coming from the Antarctic, and sealing, the first exploitation of Antarctic resources, was still not completely dead. An American sealer after sea-elephant oil operated at South Georgia in the 1912–13 season. But whaling, after years of frustration, was now the support of the Antarctic economy.

The development had taken place in an area of which the British took a possessive view. Larsen, who eventually became a British subject, acknowledged their rights by obtaining a lease of land for his shore station at Grytviken from the British colonial secretary through the British legation at Buenos Aires. The lease was for twenty-one years at a rent of £250 a year. In 1906 the whaling situation was investigated for the British government by Captain M. H. Hodges in the ship "Sappho." He charted parts of Cumberland Bay, South Georgia, on which Grytviken was located. The issuance of licenses for whaling was instituted and placed in the hands of the governor of the Falkland Islands. South Georgia, the South Orkneys, the South Shetlands, and Graham Land were all considered British by virtue of first discovery and were thought of as dependencies of the Falkland Islands. By limiting the number of licenses issued for a given location, the destruction of the whales could to some extent be controlled. Such a limitation was first placed on licenses for South Georgia. The governor of the Falklands also issued regulations to govern the actual whaling. At first he laid down a royalty payable on all whales taken, but this was soon changed to a royalty on each barrel of oil won. To control the killings, the taking of calves and mother whales accompanied by calves was prohibited. To facilitate control, Port Foster, Deception Island, South Shetlands, was made an official "port of entry" for the islands in the vicinity and nearby Graham Land. Beginning in 1910 a British magistrate who was also a postmaster was stationed at Port Foster each season. This system of licenses and regulations governed Antarctic whaling for a quarter-century.

By 1914 the value of production was £1,250,000 a year and rising. Whale oil was in strong demand for the making of glycerine and margarine. Whaling factory byproducts, bone meal and flesh meal, the one a useful fertilizer, the other when made up into cakes a good feed for cattle, both combined a kind of "guano," could well pay for the costs of rendering out the oil. The effective fishing radius of a shore or floating factory was about one hundred miles, which accounts for their multiplication over the large area under exploitation. At that time blue and fin whales accounted for 80 per cent by numbers of all taken, while humpbacks accounted for 15 per cent, and right whales were uncommonly found. The latter had never been at all common—their absence was what discouraged the whalers when they first investigated Antarctic waters—but the humpbacks had been numerous and were suffering from the attrition of excessive killings; they faced extinction. On the other hand, the supply of fins and blues seemed then to be inexhaustible. However, it was the view of an astute biologist who studied the question in 1914 that the industry might be approaching a "critical stage" on the basis of known resources; he suggested that conservation measures were very much in order.

As no one, not even the Argentines and Chileans, disputed the British right to regulate whaling, there was no immediate challenge to the Letters Patent, issued on July 21, 1908, by warrant under "the King's [Edward VII] Sign Manual" "appointing the Governor of the Colony of the Falkland Islands to be Governor of South Georgia, the South Orkneys, the South Shetlands, the Sandwich Islands and Graham's Land, and providing for the Government thereof as dependencies" of the Falklands. (Bruce's Coats Land was also included within the parallels of latitude and longitude cited, but not specifically named.) In the document it was simply and directly stated that the named places "are part of our Dominions." The basis of this claim was first discovery, for there was only partial and intermittent "occupation." It had long been the habit of British explorers to claim discoveries for the king, as indeed explorers of other nations commonly made such claims for their governments. But only if they were followed up by occupation were they meaningful in international law. The British were thus the first to assert a claim to sovereignty in the Antarctic on any basis; and they did not do it by formally claiming sovereignty but by providing for government on the assumption that they were sovereign. In this fashion Antarctica was brought into the international political arena, although political repercussions were delayed for twenty years. The economic basis of the action was remarkably clear. No further moves in the game of partitioning Antarctica were made until the 1920's and 1930's when the extension of whaling to other Antarctic waters provided a motivation. In 1917, however, the British clarified the boundaries of the Falkland Island

Dependencies when it was discovered that the northern boundary as originally laid down included a portion of the tip of South America. This overlap was a faint forecast of things to come.

It was characteristic of Shackleton that when he was invalided home by Scott he should early have resolved to return to Antarctica as leader of an expedition of his own. Shackleton was a very different man from Scott. Of Anglo-Irish origin, the son of a doctor, he was born February 15, 1874. Sanguine in temperament, romantic in outlook with a passion for Victorian poetry, of charming personality with a gift of speech which Englishmen call Irish, a big, good-looking man, but exceptional for strength of will rather than strength of body, he was very much the adventurer and hardly at all the scientist. His early years, after a not particularly brilliant schooling, were spent in the merchant marine (mostly on passenger carriers) which he entered at sixteen. By bringing a little influence to bear, he obtained his appointment to Scott's first expedition at the age of twenty-six. Here Shackleton found his real vocation, leadership of men—the power to command the loyalty of men of far more various character and talent than Scott would ever have chosen to gather about him—in great jousts with fortune in far and difficult places. By the chance that Scott took him to Antarctica, his field of action became Antarctica; it might equally well have been the jungles of the Amazon or the deserts of Central Asia. But the vocation of leadership of exploring expeditions is a hard one to follow if one has neither money, ready access to it, or a powerful patron. Shackleton was thus always open to the appeal of get-rich-quick schemes and he spent much energy upon them. He never had enough money for any of his expeditions. For his first, it was shortage all the way in spite of the generous contributions of wealthy acquaintances and contributions from the governments of Australia—£5000—and New Zealand—£1000—and much in kind. To his men he was affectionately known as "The Boss," a wonderful leader, a stupendous performer in tight places. Shackleton was par excellence the leader as popular hero. It was in keeping with his dashing character and instinct for the popular that he should have frankly declared that the principal objective of his first expedition was the South Pole, the prime sporting objective in Antarctica at that moment.

Shackleton's ship, the "Nimrod," left England on August 7, 1907, headed for Lyttleton, New Zealand, via the Cape of Good Hope. However, Shackleton and some of his men traveled out by commercial liner via Australia. Several men subsequently to prove invaluable additions to the company were recruited in Australia. The "Nimrod" sailed from

Lyttleton for Antarctica on January 1, 1908, and to save coal was towed by the steamship "Koonya" 1510 miles to the Antarctic Circle. (The "Koonya" was, incidentally, the first steel vessel to cross the circle.) Scott had warned Shackleton away from McMurdo Sound on the ground that he intended soon to return there himself, so it was Shackleton's intention to set up a headquarters either in King Edward VII Land or on the ice of the Ross Shelf, both locations having the great merit of being nearer the Pole than McMurdo. Unfortunately, it proved impossible to keep to this program for Edward VII Land proved inaccessible and the ice seemed very unsafe, so, under the pressure to make a final decision before ice prevented the ship from leaving for its wintering port in New Zealand, Shackleton perforce went to McMurdo after all. He did not, however, use Scott's site but located his hut on Cape Royds at the western end of Ross Island. As a technician of exploration, Shackleton at this stage was very much beholden to Scott, though he had developed independent ideas, particularly in the realm of organization. He had adopted Norwegian traveling equipment, but, like Scott, he was against using dogs. He was experimenting with Siberian ponies, but he was in favor of pulling the sledges by hand. His most striking technological innovation was an automobile. It was not a success as a transport vehicle on the ice, but it was demonstrated that the internal combustion engine would operate in the Antarctic cold, an important point for the future. As to food, Shackleton left this largely to his medical officer. The diet for sledging journeys proved to be inadequate in quantity and deficient in vitamins. As Scott's dietary involved slow starvation, so did Shackleton's. The plan of field work called for, in addition to the try for the Pole, a journey to the Magnetic Pole and a geological field trip to Ferrar Glacier and vicinity. The concentration of scientific work at headquarters was on meteorology.

The journey to the Pole was peculiarly Shackleton's personal project. It was the greatest undertaking in land travel in the Antarctic to that time, involving a minimum of 1600 miles out and back, including the discovery of a route from the Ross Ice Shelf onto the interior plateau on which it was assumed the Pole was located. As companions for this challenging journey Shackleton chose as his second in command, twenty-nine year-old Lieutenant Jameson Boyd Adams R.N.R., a merchant mariner like himself; thirty-year-old Eric Stewart Marshall, the expedition's doctor; and Frank Wild, a merchant mariner who had been in the Scott expedition, thirty-six years old, a direct descendant through his mother of Captain James Cook. The Pole party got away on October 29, 1908, and was accompanied by a supporting party until November 7. The start was made with four ponies, but the first had to be killed on November 21 and the last was lost down a crevasse on December 7. From that day on, it was man-hauling all the way. Scott's farthest south was passed on November 26; the men were now in sight of the mountains in country never before seen by human eyes, and when Shackleton reviewed his diary for publication he inserted this note which so well reveals an explorer's psychology:

It falls to the lot of few men to view land not previously seen by human eyes, and it was with feelings of keen curiosity, not unmingled with awe, that we watched the new mountains rise from the great unknown that lay ahead of us. Mighty peaks they were, the eternal snows at their bases, and their rough-hewn forms rising high toward the sky. No man of us could tell what we would discover on our march south, what wonders might not be revealed to us, and our imaginations could take wings until a stumble in the snow, the sharp pangs of hunger, or the dull ache of physical weariness brought back our attention to the needs of the immediate present. As the days wore on, and mountain after mountain came into view, grimly majestic, the consciousness of our insignificance seemed to grow upon us. We were but tiny black specks crawling slowly and painfully across the white plain, and bending our puny strength to the task of wrestling from nature secrets preserved inviolate through all the ages. Our anxiety to learn what lay beyond was none the less keen, however, and the long days of marching over the Barrier surface were saved from monotony by the continued appearance of new land to the south-east.

These fascinating mountains, however, had somehow to be crossed if the interior plateau was to be reached and the Pole achieved. It was with thankfulness, therefore, that on December 4, after climbing a mountain (3350 feet) to gain a view of the surrounding country, they saw a "great glacier running almost south and north between two huge mountain ranges," a kind of giant esculator into the interior. (Shackleton later named it the Beardmore Glacier after Sir William Beardmore—later Lord Invernairn—builder of battleships and maker of armor plate, chief benefactor of his expedition.) They set out to climb this glacier, 12 miles wide, 100 miles long, at 83° 30′ South, 173° East, and it took them from December 5 to December 27. They reached the plateau at an elevation of 9280 feet, and went on south. By January 1, 1909, they had beaten both the South and North polar records for high latitudes, but the inadequacy of their food and the nightmarish exhaustion induced by constant man-hauling was fatally telling on them. January 9 they reached the limit of their endurance, and the shattering decision to acknowledge defeat had to be made: "We have shot our bolt, and the tale is latitude 88° 23′ South, longitude 162° East . . . Whatever regrets may be, we have done our best." They were within ninety-seven miles of the Pole. With difficulty they made it back to base in time to catch the "Nimrod" which had returned from New Zealand to relieve them.

Before the journey to the Pole was begun, Edgeworth David, professor of geology at Sydney University, Douglas Mawson, lecturer in mineralogy and petrology at Adelaide University, and Alister Mackay, a Scottish surgeon, climbed Mount Erebus for the first time. They reached the active crater at the peak and found it to be 900 feet deep and half-a-mile across, with three openings at the bottom. They calculated the mountain to be 13,370 feet high (later ascertained to be 13,200). This was the most remarkable bit of mountaineering done in the Antarctic to that time.

While Shackleton and his party were away, the same team of two "colonials" and a Scotsman reached the area of the South Magnetic Pole. They left the hut on September 25, 1908. For the first ten miles, their stores were transported in the automobile, but thereafter they were man-hauled. They journeyed for 200 miles on the coastal ice of Victoria Land, working their way west, crossed two tortuous "ice tongues" (Nordenskjold and Drygalski) which projected athwart their path into the sea, and then turned inland and ascended Larsen Glacier (at 75° 10′ South, 162° 35′ East) to reach the plateau. The area of the Magnetic Pole was reached at 7000 feet on January 16, 1909. They then returned to the coast to be picked up near the Drygalski Ice Tongue (164° 30′ East) by the "Nimrod." All told, the party traveled 1260 miles and not only achieved an objective sought by Antarctic explorers since 1840 but, also, clarified the geography of Victoria Land and gathered specimens to illuminate its geology.

Meanwhile the expedition's twenty-three year-old geologist, Raymond Priestley, then still a candidate for a science degree in geology at Bristol, led a party to investigate the geology of Butter Point (New Harbor, McMurdo Sound), Dry Valley, and Ferrar Glacier. The "Nimrod" met them at Butter Point.

After a reconnaisance westward from McMurdo Sound, the ship finally left Antarctic waters on March 9 and arrived at Stewart Island, New Zealand, on the twenty-second. Shackleton sent an exclusive press dispatch to the London *Daily Mail* giving in 2500 words (the longest press dispatch ever sent from New Zealand up to that time) the gist of the expedition's story. The ship then moved on to Lyttleton. Shackleton himself went home by liner from Australia. Characteristically Sir Clements Markham, Scott's implacable partisan, questioned Shackleton's accuracy and honesty. The world, however, received him as a hero.

J. B. Charcot's second Antarctic voyage of 1908–10 overlapped Shackleton's stay in the south and extended a bit beyond it. Using a ship with the appropriately insouciant name of "Pourquoi Pas?" Charcot again concentrated on the problems of the area at the south of the western side of the peninsula, with special attention to charting, Charcot's specialty. The "Pourquoi Pas?" sailed from Cherbourg on August 31, 1908, and approached its field of operations from Punta Arenas, the southernmost Chilean city on the Strait of Magellan. After a call at the South Shetlands, Charcot went south beyond Adelaide Island (which he now recognized he had been mistaken to call Loubet Land and assume to be part of the peninsula); the island, he ascertained, was seventy miles long, far longer than generally supposed. Beyond Adelaide Island he discovered Marguerite Bay—named for his wife—of which Adelaide Island was one boundary and Alexander I Island another, the Fallières Coast—named for the president of France—running along the peninsula from 67° 31' South to 69° 24' South. At one stage, Charcot got within two miles of Alexander I Land, a remarkable feat in those icy seas. Returning north, he wintered at Petermann Island (which Dallman had named in 1873), from whence he made short journeys onto the peninsula. On November 9, 1909, he took the "Pourquoi Pas?" to Deception Island for coaling. He then charted the island and also Admiralty Bay, King George I Island, like Deception a whaling base. Returning south he discovered land at 70° 15' South 74° 50' West, southwest of Alexander I Land, to which it was attached by an ice shelf. He named his discovery Charcot Land after his father, but years later it was proved to be an island. The "Pourquoi Pas?" was then headed west into the Bellingshausen Sea, Peter I Island, not seen since Bellingshausen's discovery of it in 1821, was sighted, and Captain Cook's farthest south was reached. The ship thereupon turned north for Punta Arenas and home. The scientific work included contributions to hydrography, oceanography, radio-electrical studies, and meteorology in addition to the highly expert charting for which the expedition became especially famous.

Scott had resumed duty in the Royal Navy on his return from the Antarctic but his mind was soon made up that he should go back, as he had revealed to Shackleton when he asked him not to establish a base at McMurdo Sound. Scott finally got away in 1910. While the emphasis of his expedition was scientific, it was Scott's announced purpose to try to reach the South Pole, by Beardmore Glacier as Shackleton had. This led not only to the Antarctic's most cathartic tragedy but also to abrasion of the feelings of the sporting English when the prize of first at the Pole was snatched away by the Norwegian, Amundsen.

The second Scott expedition sailed in the "Terra Nova" from Cardiff, Wales, on June 15, 1910. After a call at Capetown, course was made for Melbourne in Australia where Scott received a telegram from Amundsen: "Am going South." This was the first indication that Amundsen was to be a competitor in the struggle for the South Pole; the assumption had all along been that he was preparing to return to the Arctic. Moving across to New Zealand, the "Terra Nova" was berthed at the same quay at Lyttleton as the "Discovery" earlier. Christchurch was Scott's chosen southern headquarters; a monument to his memory is erected there. The ship sailed from Lyttleton on November 26, 1910, and after a call at Port Chalmers (Dunedin), sailed south. It was a rough and difficult passage, twenty days were spent getting through the ice pack, but on January 4 they reached Cape Evans, Ross Island, where a headquarters camp was built. Almost immediately depot laying for the journey to the Pole was commenced. Before returning to New Zealand for the winter, the "Terra Nova" was sent to establish a party in King Edward VII Land, but this proving impossible it was decided, in fear that if the ship stayed south longer it would be frozen in, that the party should be put ashore on Cape Adare. While traveling along the Ross Ice Shelf front, the "Terra Nova" party had discovered Amundsen and his people established on the ice near the inlet called Bay of Whales (so named by Shackleton in 1908 when he had concluded it was unsafe to make a camp on the ice, a decision Amundsen judged to have deprived Shackleton of the prize of first to the Pole). The news was conveyed to Scott's headquarters. It made the men "furiously angry" and Scott was deeply annoyed—he had not expected Amundsen to approach the continent via the Ross Sea entryway—but he soon recovered and wrote in his diary: "The proper, as well as the wiser, course for us is to proceed exactly as though this had not happened."

Roald Amundsen had been in the Antarctic with De Gerlache in 1897–99, but his reputation rested on his later work in the Arctic. In 1903–6, he had accomplished a dream of centuries; he had traveled the Northwest Passage from the Atlantic to the Pacific across the top of North America for the first time. When Scott was assembling his expedition, it was understood that Amundsen was preparing a return to the Arctic to try for the North Pole by "drifting" his ship after the fashion of Nansen earlier. He was believed to plan his entry into the ice via the Bering Sea, this requiring him to make a journey around Cape Horn. The plan was rendered nugatory when it was announced on September 6, 1909, that the American Robert E. Peary had reached the Pole on April 6, but instead of publicly announcing a shift of plans from the North to the South Pole, Amundsen kept his intentions secret until he had reached Madeira, ostensibly en route from Christiansand—he sailed August 9—around the Horn to the Bering Sea. From Madeira he sent his telegram to Scott and sailed directly to the Bay of Whales, Ross Ice

Shelf. His knowledge of the shelf was entirely derived from "the literature"—he and his men read the books of Scott and Shackleton with particular care—but he felt he knew it well as soon as he reached it. His
planning for the journey to the Pole, done at his home in Norway in
September 1909, was extraordinarily precise and detailed, even though
it was not known in advance how the men would get from the shelf to
the plateau save it would not be by Beardmore Glacier, and the plan was
executed to the letter. It was based firmly on the use of dogs to haul the
sledges—no man-hauling for the Norwegians; the men were to use skis
all the time; the food supply was to be generous; and the concentration
was to be on the single objective with but minimum attention to scientific
work along the way, even to neglect of the cartographical record. The use
of dogs and skis was Amundsen's fundamental difference from Scott;
they gave him the advantage of speed, and speed was of the essence. But
Amundsen's extraordinary concentration on the single point of reaching the Pole was, aside from the British resentment of his unsporting conduct in challenging Scott after making what they called a feint in another
direction, the most commonly criticized aspect of Amundsen's performance. However, the Amundsen party made meteorological and ice
studies at its base on the shelf, its ship did important oceanographical
work in the South Atlantic during the winter, and while Amundsen was
away on his journey to the Pole his associate Lieutenant K. Prestrud
made a pioneer reconnaissance by land into Scott's King Edward VII
Land (later Edward VII Peninsula). The party's ship was the "Fram,"
one of the most famous of polar ships, originally built for Nansen's
Arctic expedition of 1893–96. Amundsen was entirely aware that his
outlook and procedure differed completely from Scott's. He wrote in his
book: "Scott's plan and equipment were so widely different from my own
that I regarded the telegram I sent him. . . . rather as a mark of courtesy
than as a communication which might cause him to alter his programme
in the slightest degree. The British expedition was designed entirely for
scientific research. The Pole was only a side issue, whereas in my extended plan it was the main object."

Not only had Amundsen planned to establish his base camp on the
Ice Shelf, as near the Pole as he could get by ship, but he planned to
start for the Pole as early in the season as possible. His dogs could stand
the cold much better than Scott's ponies. But he rather overdid it and
when he made a start on September 8, he was soon frustrated by excessive cold. A final start had to be postponed until October 19.

There were five men in the party: Roald Amundsen, Helmer Hans-
sen, Oskar Wisting, Sverre Hassel, and Olav Bjaaland. Traveling due
south from their base, they passed their outermost depot at 82° South

on November 6 and entered the unknown. By November 17 they were in position to start through the mountains of the Queen Maud Range at the head of the shelf which they had first seen some days earlier. It proved a tortuous and difficult task. This was the critical point in the journey and they might easily have been defeated. They took supplies for sixty days. They accomplished the passage by using the Axel Heiberg Glacier, six miles wide and thirty miles long, for their final ascent. Axel Heiberg lay between Mounts Fridtjof Nansen (13,100 feet) and Don Pedro Christophersen (12,800) at 85° 35′ South, 165° West, 250 miles east of Beardmore. They kept to the Don Pedro side. On November 22 they reduced their dog teams by selective killings and rearranged their stores. At this camp they were detained for five days, mostly by bad weather; they went on even before the weather had improved. By December 1 they were on the plateau and passed Shackleton's farthest south on the eighth. Six days later, on December 14, they were in the vicinity of the Pole at 89° 56′ South. The next two days were spent encircling the area to get as close to the actual pole as their instruments allowed them to calculate its location; they left clear indications of their visit, named the surrounding plateau for King Haakon VII, and departed for their base camp on the seventeenth. They were back on the shelf on January 6, after 51 days on land, and on January 25 reached camp. They had been out 99 days and had traveled 1860 miles. Eleven dogs of the fifty-two with which they had started survived to return to the base.

The "Fram" was back in port, and the entire party embarked on January 29, 1912. They headed for Hobart, Tasmania, and from there Amundsen sent the world the news of his great feat. Chapter I of his narrative of the expedition, dated Brisbane, Queensland, April 13, 1912, begins: "Here I am, sitting in the shade of palms . . ." His rival then lay dead on the Ice Shelf.

On May 9, 1911, Scott recorded in his diary a brief comment on a lecture he had given his men the previous evening. "I could not but hint," he wrote, "that in my opinion the problems of reaching the Pole can best be solved by relying on the ponies and man hauling." Recording his diary entry on October 31, the day before his start for the Pole, he wrote: "The future is in the lap of the gods; I can think of nothing left undone to deserve success." In his "Message to the Public," written as he lay awaiting death in his tent on the ice shelf, he began: "The causes of the disaster are not due to faulty organization but to misfortune in all risks which had to be undertaken." Thus it is apparent that Scott, with his prejudice against dogs and in favor of short rations and the punishing man-hauling, never really glimpsed the causes of his misfortune.

There was an element of pessimistic fatalism in his outlook. A melancholic sense of doom runs as an undercurrent in his diary of the journey to and from the Pole, contrasting sharply with the hearty optimism of Amundsen, a difference as sharp as the differences in their methods and performance.

The journey to the Pole started from the base camp at Cape Evans on November 1, 1911, the party for the Pole not finally selected. The starting date was later than Amundsen's because the ponies could not endure the low temperatures obtaining earlier. To get the gear and supplies forward to the foot of Beardmore Glacier all available forms of transport were pressed into use: ponies, dogs, man-hauling, and two motor sledges, a technological innovation Scott hoped forecast the end of the use of animals. Both motor sledges broke down early in the journey. (Aside from the motor sledges, the only other striking "technological innovation" of this expedition was the presence of a professional photographer, Herbert G. Ponting.) But the first true misfortune overtook the men on December 5–8 when they suffered a four-day blizzard of soft, sticky snow which kept them in their tents, buried everything, and made traveling exceedingly troublesome. On the ninth after a move forward, all the ponies were shot. Two days later the dogs were sent back. Thereafter man-hauling was the sole reliance. The soft snow of the blizzard impeded their progress on the glacier, and on December 16 they were six days behind Shackleton's schedule, the yardstick they were using, but by December 30—by this time they were past the glacier and on the plateau—they had caught up with his dates, 180 miles from the Pole. Meanwhile, one of the two remaining support parties had been sent back on December 22; on January 4 the last support party was dismissed at 87° 34′ South, 146 miles from the Pole. Instead of four men as all along intended, Scott at this point decided to have five in his party: himself aged 43; Dr. Edward Wilson, his close friend and chief of the expedition's scientists, aged 39; Lawrence Oates, a professional soldier, aged 32; Henry Bowers, an Indian army man, aged 28; and Petty Officer Edgar Evans, aged 37. Evans was the fifth man added at the final moment; he was regarded as an exceptionally strong man. On January 9, 1912, this party passed Shackleton's farthest south and on the fifteenth Scott wrote in his diary: "We left our depot today with nine days' provisions, so that it ought to be a certain thing now, and the only appalling possibility the sight of the Norwegian flag forestalling ours." The very next day Bowers detected a "black speck ahead"—a black flag left flying by Amundsen. "Great God!" wrote Scott on January 17, "this is an awful [awe-inspiring?] place and terrible enough for us to have laboured to it without the reward of priority. . . . Now for the run home and a desperate struggle. I wonder if we can do it."

The Scott party left the Pole on January 19, 1912. By the twenty-third Edgar Evans, who had suffered frostbite on his hands, was visibly weakening and four days later it was acknowledged that the men were perishingly hungry. Here was revealed a fatal menace to the enterprises: undernourishment, especially the then unknown vitamin deficiency, aggravated by exhaustion from man-hauling. Evans, by repute so strong, was weakening first—it was later decided that he had begun to falter even *before* the Pole had been reached—because his large frame was even less well nourished by the prevailing rations than those of his fellows. The men reached the head of the glacier in twenty-one days from the Pole, as contrasted with the twenty-seven they had taken from that point outward to the Pole. February 11 was their worst day—they became badly entangled by the frustrating surface conditions on the glacier. A week later they reached the camp where the ponies had been killed. The previous day, at the foot of the glacier, after appalling suffering, unbelievable disintegration, and a monumental display of the will to survive, Evans died. The shock of this to the party was very great.

On the ice shelf the survivors found the surface very bad for hauling, the weather menacing, the cold unusually intense even for the time of year, and shortages in the cached supplies of indispensable oil for their cooker. By March 11 the situation was so bad that Scott ordered Dr. Wilson to hand over to each man the "means of ending our troubles." They were fast breaking down, the measure of their disintegration being the condition of their feet. Scott's were the last to begin to go. At this stage Oates was in the worst shape, most visibly from frozen feet, and on the sixteenth or seventeenth—Scott by then was uncertain about dates—after having begged that he be left behind as a burden to his fellows, Oates walked out into a blizzard from the tent to which they were confined, saying "I am just going outside and may be some time." Scott added in his diary, ". . . we have not seen him since." On March 19 Scott summed up the predicament of the remaining three: "Sledge dreadfully heavy. We are 15½ miles from the depot [One Ton, 150 miles from the base camp, a principal depot of food and oil] and out to get there in three days. What progress! We have two days' food but barely a day's fuel. All our feet are getting bad . . . The weather doesn't give us a chance—the wind N. to N.W. and —40 temp. today." Two days later they were still eleven miles from One Ton and there they were overtaken by a blizzard which confined them to their tent. Scott's last diary entry was made on the twenty-ninth with the storm still raging. He was the last to die. From the headquarters hut to the Pole had taken 75 days, the return to their final camp 72 days; they had been out for 147 days. The bodies were not found until eight months later.

The Scott try for the Pole had ended in complete tragedy, but as Cherry-Garrard remarked when he came to make his classic assessment of the journey, "I now see very plainly that though we achieved a first-class tragedy, which will never be forgotten just because it was a tragedy, tragedy was not our business." Their business was to get to the Pole and back. Amundsen showed how that could be done. But it is nevertheless Scott who lives on most vividly in the minds of men.

"We want the scientific work to make the bagging of the Pole merely an item in the results," wrote Dr. Wilson to his father. (It was at Dr. Wilson's insistence that the Scott party dragged a collection of geological specimens weighing over thirty pounds with them to the last.) "It was his [Scott's] ambition," wrote Sir Clements Markham in his Preface to *Scott's Last Expedition*, "that in his ship there should be the most completely equipped expedition for scientific purposes connected with the polar regions, both as regards men and material, that ever left these shores. In this he succeeded." It was therefore highly ironical that the journey to the Pole, and especially its tragic ending, came to overshadow almost everything else about the expedition in the public mind.

The only really competitive event with the public has been the mid-winter journey to the Cape Crozier emperor penguin rookery, made in terrible cold and darkness by Cherry-Garrard, Wilson, and Bowers, June 27 to August 1, 1911. Their purpose was to get some penguin eggs for Wilson to study. An incredible adventure—Cherry-Garrard's "worst journey in the world"—it was a foolhardy undertaking in the interests of science, but also it has impeccable credentials as pure adventure, undoubtedly in Cherry-Garrard's mind when he observed: "Polar exploration is at once the cleanest and most isolated way of having a bad time which has been devised."

The so-called Northern Party of the Scott expedition also had a very rough time. Six men were involved. The purposes were exploration and biological and geological studies. It was out almost continuously from January 25, 1911, to January 7, 1913, hardly any part of the period under passable good conditions. This was the party intended for King Edward VII Land. For its first winter it had to be landed at Borchgrevink's campsite on Cape Adare, a peculiarly difficult place, at which Raymond Priestley carried on geological work and kept the meteorological records and Surgeon G. Murray Levick made a study of penguins. It was not a position from which exploratory ventures could readily be made, as Borchgrevink had found out, but short journeys were made, as to Duke of York Island and the western limit of Robertson Bay. On January 4, 1912, the "Terra Nova" called and moved the party to Evans Cove—charted and named for Evans of the "Koonya" by Shackleton—from whence they proposed to sledge around Mount Melbourne to Wood Bay and return to Evans Cove to be picked up and taken to the head-quarters base in mid-February. On the journey they discovered some small glaciers, found some wood fossils, formed a collection of lichens, and made a considerable geological dump for later recovery. Unluckily the ship never got within thirty miles of them on its return and the party had to improvise a shelter for a wintering place; they dug a low igloo-like affair in a snow slope. For basic food they had to be satisfied with penguins and seals, scantily supplemented by biscuits and cocoa left over from the stores of the exploratory excursion. They had only their summer clothes. Finally, on September 30, they were able to make a try for head-quarters across McMurdo Sound. With the luck of chancing upon a cache of food and clothing on October 9, they finally reached Cape Evans on November 7.

While the geologist Priestley was away with the Northern Party two geologists were at the headquarters hut, Cape Evans: Frank Debenham and Griffith Taylor, the latter a specialist in physiography. Both of them were Australians educated at Sydney University; Taylor was on leave from the Australian government service. (Debenham made his career in England, where he became professor of geography at Cambridge and head of the Scott Polar Institute, while Taylor made a career as geog-rapher in Australia, the United States, and Canada.) On Scott's instruc-tions their geological field work was done along the western coast of Victoria Land across McMurdo Sound from Koettlitz Glacier north to Granite Harbor. One of their companions was a Canadian physicist and ice specialist named Charles Wright. In December 1912, with Priestley leading, Debenham and Taylor and two others made a new ascent of Mount Erebus the occasion for further geological field work.

At Cape Evans classic work in meteorology was done by George C. Simpson. For the first time he took upper air soundings by balloons and constructed the first Antarctic weather charts.

The "Terra Nova" arrived at Oamaru, New Zealand, on February 10, 1913, with the last of the expedition's personnel. The news of Scott's fate was cabled to England, but it was not revealed to anybody locally until the ship arrived at Lyttleton twenty-four hours later.

While the Scott and Amundsen expeditions were in the Ross Sea area, a third appeared—a Japanese expedition led by Lieutenant Choku Shi-rase. The Japanese approached by way of New Zealand, sailing from

Wellington on February 11, 1911. Ross's Admiralty Range was sighted on March 6 and the ship, the "Kainan Maru," continued southeast until blocked by the ice beyond Coulman Island. No landings were made. The party wintered in Sydney, Australia (May 1—November 19, 1911), and was at Cape Adare for a second visit south on January 3, 1912. Again the "Kainan Maru" sailed southeast and proceeded east along the Ross Ice Shelf. A landing was made at what the Japanese named Kainan Bay, an identation in the shelf discovered by Ross, east of the Bay of Whales. Turning back to the Bay of Whales, a sledging party was put ashore which went south 160 miles or less in Amundsen's tracks, to 80° 05′ South, 156° 37′ West. Meanwhile the ship went east once more to King Edward VII Peninsula where a second sledging party was put ashore which traveled to the base of the Alexandria Mountains and back. After a visit to Okuma Bay, another of Ross's indentations in the Ice Shelf, now named for the prime minister of Japan, the ship returned to the Bay of Whales, picked up its sledging party, and sailed for Wellington, New Zealand, on February 4. Amundsen's associate, Lieutenant K. Prestrud, had an amusing encounter with the Japanese at the Bay of Whales. "Nice day," said the Japanese. "Plenty ice."

The idea that it might be feasible to get an expedition across the continent of Antarctica first occurred to Dr. W. S. Bruce of the "Scotia." It was thought possible that Nordenskjold's two divisions of the continent might well be joined by a strait between the Weddell and Ross seas, this promising a line of travel. However, it was not considered safe to travel from the relatively well-known Ross Sea side to the little-known Weddell coast, so the prevailing idea was that a start should be made from the Weddell side and the traveling be toward a well-known destination. (This idea continued to prevail long after much more was learned about the Weddell Sea coast.) The first man after Bruce to propose such a transantarctic journey was the German explorer, Dr. Wilhelm Filchner. Filchner's special field of study was Tibet. His proposed Antarctic adventure was to be an interlude between study trips in Asia.

While Bruce never got a chance to try out his idea, Filchner received both public and private backing in Germany. His ship was the "Deutschland." He sailed from Germany in May 1911 via Buenos Aires to South Georgia, carried out oceanographic studies on the way, and did surveys at South Georgia—for example, he resurveyed what he named Vahsel Cape after the ship's master; it had originally been roughly charted by Captain Cook. On December 11, 1911, he left Grytviken and, acting on a suggestion by Bruce, kept to the east into the Weddell Sea and after a bit of trouble with ice broke out into open water. By chance he chose a good season. On January 30, 1912, he sighted an icy coast at 70° 48′ South—Luitpold Coast (Coats Land) running from 29° West to 37° West, bounded by ice cliffs thirty to a hundred feet high. Sailing along it, he came to a great ice shelf—the Filchner Ice Shelf—which proved to be the head of the Weddell Sea. Where the ice shelf and Luitpold Coast joined he located Duke Ernst Bay (first named Vahsel Bay). Filchner followed the ice shelf for a hundred miles. He then resolved to winter on the floating ice and had his hut partly built and stores and gear ashore when on February 18 the ice began to break up and drift out to sea. While all the men were rescued, some stores and gear were lost. After this mishap, a landing was made on land-fast ice at about the same point and a sledging trip was made inland. However, it was now late in the season; in early March the ship was frozen in at 73° 43′ South, and a week later it began to drift. It drifted thereafter for nine months in a zig-zag fashion but prevailingly northwest, covering six hundred miles, until it broke out of the ice at 63° 37′ South, 36° 34′ West, in late November. During the drift Filchner established his scientists in huts on the ice where they conducted studies in meteorology, magnetism, atmospheric electricity, and oceanography—much was added to the knowledge of the ocean floor—and Filchner himself led a sledging party one hundred miles over the ice in search of an island that proved elusive. Filchner thus clarified the geography at the head of the Weddell Sea, did some useful scientific work, but never even began a transantarctic journey. A few months after Filchner's return to Europe, when he was trying to raise money for a second try, Ernest Shackleton announced in London that *his* next undertaking would be a crossing of the continent from a base on the Weddell Coast. He eventually chose Duke Ernst Bay.

The concentration on the Weddell Sea–Palmer-Graham Peninsula area on the one hand and the Ross Sea area on the other was broken up by the Australian, Douglas Mawson. Mawson began to think about a return to Antarctica early in 1910 after his service with the first Shackleton expedition. His thoughts turned to the area west of Cape Adare to von Drygalski's Gaussberg, a distance of 2000 miles, about which little was known, although he (along with David and Mackay) had traveled into it when seeking the Magnetic Pole. Balleny, Dumont d'Urville, Wilkes, Drygalski, and Scott's men had all glimpsed coasts at various places along the entire distance, and the "Challenger" company had obtained evidence that a continental land mass lay nearby. (The Scott contribution was Oates Coast, discovered in 1911 by the "Terra Nova.") This portion of the continent was in the so-called Australian sector by virtue of its relation to the Australian continent, as the Palmer-Graham–Weddell Sea area was in the American sector by virtue of its relation to South America. As Mawson remarked, "An unknown coastline lay before the door of Australia." This was a challenge, especially since Mawson believed that Australia had, from its geographical position, a large stake in the future of Antarctica. Shackleton called it the Australian "hinterland." It was nearer—1450 miles from Hobart—than any other continental landmass.

Mawson put his preliminary plans before the annual meeting of the Australasian Association for the Advancement of Science at Sydney in 1911. His scheme was to establish an outer base on Macquarie Island and two or three bases on the continental mainland at points which literally had to be discovered before being occupied. While exploration was to be a primary concern—it could hardly be otherwise in unknown country—close attention was to be given to meteorology and also to magnetism—that ancient standby—as well as biology, geology, glaciology—that is, ice studies—bacteriology, the making of tide records, and atmospheric electricity (including wireless and auroral observations), while the expedition's ship was to make oceanographical studies in the seas south of Australia and New Zealand between visits to the bases. The emphasis on meteorology was characteristically Australian. It had all along been an Australian belief that their continental weather was strongly influenced by Antarctic conditions. Professor David had used the argument that knowledge of Antarctic weather conditions was necessary to the Australian meteorologists to get money from the Commonwealth for Shackleton's first expedition. The Australian Griffith Taylor, with the second Scott expedition as a physiographer, was, in another of his several guises, a meteorologist whose work on Australian continental meteorology was to become classic. But the comprehensiveness of Mawson's scientific coverage reflected not only the breadth of his personal understanding but the growing scientific maturity of his country—and New Zealand. His expedition was eventually to be staffed largely by men from Australian and New Zealand universities. The official name of the expedition became, quite correctly, the Australasian Antarctic Expedition. Several members, notably the scientists C. T. Madigan and C. F. Laseron and the photographer Frank Hurley, then very young men, went on to distinguished careers. The A.A.A.S. appointed a committee to assist and support Mawson consisting of Professor David, Professor Orme Masson, the University of Melbourne chemist, and Professor G. C. Henderson, historian, of the University of Adelaide—Mawson's own university. Donations in support were obtained from the Commonwealth, and some of the state governments, Australian and British learned societies, and private persons and companies. Most of the money and support in kind came out of Australia, but some from the United Kingdom and New Zealand, though the latter's contribution was mostly in services. In addition Mawson got advice and counsel, especially while on a visit to London, from the leading Antarctic hands of the day, British and foreign, notably Shackleton. As second in command Mawson obtained the services of John King Davis, who had been with Shackleton as a member of the ship's staff. Davis captained Mawson's ship, the "Aurora." The outstanding technological innovation introduced was the wireless; it was proposed to establish communication between the principal continental base and Macquarie Island, possibly with Australia. Only partial success was achieved, but the end of the total isolation of Antarctic expeditions was clearly foreshadowed. Some dogs were obtained from Amundsen when he reached Hobart. The Mawson parties were at their bases by the time Scott was struggling back from the Pole.

The Mawson expedition sailed from Hobart, Tasmania, in the "Aurora" on December 2, 1911. After establishing the base on Macquarie Island, chiefly for meteorological studies, with geology and biology secondary, a main continental base under Mawson's direct command was set up on Cape Denison—named for a Sydney newspaper proprietor who had contributed generously to the funds—on the south shore of Commonwealth Bay (about 66° 40′ South, 142° 40′ East) on George V Coast (which ran from 142° to 153° East) in Dumont d'Urville's Adélie Land. A second but smaller continental base was set up 1500 miles west, 17 miles from land on the ice of the Shackleton Ice Shelf, 100 miles long (the base was at 94° to 55° East—on Queen Mary Coast running from about 92° to 100° East) bordering on Davis Sea. Commonwealth Bay was discovered and named by Mawson; the Shackleton Ice Shelf was one of Wilkes' discoveries, but named by Mawson; the Davis Sea was discovered by J. K. Davis of the "Aurora" and named for him by Mawson. The ice shelf wintering party was led by Frank Wild, Cook's descendant, who had been with the first Scott and the first Shackleton expeditions. Both bases were at points where no landings had ever previously been made anywhere near them.

The coastal area where Mawson established himself proved to be the windiest in Antarctica and one of the windiest in the world. Not only was the daily average velocity high, but on occasion gusts up to 200 miles an hour were recorded. The explanation was that there were no mountains between the coast and the interior plateau; the plateau began its rise directly from the sea; and the winds generated in the interior swept unimpeded down to the coast and out to sea. However, a compensation, probably inadequate, was that inland travelers had a ready access to the interior—there were no mountains to cross as in the Ross Sea area.

From the main base sledge journeys totaling 2400 miles were made, while from Wild's Ice Shelf base the journeys totaled 800 miles.

Three principal journeys were made from the main base. With Lieutenant R. Bage of the Royal Australian Artillery as leader, a trip was made southeast from base toward the Magnetic Pole area. The party got to within 175 miles of Professor David's position of 1909, reached from the opposite direction, and within 50 miles of the then position of the Magnetic Pole. Under the leadership of C. T. Madigan, a party proceeded eastward along the coast over the sea ice to a point just beyond the Ninnis Glacier Tongue at 147° East. But the most spectacular, dramatic, and disastrous journey was made under Mawson's own leadership, parallel to Madigan's to the east, but inland from the coast. Mawson was accompanied by Xavier Merz, a Swiss lawyer, skier, and mountaineer and Lieutenant B. E. S. Ninnis of the British army; only Mawson was an experienced Antarctic traveler. Starting on November 10, 1912, using dogs, due back by January 15, 1913, when the "Aurora" was to pick them up and take them back to Australia, the Mawson party traveled east for thirty-four days, crossing much difficult country fissured with crevasses and rough with sastrugi, as well as two glaciers—Mertz, twenty miles wide at 144° 45′ East and Ninnis, narrower, at 147° East, when they stopped to reduce their sledges from three to two to speed their progress. Mertz then took the lead on skis, Mawson followed in second place, his sledge loaded with the scientific gear and a little food, and Ninnis came on last with most of the food and the heavy camping gear. They were about 315 miles from headquarters. Suddenly as they were crossing an area where the snow was smooth, Ninnis, his dogs, and his sledge went down a crevasse to instant destruction. Mertz and Mawson thereupon turned back for base, but desperately short of food and without proper shelter. They began to eat the emaciated, fatless dogs; the last one was consumed fourteen days later. Twenty-four days after Ninnis had gone down the crevasse, when the survivors were about two-thirds of the way back to base, Mertz, after being sick and lethargic for some time, died. Mawson struggled on alone, dragging half a sledge; his strength was ebbing; he was making but four miles a day; the temptation was strong to let himself go down one of the crevasses into which he fell; he was long overdue at base. But then at thirty miles from the base he found a newly laid food cache; it had been laid down only six hours before he chanced upon it. Two days later he reached an established expedition depot and found with other food three oranges and a pineapple. The

"Aurora" was in. Mawson was now on the seaward slope of the plateau, but he was held up a week by bad weather. As he neared "home," he saw the "Aurora" steaming away, but he soon saw men at the base. The "Aurora" was recalled by wireless, but it was unable to take the men off because of heavy seas. Mawson was out ninety-one days, thirty-three days all alone, twenty-eight days beyond the appointed time of departure. Four of his associates had volunteered to stay behind and search for him in the spring and a new wireless operator had joined them. The party spent the winter on scientific work.

The ship had, however, taken off Wild's western party successfully. It reached Hobart in March 1913. The western party had, along with other journeys east and west of its vicinity, including an exploration of the ice shelf, made a trip 300 miles west to von Drygalski's Gaussberg.

The main base party was relieved after its second winter, in December 1913, and reached Australia on February 26, 1914. Mawson returned to Antarctica fifteen years later.

Shackleton sailed with his British Imperial Trans-Antarctic Expedition on August 8, 1914. He had offered his ship, the "Endurance," and its personnel to the Admiralty for war service, but First Lord Winston Churchill had replied: "Proceed." His great companions on this journey were J. M. Wordie his chief scientist, J. M. Worsley, and Frank Wild, now an exceptionally experienced Antarctic hand. Wordie subsequently gained the greatest pre-eminence in Antarctic affairs. Shackleton's first objective was Duke Ernst Bay at the meeting place of Luitpold Coast and the Filchner Ice Shelf, from where he planned to lead a party across the continent to the Ross Sea shore. A supporting expedition was dispatched to McMurdo Sound in Mawson's "Aurora" to lay depots to Beardmore Glacier and a rendezvous was appointed at the top of the glacier. It was not Shackleton's intention to do any scientific work during the crossing, following Amundsen's example, but to send one scientific party north from his landing place toward the Palmer-Graham Peninsula through unknown territory and another west through equally virgin territory toward Enderby Land (discovered in 1831 by Biscoe). A month was spent at Grytviken, South Georgia, where meteorological and biological (whales mostly) studies were made and a mapping of the island was begun. In accordance with Bruce's advice and Filchner's confirmatory experience, Shackleton entered the Weddell Sea to the east, reached Bruce's Coats Land and discovered a new stretch of coast, named Caird Coast (20° to 29° West) after a principal patron of the expedition. It was a link between Bruce's coastal discovery and Filchner's. The ship had almost reached Duke Ernst Bay—or Vahsel Bay—when it was beset by ice and forced out of sight of land. Shackleton came to regret that he had persisted toward Duke Ernst Bay and had not embraced an alternative when it presented itself, for it proved impossible to extricate the ship from the ice. It was acknowledged on January 9, 1915, that it was locked in. The "Endurance" drifted in and with the ice for nine months, following an erratic course—at one stage it was only sixty miles from Duke Ernst Bay—but prevailingly up the middle of the Weddell Sea, westward of the "Deutschland's" drift, until on October 26, 350 miles from land, it was in a dangerous condition from crushing and the men were forced off it onto the ice. It finally sank on November 21. Shackleton's first resolution was to travel over the ice, dragging three boats and food and gear to open water, but this proved impossible to do. The party had to settle down on the ice and drift with it in the expectation that when the ice finally broke up with the coming of summer the boats could be launched and land achieved. The nearest known places where huts with caches of food were to be found were Paulet and Snow Hill Islands, where Nordenskjold and the survivors of the "Antarctic" had wintered. Oddly, Shackleton himself had assembled the food with which the rescuers of Nordenskjold had stocked these huts. It proved impossible to reach either. Not until April 9, after six months on the drifting ice, was it possible, amid great peril, to launch the boats and start for land. After six perishing days and nights in the boats, they finally reached land— Elephant Island, an eastern-lying island of the South Shetlands, a good thousand miles from where they had been beset. Improvising shelter for the men, Shackleton now had one of his boats roughly reconstructed and with five companions, including Worsley, set out on April 24 for South Georgia and succor. Frank Wild was left in charge at Elephant Island. Shackleton reached South Georgia in sixteen days, but on the opposite side of the island from the objective, the whaling stations at Grytviken. The island had not at that time ever been crossed, but taking two of his companions with him and leaving the rest camped under the boat, Shackleton made a crossing in less than two days. However, it took no less than five attempts to reach the men on Elephant Island. They had had to stay there twenty weeks. Rescue was finally achieved by the Chilean ship "Yelcho," captained by Luis Pardo. Yet not a single man of the entire expedition was lost. As a fight for survival, it was a thrilling success, brilliantly managed, one of mankind's great adventure stories; but as exploration, it was a total if glorious failure. Interestingly enough, the scientists gained most from it—meteorological data and knowledge of ice movements in the Weddell Sea. Frank Hurley made some wonderful pictures.

Meanwhile, on the Ross Sea side, misfortunes also beset the expedition.

The relative chaos of Shackleton's finances and organization was the least of it, though in seeking to help the Australian government had to spend far more than it liked; Professor David had to spend lavishly of his time and energy; and Shackleton's stock in Australia fell to a low level. However, the "Aurora" got away, although it arrived late at Mc-Murdo Sound. An effort was promptly made to lay down depots on the ice shelf, but with disastrous consequences to the men. This was only the beginning. The "Aurora," locked in the ice off Cape Evans, where the scientists were ashore, was in May swept away in the ice with most of the stores and equipment still aboard. It drifted in the ice until February 13, 1916, and reached Port Chalmers, New Zealand, on April 3. The men at McMurdo Sound had all gathered at Cape Evans by June 2. During the winter the food and gear left behind by earlier expeditions were gathered together and much improvisation from discarded materials was undertaken. On September 1 a party began to move supplies to Hut Point, preparatory to the resumption of depot laying; they began the actual work on October 9, and stayed constantly at it until January 26, 1916, when they were at the foot of Beardmore Glacier. There, however, such luck as they had left ran out and scurvy descended upon them, one man dying before a return to Hut Point could be made. And shortly after their return two more men lost their lives while trying to walk from Hut Point to Cape Evans over the ice. The survivors of the depot laying party—three men out of six—reached Cape Evans again on July 15.

When Shackleton reached Wellington, New Zealand, from Chile via Panama, to lead the relief of the Ross Sea party, he found that the angry and impatient Australians had displaced him from leadership of any relief party and appointed Captain J. K. Davis. The New Zealanders were rather more favorably disposed, but unable to overrule the Australians. Shackleton could only "sign on" the ship under Davis to go south, though it was understood that he would lead any parties actually landed. The "Aurora" finally sailed on December 20, 1916; it found the men assembled at Cape Royds on January 10, 1917, and left for New Zealand again on the seventeenth. On arrival there Shackleton found his finances in much better order, thanks to the attention of a New Zealand friend; he then crossed to Australia and made his peace with his Australian critics, gave a much admired recruiting speech at Sydney, and sailed for England and war service.

Thus ended the Heroic Age in a wild burst of blazing ambition, disaster, valor, fortitude, squalor, squabbles, and tragedy.

CHAPTER XIII

Tearing at the Veil (1)

Between the world wars the interest in Antarctica was keen, persistent, many-faceted, and widespread among the nations. The rapid expansion of whaling was the major stimulant to the notion that Antarctica had an important economic potential that should not be ignored. This led in a fairly obvious fashion not only to an interest in exploration and scientific work but also to the staking of national territorial claims to specified portions of the "continent." However, not all the nations with an economic stake made claims; there was no detectable proportion between the claims and the size of the stake; and the investment in exploration and scientific work had no necessary relation to the economic stake on the one hand or the territorial claim on the other. In fact, the country whose nationals invested most in the material sense in exploration and scientific work had but a miniscule stake in the whaling and took up an attitude toward claims that made the ultimate significance of all claims rather uncertain. It was obvious enough that the status of Antarctica and the positions of the nations involved toward it required clarification but no clarification was either achieved or indeed striven for. It was only obscurely understood or admitted that Antarctica was, or was rapidly becoming, an international problem for which an internationally arranged and agreeable solution should be found. Between the wars Antarctica was, by and large, a field for competing nationalisms. The competition became fiercest around the Palmer-Graham Peninsula. The stage seemed set for a *partage* of Antarctica, but the drama never quite came off.

While to understand the history of Antarctica attention must be given to whaling and politics to enforce the idea that there has been more to it than heroic struggle in the ice and snow, the fact remains that the most memorable transactions were indeed in exploration and scientific work. In the long run they became the dominant expressions of humanity's interest in Antarctica, though the ancient serpents of economics and politics continued to lurk in the shadows.

In exploration and scientific work the technological means rapidly changed, though rather by additions than by the final subtraction of old reliances—airplanes came in but dogs and sledges did not go out. The ends of geographical and scientific knowledge and understanding remained inextinguishably constant. Adventure continued to be the primary personal motivation for going to the frozen south, but it had to be closely allied with geographical discovery or scientific accomplishment to justify itself. Individuals returned again and again; nostalgia for the tight, isolated, and dedicated kind of society an expedition represented played a large part in drawing them back. The extraordinary aesthetics of the environment, which photographs but inadequately reveal, cast a spell on many men. Although the expeditions did not swell in size and complexity with any logical inevitability as one expedition succeeded another, the general Spencerian principle was at work and there was a noticeable tendency for the major expeditions to get bigger and bigger, both as to the technology and personnel. When the Americans finally returned in the late 1920's after an absence (except for individuals) of about ninety years, they, while continuing to undertake some relatively small enterprises, were the effective agents of bigness. Only the Norwegians and the British established any connection of moment between the economics of Antarctic enterprise and the economics of exploration and scientific work.

The state of knowledge at any given time is difficult for the nonspecialist to define, not least because it has been uncommon for anybody able to handle the relatively complex data over its whole range to attempt a summary definition of a widely communicable kind. It is very noticeable, however, that it was almost routine for commentators to emphasize how little was certainly known as compared with what should be known to support anything like comprehensive understanding. Even though lacking a vagarious indigenous population to puzzle the student—hence the substitution of a fascination with the penguins—Antarctica was a difficult place to comprehend. Since the severe limitations of the accumulated knowledge have been emphasized down the years, in the face of all the data accumulated, it follows that the further back in time one goes, the greater the ignorance. Even now the cry is still for more data, and the getting of additional and new ranges of data motivates almost all the continuing work.

As the period here to be reviewed opened, the emphasis was on continued uncertainty even about the basic geographical facts and it was a commonplace that the relevant specialist sciences had made no more than useful beginnings. Such exact geographical knowledge as there was pertained chiefly to discontinuous portions of the coasts and their immediately contiguous vicinities. Though fairly numerous spot approaches had been made, the coasts had been closely studied and defined only at very occasional intervals. No circumnavigation had been made since Biscoe's of 1830–32. Some lengthy portions of the coasts had never even been seen and others had been so imperfectly seen that there was legitimate doubt that they actually existed at the points the observers specified. The coastal discoveries of the American Charles Wilkes, though they were principal evidence that there was an Antarctic continent, were especially subject to challenge. As to the interior, in spite of the traverses made by Shackleton, Scott, Amundsen, David, Mawson, and others, very little was known. The deepest penetrations of the interior had been in search of the South Pole and the South Magnetic Pole, and these journeys of necessity had been focused fairly precisely on those objectives. After the more accessible parts of the Palmer-Graham Peninsula and adjacent islands, the best-known portion of Antarctica was the Ross Sea area, from which most of the great traverses had reached out. However, at this stage—and indeed four decades later—it was still not certain that even if the coasts should finally be established in detail they would be found to enclose a continental landmass. It might well be, as had been suggested quite early, that they enclosed a vast icecap which had engulfed a group of large and small islands. As ice on land and the adjacent sea had impeded the definition of the coasts, so the ice on the land back from the coasts made it exceedingly difficult to ascertain the nature of the land presumed to be under the ice. The study of ice (or glaciology), its formation, composition, depth, movement, was therefore an important scientific undertaking in Antarctica, fully as important as geology and its allies, meteorology, magnetism, biology and its allies, or any of the other studies closely applicable to Antarctica. Correctly viewed, it, like its associated fellows, contributed to the development of a global understanding of the particular range of phenomena studied. A basic motivation for pursuing scientific studies in Antarctica was still, as it had been since such studies were initiated about a hundred years earlier, to complete certain ranges of data on a global basis. Without knowledge of the Antarctic facts, knowledge of the globe was necessarily imperfect. Men studied Antarctica that they might understand Antarctica but also so that they might assist in encompassing the entire globe.

Nordenskjold's geological theory, based on lithology and tectonics, supported by Charcot's studies, among others, dividing Antarctica into West and East provinces, the West embracing the Palmer-Graham Peninsula and linked geologically to South America and in character somewhat like New Zealand, the East apparently a continental shield with a geological resemblance to Australia, did not guarantee the conclusion that the two provinces were linked parts of one continental landmass or finally define the relations of the mountain systems. The provinces might be separated at some point by the sea, though probably deep under the ice, as by a channel running under the ice from the Weddell to the Ross seas. The Palmer-Graham Peninsula might be a series of islands, or a long island disconnected from what was apparently the main body of the continent, and the great shield of the East might be a vast icecap overlying a multiplicity of islands or a large body of land the ice on which also embraced a ring of circumjacent islands. Geographically and scientifically Antarctica was, at the beginning of this period, still much of a mystery, even without teasing one's mind about its *origin,* after the manner of the Austrian geologist Eduard Suess (1831–1914), who argued that a great landmass containing India, South America, Africa, Australia, and Antarctica had once existed but that the component parts had, ages ago, gradually drifted apart, a notion taken up and applied to the continents generally by the German meteorologist and geophysicist, Alfred Wegener (1880–1930), and, after intervals of disbelief, still debated by the geophysicists. In spite of the work so laboriously done during the fifteen decades since Captain Cook had determined by argument that Antarctica was there, the ultimate embodiment of *terra Australis incognita,* it was still not comprehended. Between the two great wars the frontiers of the unknown in Antarctica were pushed back a bit, the veil hiding it was torn here and there, but the brave adventurers, with all their new techniques of travel, observation, and study, were still at the end of their period as at its beginning, highly conscious of the speculative nature of their understanding and of the smallness of their exact knowledge as compared with the vastness of the need. They knowingly passed on to their successors a tremendous amount of work yet to be done and arguments of major import yet to be concluded. Britons, Australians, New Zealanders, Norwegians, Americans, Frenchmen, Germans, Argentines, and Chileans were, in one way and another, involved in the increasingly complicated story.

The interwar years opened with something perilously close to farce and the farce was quickly succeeded, in violation of historic if not dramatic logic, by a tragedy that removed a great figure of the Heroic Age from the scene.

John Lachlan Cope was a thirty-year-old British physician and biologist who had been surgeon to Shackleton's Ross Sea party of 1914–17. He served in the Royal Navy during the war and at its conclusion determined to lead an expedition to the area of the Palmer-Graham Peninsula. Cope was enthusiastic but totally lacked executive ability and was arrogantly tactless by habit. He put together an expedition of only four men, including himself, one of whom was an Australian, George Hubert Wilkins, whose strongest personal ambition of the moment was to fly an airplane in the polar regions. Cope engaged Wilkins' interest on this basis, but characteristically frustrated him by overspending his funds in quite other directions. Wilkins was nevertheless induced to go along. Joining the party at Montevideo where the other three had arrived on a whaler, Wilkins and his mates, after Cope had disentangled himself from the coils of debt, were taken in the whaler to the station at Deception Island in the South Shetlands. After a good deal of rather footless activity from the island, the expedition was, at the end of the season, split up and two of the men, T. W. Bagshawe and M. C. Lester, went to winter on the Danco Coast. This became in time the best remembered part of the whole curious performance, not least because it showed how men could survive on limited resources. Meanwhile Cope and Wilkins went north, Cope to look for more money which he was never to find, Wilkins to find employment for his talents in other directions.

Wilkins returned to his search for planes to fly in the polar regions. He had actually made arrangements for the use of two German planes and then had temporarily lost control of them when he heard from Shackleton. Shackleton deprecated a Britisher flying German planes at that moment in history and suggested that Wilkins join him. Shackleton had emerged from the war still beset by the strongly Victorian idea that he was under heavy moral obligation to "prove" himself—very curious in the light of his already high accomplishments. In his scheme of values, the only way to do this was by leading a successful exploring expedition. But while this was clear enough, his sense of wise objectives was rather diffuse: he tried and failed to arrange a trip to the Arctic in collaboration with the Canadians; he thought of reverting to his old fascination with tropic islands and mounting a comprehensive survey of those of possible use in modern communications; he thought of a close survey of unknown Antarctic coasts or the edge of the ice clear around the "continent," and of combining these with oceanographic work.

Shackleton, whatever his personal problem, was still the greatest living explorer, still the greatest leader in the business, and still a man of incomparable personal charm. He was, however, ill—more than he cared to admit; he was, as a matter of fact, practically worn out from the excessive demands he had already made upon himself. Yet he finally was able to put together, though with less of the close personal supervision that had always been his habit, an Antarctic expedition for a circumnavigation of the ice-edge and oceanographical work. Filling his small and ill-found ship, the "Quest," with a staggering array of the latest scientific equipment, he set out in September 1921. The magic of his name attracted a superior team to his support, old associates and new men of promise. Wilkins was one of the new men. He was to get his chance to fly, but his motivation in joining was to learn about leadership and expedition management from Shackleton. Wilkins never flew on this expedition either, for the very good reason that the airplane was never picked up. When the "Quest" was condemned to spend six weeks at Rio de Janeiro for engine repairs—an interlude that did Shackleton's health no good—Wilkins and Douglas, the geologist, obtained Shackleton's permission and flew to Montevideo and joined a whaler for South Georgia where the "Quest" would call later on. Wilkins had been photographing and collecting birds and Douglas had been studying rocks for six weeks when the "Quest" finally put in its appearance at Grytviken. Late on the night of arrival Shackleton, while actually receiving treatment from Dr. Macklin, died of heart failure, January 5, 1922. Shackleton's second in command, Frank Wild, tried to carry on but the timetable was now hopelessly off, the ship was inadequate, and little was accomplished during an oceanographical journey that covered only about one-fifth of the distance around the continent. Even the meager results cost five times the original budget estimate. Yet in the lore of Antarctica all the futility is usually ignored in the face of the tragic fact that Shackleton, one of the indisputable greats, had died still "trying" at 47. He was buried on a hillside back of Grytviken.

Shackleton's last expedition was the last British Antarctic expedition of the pattern set in the Heroic Age for several years, the last privately financed and the last for a long time, save one—that led by John R. Rymill in 1934–37—which was to be commonly remembered by the name of its leader. The British concluded that future expeditions would require government support, and gestures were made toward international co-operation beyond that arising naturally from the fraternity of Antarctic explorers. During the 1920's and 1930's the British followed a policy of continuous research conducted on a relatively small scale in any given season under the auspices of a government committee, the results to become impressive and valuable by steady cumulation. The work was to be done in close relation to the whaling industry and was mostly to involve whale biology, whale marking (to trace migrations), and oceanographical work closely related to the old, new, and discoverable habitats of the whales, exploration of the land to be very incidental, though some islands were to be charted and significant "landings" occasionally made. Charting was done in the South Shetlands,

South Orkneys, the Balleny Islands, etc., and discoveries were of Mill Island (off the Knox Coast) and William Scoresby Bay (at the junction of the Kemp and MacRobertson Coasts.) The ships also had interesting associations with exploring expeditions, British and American. The motivation for this activity was mixed, partly related to the conservation of great economic animals, partly designed to strengthen the British claim to "sectors" of Antarctica.

The British committee which directed this research was known as the "Discovery" Committee (after the ship originally employed) and was set up by the Colonial Office's Interdepartmental Committee on Research and Development in the Dependencies of the Falkland Islands (or British-claimed Antarctica). The money to support the actions was in part supplied by the fees paid to the British government by the whalers. A biological research laboratory was opened at Grytviken in 1925. The oceanographical work of the early years was also based on Grytviken. Results began to be published in 1929. At first only the ship "Discovery" was available for work at sea, but in 1926 a second, the "William Scoresby," was added and later again the old "Discovery" was replaced by "Discovery II." In the earlier years the work at sea was conducted close to South Georgia in relation to the whaling being done there to provide animals for the factories at Grytviken, with voyages to and from Capetown, South Africa, but it was early extended to the Palmer-Graham Peninsula, the west coast waters of which had other whaling grounds which were within the Falkland Islands Dependencies, and from there gradually around the continent as the whalers discovered new grounds and the politics of Antarctica spread out. Biological work was eventually done near Durban, South Africa, where shore-based whale factories were found, as well as Grytviken. First and last a good many men were employed in these activities, but outside scientific circles the best known were those associated with the ships and voyages. The pioneer leader was N. A. Mackintosh, but others to 1939 were Stanley Kemp, Dilwyn John, and G. W. Rayner. Of the circumnavigations eventually made, that of 1931–32, led by Dilwyn John in the "Discovery II," was especially notable as the first ever made by man in the winter season.

If the British concentrated on whale-related activities and politics, though not wholly as we shall see, the French exhausted their Antarctic energy in the subantarctic Kerguelen Islands. They ventured neither to the Palmer-Graham Peninsula in the tradition of Charcot nor did they follow up the discoveries of Dumont d'Urville on the continent, though politics aroused their concern for this ancient foothold. Occasionally during the 1920's but less frequently during the 1930's expeditions were in the Kerguelens to study biology, prospect for minerals, or make coastal surveys, while the last visit before the outbreak of World War II was an incident in an oceanographical cruise. One expedition of the 1920's ventured south to visit Heard Island.

The Germans, for their part, ignored the tradition of Drygalski and Filchner, at least until 1938 when they injected the malignant politics of Nazism into what had become the Norwegian sector of the continent. Up till then, however, they touched on Antarctica between the wars only in 1925–26 when Alfred Merz and F. A. Spiess led an oceanographical cruise into the Antarctic waters of the South Atlantic, in 1928–29 when Kohl-Larsen made a partial survey of South Georgia, including many of the interior glaciers, and as whalers, beginning in the mid-1930's.

The Norwegians, by contrast, very much involved in whaling, were extremely active in exploration throughout the period and also became entangled in the politics of the situation. They used their factory ships, whale chasers, tankers, and planes logistically and as bases, instruments and supports for exploratory work. The work both derived from whaling and was, fundamentally, in support of whaling. To sustain the position they won, the Norwegians were drawn into Antarctic politics.

The Norwegian exploratory work was cumulatively extensive and distinguished. It was, after claims to Bouvet and Peter I islands had been established, entirely coastal. A significance of Bouvet Island was that the nearest land to it—nearer than Capetown—was what became Princess Martha Coast on the Antarctic mainland. As whaling moved west around the continent from the old stamping ground in the Palmer-Graham vicinity, the Norwegian explorers also did so, beginning somewhat east of Enderby Land where the Australians under Mawson were working, causing some confusion about priorities and nomenclature, and more about the bases of claims, and moving from there west around the curve of the continent to Coats Land on the Weddell Sea. Even beyond Enderby Land this was not entirely virgin ground, but largely so, and the Norwegians filled in many gaps. Much of the work was done from ships but in the more formal exploration the airplane was freely employed. The only extended land journey along a stretch of coast that was planned, a scheme for traveling eastward to the Palmer-Graham area, was a failure; and no penetration of the interior was even considered in this period, though in making claims, using the sector principle, the Norwegians naturally came into "possession" of land right to the South Pole. They also occasionally recalled that Amundsen's journey to the Pole and back and Prestud's work from the camp on the Ross Ice Shelf gave them certain rights in the interior. But their activity was, except as they flew short distances inland, wholly coastal between the wars. Scientifically they were keenly interested in wireless communications and meteorology, both of obvious use in whaling and as befitted men of ships they did a good deal of oceanography, making several notable discoveries by soundings. The predominant promoter of this activity was the whaling magnate Lars Christensen of Sandefjord and his captains did much work of the kind for him. The best known of those specially employed on exploration by Christensen was the aviator, Hjalmar Riiser-Larsen who had been navigator on the plane in which Amundsen and Ellsworth had tried for the North Pole and on the "Norge" when it flew across the Arctic. Christensen himself made several trips into Antarctic waters in the 1930's, usually on one of his tankers. His wife and daughter accompanied him, the captains sometimes had their wives along, and the Christensens sometimes had women guests.

With regard to Bouvet and Peter I islands, both of which had been elusive for many years after original discovery and neither of which was certainly accessible every season, the Norwegians were chiefly concerned to use them in connection with whaling. This end was supported by building huts on them, establishing caches of supplies, and attempting to set up meteorological equipment. This was done on both between 1927 and 1930. After 1930, when highly developed factory ships could be serviced at sea, the Norwegians concentrated their interest on "continental" Antarctica where, by establishing right to coasts they could prevent others from interfering with their whaling in coastal waters during the Antarctic high summer (that is, February). On their first approach to it as explorers in 1930, with Riiser-Larsen in charge, they headed from Bouvet Island for Biscoe's Enderby Land, where they encountered the Australians at work. The Norwegians discovered Ice Bay at 67° 45′ South, 50° East and then moved west, doing oceanographical work, towards Coats Land, sighting en route the coasts they named for Prince Olav, contiguous with Enderby Land, off which was the southernmost geographical point reached by Cook on the occasion of his first crossing of the Antarctic Circle, near which they found the Gunnerus Bank by sounding, and the Princess Martha Coast abutting on Shackleton's Caird Coast at the head of the Weddell Sea. On Princess Martha Coast they sighted Cape Norvegia which marked the entrance to Seal Bay. A short distance out to sea from this point was James Clark Ross's farthest penetration into the Weddell Sea in 1843. The next season the Christensen people carried out a circumnavigation of the "continent" which started and ended at Capetown and lasted 102 days. This was the first circumnavigation in a hundred years. In the course of it Riiser-Larsen examined from the air a coast, named for Princess Ragnhild, located just beyond Prince Olav Coast toward Princess Martha Coast which had been discovered by H. Halvorsen, a Christensen whaling captain, a little earlier in the season. The 1930–31 season was, as a matter of fact, rather rich in geographical results not only for Christensen's people but also for the whalers in other employ. The latter chiefly made coastal sightings along Mac-Robertson Coast east of Enderby Land in the area where the competition with the Australians was at a maximum. Halvorsen, however, worked well outside this curiously "crowded" area, as his discovery of the Princess Ragnhild Coast shows. He spent a full month of his whaling season charting along the coasts of the Princesses Ragnhild and Martha and the Princess Astrid Coast which was discovered between them at this time.

In the 1931–32 season Lars Christensen himself visited Antarctica for the first time and between 1931–32 and 1936–37, when the work was ended, the Norwegians accomplished a great deal even though exploration continued to be secondary to whaling. 1931 was marked by the almost simultaneous discovery of Mackenzie Bay (in the Amery Ice Shelf) by the Australian Mawson and Captain Klarius Mikkelsen. Mikkelsen was investigating in that area and west along the Mac-Robertson Coast in a whale chaser on Christensen's personal orders. The next season the Norwegians suffered a reverse. Riiser-Lawson proposed to land with two companions some place in Enderby Land or vicinity and travel east by dogsled in an effort to reach the Palmer-Graham Peninsula. He proposed to keep on the sea ice along the coast, especially when beyond the Ross Ice Shelf where the coast was unknown. It proved impossible to disembark in the vicinity of Enderby Land, but the party was put on the ice off Princess Ragnhild Coast. However, the ice unexpectedly began to break up. The men were rescued by a whaler from an iceberg on which they took refuge, but their supplies and equipment were lost. In 1933–34 a near circumnavigation was made in the course of which coastal explorations by airplane were made, chiefly along the newly located Leopold and Astrid Coast behind Drygalski's West Ice Shelf. In this vicinity, which was within the Australian sphere of interest, the Norwegians under Captain Mikkelsen had something of a field day the next season. They discovered Prydz Bay, in the great indentation in the coast at about the point where the "Challenger" had approached in 1876, and named the bordering land on the east side Ingrid Christensen Coast after Lars Christensen's wife, while that on the west side was eventually named for Lars Christensen himself. Captain Mikkelsen and a large party, including his wife, were able to land. Among other famous features of the vicinity Mikkelsen discovered and named at this time the Vestfold Hills, the Larsemann Hills, and Mt. Caroline Mikkelsen. The end came in the 1936–37 season when the Christensens made their last visit to Antarctica. The purpose was to photograph the coast continuously from Mawson's

Shackleton Ice Shelf westward around to the terminus of the Princess Martha Coast. This was not accomplished in its entirety but the shores of Prydz Bay, namely the Ingrid and Lars Christensen coasts, Mac-Robertson Coast, Kemp Coast, and the coast of Enderby Land were covered. Prince Harald Coast, a newly discovered shore line between Prince Olav and Princess Ragnhild coasts, was photographed, together with the newly discovered coasts of the Havsbotn, the extreme inner portion of Lützow-Holm Bay, discovered by Riiser-Larsen in 1931, and the Sør Rondane Mountains back of the Princess Ragnhild Coast. Two new "banks" were also found this year, Four Ladies off Prydz Bay and Gribb off Drygalski's Wilhelm II Coast. The Norwegians came to call their portion of the Antarctic mainland, taken comprehensively, Queen Maud's Land.

During the first World War the whaling fleet was in large measure diverted from its usual occupations to war-related work in the carrying trade. This sharply cut down the supply of whale oil coming forward each season. At the same time there was an increasingly intense scramble for fats, particularly in war-dislocated Europe. As the rising demand for fats met the limited supply of whale oil, the price of oil rose toward unprecedented heights. The smallest quantity of whale oil was produced in 1918; the price was the highest in 1920. Under the price stimulus the industry rapidly revived and in the 1922–23 season production was actually greater than in any prewar year and was obviously going to increase further.

In 1924, however, the price began a steady decline. A double revolution in the Antarctic industry was underway, on the one side technological, on the other in the locales of whaling operations. There was a rapid change in the technology of capturing and treating the whales which made it easy to free the industry from its dependence on shore-based factories and turn it into a pelagic industry, thus allowing the migration of the whalers to any and all "grounds" around Antarctica where whales might be found. The effect of these two developments was to increase greatly the production of Antarctic oil, both absolutely and in its proportion of world supplies. Whereas in 1912 only about 50 per cent of the world's supplies came from Antarctic sources, by the early 1930's the proportion was 97.8 per cent. The economic result of this greatly intensified exploitation of Antarctic whale resources was, inevitably, especially in the economic context of the 1920's and 1930's, a price crisis induced by overproduction. This occurred in 1931 and it was worsened by the United Kingdom currency devaluation. At the same time the increased activity, which of course involved the exploitation of a wasting resource, induced a lively interest in the governance of the Antarctic whaling industry as such and also an intensified interest in the politics of Antarctica. In both fields, as indeed also in exploration and scientific investigation, Antarctic questions tended insensibly to become international questions and not the least interesting aspect of developments in the various imperfectly separable fields was the perceptible movement toward international solutions, even while the usual political actions were still decidedly nationalistic.

The way toward pelagic whaling was led by Captain Carl A. Larsen, the same who had been a leader in whaling in the Antarctic since 1892, but he himself never commanded the technology to practice it. His final great contribution to the industry was to widen its horizon with regard to locale by pioneering whaling in the Ross Sea. In 1923 he took the 13,000-ton factory ship "Sir James Clark Ross," along with five catchers, through the pack ice. This was a ship ten times larger than any that hitherto had negotiated a passage. It was, however, still technologically at the stage where it had to be anchored in a sheltered harbor in order to operate it. Since this was the case, Larsen had followed precedent as established for working around the Palmer-Graham Peninsula and had taken out a five-year lease on the Ross Sea area from the British as the claimants. The British assigned their rights to the New Zealanders. The harbor actually used was Discovery Inlet in the Ross Ice Shelf, a feature first observed by Scott in 1902. Larsen made his approach to the Ross Sea via Hobart, Tasmania, where he recruited about a dozen Australians to his crew, and Macquarie Island. He had anticipated that right and humpback whales of about forty tons each would be caught and that these could readily be hoisted on deck for flensing (cutting up) and boiling down, but actually reliance had to be placed upon the large blue whales and finbacks and they had to be flensed in the water alongside and the pieces hoisted aboard. Although Larsen got only about one-third the number of barrels of oil he had hoped for the first year, he had proved his point about the practicability of operating in the Ross Sea—a point which had been in doubt for thirty years. He had widened the horizons of the whalers once again, but technological changes were needed to widen them to the fullest extent.

The technological changes centered on the factory ship and its associated whale catchers without which it could not operate. The history of whaling shows that an uneasy and unstable relation between shore-based and ship-based operations has been characteristic. Successful Antarctic whaling began with the practice of bringing the captured whales to "factories" on shore for processing and moved on to factory ships, really floating factories, which it was customary to anchor in protected harbors while operations were carried out. Then in the late 1920's and the 1930's the factory ships were so developed that they could operate on the high seas, served by their associated whale catchers, positioning in a protected harbor no longer required. By being serviced by tankers which supplied them with fuel oil and relieved them of accumulated whale oil, the factory ships could spend a whole season on the open ocean. One technical innovation of great importance was the development of the slipway for getting even the largest whale carcase on board for flensing. This came about in 1925. It eliminated the dangerous practice of cutting up the whales alongside the ship and hoisting the pieces aboard. The Gjeldstad claw was an innovation that notably facilitated getting the carcase up the slipway. At the same time the equipment for "trying out" the carcase was markedly sophisticated and the chemical operations with the oil were improved. Also the carcase was utilized with greater and greater exhaustiveness, at once a contribution to the conservation of a resource and a positive contribution to the economics of an industry menaced by falling prices. The Japanese pioneered the freezing of whale meat for human consumption. In short, during the 1920's and 1930's the factory ships became not only free of shore ties but also became more and more complex as factories.

Both economically and politically it was important that as they became free to operate on the high seas they were also freed of the exactions as to rent, fees, and duties to which they had been subject as long as they had to use shores over which a nation could claim sovereignty. This had interesting political implications.

With regard to the associated whale catchers which actually killed the whales and brought them to the factory (and mother) ship, the technological innovations were chiefly with regard to design, engines (speed), the use of the airplane in spotting whales, the kinds of harpoons employed, techniques (such as inflation with air) for keeping killed whales afloat, and the uses of radio and radio-telephones for communications among catchers, between airplane and catcher, and with the factory (ship) and for planting an automatic signal broadcaster on a dead whale to facilitate later recovery.

Whaling remained a harsh and exceedingly odoriferous trade, but mechanization and sophistication made it a more tolerable life than it had been in the "good old days," even though the elements remained recognizably the same. In the 1930's Norway and the United Kingdom had the greatest number of factory ships and attendant whale catchers in operation, the former 14 factory ships and 131 catchers, the latter 13 factory ships and 113 catchers, or together about three-fifths of the ships in the industry. Since they collaborated, this gave them dominance. At that time Japan, which first entered the industry in the 1934–35 season, had six factory ships (shortly increased to ten) and a commensurate complement of catchers, while Germany, which came in in 1936–37, had five ships and thirty-seven catchers. There were a few of both types under other flags including the Panamanian and the American. The Japanese and the Germans had entered the industry for politico-economic reasons having to do with the intensification of the struggle to gain and save foreign exchange that occurred during the Great Depression.

Whale oil of the several kinds, and other whale products, notably whale-meat meal, whale bone, whale skin, ambergris, whale meat for human consumption, and so on, were of greatest interest to European nations and Japan. The United States had but a limited interest in producing whale oil and its consumption, involving around 5 per cent of world production, was chiefly in soapmaking and lubricants. However, special circumstances could cause American demand to be important to the world price, as occurred in 1935–36 when domestic production of cotton, corn, and hogs was forced down artificially and a search was made for substitute fats. In the European countries and Japan, however, whale oil was, after hydrogenation, a process discovered in 1915 which rendered the oil odorless and tasteless and allowed it to harden, constantly a principal source of fat, including edible fat. It was extremely important to the making of margarine, lard compounds, and soap. The principal European *producers* were Norway and the United Kingdom. The principal *consumers,* to the extent of 85 per cent, were the United Kingdom and Germany. The United Kingdom came to rate whale oil along with wheat and sugar as essential for national defense.

The shift from shore-based whaling, whether factories on land or factory ships at anchor, to pelagic whaling, and the rapid technological sophisticating of pelagic whaling, led to a vast increase in the number of whales taken each season and in the oil and other products sent to markets. The consequence of increased killings and production was to make obvious the need for regulation of the industry to achieve two ends: to conserve the supply of whales and to limit production to insure the industry's economic viability. However, the rise of pelagic whaling had the effect of largely freeing the industry from such regulations as the British had instituted in 1908, for the British regulations were based on the proposition that the whaling would be conducted in relation to factories located on land or factory ships anchored in territorial waters (within the three-mile limit). Once the industry could be conducted from factory ships on the high seas, it would not be obligatory to observe the

British rules and regulations. Then the only way to achieve comprehensive control would be by international agreement, say on the lines of the commodity agreements devised during this period.

The final significant effort to control whaling on the old basis came when the British dealt with the problem created when Captain C. A. Larsen proposed to undertake whaling in the Ross Sea. There was then demonstrated the close connection that existed between the regulation of whaling and the politics of "claims." The British had rights in the Ross Sea area and hence assumed they could and should license Larsen's operation and Larsen, for his part, was agreeable to continuing to conform to a practice which he had followed since 1905. But as the Ross Sea area was outside the Falkland Islands Dependencies as formally defined, it appeared to require a separate administration. The British assigned the area and the responsibility to the New Zealand government, thus transferring an administrative task and injecting that government into the politics of Antarctic claims. The New Zealanders did not themselves enter whaling. It was, however, a New Zealand government representative who accompanied Larsen to the Ross Sea in 1923 and it was to the New Zealand government that the income from fees, etc., went. The income never became very considerable and by the late 1930's had declined to triviality. However, the New Zealand "claim" remained. As new whaling grounds were found to the west off the coasts of the Australian sphere of interest, where the British also had rights, the Australians became keenly interested not only in the possibility of engaging in whaling themselves (which in fact they never did in Antarctica) but in gaining a bit of income from fees, etc. By this time, however, whaling was wholly pelagic in this vicinity and though the Australians experimented with the idea of extending the seaward boundary of the claim the British transferred to them far beyond the three-mile limit to create a basis for extracting fees from the pelagic whalers, they could not establish their right to do so. Nevertheless, both the Australians and the New Zealanders, as claimants to portions of Antarctica, participated in the international negotiations over whaling when they came along.

The right of a nation to regulate the actions of its own whalers wherever they might go was not in question, nor was the right of an Antarctic claimant nation to regulate anybody's whaling activity on land and in territorial waters of the claim disputed, validity of the claim being acknowledged. What was in question was how to regulate and control whaling on the high seas. Pelagic whaling was now by far the most significant kind of whaling in Antarctica and Antarctic whaling was of overwhelming importance to the industry.

As the 1920's wore on, the annual killings of whales rose to great heights and the need for conservation measures became obvious, not least because the killings appeared certain to go higher. To supplement the British regulations of conservatory effect, the Norwegian government in 1929 passed a law that prohibited the taking of right whales, calves, and cows with suckling calves, and in 1930 made an ordinance prohibiting the taking of blue whales of less than sixty feet in length and fin whales of less than fifty feet. It also required the use of the best factory techniques to insure the fullest possible utilization of carcases and reiterated this point in another ordinance in 1932. In the 1930–31 season more than 40,000 whales were taken and oil production reached its peak for the interwar period, producing a price crisis. There were now two reasons for governing the industry: conservation and control of oil production.

Late in 1931 an International Convention for the Regulation of Whaling was approved by twenty-six nations in the Assembly of the League of Nations, but as it required ratification by the governments, it was not of immediate effect. It covered the industry globally, but of course the Antarctic segment was of by far the greatest importance. As an interim measure, the Norwegians and the British, at this stage responsible for well over 90 per cent of total production, agreed to lay up their whaling fleets for the 1931–32 season to allow oil carried over to be absorbed by the market. A few ships of each nationality nevertheless went whaling, two of the surviving shore factories operated, and factory ships under other flags went out. Whales taken, however, dropped below 10,000 and oil production below one million barrels. The following season (1932–33) the Norwegian and British fleets returned to practically full operations but under a cartel-like arrangement about oil production. The number of whales taken rose 150 per cent to 24,000 (seven out of ten blues) and since the ships had been modernized while out of service, the utilization of carcases was of unprecedented efficiency. The agreement defined the length of the season, the lengths of whales that could rightfully be taken, and specified the amounts of oil each producer could market, thus aiming to advance both conservation and economic viability. But in neither respect was success achieved. About 2,000,000 barrels of oil had to be carried over. In the 1933–34 season, which by arrangement began about two weeks later than usual, the number of factory ships in operation increased and the new ships were of high efficiency in carcase utilization. This development was suggestively analogous to the agronomic progress of crop farmers subject to acreage restrictions. All told about 32,000 whales were taken this season. In mid-1934 the Norwegian government reduced the 1934–35 season to the period December 1–March 31, but announced no production quotas either for whale carcases or oil.

The League's Convention finally came into force in January 1935. In a loose way it embodied the Norwegian and British restrictions on the kinds of whales allowed to be killed and required the intensive use of carcases, but it did not limit the numbers of whales to be taken or oil to be produced. In June, therefore, the Norwegian government took power to fix, compulsorily if necessary, quotas for oil production by shore factories and factory ships operated by its nationals, and also further shortened the season. However, the industry was feeling the stimulation of a world shortage of fats and imports of whale oil into the United States promised to be larger than ordinarily because of the American effort to replace the fats not forthcoming because of production reductions in cotton and corn-hogs. While the principal producers observed the restrictions of the League Convention, Japan which had never signed it and Germany which had failed to ratify it, did not. For 1936–37 the Norwegians and the British discussed production restrictions between themselves. They again shortened the season and agreed to try the effect of limiting catchers to a specified number to each particular ship. The Japanese and Germans ignored all this. The largest fleet of factory ships since 1930 entered the field. It was now clearly apparent that the blue whale, the staple of the industry, was in grave danger of being "fished out" and that the pressure on other supplementary and substitute whales was dangerously heavy.

An International Whaling Convention of global effect was signed in London in 1937. The signatory nations were the United Kingdom, Norway, Germany, United States, Ireland, Argentina, and the British dominions with direct interests in Antarctica: South Africa, New Zealand, and Australia. The Japanese, while they attended the conference, refused to sign the Convention and proceeded to operate in disregard of it, as did a South African company by ignoring its government's signature. Canada, Denmark, and France participated in the discussions, but did not sign the Convention, though they observed its provisions. Argentina, a minor operator in Antarctic whaling, was chiefly interested in the political aspects of the Falkland Islands Dependencies claim (see below). Although a strong effort was made by the British and Norwegians to obtain them, no restrictions on oil production were arranged—the whole idea of prosperity by producing a little less was rejected, even the scheme of limiting the number of catchers per ship—and the Convention therefore emphasized conservation only: the taking of right whales was altogether prohibited and minimum lengths for others were prescribed: blues 70 feet; fins 55 feet; humpbacks 35 feet, sperms 35 feet. Some of the private operators then attempted to arrange restrictions on oil production among themselves in the hope of stabilizing the market. The

Convention was renewed in 1938 and 1939. In 1938 restrictions on oil production were again rejected and also once again the idea of limiting the number of catchers per ship, but the conservation provisions were amended to prohibit the taking of humpbacks and a whale sanctuary in Antarctica was established. In 1939 a provision was added requiring two control officers per ship, one to be a biologist if possible. The signatories this year were the principal producers only: Norway, the United Kingdom, Germany, and, for the first time, Japan.

World War II had a heavy impact on Antarctic whaling. At the outbreak of war both Britain and Germany, the principal European consumers, had considerable stockpiles of oil and in the early years of the war the British, in addition to some normal increments, added some windfalls from Norwegian suppliers whose homeland and usual markets fell under Nazi domination. The result was that the British, partly by the fortunes of economic warfare, came out of the war still in possession of small reserves of whale oil while Germany's stocks were all but exhausted by 1943. However, this is not to discount the effect of German action on the whaling industry.

Production of oil, as a matter of fact, quickly and drastically declined and the whaling fleets were in the course of the struggle decimated or worse. The Nazi fleet did not operate in the 1939–40 season, but the other fleets did and oil production was close to the average of the early 1930's. The British stockpiles were benefited by this production. However, it was the British who first suffered the loss of a ship by enemy action; it lost a factory ship on July 27, 1940. The vessels, moreover, had begun to be requisitioned for war service as bulk-carriers of inflammable liquids, general cargo carriers, antisubmarine vessels, and so on, this directly exposing them to the enemy action directed at merchant shipping and ships of war generally. Fear of possible Nazi raider action against the whalers if they were sent to the Antarctic grounds was strong when the 1940–41 season came around. The Norwegians sent out only three factory ships and the British but two. Only the Japanese fleet, having no fear of the Nazis, was out in full force. Two of the Norwegian factories and all their catchers but three were captured by Nazi raiders off Queen Maud's Land and, together with another factory serving as a transport for the operating fleet, were taken by the Nazis to French ports. Only one Norwegian factory survived; its oil went to the British. In addition the British and Norwegians lost factory ships elsewhere by enemy action. Oil production dropped to 50 per cent of the previous year's total and half of this was obtained by the Japanese. However, this was the last season the Japanese were able to operate and factories of other flags now ceased to operate also. While the shore station run by La Compañía

Argentina de Pesca at Grytviken, South Georgia, continued to operate throughout the war, no pelagic whaling operations were conducted after the 1940–41 season until they were resumed by the Norwegians with only one ship in 1943–44 and in 1944–45 also a Norwegian ship was the sole pelagic operator. In 1944 official discussions of the future of whaling were resumed. A fat famine such as that after World War I was definitely likely. The poor whales had a rest from their human predators for only two of the wartime years.

The invasion of the Ross Sea for whaling set in motion a cycle of developments in the matter of claims which was not completed until 1959, assuming that the arrangement arrived at in that year was more than a temporary pause in the struggle for sovereignty over the Antarctic wastes. Here we are concerned with developments to around 1945.

As noted, the British, who had initiated the assertion of sovereignty over Antarctic territory in 1908 to give a firmer base to their regulation of whaling using shore-based facilities or conducted within territorial waters, acted as though they regarded first discovery as an adequate foundation for the assertion of sovereignty. This continued to be their position up to World War II. It was certainly the basis of their response to the initiation of whaling in the Ross Sea. On this occasion they were referring to James Clark Ross's ceremonies at Possession Island near Cape Adare when he claimed by virtue of discovery, and named for Queen Victoria, all the land he had seen in the general vicinity.

The innovation the British introduced in 1923 was the transference of administrative responsibility for the claimed area from one part of the British Empire to another, from the United Kingdom to New Zealand. In this fashion the Ross Sea area became a dependency of New Zealand. The transfer was made by an Order in Council dated July 30, 1923, under the British Settlement Act of 1887, an imperial act which, as its title implies, had to do with regularizing the position of settlements of Britons which had grown up outside the Queen's dominions. No such settlements existed in Antarctica, least of all in the Ross Sea area. But nevertheless under the Order in Council the Ross Dependency, so-called, was put under the control of the New Zealand government and the governor was designated chief administrator, the nominal promulgator of such regulations as might be required. By this machinery the British-devised regulations governing whaling were applied in the Ross Dependency.

At the same time the question was at least implicitly raised as to how Antarctic claims were to be founded, especially since knowledge of geographical features was extremely limited. The earlier British claim was in effect an administrative attachment of Antarctic territory to an existing possession—the Falkland Islands—clearly outside Antarctica. (Especially with regard to the Falkland Islands Dependencies this matter of where Antarctic territory was administratively attached turned out to be important.) As it happened the northern boundary of the F.I.D. was defined so as to include South Georgia and therefore was north of any conventional northern limit of Antarctica, such as 60° South. To establish eastern and western boundaries, degrees of longitude were selected. Borrowing the sector principle which the Canadians had developed as a weapon in their struggle to gain control of the Arctic contiguous with their territory, the east and west meridians were traced to the South Pole, where all meridians converged, this giving the southern boundary, or terminal point. Whereas in the Arctic it was not possible to use the Pole as a terminal point because it was in the open ocean, in Antarctica it was possible because the Pole was presumed to be on land. The new Ross Dependency was administratively of a comparable nature, the attachment for convenience of Antarctic territory to a possession outside Antarctica, but no sound ground existed for drawing boundaries of the dependency so as to include land outside the conventional northern limits of Antarctica. Therefore the northern limit of the Ross Dependency was defined as 60° South, leaving the subantarctic islands of New Zealand as they were before. An alternative would have been to use the so-called Antarctic Convergence "where the cold, northward-flowing Antarctic waters sink beneath the relatively warmer waters of the sub-Antarctic," a line of fluctuating position between 48° and 60° South, often chosen by geographers as the correct northern limit of Antarctica. Since 1923, however, 60° South has always been the selected northern political boundary of Antarctica except in the Falkland Islands Dependencies where the boundary bulges a good bit to the north. Eastern and western boundaries for the Ross Dependency were, on the Falkland precedent, defined as degrees of longitude and the southern limit was the South Pole. The effect of this has been to cut up Antarctica like a pie with an ineptly made edge. The slices, as we shall see, have been of an uneven size. However, 60° South is in the high seas far beyond the conventional three-mile limit of territorial waters, a twelve-mile limit, or the edge of the continental shelf. After a rather weak effort to assert an obviously ill-founded jurisdiction over the icy high seas within the 60° South boundary in an effort to get control of pelagic whaling, it became the usual practice to limit the assertion of sovereignty to the islands already or subsequently to be discovered within the defined area of ocean. Even this left the New Zealanders asserting sovereignty over a large extent of "sea," though *permanently* ice-covered, as far as anyone could know, namely, the Ross Ice Shelf. The Ross Dependency came to be defined as "the sector of the Antarctic continent between 160° east and 150° west longitude, together with the islands lying between those degrees of longitude and south of latitude 60° south."

The British action to bring an additional large segment of Antarctica under sovereignty set other nations to thinking about their positions. The next year, 1924, the French, noting the direction of the British drift and well aware that their stake on the Antarctic continent was in effect "encircled" by areas which the British might take by virtue of first discovery, made a claim. They referred to Dumont d'Urville: "Dumont d'Urville prit possession au nom du roi Louis-Philippe, de tous les territoires compris entre le 136° et le 142° méridiens de longitude Est de Greenwich, auxquels il donna, en l'honneur de sa femme, le nom de Terre Adélie. La publication de cette découverte fut faite dans les journaux de l'époque, notament le 'Sydney Herald' du 13 mars 1840, le 'Moniteur', les 'Annales Maritimes et Coloniales', ainsi que le 'Voyage au Pole Sud publié par Ordonnance du Roi'." It was on this first discovery basis that by decree on March 27, 1927, the French "réserva aux citoyens français les droits miniers, de pêche et de chasse. Un autre décret du 21 avril 1924, rattacha la Terre Adélie (ainsi d'ailleurs que les archipels voisins, Kerguelen et Crozet et les îles Saint-Paul et Amsterdam) au Gouvernement général de Madagascar [thus getting far more incongruously far afield than the British]. Le 2 avril de la même année, une décision du Ministère de la Marine avait placé cette région dans le zone de surveillance des forces navales françaises. Quant aux limites mêmes de la Terre Adélie, elles furent fixées, après une négociation avec la Grande-Bretagne, par un décret du 13 avril 1938 . . . dont l'article est précise: 'Les îles et territoires situés au sud de 60° parallèle de latitude sud [note this] et entre les 136° et 142° méridiens de longitude Est de Greenwich relèvent de la souveraineté française'. . . . Par la suite, un traité aérien fut signé par la France, la Grande-Bretagne, L'Australie et la Nouvelle-Zélande, le 25 octobre 1938, autorisant le navigation aérienne des puissances signataires sur les territoires antarctiques." All this without the slightest effort even to revisit Terre Adélie!

In 1925 the Argentines began a challenge to British sovereignty in the Falkland Islands Dependencies (as they had long contested British possession of the Falkland Islands), in which they had apparently acquiesced since 1908. This contention was to grow by stages into the most heated political quarrel in Antarctic history, though how it was going to go was hardly clear at its beginning. The Argentines generated by far the most considerable head of nationalistic steam in support of their claim of any nation involved in the Antarctic arena.

The French invocation of Dumont d'Urville stirred memories of Charles Wilkes in American minds. The Americans had been absent from Antarctica as long as the French, indeed if account is taken of Charcot's expeditions to the Palmer-Graham area in 1908 and 1910, rather longer. There were four years yet to go before the Americans would return. But Charles Wilkes had made discoveries in 1840; he had indeed established that an Antarctic continent existed, or asserted circumstantially that he had. So why should not the United States now claim what Wilkes had discovered? The agitation led Secretary of State Charles Evans Hughes to make a statement about the matter. The position he took unsettled *all* claims. Hughes said in 1924: "It is the opinion of this department that the discovery of lands unknown to civilization, even when coupled with the formal taking of possession, does not support a valid claim to sovereignty unless the discovery is followed by actual settlement of the discovered country." From this statement, apparently impeccable in international law, but ignoring the problem of how settlement could in fact be made in a place like Antarctica, was derived an American position toward Antarctic claims: it was that the United States would make no claims, because Hughes' condition could not be fulfilled even though first discovery could be proved, and it would recognize no claims by others because the condition was not fulfilled, first discovery constituting no adequate basis for a claim to sovereignty. This remained the official American position and though it did not prevent the making of claims, it kept alive the question of their validity. The claimants had only the support arising from mutual recognition of their positions. The American official position did not, however, prevent private American citizens from making claims on the basis of first discovery, beginning with the first Byrd expedition. Both Byrd himself and Laurence Gould, his second in command, made claims to what became known as Marie Byrd Land. Their American successors in Antarctica did likewise when they made first discoveries, notably Lincoln Ellsworth in a variety of places west of the Falkland Islands Dependencies. Indeed, on Ellsworth's 1939 expedition while he made claims as a private American citizen, his associate Sir Hubert Wilkins made them in the same area on behalf of the Australian government. However, until 1938 not the faintest official countenance was given to the claims of private American citizens. In that year a certain ambiguity was introduced into the situation, less because of any actual change of policy than because the instructions on the point first given to Ellsworth in 1938 before he left Capetown were not made public.

What President Roosevelt actually wrote to Byrd the next year when he was commander of the USASE (or the State Department caused him to write) was (italics added):

The United States has never recognized any claims to sovereignty in the Antarctic regions asserted by any foreign state. No member of the United States Antarctic Service shall take any action or make any statements tending to compromise this position.

Members of the Service may take any appropriate steps such as dropping written claims from airplanes, depositing such writings in cairns, et cetera, which *might* assist in supporting a sovereignty claim by the United States Government. Careful record shall be kept of the circumstances surrounding each such act. *No public announcement of such act shall, however, be made without specific authority in each case from the Secretary of State.*

Although claims were rather frequently made during the USAS Expedition in a form prescribed by the State Department and ordinarily are detailed in the published accounts of the USASE, the secretary of State never took official cognizance of them because the United States government did not in fact make a claim and therefore never had to invoke a support which it had publicly stigmatized as of little substantive value. It came to be widely assumed, however, that if the United States ever did make a claim it would be to Marie Byrd Land, the vast ill-defined territory lying between the British Falkland Islands Dependencies and New Zealand's Ross Dependency fronting on the Bellingshausen and Amundsen seas. A fascinating by-blow of the claims which affected the United States expeditions was that when they were conducted from bases in claimed areas, permission to enter those areas was extended by the claimants even though such permission, being an acknowledgment of the claim, was never asked. Thus Byrd's famous Little America bases which were in the Ross Dependency were technically there by permission of the New Zealand government. (For accounts of the expeditions mentioned, see Chapter XIV.)

The political developments of the middle 1920's stirred the Australians deeply. They saw in them evidence that Antarctica was slipping away from them, and in the light of the belief that Australia had a special and unique stake in Antarctica, this was nothing short of a calamity. For forty years it had been argued by Australians that at least that portion of the continent to which the Australian continent stood in close geographical relationship should be British. This position was derived from and supported by the Australian position with regard to the Pacific islands south of the equator; the postion was an extension to the south polar regions of the doctrine that any land within a conveniently undefined distance of Australia should be in British possession to insure Australia's insulation from the attentions of hostile powers. This doctrine, or notion, as we have seen, justified both campaigns against allowing foreign powers to take possession of territories near Australia and in favor of Britain's taking possession of hitherto unclaimed territories within the elastically defined limits. With regard to Antarctica (as indeed it had been with regard to the islands) the situation was confused, especially as to where in the British constitutional system the right to annex really resided, in spite of what should have been learned from experience in the islands. Even so distinguished a spokesman as Sir Douglas Mawson was unclear on this point. Mawson's remarks could sometimes be taken to mean that Australia should act in Antarctica, sometimes that the London government should act. (In either case, in Mawson's mind, it would be an action on the basis of first discoveries, mostly imperial British but latterly Australian British, including Mawson's own.) At his most chauvinistic Mawson was of the opinion that *all* of Antarctica should be British with responsibility for portions shared out to the United Kingdom and the geographically related dominions, New Zealand, Australia, and South Africa, a position identical with that of those who argued that Britain should have taken *all* the islands. In his more moderate moods Mawson's concern was that Australia at least should get a very commodius sector embracing everything from the western limit of the Ross Dependency to a defined western limit of Enderby Land, come what may otherwise. When France claimed Adélie Land she cut a narrow slice out of what was felt to be the Australian sector and the Australian popular reaction to this was comparable in kind to the earlier Australian reactions to the taking of sovereignty by the French in Tahiti and New Caledonia. As earlier, the matter was handled, as noted above, by negotiations between France and the United Kingdom in the light of international considerations to which the Australians were still not at all sensitive. And before the whole question of Australia's position in Antarctica was settled, the Australians were upset by the activities of the Norwegians in whaling and exploration in the "Australian" sector and even were dubious about the activities of the nonclaiming Americans outside the Australian sector, though the New Zealanders were quite undisturbed.

Insofar as pressure for action was directed at the Australian government of S. M. Bruce, it was directed at a government aware of its constitutional incapacity to act to the end sought. Such action was an imperial prerogative and all Australia could do was to consult with the imperial authorities about the whole Antarctic problem. What the preliminaries of consultation amounted to is not yet known, but in the *Summary of Proceedings* of the Imperial Conference of 1926 it is recorded:

XI.—British Policy in the Antarctic.

The question of Antarctic exploration was discussed between representatives of the Governments interested. There are certain areas in these regions to which a British title already exists by virtue of discovery. These areas include:

(i) The outlying part of Coats Land, viz., the portion not comprised within the Falkland Islands Dependencies.

(ii) Enderby Land

(iii) Kemp Land

(iv) Queen Mary Land

(v) The area which lies to the west of Adélie Land and which on its discovery by the Australian Antarctic Expedition in 1912 was denominated Wilkes Land.

(vi) King George V Land

(vii) Oates Land

The representatives of the Governments concerned studied the information available concerning these areas with special reference to their possible utilization for further developing exploration and scientific research in the Antarctic regions.

In this fashion a reassertion was made of the doctrine that first discovery created a valid title, a list of areas to which it applied was compiled, and then the focus was shifted to exploration and scientific work. For Australia the first fruit of this statement of policy was a renewal of Mawson's work in Antarctica (see Chapter XIV). In due course, however, action was taken to insure that Australia received a substantial claim in Antarctica on the basis of discovery by British subjects. It proved to be the largest single claim of all.

The Australian claim was in legal character much like New Zealand's with the difference that it had been actively solicited and New Zealand's had not. On February 7, 1933, the imperial government issued an Order in Council affirming on the basis of discovery by British subjects the king's sovereign right over that part of Antarctica south of 60° falling between 160° East, the western boundary of the Ross Dependency, and 45° East, a conventional western boundary of Enderby Land, excepting the French claim of Adélie Land (which thus was completely surrounded). Embraced in this claim were all those areas except (i) enumerated in XI of the *Summary of Proceedings* of the Imperial Conference of 1926. The earliest discovery involved was Biscoe's of Enderby Land in 1831, the latest were Mawson's of 1912, but within the limits now defined were also included Mawson's of 1929–1931 and certain Norwegian discoveries of recent years. The claim very generously interpreted —more generously than the Australians had suggested was satisfactory as recently as 1925—what of Antarctica might be considered to be geographically the Australian sector on the ground that it was positioned in obvious relation to the Australian continent. By the Order in Council it was passed to the control of the Commonwealth of Australia if and when the Commonwealth accepted it by formal parliamentary action. The formal acceptance was signified by the Australian Antarctic Territory Acceptance Act, assented to June 13, 1933. This was brought into force when the governor general proclaimed it on August 24, 1936. In this fashion the Australians acquired territory in Antarctica much as they had acquired the colony of Papua in New Guinea and much as the New Zealanders had acquired the Ross Dependency—that is, by transfer to them of what was alleged to be part of the imperial domain. Australia's title was therefore no better and no worse than the imperial title.

In the parliamentary debates on the Acceptance Act it emerged clearly enough that the Australians had solicited this solution of their Antarctic problem from mixed motives, as mixed as their motives with regard to the islands. The most authoritative pronouncements were made by Sir John Latham, the attorney general, and R. G. Casey, who had been knowledgeable about Antarctic affairs since he had assisted Sir Hubert Wilkins in London in 1928. Both confused highly optimistic views of the economic potential of the acquisition and the exploration and scientific aspects. Economically the precedent of Alaska was bandied about. It was freely predicted that control of whaling would immediately bring in considerable income, the fact that whaling throughout the Australian sector was pelagic misunderstood, and it was alleged that dreams of avarice were in order with regard to the future. It was these dreams that drew the Australians on. Antarctica was part of their economic heritage from Britain. It was only very unclearly perceived that rather they were assuming heavy material and moral obligations far more readily to be expressed in outgo than income. Even after this became much clearer than it was in 1933, the Australians remained strongly possessive about their sector.

The United States, of course, did not recognize the Australian claim, particularly since it obviously derived from a British claim based on first discoveries, some of which were remote in time and one—Kemp's—was as contingent as anything in the Wilkes repertory. When in 1939, however, Lincoln Ellsworth, the first American since Wilkes to operate within the boundaries of the Australian sector, claimed as a private citizen what he called American Highland back of the Ingrid Christensen Coast, the Australian public was a bit upset, though the Australian government took comfort in the expectation that the United States government would take no official notice of the claim. It did not. The ground for thinking that Ellsworth's claim might possibly receive official support was the action of the Congress in 1936 awarding Ellsworth a gold medal and formally thanking him for having claimed James W. Ellsworth Land during his trans-Antarctic flight. However, the State Department had, simultaneously, reiterated its stand on the Charles Evans Hughes position of 1924. The Australians knew nothing of what Hull had cabled Ellsworth at Capetown.

The Norwegian attitude was different. Unlike the Americans, they were disposed to recognize and make claims. As early as 1905 the Norwegian government had accepted a British assertion of sovereignty over South Georgia, the South Shetlands, the South Orkneys, and the northern part of Graham Land. On January 23, 1928, they had brought Bouvet Island under Norwegian sovereignty and on May 1, 1931, Peter I Island, the former north of 60°, the latter south of it. Both were created dependencies of the Norwegian kingdom. This was done to effectuate purposes explained earlier. Neither island was a first discovery of Norwegian nationals. Bouvet was discovered by a Frenchman in 1739, Peter I by a Russian in 1821, but the Norwegians had first occupied (although hardly "settled") them. In 1929 the Norwegians promised the British that they would not claim sovereignty over any Antarctic territory over which the British had asserted rights (see the British list of 1926). When in 1930 the Norwegians began to engage in exploration on the coasts of the Antarctic mainland, the situation was that the British had formally asserted sovereignty over the Falkland Islands Dependencies and the Ross Dependency and had in an official document notified that other areas specified were places in which "a British title already exists by virtue of discovery." These other areas were mostly discontinuous stretches of coast west of the Ross Dependency in what the Australians already regarded as "their" sector. It was there and beyond that the Norwegians now began to prosecute investigations and make discoveries clear around to the boundary of British Coats Land, in close association with their whaling in off-shore waters. They thus came to make discoveries both within and outside the "Australian sector" without, however, encroaching upon areas to which a British title had been asserted. The popular Australian and British feeling was that the Norwegians were nevertheless intruding into a British preserve. The British government took a rather more benign attitude. The first effort to exclude the Norwegians from the "Australian sector" in disregard of whether or not a British title to a particular coast had been asserted to exist was made in private negotiations in 1930 between Sir Douglas Mawson and Hjalmar Riiser-Larsen off the coast of Enderby Land. It was agreed between the explorers that the Norwegians would confine their attentions to the coasts beyond 45° East, around to Coats Land, while the Australians would work from

45° East, eastward to the boundary of the Ross Dependency. When three years later the British finally defined the boundaries of what was to become the Australian sector they found them to run from the western boundary of Ross Dependency precisely to 45° East, thus embracing many features and stretches of coast the Norwegians had discovered during and after 1930. Whether or not the Norwegian government was disturbed by this is unclear, but Lars Christensen, as the leading promoter of Norwegian Antarctic exploration (and whaling), certainly was. This, of course, was not the first time a claim based on first discovery had included within its lines of longitude the first discoveries of others. The Falkland Islands Dependencies included a great many first discoveries by nationals of other than British countries and so also did the Ross Dependency. The Norwegians were thoroughly alive to the fact that the discoveries of Roald Amundsen had been included within the Ross Dependency. It was already becoming an American habit not only to establish bases within claimed areas but to prosecute exploration within them and make first discoveries. Considering the history of Antarctic exploration it is difficult to see how, if the precedent for bounding claims set by the British in 1908 was to be followed, the consequence of arbitrarily attempting to extinguish the first discovery claims of others could be avoided. The only visible alternative way of dividing up Antarctica was the method practiced in partitioning Africa south of the Sahara—which would have produced an even less sensible political geography. Nevertheless, the inclusion of coasts *recently* discovered by Norwegians within the Australian claim upset Lars Christensen. His feeling was not only that the action dispossessed Norwegians of territory legitimately theirs by virtue of first discovery but also that the boundary of 45° East represented an excessive extension of the Australian claim and compounded the offense. However, Christensen's grumblings seem not to have gone beyond the newspapers and his book about Antarctica. The Norwegians accepted the Australian claim and indeed their acceptance was a factor in establishing it. On the other hand, they successfully resisted the Australian effort to regulate and levy tribute on pelagic whaling conducted within their claim on the high seas south of 60°.

The Norwegians, indeed, were not immediately stimulated to make a claim to protect their numerous and still multiplying coastal discoveries from 45° East, the Australian western boundary, around to Coats Land, the western boundary of the Falkland Islands Dependencies. It was the fear of what the Nazi exploring expedition of 1939 (see Chapter XIV), directed to territory behind the coasts the Norwegians had found, portended that moved them to action to protect those discoveries. Queen

Maud's Land was brought under Norwegian sovereignty by an Order in Council on January 14, 1939, but unlike Bouvet and Peter I islands it was not made a dependency of the kingdom.

The claims of the British, the New Zealanders, the French, the Australians, and the Norwegians were supported chiefly by mutual recognition and they were unsettled by the United States policy of nonrecognition. The United States did not, however, actively dispute anybody's claim to a particular territory in an effort to establish a counterclaim to the same territory. This was precisely what the Argentines did, beginning in 1925. Over a period of a dozen years they worked up to a counterclaim to the Falkland Islands Dependencies in their entirety. From a rather simple beginning the dispute developed unparalleled complexity, largely by the introduction of arguments in support of the Argentine position which had not hitherto been employed in discussions of Antarctic claims. The argumentation was not fully developed until after World War II. In various complicated ways, moreover, the Argentine claims in and to the Falkland Islands Dependencies were entangled with the Argentine dispute of the British claim to sovereignty over the Falkland Islands themselves—known to the Argentines as Las Islas Malvinas— which had been intermittently prosecuted since 1820 and as between the Spanish and the British for fifty years before that date. The British had, however, uninterruptedly occupied and administered the Falklands since 1833 and they had begun as early as 1843 to use the expression "Falkland Islands and their Dependencies," though not until 1887 did they name any of the so-called dependencies. They then named South Georgia. A little over twenty years later, in 1908, for reasons and in a form already discussed—the effective *reason* was developments in whaling (see Chapter XII)—the British formally specified more of the dependencies by name; to South Georgia they added the South Orkneys, the South Shetlands, the Sandwich Islands, and Graham Land. Other territories not immediately specified were then included within the lines of latitude and longitude cited as the boundaries of the Dependencies, notably Coats Land.

The Argentines had been interested early in sealing south of 60° and were associated with Captain C. A. Larsen's pioneering of whaling at South Georgia. The Argentine government began to show an interest in the far south in 1902 when, in response to the resolution of the International Geographical Congress of 1895, it set up a meteorological and magnetic station on Staten Island off the eastern tip of Tierra del Fuego within Argentine territory on the northern subantarctic fringes. At the end of 1904 the Argentine government accepted the proposal of W. S. Bruce that it take continuing operating responsibility for the meteorological and magnetic station the Bruce expedition (see Chapter XII) had established on Laurie Island, just *south* of 60°, in the South Orkney group. Laurie Island was recognizably outside Argentine territory as then defined but acceptance of responsibility for the station on it, which the Argentines continued to operate down the years, raised the question of sovereignty only implicitly. However, the British with good reason continued to assume that the Argentines accepted their sovereignty over Laurie and the South Orkneys generally. (Incidentally, in claiming sovereignty over the South Orkneys the British unilaterally extinguished any American rights in the group that might have arisen from the fact that Nathaniel Brown Palmer was the coadjutor of the British subject, George Powell, in the discovery of the group in 1821, just as in other parts of the Dependencies they unilaterally extinguished other first discovery "rights" of Palmer and other Americans.) Neither in 1904 nor for some years after did the Argentines cause the assumption to be questioned. Indeed, by their conformance with the British regulations with regard to whaling both before and after the crucial year of 1908, and their acquiescence in what the British called sovereign acts in the Dependencies in connection with the administration of the whaling regulations, they showed that they at least tacitly accepted the British position.

The Argentines appeared to accept the situation as the British defined it over a twenty-year period, but in 1925 they veered off their apparently settled course. Whether they took the new tack by suggestion from the then rising interest in sovereignty in Antarctica or in response to some nationalistic current of opinion in Argentina is not clear. It is rather obvious, however, that their new position regarding the South Orkneys was related to, or derived from, their traditional position of nonrecognition of British sovereignty in the Falkland Islands. At any rate, the British first heard of the new direction of Argentine Antarctic policy when, learning that the Argentine government was erecting a wireless station at the Laurie Island installation, they informed the Argentines that since Laurie was British, application for a "call sign" for the station should, to accord with the relevant international convention, be made through the British government. To this the Argentine government replied very ambiguously and when pressed the next year about the sovereignty question, fell silent altogether. The station finally came into operation in 1927 and the British then learned from the International Telegraph Bureau at Berne, Switzerland, that the Argentines had applied for a "call sign" and in doing so had implied that they had sovereignty over the South Orkneys. Replying to the British objection to this implication on January 20, 1928, the Argentines openly laid claim to the South Orkneys on the ground of first *occupation* (that is, "settlement"). However, the Argentines were not too sure of themselves and offered to resume a discussion, aborted earlier, to exchange the South Orkneys for a new site for a British embassy in Buenos Aires. Also in 1927 the British learned, this time from the International Postal Bureau at Berne, that the Argentines had in dealings with the bureau claimed sovereignty not only over the South Orkneys *but also South Georgia*. This proposition arose from the Argentine refusal to recognize Falkland Islands stamps, then in use in the Dependencies also, a deduction from their non-recognition of British sovereignty in the Falkland Islands. For some years, however, the Argentine government had contributed to the support of a meteorological station maintained at Grytviken in connection with the Argentine-owned whaling operation. Taxed with this, the Argentines dropped South Georgia but affirmed their position with regard to the South Orkneys. The British, however, told the Postal Bureau that the United Kingdom postmaster-general represented both the South Orkneys and South Georgia. There the rising argument rested for ten years. Neither side conceded anything in the interval.

In 1937 the Argentine government by two actions made it clear that during the preceding decade, far from retreating to a diffidently advanced claim to the South Orkneys only, it had advanced to an implied claim to all the Falkland Islands Dependencies. On the occasion of the Whaling Conference in London in 1937 at which an International Whaling Convention was negotiated (see above), the Argentine ambassador drew the attention of the Foreign Office to a statement made to the Conference by the British minister of Agriculture and Fisheries to the effect that the Falkland Islands Dependencies were under the jurisdiction of the Falkland Islands government. The ambassador then "reserved" all rights Argentina claimed over the Dependencies. This was tantamount to notifying Great Britain that Argentina challenged British pretentions in the Dependencies in their entirety. The position was reiterated by the Argentines on September 22, 1938, when in promulgating the ratification of certain international postal conventions which Britain had signed on behalf of the Falkland Islands and Dependencies, they again "reserved" their rights comprehensively. However, the Argentine claim was still more implicit than explicit and the British treated it as a nuisance rather than a threat.

With the outbreak of World War II the affair took a new turn. Because of the war the "Discovery" Committee's people and ships ceased their activities, the whalers ceased operations, and those officials who in association with one or the other were the agents of activities demonstrating British sovereignty disappeared from the scene. In 1940 the Argentines signalized that they were about to take a more aggressive stance by setting up a Comisión Nacional del Antárctico in the Ministry of External Relations. And then, in 1940 also, the government of Chile projected itself into the already complicated situation in the Falkland Islands Dependencies. On November 6, 1940, a decree was issued which, after recalling that the matter of Chile's position with regard to Antarctica had been under (presumably desultory) study from 1906 to 1939, declared:

I [the President] decree:

All lands, islands, islets, reefs and rocks, glaciers (pack-ice), already known or to be discovered, and their respective territorial waters, in the sector between longitudes 53° and 90° West, constitute the Chilean Antarctic or Chilean Antarctic territory.

The Chilean claim overlapped both the British and the Argentine claims, but the Argentines and the Chileans nevertheless came to an accommodation about pushing their conflicting claims against their common opponent, the British. The Chileans had even longer than the Argentines acted as if they acquiesced in the British pretention to sovereignty in the claimed area, though allegedly significant acts and statements to the contrary were now recalled. Like the Argentines the Chileans had conformed to British whaling regulations. They had not, in fact, shown any particular restlessness about the situation at any time in the past. Unlike the Argentines they had no precedent like the question of the Falkland Islands for an anti-British stand. They may have been encouraged to act in 1940 by Secretary of State Cordell Hull's innocent sounding remark to the effect that the sovereignty question in the American sector ought to be cleared up. They may have acted from a realization of the strategic risks they were running. Hostile ships *might* be based in such Antarctic ports as Deception Island. (The Argentines may also have had this on their minds.) Or the Chileans (and the Argentines) may have been stimulated to move simply by the war-explained absence of the British.

With the Argentines taking the lead, the ensuing campaign against the British took the form of expeditions into the islands on the west side of the Palmer-Graham Peninsula. They were directed by the Comisión Nacional del Antárctico and the ship was provided by the Ministry of Marine. In 1942 the Argentine naval vessel "Primero de Mayo," Captain A. J. Oddera commander, with Chilean "observers" aboard, made a voyage into the area. It went south to the vicinity of the Melchior Islands, Palmer Archipelago, a considerable collection of small islands individually named for letters of the Greek alphabet, in Dallman Bay. The Germans had originally discovered the group; the French and the British had surveyed it. The Argentines now resurveyed it. On one of the islands they set up a light beacon as a navigation aid. They did some oceanography. But the real point of the expedition was finally made clear at Deception Island. Here the abandoned whaling installations were closely examined and a bronze cylinder was left in which was a statement of a claim to all lands south of 60° between 25° West, and 68° 34′ West. This was the most explicit declaration of a position yet.

The British became aware of what the Argentines and Chileans had done at Deception Island when in January 1943 H.M.S. "Carnarvon Castle," Lt. Commander E. W. Kitson, visited the island to follow up the British check on the possibility that German raiders were using the facilities, initiated earlier by the merchant cruiser "Queen of Bermuda." The "Carnarvon Castle" crew found the Argentine cylinder. They systematically obliterated all traces of the Argentine-Chilean visit, hoisted the flag, and left a record of *their* visit. The flag-raising and record-leaving ceremonies were repeated on Signy Island in the South Orkneys. A visit was then made to the meteorological station on Laurie Island to notify the Argentines of the British presence. The bronze cylinder was returned to the Argentine government through the British Embassy at Buenos Aires. The British were now worried; they suspected that the Argentines planned a coup in the Dependencies.

The Argentines certainly responded as though they did. That same season they sent the "Primero de Mayo," Captain Silvano Harriague commanding, into the area again. Oceanographic work was resumed around the Melchiors. The USAS base at Stonington Island in Marguerite Bay (see Chapter XIV) was visited—incidentally an Argentine farthest south. A bronze cylinder containing a restatement of the claim was deposited, this time at Port Lockroy on Wiencke Island. Deception Island was visited and all evidences of the "Carnarvon Castle" visit were systematically obliterated. The challenge was thus underscored.

In spite of the war and its heavy absorption of British energies and resources, the response was vigorous. It took the form of Operation Tabarin, a military operation organized by the Admiralty acting on behalf of the Colonial Office. As originally planned two bases were to be established, an administrative base at Deception Island at which meteorological work would be carried on and a second on the peninsula at which meteorology and other scientific work would be done and some exploration essayed toward the Rymill expedition's marks (see below). At Deception the hypothetical German raiders would be foiled and a watch would be kept on ships of other nationalities. Recognizing that Operation Tabarin was an emergency expedition, it is nevertheless the case, at least as viewed ex post facto, that the British were coming around to permanent occupation, or "settlement," to hold their claim. Tabarin proved to be the initiating stage of what was the very next season to become the Falkland Islands Dependencies Survey, under the Colonial Office, successor to the "Discovery" Committee operation, characterized by the establishment and maintenance of permanent bases at most of which symbolic acts of sovereignty were to be executed.

Operation Tabarin was led by Lt. Commander J. W. S. Marr, R.N.V.R., who had been initiated into Antarctic work as the Boy Scout of Shackleton's last expedition, and who had been with Mawson's expeditions of 1929–31 as a specialist in oceanography. The party arrived at Port Stanley, Falkland Islands, on January 26, 1944. Two ships were used, the Discovery Committee's "William Scoresby," called off minesweeping duties, and the "Fitzroy," owned by the Falkland Islands Company, a private commercial concern. The two ships arrived at Deception Island on February 3 and set up the administrative base as planned, obliterating the Argentine signs and symbols. The other base was now planned for Hope Bay at the northern tip of the peninsula where one of Nordenskjold's scattered parties had wintered, but the "Fitzroy" could not enter the bay because of ice and after prospecting for an alternative site the base was actually established at Port Lockroy, where the second Argentine cylinder had been left. At Port Lockroy meteorological work was also done and geological, biological, and topographical work was undertaken, but as no provision had been made for traveling, the studies were prosecuted only on Wiencke Island.

The next season, under the name Falkland Islands Dependencies Survey, the two established bases were visited, reprovisioned, and freshly staffed and a third base at Hope Bay was established, though just barely. Preliminary work was done for a fourth base on Coronation Island in the South Orkneys. All bases were to participate in the emerging meteorological network heading up in Port Stanley and at the Hope Bay base geological and biological studies were to be prosecuted, as at Port Lockroy, and additionally, being supplied with dogs, the Hope Bay men were to travel south on the east side of the peninsula. The first year their farthest south was Nordenskjold's Cape Longing, 64° 33′ South. The British pattern of reply was entirely clear: a network of bases was to be established and continuously operated in the Dependencies. Meanwhile, neither the Argentines nor the Chileans had been south since the 1943 season. The first energies of the Comisión Nacional de Antártico had apparently been exhausted. But in January 1947 both Argentina and Chile sent politico-exploratory-scientific expeditions south.

CHAPTER XIV

Tearing at the Veil (2)

In 1928 G. H. Wilkins, now Sir Hubert Wilkins, finally reached Antarctica with an airplane—two of them, in fact, Lockheed-Vega's—and for the first time in history carried out exploration there by air. Wilkins was born on a station in the dry country of South Australia and studied both engineering and music in Adelaide. He launched a fruitful career of adventure by stowing away on a ship he thought was going to Sydney but which took him to North Africa. Eventually arriving in London, he became a photographer, both movie and still, covered the Turco-Bulgarian war of 1912 from the Turkish side, had a tour of duty in the West Indies, and when World War I began was with Stefansson in the Arctic. Already fascinated with airplanes, he tried to become a flyer in the Australian service but was assigned instead as a photographer on the Western Front. After the war, failing in the United Kingdom-Australia air race, he joined Cope's Antarctic expedition and then Shackleton's last, expecting both times to fly. Following a mysterious trip into Russia, he next led a natural history expedition into North Australia and only after that began exploratory flying in the polar regions. He had a strong conviction of the practicability of this, including the feasibility of safely landing on ice, stronger than Stefansson's, Amundsen's, or Byrd's, for instance, and it was associated with a fixed belief in the importance of the establishment of meteorological stations in the polar areas. This idea he had apparently picked out of the air in Australia, where the conception that the domestic weather, particularly the cruelly fluctuating rainfall, was somehow under Antarctic influences had been current since the 1880's. Wilkins' first polar flying was in the Arctic beginning in 1926 (the year Byrd had flown to the North Pole) and in 1928 he flew in twenty hours from Point Barrow, Alaska, 2500 miles east to Spitzbergen, a superb feat. This climaxed fifteen years of work as an explorer-scientist, and he was then honored with his knighthood.

Wilkins entered Antarctica with a rather miscellaneous group of backers ranging from the Vacuum Oil Company of Australia to William Randolph Hearst to British well-wishers. He believed in small expeditions, though shortly he was to recognize that their day was fading. He believed in the airplane as an ideal instrument for fast coverage of unknown territory, he was deeply impressed with the protective importance of radio communications between plane and base, and he had an overly strong conviction that accurate observations could be made by eye from a plane and satisfactorily recorded by the single-focus camera then available. In 1928 his men and planes were taken to Deception Island from Montevideo in the British factory ship "Hektoria." After some short reconnaissance flights, Wilkins and his pilot Carl Eilson (who had piloted the plane across the Arctic), took off on December 20, 1928, on the historic pioneer exploratory flight, staying in the air ten hours. From Deception Island they flew toward Trinity Island and thence across the Palmer-Graham Peninsula. Turning south they flew, largely over hitherto unseen country, until they reached the point where the peninsula appeared to join what was assumed to be the mainland. This area they named Hearst Land. Here they saw what seemed to be channels severing the peninsula, turning it into islands. This was not the first time the peninsula was thought to be insular. As recently as 1924 some British whalers had made similar observations. Later exploration on the ground showed conclusively that Wilkins' observations were in error. The name Hearst Land was then transferred to the sizable Hearst Island in the ice of the Larsen Ice Shelf and the name Stefansson which had been applied to the principal channel across the peninsula was assigned to the strait separating Hearst Island from the peninsula. In sum it was in a few years shown that the airplane, while invaluable for reconnaissance and also logistically, rather prepared the way for the hard, slogging work on the ground or was an ideal support for advanced bases from which ground work could proceed farther into the field; it did not serve to eliminate the need for ground work. Even the pictures taken from a plane were reduced in worth if carefully made "fixes" of ground positions were not available to establish points of reference for reading them. After a short confirmatory flight over the northern segment of their great flight, Wilkins called the season's work complete.

Returning to the field again the next season, having meanwhile made the flight around the world in the Graf Zeppelin, Wilkins and his people again reached Deception Island via Montevideo on the "Hektoria" intending to explore southward along the west side of the peninsula (or island chain). To reach as far south as possible by plane, they proposed to set up a base on the ice just within flying distance from Deception

Island but this season the ice proved to be "out" unusually far south, beyond flight reach. Wilkins enlisted the help of the "Discovery" Committee's ship the "William Scoresby" which took them to Port Lockroy. From there they flew farther south and finding what seemed to be solid ice serviceable for a take-off, they started out to reach it in the "Scoresby." Unfortunately this ice broke up before a take-off could be managed. However, at a point somewhat north of Charcot Land, pontoons were installed on the plane and a take-off was made from the water. The first flight ended in fog short of Charcot Land, but a second flight next day (December 29, 1929) enabled them to encircle Charcot Land and demonstrate that it was an island. This was the great accomplishment of the season. On later flights to the southwestward no land was seen—nothing but the ice of Bellingshausen Sea.

After this Wilkins was in and out of the Antarctic for a decade as adviser to and in charge of the base ship of Lincoln Ellsworth (1880–1951). Ellsworth was born to wealth in Chicago, but the strenuous life appealed and after training as an engineer, he chose to work on railroad and mining projects in remote places. By 1921 he was convinced that his proper business was exploration. There was a strong romantic strain in him. In the middle 1920's he became fascinated with airplanes and in 1925 he made a famous flight toward the North Pole with Amundsen. The following year he was a principal in the Amundsen-Nobile-Ellsworth flight of the dirigible "Norge" from Spitzbergen to Alaska. (Wilkins was at Port Barrow when the "Norge" passed over.) He met Wilkins in the late 1920's and in 1931 was associated with his project for taking the submarine "Nautilus" under the Arctic ice. By that time Ellsworth was actively planning a transantarctic flight—from the Ross to the Weddell Sea and back, or perhaps to some point in the Palmer-Graham area, or vice versa. By this time not only Wilkins but also Riiser-Larsen, Mawson, and Byrd had demonstrated the feasibility of flying in the Antarctic, yet as no one had done exactly what Ellsworth proposed to do the hazards involved had to be considered anew.

The whole affair was not sheer adventure; it was designed by Ellsworth to contribute to the solution of two geographical problems: whether or not the so-called Andean mountains of the Palmer-Graham "peninsula" (for Ellsworth accepted Wilkins' idea that the peninsula was insular) connected with the mountains back of the Ross Ice Shelf, and was there a below-sea-level channel connecting the Weddell and Ross Seas? In preparing for the flight, Ellsworth assumed that it was unlikely he would be able to fly the whole distance in one hop, but must expect to land occasionally en route if only to wait out bad flying weather. By studying the narratives of Scott, Shackleton, Amundsen, and Mawson he concluded that such landings would be feasible even though his witnesses had not been thinking in terms of airplane landings. This was correct. He knew, of course, that meteorology was too undeveloped to permit weather forecasts for the whole line of flight. He reckoned that aside from blizzards the weather menaces would be high winds and the dreaded "whiteouts" of blowing snow which destroyed visibility. With wind in mind he decided that a low-wing plane would be best both in the air and on the ground and he had one specially built for him, dubbed the "Polar Star." It was large enough to carry a pilot and himself, around 500 gallons of gasoline, a reserve of oil, and equipment and supplies for fairly long stays or journeys on the surface. He carried a camera to record landscape features observed. He installed radio equipment to keep close contact with his base ship. The ship's name revealed his romanticism; it was called the "Wyatt Earp," after the famous western frontier marshal.

Ellsworth tried twice to make his flight before he succeeded. His first effort was to fly from the Bay of Whales in the Ross Ice Shelf to the Weddell Sea and back. The approach was made via New Zealand and the bay was reached on January 6, 1934. Byrd was on his way south with his second expedition and Ellsworth was in touch with him by wireless. A week later the plane was seriously damaged when the ice unexpectedly broke up and the flight had to be abandoned. On the next attempt the approach was made via New Zealand to Deception Island, Wilkins' old stamping ground, where the party arrived on October 14, 1934. The shift of starting point was made to take advantage of earlier favorable seasonal conditions. The Bay of Whales was now the *destination*. However, not only did they run into mechanical troubles with the plane but, ironically, the thorough melting of the snow on Deception Island made a take-off impossible. They tried Port Lockroy but finally had to move to Snow Hill Island on the other side of the peninsula where, incidentally, they found Nordenskjold's old hut still intact. On January 3, 1935, they flew south as far as the Seal Nunataks (discovered by C. A. Larsen in 1893) in the Larsen Ice Shelf where they were turned back by bad weather. This terminated the season's effort. On their way north they selected Dundee Island, a discovery of the Dundee whalers in 1893, as the site of next season's take-off point.

The party arrived at Dundee Island via Montevideo and Deception Island on November 11, 1935. As pilot they had the Canadian Arctic flyer Herbert Hollick-Kenyon. It was calculated that the flight could be made in fourteen hours. The first try on November 21 was a failure for after they had flown 600 miles and had reached new country beyond Wilkins' Stefansson Strait and Hearst Land they suffered a clogged fuel gauge and had to turn back. The next day they started again. This time they flew south along the coast to Mobiloil Inlet in the Larsen Ice Shelf (one of Wilkins' discoveries, named for the product of the Vacuum Oil Company of Australia) and then turned inland, flying southwest. They were on their way. New mountains dubbed the Eternity Mountains, one peak of which was over 12,000 feet high, loomed up. The radio broke down and unknown to them Wilkins on the "Wyatt Earp," aware as always of how vital contact was, broadcast the fact and thus set going elaborate search and rescue operations. Three hours later Ellsworth and Hollick-Kenyon were over a polar plateau, later called Ellsworth Highland, beyond the limits of the Falkland Islands Dependencies sector, with considerable mountains visible on both sides of the plane. However, the country was becoming more and more featureless and when they saw and photographed the Sentinel Mountains, of which the central peak was Mount Ulmer (after Ellsworth's wife), it was an isolated feature they were observing. (The relation of the Sentinels to the Filchner Ice Shelf was unperceived.) They were now rather uncertain of their position, visibility was getting poor, and they had been flying fourteen hours, so they came down for a landing, succeeding fairly easily but crumpling the fuselage in the process, this to slow their air-speed in the future. They spent nineteen hours on the ground. Starting again they flew but half-an-hour when bad visibility forced another landing, this time for three days. They were still uncertain as to just where the Bay of Whales lay. Starting again they flew but ninety miles when they were forced down by fog and soon a blizzard came up which kept them on the ground for eight days. They were probably 600 miles from Byrd's Little America camp, fuel was getting short, and they could not make radio contact with the "Wyatt Earp." The outlook was bleak. However, they got in the air again on December 4 in beautiful weather and flew out of the plateau country over the Ross Ice Shelf to within 145 miles of Little America well within the territory explored by Byrd. The next day they were able to see the waters of the Ross Sea from the plane, but exhaustion of the gasoline brought them gliding down an estimated sixteen miles short of Little America at what they learned later was the north end of Roosevelt Island. After two days largely spent in securing the plane which was still air-worthy, they set out on foot to reach Little America and shelter. All told it took them five days and sixty miles of hard travel to accomplish this. First they chose a course too far west and came to open water, this indicating that they were north of the camp, and so they ended up traveling south to reach their destination. They were able to break through a skylight and drop into what proved to be the radio shack. Establishing a marker at Byrd's unloading place on the bay six miles away, they settled down to await the arrival of their relief, the "Wyatt Earp." Ellsworth always insisted they were not lost and required no "rescue." Relief finally came a month later in the shape of the "Discovery" Committee's ship "Discovery II" from Melbourne, called off its regular work at the instance of Prime Minister Lyons of Australia, supported by the governments of New Zealand and the United Kingdom, after Wilkins' broadcast that radio contact had been lost. Three days later the "Wyatt Earp" with Wilkins arrived. The "Polar Star" was flown to the bay and loaded on the "Wyatt Earp," while Ellsworth went off on the "Discovery II" to make a twelve-day visit to Australia as guest of the government. The great adventure was over, but the direct contribution to the solution of the geographical puzzles that had engaged Ellsworth's mind was negligible.

Ellsworth's final voyage into Antarctica, again accompanied by Wilkins, was made in 1938–39. Leaving Capetown in the "Wyatt Earp" on October 29, 1938, they spent an exceptionally long time getting through the ice, not emerging until January 2, 1939, off the Ingrid Christensen Coast. Here the Norwegians and the Australians had been active in coastal exploration, but Ellsworth's objective was to survey back country from the air. After carefully searching the coastal ice between Mikkelsen's Vestfold Hills and his Rauer Islands for a takeoff place for the larger of their two planes, they found one just east of the hills. From this site on January 11, 1939, they flew inland over the elevated continental plateau (7500 feet), eventually covering 77,000 square miles of territory in a block 288 miles north and south and 300 miles east and west. To this territory Ellsworth gave the name American Highland. Two days later a member of the expedition sustained an injury which required more treatment than the doctor could manage. Leaving the coast immediately, the "Wyatt Earp" arrived at Hobart on February 4. The ship, the two planes, and the stores were sold to the Australian government which was then seriously thinking of establishing a meteorological station in its Antarctic claim. However, the war supervened and the "Wyatt Earp" passed into the Royal Australian Navy.

Toward the end of 1928 Richard Evelyn Byrd arrived at the Bay of Whales, Ross Ice Shelf, with a large expedition of eighty men, of whom forty-two were to stay in a wintering-over camp, christened Little America, for fourteen months. This was the largest single wintering-over party in Antarctica to date. This expedition is usually taken to mark the return of the Americans to Antarctica for the first time since Charles Wilkes's visit in 1840.

Richard Evelyn Byrd (1888–1957) was Virginia-born of a "first family," younger brother of Harry Flood Byrd, politician, at this time governor of the state, soon (1933) to become and long remain a conservative Democratic United States Senator. Richard Evelyn was a graduate of the United States Naval Academy (1912), a career officer in the service. He had been a pioneer of naval aviation and had commanded the United States Air Force in Canada during World War I. He had always had a strong bent toward adventure and in boyhood had shown a harum-scarum streak; heroes of his youth were Robert F. Scott and Robert E. Peary. In 1925 he was in charge of aviation with the Navy-MacMillan Arctic expedition and the next year he and Floyd Bennett had flown from Spitzbergen to the North Pole and back. In 1927 Byrd and three companions flew the Atlantic from New York to France. He first consciously formulated the idea of actually going to Antarctica when, the evening after his flight to the North Pole, Amundsen—Ellsworth was also there—said to him, "Well, Byrd, what shall it be now?" and Byrd had replied, "The South Pole." He began to plan this adventure before he flew the Atlantic. It was entirely logical that he should fix upon the Bay of Whales as his "port of entry," for talking to Amundsen inevitably suggested it, but while Byrd's personal project of flying to the South Pole and back was in the tradition of Amundsen's own journey to the Pole, the expedition Byrd put on, with its strong emphasis on geographical work and concern for scientific knowledge, was in the tradition of Scott, Shackleton, and Mawson and the narratives of these and other prior workers in Antarctica were closely studied for cues and information. (At Byrd's request, Mawson consulted with him in New Zealand.)

The Byrd expedition not only had an unprecedented number of personnel but it was also founded on the most advanced technology. But while it gathered up the accumulated technology that seemed applicable to polar exploration for use in Antarctica, it was also rooted firmly in tradition and had "reserves" of methodological means, such as dogs and sledges, should the advanced but still experimental technology fail. It was enormously costly and though Byrd managed to finance it privately, with John D. Rockefeller, Jr., and Edsel Ford the principal backers, and indeed to repeat the performance, though with very great difficulty, a few years later, the first Byrd expedition made it quite obvious that only with government support could geographical and scientific work on this scale be carried on in the future. In addition to the support and assistance of individuals, Byrd also commanded aid from a variety of institutions, like his predecessors, notably perhaps the American Geographical Society, the National Geographic Society, the *New York Times,* and, by way of assigned personnel, departments of the United States government.

Of the two ships serving the expedition, one, the "City of New York," was traditional, a fishing boat obtained in Norway by Amundsen, while the other, the "Eleanor Bolling," was an iron-hulled freighter of World War I vintage of a type never before taken by an explorer through the ice pack. In a fairly exact way the expedition foreshadowed the coming of an era when logistics would be promoted from a secondary, even catch-as-catch-can, position in expedition planning to a more primary position than it had had even in the great pioneering days. However, Byrd was still dependent upon the assistance of the whalers, as we shall see. He took three planes (and a fourth had to be left behind) accompanied by the requisite operating and maintenance personnel, a commitment made on analogy to Arctic successes before Wilkins made his pioneering Antarctic flight. (Byrd communicated by wireless from the "City of New York" with Wilkins while he was actually in the air on his great flight.) Regarding radio communications as basic to safety and control, Byrd not only provided equipment for ground to air and ground to ground communications but also a station capable of direct contact with New York City. The radio telephone was also employed. Direct contact with New York justified the presence of a newspaper correspondent, a "first" on the personnel roster; he won a Pulitzer Prize. No less than five expert radio engineers were in the party. Elaborate provision was made for aerial photography, still in its World War I stage and therefore only possible from one side of a plane at a time or straight down, the overlapping pictures in the former case taken at an oblique angle that included an horizon at 10,000 feet 132 miles away, giving a "visible world" of 50,000 square miles; and for the development, printing, and immediate study of the pictures at the base. Ground "fixes" were indispensable to correct interpretation. The expedition had a motorized vehicle to continue the experimentation with mechanical transport begun by Shackleton two decades earlier. The machine-shop was exceptionally elaborate, allowing not only the maintenance of equipment but the making of immediate improvements in standard equipment—even so sacred an item as Nansen's cooker was tinkered with—as well as the building of additional items (like field radios) as required and the making of new devices or mechanical supplements to devices in use for the first time which developed "bugs" in the Antarctic environment. There was a complement of traditional scientists along; their leader was second in command of the expedition. Nevertheless, all this did not imply the easy, automatic elimination of the traditional problems of Antarctic explorers, such as those deriving from "the weather," including moisture in the buildings, the hazards of crevasses in surface travel, or the personality problems of the men. Nor did it eliminate fundamental reliances of an inherited kind. The food might now be calculated by a research medical doctor in terms of vitamins, but on the trail diet was still well within the established limits. And, as remarked, dogs and sledges were included. Indeed, Byrd concluded that the ideal combination for Antarctic exploration was airplanes and dogs.

What polar experience any of the members had was of the Arctic, but one man, Martin Ronne, had been at the Bay of Whales with Amundsen. Great talent was brought to the expedition and it contributed largely to the development of a pool of American Antarctic expertise. In addition to Byrd himself, who became closely identified with Antarctica, men on Byrd I who then and later made great contributions to Antarctic work were Laurence M. Gould, University of Michigan geologist and Arctic hand, second in command, Lloyd Berkner, radio engineer, Berndt Balchen, airplane pilot, A. D. McKinley, aerial photographer, Victor Czegka, master machinist, Paul Siple, dog driver and Boy Scout representative, and Russell Owen, the *New York Times* correspondent. Of the wintering party thirty-three were Americans, five Norwegians, a Greek, a Czech, a Newfoundlander, and a Welshman.

The jumping-off place for the expedition was Dunedin, New Zealand. They sailed south on December 2, 1928. The "City of New York" was towed to sea by a tug and then picked up and towed to the edge of the ice pack by the "Eleanor Bolling" where the Norwegian factory ship, the "C. A. Larsen," picked it up on December 15 and towed it through the pack to the open waters of the Ross Sea. The "Eleanor Bolling" returned to Dunedin from the edge of the pack to load cargo for the Bay of Whales. It eventually made two round trips to that "port" and was frustrated with regard to a third only by heavy ice. The "City of New York" reached the Ross Ice Shelf at 177° 25′ West, moved along the face, visited Discovery Inlet, and reached the Bay of Whales on the twenty-ninth. An inlet in the bay, dubbed Ver-sur-Mer after the village in France at which Byrd had landed on his transatlantic flight, became the point of disembarkation and Little America camp was built in a kind of basin in the ice a few miles "inland." It was 792 miles north of the geographical Pole and 820 miles east of the Magnetic Pole.

Work away from Little America was initiated even before the camp, an extensive collection of buildings well scattered to reduce the fire hazard, was completed. On January 27, 1929, probing of the country to the eastward was begun by air. With Balchen as pilot and Harold June as radio operator in constant touch with Little America, Byrd flew east into King Edward VII Land to above Scott's Nunatak (discovered in 1902 and visited by Prestrud in 1911), Scott's low Alexandra Mountains, which the Japanese had visited in 1912, visible to the south. Encountering a whiteout, they swung north over the sea and after a short while turned south over the land again, frustrated from determining at this time the true character of King Edward VII Land but rewarded by the sight of a new cluster of mountain peaks and ridges which they named the Rockefeller Mountains. They then returned to base. On February 18 two planes went east, Byrd in one of them with Balchen as pilot again and Berkner as radio operator. They headed again for Scott's Nunatak. Encountering snow storms on their route east, they turned southeast, ascertained that the Rockefeller Mountains were more extensive than had first appeared, and then east again toward a conspicuous peak which Byrd took to be on the border (the 150th meridian) of the Ross Dependency. Beyond was unknown, unclaimed territory and its lure to Byrd was strong. Clouds blotted out their landmark and they flew south for sixty miles seeing nothing but a flat, monotonous surface. On March 7 Balchen and June flew Laurence Gould, the geologist, to the Rockefeller Mountains for a preliminary topographic and geographic survey. They were to fly in, make a camp, retain the plane, do the work, and fly out again, the first time this scheme of operations had been attempted. Regular touch with Little America was to be maintained by radio. They were able to fly in, land, and set up their camp, but they were then plagued by high winds such as Mawson encountered. The winds eventually damaged the plane beyond use. (The engine and the instruments were recovered during the Byrd II expedition.) Radio communications broke down with the failure of the field set. Gould's work nevertheless revealed that the mountains were granite, not sandstone as he had hoped; he discovered some lichens and some moss; and his "fixes" of ground locations enabled the accurate interpretation of some photographs McKinley had made on another occasion. Byrd flew to locate the marooned men and, if possible, rescue them and in the end they were brought out by plane, though as a precaution dog teams were started to get them. While the contretemps in the mountains was transpiring the work of establishing depots on the road south to the Queen Maud Mountains was begun. But by March 23 the flying season was over and the wintering-over period had begun.

As Byrd planned to leave Antarctica early in 1929 the second period of field work was planned to begin as early as possible. It was to consist of the flight to the Pole and back, a geological field trip south to the mountains at the head of the ice shelf, more flights east into the unknown country, and possibly a flight west toward McMurdo Sound. The men actually began to dig the airplanes out of their winter snow-cover in mid-September and the dog teams began to work on depot-making in mid-October. Between the end of March and this resumption of outside activity the time was given to scientific work and to planning and preparation for the field work. A vital element of the planning of Antarctic trips is the closest calculation of the weight of the equipment and supplies to be taken on a journey, whether by dog-sledge, tractor, or airplane.

Laurence Gould was leader of the geological party going to the southern mountains. It was proposed to strike Amundsen's Queen Maud Mountains in the vicinity of Mount Fridtjof Nansen, climb that mountain and attempt to work out a cross-section of the range, and then to travel east along the face of the range to verify Amundsen's opinion of its direction trend or establish the true trend. On the return trip to Little America an effort was to be made to investigate the high land Amundsen had reported to the east between latitudes 81° and 82°.

Gould's party of six men made its final departure on November 4. The technical personnel included Gould as geologist, a topographer, a surveyor (civil engineer), and a radio operator. Like its "supporting party" (that is, the party designated to assist the Gould party forward into the field) and the tractor party, Gould's had been out earlier helping with the laying of depots of food and fuel. It was planned that seven be established in a soldierly file between Little America and the mountains, a distance of about 400 miles. The supporting party went to number four; Gould and his men were to make the other three. From number seven Gould would tackle the mountain assignment. The geological party, as the group farthest into the field toward the Pole, was to assist Byrd's flight (which would pass over them) by returning regular weather reports by radio to Little America—they proved to be of the greatest worth—and by standing by at their seventh depot on the day of flight, to serve as a rescue party if the plane should be forced down in that vicinity. (The plane party had a fuel dump of its own at the base of the mountains, but no men were stationed at it.) Gould's party drove dogs and this was a traditional dependence in which Gould took great satisfaction, even though in fact it was in part made necessary by the loss of that airplane in the Rockefeller Mountains. He was positively gleeful when on the outward journey he encountered the tractor party walking back to Little America, their vehicle having irremediably broken down between depots one and two, another failure in the effort to use motorized transport in Antarctica. (The tractor was recovered by the Byrd II expedition.) He was infinitely more sympathetic toward the supporting party, using dogs, when it was encountered homeward bound from depot four. All told the geological party was in the field for three months, not arriving back at Little America until January 19, 1929.

The geological party reached the mountains at the foot of Liv Glacier up which Byrd had flown to the interior plateau, in the very shadow of Mount Fridtjof Nansen, on November 30. The foothills were identified as pre-Cambrian rocks, the world's oldest, but the mountain itself was found to be capped with sandstones which embodied coal-like material, this linking Nansen with the mountains to the west of the Ross Sea which the British and Australian geologists had studied, and extending the area of the great coal field presumed to be under the ice. Mount Nansen was, then, part of the great "uplifted fault block" mountain system, perhaps the largest of its kind in the world. Lichens were found, the most southerly lying of living things, even at the party's farthest south, 85° 27′. While Gould did his geological work, the surveyor and the topographer did theirs, providing, with McKinley's photographs made on the flight to lay the fuel dump, the data for maps. Turning east, the party sought to ascertain exactly the trend of the mountains to prove or disprove the existence of Amundsen's Carmen Land and possibly to cast some light on the land beyond the 150th meridian Byrd had glimpsed to the north. They disproved the existence of Carmen Land and established that the mountains continued in an easterly direction beyond the limits of their vision at their easternmost camp, though with diminishing elevation (by perhaps 10,000 feet from the highest peaks to the west) and without the sandstone cover which, it was speculated, had been removed by glacial action. Composed of pre-Cambrian rocks, they were like the foothills earlier examined. To the east also they found glaciers such as Leverett, seemingly as vast as those to the west. Their farthest east was well inside Byrd's new territory; their mark was Supporting Party Mountain at about 85° 27′ South, 147° 50′ West. They had examined the mountains over a distance of 175 miles and incidentally proved that the eastern limit of the Ross Ice Shelf was a hundred miles beyond its earlier-assumed boundary. On their return journey they found on Mount Betty at the head of the ice shelf the cairn that Amundsen had erected on his way back from the Pole and in a tin can a paper on which he had written a brief account of his achievement. They had seen no evidence one way or the other with regard to the suppositious channel between the Weddell and Ross seas.

Accompanied by Balchen as pilot, June as radio operator, and McKinley as photographer, Byrd took off from Little America on his flight to the Pole in the Ford plane, the "Floyd Bennett," at 3:29 P.M. on November 28, 1928. They flew south along the line of the trail to the mountains, punctuated as it was by depots, and passed over the Gould party at depot seven, 325 air miles from home base, at 8:15 P.M. While intending to fly the Axel Heiburg Glacier, up which Amundsen had toiled on his way to the Pole, by a last minute decision they actually flew the Liv Glacier (named by Amundsen for Nansen's daughter), and to make the altitude they needed to get up onto the plateau through the strong downcurrents of air in the narrow pass they threw overboard at brief intervals two bags of food of a total weight of 250 pounds. It was either food or gasoline and Byrd chose food. They went over the hump of the pass with only 500 feet to spare. This was about 9:15 P.M. McKinley was photographing from the east side of the plane.

Laying a line of flight on the 171st meridian they headed south directly for the Pole, leaving behind that great line of mountains trending eastward which impressed them as deeply as it had impressed their land-bound predecessors. The plane drifted slightly under the influence of a wind from the east and a correction had to be made. Their height above the snow they could not accurately determine but they were flying at 10,000–11,000 feet above sea level and at one point quite near the Pole they calculated that they were about 1400 feet above the snow. They made their air speed 100 miles an hour, their ground speed 90. By 12:30 A.M. the mountains had faded out of sight behind them. At 1:14 A.M. they calculated that they were over the Pole, but they flew a little beyond before turning back. As they passed over the presumed position on the return flight Byrd dropped an American flag weighted by a stone from Floyd Bennett's grave, an act of patriotism and personal loyalty which put the flag 1500 miles south of the most southerly point it had ever achieved prior to the arrival of the expedition at the Bay of Whales. But whereas neither Amundsen nor Scott had exactly lingered at the Pole, once achieved, by this new means of achieving it Byrd was actually present only a few *seconds* out of the ten minutes spent in the general vicinity. In honor of the great predecessors the plane carried the Norwegian and British flags.

Leaving the Pole at 1:25 A.M. following the 168th meridian, McKinley photographing on the west side, they watched for the great mountains to come majestically into sight again. They intended to go *down* Axel Heiberg Glacier. They climbed higher and with a tail wind reached an air speed of 125 miles an hour. Mount Fridtjof Nansen was their landmark. By instant choice they went down a pass between Mount Ruth Gade and Mount Don Pedro Christophersen (both Amundsen discoveries), but this pass led into Axel Heiberg and they emerged from the mountains via that glacier at 4:00 A.M. Having a satisfactory reserve of fuel they flew east along the face of the mountains, disposing of the Carmen Land idea, and then turned west for the fuel dump, where they landed at 4:47 A.M. After refueling they left about six o'clock and flew straight for Little America, landing there at 10:08 A.M., November 29. Byrd's diary entry next day began "Well, it's done." In about seventeen hours in the air they had done what it took Amundsen ninety-nine days to accomplish and Scott had laid down his life attempting—they had been to the South

Pole and back. However, Byrd came to think of the adventure as a mere tour de force, hardly in a class with his discoveries to the east.

The unknown land to the east beyond the boundary of the New Zealand sector continued to exert a special fascination over Byrd's mind not only because it was unknown and unclaimed but also because it probably contained the answer to the great question of the Weddell-Ross channel. On this latter matter Byrd was able to gain no light, but on his final eastward flight on December 5 he began the uncovering of the general geography of at least the northwestern portion of the presumably vast area. In the "Floyd Bennett" with Alton Parker as pilot, June as radio operator, and McKinley as photographer, a flight of seven hours was made during which, after getting their bearings on Scott's Nunatak and the Rockefeller Mountains, they discovered the icebound Sulzberger Bay to the east and thus laid a tentative foundation for the determination that King Edward VII Land was in fact a peninsula. At the head of the bay they found Mount Grace McKinley (named for the photographer's wife) and stretching from it northeast along the eastern shore of the bay the extensive and complicatedly formed Edsel Ford Ranges, apparently running north-south, on features of which names of expedition members and backers were freely scattered. Toward the sea a survey of the ice gave a limited insight into the way in which the land geography conspired to keep the coastal ice from working free and floating away north; and thus into why explorers by ship had always been frustrated from working east of the Ross Ice Shelf along the shore. Landward they glimpsed what appeared to be a vast plateau, in general character resembling the polar plateau. To the land beyond the New Zealand boundary—roughly speaking beyond Mount Grace McKinley—Byrd gave the name "Marie Byrd Land," after his wife.

Byrd's final flight of the expedition was to the west on January 21. Its principal feature was an air survey of Discovery Inlet. For the others the time was spent examining the ice shelf in areas they had not otherwise seen.

Ice conditions in the Ross Sea were unusually severe in the 1929 season and for a while it looked as though the party would get away only if the whalers, with whom the Little America wireless operators were in constant touch, took them out in their factory ships. However, the "City of New York" finally got through, though the "Eleanor Bolling" failed to make it, and they left on February 19, 1929. Concluding his account of the expedition Byrd expressed the "wish to put an end, once and for all, to the journalistic practice of referring to our efforts as the 'conquest' of the Antarctic. The Antarctic has not been conquered. At best we simply tore away a bit more of the veil which conceals its secrets. An immense job yet remains to be done. [It is] one of the great *undone* tasks of the world."

As the 1920's wore on the Australians became restless about the increasing activity in Antarctica: with regard to claims, whaling, the probable but highly speculative general utility of the "continent," and even about the exploratory and scientific activities of expeditions other than British. Their close geographical relation to Antarctica was heavily emphasized as justifying the concern about what was going on. The central figure in the discussion was Sir Douglas Mawson but he was not alone. Many different persons spoke and wrote on the various points and variously emphasized them. The economic values of whaling were given particular attention and Australia's failure to share in them deplored.

A turn toward action began after the discussion of the Antarctic problem at the Imperial Conference of 1926. In June 1927 an Antarctic Committee was set up under the National Research Council, the central organization for university research, including in its membership Mawson (professor of geology and mineralogy at Adelaide), Sir David Orme Masson (professor of chemistry at Melbourne), David Rivett (chief executive of the government's Council for Scientific and Industrial Research), and Captain J. K. Davis, late of Mawson's "Aurora." This body was to advise Prime Minister Bruce as to what should be done to protect Australia's position. The obvious tactic was to send an expedition to Antarctica. In 1928 the government intimated that it was interested in an expedition in collaboration with the British and New Zealand governments, to be partially supported from private sources. It would concentrate on a program of discovery and rediscovery along the coasts to the west of the Ross Dependency to the limits of Enderby Land, the general area to which Mawson had specifically directed Australian attention by his expedition of 1911–14 and which was now regarded as the Australian sector (though the Norwegians felt free to work in most of it). Whale resources would be closely studied. Oceanography would be emphasized. The airplane would be employed. Mr. Bruce announced the government's official commitment on February 21, 1929; Labor's support was expressed by J. H. Scullin. It was an Australian national enterprise in spite of the fact that it was officially known as the British, Australian, and New Zealand Antarctic Research Expedition (BANZARE), partly, one assumes, because Australia did not feel itself in a constitutional position to make the intended claims to territory, still the imperial government's prerogative.

The enterprise was carried on through two seasons, 1929–30 and

1930–31, in spite of the intervention of the depression. The ship "Discovery" was hired from the "Discovery" Committee and Captain J. K. Davis took charge of it. It was brought out from England to Capetown where Mawson, the scientists, Australian, New Zealand and British, and the aviators, Australian, joined her. The party sailed for Antarctic waters on October 19, 1929, and, after visits to the Crozet and Kerguelen islands and to Heard Island, went on toward the continent through seas the "Challenger" had traversed in 1876. For 300 miles they moved through waters copiously strewn with ice and at 65° 5′ South, 81° 5′ East, came to impenetrable pack. It was a bad ice season. They worked west.

The first of rather numerous flights was made on December 29 with Flight Lieutenant S. A. C. Campbell, senior aviator, at the controls, accompanied by Flying Officer Douglas. Beyond the icefield which kept the ship from the land they ascertained that a coast did indeed exist and in the ice they saw rocky islands. The islands were named for Douglas; the coast in time was, with its extensions, called the Mac-Robertson Coast after the principal private supporter of the expedition, Macpherson Robertson, confectionery maker of Melbourne. (The nearest coastal feature to the islands was the subsequently located Cape Daly.) Forced northwest by the ice and bad weather, it was not for some days that the new coast was again seen. This time rocky mountain ranges were observed behind it. They moved on west and on January 12 they identified coastal land in the vicinity of Kemp's claimed discovery of 1833 and named it Kemp Coast. Still working west, the next day they saw Cape Batterbee, northernmost point of Enderby Land, and three miles to the west, Proclamation Island. Here the scientists were able to make a brief visit in the launch. Still continuing west they passed Cape Close where the land turned south and shortly came upon a cape surmounted by a 1500-foot peak. The cape was assumed to be Biscoe's landmark of 1831 and was given his name of Ann, while the peak was named Mount Biscoe. Ice now forced them out to sea, but working landward soon after at Ice Bay (discovered by Riiser-Larsen a little earlier) they were able to see and name the Tula Mountains (for Biscoe's ship) to the northeast and the Scott Range at the head of the bay. Just west of the bay they came upon the Norwegian Riiser-Larsen and his party, and at a conference aboard the "Discovery" it was agreed that the Norwegians, Lars Christensen concurring, should concentrate their efforts beyond 45° East, the approximate limits of Enderby Land, toward the Weddell Sea, while the Australians should work east toward the Ross Dependency. Christensen had already notified Riiser-Larsen that Norway recognized Enderby Land as British. Although Christensen and the other interested Norwegians did not in future invariably observe the division as it applied to coasts *east* of what was conventionally considered Enderby Land, Mawson sealed what he considered to be a bargain by naming the highest peak in the Tula Range after Riiser-Larsen and an ice-covered dome mountain southwest of Ice Bay after Christensen. Mawson went to 45° and then turned back east with the intention of taking a closer look at Ice Bay and the Scott Range, but the weather turned bad and the "Discovery" was driven west-south-west out to sea for 150 miles. Recovering their position at Ice Bay, it was found that coal was getting short, so after a few flights from the vicinity of Proclamation Island during which numerous considerable peaks were seen on the mainland, they retreated to their coal depot at the Kerguelen Islands and from there went on to Australia, arriving at Albany, Western Australia, on March 21, 1930. The "Discovery" had observed rich "new" whaling grounds (of which, however, the Norwegians were well aware) and as Mawson arrived in Australia reports were coming in of phenomenal successes of the Norwegian factory ships. This intensified Australian respect for Antarctica's economic potential but it was nevertheless the enthusiasm of the scientists rather than economic expectations that sustained the plan to send Mawson back the next season.

The "Discovery" sailed from Hobart on November 22, 1930, planning to call at Macquarie Island and reach the Antarctic continent in the vicinity of the Balleny Islands. The island was visited but bad weather kept the ship away from the Ballenys and the landfall was made at Mawson's Cape Denison on the George V Coast. Scientifically the concentration continued to be oceanographical, with meteorological and solar radiational studies additional, while geographically the central purpose was coastal survey work. A distance equal to about a third of the way around the continent was covered, with special attention to the Adélie and Claire coasts, Dumont d'Urville's discoveries of 1840. Proceeding west beyond Claire Coast, Mawson discovered and named Banzare Coast, named after the expedition, and Sabrina Coast, named in recognition of Balleny's sighting of land in 1839 from his ship, the "Sabrina." Then followed attention to the Budd and Knox coasts, discovered and named by Wilkes in 1840, which led on to the Queen Mary Coast, discovered and named by Mawson in 1912. (The land behind all the coasts from Claire to Queen Mary had already been designated Wilkes Land.) Beyond Queen Mary Coast the coasts Norwegians had been discovering and naming in recent years were observed up to Lars Christensen Coast (bordering the western side of Amery Ice Shelf). They believed the Mac-Robertson Coast began at that point and ran on west to the Kemp Coast, beyond which was Enderby Land. Along the Norwegian-named coasts of this sequence and along Mac-Robertson Coast (of which part was at one stage called Lars Christensen Coast) many of the particular features were discovered by the Norwegians and the Australians either simultaneously or at so closely related times that the name of a feature had not become generally known before it was rediscovered and named again. A great many Norwegian names survived, but in some instances a shift to an Australian name was made—illustratively part of Mac-Robertson Coast and Scullin Monolith on that coast. Scullin Monolith (named after the Labor prime minister) was originally Mount Klarius Mikkelsen. The latter name survived only as the designation of the highest peak of the formation. Mawson landed at the Scullin Monolith on February 13, 1931, shortly after Mikkelsen had first seen the feature. On February 18 he landed at Cape Bruce (named after S. M. Bruce whom Scullin had displaced as prime minister), also on the Mac-Robertson Coast, and from there he sailed from home, impelled by the imminent exhaustion of the ship's coal. Hobart was reached on March 19. There was no further Australian activity in Antarctica until after World War II. Mawson's journeys were immensely productive geographically and scientifically.

Byrd's second expedition was essentially a continuation and elaboration of the first, designed to extend its accomplishments, geographical and scientific, by building upon the knowledge and expertise so laboriously acquired on that occasion. It was marked, like its predecessor, by the intensive use of the most advanced technological means and by an even heavier emphasis on scientific work than before, this pointing the way in which work in Antarctica was to go. Occupying the buildings of the first expedition, they added eight more. There were fourteen more men in the wintering-over party than before. A few "old hands" returned but more of the men were in Antarctica for the first time.

Perhaps the most interesting advance technologically was with regard to motorized surface transport, though the problems involved were not finally solved, if they ever could be. The expedition had four tractors. Byrd concluded from experience in operating these that such transport would be the principal reliance of the future. Dogs would become supplementary. The present expedition, however, had no fewer than 150 dogs. The pattern now emerging was of the airplane for reconnaissance and point to point transport with the absolutely indispensable follow-up work on the surface largely dependent upon motorized vehicles. The expedition had four planes, though flying was dependent on weather conditions. Radio, extended to voice broadcasting where appropriate, was even more firmly established as the essential instrument of communication and control. Voice broadcasting to New York was proved feasible.

Progress with food, clothing, and shelter was made. Yet it was still obvious that there was an enormous amount of work to be done with regard to men and machines in low temperatures and on snow and ice.

Byrd II carried forward the traditional Antarctic sciences such as meteorology, biology, botany, geology, terrestrial magnetism, oceanography, and added others, including physics (both astronomical and geophysics), paleontology, and glaciology. In all, provision was made for twenty-two divisions and subdivisions of scientific research. Often it was not so much a case of adding an absolutely "new" science as initiating an innovation in methodology, such as the obtaining of high altitude data by airplane for the study of meteorology. Byrd himself was more intelligently sympathetic to scientists than personally keen about any science. Nevertheless, he attempted a personal contribution to meteorology by isolating himself for six months at an observation post 123 miles south of Little America on the ice shelf at 80° 08′ South, 163° 57′ West, the excuse for this high risk performance—he very nearly lost his life—being the need to supplement the coastal meteorological data with data obtained inland. Byrd II initiated the use in Antarctica of seismic soundings to determine ice thickness, hitherto a matter of speculation only. The technique was borrowed from petroleum geophysics and had before this been used in polar ice studies by the German Alfred Wegner only in Greenland. It also carried cosmic ray studies into the air and by this means to the highest southern latitudes yet achieved. Its meteor studies were synchronized with those of observatories around the world.

Geographically the concentration of interest was on Marie Byrd Land beyond the 150th meridian, the eastern boundary of New Zealand's dependency. Byrd was concerned to disclose the geography of this area, to establish if possible the relation of the Andean mountains of the Palmer-Graham Peninsula and those on the "continent," and to prove or disprove the notion that there was a channel running from the Weddell to the Ross Sea. Using the airplane, particular attention was to be given to filling in the gap between the Rockefeller and Edsel Ford mountains in the north and the Queen Maud Range in the south.

The expedition had its United States headquarters in Boston, Massachusetts. Its two ships were closely similar to those used on Byrd I, the "Bear of Oakland" being an old ice ship, while the freighter employed was an ancient lumber-carrier renamed the "Jacob Ruppert." Sailing from Boston via the Panama Canal, the ships made a rendezvous at Wellington, New Zealand, though Dunedin was, as traditionally, the winter headquarters.

First item on the program was the probing by air from a ship of the vast area of unknown ocean north of the continental coast between the Palmer-Graham Peninsula and the Ross Ice Shelf, involving the Bellingshausen and Amundsen seas. The objective was to locate and define the continental coast in this area, presumptively the coast of Marie Byrd Land, and to prove or disprove a theory that the heavy ice congestion perennial in the area was in part caused by the ice being held tightly in place by islands (possibly an archipelago) or a considerable peninsula. The flights were made from the "Ruppert," with Byrd aboard, when en route from New Zealand to the Bay of Whales and Little America. The first flight was made from a point about 150 miles beyond Captain Cook's famous farthest south, due south along 150° to 69° 51' South, 149° 45' West. No coast was seen and no islands. The ship then moved west, keeping as far south as possible and two more probing flights were made with similarly negative results as to new land. A proposed flight from the ship to Little America, from whence Ellsworth was to advise on weather conditions, was abandoned. The worth-while results of these efforts were that the Pacific Ocean was extended south beyond limits hitherto speculatively assigned and an hypothesis was advanced that the continental coast was probably in the vicinity of 75° South, which, if true, would considerably reduce the presumed area of the "continent." (This hypothesis was subsequently shown to be wrong.)

Later, after reaching the Bay of Whales, this probing for the coast of Marie Byrd Land was continued in the "Bear of Oakland." An attempt was made to get east beyond the limit of the ice shelf and King Edward VII Land in an effort to exceed the marks set by Ross, Scott, Shackleton, Shirase, and the Byrd I ship, the "City of New York." Byrd and a complement of scientists went in the "Bear." They got a considerable distance beyond the earlier eastward marks but were forced away from the coast by the ice and arrived at the conclusion that this was indeed a kind of "ice-breeding" area. What they saw confirmed the idea that no islands which held the ice in place existed. After a narrow escape from being trapped in the ice, they worked free and regained the Bay of Whales. Beyond Sulzberger Bay the coast came to be known as the Ruppert Coast.

The exploratory work from Little America was carried out by three major surface parties—the Geological Party, the Plateau Party, and the Marie Byrd Land Party—and fairly numerous reconnaissance flights designed to link the known features and extend the area of the known to the east. All the probing eastward was supposed to contribute to illuminating the channel hypothesis and the scientific workers would throw light on the relationships of the known mountains. Scientists went on all the major surface expeditions; they themselves set up minor ones for work in the immediate vicinity of Little America and they were able to use an airplane to facilitate their work.

The Geological Party consisted of three men using three dog teams, led by a geologist, Q. A. Blackburn. It was to make a geological and paleontological survey of the eastern reaches of the Queen Maud Mountains, building on the work of Gould's party of Byrd I. The Blackburn party traveled 1410 miles, the longest journey of the expedition, and was out three months. Its most productive work was done at the eastern limits achieved by Gould. Ascending for the first time what was then called the Thorne Glacier (later renamed the Robert Scott Glacier), one of the largest in the Queen Mauds, five to fifteen miles wide and ninety miles long, the party discovered and climbed Mount Weaver, a 10,000-foot peak at 86° 57' South. At this point they were but 207 miles from the Pole and from the mountain's top could see half that distance toward the Pole. They actually set foot on the Polar Plateau and were the first to fly the United States flag on that great feature. Mount Weaver they examined in considerable detail, gathering quantities of specimens (nearly a quarter-ton). And here in relatively close proximity to the Pole they found quantities of plant fossils and fossil evidences, traces of coal, and, perhaps most remarkably of all, patches of lichens. When climbing the glacier they had hundreds of hitherto unseen peaks under observation. Particular attention was given to fixing the locations of these and to the accumulation of data, including photographs, for accurate mapping. They arrived at the opinion that Leverett Glacier was not a true glacier but a kind of subplateau lying between the Polar and Marie Byrd Land plateaus.

The Plateau Party, of which Drs. C. G. Morgan, geologist, and E. H. Bramhall, physicist, were the co-leaders (and Finn Ronne, Martin's son, was a member), was supposed to conduct a series of magnetic observations and seismic soundings along a line well eastward of Little America to the Queen Maud Mountains and up to the Polar Plateau. It was to use dogs to haul the heavy magnetic and seismic instruments but was to be accompanied by a tractor party carrying supplies on which it would be dependent once it had passed depots laid down earlier. However, this program proved impossible to carry out because of the extreme difficulties experienced with the tractors in the known but still incompletely assessed belt of crevasses across the line of travel in 80°–82°. Dog teams could manage fairly well but tractors would break through "covers" the dogs could cross without any trouble. A loaded tractor weighed about 16,000 lbs., 60 per cent of the weight gasoline and its containers. Great efforts were made to get east onto the plateau and around the end of the crevassed region. This fitted in well enough with the intention to follow an eastern line of approach to the mountains and go up a glacier in the eastern reaches. However, once on the plateau it was decided to travel not south but north along the plateau edge to the Rockefeller Mountains and in spite of troubles the scientists were able to maintain a schedule of work, magnetic and seismic. They struggled through country that was as new as any and scientifically the results were satisfactory, but as they were not obtained where planned there was a slight feeling that full value had not been achieved.

The third surface party, that into Marie Byrd Land, was led by Paul Siple, the Boy Scout of Byrd I, acting as biologist and botanist, with Alton Wade as geologist, and three dog drivers, one of whom was the radio operator. The party spent seventy-seven days in the field and traveled 862 miles. A tractor party had earlier laid depots along its line of march from Little America. The purpose was to examine the front range, or western face, of the Edsel Ford Mountains discovered from the air by the Byrd I expedition. Geologically it established by studies along a line from Mount Grace McKinley to Mount Saunders that the mountains were ancient and consisted of granites—the softer rocks had apparently been eroded away—which had been highly metamorphosed and severely folded. The topping of sedimentary beds characteristic of the southern mountains was absent. The rocks were chemically different from those of the Palmer-Graham Peninsula. Therefore, it could not be argued that in terms of geology there was any association between the Edsel Ford Range and the Palmer-Graham mountains and neither could it be argued that they were related to the mountains at the head of the ice shelf. Siple found ninety-four species of lichens, eighty-six never before seen, and located skua gull and snowy petrel rookeries.

Byrd's strongest personal commitment was to the exploration by air. He was deeply concerned to fill in the 500-mile gap between the Edsel Ford and the Queen Maud ranges and in so doing to "settle" the channel theory. It was also likely that at last a tentative definition of the eastern limits of the ice shelf would be made.

The tractor party that laid depots for Paul Siple's party was the first to cast new light on the problem to be tackled by the aviators. By ascending Mount Grace McKinley it had ascertained that, far from simply running north and south as had been concluded from air observation during Byrd I, the Edsel Ford Range actually "streamed" off to the northeast. What had really been seen earlier was the western face of the range. From the top of Grace McKinley it had further appeared that to the south and east was a great plateau. (Ellsworth was to fly across it from east to west that year.) The question was whether or not it rolled inexorably to the foot of the Queen Maud Range. If it did, then presumably the channel speculation would collapse.

Byrd directed a series of flights to deal with the problems of the gap. As he was not fully recovered from the physical beating he had taken while at the isolated meteorological station, most of the flights were made without him. However, he went on the first, with Harold June as pilot. They saw and speculated on the meaning of the belt of crevasses in the ice shelf and confirmed that the Edsel Ford Range indeed trended east. Harold June then made a flight without Byrd specifically to study the crevasses and if possible to find a passage through for the Plateau Party's tractors. He established that the belt seemingly ran clear across the ice shelf and, as an incidental result, defined a new portion of the eastern shore of the shelf, and he was able to direct the tractors onto the plateau. The meteorologists had now established that Marie Byrd Land was a "weather breeder" which made aerial exploration a matter of seizing opportunities for flight, not scheduling them. With June in charge again a short-notice flight confirmed the new conception of the trend of the Edsel Ford Range, established that the plateau was unquestionably a major feature, and that Marie Byrd Land was "continental" in character, but failed in an effort to trace the coast of the area. Following this, June made a flight to the southeast from Little America which reached 83° 05′ South, 119° 00′ West. At this farthest point mountains were observed farther east than any previously seen. (This observation was confirmed by the Geological Party.) These were named the Horlick Mountains, probably an eastward extension of the Queen Maud Range. The plateau was established to reach south of 81°. More of the eastern margin of the shelf was defined. Now only two small subgaps remained over the whole distance between the known points and Byrd concluded that, when they were filled up, the fate of the channel theory would be determined. He therefore went on the flight to close the subgaps. It was successful and appeared to establish that there was an unbroken, elevated plateau, saucer shaped, with the lip at the north higher than that at the south, extending from the Edsel Fords to the Queen Mauds. Byrd named it the Rockefeller Plateau. At the same time the definition of the eastern margin of the shelf was completed, in itself a major accomplishment, liquidating a long-standing mystery. The margin was the western edge of the Rocke-feller Plateau. There was now but one place the channel might con-ceivably be, a small, imperfectly studied area just north of the Horlick Mountains, but Byrd did not believe a channel could possibly be there. In his mind it was entirely certain that Antarctica was "one continent," though at this stage he still thought Wilkins had established that the Palmer-Graham Peninsula was actually an island cut off from the continent by channels. There but remained the question of the *coast* of Marie Byrd Land. In an effort to establish it, a flight (on which Byrd did not go) was made eastward across King Edward VII Land and Sulzberger Bay. It was defeated by cloud. No new geography was uncovered. The notion that the coast was at about 75° continued to be entertained.

In addition to their sedentary labors at Little America, the scientists made excursions on the ice shelf from the settlement in pursuit of their interests. Dr. E. B. Perkins, the biologist, for example, studied life in the accessible ocean waters. But none was as indefatigable in this regard as Dr. T. C. Poulter, chief scientist and second in command of the expedition, who steadily pursued the task of redefining the character of the shelf by using seismic shots. In a sense the original program of the so-called Plateau Party was essentially an extension of Poulter's project farther afield on the shelf and onto land up to the edge of the Polar Plateau. At any rate by dog-sledge and airplane Dr. Poulter succeeded in rather radically revising the conception of the shelf, theoretically one of the best-known portions of Antarctica. He established a tentative distribution of the areas which were afloat on water—Little America itself was on one of these—and those which were grounded on land. His most spectacular single accomplishment was to locate and define a great island, named Roosevelt Island (after F.D.R.), under the ice. That there was a dome-shaped formation in the ice at that point had been noticed by Amundsen. When the dome was probed an island ninety miles long and forty wide was revealed, its northernmost point but three miles from Little America.

As it approached Bay of Whales to relieve the party the "Bear of Oakland," which had already done extensive oceanographical work during its earlier voyages on the Ross Sea, undertook a survey of the front of the shelf from some point to the west, east to the Bay of Whales. Ice prevented it from getting into McMurdo Sound, but a fine view of Ross Island and Mount Erebus was had and the crew took up survey work at Cape Crozier, the eastern tip of Ross Island. The oceanographer in charge was J. E. Roos; the ship's master was Lieutenant R. A. J. English, USN. Previous surveys—those of Ross, Scott, Shackleton, and Pennell (of Scott's 1912 expedition)—had raised the question as to whether the shelf was advancing or receding at its coastal limits. English and Roos, using a full panoply of modern equipment, found that for 400 miles on east from Cape Crozier the ice had advanced seaward beyond previously recorded limits and appeared to be advancing at the approximate rate of half a mile a year.

After a visit to Discovery Inlet, where it picked up Dr. Poulter and a seismic party, the "Bear" arrived at Bay of Whales on January 19, 1935. The "Ruppert" arrived a few days later. The entire party sailed on

February 5, headed for New Zealand. The "Ruppert" visited Discovery Inlet to pick up some live penguins, while the "Bear" resumed its oceanographical work. Little America lay undisturbed for ten months or until Ellsworth and Hollick-Kenyon arrived in December.

While Byrd II was ending its work preparatory to departure, the only important British Antarctic expedition of the interwar period, aside from the "Discovery" Committee's activities, was getting into the field. This was the British Graham Land Expedition, led by John Rymill. Scientifically it was concerned with meteorology, geology, glaciology, biology, and ornithology, while geographically it was concerned with unravelling the complicated land-ice-water relationships at the base of the Palmer-Graham Peninsula on the western and eastern sides. It therefore worked in a locality rich in associations with earlier British, American, Russian, Belgian, and French explorations and also with the more recent activities of Sir Hubert Wilkins and Lincoln Ellsworth. A consequence of its work was the reattachment of the peninsula to the continental landmass.

The Rymill expedition was a fruit of the interest in polar activities sustained and fed during these years by participants in earlier British Antarctic expeditions, notably such men as Frank Debenham, J. M. Wordie, and R. E. Priestley. An institutional expression of these same interests and impulses was the Scott Polar Research Institute at Cambridge University, founded 1925, of which Debenham was the founding director. Up to the Rymill expedition the energy of the young Britons responding to the call of the polar regions was (except for the "Discovery" activities) expended in the Arctic, particularly Greenland, where Americans led by Professor William H. Hobbs of the University of Michigan and Germans led by Professor Alfred Wegener were also at work at this time. The principal British expedition was the Arctic Air Route Expedition, designed to prepare the way for an air route from the United Kingdom via Greenland and Canada to the Pacific coast. The exemplary figure in this activity was Gino Watkins, something of a culture-hero, who was drowned in Greenland waters. Watkins had had Antarctic ambitions. Rymill had worked with Watkins and was in a sense dedicated to carrying out his Antarctic purposes. John Riddoch Rymill was an Australian, born in 1905 in the same part of South Australia that had produced George Hubert Wilkins (in which there is an element of irony). Rymill's people were very substantial pastoralists, as he himself was later. He was educated at the socially prestigious Melbourne Church of England Grammar School and Cambridge. He served in the Australian Navy during World War II. The Rymill expedition enjoyed widespread support from British scientific societies and had assistance from the "Discovery" Committee.

The expedition sailed from Port Stanley, Falkland Islands, in the three-masted, French-built schooner "Penola," so named for Rymill's birthplace, on December 31, 1934, bound for Port Lockroy, Wiencke Island, in the Palmer Archipelago. At Port Lockroy the party found the "Discovery II" which had brought down equipment and stores. Because of trouble with the "Penola's" engines, the intention to establish the base at Marguerite Bay 200 miles south had to be given up and instead, after scanning possibilities by air, a site was chosen at the Argentine Islands, forty miles southwest. Here the shore party of but nine men wintered. The ship was frozen in. The winter was chiefly devoted to scientific work with special attention to the richly available bird life, lichens, and mosses. As one item on the program was a crossing of the peninsula, an air survey of the nearby coast was made, but no suitable place for a start was found. A coastal survey by sledge confirmed this finding.

The ship was free of the ice early in January 1936; its engines had been repaired during the winter; and preparations were therefore put in hand for a southward move. While awaiting favorable conditions, a combined survey—biological, geological, and cartographical—was made by sledge in the Grandidier Channel. The move south began on February 16, the objective Marguerite Bay, and with the help of the expedition's plane a site was found on Barry Island in a newly discovered group of islets collectively named for the Debenhams—individually for Frank Debenham's numerous children. The "Penola" then left to winter at Port Stanley. The party was now in position both to do its exploratory work and to continue fruitfully with its scientific studies. The primary geographical efforts were to be toward Alexander I Land, suspected since the Wilkins and Ellsworth flights to be an island, and across the peninsula to the Weddell Sea coast. Much survey work of a combined type was to be done around Marguerite Bay.

The great accomplishment with regard to Alexander I Land was to locate and begin the penetration of the arm of what proved to be a J-shaped channel separating the land from the peninsula and also from the continent to the south, this requiring the substitution of "Island" for "Land" in the nomenclature. The channel was subsequently named King George VI Sound. It was tentatively established that Alexander I Island was geologically different from the peninsula. The penetration of the channel was made both on the ice and in the air. First try on the ice after the feature was located resulted in the loss of the expedition's only tractor when the ice broke up. The longest journey on the ice extended 200 miles south of the entrance to 72°, while by airplane the mountains overlooking the channel from the peninsula at 71° 23′ South were reached. The northernmost reaches of these mountains had been surveyed by the party on the ice and named the Batterbees. This created confusion which had to be sorted out later, for the Batterbees possibly were identical with the Eternity Range Ellsworth had seen, photographed, and named about a year earlier. On the other hand, the explorations allowed the disproving of the existence of Sir Hubert Wilkins' several channels and his Stefansson Strait which allegedly cut off the Palmer-Graham Peninsula from the continent. Neither the channels nor the strait existed. Wilkins and his camera had probably been deceived by fog.

Meanwhile Rymill and a companion had made a journey across the Peninsula by dog-sledge. Assisted by a depot laid down on an ice shelf later named for Wordie, they crossed from the shelf at about 69° 50′ South, traveling along the south sides of the later-named abutting Fleming and Bingham glaciers which filled a major depression of the peninsula, reaching a maximum height of 7000 feet. While crossing they discovered and named Mount Wakefield which, with associated peaks, also might be Ellsworth's Eternity Range. They reached the east coast at the later-named Cape Rymill opposite Hearst Island and surveyed 140 miles south to 70° 40′ South, short of the Weddell Sea. The party returned to Barry Island on January 5, 1937.

The expedition finally left the field in the "Penola" on March 12, 1937, and returned via South Georgia and the Falkland Islands to England. It became something of a model for showing what could be done by a very small party with but a limited quantity of modern technological equipment, especially for the Australians.

Late in 1938 the Nazis, already implicated in Antarctic whaling for fairly obvious reasons, as has been noted, suddenly showed an interest in continental exploration. They chose to investigate along and behind the Princess Martha and Princess Astrid coasts the Norwegians had located. As the Nazi action was assessed to be political in essence, a preliminary to lodging a claim, it had politico-strategic implications. Sponsored by the Nazi government, Herman Goering as commissioner of the Four-Year Plan, and the Deutsche Forschungsgemeinschaft (Research Society), staffed by naval and air force personnel and led by Captain Alfred Ritscher, the expedition sailed from Hamburg on December 17, 1938, in the catapult ship "Schwabenland" carrying two flying boats. The tradition of Drygalski and Filchner was invoked. Ritscher had Arctic experience. The party was back in Germany on April 11, 1939, having spent three weeks probing in Norway's Queen Maud Land between 4° 20′ West, and 14° East.

While meteorological, oceanographical, biological, and geophysical data were collected, the basic method of survey was from the planes by cameras. A technique of aerial photography more advanced than that in general use was employed. The coasts were photographed, the coastal forelands, and then territory inland to some point on the continental plateau. The deepest southerly penetration was to 74° 25′ South, 0° 20′ West, this involving a flight of 300 miles. All told seven major flights were made inland. Since this area had never been penetrated before, striking discoveries were alleged. Impressive mountain ranges, great and sudden rises in the plateau level, numerous lakes, and an ice-free area were reported to have been seen. Ritscher and his specialists claimed that they had picture-mapped 350,000 square miles and reliably observed 250,000 square miles more. By way of filing a claim to the territory the flyers dropped at intervals spearlike, swastika-topped markers. Dubbed Neu-Schwabenland, the area was alleged to be the first Nazi colony. However, Hitler never formally challenged the Norwegian claim to the same area. The 11,600 pictures taken disappeared during World War II. What the successor German government concluded about the matter has not been made public; it would have been grossly impolitic to try to establish Hitler's claim.

United States action in the Antarctic at this time appeared to be a response to the Hitler adventure at least analogous to that of Norway but, while there was a connection with the question of claims, neither the American interest in the claims question nor its interpretation of the Antarctic situation of the moment led it, in the end, to make an actual claim. As we have noted, an element of ambiguity was introduced into the American attitude toward claims largely because the instructions on the matter were not made public at the time. The United States government's concern about the political and general drift in Antarctica (and also in the Arctic) had been rising in recent months. Early in 1938 President Roosevelt had asked the State Department to study the whole matter and obvious points early established were that the claimant nations both in the Antarctic and the Arctic were seeking ways to strengthen their claims and that the Germans and Japanese were keenly interested in what was being attempted and curious about what the United States intended to do. In reporting to the president at the beginning of 1939 the State Department recommended that two linked expeditions be sent to Antarctica that autumn to establish bases which should be made permanent. This would strengthen the American position in Antarctica. Strengthening the position was the primary concern and purpose in mind. Management of the expeditions was to be in the hands of the government, which would largely but not wholly finance them. To deal with the matter an agency called the United States Antarctic Service was set up—apparently this form of organization was suggested by Lt. Commander Richard D. Black, who had been with Byrd II—and lodged in the Division of Territories and Island Possessions, itself enough to stir foreign suspicions about an imminent claim. The agency was to be governed by an Executive Committee of representatives of the departments of State, the putative fount from which the whole idea flowed, Interior, Navy, War, and Treasury. The business in one sense recalled the Wilkes expedition of 1840, in another it was an administrative improvisation characteristic of the New Deal. The personnel, it was intended, should be both "service" and civilian but, since the government was running the show, rules of government procedure would be followed, this inevitably insuring that some not at all funny "snafus" which had little to do with exploration and scientific work but a good deal to do with bureaucratic red-tape, inter-service and personal rivalries, and so on would plague the work. At President Roosevelt's personal intervention his old friend Richard Byrd was appointed commanding officer, but this meant he would have but limited time in the field and would be mostly in Washington dealing with paper work. Byrd was at the time actively planning a new expedition of his own. In a significant sense the USAS expedition was Byrd III. It was built in large measure on Byrd I and Byrd II.

The governing idea became to tighten the American grip on Marie Byrd Land (by universal opinion the most likely locale of a formal American claim) and to incorporate with it the supposedly contiguous James W. Ellsworth Land to the east and possibly also Sir Hubert Wilkins' Hearst Land (if any of it should fall outside the Falkland Islands Dependencies), though Hearst Land was fading into the limbo of geographical errors. The work of consolidation was to be carried out mostly by aerial photography, though from the west base effort was to be made to get as far east as possible on the surface, and from the east base an effort was to be made to penetrate the eastern reaches of the vast area and perhaps get some distance west. At the same time an effort was to be made to define the coast of Marie Byrd Land at which Byrd had so frustratedly been persisting. The fairly elaborate scientific program, designed by the National Research Council of the National Academy of Sciences, was to be executed mainly in Marie Byrd Land, though with parallel and complementary activities at East Base. And finally the bases were to be established permanently, to be continuously operated in the future, and thus designed to be "settlement" within the meaning of international law.

Two ships were employed, the "Bear of Oakland" which Byrd more or less donated and the "North Star" from the Department of Interior's

Alaska service. West Base turned out to be Little America III, near the old Little America, now effectively wrecked by the movement of the ice, and East Base was established on Stonington Island (newly named for what was Captain Nathaniel Palmer's home port when he was a sealer) far to the south on the west side of the Palmer-Graham Peninsula in Marguerite Bay. Neither was set up where originally planned; both were in other nations' claims. It was intended that Little America III be in King Edward VII Land (or Peninsula) and the Stonington Island establishment be on Charcot Island conveniently near the largely unknown mainland to the south which was presumably contiguous with Marie Byrd Land, near enough its fellow to make an air shuttle between them feasible. However, men propose and the Antarctic disposes.

The ships left the United States in November 1939. The "North Star" reached the Bay of Whales, followed shortly by the "Bear," on January 9, 1940, having visited isolated Pitcairn Island en route and voluntarily replenished the island's depleted food supplies. The conspicuous technological innovation was a so-called snowmobile, a vast contraption intended to solve the problem of motorized transport in Antarctica. It was, in fact, a mobile base. Designed by Dr. Thomas Poulter at the Armour Institute in Chicago, it was built in the Pullman Company's shop. Dr. Alton Wade, the geologist, was in command. The thing was 35 feet long, 20 feet wide and 15 high and fully loaded it weighed 33.5 tons. The wheels were 10 feet high and retractable so that on suitable slopes the vehicle could be worked like a sled. It carried a small airplane on its roof. A year's supply of fuel for vehicle and plane could be carried and supplies for the same period for a complement of four men. Its range was calculated to be 5000 miles. It was hoped to get to the South Pole in it with ease. But, alas, this creation, by Rube Goldberg out of a passionate scientific gigantism, could not be successfully operated on Antarctic surfaces. With difficulty it went from the edge of the ice to Little America III. It sank into the snow and could not readily surmount the "chocks" of snow that built up in front of the wheels. Wade finally put his plane, his men, and himself at the general service of Paul Siple, now a Ph.D. in geography from Clark University, in charge at Little America III.

En route in the "Bear" from Little America III to the Palmer-Graham Peninsula to establish East Base, Byrd resumed his assault on the problem of the coast of Marie Byrd Land. (Incidentally the "Bear" was commanded by Richard Cruzen and its navigator was George Dufek, both USN men who were to play important roles in Antarctic activities after World War II.) On this occasion Byrd's luck was in. Before the "Bear" was forced away from the coast by ice, it got 140 miles east close to the coast beyond any mark previously set and the airplane flights from the ship toward shore were productive too. Sulzberger Bay was found to be much more extensive than hitherto supposed. Beyond the Ruppert Coast, the eastern terminus of which came to be Emory Land Bay into which the Emory Land Glacier descended from both sides of table-topped Mount McCoy, Hobbs Coast (named for the redoubtable Professor W. H. Hobbs of the University of Michigan) was later revealed. It was later defined to run northeast as far as the Getz Ice Shelf in Wrigley Gulf (so named for the gum magnate). Beyond the ice shelf Byrd found the Walgreen Coast, named for the Chicago druggist, bounding which on the east he saw what appeared to be a tremendous peninsula thrusting 100 miles beyond the prevailing trend of the shore into the ocean, providing a convenient dividing mark between the Bellingshausen and Amundsen seas. This was Thurston Peninsula, named for a textile manufacturer who had made Byrd some "wind-proof" cloth. Just beyond the peninsula was Seraph Bay, named for the ship of the early American sealer Captain Benjamin Pendleton and the farthest east of this remarkable effort. Some of the features named for clarity of understanding were not seen by Byrd but by fliers from Little America III later on (see below). But Byrd established the general position of the coast from Sulzberger Bay to Seraph Bay, though details and revisions came later and are still to come. The coast proved to be definitely north of the speculative location of 75° South, this adding to the presumptive size of Marie Byrd Land.

The "Bear" met the "North Star," which had been from Bay of Whales to Valparaiso, Chile, to pick up equipment and supplies, at Marguerite Bay and, after it had been established that Charcot Island could not be reached, established a party of thirty-three men under Lt. Commander Richard B. Black on Stonington Island. This was 1700 miles east of Little America III. In effect East Base of USASE was in a position to pick up and carry forward the geographical work of the Rymill expedition which, in a sense, is exactly what was done, though the ostensible objectives were farther south and west.

From Stonington Island Black's men went south along both the west and east sides of the peninsula, probing for the eastward continental extension of Marie Byrd Land. They worked both on the surface and in the air. On neither coast did they get much beyond the northernmost outer edge of their objective, and there was necessarily a wide gap between their westernmost reach and the easternmost reach from Little America III. No attempt was made to fly between the two bases.

To get from Stonington Island to the east coast involved crossing the peninsula, always a difficulty. It was done by Black's men considerably north of the passage used by the Rymill party. Stonington was very close to the peninsula and actually linked to a steep, stagnant glacier at 68° 09′

South, dubbed Northeast Glacier because it was northeast of camp, by a snowbridge. The snowbridge and glacier, which Rymill had surveyed but not used, were used by Black's party to get up to the top of the peninsula. Here they established a flying field and a weather station and from here reached a glacier which led down to the east coast at Trail Inlet, a feature first noted by Wilkins in 1928, at 68° 05′ South. At this point the peninsula is only twenty miles wide but a mile high. Paul Knowles, geologist, Donald Hilton, surveyor, and Harry Darlington, radio operator, made up the party to go down the east coast. They used dogs. Like Rymill, their objective was the Weddell Sea Coast; like Rymill they did not reach it. They did, however, get somewhat south of Rymill's mark. Their farthest south was 71° 51′ South. Their southernmost landmark was Hilton Inlet, the southern boundary of which, Cape Darlington, they took to be an island. They were out fifty-nine days and covered 683 miles. Since it was an expedition objective to get as far south as possible, Black made a flight to get well beyond the trail party's limit. He flew south on the west side of the peninsula and crossed through a gap in what were thought to be the Eternity Mountains, hit the east coast south of Cape Darlington and flew on south to 74° 37′ South. From there he could see the mountains continuing on south, apparently as far as 77° South. His chief southernmost landmark was Mount Tricorn at 73° 58′ South, at the head of Wright Inlet. He saw and named New Bedford and Nantucket inlets as though full of nostalgia for the old whaling days.

On the west coast the performance was rather more spectacular but an extension of Rymill's nevertheless. Two dog-sledge parties went south from Stonington, ascended onto the peninsula up Fleming Glacier from Wordie Ice Shelf and went south along glaciers to the Batterbee Mountains where a depot had been laid by air. Here the parties separated, one under J. Glenn Dyer to make a survey of the country hereabouts, the other, consisting of two men, Finn Ronne and Carl Eklund, to continue the exploration of the channel between the peninsula and Alexander I Land.

Ronne and Eklund reached the ice of the channel south of Rymill's limit. They sledged on south until it was clear that the channel was going to veer west, indicating its J-shape, at which time they cut across the corner of Alexander I Island and, entering upon the ice again, crossed to the south, or continental, shore, only glimpsed hitherto. This shore was eventually called the Robert English Coast after the executive secretary of the Executive Committee of the USAS, who had been captain of the "Bear" on Byrd II. They caught sight of Mount Vang, an isolated peak on the mainland. Continuing west they discovered the rocky Eklund Islands, though at this time they actually located only the highest of them, and terminated their journey at the edge of Ronne Entrance where the channel met the Bellingshausen Sea. Here they reached their farthest west but were still within the Falkland Islands Dependencies and there was a long coastal gap between their position and Seraph Bay to the east. On the return journey their first objective was the depot at Batterbee Mountains. They had a tough time of it but reached the depot and after a rest continued on until at the Wordie Ice Shelf they encountered a relief party coming to meet them. They had been out eighty-four days and had traveled 1200 miles. They had proved conclusively that Alexander I "Land" was indeed an island and that King George VI Sound separated it both from the peninsula and the southern mainland.

Meanwhile the Dyer party had discovered the extensive, high-lying Dyer Plateau, made numerous "fixes" for locating the mountains on and around it, and discovered Mount Andrew Jackson, named for the president who had signed the bill authorizing the Wilkes Expedition, 13,750 feet high, the dominant feature of this elevated portion of the southern Palmer-Graham Peninsula. Its identification of Ellsworth's Eternity Range proved only tentative.

The discoveries of both the Ronne-Eklund and the Dyer parties were surveyed from the air shortly after they were reported.

Before the winter set in at West Base—Little America III—a flight was made to try to fill in a gap in the knowledge of the mountains at the head of the ice shelf. This was the stretch between Beardmore Glacier, up which Scott had traveled on his way to the Pole, and Axel Heiberg Glacier to the east up which Amundsen had made his way en route to the Pole. By the accidents of purposes and interests nobody had had occasion to survey the ground between the two glaciers. It was now found by air to be a practically continuous escarpment in which the most spectacular break was a very large glacier debouching onto the shelf by the side of Mount Wade (which Byrd had glimpsed from the air in 1929), 12 miles wide at its mouth and up to 100 miles long. At first called Wade Glacier, it was eventually named for Shackleton.

However, the primary focus of the expedition's interest was to the east in Marie Byrd Land. An exploratory flight to photograph the area in which the surface parties were to work was made. From Little America III it was hoped to reach at least 600 miles east, if not on the surface, then by air. It was about 200 miles to the eastern border of the New Zealand claim and Byrd had flown about 160 miles beyond that, so a farther penetration of about 250 miles was hoped for. Much energy went into laying down depots for both the trail parties and the planes, for the latter chiefly fuel dumps designed to give them increased flying range.

Dogs, tractors, and planes were all employed at depot laying. The three major depots were made at the Rockefeller Mountains (105 miles out), Mount Grace McKinley at the head of Sulzberger Bay, 130 miles farther out, and at Mount Rea to the northeast facing the Bay, 75 miles beyond Grace McKinley.

Five surface parties were sent out, each with an assigned area to investigate and with a variety of geographical and scientific purposes. Three were definitely major efforts. The surface parties were dependent upon dogs. One party, led by Leonard Berlin, surveyor, was assigned to reach Mount Hal Flood far to the east on the high plateau beyond the Edsel Ford mountain complex. Byrd had glimpsed it from a distance in 1934. "Mount Hal Flood" turned out to be a line of mountains extending 80 miles farther east; it therefore became the Hal Flood Range and the first detected peak became Mount Berlin (76° 04′ South, 135° 50′ West). To establish this involved a journey out and back of 1200 miles lasting 83 days, by 400 miles the longest surface journey made. A geological party led by Lawrence Warner examined the central Edsel Ford Ranges, up to then chiefly known by their western fronts, and discovered behind the fronts a vast tangle of peaks and ranges. No fewer than fifty-nine peaks were visited and geologized. A biological party led by J. E. Perkins examined the northern, or seaward, portion of the Edsel Ford front in the *New York Times* sector (so called from the many features named for *New York Times* people) centering on Mount Iphigene. The party made an especially rich find of lichens at Mount Marujupu. R. C. Fitzsimmons, physicist, and two others set up seismic equipment in the Rockefeller Mountains near the depot and recorded earth tremors for the first time in Antarctica, while Alton Wade, detached from his snowmobile, extended the geological survey of the Rockefellers Laurence Gould had initiated on Byrd I and Wade himself had continued on Byrd II. Because of soft snow, the tractors had great difficulty in hauling the accumulation of specimens and records from the collecting point at the Rockefeller Mountains depot to Little America III. At the camp particular satisfaction and interest were taken in auroral studies and pioneering physiological studies of the effect of cold upon the human body.

But aside from Berlin's eastward thrust to the Hal Flood Range, the farthest east marks were made by plane. The little plane off the snowmobile, relying on the depots and the scattered surface parties for assistance in a possible emergency, flew northeast beyond the Hal Flood Range and observed mountains, named the Executive Committee [of USAS] Range of which the highest peak was Mount Sidley, first noted from a long way off by Byrd in 1934. On the return flight Mount Petras, separate from but in line with the Hal Flood Range, was seen. In a larger plane Paul Siple and a party made a coastal flight east; they discovered the Emory Land Glacier, Wrigley Gulf mostly occupied by the Getz Ice Shelf, and in the far distance, with a summit resembling that of Mount Erebus, saw Mount Siple (73° 15′ South, 123° 00′ West), the easternmost feature seen, around 250 miles short of Byrd's easternmost sighting from the "Bear" but well over 600 miles east of Little America III.

The Little America party was evacuated on February 1, 1941, by the "Bear" and the "North Star." The ships then went north to Scott Island and east to Marguerite Bay where ice prevented them from getting to Stonington Island. After waiting a month for the ice to break up, the East Base party was taken by air to Watkins Island (named for Gino Watkins) in the Biscoe group where the ships were boarded. This involved leaving behind instruments, gear, notes, and specimens, but these were either forwarded to Washington eventually by Chilean and Argentine visitors to Stonington or recovered after the war by Americans. Because of the war USAS was terminated, but the idea of continuous operation of permanent American stations in Antarctica survived for use another day.

CHAPTER XV

A Scientific Preserve

The fifteen years between the end of World War II and 1960 were marked by the climactic episodes so far in the nationalistic struggle over claims to Antarctic territory, the continuation of the efforts to bring whaling under rational international control to conserve a wasting resource, continuation of the interest in exploration, increasingly in close association with exact mapping, and the movement to a position of substantial dominance of the emphasis on the accumulation of scientific knowledge and understanding. The scientific approach in the end provided the sustaining rationale for the effective but limited internationalization of Antarctica. Adventure remained an ineradicable personal motivation for participation in Antarctic work.

While the nationalistic contention was most marked around the Palmer-Graham Peninsula between the United Kingdom on the one hand and Argentina and Chile on the other, these nations were not alone in taking up nationalistic positions of varying intensity. Australia, Norway, and France, while never provoked to extravagance by counterclaims, clearly revealed nationalistic positions toward what they held. Only one claimant nation developed an internationalist approach prior to the actual achievement of internationalization in 1959. This was New Zealand, of all the claimants the nation least able to "find" material resources on a scale commensurate with properly sustaining the claim it had by transfer acquired. Among the directly interested nonclaimants the United States continued to maintain its ambiguous position of recognizing no claims and making none, thus contributing to keeping the situation fluid. However, its "special interest" in Marie Byrd Land was widely acknowledged. The Japanese were obliged by treaty (Article 2e), on Australian initiative, to renounce whatever basis for a claim they had. The Germans never achieved a position to enter the field on the basis of the Ritscher adventure, if they ever had the disposition—they had by implication re- nounced any claim based on earlier first discoveries at the end of World War I. And the Russians, returned to Antarctica after an absence of 125 years, asserted that no settlement of the matter, nationalistic or inter- nationalistic in essence, could be made without their participation and agreement, this interpreted to mean that they asserted "floating" rights, geographically even less specific than the American interest in Marie Byrd Land; the position was, of course, nationalistic in substance. In this complicated situation significant pressure in favor of some scheme of internationalization, the logical solution as the material value of Ant- arctica became increasingly hypothetical and its principal value as a scientific preserve more obvious, could only come either from one or several of the non-Antarctic nations acting through the United Nations or from an involved nation sufficiently interested and prestigious to take a very strong lead. In the end the decisive assertion of leadership toward internationalization came from the United States.

The differences between the United Kingdom and Argentina and Chile found expression in a struggle to establish and maintain bases on the one hand and diplomatic exchanges on the other. The bases being, by inten- tion though not always for one reason or another in practice, permanently occupied would constitute "settlement" and the performance of functional acts like the maintenance of postal service and the sale of stamps with special designs on them indicating a claim, and the appointment of per- sons to be magistrates, etc., would demonstrate the actuality of the sovereignty asserted. For the British the "chosen instrument" with regard to bases was the Falkland Islands Dependencies Survey, for the Argen- tines it was the Comisión Nacional del Antártico of the Ministry of External Relations, while the Chilean bases were at first in charge of the armed forces, particularly the navy, latterly an Antarctic Commission. (In 1962 the British constituted the FID a separate colony with the Survey under its auspices.) Diplomatic exchanges brought the foreign offices of the three nations now and again into the forefront and in 1948 there was a crisis of relations in which other nations, including the United States, were at least tangentially involved. In 1955 the United Kingdom brought the whole business to the attention of the International Court of Justice at The Hague, but as neither Argentina nor Chile would submit its case to the Court, the matter was removed from the Court's list in 1956. Shortly the pacifying influences of the International Geo- physical Year were at work and in 1959 the whole question of claims was suspended, so to speak, for as long as a treaty should last. The affair was not so much settled as swept under a convenient rug. It was plain, how-

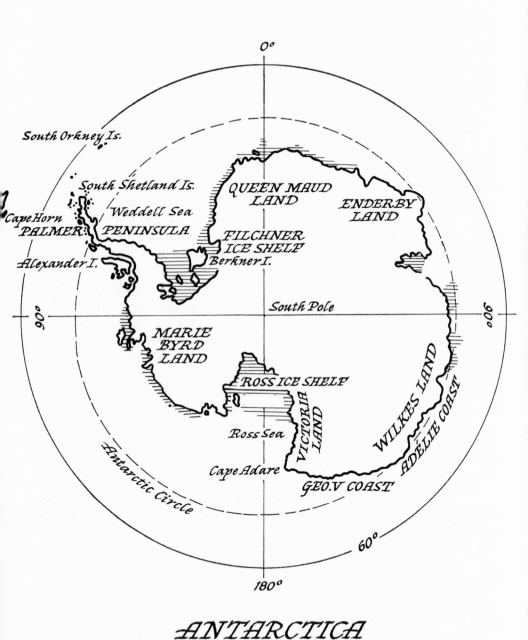

ANTARCTICA

ever, that the rug might be lifted in the future to uncover who knows what?

Most of the British bases were at sites occupied for the first time for the specific purpose of supporting the claim, but some represented re-occupations of sites and even buildings used on earlier occasions of clearly nonpolitical import. All were small and could be operated by a dozen men or less. While the political significance was patent, as shown for example by location, all were also justifiable by the scientific work carried out—science was the rationalizing purpose of the FIDS, and the journeys for survey work carried out from them. However, there was no scientific justification for the considerable multiplication of bases which politics brought about within the rather confined area. In sequence of founding the British bases were at Deception Island and Port Lockroy (1944); Coronation Island in the South Orkneys and Hope Bay on the Palmer-Graham Peninsula (1945); Laurie Island in the South Orkneys, Stonington Island (where the USAS East Base had been) and Barry Island in the Debenhams (where Rymill's second base had been), both in Marguerite Bay (1946); Signy Island in the South Orkneys, King George Island in the South Shetlands, and the Argentine Islands (the first Rymill location) (1949); and at Druse Bay on the Palmer-Graham Peninsula (1953). While not all the bases were occupied every season after original establishment, whether by plan or as a consequence of an accident such as a fire which destroyed the facilities, the British were continually active in the area from 1944. There was an annual turnover of personnel at each base during its occupation and in this fashion there was developed a relatively large corps of Britons with Antarctic experience. Of the many men who served at one or another of the bases, Vivian Fuchs eventually acquired the widest fame. The scientific work done was various. The most widely dispersed interest was meteorology, the communications center of which was Deception Island, though eventually weather forecasting was centered at Grytviken, South Georgia. Geological studies were carried on at several bases, work in glaciology was done at several, while ionospherics, physiology (effect of cold on human beings), ornithology (with special attention to penguins), biology (with special attention to elephant seals), and other specialities were distributed around. One base specialized in breeding dogs and accumulating stocks of seal meat to service the other bases. While journeys were usually organized as "combined surveys," the primary intent was to gather data for exact mapping. They were carried out at the island bases but the most extensive journeys were made southward on the peninsula plateau from the Hope Bay base. Hope Bay was, with some help from the Ronne expedition (see below), eventually linked with the Stonington Island base. Fuchs made a journey from Stonington the full length of the King George VI Sound and corrected some of Ronne's earlier findings. This was the farthest south reached.

The work at these bases represented by far the greater part of the United Kingdom's contribution to Antarctic studies until the Geophysical Year. However, in 1946–47 there was a three-man British expedition to South Georgia to photograph wild life, and the same year a combined whaling and scientific expedition was made to the Queen Mary and Wilkes coasts in the Australian sector where a special study was made of the uses of whale meat for human consumption and attention was given to meteorology, glaciology, ornithology, and the physiology of whales. The British collaborated in the Norwegian-British-Swedish expedition of 1949–52 to Queen Maud Land (see below). In 1950–51 the newly established British National Institute of Oceanography undertook to continue and complete the oceanographic work of the old "Discovery" Committee, basing the ship in Australian or New Zealand ports and chiefly studying the seas to the south. A climax of this effort was a circumnavigation of Antarctica in the winter of 1951. South Georgia was given additional attention by a private undertaking led by Verner D. Carse in the seasons 1951–52 and 1953–54, the primary interests of which were geographical survey and ornithology.

The Argentine bases (counting the old Laurie Island base as one) were established as follows: on Deception Island and on Gamma Island in the Melchior group (1947); at Hope Bay and on the Danco Coast of the Palmer-Graham Peninsula and on Barry Island in the Debenhams (1951); on Half Moon Island in the South Shetlands and on Dundee Island (1952); on King George Island in the South Shetlands (1953); at another site on King George Island, on Nelson Island also in the South Shetlands, and at Brialmont Cove on the peninsula (1954); Petermann Island off the west coast of the peninsula and far to the south facing the Weddell Sea on the Filchner Ice Shelf in Coats Land (1955). Some of these were refugios [refuges] rather than true stations. The frequency with which the Argentines located in close proximity to British stations earlier established illustrates the pertinacity of their challenge. The sudden swoop south to Coats Land, a move against a vulnerable flank, accomplished with the aid of a German-built icebreaker, was an acute embarrassment to the British. Although the Argentines were obviously strongly motivated by political considerations in all they did, they were not without an interest in science, particularly meteorology (since the weather of southern South America, like that of Australia, was believed to be strongly influenced by Antarctic conditions), oceanography, and the problems of ocean navigation and aviation under polar conditions.

They did some significant aerial photography. They took no interest in exploratory journeys on the surface, ordinarily not stirring from the close vicinity of their stations.

The Chilean stations were located in studied relation to British and Argentine bases to emphasize that the Chileans were claiming the same ground as the others. In 1947 the first Chilean base was set up at Discovery Bay, Greenwich Island, in the South Shetlands. The next two bases were set up on the main peninsula, the first at Trinity Peninsula in 1948, the other at Paradise Harbor in 1951. A fourth base was formed on Deception Island in 1955 at a location near the British establishment. Meteorology was the principal scientific interest at all these stations. Like the Argentines the Chileans did not go in for travel on land.

The British maintained, of course, that the Argentines and Chileans were intruders into an area where British sovereignty had long been acknowledged by, among others, the Argentines and Chileans themselves. Founding their case ultimately on the first discoveries of such men as Cook, Smith, Bransfield, and Powell, they pointed to an implicit assertion of sovereignty that dated back to 1843 and to the explicit assertion followed by a variety of sovereign acts beginning in 1905. While their own actions with regard to bases in 1944 and after were asserted to be in the nature of "settlement" or at least by way of demonstratively emphasizing the sovereignty they claimed, they denied that in establishing bases the Argentines and Chileans were bolstering *their* claims. Rather they were only, as base followed base, compounding their trespass.

On their side the Argentines and Chileans developed a variety of arguments in support of their positions, most of them closely similar in substance, the chief difference being that the Argentines also exploited their position with regard to the Falkland Islands. While the Chileans maintained their own bases and sometimes indicated that they disputed the Argentine claim, they nevertheless maintained a united front against the British with the Argentines. The British, however, tried to exploit the point that since the Chilean and Argentine claims so extensively overlapped, it was obvious that both could not be right. The Argentines claimed the South Orkney Islands, South Georgia, and the South Sandwich Islands to which the Chileans made no claim, while the Argentines ignored everything in the western reaches of the Chilean claim which extended almost to Peter I Island and embraced a portion of Alexander I Island and all of Charcot Island, beyond the Argentine western boundary. The focus of common interest was thus the South Shetlands, the Palmer-Graham Peninsula (called Tierra O'Higgins by the Chileans and Tierra San Martin by the Argentines), the numerous islands on both sides of the peninsula, and the territory within the selected degrees of longitude to the South Pole. The Argentine claim was wholly within the boundaries of the British claim, but the Chilean claim extended beyond it to the west. The British were thus in the position of resisting both Argentine and Chilean pretentions to sovereignty over some of the same territory within the Dependencies and also Argentine pretentions to some and Chilean pretentions to other territories.

Both the Argentines and the Chileans took the position that their claims were in effect definitions of extensions of the national territory and as national territory the question of title could not be submitted to any *ad hoc* arbitral authority or to the International Court of Justice. The titles, they said, were incontrovertible. Both the Chileans and Argentines regarded the British as having encroached on their national territory. The bases for arguments that the territory was national and always had been, ignoring or countering apparent Chilean and Argentine acquiescence in British acts of sovereignty in times past, were geographical and historical but did not include first discovery which neither could assert. Geographically the argument turned in part on whether or not the portion of Antarctica in dispute was a continuation of South America or a separate and distinct continent and in part, making the decision that it was in fact a continuation of South America, on the argument that as the nations were contiguous to an extension of the continent on which they were located, their boundaries necessarily ran southward to the far limits of the extension. That there was a geographical connection between South America and Antarctica had been the opinion of geologists and oceanographers since the time of W. S. Bruce. The connection was argued from the character of the mountains which both on the Palmer-Graham Peninsula and in South America were *Andean,* and from the existence of a submarine formation actually connecting the two land masses, known as the Scotia Arc. However, the fact that the land masses were separated, in spite of their submarine connection, by 600 miles of ocean rather weakened the idea of contiguity as a politically useful idea and therefore also the argument for sovereignty by contiguity. And anyhow, as the British pointed out, contiguity was a weak reed, for in the Island of Palmas case (1928) the judge had declared: "Nor is this principle of contiguity admissible as a legal method of deciding questions of territorial sovereignty; for it . . . would . . . lead to arbitrary results." The Chileans and Argentines therefore tried to buttress their positions by appeals to history in an attempt to establish that they were speaking and acting in the light of their inheritance from Spain. The difficulty with the "inheritance" argument with regard to Antarctica as contrasted with its use by Argentina with regard to the Falklands was that the territories in dispute had barely been discovered in Spain's day and had in no instance ever been part of any Spanish dominions and therefore could with difficulty be alleged to have been inherited from Spain by the successor nations. However, the Chileans declared in 1955 that in their view their claim was "une portion du territoire national où le Chili exerce une souveraineté complete et absolue, en vertu de titres incontestables de caractère juridique, politique, historique, geographique, diplomatique et administratif." At the same time the Argentines took essentially the same position, adding some grace notes peculiarly their own, and in the same year emphasized their position by establishing as a province Patagonia below 46° South, Tierra del Fuego, the Argentine Antarctic sector, and "islands of the South Atlantic" (including the Falklands). Two years later Ushuaia was designated the capital of this province.

The failure of the British to get the dispute before the International Court of Justice in 1955, caused by Argentine and Chilean intractability, occurred seven years after the first crisis the dispute had evoked. The failure of the powers to solve the problem in 1948 was attributable in large measure to the strength of nationalistic sentiment among the Antarctic claimants at the time. By 1955 the strength of the sentiment had materially lessened, though it was far from exhausted, as will be explained later. It was shortly possible to circumvent and contain it. The ex post factor significance of the 1948 crisis was that it provoked the United States to introduce into the situation the idea of internationalization.

The so-called crisis of 1948 was a peculiarly tangled affair, a snarl of discordance, which at its most extreme expression pointed to the possibility of armed conflict over a claim between Argentina and the United Kingdom. In 1948 the Argentines sent a naval task force to carry out maneuvers in the vicinity of Deception Island. In the existing context of conflict this could not fail to be regarded as rather more than a scheme for giving the Argentine navy some polar experience as other navies were seeking it at this time. In reply the British sent a ship of war to the scene which, fortunately, arrived after the Argentines had left and the Australians offered to support the British by assigning units of their navy to the area. That same season ships of the Chilean navy carried the president of the Republic on a formal visit to two of the Chilean bases, the ceremonies in which he participated emphasizing that the Chilean claim must be taken seriously. If these things were to become common, an armed conflict might eventuate if only by one of those "accidents" of which history has numerous examples. To avoid the chance the British took the initative in inducing the Chileans and Argentines not to send *warships* south of 60° except on relief expeditions, though the ships and personnel of the armed services could be used in Antarctic work. Once made (in November 1948) it was possible to renew this agreement annually. This was by way of taking the warhead out of the argument without really moderating it in any other respect.

In casting about for support of their common positions vis à vis Britain, the Chileans and Argentines tried to involve the other nations of the Americas who participated in the Organization of American States, believed in Pan-American solidarity, and supported the Monroe Doctrine. The effort was based on the assumption that all these nations would support the contention that the American sector of Antarctica was properly to be considered a geographical extension of Andean America and that contiguity soundly supported a claim to sovereignty. An effort was made to have it accepted by the associated states that since the Antarctic (and the Arctic) had been declared to be within the area of defensive interest to the Pan-American countries, it was vital that American Antarctica be under American sovereignties. And Monroeism was brought up by seeking acceptance of the proposition that all non-American states should be forthwith expelled from their possessions in the Americas which, if accepted, would have required the expulsion of the British from the American sector of Antarctica (as well as the Falkland Islands). These efforts were frustrated for a variety of complicated reasons, not least of which was that not only did the United States not accept the geographical argument, rather taking the line that Antarctica was a separate and distinct continent, but also and more importantly did not recognize any claims whatever. It could not, therefore, support a move to expel the British from a claim it did not in any case recognize to install the Chileans and Argentines in claims it would not recognize. The traditional American position had been reiterated by Undersecretary of State Dean Acheson in 1946 and while there was popular and Congressional opinion to the contrary and the postwar government-supported expeditions (see below) had as a purpose the strengthening of the foundations of possible United States claims, none was in fact ever made.

Instead, in 1948 the United States turned toward internationalization as a way out of an increasingly exasperating situation. The general idea of an international approach to Antarctica had been in the air since the scientists had agitated for a revival of study of Antarctica at the end of the nineteenth century. What the scientists had in mind was less a political idea than a professional notion that since Antarctica was a no-man's-land posing tremendous problems it could best be handled if the scientists of all nations acted in a co-operative and co-ordinate fashion in accordance with the widely entertained idea that the world of science was a supra-national world. The idea of co-operation and co-ordination survived among the scientists down the years. It was, for instance, formally re-formulated by Dr. H. R. Mill of the United Kingdom in 1905 as the Heroic Age was beginning and again in the 1920's by the Australian Briton Frank Debenham. Between Mill's time and Debenham's the politicalization of Antarctica had begun. By the late 1940's the political factor in the equation was in many ways the most important of all. Only an occasional voice suggesting that internationalization was a politically feasible way out of an increasingly difficult situation was then to be heard. To be sure, on the basis of a suggestion advanced by a private group, the Trusteeship Council of the United Nations discussed the idea of an inter-national regime under the UN in 1947 but it was unable to arrive at any firm opinion about the matter.

The American proposal of 1948, revealed to the public on August 28, was for discussions of the general situation among the interested nations in which internationalization would be considered as a possible solution of the Antarctic tangle. The American idea was to throw the emphasis on "scientific investigation and research" and off the claims to national sovereignty. No *conference* was contemplated until the discussions had uncovered some generally acceptable internationalist solution. The dis-cussions, as a matter of fact, foundered on the recalcitrant nationalism of the participants. Seven nations were invited to participate: Argentina, Australia, Chile, France, New Zealand, Norway, and the United King-dom. Nationalism was then so decidedly dominant that only New Zea-land and the United Kingdom would agree even to talk about interna-tionalization. Not unexpectedly Chile and Argentina categorically re-fused to talk about the possibility. Dr. H. V. Evatt of Australia neatly combined a nationalistic with an international approach, suggesting, ". . . the Australian view was that what was required was a reasoned agreement retaining sovereignty, including Australian sovereignty over Australian Antarctic Territory, but with the interested states also agree-ing to assist each other in the development of Antarctica." In 1950 the U.S.S.R., which had been skirmishing around the Antarctic question in recent years, entered the discussion with a note addressed to all the nations involved. Invoking the name of Bellingshausen and placing the most dogmatic possible interpretation on what he had discovered, re-ferring to its participation in Antarctic whaling since 1946 and to the work of its scientists on the whalers, with a bow to the amenities of international intercourse in the form of an accusation that the United States had imperialist designs on Antarctica, the Soviet Union stated that

the Soviet Government cannot recognize as legal any decision on the regime for the Antarctic taken without their participation. They consider that because the fate of the Antarctic is of interest to many countries it would be expedient at the present time to discuss internationally the question of the regime of the Antarctic, having in view the achievement of an agreement such as would accord with the legitimate interests of all interested states.

What in fact this meant was difficult to determine, but it was widely assumed that the U.S.S.R. was asserting rights in Antarctica on the basis of first discoveries by Bellingshausen and its recent whaling and scientific activities and while apparently favoring the national sovereignty principle was yet not ready to specify a claim or claims, preferring to leave the idea of a claim "floating" in the minds of all. Meanwhile, enough had been said and implied to allow it to demand a seat at any table at which Antarctica and its future were under discussion. In spite of all the cold water thrown around at this time, the idea of internationalization did not die; it was simply shelved for a while. The United States turned again to the idea of making claims on its own behalf.

The postwar return of the United States to Antarctica, which occurred before the short-lived American turn to internationalization, was closely related to the navy's effort to prepare itself for possible armed conflict in the polar regions rather than a straightforward renewal of geographical-scientific activity. It was, that is, a by-product of the cold war with the U.S.S.R. which was then taking shape. Already in 1946 the navy had carried out Operation Nanook in the Arctic when a weather station and airstrip had been established at Thule, Greenland (later transferred to the Air Force and very elaborately developed as a research center). On August 26, 1946, in this context, Admiral Chester Nimitz, then chief of Naval Operations, issued a directive for an elaborate expedition to the Antarctic. It has been suggested that this turn was decided on because an incursion into the Antarctic seemed less provocative than an immediate return to the Arctic and because the navy was anxious to get as much polar experience as possible before the already initiated economy in defense expenditures could eliminate funds to support such an undertaking. It seemed best to act while men and equipment were still available. At any rate the preplanning of the expedition was hurried and the execution while able was a bit ragged. The primary objective was to train men and especially to test equipment under polar conditions and to establish whether it was feasible to build an airfield for wheeled aircraft on ice (with a view to establishing such a field in Greenland). Provision was made for carrying out some purely scientific investigations, but the emphasis was to be on geographical exploration—particularly along the coasts—by air using the new trimetrogon cameras as recorders, this throwing the equipment-testing emphasis on the airplanes and the ships.

The scientists came to feel like also-rans, although useful work was done in ionospherics and magnetism (some observations correlated with Thule's). An important study of "ice deformation" in the Ross Ice Shelf, aimed at understanding what was happening at Bay of Whales which was being destroyed by natural forces, was initiated. The political purpose, obviously of prewar derivation, was phrased as "consolidating and extending United States sovereignty over the largest practicable area of the Antarctic continent," exactly what in the end the State Department chose not to do.

The expedition was officially called The Antarctic Development Project, 1947, but was to become more widely known as Operation Highjump and the thirteen ships carrying 4700 men and an assortment of planes as Task Force 68. Admiral Richard E. Byrd, fresh from wartime service in the Pacific, was "Officer-in-Charge" but "tactical command" was given to Rear Admiral Richard Cruzen. Byrd's primary interest was in the adaptability of equipment developed for war purposes to exploratory work, a slightly different emphasis from the navy's, but complementary. Cruzen had been with Byrd in Antarctica in 1940 and had just led Operation Nanook to Greenland.

The task force was divided into three groups, Central, Eastern, and Western. The Central Group, directly under Cruzen, with which Byrd also worked and to which Lt. Colonel Paul Siple was attached in the capacity of army observer, was to carry on its activities from a Little America (No. IV) on the Ross Ice Shelf. It alone would test equipment for surface travel; half of the scientists would be assigned to it; its land planes, equipped with a ski-wheel arrangement, would be flown in from an aircraft carrier stationed outside the pack ice. The East Group, commanded by George J. Dufek, also a veteran of Byrd's expedition of 1940 and of Operation Nanook, was wholly a ship-based operation. It was first to direct its attention to the still inadequately known coast of Marie Byrd Land and was then to work eastward around the coast until it met the Western Group. The Western Group, also ship-based, Captain Charles Bond in charge, was to begin its work on the coast in the vicinity of the Balleny Islands and work west until it met Dufek's Group. The sea planes of both the Eastern and Western groups were to fly over the ice to the coasts they were to photograph. The expedition reached Antarctica just before Christmas 1946 and all units were out and away during March 1947. All told, sixty-four mapping flights, most by the Central and Western groups, accumulating 70,000 mapping pictures, were made. The critical natural limitation on carrying out the assignment was foul weather.

Dufek's Eastern Group was the first to get into action. The command ship was the seaplane tender "Pine Island." To begin with, the coastal landmark was Thurston Peninsula over which Dufek had flown with Byrd in 1940; the concentration of interest was then from the peninsula westward. In a series of flights, one of which came to grief on the inland ice with the death of three men, a camera record of coastal features from 95° 30′ West to 127° 30′ West, or roughly from Seraph Bay to Mount Siple, was made. This included the large Wrigley Gulf bordered by Getz Ice Shelf. The flights revealed a much indented coast fringed by mountains, some very high, apparently situated around seventy miles south of its previously calculated position. It appeared probable that Thurston Peninsula was actually a large island (as it was subsequently shown to be) and on examining the accumulated evidence Byrd speculated that the coastal mountains were on islands separated from the mainland of Marie Byrd Land by a water-channel running from someplace in the Wrigley Gulf to the Ross Ice Shelf. An observation of water-sky by Ellsworth on his flight back of this coast was cited in support of this. This clever guess was partially supported by later research on the elevation of the Antarctic land under the ice. Dufek formed the opinion that the coast, hitherto utterly inaccessible, would one day be reached by ship. This was done in 1960. Driven east by bad weather, Dufek next concentrated on the north shore of Alexander I Island and Charcot Island. The closest approach to Charcot yet made by ship was achieved, but an attempt to land was stopped by shore ice. While awaiting an opportunity to enter Marguerite Bay, orders were received from Cruzen to proceed to the Weddell Sea. A Russian whaler was passed en route. The weather outside the Weddell Sea ice-pack made flying toward the coast impossible. This proved to be the major coastal gap of the expedition. The group sailed to South America and home from the Weddell Sea.

The principal ship of Captain Bond's Western Group was the seaplane tender "Currituck." The group turned in over half of the mapping photographs taken on Highjump. Its work was mostly done on the Australian and Norwegian sector coasts but its deepest penetration inland was in the French sector, 425 miles to 72° 30′ South, 135° East.

Flights began on January 4. The first round of photographs covered the coast south of the Balleny Islands from James Clark Ross's Smith Inlet just west of Robertson Bay in Victoria Land to Cape Freshfield on George V Coast, possibly Wilkes' Cape Hudson of 1840 but definitely discovered and named by Mawson in 1912. This coast was found to be much indented and fringed by mountains, some of considerable height, with numerous glaciers flowing into the ocean from the plateau behind. Scott's Rennick Bay on Oates Coast, of which only the entrance had been seen hitherto, was found to make a deep penetration inland. Because of bad weather experienced while offshore in the vicinity of the Nennis and Mertz Glaciers, continuous photography had to be abandoned and a move westward made. It then proved possible to cover 1000 miles of coast from a little east of Adélie Land on west, along which Wilkes, Dumont d'Urville, and Mawson had operated. Numerous flights into Wilkes Land back of this coast, averaging 100 miles in penetration, were made. The inland flights disclosed a characteristically featureless high (six to ninety-five hundred feet above sea level) plateau. For a long distance few mountains were seen but two features of considerable current and future interest were discovered on the Budd and Knox coasts, the Windmill Islands in Vincennes Bay, where there was much ice-free rock, on the former, and Bunger's Hills on the latter. The Bunger Hills area, originally called Bunger's Oasis, was an ice-free "dry valley" of a type first discovered in Antarctica by the first Scott Expedition (e.g., the Taylor Glacier Dry Valley) which received a good deal of miscomprehending publicity before its true character was established. To the west again the photographers surveyed the entire length of the Mac-Robertson Coast. At about 63° East, they picked what seemed an exceptionally good site for a station. It proved to be the only good site for many hundreds of miles in either direction. As the group moved west toward Enderby Land, already suspected of being highly mountainous, they began to note mountain ranges in the interior of which the most impressive was just west of the Lars Christensen Coast bordering the glacier-ice shelf complex called Amery. These mountains were definitively located by the Australians later on and named for Prince Charles. In the Norwegian sector the coast was found to be bordered over long stretches by ice shelves, collectively perhaps as vast as any known, while in the interior were spotted mountain ranges that appeared to extend the mountains seen earlier by Lars Christensen's people into one of the great systems of the continent and the world. Icing conditions in early March dictated a retreat and course was set for Sydney in Australia. The passage was unusually rough. No link with Dufek's Group had been made nor any with the exploratory work of the Central Group.

The Central Group at Little America IV had an airfield in operation within a week of arriving at the Bay of Whales. Although it was intended to pave the strip with pierced planking to provide a hard surface usable by wheeled planes, a quick construction practice developed during World War II, this was not done. The planes sent in from the "Philippine Sea" standing 700 miles away outside the pack ice landed and took off at Little America on their skis. It was concluded in the end, and tested experimentally, that planes could use their wheels on a snow surface that had been thoroughly compacted.

Most of the important exploratory flights of the Central Group were made within fifty hours beginning on February 13. The first effort was to deal again with the Ross-Weddell channel problem, not by flying a course from the ice shelf to the Weddell and back again, as was feasible in planes of proper range, but by attempting to trace the eastward course of the horst mountains beyond the point already seen—that is, beyond the Horlick Mountains, sighted from a distance in 1934. A close approach to the Horlicks was made and new high mountains about 200 miles farther east were sighted. The mountains were not only examined along their "fronts" but, by flying up a glacier, also from the Polar Plateau side, or "backs." Byrd himself participated in one of these flights. In his mind the results still left open the question of a channel north of the mountains. Flying southwest from Little America efforts were made to find out what was behind the horst mountains in that direction. The identified (1940) but unexplored Shackleton Glacier was used as an avenue into the interior, with Mount Wade as the landmark, while the return was made down Beardmore with Mount Kirkpatrick (a Shackleton discovery) the landmark. Beyond the mountains it was found that the great Polar Plateau, here reaching perhaps 11,500 feet above sea level, trended away toward the Indian Ocean, as Scott had long ago ascertained on the surface. The Shackleton Glacier, never before traversed, proved to be a formation of unexampled grandeur and extent with a most impressive medial moraine riding it. Using the Shackleton Glacier again, this time with Byrd along, a two-plane flight was made to and 100 miles beyond the South Pole into the area containing the so-called Pole of Inaccessibility, located 1000 miles from the sea in all directions. This was Byrd's second trip over the Pole. As far as could be seen the featureless plateau reigned supreme beyond the Pole, but en route evidence was found that the maximum height of the plateau—10,000 to 11,500 feet— occurred at about 88° South, probably indicating the presence of a submerged mountain range under the ice at that point. Turning to the west, flights were made over and beyond the mountains into Victoria Land, named by Ross in 1840. On one flight from south to north the "back" of these mountains was for the first time extensively observed. Mount Markham was closely observed. A great new glacier emptying into Shackleton Inlet of the Ross Ice Shelf was found, later named Nimrod for one of Shackleton's ships. At Royal Society Range, which Scott had named, the return flight was begun, calculated to pass over Mount Erebus. On another flight west, of which Mount McClintock was the southern landmark, a flight north farther to the west than its predecessor (155° East) but not as far west as Scott had penetrated was made, during which the "dry valleys" near the Ferrar Glacier were seen from the air for the first time, and by communicating with another plane, an aerial survey of this remarkable region was made at both the lower and upper ends. Eastward a flight was made with Siple aboard in an effort to link up with Dufek's work. The attempt to reach Mount Siple and Wrigley Gulf beyond was frustrated by cloud but the Executive Committee Range, dominated by Mount Sidley, was for the first time seen close up. The Central Group was evacuated by the icebreaker "Burton Island" on March 3.

All this photographic work was, in the final analysis, only useful insofar as reliable "fixes" of ground positions allowed the establishment of firm points of reference for exact interpretation of the pictures. The "fixes" (or more formally, astrofixes) could be specially made for the occasion, as the Western Group tried unsuccessfully to do, or earlier discoveries, the positions of which had been precisely determined, could be used if they appeared in the new photographs. Unfortunately "fixes" were scarcest or unavailable altogether just where the photographers were able to do their most original work. The result was that a high percentage of the Highjump pictures were unusable for mapping. In an effort to repair the deficiency, a supplementary expedition, using the icebreakers "Edisto" and "Burton Island" and helicopters, so useful in landing at otherwise inaccessible points, was sent out December 1947–February 1948 to obtain the needed control data and carry out some other useful chores. This became known as Operation Windmill. Among other useful things, a very careful geological study was made of Bunger Hills during which two and a half tons of specimens were accumulated and the Windmill Islands were closely examined. West of the Ross Ice Shelf, Windmill was partially successful in getting "fixes" it was sent out for, but east of the shelf it was not. Many pictures remained enigmatic. According to Dufek, as late as 1956 only about one-third of the 70,000 pictures had been used in mapping by the Americans or the French and Australians to whom prospectively useful copies had been presented. But after that date surface exploration along the coasts photographed by Highjump continued, and more of the pictures became usable.

Nor in spite of the enormous extent of the ground covered were all the planes used ideally adapted for the work. Because of the failure to pave the Little America airfield with pierced planks it was impossible to bring in planes of continental range. And not only were the planes actually used of limited range, but, also, in the case of the seaplanes, they were difficult to prepare for flight. Much of the range was exhausted at Little America in getting beyond the known area into truly new country. The usefulness of the Little America planes was further reduced by the removal of the oxygen equipment which made high flying over the mountains dangerous because of the risk of inducing anoxia. On the other hand, Highjump confirmed the great utility of planes in reconnaisance work; and the scheme of flying in from beyond the pack proved, ex post facto, to be a step toward flying in from a land base outside the continent, such as New Zealand. Highjump taught a good deal about types and equipment of planes most useful in Antarctica and it also taught something about the inherent risks, including "icing," and the possibility, with good weather forecasting, of taking off in poor weather and flying into favorable weather, a technique suggested by Byrd. It iterated the difficulties of aerial navigation under Antarctic conditions where ground landmarks were scarce, magnetic interference with instruments like compasses strong, and the winds devastating. Windmill demonstrated the great utility of the helicopters for placing surface workers in otherwise inaccessible positions. However, it remained obvious that travel and work on the surface was never to be dispensable.

Of the ships employed, the strikingly successful innovation was the icebreaker—two of these, the "Northwind" and the "Burton Island," were used. It proved possible to take naval ships into and through the ice only under the care of icebreakers (and even then at considerable risk). So valuable did the icebreaker prove that an Antarctic specialist suggested later on that a nation lacking an icebreaker was not really in the Antarctic swim. In surface travel, of which there was comparatively little on Highjump, the wartime "weasel" proved to be a successful general utility motorized vehicle—its "tracks" were, however, not too easy to keep operative—while the sixteen-ton combat motorized vehicle known as the LVT proved successful for long-distance travel. A journey from Little America to Mount Helen Washington in the Rockefellers was made in two LVT's. This success was taken to be a posthumous justification for Dr. Poulter's celebrated snowmobile of 1940. But not all the technology proved so useful. The magnetometer, designed to record the nature of the rocks under the ice, proved to be of limited utility because it could not detect nonmagnetized rock, could not differentiate between nonmagnetized rock and snow and ice, and could not report at what depth rocks actually lay.

On March 12, 1947, as Highjump was pulling out, an expedition led by Finn Ronne landed to occupy the old USASE East Base on Stonington Island. The expedition was private, though it had governmental assistance in one way or another, and it was small, both of which characteristics were much cherished by its leader. Ronne was returning to an area in which he had had great triumphs in times past, of which the most spectacular was the demonstration that Alexander I was an island. Long associated with Byrd's activities, Ronne had had the notion of an expedition of his own since 1934 when he had planned a small sledging party to explore and map the continental coast from a point opposite Charcot Island on the Robert English Coast to the Ross Ice Shelf. Now he was proposing to probe south of the farthest south yet achieved on the Weddell Sea Coast, to attempt to determine the direction of the Peninsula mountains in their continental extension, and to contribute to the solution of the standing question of the Weddell-Ross channel.

Ronne was, of course, proposing to work in an area disputed by the United Kingdom, Argentina, and Chile. His justification was the State Department's position that its policy of no claim and no recognition of claims allowed Americans to go anyplace in Antarctica on scientific-geographical errands. Ronne was, however, involved in the department's current solicitude for building up a foundation for possible future claims. He was to fly the American flag and he was to operate a United States post office. The British made the most serious objection to Ronne's expedition. They challenged his right to land on Stonington, questioned his right to hoist the flag, and questioned his right to operate a post office. The British wanted him to go elsewhere, but Ronne made the point that he was reoccupying an old United States base—he found it considerably damaged by visitors, apparently including British visitors as well as Argentines and Chileans—thus evading the charge that the act implied a claim, and he kept his postal activities under cover. In the end Ronne and the British worked out a basis for co-operation in both geographic work on the ground and science, particularly after he had had conversations with Sir Miles Clifford, governor of the Falkland Islands and Dependencies, who visited Stonington while on one of his periodic visits of inspection of the British bases. Ronne's immediate collaborator was Major K. S. P. Butler, in charge of the FIDS base at Stonington. The British particularly admired Ronne's ship, a wartime ATA; they eventually obtained one and named it the "John Biscoe." Ronne had three planes. The exploratory plane was equipped with a trimetrogon camera unit and had a cruising time of nine hours. For surface travel dogs were used, chiefly British dogs since Ronne's had been decimated by sickness. The British eventually took over the seismographic installation that Ronne established. In a reversion to earlier practice, Ronne froze in his ship in what was known as Back Bay.

Primary interest was taken in probing south along the east coast. To facilitate operations, a meteorological station was established on the peninsula plateau 6000 feet up. An advance base for both ground and air exploration, also equipped for meteorological work, was established at Cape Keeler in the Larsen Ice Shelf, directly east of Stonington

Island. A primary purpose of surface operations south from Cape Keeler was to establish "fixes" to make accurate interpretation of the aerial photographs possible. An American-British team, using dogs, first crossed the peninsula to the Cape Keeler base and then went south toward Mount Tricorn at the head of Wright Inlet, which the party was the first to reach on the surface. Lichens and moss were seen as far south as Cape Darlington, Hilton Inlet. From Mount Tricorn the party went on to establish the expedition's farthest south on the surface at Gardner Inlet, earlier found from the air by Ronne, at the northernmost reach of the vast ice shelf of which Filchner had discovered the southern portion in 1912.

Three southward flights were made by the exploratory plane accompanied by a cargo carrier with a reserve supply of gasoline. On the first flight from Cape Keeler revisions were made in the configuration of the coast, but the first significant discoveries were mountains south of Mount Andrew Jackson: Mount Russell Owen (71° 50' South), the Gutenko Mountains (72° 19' South), and Mount Coman (74° 02' South). Gardner Inlet was discovered south of Mount Tricorn and a landing was made on the slopes of Mount Austin in the inlet where Ronne calculated positions, correcting the location of Mount Tricorn, and the exploratory plane was refueled from the cargo carrier. This expedition was notable for the number of impromptu landings in the field, a highly significant innovation. At Mount Austin the party was about 250 miles south of the farthest south achieved on the surface up to that time. The exploratory plane went on south, using Cape Schlossbach, the southern boundary of Gardner Inlet, as a point of departure. The coast was found to trend off to the west, and equally important was that the axis of the Peninsula Mountains appeared to be shifting southwestward, the mountains gradually spacing out, and as the elevation of the Joerg Plateau rose, the mountains diminished in height. Among the newly seen mountains were the [Sir Hubert] Wilkins Mountains (75° 54' South, 64° West), the Lowell Thomas Mountains (76° 30' South, 70° 45' West), and, most southerly of all, isolated Mount Haag (77° 40' South, 79° West) only eighty-five miles east of Lincoln Ellsworth's Mount Ulmer. Beyond Mount Haag—the visibility allowed Ronne to see to about 81° South—a gradually rising, unbroken plateau was to be seen. Ronne concluded that by all signs now known a Weddell-Ross channel was an impossibility. With a stopover at Mount Austin to refuel the exploratory plane, a return to Stonington Island was made. After having been immobilized for several weeks by bad weather, a second southern flight was made. This time a refueling stop was made at Cape Wheeler, the northern headland of Wright Inlet (seaward from Mount Tricorn) where the sledging party then was. The plane then went on, but, frustrated by heavy cloud, was back two hours later, nothing new seen. The sledgers had gone on toward Gardner Inlet, their southernmost objective, making "fixes." Next day the final southward flight was possible—the objectives to reach Filchner's Moltke Nunatak, Bruce's Coats Land, and, if possible, to go beyond these old landmarks. Gould Bay (named for Laurence Gould), an indentation in the face of the ice shelf caused by land under the ice, was discovered. Moltke Nunatak was not seen because of overcast. It was established, however, that the ice shelf which began at Gardner Bay was continuous to Coats Land and that there was at least one very considerable island under the ice. Ronne reached 78° 30′ South, 42° West. As one traveled south, the elevation of the ice appeared to increase. The mainland to the west Ronne named Edith Ronne Land for his wife. This, it seemed, was the long elusive head of the Weddell Sea, but much work still remained to be done to link it up firmly with the rest of the apparent continent.

On the west coast several flights to obtain trimetrogon photographs were made north and south of Stonington Island, but perhaps the most significant was that down George VI Sound and along the Robert English Coast of the continent in late December 1947. Here Ronne had made a series of "fixes" in 1940. Flying along the Robert English Coast to beyond Ronne Entrance, where the Sound met the Bellingshausen Sea, they passed the Ashley Snow Nunataks (a USASE discovery) and to the south saw Mount Rex (74° 57′ South, 76° 55′ West) and farther west Mount Tuve (74° South, 85° West), approximately on Ellsworth's track but unseen by him. At about the point where these sightings were made, the airplane was landed briefly and a "fix" was made. A course was then set for the Stonington base. They flew toward Alexander I Island, observing a new mountain range, and then varied course to pass over Charcot Island where an opportunity was taken to make a landing, the first in history. Taking to the air again they flew over Alexander I Island, discovering and flying along Tufts Valley. Approaching Marguerite Bay they ran into overcast and were advised from base that foul weather was closing in, so they made for home, at considerable risk but nevertheless safely. Earlier a sledge party of geologists had visited Mount Nicholas (for Czar Nicholas, so named after having been called an island by Charcot and a cape by Rymill) on the east side of Alexander I Island where specimens of sedimentary rocks were obtained.

In early January the planes were dismantled and loaded aboard ship. The ship was, however, still firmly held in the ice and it began to look as though a bad ice season was in prospect and they would not get away, but on February 19 the icebreakers "Edisto" and "Burton Island" of the

Windmill expedition arrived and broke out an escape route to the open sea.

The war had frustrated the Australian intention to set up a meteorological station some place in its sector of continental Antarctica, for use in connection with which Ellsworth's "Wyatt Earp" had been purchased, but the war intensified rather than diminished the government's sense that work in Antarctica was a necessary undertaking and to meteorology, which remained a central concern, it was early persuaded to add a constantly widening range of geophysical and other sciences as well as a commitment to exploration and mapping, chiefly coastal. With Sir Douglas Mawson still the exemplary exponent of Antarctic studies, the question of what should be done was mooted again in government circles in 1946 and early in 1947 the Labor government authorized the Australian National Research Expeditions with a life expectancy of five years. From the beginning ANARE was loosely attached to the Department of External Affairs, with scientific plans in the hands of C.S.I.R., but in January 1949 its status was improved and its continuity better assured when an Antarctic Division of the department was created and Dr. Phillip Law was appointed director. Law was an Australian-born physicist, trained under T. H. Laby at Melbourne, and was a lecturer in physics with a special concern for cosmic ray studies at the time of his appointment. He had graduated into an interest in Antarctica from mountaineering, into which he had been initiated in his high-school days, and had first been in Antarctica in 1947–48. The ANARE was not, however, only the concern of the Antarctic Division for through a Planning Committee established in 1947 with the minister of External Affairs as chairman a wide range of government departments, scientific institutions as well as veteran Antarcticists like Mawson and Captain J. K. Davis had a say in the proceedings. Among the departments concerned in addition to External Affairs were in due time Navy, Army, Air, Interior (meteorology), National Development (mineralogy, mapping), and Primary Industry (ocean resources) and among the institutions were CSIRO and the Academy of Science. Parliament was represented by a member of the Foreign Affairs Committee of the House. The universities were drawn into the planning of the gathering and processing of data, and helped by training and lending personnel. The activity had a political import for once a station was established on the continent with the prospect of permanence it would constitute "settlement." Machinery of government was provided in 1954 when the laws of the Australian Capital Territory were made applicable in the Antarctic Territory and the governor-general was given power to make ordinances. This way of dealing with the situation had been evolved the previous year when government was so provided for Heard Island which had been transferred to Australia by the United Kingdom in 1951. Macquarie Island, of course, was a part of the Commonwealth of long standing, attached to and governed by Tasmania.

While the Australians used Heard and Macquarie islands as weather and scientific stations and stepping stones to the Antarctic mainland, the New Zealanders and the South Africans also moved into the subantarctic islands. After a rather protracted interval, the New Zealanders and South Africans went on to establish themselves on the continent. The New Zealanders had recognized their responsibilities to their subantarctic islands for many years, chiefly from 1860 to 1930 by providing shelters and food caches for mariners who might be cast away on them—a fairly frequent and often highly dramatic occurence while the route of sailing ships from Australia to Cape Horn passed in their vicinity. From Wilkes on, the explorers of Antarctica had called at one or another of the groups when outward or inward bound, but only three of the groups had ever been exploited economically by anybody but sealers: the Aucklands, the Campbells, and the Chathams, and only the Chathams, the sole group which had an indigenous people, the Mariori, had ever had a permanent economy. The Chathams had long been an extension of the wool-growing economy of the main islands of New Zealand. For forty years (1895–1935) sheep had also been run on Campbell Island but abandoned during the depression, the enterprise was not resumed. The Auckland Islands had been transiently occupied by Maoris from the Chathams (after their conquest of the Marioris) and even more transiently by a European settlement promoted by the Enderbys (1850–52) as a base for whaling operations. Thus aside from the Chathams, the New Zealand subantarctic islands had had, after the sealers had finished with them, little utility and when the sailing ships ceased to pass through them, they had mostly reverted to an isolation as effective as any they had ever known. During World War II, however, the suspicion arose that German raiders might be using the harbors and the New Zealanders set up coastwatching and meteorological stations in the Auckland and Campbell groups. At the end of the war the Campbell Island meteorological station was made permanent as an effective contributor of data for weather forecasting on the main islands. South Africans also recognized the influence of Antarctic conditions on their weather. Marion du Fresne had discovered the Prince Edward Islands in 1772 and Cook had rediscovered them five years after, but on learning of the French priority had given Marion's name to the principal island. The group had been visited by Antarctic expeditions from the time of Ross. In 1947 the South Africans, on the initiative of Field Marshal Smuts, then prime minister, took sovereignty over the Prince Edwards and proceeded to set up a permanent weather station on Marion Island.

The Australians began their postwar work in Antarctica in the 1947–48 season. With Group Captain S. A. C. Campbell, an associate of Mawson in prewar expeditions, as executive officer, ANARE began its career by setting up stations at Heard and Macquarie islands. Heard Island, almost equidistant from Australia and South Africa, 900 miles from the western end of the Australian sector of the continent, located at 53° 06′ South, 73° 30′ East, is south of the Antarctic Convergence and truly Antarctic in character, though it supports some grasses. British-discovered in 1833, it was long thereafter in obscurity and a no man's land. In the 1850's its animal resources were freely exploited by American sealers, but the British Colonial Office asserted the right to issue licenses and in 1910 formally reasserted sovereignty by raising the flag although no permanent occupation was attempted. Several expeditions to the continent— e.g., those of Drygalski and Mawson—used Heard as a kind of way station, but nobody had attempted a lengthy stay. The island is volcanic in character, mountainous, and dominated by Big Ben, an American-named peak of 9000 feet. The Australian station, with a complement of fourteen men, was built on a flat, narrow isthums connecting Laurens Peninsula (so named in 1855 after a visiting American sealing vessel) and the main bulk of the island. The Australians maintained their station from December 1947 until the end of 1954 when it was closed in favor of a continental station. In the first instance a weather station, provision was made from time to time for the accumulation of seismographic, magnetic, and cosmic ray data, the great desideratum in these fields being continuous observations over an appreciable period of time. Biological studies of the elephant seals and the bird life were carried out, a geological survey was made, and the island was accurately mapped for the first time, this involving pioneer circuits of the island on land. Macquarie Island, discovered by a sealer out of Sydney in 1810 at 54½° South, 159° East, 900 miles north of the continent is north of the Antarctic Convergence and supports a far lusher vegetation and a more varied animal and bird life than Heard. It has been a "sanctuary" since 1933. Much better known than Heard, it had a more complex history and had been more elaborately studied when the Australians went there in 1948. It had, for example, been the site of a weather station and wireless relay point for Mawson from 1911 to 1915. The ANARE scientific station was established in March 1948 for continuous operation indefinitely, a policy which has been adhered to. The sciences cultivated have been meteorology, geophysics in its various branches, and biology. The meteorological observations at both Heard (while it operated) and Macquarie have been transmitted not only to Australia but also to New Zealand and South Africa.

Although it was the intention to proceed immediately to the establishment of a base on the continent in 1947 this proved impossible. With Group Captain Campbell and senior scientific officer P. G. Law aboard, the old "Wyatt Earp" was taken south early in 1948 to locate a site, but not only did the "Wyatt Earp" prove by mechanical breakdowns and otherwise that it was no longer adequate to Antarctic service—it was renamed and retired to the Australian coastal service—but the trip was made too late in what appeared to be a difficult ice year. Little flying could be done and no exploratory landings could be made. The most useful work accomplished was in meteorology in collaboration with the ships of Highjump, the Japanese whaling fleet, and the ANARE ship at Macquarie Island. The Heard and Macquarie Island stations had been established by using a wartime LST, but it was not to last long and using ordinary merchant ships involved heavy risks in the stormy seas that environed both islands. The Achilles' heel of ANARE proved to be logistics, not national will nor, up to a point, the government's pocketbook, least of all scientific capacity.

It was lack of a suitable ship that kept the Australians from establishing a continental station until 1954 when a Danish-built and owned polar ship became available on charter. This was the "Kista Dan." (Later on the Norwegian "Tottan" was also used.) A plan to build a proper vessel in Australia had to be abandoned because of the great cost. Resort to charter was a necessary but not completely satisfactory solution of the problem. By 1954 the Australians felt more keenly than ever that they were under challenge to make good their claim to their vast sector of the continent. Since the failure in 1948 of the American effort to compose the situation in Antarctica by internationalization, a failure to which the Australians had contributed, they had felt their position insecure, not least because they suspected the designs of the United States. They tended to interpret all expressions of American intent to mount expeditions as preludes to the making of claims. To the repertory of reasons for hanging on to their claim they now added a conception of its utility to the defense of Australia if only in the sense that they should interdict its use by somebody else who might be or turn hostile. After all, even in the old days the Australian naval station had had responsibilities down to the Antarctic Circle. On the other hand they had shown themselves receptive to the exchange of observers with expeditions of other nationalities and in due course were prepared to admit foreign expeditions to work in their sector, this in the interest of the internationalism of science.

They were well prepared for a continental adventure by 1954. Not only had Heard and Macquarie proved excellent training grounds for personnel, but the observers had acquired useful knowledge. On January 4, 1954, the "Kista Dan" sailed from Melbourne for Heard Island en route to the continent. Philip Law was in charge. After a visit to the Kerguelen Islands to pick up French observers, the continent was reached, after great difficulty with ice and wind, on February 11. A station was established at 67° 36' 21" South, 62° 52' 48" East, in Mac-Robertson Land. Although an aerial survey over 250 miles of coast from Scullin Monolith to Stefansson Bay was made in search of a site, that actually occupied had been chosen earlier from a Highjump photograph. Located on a small bay west of the Douglas Islands, discovered by S. A. C. Campbell in 1929, with the Casey, David, and Masson ranges and isolated Mount Henderson, all named by Mawson, just behind, the station was far to the west of the George V Coast where it had earlier been intended to establish it. It was 1500 miles from the South Pole. It was named Mawson. In charge was an old Heard Island hand, R. G. Dovers, who had been with the French to Adélie Land (see below). In January 1957 a second, smaller, station was established at the Vestfold Hills on the Ingrid Christensen Coast (68° 34' 6" South, 77° 58' 6" East), 400 miles east of Mawson. It was named Davis. P. G. Law supervised the establishment. The two continental stations were shortly linked by air. The equipment at Heard Island was transferred to Mawson and the Heard station abandoned. The Macquarie Island station was continued.

Although the scientific equipment at Mawson became much more extensive than anything Rymill had had, the Rymill expedition was still the model for the Australians as showing what could be done on a small scale (as things had come to be measured in Antarctica). By 1957 Mawson was equipped to handle studies in meteorology (to a high degree of sophistication), the aurora, ionospherics, cosmic rays (including two meson telescopes), magnetism, seismology, gravity, and glaciology (including ice-boring to investigate the composition of the snow and ice and seismic depth measurements designed to map the land under the ice). Provision was also made for geological work on new-found features and biological work also. At Macquarie Island meteorology was also highly developed and magnetism, gravity, and ionospheric studies were also pursued, together with geological and biological studies. Davis was primarily a meteorological station but was equipped for auroral studies in close collaboration with Mawson and usually had a geologist in the occupying party. The meteorological work at the stations was supplemented by automatic weather stations at points on the mainland and offshore islands.

Geographical work was initiated almost as soon as Mawson station was established and was vigorously continued in succeeding seasons. It was in connection with this work that the geologists and biologists found their most rewarding employment. The relieving ship was consistently used in coastal surveys (and to do oceanographical work) and in 1956 the Air Force provided two planes not only for use from the ship but from Mawson during the ensuing season. The first surface journeys were made under Dovers' leadership eastward from Mawson along the coast to the Scullin Monolith and westward to Edward VIII Bay (discovered in 1936 by the "William Scoresby"), on which latter journey an emperor penguin rookery (the fifth ever to be found) was discovered near Taylor Glacier, just east of Cape Bruce. Dovers also initiated inland exploration by leading a party which saw and named but did not reach the Prince Charles Mountains 200 miles south of Mawson. The next season, with John Bechervaise as leader, a visit was made to the emperor rookery when a census revealed 5000 birds, the Prince Charles Mountains were reached for the first time, and a visit was made to the Framnes Mountains (in which were the Masson, David, and Casey ranges), a "simultaneous" discovery of Mawson and Norwegian whalers in 1931 and mapped aerially and named by Lars Christensen in 1937. Several peaks were climbed, growths of lichens and mosses were seen, and a multitude of nests of the snowy petrel were observed. On the 1956 relieving visit of the ship, an aerial survey of the Queen Mary Coast of Wilkes Land was made and when established at Mawson the planes took trimetrogon photographs of much of Mac-Robertson, Kemp, and Enderby lands while ground teams (placed in position by air) made the indispensable "fixes" and carried on geological, biological, and magnetic studies. "Fixes" were made at strategic points from Prydz Bay westward around to Amundsen Bay. Work on the study of the Prince Charles Mountains was continued.

One hundred and eight years after its discovery by Dumont d'Urville the French again gave attention to Adélie Land. Their first attempt to establish a station was frustrate. Sponsored by Expéditions Polaire Françaises, a government-supported organization directed by Paul-Emile Victor which up to the time had been active only in Greenland, the "Commandant Charcot," formerly an American net-tender like Ronne's ship, sailed from Brest on November 25, 1948, with a wintering-over party of eleven led by André-Frank Liotard. Calling in at Hobart the

"Charcot" sailed for the Adélie Coast but never got nearer than forty miles of it because of heavy ice. The ship and party then visited the Balleny Islands and charted several of them; a landing was made at Sabrina Islet; meteorological and oceanographical observations were made; but these were gestures, for a retreat had to be made. Via Macquarie Island they returned to Hobart where much of the equipment for the station was stored against a later attempt at establishment while the dogs were sent to the Melbourne zoo. (Some of them were taken over by ANARE and, bred on Heard Island, became the ancestors of the dogs the Australians eventually took to Mawson.)

The "Commandant Charcot" left Hobart for a second attempt to establish a station on December 21, 1949, Liotard again the leader. The coast was successfully reached on January 18, 1950, and two days later a base was established at Port Martin on Cape Margerie (66° 49' South, 141° 24' East) about forty miles from Mawson's old establishment at Commonwealth Bay. In fundamental intent this was a research unit. Provision was made for the study of meteorology, seismology, cosmic rays, hydrography, geology, and biology. However, exploring parties were also provided for and equipped with dogs and sledges and weasels but not an airplane. The chief objective of the exploring parties, aside from the finding and describing of geographical features, was to make "fixes" which would enable use to be made for mapping of the Highjump photographs the Americans had supplied. All told, eleven important "fixes" were made the first season. The western boundary of Adélie Land was reached. An emperor penguin rookery was found forty miles west of the base at the southern end of Géologie Archipelago, off Cape Géodésie, the fourth such rookery ever discovered. In January 1951 a party of fourteen led by Michel Barré relieved Liotard and his group. An Australian observer, R. G. Dovers, accompanied the Barré group. Auroral studies were added to the scientific repertory. The "Commandant Charcot" reconnoitered along the coast, established a depot at the Géologie Archipelago, and made scientific observations east to Cape Denison, Commonwealth Bay. A surface journey to the South Magnetic Pole failed when the weasels broke down, but a trip south for 200 miles allowed a successful beginning in seismic soundings of ice depths. A dog-sledge journey was made west to Cape Pépin, one of Dumont d'Urville's identifications. The next season the Norwegian sealer "Tottan" was employed to relieve the Port Martin station and take in a special party, led by Mario Marrett, to establish itself at the Géologie Archipelago for a close study of the emperor penguins during the breeding season. The "Tottan" sailed from Melbourne (where the French found the Australians at least as odd as the mysterious English), the Frenchmen reaching Melbourne

by various routes, one party via Indo-China. After stopping at Port
Martin and then going on to debark Marrett and his fellows at the
Archipelago, the "Tottan" returned to Port Martin for the change-over
of personnel to find that the station had suffered a devastating fire (January 23, 1952). The station was evacuated and the "Tottan" visited the
penguin party prepared to take it off too, but not only did all the members choose to stay but they were joined by three of the Port Martin
party, including the Australian Dovers. The penguinists made a very
notable contribution to penguinology (or ornithology or biology) and
moreover by "raiding" the ruins of Port Martin for supplies and weasels
made a successful journey west and Rock X (136° 42′ East), hitherto
only a cross on a Highjump photograph, was located. The party was
finally taken off by the "Tottan" in January 1953.

Meanwhile in 1949 a scientific station had been set up at Port-aux-
Française on the principal island of the Kerguelens where, beginning with
meteorolgy and radio science, research in the full range of the geophysical
sciences, oceanography, biology, and botany was developed. The following year work was begun at Camp Heurtin on New Amsterdam Island
to the north—and enjoying a milder but still unpleasant climate—where
a radio-meteorological station was established and biological studies were
undertaken and, emphasizing that this was not Antarctica, though related
to it, a cattle-raising station and a horticultural center were set up.

On August 6, 1955, as a phase of the recurring tidying up of the
shrinking empire, the French subantarctic and Antarctic possessions were
taken out of the hands of the governor of Madagascar (shortly to become the independent Malagassy Republic) and given administrative and
financial autonomy with a seat of government for its high commissioner
at Paris. The high commissioner had a consultative council. Finance
came from metropolitan France.

From February 1950 to January 1952 a joint Norwegian-British-
Swedish expedition was active at a station called Maudheim at 71° 03′
South, 10° 55′ West, built on a stable place on the ice shelf about forty
miles beyond Cape Norvegia, Princess Martha Coast, Queen Maud Land.
This station pioneered surface work in this part of the continent. The
coast had first been seen by Riiser-Larsen on a flight from the ship
"Norvegia" in 1930, and the Nazi expedition under Ritscher had made
its air survey hereabouts in 1939. Norwegian whalers had worked the
offshore waters since the early 1930's.

The idea of an expedition to this area had first been suggested by
Professor Hans Ahlmann, professor of geography at Stockholm early in
the war years. He had been studying some of the photographs taken by

Ritscher's flyers, with particular attention to those of mountains and glaciers. Ahlmann was a world-famous glaciologist who had mostly worked in Greenland. It occurred to him that his understanding of ice would be improved if he had data from Antarctica. He therefore proposed a joint expedition to the Norwegians and the British, but in the end it was the Norwegians who took the essential initiative, though Ahlmann was the active promoter as long as the war lasted. The oceanographer, Dr. H. U. Sverdrup, an experienced Arctic hand, returned to Norway from the United States in 1948 to take charge of the Norwegian Polar Institute and shortly he persuaded the Norwegian Parliament to allot money for actual preparations for Ahlmann's proposed expedition. The Swedes and the British were to be active collaborators and the undertaking was to be governed by an international committee consisting of Sverdrup, Ahlmann, and (for Britain) J. M. Wordie. Expert advisers were chosen by each national committee—the British committee drew on the membership of the Royal Geographical Society and the Scott Polar Research Institute—and the expedition members were specialists and helpers recruited by the national committees. A wintering-over party of fifteen was assembled, nine of whom were scientists. The majority of the group had polar experience either in the Arctic or Antarctic. The British members, of whom two were Australians and one a Canadian, had either FIDS or ANARE experience. The Swedes had charge of the glaciological and physiological studies, the British of the geological, the Norwegians of the meteorological and topographical as well as the logistics of the operation. The British provided air assistance in establishing the station and making a preliminary reconnaissance; the Swedes later sent out a two-plane air photography team. The FIDS provided half of the dogs; the Norwegians obtained the rest from Greenland. Weasels were the mechanical transport. The leader of Maudheim was Captain John Giaever of the Norwegian Polar Institute who had had considerable experience in the Arctic. Giaever used Mawson's *Home of the Blizzard* as his guide with additions from Amundsen, Scott, Shackleton, Byrd, and Nordenskjold.

Each national group contributed to the supplies, and the ship, provided by the Norwegians, was an ocean-going icebreaker constructed by the Germans in Norway during the war and reconstructed in a German yard for Antarctic service. It was named the "Norsel." Loaded in Sweden, Norway, and England in turn, the "Norsel" traveled to Capetown where it was joined by observers for Australia (P. G. Law) and South Africa (J. A. King) who were to return to Capetown in the ship after the station had been established. The approach to the Princess Martha Coast was made via Bouvet Island, the South Sandwich Islands, and the Weddell Sea. In the Weddell Sea a rendezvous was kept with the Norwegian factory ship "Thorshøvdi" which had brought out the expedition's three weasels, its two-ton ice-boring machine (obtained in Canada), and its forty-seven dogs. These were now transferred to the "Norsel" along with twenty tons of whale meat in eleven-pound packages for the dogs. From then on the "Norsel" was on its own. Maudheim was established about two miles from the seaward edge of the ice shelf.

The emphasis of the work of the expedition both at the station and in the field was on science. At Maudheim in addition to the meteorological work and the operations of the glaciologists with the ice-borer (by which a maximum depth of 330 feet was reached, determining that the compacted snow, or névé, turned to ice at 200 feet), work was done in aurora observations, magnetism, and the physiology of man under polar conditions. Very little new was uncovered by exploration on the scientific field trips though since the Ritscher flyers had had no ground "fixes," errors in the interpretation of the photographs were detected and corrected, both as to the exact location of features and their true character (height, extent, etc.). (Nevertheless, the photographic work was judged excellent.) The field workers established an advanced base at an elevation of 5000 feet in the interior 185 miles from Maudheim at 72° 16′ South, 3° 49′ West. The mountains and nunataks examined by the geologists were chiefly in the Regula Range south of the Boreas and Passat Nunataks at the edge of the ice shelf and including the great Penck Trough, to the Neumayer Escarpment, beyond which was the interior plateau, together with a few of the features of the Mühig-Hofmann Mountains behind the Princess Astrid Coast just beyond, the features straddling 0° longitude. This was working away from, rather than toward, the parties reaching southward along the Weddell Sea coast, like Ronne's. Like the mountains on the opposite and so much better known coast, these mountains lay between the coastal ice and the interior plateau. Here the geologists did almost all their work; they were in doing so dealing with the first "land" ever touched by man in Queen Maud Land. They found lichens, moss, and arachnids (mites), the vegetable and animal life of Antarctica, on Passat Nunatak. In their field work the glaciologists were concerned with measuring the accretion of snow, the movement of the ice, and, by the use of seismic shots, determining the depth of the ice and the profile of the underlying land. They pursued their seismic work as far south as 74° 20′ South, beyond the Neumayer Escarpment on to the interior plateau. This was the most extensive and illuminating seismic program since Byrd's people had first used the technique in 1934 and the effective beginning of the protracted task of determining Antarctica's under-ice profile. The topographers, working in the field with both the geologists and the glaciologists, triangulated 23,000 square miles of territory. By air about 15,000 square miles additional were surveyed. All in all, the expedition was a great scientific success. In character it foreshadowed the IGY expeditions.

Antarctic whaling revived after World War II in an economic environment of an acute world shortage of fats and therefore of active demand and a high price (about ten times prewar) for whale oil. There was great uncertainty about the probable future contributions to the world's stock of fats from such alternative and, for whale oil, competitive sources as soybeans, peanuts, cotton-seed, corn, copra, animal fats, etc. In this environment the future of whaling looked good. Whale oil appeared likely to be in strong and continuing demand for the making of margarine, artificial lard, soap, and specialized lubricants, not to mention such of its byproducts as could be used for animal and fowl feed and as a source of a rapidly widening range of pharmaceuticals and cosmetics, not to forget whale meat for human consumption. The position of whale oil in the fats spectrum would, of course, change as other sources of supply were revitalized and extended, but nothing seemed really to menace its position except possibly the decline of the stock of whales. (However, the price of whale oil began to decline in the early 1950's.) The questions at the end of the war were: who was going to get the whale oil and under what conditions?

Even before the war was over it was apparent that postwar whaling was going to be a controlled industry, that the pattern of control evolved under pressure in the 1930's was going to be extended to the future. At the conference on whaling in London in 1944, when only the United States, the United Kingdom, Norway, New Zealand, Australia, Canada, and South Africa were represented, the delegates, while fully aware of the fats situation, nevertheless warned against any ill-considered or panic relaxation of the controls worked out in 1937 and 1938. In fact, they fixed a quota for maximum seasonal killings that was but two-thirds of the prewar seasonal average. Defining the quota for Antarctic pelagic whaling as 16,000 Blue Whale Units (that is, 1 blue whale equals 2 fins, $2\frac{1}{2}$ humpbacks or 6 sei), they clearly indicated that no reversion to unrestricted whale killing was to be tolerated, emergency or no emergency. The next year with more nations represented—Denmark, France, Mexico, The Netherlands, and Newfoundland—the same line was taken and the only relaxation was a liberal interpretation of the rule about the length of the ensuing Antarctic pelagic season. And in 1946 at Washington when a permanent machinery for governing whaling was worked out, it was clear that what was sought was to put the industry on a "continuous yield" basis, an impossibility without close control over the use of the whale stocks. Argentina, Australia, Brazil, Canada, Chile, Denmark, France, The Netherlands, New Zealand, Norway, Peru, U.S.S.R., the United Kingdom, and the United States (not all likely to be involved in *Antarctic* whaling) took part. Out of the discussions came an International Convention for the Regulation of Whaling of global coverage, of which the executive body was to be an International Whaling Commission with its headquarters in London. The Convention included the principles embodied in the agreements of 1937, 1938, and 1944, including the over-all BWU limitation on Antarctic killings. For administrative purposes Antarctica was defined as beginning at 40° South. The Commission's task was to control the industry to achieve the "intelligent *optimum* use of resources" but also to conserve whale stocks. It was given authority over such matters as the duration of the Antarctic pelagic season, the length and condition of whales legally to be taken, the definition and governance of the whale "reserve" (in effect the Bellingshausen and Amundsen Seas), the matter of which species could be killed and when, and so on. The Commission was to have the assistance of a statistical service, vital to control, to be provided by the Norwegians, and a biological research service, equally indispensable to control, to be provided by several of the associated governments. As it turned out, the scientists and statisticians came to have more influence in the whaling industry than in any other world-wide economic activity. The Commission was to exercise control both from headquarters and through an inspectorate. Each Antarctic factory ship was to carry two inspectors of different nationalities, one a biologist. The Commission began its work in 1948. Fundamental decisions came to be taken in the annual conferences that began in 1949. This was not international government but government based on agreement among states that retained disciplinary powers over their citizens, and, in the end, final initiative as to whether or not the Commission's rules were to be observed.

The Norwegians, as noted earlier, were the first to resume pelagic whaling in Antarctica after the war. The British were the first to join them. In the 1945–46 season the Norwegians sent out six factory ships, the British three. These included the three German ships that had survived the war and had been taken as reparations; the British got two (one of which they had sold the Germans in 1938), the Norwegians one—the worst damaged one as it happened. By the 1946–47 season the postwar pattern of national participation began to be clear. There were seven Norwegian factories in the field, four United Kingdom, two Japanese, one The Netherlands, and one U.S.S.R. Though other nations, for example, the Union of South Africa and Panama, were later to send out factories, the five nations just mentioned became the consistent participants in Antarctic pelagic whaling. In addition three shore factories were operated on South Georgia, one by the British, one by the Norwegians, and one by the Argentines. While more factory ships were built, and more catchers, the total fleet never reached prewar size in either respect. But the new ships were larger than their predecessors and more efficient qua factories in their utilization of the whales, this involving close control of oil and by-product production by trained chemists and skilled technicians. The navigational equipment also became more elaborate: radar became standard as an iceberg detector. The catchers were given greater engine power to increase their speed. There was, in short, intense technological competition and, as earlier, advanced technological standards became required to support the interests of the conservationists. The return of the Japanese to Antarctic whaling occasioned opposition, especially from the Australians off whose sector the Japanese customarily worked, but the occupation authorities overrode it on the ground that it was required to bolster the Japanese economy. By the late 1950's the Japanese were the leading producers of the industry. The Russians, prewar only in Arctic whaling, came into the Antarctic with one of the old German factory ships, transferred to them by the British on reparations account, and named the "Slava" (of Odessa). They early took an interest in research, carrying scientists on their factory ship to study meteorology, oceanography, and hydrology and took a special interest in the distribution of plankton, the food of the favorite food of the whales (*krill*), as an index to the probable whereabouts of the whales. In terms of personnel employed in the industry, the Norwegians retained paramountcy. They even sailed with the Russians for a few seasons. The Antarctic pelagic industry came to constitute about 70 per cent of the world whaling industry and to produce about four-fifths of the world's oil, less dominant than prewar, but still paramount.

Under the close regulation of the Whaling Commission with its BWU ceiling on the season's catch, the tendency was, as efficiency in capture improved, for the season to shorten. It was fixed to open later, useful in that this allowed the whales to feed and become fatter and richer in oil than they were on arrival from tropical parts, and to close earlier because the annual quota had been taken, a point determined by the Norwegian statisticians in regular touch with factory ships by wireless. Over the years the trend of the BWU limitation was downward and by the late 1950's it was 14,500. The proportion of fins in the catch tended to rise; they became the primary quarry of the industry. Blue whales became scarce and it was directed that none be killed before February 1 in any season. No right whales, the classic whale of the elder days in both the northern and southern hemispheres, could be taken and from 1938 to 1949 no humpbacks could be taken in Antarctica so that stocks might be replenished. The ban was lifted, with a top limit for killings, in 1949, but shortly killing of humpbacks was limited to four days each season. Only sperm whales could be killed outside the quota in Antarctica, but there were few of them and all of them males, for the sperms lived mostly in tropical waters. But with all the attention to conservation the possibility of "over-fishing" was constantly on the minds of the experts, notably the biologists. Little was known about the dynamics (or replacement power) of the whale populations and while the fins, as chief victims, seemed to bear the numerous killings they suffered in a satisfactory way, it was not certain that even they were not experiencing an erosion of total numbers because killings were exceeding replacements. The possibility that the largest of surviving mammals might end its terrestrial career in our time was canvassed by pessimists, but closer to probabilities was that the requirements of conservation would reduce allowable killings to such a low level that the industry would become uneconomic to competitive participants. A crisis in the industry in the late 1950's indicated the drift. Since the over-all quota for whales in Antarctic pelagic fishing was not shared out among the nations in any agreed fashion, the struggle for whales became very fierce, this not only increasing the cost of getting a whale but causing the competitors in their anxiety to get what they thought a proper share to burst through the ceiling on total killings and so increase the ever-present danger that whale stocks would be fatally reduced and the industry destroyed by exhaustion of resources. This led some of the nations to revert to the practice of the 1930's and impose a quota of killings on their own nationals. This, of course, did not solve the problem. So the Norwegians and the Dutch took the lead in advocating the negotiation of quotas within the over-all quota under the auspices of the Whaling Commission. Such an agreement was first reached in 1961 for the 1962–63 season when the percentage allowances (revelatory of the status of the nations in the industry) were Japan 33, Norway 32, U.S.S.R. 20, United Kingdom 9, The Netherlands 6. In 1962 an agreement on this basis was made which was to be in effect for four seasons. But whether the future of Antarctic pelagic whaling was thus made secure was problematical. Would the stocks of economic whales hold out much longer?

A by-blow of the postwar story of whaling was the Australian experience. The idea that the economic potential of Antarctica was the important thing about the place was a cardinal belief of many, but not all, Australians for many years. The clearest proof that the potential was considerable was the whaling industry. For years Australian Antarcticists had advised the capitalists to get into whaling and bring to Australia its proper share of the profits of the pelagic industry. There was something in this but the Australian capitalists had never felt moved, or able, to find the necessary money to invest in the required equipment. When the argument was revived after the war, the possibility was canvassed that a factory ship might be extracted from the Japanese by way of reparations (as the United Kingdom had come by German factories). This never proved possible and to have such a ship built would cost nearly two million pounds which neither private investors nor the government was prepared to put up. Instead in 1949 the federal Labor government, as one of its last significant acts, created an Australian Whaling Commission, an operating body eventually capitalized at £1,375,000, to demonstrate if possible the profitability (more than the feasibility) of a domestic shore-based whaling in the hope of stimulating a moribund traditional industry. In the twentieth century Australian shore-based whaling had had a very checkered history and by 1929 had faded out altogether. It was known that humpbacks traveled inshore from Antarctica for patruition and mating along the Indian and Pacific ocean coasts of Australia and that while the taking of humpbacks was prohibited in Antarctica it was not in Australian waters. The Whaling Commission set up a factory on Babbage Island, near the town of Carnarvon on the Western Australia coast. It put two catchers into service. Norwegians were employed as advisers and instructors. Almost simultaneously a private company, the Nor' West Whaling Company, also entered the industry on the same coast, basing at Point Cloates. The Commission's venture was a huge success, financially and otherwise, but in 1956, after six years of profitable operation, the venture was sold by the Menzies government in accord with its "antisocialist" policy of not keeping in government ownership and operation commodity-producing enterprises. At a financially advantageous price, the Babbage Island factory was sold to the Nor' West Whaling Company which thereupon ceased operation at Point Cloates. By that time other private ventures were in operation at Albany in Western Australia, Byron Bay in New South Wales, and Moreton Island in Queensland, the latter two on the Pacific coast. While the profitability of shore-based whaling had been demonstrated, the Australians were still not in Antarctic pelagic whaling. It was unlikely that they ever would be.

Between 1950 and 1960 there was a striking shift of emphasis in the general attitude toward Antarctica, the import of which was to take the stress off the politics of claims and place it on scientific studies, exploration, and mapping. An important effect of this was to encourage an internationalist as opposed to a narrowly nationalist approach to the region, an attitude which was given formal expression in a treaty in 1959. The effective turntable was the International Geophysical Year (July 1, 1957 to December 31, 1958).

During the Year geophysical studies occupied workers in far more countries than had any interest in Antarctica, but Antarctica was nevertheless a region of major concern. The objective was world-wide coverage, but, as comparatively little had been done in many of the sciences in Antarctica, work in them there was regarded as of the first importance. Even after over a hundred years of scientific endeavor, there was still a very wide gap between what was known and what it was considered indispensable to know about Antarctica. It was rated along with outer space as a geophysical province in which concerted effort could very likely achieve exceptionally significant results. It had, of course, been recognized for years that a variety of data from Antarctica were indispensable to a fuller understanding of global phenomena. The IGY provided an opportunity to have relevant data accumulated by the most advanced means. To the geophysicists Antarctica appeared to be

a region of almost unparallel interest to the fields of geophysics and geography alike. In geophysics Antarctica has many unexplored aspects; for example, the influence of this huge ice mass on global weather; the influence of the ice mass on atmospheric and oceanographic dynamics; the nature and extent of the aurora australia, for, although the aurora borealis has received considerable attention in recent years, the detailed characteristics of Antarctic aurora remain largely unknown; the possibility of conducting original ionospheric experiments northward from the South Polar Plateau during the long total-night season to determine the physical characteristics of the ionosphere during prolonged absence of sunlight. These and similar scientific considerations lead the CSAGI to recognize that Antarctica represents a most signficant portion of the earth for intensive study during the International Geophysical Year.

The International Geophysical Year originated out of an evening of sociability and shoptalk between some American geophysicists and Professor Sydney Chapman of England, regarded by many as the greatest geophysicist of the age, at the home of James A. Van Allen in Silver Spring, Maryland, on April 5, 1950. At that gathering Lloyd Berkner, who had been in Antarctica as a radio engineer with Byrd I, stimulated by the talk about what was known and what was unknown and the new means of changing the latter into the former, including rockets, suggested that the time was ripe for another "polar year," as the ventures in international co-operation in geophysical research had hitherto been called. The first of these had been held in 1882–83 at the instance of Karl

Weyprecht (1838–81), a German Arctic explorer in the Austrian service, and had involved the Antarctic only to the extent of a French station at Cape Horn and a German station at South Georgia. The second "polar year" was suggested in 1927 by Johannes Georgi, a German meteorologist and Arctic hand, and carried out in 1932–33. It suffered badly from the Great Depression. Antarctica figured in it only peripherally, although at one stage Professor Harald U. Sverdrup had said that the Norwegian whalers were willing to take out scientists and bring them home at the end of the whaling season. Many of the data collected were subsequently lost. However, American, German, Russian, and British scientists worked up some of them into published papers. The impact was principally on radio communications. Berkner had worked on a project in Washington during this Year. Now he was suggesting a new and more ambitious "polar year," this time but twenty-five years after its predecessor. An argument for holding it in 1957–58 was that this would be a period of maximum sunspot activity and the inter-relations of the earth and the sun were central to geophysics.

Professor Chapman joined with Berkner in submitting the idea to the International Joint Commission on the Ionosphere, the link between radio science, geodesy, geophysics, and astronomy. It was accepted by this body and passed on to the International Council of Scientific Unions which also accepted it. In 1952 the ICSU appointed a special committee to organize and administer the Year which was to become known as the CSAGI, Comité Spécial de l'Année Géophysique Internationale. Chapman became president, Berkner vice-president. The work program was given final form in a series of international conferences. The scientific branches involved became meteorology, geomagnetism, aurora and airglow, ionosphere, solar activity, cosmic rays, longitudes and latitudes, glaciology, oceanography, seismology, gravity measurements, and nuclear radiation. None of these was irrelevant to Antarctica, all were incomplete on a global view if data from Antarctica were missing.

The outcome was that eleven nations operated stations in Antarctica during the IGY: Argentina (8), Australia (2), Belgium (1), Chile (4), France (2), Japan (1), New Zealand (1, plus another jointly with the United States), Norway (1), the United Kingdom (14), the United States (8, including the one operated jointly with New Zealand), and the U.S.S.R. (6). Of these nations Argentina, Australia, Chile, and the United Kingdom had had stations continuously in operation for a few to several years before the IGY was thought of. Argentina, Australia, and the United Kingdom added stations to their existing lists, while Chile increased the number of scientists at its four stations. France and the United States resumed their Antarctic work after brief absences; Belgium and Japan after rather extended absences; Norway took the occasion to set up its first independent station; and New Zealand and the U.S.S.R. entered upon research on the "continent" for the first time. In terms of manpower and lavishness of expenditure on logistics and scientific research, the United States and the U.S.S.R. led the field and the United States established itself as the premier investor in Antarctica by a substantial margin.

Argentina, Australia, Chile, France, New Zealand, Norway, and the United Kingdom placed their IGY stations within the portions of Antarctica they claimed. Belgium and Japan set up stations within the Norwegian claim, the U.S.S.R. operated within the Australian claim, while the United States placed its stations in the New Zealand, Australian, and United Kingdom-Argentine claims, as well as in its area of "special interest," unclaimed Marie Byrd Land, and at the South Pole, the point where all claims met and therefore where the United States was an intruder on all claims. Not unexpectedly the Argentines at first challenged the United Kingdom's right to locate stations where it did and the Australians were uneasy hosts to the Russians, but in general the position was established that the internationalism of science should override the possessiveness of nationalism. However, there was no immediate abatement of the firmness with which claims and rights were, in the diplomatic phrase, "reserved."

In most of the countries there was an established machinery for dealing with the obligations assumed in Antarctica, linked to or an integral part of the machinery of government, and if not directly related to Antarctica (like the Australian, the Chilean, the Argentine, and the British), then to polar activities (like the Norwegian, the Russian, and the French), and, or also, to scientific research. In any case governments necessarily assumed primary responsibility for finance. The IGY activities in Antarctica clearly illustrated that the era of privately financed and led expeditions was over and that publicly financed and directed enterprises had replaced them. This insured that considerations of intergovernmental competition and national prestige were injected into the situation. As the IGY proceeded, however, the strictly political notes modulated a great deal and national competition and prestige came more and more to be expressed in technological and scientific terms. Even in these realms, international co-operation and collaboration tempered the possible asperities.

The Americans, however, not having succeeded in establishing a policy of continuous activity in Antarctica in spite of a great deal of talk about the principle, had to improvise organization to control what proved to be their biggest effort yet. They had been planning to resume work in Antarctica when the IGY proposals began to be discussed. Admiral Byrd was still the leader in Antarctic affairs and the administrative head of what governmental organization there was. That organization, from 1955 known as the United States Antarctic Programs, was, in the early 1950's, in a weak position as far as actually putting an expedition in the field was concerned. For political and financial reasons—that is, "economy"—a Highjump II, scheduled for 1949–50 had been canceled after preparations had been carried to an advanced stage. The most immediate spur to activity was the State Department's interest in the matter of claims. The failure of the department's internationalization proposal of 1948 and the obvious strength of the opposing nationalism caused it to encourage the assembling of the widely dispersed evidence possibly supporting American claims that had accumulated over the years. This led logically to an interest in a possible program of further exploration and mapping to give additional support to American claims. In 1949, also, the Department of State had asked the National Academy of Sciences to have a scientific program prepared; this was done under the chairmanship of Dr. Isaiah Bowman. Byrd, his close associate Siple, and other interested persons within the government were, at this time, mostly thinking in terms of exploration and mapping when the IGY program, wholly scientific in emphasis, began to be discussed. Siple (but not Byrd) was directly involved in the IGY scientific discussions. The over-all United States IGY program was in the hands of a committee of the National Academy of Sciences-National Research Council called the United States National Committee for the IGY, Professor Joseph Kaplan of the University of California chairman. A special committee on Antarctica, called the USNC Antarctica Committee, functioned under Kaplan's committee. Siple was a member of both these committees. Specifically to deal with the scientific work in Antarctica there was established a USNC Antarctic Program Direction. Dr. Laurence M. Gould, president of Carleton College, who had been in Antarctica with Byrd I, was chairman of both the committees dealing with Antarctica. These committees linked the government scientists—no fewer than fourteen federal departments and agencies had specific Antarctic interests—the university scientists, and the scientists in private research institutions who were concerned with geophysical problems. As the scientific program of the IGY for Antarctica developed, interest in exploration and mapping for a political purpose tended to diminish—it disappeared from official instructions after Deepfreeze I in the 1955–56 season—and in the end the special appropriation for the purpose was eliminated to effect a minor economy. Exploration, however, continued to be an incidental activity of the logistics people and of the scientists in connection with their "traverses." The strictly political approach survived in the minds of the old Antarctic hands like Byrd and Siple, certain senators, and some publicists.

As the number of bases it was proposed to establish and the number of persons needed to build, operate, and maintain them and carry out scientific research at them increased, the importance and magnitude of the logistics of the program increased. In the end logistics often appeared to dominate the picture even though in actuality its fundamental rationale, however spectacular and brilliant it was in execution, was to place the scientists in positions to do their work. To deal with the logistical problems, the Department of Defense was consulted. The Department assigned primary responsibility to the Navy and the Navy established the United States Naval Support Force Antarctica in August 1954. This was, in a way, a fruit of Highjump. On Byrd's nomination, Rear Admiral George F. Dufek was appointed commander of Naval Support.

With the initiative with regard to both science and logistics effectively out of his hands, Byrd's position as leader in Antarctic affairs and head of Antarctic Programs began to be eroded, though his personal prestige could not be impaired. Byrd last visited Antarctica in the season of 1955–56 when he participated in the dedication ceremonies at Little America V and flew over the Pole for the third and last time. On March 11, 1957, he died. Rear Admiral Dufek took charge of Antarctic Programs (redesignated Projects) in August. In April 1959 Dufek was succeeded by Rear Admiral David M. Tyree.

All the Antarctic stations especially set up for the IGY were established on the main "continent"—that it was a continent was still a matter of debate—where Argentina already had one on the Filchner Ice Shelf and Australia one in Mac-Robertson Land. The numerous stations established earlier on the Palmer-Graham Peninsula and in its vicinity amply—even over—covered that part of the continent. The only stations added in subantarctica were those of South Africa on Tristan da Cunha and Gough islands. After the IGY was concluded, South Africa in the 1959–60 season borrowed the use of the Norwegian station and thus became the twelfth nation to work on the continent.

The Americans began their investigation of possible sites early in the 1954–55 season when the icebreaker "Atka" visited the Ross Ice Shelf, approaching by way of New Zealand, and ascertained that the Bay of Whales had been destroyed by ice movement and that the old Little Americas nearby had either floated away on icebergs or been rendered unusable. After failing to get beyond Sulzberger Bay to the east—the objective was Mount Siple—the "Atka" crew decided that Kainan Bay (named by the Japanese in 1912) was a suitable port of entry for a base on the shelf and then went around the Palmer-Graham Peninsula en route to the Queen Maud coast. They examined the coast for some distance either side of Cape Norvegia. Several useful points of accessibility were found, but in the end the United States did not establish a base in this vicinity.

Actual base building got underway in the 1955–56 season when Operation Deepfreeze I, led by Dufek, was carried out and during Deepfreeze II the following season the task was carried to completion. Hitherto Antarctic stations had always been located at points on the coast or on nearby islands, but now it was proposed to build bases in the interior, established and serviced from a coastal base. It was reasoned that until data were cumulated in the Antarctic interior over an extended period of time it would be impossible to understand Antarctica and on a global basis data would be incomplete. Many of the data already accumulated at coastal points supported the expectation that full understanding could be achieved only if data were gathered in the interior. Trail parties on the move could neither carry about the most important equipment it was now proposed to use nor establish themselves for continuous observations for any significant length of time. On their own the Americans had determined upon establishing a station in the interior of Marie Byrd Land and they had been solicited to establish a station at the South Pole, logistically the most difficult proposition of all. Although reluctant to commit themselves, they were jockeyed into undertaking it by the exigencies of competition with the Russians, while the Russians undertook to place stations at the comparably difficult points of the South Magnetic Pole and the Pole of Inaccessibility (the point in the interior equidistant from the ocean in all directions, hitherto unseen). The principal American coastal staging point, serviced both by sea and air, was established at McMurdo Sound, a location fixed upon after consultations about local geography with Frank Debenham of the Scott Polar Institute.

Although scientific work was developed at McMurdo after IGY, in genesis it was in emphasis logistical. During the Deepfreeze I an airfield was built on the ice and for the first time planes were flown into Antarctica from New Zealand (2400 air miles), a pioneering achievement of the first order, significant as greatly facilitating entry into Antarctica and confirming New Zealand's position as a principal waystation to Antarctica for the Americans. Christchurch now became the base for American Antarctic operations in New Zealand. Planes were brought out from the United States via Hawaii, Canton Island, and Fiji. (Late in 1958 New Zealand-American relations with regard to the Christchurch base and Antarctic logistics were formalized by an exchange of diplomatic "letters.") During Deepfreeze I also a Little America V was built on the Ross Ice Shelf near Kainan Bay, a dual-purpose station to serve as a scientific center and a coastal base from which to establish the station in the interior of Marie Byrd Land. A route to the proposed inland station was prospected over the ice. During Deepfreeze II the Marie Byrd Land station, wholly scientific in purpose, was established over the ice at 80° South, 120° West, 646 miles from Little America V, using heavy tractors. Little America V was host to an international weather analysis station which released synoptic reports on Antarctic weather patterns. After IGY the center was transferred to Melbourne, Australia. During Deepfreeze II also the South Pole station, wholly scientific, was established by air from McMurdo. It was named Amundsen-Scott. Because of the difficulties involved in landing and taking off at the Pole, the station was provided with most of its construction material and much of its equipment by airdrop. Only personnel and the most delicate equipment were landed by plane at the Pole. To facilitate the operation, which was enormously difficult, a subsidiary air station was established near the foot of Liv Glacier and another in collaboration with the New Zealanders at Cape Hallett (one of Ross's discoveries in 1841) on the Victoria Land Coast, eighty miles south of Cape Adare, partly as a protective station on the air route from and to New Zealand but also as a jointly operated scientific station. A station wholly scientific in purpose, named for Charles Wilkes, was placed in the Australian sector 2400 miles west of McMurdo on one of the Windmill Islands in Vincennes Bay on the Budd Coast. After IGY it was given to the Australians. And a scientific station named for Ellsworth was built on the Weddell Sea Coast on the Filchner Ice Shelf, largely on the initiative of Finn Ronne who was appointed leader —he had a strong personal interest in the area it served, partly to quiet the Argentine suspicion of two British neighbors. Ellsworth station was only thirty miles from the Argentine Filchner Shelf station and fifty miles from the nearest British station. After IGY it was turned over to the Argentines.

The Russians were equally as determined as the Americans to set up stations in the interior. They began their base building in 1956 by establishing a coastal station at the Haswell Islands in the Davis Sea (66° 33′ South, 93° East) on February 13, a location the Australians had once thought of using for Mawson. Originally the Russians had intended to approach the continent by using an Australian port as a way station, but in the end they achieved their objective direct from Soviet Russia by using two vessels especially equipped for research in polar seas, the "Ob" and the "Lena." The vessels were supplied by the North Sea Route Administration of the Merchant Marine Ministry, while Antarctic scientific work was the responsibility of the Academy of Sciences. The initial coastal base was named Mirnyi after one of Bellingshausen's ships. A much smaller, subsidiary, coastal base, wholly scientific in purpose, was also set up at the Bunger Hills to the east. From Mirnyi it was proposed to achieve the objectives in the interior by stages, setting up bases (and using mobile bases) on the way. The first of the interior bases was Pionerskaya at 69° 44′ South, 95° 30′ East, and when a second expedition arrived from the Soviet Union at the end of 1956, a second interior station named Vostok (after Bellingshausen's other ship) was set up in March 1957 beyond Pionerskaya and in November a station called Komsomolskaya was established at 74° 5′ South, 97° 29′ East, beyond Vostok. This leapfrogging was continued until the interior objectives were reached and involved the Russians in a good deal of pioneer traveling which was in the nature of exploration. The station at the Pole of Inaccessibility, named Sovietskaya, was established on February 16, 1958.

When the French resumed their work in Terre Adélie in 1956 they set up a new principal base on Petrels Island in the Géologie Archipelago off Cape Géodésie at the penguin rookery, and named it for Dumont d'Urville. The next year a much smaller base 165 miles inland was set up and named for Charcot. The Australians, the Norwegians, the Japanese, the Belgians, and the New Zealanders, however, confined themselves to coastal stations, though they made excursions into the interior, both on the surface and in the air. Of the two Australian stations, only Davis was established especially for IGY and it would probably have been established in due course in any event. The Norwegian station (later, as noted, taken over by the South Africans) was established on the Princess Martha Coast at 70° 30′ South, 2° 32′ West. Fourteen men, led by a staff member of the Norwegian Polar Institute, constituted the party. An eleven-man Japanese party, led by Professor Takesi Ngata, established itself on Ongul Island off the Prince Harald Coast in Lützow-Holm Bay in a station called Showa. Because of bad ice conditions in this vicinity it was maintained with difficulty, but the Japanese persisted. The Belgians, led by a son of De Gerlache of the "Belgica," located their station between the Norwegian and Japanese locations on the ice at Breid Bay on Princess Ragnhild Coast (70° 26′ South, 24° 18′ 6″ East) and named it for King Baudouin. The New Zealanders, early in 1957, in addition to helping staff Hallett, established a dual purpose base of their own (with logistical assistance from the Americans) at Pram Point, Scott Island, near the American installations at McMurdo. On the one hand it was the station for New Zealand's IGY scientific studies in Antarctica, on the other it was the point of assembly and departure for a depot-laying, route-prospecting expedition from the Ross Sea toward the South Pole in conjunction with the Commonwealth Trans-Antarctic Expedition (see below) which was to proceed toward the Pram Point base from the Weddell Sea coast.

The only scientific station the United Kingdom specially established for IGY purposes was also coastal—the Royal Society's station at Halley Bay, Caird Coast, on the Weddell Sea. It was serviced by the FIDS; the scientists came from the Air Ministry (meteorology), the U.K. Radio Research Station (ionospherics), and Manchester University's Jodrell Bank establishment (radio-astronomy). Two hundred miles east, however, was the station of the Commonwealth Trans-Antarctic Expedition (see below) called Shackleton, point of departure for Britain's contribution to the investigation of the Antarctic interior. Not related to IGY, this undertaking was simultaneous with it by an accident of scheduling. Led by Vivian Fuchs, it had been conceived by him while working at the Stonington Island station of the FIDS in 1948, enjoyed the support of Sir J. M. Wordie, and eventually was financed by the governments of the United Kingdom, Australia, South Africa, and New Zealand and manned by a mixed Commonwealth team.

The logistics of station building and maintenance proved not only difficult, because of the ice conditions and weather, but also extremely costly, with a great increase in costs for stations in the interior. The IGY cost the United States $250,000,000—$245,000,000 of it for logistics, only $5,000,000 for science. Fuel for power and heat was estimated to be 60 per cent of all Antarctic cargo wherever delivered for use. At the South Pole station (of eighteen men) fuel could cost a quarter of a million dollars a year. The escape from this large fraction of the difficulties was atomic power plants for permanent stations. The first of these, pioneered under polar conditions at Thule, Greenland, was established in Antarctica at the American McMurdo Station. It was built on the slope of Observatory Hill, below the peak on which stands a cross commemorating Scott and his men of the 1912 disaster. The plant came into operation in March 1962. Others were then in prospect.

The scientific work in Antarctica during IGY was of comprehensive range within the ambit of geophysics and while all participants by agreement contributed to geophysical studies, some of them continued or initiated studies outside the field. Not all the geophysical disciplines were studied at all the stations, either in general or among the stations of any nation having several, but in total the coverage was exhaustive. As the IGY passed and it became apparent that the general disposition was to continue scientific work at permanent stations into the future, non-geophysical studies, notably biology, geology, and cartography, were added. The scientists were well satisfied with the results of their IGY efforts even before they were completed. It was concluded that scientific data would be the only important "export" from Antarctica indefinitely into the future, and they acquired a powerful vested interest in the trade. In spite of the fact that the geologists had then studied no more than 1 per cent of the "continent," the prospect of discovering resources of economic significance was heavily discounted and the prospect of finding any which would justify the enormous cost of recovering them and delivering them to national and world markets was even more heavily discounted. Not only were data vital to comprehending Antarctica obtained in generous quantity during IGY, but data indispensable to global and even extraglobal understanding were cumulated. The data were, by and large, freely delivered to previously designated data centers for analysis and general dissemination. While post-IGY analyses of the situation emphasized that there was considerable variation in the richness of the data between the geophysical disciplines, and therefore some variation in the extent of the need to supplement them by further work, in no discipline were the results considered conclusive. Given the fact that historically enduring conclusive results are uncharacteristic of the sciences—they have always had unexplored frontiers—this was not unexpected. The point was that the IGY experience, even before its conclusions, convinced the scientists that Antarctica was a locale peculiarly useful not only for cumulating supporting and explicating data for existing ideas but for skirmishing on the frontiers of the disciplines. Some of the activities, such as geographical exploration, might be subject to the law of diminishing returns, but that was unlikely to be true of any scientific work into the predictable future. The big question was whether they could continue to carry out their operations unvexed by nationalistic political contention.

In 1957, at a meeting in Paris to discuss IGY Antarctic research the American delegates proposed that it be planned to continue the work after the Geophysical Year had ended. This was agreed to and SCAR—Special Committee on Antarctic Research—was constituted with the approval of the International Council of Scientific Unions. SCAR first met in formal session at The Hague in February 1958. American participation in SCAR was through the Committee on Polar Research of the National Academy of Sciences, which was established in 1958 to replace the old Antarctic research committee. The political problem was then, of course, still unsolved, but the Americans were shortly to make a significant and in the end fruitful move.

By plan geographical discovery was not to be a part of the IGY, but it was impossible not to make contributions to it. The Americans made nine exploratory flights during Deepfreeze I in the 1955–56 season. Probably the most important discovery was of what came to be called the Pensacola Mountains on the edge of, and inland from, the Filchner

Ice Shelf, but significant aerial probes were also made toward the Pole of Inaccessibility. (The extent of the Pensacolas was determined later from Ellsworth Station.) During the IGY incidental to the traverses to carry out geophysical purposes (glaciology, especially in its seismic aspect, gravity, magnetism, etc.) from Little America V and the Byrd and Ellsworth stations—nothing of the sort was done from the South Pole and McMurdo stations—geography ineluctably raised its head. The traverses, made in heavy, powerful Sno-cats, were usually but not always roughly triangular in design, with the station the apex. A great roughly triangular traverse was made on the Ross Ice Shelf during which much was learned about the varying thickness of the ice and the contours of the sea bottom; while on another occasion a differently designed journey was made west from Little America V across the horst mountains into Victoria Land where ice-thickness was systematically studied and that the land beneath was on occasion below sea level was determined. It appeared likely that beyond the mountains was a great ice reservoir, the mountains serving as a dam to it. From Byrd Station the nature of Marie Byrd Land was illuminated. It was ascertained that the land behind the coastal mountains was below sea level and that instead of being a land plateau, Marie Byrd Land was an ice plateau resting in a great basin. On the Byrd Station traverses Ellsworth's Sentinel Mountains and the Horlick Mountains were visited, lichens in great variety being discovered in the former, while the latter proved rich in fossils and indications of coal. From Ellsworth Station it was established that the Filchner Ice Shelf was even larger than had hitherto been assumed, though still smaller than the Ross Shelf. At one point it extended inland to the base of Ellsworth's Sentinels. Under the Filchner ice was an island, named for Lloyd Berkner, much larger than Roosevelt Island under the Ross Shelf. In 1958 during a scientific traverse from Ellsworth Station via Byrd Station to Little America V it was found that it was necessary to reduce the Sentinels to the status of a "range" and upgrade the total complex to "mountains"—eventually named for Ellsworth. Ice soundings on this journey confirmed that Marie Byrd Land was indeed underlain by a vast basin below sea level and suggested that the Bellingshausen and Ross Seas were connected by a channel of similar depth under the ice, leaving the coastal mountains insular, constituting a vast archipelago, in line with Byrd's speculation of 1947. However, at the end of the IGY large parts of this general area were still unseen.

An effect of these discoveries, the implications of which were pursued after the IGY, was to make it likely that if any channel connected the Weddell and Ross Seas it was very narrow and lay between the terminus of the Peninsula Andean mountains and the starting point of the horst mountains. The terminus of the peninsula mountains was thought to be either the Ellsworths or the Pensacolas, the easternmost horst mountains the Thiels. It might also be that the Andean mountains divided when they left the narrow peninsula, for the mountains of the Marie Byrd Land coast were mostly Andean in character. Or it might be that all this was misguided speculation and the Antarctic mountains were independent chains. It might also be that the portion of Antarctica almost pinched off by the Filchner and Ross shelves was the somewhat bulbous base of the peninsula and considerably enlarged it; that the peninsula actually embraced far more than the portion of Antarctica that had traditionally been assigned to it. If so, perhaps a new definition of the so-called West and East provinces of Antarctica was called for and perhaps a new terminology for them as well. All this was quite apart from the question of "continent" versus "islands" which was now insistently raised as it was found that so much of the under-ice rock was below sea level. The Russians also appeared to be moving definitely toward the "islands" conception.

The Russians had been active in geographical discovery since their arrival on the "continent" in 1956. At first they had engaged in the old Antarctic pastime of correcting errors and misconceptions of their predecessors along the coast they examined, using aerial photography, but perforce as they pursued their course toward inland bases, making seismic soundings and taking gravity readings in the interest of geophysics, they developed geographical ideas of larger import. In fact, *all* trips into the interior had in some degree a geographical aspect. This was true not only of the Americans and the Russians, but also of the work of the Australians in the Prince Charles Mountains, the French in the featureless interior of Adélie Land, the Belgians in the Sør-Rondane Mountains, the Norwegians in the Muehlig-Hofmann Mountains, the New Zealanders in the mountains to the west of the Ross Shelf.

However, only the British undertook an expedition primarily geographical in purpose—the Trans-Antarctic Expedition from the Weddell to the Ross Sea—but even on it great attention was given to geophysical tasks, often under difficult conditions: gravity readings every fifteen miles, seismic shots every thirty miles. Because it represented an attempt to realize an old ambition—to cross Antarctica—this expedition attracted great attention and its success brought fame to its leader Sir Vivian Fuchs and added lustre to the fame of Sir Edmund Hillary, conqueror of Mount Everest, who led a supporting expedition. The plan was for Fuchs to lead a party over the entire distance to be traversed while Hillary was to lay depots into the interior from New Zealand's Ross Base. The two parties would meet on the plateau.

A party set up a primary base called Shackleton in the 1956–57 season, one mile inland from Duke Ernst Bay on the Filchner Ice Shelf. Immediately the men set about establishing, partly by air and partly over the ice, an inland advance base called South Ice. This was located near the Whichaway Nunataks and would be the point of final departure for the Ross Sea coast. Basic reliance for surface travel was to be Sno-cats, with weasels and dog teams in support. Shackleton was left by the transcontinental travelers on November 24, 1957, South Ice was reached on December 21 after great trouble with crevasses, and a course was set for the South Pole on the evening of Christmas. Meanwhile Hillary had left the dual purpose New Zealand base on Ross Island with a team of converted farm tractors on October 14. He reached the interior plateau by way of the Skelton Glacier to the west and reached the site of the last planned depot, number 700, by December 15. He was 730 miles from Scott Base, 521 miles from the Pole, 200 miles south of the point originally selected for the final depot. Although by plan this completed Hillary's assignment and he was expected to be at Depot 700 when Fuchs arrived and to accompany him to Scott Base, he decided to make a dash for the Pole and the Amundsen-Scott Station. Leaving Depot 700 on December 20 with three companions riding three tractors, he reached the Pole on January 4, 1958. This party was the first to achieve the Pole overland since Scott in 1912 and the first party ever to reach it by motorized vehicles. The Fuchs party reached the pole on January 19, 900 miles out from Shackleton base, the first ever to reach it from that direction, and were greeted by the Americans, including newspaper correspondents, and Hillary. The Pole, Fuchs established, was in a great ice-filled basin. The transcontinental party left the Pole on January 24 and headed for Depot 700. Hillary joined them there. Scott Base was reached at 1:57 P.M. on March 2. The journey of 2158 statute miles from the Weddell to the Ross Sea via the South Pole at an average speed of twenty-two miles a day had taken ninety-eight days.

On May 3, 1958, it was announced in Washington that on the previous day the United States had, in anticipation of the end of the IGY, initiated discussions about how to reserve Antarctica "only for peaceful purposes" in the future. How this was related to the American initiative in favor of continuing scientific programs beyond the termination of the IGY, which led to the formation of SCAR, was not stated. The initiative was in the form of a fairly long letter addressed to the governments of the eleven other nations active in Antarctica during the IGY: Argentina, Australia, Belgium, Chile, France, Japan, New Zealand, Norway, the Union of South Africa, the U.S.S.R., and the United Kingdom, currently the members of the Antarctic club. The letter was signed and delivered by the American ambassadors to the several countries. *Inter alia* the letter said:

It is the opinion of my Government, however, that the interests of mankind would best be served, in consonance with the high ideals of the Charter of the United Nations, if the countries which have a direct interest in Antarctica were to join together in the conclusion of a treaty which would have the following peaceful purposes:

A Freedom of scientific investigation throughout Antarctica by citizens, organizations, and governments of all countries; and a continuation of the international scientific cooperation which is being carried out so successfully during the current International Geophysical Year.

B International agreement to ensure that Antarctica be used for peaceful purposes only.

C Any other peaceful purposes not inconsistent with the Charter of the of the United Nations.

The Government of the United States is prepared to discuss jointly with the Governments of the other countries having a direct interest in Antarctica the possibility of concluding an agreement, which would be in the form of a treaty, for the purpose of giving legal effect to these high principles.

The stumbling block of national claims, rights, and interests was dealt with in two passages, the first of which restated the American position (italics added):

The United States for many years has had, and at the present time continues to have, direct and substantial rights and interests in Antarctica. Throughout a period of many years, commencing in the early eighteen hundreds, many areas of the Antarctic region have been discovered, sighted, explored and claimed on behalf of the United States by nationals of the United States and by expeditions carrying the flag of the United States. During this period, the Government of the United States and its nationals have engaged in well-known and extensive activities in Antarctica.

In view of the activities of the United States and its nationals referred to above, *my Government reserves all of the rights of the United States with respect to the Antarctic region, including the right to assert a territorial claim or claims.*

The second passage proposed a way of handling, pro tem, the claims, rights, and interests of all nations without facing up to the difficult (perhaps impossible) task of dealing forthrightly with them in an effort to achieve complete internationalization.

It is believed that such a treaty can be concluded without requiring any participating nation to renounce whatever basic historic rights it may have in Antarctica, or whatever claims of sovereignty it may have asserted. It could be specifically provided that such basic rights and such claims would remain unaffected while the treaty is in force, and that no new rights would be acquired and no new claims made by any country during the duration of the treaty. In other words, the legal status quo in Antarctica would be frozen for the duration of the treaty, permitting cooperation in scientific and administrative matters to be carried out in a constructive manner without being hampered or affected in any way by political considerations.

The letter set going a long series of discussions designed to be preliminary to a conference at which the sought-for treaty would be put into final form. Beginning in June 1958 no fewer than sixty such discussions took place, and a multiplicity of "working papers" were produced, but exactly what transpired was not made public. It may be speculated, however, that there was reasonably ready acceptance of the principle of internationalization for scientific purposes, though with the expected diplomatic quibbling over the language of proposed articles of a treaty, but rather vigorous expressions of skepticism about the possibility of finding a generally agreeable formula for surmounting the problem of territorial claims, rights, and interests, particularly on the part of the Australians—they later publicly confessed as much—and even more vigorously on the part of the Argentines and Chileans who would conceive of themselves as being asked to internationalize national territory rather than "colonial" possessions. The French, the Russians, and the Norwegians had also not publicly modified their strictly nationalistic positions since 1948. But on the other hand the United Kingdom and New Zealand had been willing to discuss internationalization in 1948 and New Zealand had since publicly declared its willingness even to "consider the relinquishment of national rights and claims in Antarctica if such a step towards the establishment of a wider regime were generally agreed." At any rate, on May 28, 1959, it was announced that the hoped for conference would convene in Washington on October 15.

Between October 15 and December 1 a treaty was indeed drawn up, and in due course it was ratified and brought into force. Drawn up by the twelve nations active in Antarctica, provision was made for other nations actually undertaking research there to associate themselves with it. Antarctica was defined (Article VI) as "the area south of 60° South Latitude including all ice shelves," but, in a general renunciation of past pretensions, the high seas were carefully excluded and left to the care of international law. The treaty provided:

Article I. 1. Antarctica shall be used for peaceful purposes only. There shall be prohibited, *inter alia,* any measures of a military nature, such as the establishment of military bases and fortifications, the carrying out of military maneuvers, as well as the testing of any type of weapons.

2. The present Treaty shall not prevent the use of military personnel or equipment for scientific research or for any other peaceful purpose.

Article II. Freedom of scientific investigation in Antarctica and cooperation toward that end, as applied during the International Geophysical Year, shall continue, subject to the provisions of the present Treaty.

Article III. 1. In order to promote international cooperation in scientific investigation in Antarctica, as provided for in Article II of the present Treaty, the Contracting Parties agree that, to the greatest extent feasible and practicable:

(a) information regarding plans for scientific programs in Antarctica shall be exchanged to permit maximum economy and efficiency of operations;

(b) scientific personnel shall be exchanged in Antarctica between expeditions and stations;

(c) scientific observations and results from Antarctica shall be exchanged and made freely available.

2. . . .

Article V. 1. Any nuclear explosions in Antarctica and the disposal of radioactive waste material shall be prohibited.

2. . . .

The vexed question of claims, rights, and interests was dealt with in

Article IV. 1. Nothing contained in the present Treaty shall be interpreted as: (a) a renunciation by any Contracting Party of previously asserted rights of or claims to territorial sovereignty in Antarctica; (b) a renunciation or diminution by any Contracting Party of any basis of claim to territorial sovereignty in Antarctica which it may have whether as a result of its activities or those of its nationals in Antarctica, or otherwise; (c) prejudicing the position of any Contracting Party as regards its recognition or non-recognition of any other State's rights of or claim or basis of claim to territorial sovereignty in Antarctica. 2. No acts or activities taking place while the present Treaty is in force shall constitute a basis for asserting, supporting or denying a claim to territorial sovereignty in Antarctica or create any rights of sovereignty in Antarctica. No new claim, or enlargement of an existing claim, to territorial sovereignty in Antarctica shall be asserted while the present Treaty is in force.

As the treaty was to have a life of thirty years, the claims, rights, and interests were thus "frozen" for that period.

The treaty was plainly made possible by the general recognition that the economic potential of Antarctica was low and would probably continue to be in the predictable future, and that the strategic importance of Antarctica was, in global perspective, very small in contrast, say, to the Arctic. Apparently because the sovereignty question was elided or evaded rather than faced frontally and "solved," Antarctica was left a kind of administrative vacuum. While provision was made for consultation among the parties at periodic intervals—the first consultative meeting was held at Canberra, Australia, in July 1961—it was not provided, as in other post-World War II treaties, that any permanent organizational structure for administration be developed. No provision was made for a secretariat, although Australia was ready to provide a home for one. Even much of the scientific planning was left in the hands of the national committees with the basic international co-ordination left to a nongovernmental outside organization, SCAR. Plainly Antarctica was in effect internationalized so long as the only changes in the status quo were in the realm of science. Should there be a decisive change in either the idea of the economic potential (e.g., through mineral discoveries) or the military strategic uses, this very clever "rug" could be lifted and nationalistic contention resumed, probably at a higher level of intensity than ever before. Even the self-denying provision of Article IV, 2, would then hardly prevent powers like the United States and the U.S.S.R., heavy investors in Antarctica science, from acting to protect their acquired rights and interests in the light of the facts existing then, not the facts of 1959. Alternatively, however, the scientific uses of Antarctica might prove over the ensuing thirty years to be the only uses worthy of consideration, this intensifying the internationalist factor and contributing to the effective "withering away" of claims, rights, and interests of a nationalistic character worth "bucking" the world to assert. In the face of the potentially destructive variables, this was the "hope" upon which the Antarctic Treaty was founded. And so in the sixth decade of the twentieth century the "coast" which Captain Cook in the seventh decade of the eighteenth century had thought would not be "of the least use, either to navigation or geography or, indeed, to any other science," was in the wisdom of the world's governors chiefly to be valued precisely as one of the most fruitful sources of scientific knowledge and understanding on the globe, though still of doubtful value otherwise.

SUGGESTED READINGS

AUSTRALIA

I. COMMONWEALTH AND COMMON WELFARE

In addition to general histories cited in *The Southwest Pacific to 1900*, of particular relevance (usually in sequential chapters) are H. G. Turner, *The First Decade of the Australian Commonwealth 1901–1910* (Melbourne, 1911); A. N. Smith, *Thirty Years: The Commonwealth of Australia 1901–1931* (Melbourne, 1933); G. Sawyer, *Australian Federal Politics and Law 1901–1929* (Melbourne, 1956); and B. Fitzpatrick, *The Australian Commonwealth 1901–1955* (Melbourne, 1956). Very useful biographies of varying merit are John Reynolds, *Edmund Barton* (Sydney, 1948); Walter Murdoch, *Alfred Deakin* (London, 1923); L. F. Fitzharding *et al., Nation Building in Australia: Life of Sir Littleton Ernest Groom* (Sydney, 1941); W. F. Whyte, *William Morris Hughes* (Sydney, 1957); H. V. Evatt, *Australian Labor Leader: W. A. Holman* (Sydney, 1940); N. Palmer, *Henry Bournes Higgins* (London, 1931); F. H. Sugden and F. W. Eggleston, *George Swinburne* (Sydney, 1931); Harold Nicolson, *King George V: His Life and Reign 1865–1936* (London, 1953); T. H. Smeaton, *From Stone Cutter to Premier: Life of Tom Price* (Adelaide, n.d.); Paquita Mawson, *A Vision of Steel: Life of G. D. Delprat* (Melbourne, 1958). A miscellany of special studies, not all of them organized as histories, which are relevant here are J. A. La Nauze, *The Hopetoun Blunder* (Melbourne, 1957); L. F. Crisp, *The Australian Federal Labor Party 1901–1951* (Melbourne, 1955); L. F. Crisp, *The Parliamentary Government of the Commonwealth of Australia* (Adelaide, 1949); Louise Overacker, *The Australian Party System* (New Haven, Conn., 1952); R. S. Parker, *Public Service Recruitment in Australia* (Melbourne, 1942); F. W. Eggleston, *State Socialism in Victoria* (London, 1932); J. M. Garland, *Economic Aspects of Australian Land Taxation* (Melbourne, 1934); S. Mills, *Taxation in Australia* (London, 1935); B. U. Ratchford, *Public Expenditures in Australia* (Durham, N.C., 1959); J. H. Portus, *The Development of Australian Trade Union Law* (Melbourne, 1958); L. C. Jauncey, *Australia's Government Bank* (New York, 1934); C. C. Faulkner, *The Commonwealth Bank of Australia 1912–1923* (Sydney, 1923); M. H. Ellis, *The Beef Shorthorn in Australia* (Sydney, 1932); *Tom Mann's Memoirs* (London, 1923); E. H. Lane, *Dawn to Dusk: Reminiscences of a Rebel* (Brisbane, 1939); C. Joyner, *Holman Versus Hughes: Extension of Australian Commonwealth Powers* (Gainesville, Fla., 1961); Fredk. Watson, *History of Canberra* (Canberra, 1927). And most of the economic and industry histories cited in *The Southwest Pacific to 1900* are relevant here. On cultural affairs, see references there, and add as specifically pertaining to this chapter Miles Franklin and Kate Baker, *Joseph Furphy: The Legend of a Man and his Book* (Sydney, 1944); V. Palmer, *Frank Wilmot* (Melbourne, 1942); F. T. Macartney, *Furnley Maurice* (Sydney, 1955); Victor Kennedy and Nettie Palmer, *Bernard O'Dowd* (Melbourne, 1954); E. M. Higgins, *David Stewart and the W.E.A.* (Sydney, n.d., c. 1954); *The Mitchell Library: Historical and Descriptive Notes* (Sydney, 1936). As hitherto, no effort to provide bibliographies of the works of writers mentioned will be made.

II.   WORLD WAR I

Most of the histories and biographies cited in the previous chapter and some of the special studies remain relevant here. The comprehensive history of Australia in World War I is *Official History of Australia in the War of 1914–1918*, of which C. E. W. Bean was the editor and part author. It was published volume by volume over many years. Most of the volumes deal in elaborate detail with the combat side of the war and the preparation of the services for war, but Vol. XI by Professor Ernest Scott, *Australia During the War* (1936) deals with the home front. A single-volume summary of this tremendous work is C. E. W. Bean, *Anzac to Amiens* (Canberra, 1946). W. M. Hughes's *The Splendid Adventure* (London, 1929) is his principal book on the war and after. There are paperback collections of his wartime speeches, and Low's *The Billy Book* (Sydney, 1918) is wholly devoted to Hughes, though it does not include some of the best of Low's cartoons dealing with Hughes. It has already been said that Whyte's biography is unsatisfactory, not least so in dealing with Hughes and the war and the peace-making. For light on the conscription referenda see L. C. Jauncey, *The Story of Conscription in Australia* (London, 1935). General Monash contributed *The Australian Victories in France in 1918* (2d rev. ed.; Melbourne, 1923). On the navy, G. L. Macandie, *The Genesis of the Royal Australian Navy* (Sydney, 1949) and Frances McGuire, *The Royal Australian Navy* (Melbourne, 1948), which continues the story through World War II. On Duntroon, see J. E. Lee, *Duntroon* (Canberra, 1952). Alan Moorhead's *Gallipoli* (New York, 1956) must unfailingly be read. P. Magnus, *Kitchener* (New York, 1959) gets his visit to Australia and New Zealand into perspective. For an idea of how Australia now figures in a sound history of World War I look into Cyril Falls, *The Great War 1914–1918* (New York, 1959). On the peace conference, the Scott volume of the *Official History* is still the standard Australian reference. The enormous literature of the conference, British, American, French, etc., can profitably be combed for perspective on Hughes's performance. A first-rate afterview which takes notice of Hughes's performance is Paul Birdsall, *Versailles Twenty Years After* (New York, 1941). A history of Japan that takes care to refer to Australia's relations is A. L. Sadler, *A Short History of Japan* (Sydney, 1946).

III.   INSECURITY, UNCERTAINTY, DEPRESSION

While several of the histories and biographies already mentioned continue useful into this period and beyond, it should be mentioned that Gordon Greenwood, ed., *Australia: A Social and Political History* (Sydney, 1954) is especially useful. R. H. Barrett, *Promises and Performances in Australian Politics 1928–1959* (New York, 1959) is chiefly useful for its carefully accumulated detail. No really good book-length study of Bruce and the Bruce-Page era has yet been published. Page's autobiography, *Truant Surgeon: The Inside Story of Forty Years of Australian Political Life* (Sydney, 1963), unfortunately reached me long after I had fixed my text. Ulrich Ellis, who has published a history of the Country party in New South Wales: *The Country Party* (Melbourne, 1958), has a study of the federal Country party in progress. Don Whitington, *The House Will Divide* (Melbourne, 1954) is a political journalist's survey of federal politics from the end of the war to the middle 1950's, loosely written and marred by eccentric judgments on policy. Although focused on the succeeding Scullin government, Warren Denning, *Caucus Crisis: The Rise and Fall of the Scullin Government* (Parramatta, N.S.W., 1937) has perceptive things to say about Bruce-Page. J. G. Latham, *Australia and the British Commonwealth* (London, 1929), with a preface by Bruce, adequately reflects the Australian outlook of the time. For Hertzog on Bruce, Oswald Pirow, *J.B.M. Hertzog* (Capetown, n.d.). How Bruce appeared to the Canadians, R. MacG. Dawson, *William Lyon Mackenzie King,* Vol. 1 (Toronto, 1958). On Australian policy in the League, see G. Carter, as cited earlier. While Australian writers do not like the presentation, the differences over the Japanese treaty in 1921 are treated in J. B. Brebner, *North Atlantic Triangle* (New Haven, Conn., 1945) and in his classic article in the *Pol. Sci. Quarterly,* March 1935. For the Commonwealth background in general, see W. K. Hancock's three volumes, *Survey of British Commonwealth Affairs* (London, 1937, 1940). Characteristic symposia of the twenties are M. Atkinson, ed., *Australia: Economic and Political Studies* (Melbourne, 1920) and P. C. Campbell, R. D. Mills, G. V. Portus, editors, *Studies in Australian Affairs* (Melbourne, 1928). A survey of the economic position *circa* 1930 by Australian writers is the November 1931 number of *The Annals* (Philadelphia, 1931). Nancy Windett, *Australia as Producer and Trader 1920–1932* (London, 1933) and W. M. Smith, *The Marketing of Australian and New Zealand Primary Products* (London, 1936) are useful books. F. C. Benham, *The Prosperity of Australia* (London, 1930) is a contemporary critical analysis of Bruce-Page economics. There is some intelligent writing about manufacturing in *The Annals* number. A good specialized study is F. R. E. Mauldon *et al., Mechanisation in Australian Industries* (Hobart, 1938). On the BHP see Roy Bridges, *From Silver to Steel: The Romance of the Broken Hill Proprietary* (Melbourne, 1920) and the Jubilee Number of *The BHP Review,* June 1935. A contemporary study of the immigration problem is P. D. Phillips and G. L. Wood, eds., *The Peopling of Australia, First Series* (Melbourne, 1930), *Second Series* (1933). A contemporary study of the non-British elements, based on "phony" anthropology, is J. Lyng, *Non-Britishers in Australia* (Melbourne, 1927). W. M. Hughes was one of the worst traducers of the Italians. The famous study of the tariff was published in Melbourne in 1929, *The Australian Tariff: An Economic Analysis;* it was prepared by J. B. Brigden, E. C. Dyason, C. H. Wickens, Copland, and Giblin. On the exploitation of Victorian brown coal, the lavishly illustrated *Three Decades: The Story of the State Electricity Commission of Victoria* (Melbourne, 1949). On black coal, F. R. E. Mauldon, *A Study in Social Economics: The Hunter River Valley* (Melbourne, 1927) and F. R. E. Mauldon, *The Economics of Australian Coal* (Melbourne, 1929). On Mt. Isa, see Geoffrey Blainey, *Mines in the Spinifex: The Story of Mount Isa Mines* (Sydney, 1960). On the wheat industry, see Dunsdorfs and Callaghan and Millington. On wool the basic figures are in *Statistical Handbook of the Sheep and Wool Industry* (Canberra, 1956). Reference has been made earlier to sources of historical information about other industries, but the truth is that the data are scattered and unorganized except as they enter into economic histories. There is little historical analysis of transport. A review of about this time is a supplement to *The Economic Record, The Economics of Transport* (1935). See also E. Harding, *Uniform Railway Gauge* (Melbourne, 1958); K. Winser, *Story of Australian Motoring* (Melbourne, n.d.), a scrappy scrapbook full of wonderful pictures; and if really interested the fairly numerous government papers. On aviation there is, however, a good book, D. M. Hocking and C. P. Haddon-Cave, *Air Transport in Australia* (Sydney, 1951). L. F. Giblin, *The Growth of a Central Bank 1924–1945* (Melbourne, 1951) picks up the story of the Commonwealth Bank at the point discussed in this chapter. For additional light on banking, see G. Blainey, *Gold and Paper* (Melbourne, 1958), S. J. Butlin, *Australia and New Zealand Bank* (Melbourne, 1961). On grasslands study in Australia, see H. C. Trumble, *Blades of Grass* (Melbourne, 1946). For the irrigation country on the Murray, E. Hill, *Water into Gold* (Melbourne, 1937). A reference on the sugar industry has already been given, but on white settlement in the tropics, see A. G. Price, *White Settlers in the Tropics* (New York, 1939). On Northern Territory at this time see A. G. Price, *History and Problems of the Northern Territory* (Adelaide, 1930); for another view of the Territory, E. Hill, *The Territory* (Sydney, 1951); but there is a very copious pamphlet and hardcover literature and an accumulating volume of official "papers" of which the best of this general time is W. L. Payne *et al., Report of the Northern Territory Investigation Committee* (Canberra, 1937). On "New States" there is a voluminous pamphlet literature but see as a history, U. R. Ellis, *New Australian States* (Sydney, 1933). The basic study of the arbitration system of this time is George Anderson, *Fixation of Wages in Australia* (Melbourne, 1929). A later study which reviews the complicated story from its beginnings is O. deR. Foenander, *Towards Industrial Peace in Australia* (Melbourne, 1937). A volume on the referendum that Bruce lost and the election that was fatal to him, A. Wildavsky & D. Carboch, *Studies in Australian Politics: The 1926 Referendum; The Fall of the Bruce-Page Government* (Melbourne, 1958), studies in political science, not history. There is a good deal of writing about Labor's 1921 objective, but no book. See especially the essays by Lloyd Ross in various magazines and his lecture "Workers' Participation in the Ownership and Control of Industry" (Chifley Memorial Lecture, Melbourne, 1929); Arthur Calwell's essay in S. R. Davis, ed., *The Australian Political Party System* (Sydney, 1954); the relevant passage in L. F. Crisp, *The Australian Federal Labour Party* (Melbourne, 1955); and E. H. Lane, *Dawn to Dusk* (Brisbane, 1939). There appears to be little but partisan writing about the coming and career of the communists, e.g., the party document with the imitative title, L. L. Sharkey, *An Outline History of the Australian Communist Party* (Sydney, 1944). On Mr. Moore-Wicks see Theodore Draper, *The Roots of American Communism* (New York, 1957). V. G. Childe, *How Labour Governs* (London, 1923) is a famous study of Labor politics in New South Wales in the early 1920's when Childe was a Labor premier's secretary, long before he became a world-famous prehistoric archaeologist. Nobody has yet thought to write a "life and times" of Scullin; hence his reputation is obscured today by clouds of depression-generated suspicions and hostilities. The newly organized (1961) Australian Society for the Study of Labor History might put such a book on its agenda and plan also a study of E. G. Theodore as well as consider what should be done about such a minor but strategically very important figure as Frank Anstey. Of the three principal books by economists on the depression (which of course cast light on the Bruce-Page past), that by W. R. MacLaurin, an American, *Economic Planning in Australia 1929–1936* (London, 1937) is perhaps the best. The other two are E. R. Walker, *Australia in the World Depression* (London, 1933) and D. B. Copland, *Australia in the World Crisis 1919–1933* (Cambridge & New York, 1934). Books of documents produced in the period are E. O. Shann and D. B. Copland, eds., *The Crisis in Australian Finance 1929–1931* (Sydney, 1931); Shann and Copland, eds., *The Battle of the Plans 1931* (Sydney, 1931); and Shann and Copland, eds., *The Australian Price Structure 1931–1932* (Sydney, 1933). J. T. Lang's career deserves a thorough critical study. J. H. C. Sleeman, *The Life of John T. Lang* (Sydney, 1933), the only existing book, is rubbish. Lang has written prolifically about himself and his ideas, e.g., in hardcovers, *Why I Fight* (Sydney, 1934) and *I Remember* (Sydney, 1956), but this fascinating stuff is to be used with great caution. In 1962 Lang, now 84, published *The Great Bust* (Sydney), his own story of the great depression, but I had not seen it when the passages here were written. James Bryce's account of Australia is in volume 2 of *Modern Democracies* (New York, 1921). For D. H. Lawrence: his letters in Aldous Huxley, ed., *The Letters of D. H. Lawrence* (New York,

1932); his fiction: D. H. L. and M. L. Skinner (an Australian writer), *Boy in the Bush* (1924) and D. H. Lawrence, *Kangaroo* (1923). The Wilkins quote comes from *Undiscovered Australia* (New York, 1929). A survey of Australian public school education as it was and was evaluated in the 1920's is G. S. Browne, ed., *Education in Australia* (London, 1927). The publications of the ACER are too numerous to list; included are books on Tate and Board. A collection of New Education Fellowship Conference papers is K. S. Cunningham and W. C. Radford, eds., *Education for Complete Living* (Melbourne, 1938). On the universities, see the references earlier. See also D. H. Drummond, *A University is Born: The Story of the Founding of the University College of New England* (Sydney, 1959). There is no general survey, but see *Report of Proceedings, Australian and New Zealand Universities Conference 1937* (Adelaide, 1937). The report on the libraries is R. Munn and E. R. Pitt, *Australian Libraries: A Survey of Conditions and Suggestions for Their Improvement* (Melbourne, 1935). For Griffith Taylor, see his *Australia: A Study of Warm Environments and their Effect on British Settlement* (London, 1940) and his autobiography, *Journeyman Taylor* (London, 1958). Re the economists, see *The Economic Record* No. 73 (March, 1960); "Essays in honour of Sir Douglas Copland"; and Douglas Copland, ed., *Giblin: The Scholar and the Man* (Melbourne, 1960). On economists in the federal public I have relied on casual references in a variety of books and articles. There is no account of the rise of the AIPS I know of, nor any historical sketch of public administration as a university subject or as promoted by Mr. Remington. Much of the material published as "data papers" (which is most valuable) was in mimeographed form and hence rather perishable. On foreign policy much of the material was in pamphlet form. On expatriation, see J. C. G. Kevin, ed., *Some Australians Take Stock* (London, 1939) and W. K. Hancock, *Country and Calling* (London, 1954). As remarked, there is no history of science in Australia, but see the annual reports of CSIR and the symposium, *Science in Australia* (Melbourne, 1952). On the prickly pear affair, A. P. Dodd, *The Biological Campaign Against the Prickly Pear* (Brisbane, 1940). This affair was given wide publicity by its use in H. G. Wells, J. S. Huxley and G. P. Wells, *The Science of Life*, 2 vols. (New York, 1931). On adult education in this period see the Higgins book on Dave Stewart referred to earlier and G. V. Portus' autobiography, *Happy Highways* (Melbourne, 1953). A bibliography of the writings of Sir Frederick Eggleston is to be found in his *Reflections on Australian Foreign Policy* (Melbourne, 1957). Additional to books cited elsewhere in this bibliography, mention may be made here of *Reflections of an Australian Liberal* (Melbourne, 1953) and *Search for a Social Philosophy* (Melbourne, 1941). The *Australian Encyclopedia* (Sydney, 1927) was edited by A. W. Jose (1863–1934), author of several useful books on Australian affairs, long Australian correspondent of the London *Times*. One suspects that a study of Jose's career would cast much light on Australian intellectual and public life from around 1880 through the first third of this century. It should be noticed that W. K. Hancock's classic book, *Australia* (London, 1930) is culturally situated in the Bruce-Page era and perhaps I may be permitted to say that my *Introducing Australia* (New York, 1942) is related to my experiences in Australia in 1927 and 1936–38. As it is impossible to supply a full bibliography for the discussion of literary developments, and selection is necessarily invidious, the following items should be taken as indicative of what can be found and no more. For a sense of what the literary life was like, Nettie Palmer, *Fourteen Years: Extracts from a Private Journal 1925–1939* (Melbourne, 1948). Contemporary evaluations include Nettie Palmer, *Modern Australian Literature, 1900–1923* (Melbourne, 1924); C. Hartley Grattan, *Australian Literature* (Seattle, 1929); H. M. Green, *An Outline of Australian Literature* (Sydney, 1930); P. R. Stephensen, *The Foundations of Culture in Australia* (Sydney, 1936); Barnard Eldershaw, *Essays in Australian Fiction* (Melbourne, 1938); T. I. Moore, *Six Australian Poets* (Melbourne, 1942). The most highly regarded anthology of the poetry in this period is Percival Searle, *et al.*, *An Australasian Anthology* (London, 1927). Some books about writers of this time are Nettie Palmer, *Henry Handel Richardson* (Sydney, 1954); Leonie J. Gibson, *Henry Handel Richardson and Some of Her Sources* (Melbourne, 1954); Edna Purdie and Olga Roncoroni, *Henry Handel Richardson: Some Personal Impressions* (Sydney, 1957); James Devaney, *Shaw Neilson* (Sydney, 1944); and John Hetherington, *Norman Lindsay* (Melbourne, 1961). On painters, Moore and Smith, cited in *The Southwest Pacific to 1900,* are important—Moore barely reaches this period. The traditionalists put their best foot forward in *Australian Landscape Painters of Today* (Sydney, 1929). For Basil Burdett on "modernism" in 1929 see text of the book of color reproductions, *A Contemporary Group of Australian Artists* (Sydney, 1929). On Macqueen, see K. Macqueen, V. Lahey and J. V. Duhig, *Adventure in Water-color* (Sydney, 1949), text and color reproductions. On the assimilation of the early experimentalists to the tradition, see R. H. Gordon *et al.*, *A Memorial Volume to Howard Hinton, Patron of Art* (Sydney, 1951), text, color reproductions, and catalogue, and Australia's *Achievement in Art* (Sydney, 1937), color reproductions with a prefatory note by Lionel Lindsay. For an account of the row over the academy proposal embedded in a general "modernist" foray against the traditionalists see Adrian Lawlor, *Arquebus* (Melbourne, 1937). For a traditionalist foray against the modernists, see Sir Lionel Lindsay, *Addled Art* (Sydney, 1942). On the *Herald* show of 1939, see S. Ure Smith, ed., *Australian Art Annual* (Sydney, 1939). A record of a well-chosen retrospective exhibition of Australian art 1788–1941 is *Art in Australia 1788–1941, An Exhibition of Australian Art Held in the United States of America and the Dominion of Canada under the auspices of the Carnegie Corporation* (New York, 1941). On the aboriginals, see for public policy the Foxcroft and Hasluck books, and for anthropology, in addition to the Elkin and Berndt books cited in *The Southwest Pacific to 1900,* F. McCarthy,

Australia's Aborigines: Their Life and Culture (Melbourne, n.d., but in the 1950's), particularly notable for the color photographs, and the series of linked articles in the *Australian Encyclopedia,* vol. 1. The McCarthy book and the *Encyclopedia* articles have good bibliographies. For a fascinating history of the "abo" country in Northern Territory, see R. and C. Berndt, *Arnhem Land: Its History and Its People* (Melbourne, 1954). W. E. H. Stanner's essay "The Aborigines" in Kevin's *Some Australians Take Stock* is an anthropologist's reaction to the general situation *circa* 1938. An invaluable two-part essay is D. J. Mulvaney, "Australian Aborigines 1606–1929: Opinions and Fieldwork" in *Historical Studies,* Nos. 30–31 (1957–58). A good idea of what was being thought about the problem just before World War II can be gained by reading books published at the time, e.g., for missionary opinion J. R. B. Love; for humanitarian opinion, Daisy Bates; for anthropologists' views, Lloyd Warner, H. Basedow, F. Wood Jones, and so on. The Canberra conference is reported in fair detail in *Aboriginal Welfare: Initial Conference of Commonwealth and State Aboriginal Authorities* (Gov. Printer; Canberra, 1937). The conference was, of course, dominated by the "protector" point of view. The "protector" point of view of this time appears to have been given classic expression in J. W. Bleakley's posthumous book, *The Aborigines of Australia* (Brisbane, 1961). On Canberra, for the historical background to 1927, see the Fredk. Watson book already cited and for information about the city's development see H. L. White, ed., *Canberra: A Nation's Capital* (Sydney, 1954). A sense of what Canberra was like in the late 1930's can be gained from Warren Denning, *Capital City* (Sydney, 1938).

IV.   INTO AND THROUGH WORLD WAR II

Understanding of this period of conservative dominance in federal politics is, as is true of the earlier conservative periods, considerably impeded by the fact that most of the substantial writers on public affairs, including the historians, are normally out of sympathy with the conservatives, favoring Labor. Only in the 1960's is a nonlaboristic school of historians beginning to influence understanding of the story. No biography of Lyons has yet been written. A life of John Curtin by Lloyd Ross can be expected in the near future. For the time being see Alan Chester, *John Curtin* (Sydney, 1943). On the wheat industry in this period, in addition to Dunsdorfs and Callaghan & Millington, see also the *Reports* (5) of the Royal Commission on the Wheat, Flour and Bread Industries, published by the government printer 1934–1936. For documentation for the passages on finance, trade, and marketing, see D. B. Copland & C. V. Janes, eds., *Cross Currents in Australian Finance: A Book of Documents* (Sydney, 1936); Copland & Janes, eds., *Australian Trade Policy: A Book of Documents 1932–1937* (Sydney, 1937), and Copland & Janes, eds., *Australian Marketing Problems, A Book of Documents 1932–1937* (Sydney,

1938). See also D. F. Nicholson, *Australia's Trade Relations* (Melbourne, 1955). Reitsma, as cited above, reviews Ottawa in relation to the Australian tariff. We still await competent state histories to understand state politics and their impact on federal affairs (and vice versa). Currently F. K. Crowley on Western Australia is the most useful volume available. In addition to Crowley on the secession movement, see the movement's book, *The Case of the People of Western Australia* (Perth, 1934). I know of no book on the Grants Commission, a study of which would give much light on federal-state relations, but there are fairly numerous articles and a Canadian monograph is E. J. Hanson, *Australian Grants Commission: A Quarter Century of Fiscal Judgment* (Toronto, 1960). On banking, see the Royal Commission on Banking, *Report* (Canberra, 1937); Giblin's *The Growth of a Central Bank, 1924–1945* (Melbourne, 1951); and the histories of two trading banks by Blainey and Butlin cited above. The best studies of external (or foreign) affairs and defense for this period are the opening, retrospective chapters of the volumes of the great series *Australia in the War of 1939–1945,* published by The Australian War Memorial, Canberra. Particularly useful at this point are the opening chapters of Paul Hasluck, *The Government and the People 1939–1941* (Canberra, 1952); S. J. Butlin, *War Economy 1939–1942* (Canberra, 1955); Gavin Long, *To Benghazi* (Canberra, 1952); and D. P. Mellor, *The Role of Science and Industry* (Canberra, 1958). There is a very considerable body of material in both hard and paper covers that should be examined by any thorough student. Some of it—I emphasize, some of it—is listed in the bibliography of my *The United States and the Southwest Pacific* (Cambridge, Mass., 1961). If to be found, the data papers for IPR and Commonwealth Relations conferences should be looked at. Among the hard-cover books perhaps attention should be specially directed to I. Clunies Ross, ed., *Australia and the Far East* (Sydney, 1936); J. Shepherd, *Australia's Interests and Policies in the Far East* (New York, 1940); H. L. Harris, *Australia's National Interests and National Policy* (Melbourne, 1938); and W. G. K. Duncan, ed., *Australia's Foreign Policy* (Sydney, 1938). For the imperial context see W. K. Hancock, *Survey of British Commonwealth Affairs,* 2 vols. (London, 1937–42); and Nicholas Mansergh's continuation of the work, *Problems of External Policy 1931–1939* (London, 1952), together with Mansergh's two volumes of documents for 1931–1952, cited above. Also see Gwendolyn Carter as cited above. On the first two years of the war see, of course, the Hasluck, Butlin, Mellor, and Long books just cited. Long covers the first phase of the combat in the Middle East. Long's *Greece, Crete and Syria* appeared in 1953. Chester Wilmot, who gained a world-wide reputation with his *The Struggle for Europe* (New York, 1952) was to have written *Tobruk and El Alamein* but was killed in an airplane accident and to 1962 this gap in the story has remained unfilled. However, see Wilmot's remarkable book, *Tobruk, 1941, Capture-Seige-Relief* (Sydney, 1944). The critical literature on the Middle Eastern or Mediterranean campaigns should be read for better understanding, e.g., Correlli Barnett, *The Desert Generals* (New York, 1961) and the books on Greece and Crete. With regard to domestic developments during the first two years of war see additionally Warren Dennings documentary pamphlet, *Australian National War Council* (Canberra, 1940), and with the remark that they go forward beyond this period to the end of the war, J. G. Crawford *et al.*, *Wartime Agriculture in Australia and New Zealand 1939–1950* (Stanford, Calif., 1954) and E. R. Walker, *The Australian Economy in War and Reconstruction* (New York, 1947). Walker's *War-Time Economics* (Melbourne, 1939) appears to have been an influential treatise, especially after 1941. On the imperial context in wartime and after, Nicholas Mansergh, *Problems of Wartime Cooperation and Postwar Change 1939–1952* (London, 1958). With the outbreak of war in the Pacific and the emergence of Australia from behind the British arras, attention should perhaps be directed to American and British memoirs and other works in which Australia figures, but to list this material exhaustively is impossible. The reference is, of course, to Churchill's memoir-disguised-as-a-history, *The Second World War*, 6 vols., Cordell Hull's *Memoirs,* 2 vols. (New York, 1948); Sherwood's *Roosevelt and Hopkins* (New York, 1948); Arthur Bryant's narrative based on the diaries of Field-Marshall Lord Alanbrooke, the CIGS, 2 vols. (London, 1957 & 1959) etc., while "other works" would be, e.g., Herbert Feis's various volumes on the Pacific war, but attention should be directed to the accumulating critical literature on the politics, strategy, and fighting of the Pacific war which is beginning to be published, for almost anything said is helpful in "placing" Australia in relation to the war. Not the least useful source on the preliminaries of the war is the multivolume *Reports and Hearings of the Investigation of the Pearl Harbor Attack,* in which both the direct references to Australia and the failures to refer to it are significant. See F. C. Jones, *Japan's New Order in East Asia: Its Rise and Fall 1937–1945* (London, 1954) and, e.g., F. W. Schroeder, *The Axis Alliance and Japanese-American Relations, 1941* (Ithaca, N.Y., 1958) and the works of American and Japanese authorship on the origin, prosecution, and ending of the war. On the war in its organizational and fighting aspects see the official and unofficial histories, American, British, and Australian of which more is said in the bibliography for Chapters IX–XI. On Singapore a definitive work tracing the story from the genesis of the idea of the base through the tortuous course of its construction to its fall has yet to be written. On the fall see Lionel Wigmore, *The Japanese Thrust* (Canberra, 1957), a volume of the Australian official war history, and the account in the British official war history, S. W. Kirby, *The War Against Japan,* vol. 1 (London, 1957). My earliest opinions about the fall of Singapore were much influenced by Ian Morrison, *Malayan Postscript* (Sydney, 1943). Morrison, son of "Chinese" Morrison, was the London *Times* correspondent in Malaya. An important Australian version is Lt.-Gen. H. Gordon Bennett, *Why Singapore Fell* (Sydney, 1944). Bennett was commander of the Australian forces and escaped home into a violent service controversy about the military ethics of his action. Other British efforts to "digest" the defeat and retell the story, neither exactly good, are Kenneth Attiwill, *The Singapore Story* (London, 1959) and Frank Owen, *The Fall of Singapore* (London, 1960). A Japanese account is Masanobu Tsuji, *Singapore: The Japanese Version* (Eng. language ed.; Sydney, 1960). There is no good book yet on MacArthur in Australia, nor of American-Australian relations of the time. Perhaps the best book on MacArthur for the present purpose is C. A. Willoughby and John Chamberlain, *MacArthur 1941–1951* (New York, 1954). We will have much more data relevant to American–Australian relations when Hasluck and Butlin publish their second volumes. An American retelling of the coming of the war to the Pacific is John Toland, *But Not in Shame* (New York, 1961), but I do not find it particularly good. Important serial publications carrying indispensable data on the Curtin administration are *Digest of Decisions and Announcements and Important Speeches,* no. 1, Oct. 2, 1941 to 104, July 5, 1945, and *Facts and Figures,* no. 1, June 1943 to no. 10, September 1945. On the Commonwealth Bank in wartime, Anon., *Commonwealth Bank of Australia in the Second World War* (Sydney, 1947). As I am in doubt about how profitable it is to cite "source material" in this kind of book, I confine myself in this chapter-bibliography to the following sampling: *Statute of Westminster Adoption Bill: A Monograph,* Circulated by the Attorney-General (Canberra, 1942); *Post-War Reconstruction: A Case for Greater Commonwealth Powers,* Prepared for the Constitutional Convention by the Attorney-General (Canberra, 1942); *Report of the Convention Proceedings* (Canberra, 1942); the *Reports* (10) of The Rural Reconstruction Commission (Canberra, 1943); the *Report . . . on Standardization of Australia's Railway Gauges* (Canberra, 1945); J. G. Allen, ed., *Editorial Opinion in the Contemporary British Commonwealth and Empire* (Boulder, Colo., 1946); *Report by the Australian Delegates to the United Nations Conference on International Organization* (Canberra, 1945); the parliamentary paper, *Full Employment in Australia* (Canberra, 1945). Dr. Evatt's foreign policy speeches are collected in *Foreign Policy of Australia* (Sydney, 1945) and *Australia in World Affairs* (Sydney, 1946). There are two volumes of Mr. Menzies' wartime speeches, *To the People of Britain at War* (London, 1941) and *The Forgotten People* (Sydney, 1943). And from among the many useful pamphlets, I select as indicative of what can be found, Anon., *Australian Home Front 1939–1941* (Melbourne, 1941) and A. P. Elkin, *Our Opinions and the National Effort* (Sydney, 1941).

V.   A MIDDLE POWER IN THE PACIFIC

L. F. Crisp's *Ben Chifley: A Biography* (Melbourne, 1961), though occasionally hagiographic, is a first-class political study, highly illuminating on political developments right up to Chifley's death in 1951.

For Chifley's speeches, see A. W. Stargardt, ed., *Things Worth Fighting For* (Melbourne, 1952). See also the memorial volume *The Light on the Hill* (Sydney, 1951). The publication *Digest of Decisions and Announcements* covers the Chifley administration (nos. 105 to 149), at the end of which it was discontinued. See also *Facts and Figures* for the Chifley years. Nobody has yet thought to write any kind of book about R. G. Menzies. Some of his speeches of recent years were collected in *Speech is of Time* (London, 1958). *Facts and Figures,* now much elaborated and improved, provides the principal running record of the Menzies' years. See also the political chronicles in *The Australian Quarterly* and *Politics and History* and the recurrent running reviews of economic developments in *The Economic Record*. R. H. Barret's political study cited above reaches 1959, Whitington's 1954, B. Fitzpatrick's somewhat eccentric book, *The Australian Commonwealth* (Melbourne, 1956) 1955, J. C. Horsfall's *Australia* (New York, 1955) to the middle 1950's. On the controversies over economic policy, see Copland and Barback, *The Conflict of Expansion and Stability: Documents Relating to Australian Economic Policy 1945–1952* (Melbourne, 1957).

On politics there has been a good deal of writing in recent years, for political science has come into its own in the universities. Much of the academic writing is too specialized for citation here but readers should be aware of its existence. A sampling of writing on politics in hardcover form would include Louise Overacker, *The Australian Party System* (New Haven, Conn., 1952); F. W. Eggleston, *Reflections of an Australian Liberal* (Melbourne, 1953); Anon., ed., *The Australian Political Party System* (AIPS; Sydney, 1954); J. D. B. Miller, *Australian Government and Politics* (London, 1954, and later eds.); A. F. Davies, *Australian Democracy* (Melbourne, 1958); D. W. Rawson, *Australia Votes: The 1958 Federal Election* (Melbourne, 1961); S. Encel, *Cabinet Government in Australia* (Melbourne, 1962). There is a good deal of material on state politics in S. R. Davis, ed., *The Government of the Australian States* (Melbourne, 1960). No book-length study of what happened in the Labor party after 1949 has yet been attempted. Crisp's history of the party ends in 1951. Although there are men in Australia who thoroughly understand communism in its international and domestic phases and have written excellently about it in periodicals, there seem to be no really good books of a scholarly kind about Australian communism. Book length anticommunist exposés include J. T. Lang, *Communism in Australia* (Sydney, n.d.) and E. J. Hogan, *What's Wrong with Australia* (Melbourne, 1953). On the 1951 referendum on proscribing the Communist party, Leicester Webb, *Communism and Democracy in Australia* (New York, 1955). On Soviet espionage in Australia, see *Report of the Royal Commission on Espionage* (Sydney, 1955). On the trade unions, see J. H. Portus, *The Development of Australian Trade Union Law* (Melbourne, 1958); Wilkes and Benson, eds., *Trade Unions in Australia* (AIPS; Sydney, 1959); and on arbitration, Mark Perlman, *Judges in Industry* (Melbourne, 1954). On the Roman Catholics and politics, in addition to what is said in the periodical literature and in certain of the more recent books on politics, see the pamphlets, *Socialisation,* published with the authority of the Archbishops and Bishops (1949); Brian Doyle, *Catholics and Labor's Socialist Objective* (Sydney, 1949); *Spotlight on Santamaria* (Melbourne, 1960); and the books, Tom Truman, *Catholic Action and Politics* (Melbourne, 1959) and the reviews thereof; Henry Mayer, ed., *Catholics and the Free Society* (Melbourne, 1961); and J. G. Murtagh, *Australia: The Catholic Chapter* (rev. ed.; Sydney, 1960).

General economic discussions include D. A. S. Campbell, ed., *Post-War Reconstruction in Australia* (AIPS; Sydney, 1944); Anon., ed., *Australia's Postwar Economy* (AIPS; Sydney, 1945); Anon., ed., *Australian Production at the Crossroads* (AIPS; Sydney, 1952); J. Wilkes, ed., *Productivity and Progress* (AIPS; Sydney, 1957); and J. Wilkes, ed., *Economic Growth in Australia* (AIPS; Sydney, 1962). The very best comprehensive account of the Australian economy is P. H. Karmel and M. Brunt, *The Structure of the Australian Economy* (Melbourne, 1962). The maps and accompanying texts of *Atlas of Australian Resources,* a publication of the Department of National Development, Canberra, must unfailingly be consulted. Specifically on the land industries up to the early 1950's, see J. G. Crawford, *et al., Wartime Agriculture in Australia and New Zealand* (Stanford, Calif., 1954) and *Rural Australia: A Graphic Summary,* a publication of the Bureau of Agricultural Economics, Canberra (Canberra, 1952). For subsequent developments see the Bureau's quarterly magazine, *Review of Agricultural Economics,* and its occasional papers on particular land industries. See also Ian Shannon, *Rural Industries in the Australian Economy* (Melbourne, 1955), and Drane and Edwards, eds., *The Australian Dairy Industry* (Melbourne, 1961). On the specifics of factory industry development resort must be had to studies periodically issued by federal government departments and the financial press. The position in 1952 was elaborately reviewed in *The Structure and Capacity of Australian Manufacturing Industries,* issued by the Department of National Development (Canberra, 1952). A useful pamphlet is F. G. Davidson, *The Industrialization of Australia* (Melbourne, 1957). To supplement P. H. Karmel's remarks about the business community, see such books as E. L. Wheelwright, *Ownership and Control of Australian Companies* (Sydney, 1957); A. R. Hall, *Australian Company Finance, 1946–1955* (Canberra, 1956); and J. A. Bushell, *Australian Company Mergers 1946–1959.* On Australia and the Sterling Area, see e.g., *The Sterling Area: An American Analysis* (London, 1951), but of course Australia figures in all the many books about the Sterling Area. An international survey of inflation in which Australia figures is A. J. Brown, *The Great Inflation 1939–1951* (London, 1955). D. F. Nicholson on trade policy ends with an analysis of GATT. A specialized economic study is J. O. N. Perkins, *Britain and Australia . . . in the 1950s* (Melbourne, 1962). On government finance, Ratchford's *Public Expenditures* continues to 1955–56. At the time of the annual budget speech there is regularly distributed a paper on

National Income and Expenditure. On Commonwealth-State financial relations, see the government paper *Commonwealth Payments to or for the States,* issued first in 1961. There is an annual report of the National Debt Commission. Surveys of the economy prepared in the Treasury are normally issued each year. These should be read in the light of the comments by the professional economists and the financial journalists. On immigration see W. D. Borrie, *Immigration, Problems and Prospects* (Sydney, 1949); W. D. Borrie, *Italians and Germans in Australia: A Study of Assimilation* (Melbourne, 1954); C. A. Price, *German Settlers in South Australia* (Melbourne, 1945); J. A. Hempel, *Italians in Queensland* (Canberra, 1959); Jerzy Zubrzycki, *Immigrants in Australia* (Melbourne, 1960), with its *Statistical Supplement* (Canberra, 1960); Anon, ed., *Australia and the Migrant* (AIPS; Sydney, 1953); Anon., ed., *A White Australia* (AIPS; Sydney, 1947). The most substantial case for a drastic revision of the White Australia policy is probably the pamphlet, *Control or Colour Bar?* (Melbourne, 1960), issued by The Immigration Reform Group. Recent studies in federalism are Anon., ed., *Federalism in Australia* (AIPS; Melbourne, 1949) and G. Sawer, ed., *Federalism: An Australian Jubilee Study* (Melbourne, 1952). G. Greenwood, *The Future of Australian Federalism* (Melbourne, 1946) is the argument of a convinced unificationist. It tells much about the climate of opinion that no solid and convincing statement of the states' rights position has been made. What the politicians are currently thinking comes out in *Report from the Joint Committee on Constitutional Review* (Canberra, 1959). On the public administration, or the bureaucracy, see in addition to the Spann book noticed earlier, H. A. Scarrow, *The Higher Public Service of the Commonwealth of Australia* (Durham, N.C., 1957); L. Blair, *The Commonwealth Public Service* (Melbourne, 1958); and *Report of the Committee of Inquiry into Public Service Recruitment* (Canberra, 1959). Re banking, the pamphlet on nationalization mentioned in the text is *The Case for Bank Nationalization,* N.S.W. Fabian Society, Pamphlet No. 1 (Sydney, 1947). For the struggle over banking as seen by the private trading banks, see the Blainey and Butlin volumes cited above. For a general analysis of the private trading banks see H. W. Arndt, *The Australian Trading Banks* (Melbourne, 1947). For banking techniques, Gifford, Wood, Reitsma, *Australian Banking* (4th ed.; Brisbane, 1960). The annual reports of the Commonwealth Bank to 1959 and of the Reserve Bank from 1960 contain statements of the changes in the legal status of the government's banking institutions as well as informative reviews of the economy from the banker's standpoint. On transport, Hocking and Haddon-Cave, *Air Transport in Australia* (Sydney, 1951); J. Wilkes, ed., *Australia's Transport Crisis* (AIPS; Sydney, 1956); and E. Harding, *Uniform Railway Gauge* (Melbourne, 1958). On power, N. R. Wills, ed., *Australia's Power Resources* (AIPS; Melbourne, 1955). On urbanization, a general treatise on planning which constantly refers to the Australian scene is Brown and Sherrard, *Town and Country Planning* (Melbourne, 1951). On the Sydney problem, Denis Winston, *Sydney's*

Great Experiment (Sydney, 1957) and the publications of the Cumberland County Council, e.g., *Economics of Urban Expansion* (Sydney, 1958); on Melbourne, see the last three selections in Grant and Serle, *The Melbourne Scene 1803–1956* (Melbourne, 1957); on Brisbane there is some light in the Greenwood and Laverty book cited above; on Perth, J. R. H. Johns, *Metropolitan Government in Western Australia* (Perth, 1950); and on the development of Canberra, see the publications of the National Capital Development Commission, e.g., *Planning Survey Report of the Canberra City District* (Canberra, 1959).

On the cultural situation probably the best single source is *Meanjin Quarterly* in which, sooner or later, somebody discusses "the issues." On building, architecture, and associated matters the most lively writer is Robin Boyd, author of *Australia's Home: Its Origins, Builders and Occupiers* (Melbourne, 1952) and *The Australian Ugliness* (Melbourne, 1960). For pictures and plans of houses, the money put into which is a major item of private capital investment, the building of which is a major industry, see Neil Clerehan, ed., *Best Australian Houses* (Melbourne, 1961)—best in the sense of architectural modernity, as contrasted with Spooner and Eeles, *Practical Homes* (Sydney, 1947) or the inbetween values of K. McDonald, *The New Australian Home* (Melbourne, 1954). On painting see the color reproductions and the black-and-whites in *Modern Australian Painting and Sculpture: A Survey of Australian Art from 1950–1960* (Adelaide, 1960) and the catalogue of the Whitechapel Gallery show in London, *Recent Australian Painting* (London, 1961). On Sidney Nolan see the sumptuous monograph, Clark, MacInnes, and Robertson, *Sidney Nolan* (London, 1961). On Russell Drysdale, *Russell Drysdale: A Retrospective Exhibition 1937–1960* (Sydney, 1960). Both men and many others will eventually be presented in Australian Art Monographs, of which the first was Noel Macainish, *Clifton Pugh* (Melbourne, 1962). A comprehensive restudy of the history of Australian painting which appeared too late to be profited from by me is Bernard Smith, *Australian Painting 1788–1960* (Melbourne, 1962). A Penguin by Robert Hughes entitled *Australian Painting: A Critical Survey* is to be expected. Most recent books on "primitive art" that pretend to comprehensive coverage now include something about aboriginal art in Australia. See also A. P. Elkin and R. and C. Berndt, *Art in Arnhem Land* (Melbourne, 1950); the elaborate UNESCO volume, introduction by Sir Herbert Read, *Australia: Aboriginal Paintings–Arnhem Land* (New York, 1954); and Volume 1 of the Records of the American-Australian Scientific Expedition to Arnhem Land: Charles P. Mountford, *Art, Myth and Symbolism* (Melbourne, 1956). For the work of untrained aboriginal children, see Miller and Rutter, *Child Artists of the Australian Bush* (London, 1952). On the European-style painting of adult aborigines, see Rex Battarbee, *Modern Australian Aboriginal Art* (Sydney, 1951). The most prolific anthropological writers in this period are Ronald and Catherine Berndt, separately or in collaboration. See, e.g., *Kunapipi* (Melbourne, 1951) and

Djanggawul (London, 1952), both studies in aboriginal religion; *Sexual Behavior in Western Arnhem* (New York, 1951); and *From Black to White in South Australia* (Melbourne, 1951) for the situation today of the aborigines of one state. See also C. P. Mountford, *Brown Men and Red Sand* (Adelaide, 1950) and *The Tiwi, the Art, Myth and Ceremony* (London, 1958); D. F. Thomson, *Economic Structure and the Ceremonial Exchange Cycle in Arnhem Land* (Melbourne, 1949); T. G. H. Strehlow, *Aranda Traditions* (Melbourne, 1949); A. P. Elkin, *Aboriginal Men of High Degree* (Sydney, 1944). A "travel" writer's impressions, beautifully illustrated, is C. Simpson, *Adam in Ochre* (New York, 1953). An account of what happened to a detribalized aboriginal who murdered a white child is K. S. Inglis, *The Stuart Case* (Melbourne, 1961). Most of the useful material on the theatre and drama is in newspaper and periodical articles. The successful plays are normally published in book form shortly after production. On the Elizabethan Theatre Trust, see *The Australian Elizabethan Theatre Trust: The First Year* (Sydney, 1956) and the views of the first executive director, Hugh Hunt, *The Making of Australian Theatre* (Melbourne, 1960). I know of no comprehensive, critical review of education below the university level, but there is some periodical and pamphlet literature on the subject and occasionally the matter is touched upon in the evaluatory symposia listed below. In addition to the ACER publications, see also the publications of The Australian College of Education (founded 1959) and of the Melbourne University specialists in education. On the universities, there are numerous articles in symposia and periodicals. G. Blainey's "Centenary History" of the University of Melbourne reaches into the post-World War II years. A. P. Rowe's *If the Gown Fits* (Melbourne, 1960) presents his often sour and disillusioning experiences as a vice-chancellor. An effort to forecast the student populations which erred on the side of modesty is Borrie and Dedman, *University Enrolments in Australia 1955–1970* (Canberra, 1957). See the Commonwealth document, *Report of the Committee on Australian Universities* (Canberra, 1957). The report of a seminar is *Science in Australia* (Melbourne, 1952). There is an account of the cultural institutions in the federal capital in H. L. White, ed., *Canberra* (Sydney, 1954). The universities regularly publish "calendars," handbooks of general information, and so on, which give light on their activities. On the humanities, see A. G. Price, ed., *The Humanities in Australia: A Survey with Special Reference to the Universities* (Sydney, 1959). The library situation has been under constant study since the war and the pamphlet literature is voluminous but there seems to be no comprehensive book. Adult education has also been much written about. In addition to pamphlets such as W. G. K. Duncan, ed., *The Future of Adult Education in Australia* (Sydney, 1944); F. Alexander, *Adult Education in Australia* (Melbourne, 1959); and Paul Sheats, *A Report on University Adult Education in Australia and New Zealand* (Chicago, 1960); a useful source of information is the periodical *Adult Education* published quarterly by the Council of Adult

Education, Victoria. On the press, about which too little is said in
the text of this book, see W. S. Holden, *Australia Goes to Press* (De-
troit, 1961) and K. S. Inglis' superior essay on "The Daily Papers"
in the Coleman symposium cited below. This may be the proper place
to call attention to the biweekly *Nation* (Vol. 1, no. 1, 1958) and
to the fact that *The Bulletin* reached the end of its historic road in
1961, was taken over by *Observer,* a fortnightly of recent vintage,
and rather rapidly transformed in character. In a way, this symbolizes
that not only is Australia changing but that its conception of itself
has radically changed, leaving the old *Bulletin* stranded in a shrinking
billabong. The best way to gain an understanding of Australian literature today is to read the writings of the poets, critics, and fiction
writers. Since it is not my practice to provide bibliographies of the
individual writers, perhaps it will suffice if I call attention, with regard to the poetry, to three recent anthologies: George Mackaness,
ed., *An Anthology of Australian Verse* (rev. ed.; Sydney, 1952);
Judith Wright, ed., *A Book of Australian Verse* (Melbourne, 1956);
and Thompson, Slessor, and Howarth, eds., *The Penguin Book of
Australian Verse* (Mitcham, South Australia, 1958). With regard to
the prose writers there have been a good many anthologies since the
war, e.g., T. A. G. Hungerford, ed., *Australian Signpost* (Melbourne,
1956); T. I. Moore, ed., *Australia Writes* (Melbourne, 1953); and
Lionel Wigmore, ed., *Span* (Melbourne, 1958); as well as the several
anthologies edited by Colin Roderick dealing historically with the
short story and the novel, published in Sydney at various dates. Most
of the critical writing is still in the periodicals but Vincent Buckley
has published two books, A. A. Phillips one, and James McAuley
one. On Patrick White, a not entirely satisfactory pamphlet is G. Dut-
ton, *Patrick White* (Melbourne, 1961). How an Australian academic
sees the literature is apparent from C. Hadgraft, *Australian Literature*
(London, 1960). An American attempt to define the cultural image
of Australia is J. Jones, ed., *Image of Australia,* a special number of
The Texas Quarterly in hardcover form (Austin, Texas, 1962). An
even more comprehensive attempt is Norman Macgeorge, ed., *The
Arts in Australia* (Melbourne, 1948). There is currently in North
America an effort to build the literatures of the Commonwealth
countries into the academic English curriculum. This has resulted
thus far in the publication of some pretty bad books, e.g., A. L. Mc-
Leod, ed., *The Commonwealth Pen: An Introduction to the Literature
of the British Commonwealth* (Ithaca, N.Y., 1961) and the comparative study of Australian and Canadian poetry, J. P. Matthews,
Tradition in Exile (Toronto & Melbourne, 1962). For fascinating
personal statements of the expatriation theme see Alan Moorehead's
opening essay in his book *Rum Jungle* (London, 1953); W. K.
Hancock's *Country and Calling* (London, 1954); and the rather silly
essay by Murray Sayle in T. O'Keefe, ed., *Alienation* (London, 1960).
Memorial volumes on home-staying intellectuals of the generation
just now passing are *Ian Clunies Ross: Memoirs and Papers* (Melbourne, 1961) and Sir Douglas Copland, ed., *Giblin: The Scholar*

and the Man (Melbourne, 1960). The trade problem is, of course, earnestly discussed by the economists in their professional journals and the popular press. The very best writing on the subject is that of Sir John Crawford. Probably the best single statement of Australia's relation to the Commonwealth is that by J. D. B. Miller in his *The Commonwealth in the World* (London, 1958), but for full understanding of the complexly various views of this one must pursue the matter in the books on "foreign relations" and the newspaper and periodical press. How a "loyal" Australian sees Australia's relation to royalty, see Rex Ingamells, *Royalty and Australia* (Melbourne, 1954). On Queen Elizabeth's visit of 1954, see the "official commemorative volume," *Royal Visit to Australia of Her Majesty Queen Elizabeth II and His Royal Highness the Duke of Edinburgh* (Sydney, 1954). The pictures should be studied as carefully as the text. On foreign policy, the best continuing chronicle appears in *Politics and History,* but latterly the *Australian Quarterly* has also provided one and important articles on foreign policy and foreign political affairs appear in *The Australian Outlook.* In the early 1960's complaints about the poor quality of Australian thinking and writing on foreign policy began to be made, but this generalized indictment should not deflect attention from the good work that has been and is being done, lacking in sophisticated realism as much of it is. Dr. Evatt's speeches subsequent to 1946 have not been collected but he wrote two books about the United Nations and its work, *The United Nations* (Cambridge, Mass., 1948) and *The Task of Nations* (New York, 1949). Books by men who worked with Dr. Evatt as diplomats with greater or lesser success include F. W. Eggleston, *Reflections on Australian Foreign Policy* (Melbourne, 1957); P. Hasluck, *Workshop of Security* (Melbourne, 1948); J. A. Alexander, *In the Shadow: Three Years in Moscow* (Melbourne, 1949); W. Macmahon Ball, *Japan: Enemy or Ally?* (Melbourne, 1948); and *Nationalism and Communism in East Asia* (Melbourne, 1952). See also Professor Ball's significant essay in J. Wilkes, ed., *Asia and Australia* (AIPS; Sydney, 1961). An important pioneer book on postwar Asia written by Australians is Gilmore and Warner, eds., *Near North* (Sydney, 1948). Mr. Warner has continued to be the best of the Australian journalists writing on Asia. A review of Australian opinion of Asia is Werner Levi, *Australia's Outlook on Asia* (Sydney, 1958). For a review of foreign policy 1950–55, Greenwood and Harper, eds., *Australia in World Affairs* (Melbourne, 1957), presumably the first volume of a continuing series. For the relation with the United Nations, see Harper and Sisson, *Australia and the United Nations* (New York, 1959). The most important special study thus far is R. N. Rosecrance, *Australian Diplomacy and Japan 1945–1951* (Melbourne, 1962). An Australian study of SEATO was announced for late 1962, G. Modelski, ed., *SEATO: Six Studies.* W. C. B. Turnstall, *The Commonwealth and Regional Defence* (London, 1959) is a valuable study. Percy Spender never collected his several important speeches, but R. G. Casey offered *Friends and Neighbors* (East Lansing, Mich., 1955). See also the printed version of Casey's Roy Milne Memorial Lecture, *The Conduct of Australian Foreign Policy* (1952). A source for Menzies and the Suez crisis is *The Memoirs of Anthony Eden: Full Circle* (London & Boston, 1960). On the American involvement in the Southwest Pacific, see C. Hartley Grattan, *The United States and the Southwest Pacific* (Cambridge, Mass., 1961). Some evaluations of Australia, more or less comprehensive in coverage, published in recent years are W. V. Aughterson, ed., *Taking Stock* (Melbourne, 1953); Ian Bevan, ed., *The Sunburnt Country* (London, 1953); Geo. Caiger, *The Australian Way of Life* (New York, 1953); J. D. Pringle, *Australian Accent* (London, 1958); Colin Clark, *Australian Hopes and Fears* (London, 1958); R. M. Crawford, *An Australian Perspective* (Madison, Wisc., 1960); Jeanne MacKenzie, *Australian Paradox* (Melbourne, 1961); Blaxland, Mayor, and Phillips, eds., *Australia: 1970 and Beyond* (AIPS; Sydney, 1961); P. Coleman, ed., *Australian Civilization* (Melbourne, 1962); and James Morris, a series of twelve articles in the *Manchester Guardian Weekly,* July 26–October 11, 1962.

NEW ZEALAND

VI. BRITAIN'S OUTLYING FARM

For political and economic developments, see *The Southwest Pacific to 1900.* There is as yet no life of Massey but one would seem to be in progress from the excellent articles on him appearing in *Political Science.* While there does not appear to be a book about the 1913 labor upheaval, it is discussed in all general histories, the biographies of contemporaries, such as James Thorn, *Peter Fraser* (London, 1952), and in a scattering of journal articles including those which deal with the percolation of radical thought into New Zealand. On the Maori in this and the next chapter in addition to what is to be found in the general histories, see I. L. G. Sutherland, *The Maori Situation* (Wellington, 1935); I. L. G. Sutherland, ed., *The Maori People Today* (Wellington, 1940); Ernest and Pearl Beaglehole, *Some Modern Maoris* (Wellington, 1946); the relevant passages in Raymond Firth, *Economics of the New Zealand Maori* (Wellington, 1959); J. F. Cody, *Man of Two Worlds: A Biography of Sir Maui Pomare* (Wellington, 1953); Eric Ramsden, *Sir Apirana Ngata and Maori Culture* (Wellington, 1948); as well as Ngata's own writings—e.g., his essay "Anthropology and the Government of Native Races" in *New Zealand Affairs* (1929); the reminiscent writings of Sir Peter Buck, e.g., his "Introduction" to the book by E. and P. Beaglehole and H. B. Hawthorne, *The Maori: A Study in Acculturation* (Menasha, Wisconsin, 1944); the relevant passages in H. Belshaw, *et al.,* eds., *Agricultural Organization in New Zealand* (Melbourne, 1936); the chapter in Thorn's biography of Peter Fraser; and the relevant essays in J. D. Freeman and W. R. Geddes, *Anthropology in the South Seas* (New Plymouth, N.Z., 1959). On New Zealand and World War I, in addition to the general histories, there is a four-volume

Official History of New Zealand's Effort in the Great War (Wellington, 1919–23) and see the relevant biographies, such as those of Bell and Fraser; Wood's study of *New Zealand in the World;* and the specialized material listed in C. E. Dornbusch, *The New Zealand Army: A Bibliography* (Cornwallville, N.Y., 1961). Some documentation on New Zealand and the Empire is to be found in R. McG. Dawson, *The Development of Dominion Status 1900–1936* (London, 1937).

VII. INSECURITY AND EXPERIMENT

Nobody has yet thought to write a life of J. G. Coates, or even to do some thoroughly researched articles about his career, yet he was undoubtedly the ablest conservative politician of his time and should attract a comparably able biographer. The general histories written after World War II tend to skimp the period 1919–35, its importance unperceived, and hurry on to get to the Labour victory of 1935, regarded as a climax of New Zealand history, as the Ballance Liberal victory was so long regarded earlier. Harold Miller, *New Zealand* (London, 1950) is an almost classic illustration of this. The most vivid, if not the wisest, writing about the 1920's and 1930's is in Beaglehole, *New Zealand: A Short History* (London, 1936). How the general situation appeared in the late 1920's is apparent from *New Zealand Affairs* (Christchurch, 1929). A more comprehensive review of a few years later is *Handbook of New Zealand* (prepared for an ANZAAS meeting) (Wellington, 1936). An economic review is the "New Zealand Centennial Number" of *The Economic Record* (Melbourne, 1939). J. B. Condliffe, *The Welfare State in New Zealand* (London, 1959) picks up the economic history at the depression; the book's interpretations have been severely criticized in New Zealand. See, too, W. B. Sutch, *Recent Economic Changes in New Zealand* (Wellington, 1936). A very superior example of government publicity, well-written, excellently illustrated, is *Introduction to New Zealand* (Wellington, 1945). A rich mine of information about the land industries in all their aspects is H. Belshaw, *et al.*, eds., *Agricultural Organization in New Zealand* (Melbourne, 1936). Specifically on marketing is W. M. Smith, *The Marketing of Australian and New Zealand Primary Products* (London, 1936). A classic book on the grasslands is Sir E. Bruce Levy, *Grasslands of New Zealand* (2d ed.; Wellington, 1955). A historical essay of great usefulness is B. L. Evans, "Grassland Research in New Zealand" in the *Official Yearbook* for 1960. Robert Wallace's impressions are in his *The Rural Economy and Agriculture of Australia and New Zealand* (London, 1891); R. G. Stapleton's in *A Tour in Australia and New Zealand* (London, 1928). On Bell in forestry, see his biography. On the history of the social services see W. B. Sutch, *Poverty and Progress in New Zealand* (Wellington, 1941), really a rather thin history of the harsh underside of New Zealand life. Two of the more memorable public documents

of the early depression years are *Report of the Economic Committee*
(Wellington, 1932), which reflects Australian thinking as carried to
New Zealand by D. B. Copland, and *Report of the Monetary Committee 1934* (Wellington, 1934). The literature on the Labour government 1935–49 is enormous but much of it is in the form of topical
pamphlets and articles and is often more publicity than anything else.
Attention has already been called to how the arrival of Labour in
office figures in the general histories. The sympathy of the New
Zealand intelligentsia for Labour is an important fact about the New
Zealand situation. A wide-ranging assessment of New Zealand which
naturally has much to say about Labour's innovations is H. Belshaw,
ed., *New Zealand* (Berkeley, Calif., 1947). John Lee, *Socialism in
New Zealand* (London, 1938) is factually rich if not impeccably accurate about what is socialism; it reflects directly his own odd ideology. In his *New Zealand: A Working Democracy* (New York, 1943)
Walter Nash offers a bland semi-official "case for Labour." Thorn's
life of Fraser is irritatingly hagiographic but it must be read. Condliffe's *The Welfare State in New Zealand* reflects his strong skepticism
of Labour. C. Westrate, *Portrait of a Mixed Economy: New Zealand*
(Wellington, 1960) is more concerned with results and analysis thereof
than with historical development, but it must unfailingly be read; it
is a very important book. The impact of Labour on the social services
is made abundantly clear in the official history, *The Growth and Development of Social Security in New Zealand* (Wellington, 1950). A
review of the developments in legal terms is to be found in the relevant sections of J. L. Robson, ed., *New Zealand: The Development
of its Laws and Constitution* (London, 1954). E. H. McCormick in
New Zealand Literature (London, 1959) is authoritative on the
writing of this period. What McCormick says can profitably be contrasted with a statement of the position as it appeared in 1943 to a
man of a previous generation, Alan Mulgan, *Literature and Authorship in New Zealand* (London, 1943). On the novel in New Zealand,
see Joan Stevens, *The New Zealand Novel 1860–1960* (Wellington,
1961). There is no history of "fun and games" in New Zealand,
though an enormous casual literature about them, but see the pictorial surveys in *Making New Zealand* (Wellington, 1940). On Guthrie-
Smith see A. E. Woodhouse, *Guthrie-Smith of Tutira* (Wellington,
1959) and for a bibliography of Fairburn which illustrates the nature
of a writing life in New Zealand see G. A. Johnson, *A. R. D. Fairburn
1904–1957* (Auckland, 1958). A study of Satchell's career is Phillip
Wilson, *The Maorilander* (Christchurch, 1961). M. H. Holcroft eventually wrote a three-book essay and collected the three in *Discovered
Isles* (Christchurch, 1950). A pioneering effort to investigate its subject is S. J. Baker, *New Zealand Slang* (Christchurch, 1941).

VIII. A SMALL NATION IN THE PACIFIC

From the point of view taken in this book, the most important book
on New Zealand and World War II is F. L. W. Wood, *The New*

Zealand People at War: Political and External Affairs (Wellington, 1958), an excellent job. (This is a volume of the series, "New Zealand in the Second World War 1939–1945" to which readers may be referred *passim* for works dealing with combat activities.) For the context and background of prewar New Zealand in international politics see G. Carter as earlier cited. Attention should also be directed to Nicholas Mansergh's historical and documentary works cited earlier, both of which span the war and continue to 1952. For light on New Zealand attitudes toward foreign affairs in the 1920's, see W. D. Stewart, *Sir Francis H. D. Bell* (Wellington, 1937). See also Wood, *New Zealand in the World;* I. F. G. Milner, *New Zealand's Interests and Policies in the Far East* (New York, 1940); the symposium, *Contemporary New Zealand: A Survey of Domestic and Foreign Policy* (Wellington, 1938), plus the supplementary pamphlet, F. L. W. Wood, *New Zealand in Crisis May 1938–August 1939* (Wellington, 1939) and the news-letter, *New Zealand Affairs*, issued from 1940 to 1942; and B. K. Gordon, *New Zealand Becomes a Pacific Power* (Chicago, 1960), but this book was severely criticized in New Zealand and should only be read in the light of those criticisms. An early discussion of New Zealand at war is to be found in W. Y. Elliott and H. Duncan Hall, eds., *The British Commonwealth at War* (New York, 1943), a book much disfigured by Elliott's pro-British silliness and Hall's outrageous prejudices. See also the British and American writing on the war discussed in the bibliography of Chapter IV. On domestic politics during the war—the writer observed the political situation first-hand in 1940—Wood's narrative is basic, but such general histories as cover the war years can profitably be read. Kippenberger's personal account of his soldiering is *Infantry Brigadier* (London, 1949). On the economic history of the time, Wood should again be read first; there is something in Condliffe's *Welfare State;* there are indispensable data in the official document *The New Zealand Economy 1939–1951* (Wellington, 1951); there is J. W. Williams, *The New Zealand Economy in War and Reconstruction* (New York, 1948); and there is, for the land industries, A. A. Ross, "Wartime Agriculture in New Zealand 1939–1950," in J. G. Crawford, ed., *Wartime Agriculture in Australia and New Zealand 1939–1950* (Stanford, 1954). On the coming of war in the Pacific see Wood, Thorn, Nash, Gordon, and the relevant references in Chapter IV above. There is a dearth of material on postwar New Zealand in hardcover form, even some of the lately published general histories skimping it in favor of general interpretation of the country, its predicament, etc. It may be noted, however, that Oliver does better than Sinclair. On economic affairs Condliffe's *Welfare State* has its uses, but Westrate is indispensable. See also for light on politico-economic matters from the angle of public administration, R. S. Parker, ed., *Economic Stability in New Zealand* (Wellington, 1953); K. J. Scott, ed., *Welfare in New Zealand* (Wellington, 1955); and T. C. Larkin, ed., *New Zealand's External Relations* (Wellington, 1962). In a country such as New Zealand public administration is of peculiar importance. See, therefore, R. J. Polaschek, *Government Administra-*

tion in New Zealand (Wellington, 1958). On the economic future, see *Industrial Development Conference, 1960, Background Papers* and *Report,* particularly the former. On the waterfront strike of 1951, see Dick Scott, *151 Days* (Abridged ed; Auckland, 1954), definitely a "red" version of the affair. On communism in New Zealand, there is a flood of light in Sid Scott, *Rebel in a Wrong Cause* (Auckland, 1960). The first New Zealand study in psephology is Chapman, Jackson, & Mitchell, *New Zealand Politics in Action: The 1960 General Election* (London, 1962). At this point attention may profitably be called to two magazines of comment and information additional to the journals mentioned earlier, *Comment,* a quarterly, Vol. 1, no. 1 (Wellington, 1959) and the fetidly leftist *Monthly Review,* Vol. 1, no. 1 (Christchurch, 1960). Much can be learned from geographers' assessments of various situations in the country such as appear in the *New Zealand Geographer* and such collections of papers as *New Zealand: Inventory and Prospect* (Wellington, 1956). There appears to be no study of the actual adoption of the Statute of Westminster, but preliminary examinations of the matter are J. C. Beaglehole, *et al., New Zealand and the Statute of Westminster* (Wellington, 1944) and A. E. Currie, *New Zealand and the Statute of Westminster* (Wellington, 1944). A discursive account of the abolition of the upper house is H. J. Benda, "The End of Bicameralism in New Zealand" in S. D. Bailey, ed., *Parliamentary Government in the Commonwealth* (N.Y., 1952). An up-to-date study is K. J. Scott, *The New Zealand Constitution* (Oxford, 1962). There is no comprehensive study of the position of the Maoris in postwar New Zealand comparable to Sutherland's symposium of 1940, but see the discussions in the general histories which reach this period, especially Oliver's, the valuable essay by E. G. Schwimmer, "Government and the Changing Maori" in the *New Zealand Journal of Public Administration,* March, 1960, and the essays by Booth and Borrie in Freeman and Geddes, eds., *Anthropology in the South Seas.* J. K. Hunn, *Report on Department of Maori Affairs* (Wellington, 1960) must also be read. On education in New Zealand see A. E. Campbell, *Educating New Zealand* (Wellington, 1941); Beaglehole's history of the university listed earlier and his *Victoria University College* (Wellington, 1949); L. Webb, *The Control of Education in New Zealand* (Wellington, 1937); G. W. Parkyn, ed., *The Administration of Education in New Zealand* (Wellington, 1954); H. Roth, *George Hogben: A Biography* (Wellington, 1952); and the *Report of the Committee on New Zealand Universities* (Wellington, 1960). The report on the libraries so freely quoted is A. D. Osborn, *New Zealand Library Resources* (Wellington, 1960). McCormick's *New Zealand Literature* (London, 1959) continues indispensable. A stimulating book-length essay on poetry is J. K. Baxter, *The Fire and the Anvil* (Wellington, 1960). Joan Stevens' book on the novel is, of course, still useful. A sketch of New Zealand literary development is to be found in A. L. McLeod, ed., *The Commonwealth Pen* (Ithaca, N.Y., 1961). For a general survey or directory of all the arts see E. C. Simpson, ed., *Survey of the Arts in New Zealand* (Wellington, 1961).

Since it is manifestly impossible to provide a bibliography for each writer mentioned, one may refer, for the poets, to Robert Chapman and Jonathan Bennett, eds., *An Anthology of New Zealand Verse* (London, 1956) and Allen Curnow, ed., *The Penguin Book of New Zealand Verse* (Hammondsworth, 1960). There is no comparably easy approach to the fiction writers but the Government Printer has been issuing pamphlets under the collective title *Writing in New Zealand* of which two deal with the novel and two with the short story. From these one can proceed to search out the books excerpted. Many of the fiction writers mentioned are represented in D. M. Davin, ed., *New Zealand Short Stories* (London, 1953), The World's Classics, No. 534. A good many of the novelists mentioned have found publication in New York as well as London in recent years. A retrospective anthology covering the first fifteen years of *Landfall* is Charles Brasch, *Landfall Country* (Christchurch, 1962). With regard to painting and painters, attention should be called to the pamphlets published by the Auckland City Art Gallery. The only book devoted to a New Zealand painter resident in New Zealand of which I have knowledge is E. H. McCormick, *Eric Lee-Johnson* (Hamilton, 1956). An effort to get New Zealand pictures into the world gallery of reproductions is *Caxton Prints: Paintings by New Zealand Artists* (Christchurch, 1958–). The artists represented to 1960 were Eric Lee-Johnson, W. A. Sutton, and Doris Lusk.

As to "verdicts" on New Zealand, in addition to F. L. W. Wood's *This New Zealand* cited earlier, the books of the historians almost invariably end up with interpretative essays. See also Desmond Stone, ed., *Verdict on New Zealand* (Wellington, 1959), covering the field from Samuel Butler to *Réalités* and including several that enraged the easily enraged New Zealanders; Oliver Duff, *New Zealand Now* (Wellington, 1941 and later eds.); Oliver Duff, *Ourselves Today* (Christchurch, 1959), with its amusing reflections on the effect of the overwhelmingly numerous economic animals on the human beings; Roderick Finlayson, *Our Life in this Land* (Auckland, 1940), a rejection of the results of the whole adventure; David Ausubel, *The Fern and the Tiki* (Sydney, 1960), really a portrait of an American with his foot in his mouth; and the wise and witty topical verse commentary on this, that, and the other. *The Best of Whim Wham* (Hamilton, 1959), a product of the genius of Allen Curnow. A specialized look at New Zealand is K. Sinclair, ed., *Distance Looks Our Way: The Effects of Remoteness on New Zealand* (Auckland, 1961).

THE ISLANDS

IX–XI.

GENERAL: As this book was being completed there came to hand F. M. Cammack and Shiro Saito, *Pacific Island Bibliography* (New York, 1962). In the "Introduction" it is stated that "This bibliography is based on a selection of materials in the Pacific Collection of the University of Hawaii's Gregg M. Sinclair Library," and that ". . . the majority of entries for printed works are limited to titles published since the completion in 1948 of C. R. H. Taylor's *A Pacific Bibliography* [cited in *The Southwest Pacific to 1900*]." As often with bibliographies, no critical evaluation of the items is attempted. It is obvious the work was not planned for the use of a historian, though much of interest to a historian is listed. However, even a preliminary study of it reveals some odd aspects, such as the inclusion of Nauru under the Gilbert Islands and under "New Zealand and the Maori" of much material that deals largely or exclusively with pakeha New Zealand and only incidentally if at all with the Maoris. The need of the historian for a critical bibliography of the materials on the islands remains unsatisfied.

A writer who attempts to continue his narrative into the twentieth century is under a handicap in that very few historians before him have done so either with regard to any particular island group, islands under a particular sovereignty, or the islands in general. The tendency has been to end a historical narrative *circa* 1900 (and often earlier). For example, while G. H. Scholefield ostensibly extends his narrative to around 1918, actually he is most unsatisfying about what happened after 1900, while Morrell, whose book is so superior to Scholefield's, puts the twentieth century into an "Epilogue" which occupies but 18 out of his 441 pages.

A writer who tries to carry his narrative up to the present day in any degree of amplitude therefore feels that he is not getting the aid and comfort he should and that he is conducting a catch-as-catch-can operation, becomes unsure about his perspective, terribly self-conscious about the gaps in his knowledge, and inevitably begins to wonder why he ever got involved in so perilous an undertaking.

Since even the most casual student must try to understand the physical character of the islands and their environments, mention should be made of the following books, some of which incidentally include historical information: E. H. Bryan, Jr., *American Polynesia and the Hawaiian Chain* (Honolulu, 1942); E. G. Mears, *Pacific Ocean Handbook* (Stanford, Calif., 1944); Fairfield Osborn, ed., *The Pacific World* (New York, 1944); W. H. Hobbs, *The Fortress Islands of the Pacific* (Ann Arbor, 1945); K. B. Cumberland, *Southwest Pacific: A Geography* (Wellington, 1954); M. Bates and D. Abbott, *Coral Island* (New York, 1958); and Herold J. Wiens, *Atoll Environment and Ecology* (New Haven, 1962). Since the island environments are tropical, the following books are helpful, even though they are not always concerned specifically with the islands: Pierre Gourou, *The Tropical World* (2d ed.; New York, 1958); M. Bates, *Where Winter Never Comes* (New York, 1952); E. P. Hanson, *New Worlds Emerging* (New York, 1949); D. H. K. Lee, *Climate and Economic Development in the Tropics* (New York, 1957); A. G. Price, *White Settlers in the Tropics* (New York, 1939).

With regard to the natives anthropologically considered, see the

Keesing and Elkin bibliographies cited in *The Southwest Pacific to 1900*, and in the context of "primitives," such books as M. J. Herskovits, *Man and His Works* (New York, 1951); R. Linton, *The Tree of Culture* (New York, 1956); and F. M. Keesing, *Cultural Anthropology* (New York, 1958). A fascinating paperback on the Polynesian background is R. C. Suggs, *The Island Civilizations of Polynesia* (New York: Mentor, 1960). Professor Herskovits' *Economic Anthropology* (New York, 1952) can also be read with profit, though preferably with regard to the controversy it generated. Because so much of the illustrative material is drawn from Melanesian situations, H. I. Hogbin, *Social Change* (London, 1958) is a very useful book to read on this important topic. Other books helpful in understanding the native peoples surely include J. Barrau, *Subsistence Agriculture in Melanesia* (Honolulu, 1958)—a companion volume on Polynesia is promised —Murai, Pen, and Miller, *Some Tropical South Pacific Islands Foods* (Honolulu, 1958); R. Linton and P. S. Wingert, *Arts of the South Seas* (New York, n.d.; a Museum of Modern Art publication); and P. S. Wingert, *Primitive Art: Its Traditions and Styles* (New York, 1962), which has a good bibliography of this fascinating subject; P. Worsley, *The Trumpet Shall Sound* (London, 1957), the most comprehensive book yet on the "cargo" cults. Anthropological studies relating to particular islands or portions of islands will be listed below as relevant. Most books on the islands are illustrated, but two books of pictures which specialize in the natives are H. I. Hogbin, ed., *Peoples of the Southwest Pacific* (New York, 1945) and L. Rose, ed., *People in the Sun* (Sydney, 1961).

Finally, there is a group of books, none specifically organized historically but all containing historical information: R. W. Robson, ed., *Pacific Islands Year Book*, first issued in 1932 (8th ed.; Sydney, 1959), covering the islands comprehensively but not according to any satisfactory system; J. C. Furnas, *Anatomy of Paradise* (New York, 1948), which is organized topically but refers to a wide range of island groups and treats everything intelligently and often amusingly as well; W. E. H. Stanner, *The South Seas in Transition* (Sydney, 1953), which deals with Papua–New Guinea, Fiji, and Western Samoa; F. M. Keesing, *The South Seas in the Modern World* (New York, 1941), a classic area survey of comprehensive coverage; L. A. Mander, *Some Dependent Peoples of the South Pacific* (New York, 1954), covering Western Samoa, Papua–New Guinea, the Solomons, Tonga, Fiji, the New Hebrides; F. J. West, *Political Advancement in the South Pacific* (Melbourne, 1961), covering Fiji, Tahiti, and American Samoa; J. A. Decker, *Labor Problems in the Pacific Mandates* (New York, 1940), covering the Japanese mandate, the Territory of New Guinea, Nauru, and Western Samoa; two books by C. S. Belshaw, *Island Administration in the South-West Pacific* (New York, 1950) and *Changing Melanesia: Social Economics of Culture Contact* (Melbourne, 1954), both covering the Solomons, the New Hebrides, and New Caledonia; and S. M. Lambert's "personal history," *A Yankee Doctor in Paradise* (Boston, 1941), invaluable for information and insight into the health problems and practices in Fiji, the High Commission Territories, Papua, Western Samoa and the Cook Islands in the 1920's and 1930's. Attention should also be called to the updated version of D. Oliver's *The Pacific Islands,* which appeared in 1962 in hardcovers and paperback. On the economic situation in the British islands in the middle 1930's, including the New Hebrides, see *An Economic Survey of the Colonial Empire* (London: HMSO, 1935). (And as a by-the-way I may here note that Hancock in his two volumes on *Problems of Economic Policy 1918–1939* [London, 1940, 1942], while writing copiously about the African colonies, mentioned only Fiji among the Pacific colonies, once in a footnote and once in the text, both mentions being illustrative of some general point. I suspect that this is an indication of how the Pacific island colonies figured in the British mind between the wars.)

There are government reports, annual, every-other-year, and those specially issued, some of which will be listed below. These are ordinarily very bland in character, but often factually rich. The articles on the Pacific ocean colonies printed in *The Times Survey of the British Colonies,* of which thirty-eight numbers were produced between 1950 and 1960, are useful enough but very few, indicating that these islands did not in that decade figure very prominently in the London mind. The South Pacific Commission publishes papers both of very specific and general reference. Of the latter I may cite as examples, V. D. Stace, *The Pacific Islander and Modern Commerce* (Nouméa, 1954); K. H. Danks, *Industrial Activity in Selected Areas of the South Pacific* (Nouméa, 1956); and E. J. E. Lefort, *Economic Aspects of the Coconut Industry in the South Pacific* (Nouméa, 1956). The only news and opinion magazine dealing with the islands is *Pacific Islands Monthly,* founded in 1930 and issued in Sydney. Its news is not always as full as one would like but it directs attention to what is going on; its opinions are often alarming but always put with exceeding self-confidence and vigor. In addition to the magazines referred to earlier as carrying articles on the islands from time to time, attention may here be called to *Pacific Viewpoint* (Vol. 1, no. 1; Wellington, N.Z., March 1960) and the IPR publications, *Pacific Affairs* and *Far Eastern Survey.* Studies of the islands normally figure in the "data papers" of the IPR international conferences.

In conclusion a few words may profitably be said about the absence from this "Reading List" of any reference to books such as Thor Heyerdahl, *Kon Tiki* (New York, 1950) and Andrew Sharp, *Ancient Voyagers in the Pacific* (Wellington, 1956). They are absent because, while I know they are widely read and have sparked fascinating controversies, they are concerned with the history of the island peoples before the arrival of Europeans and my concern is with the impact of the Europeans on the islands.

The following bibliographical notes on the island groups refer to the time-span of Chapters IX–XI taken together; that is, 1900–1960, roughly speaking. Some of the most knowledgeable students of island history have yet to publish books. Our understanding will be much enriched when such men as Mr. Harry Maude and Professor J. W. Davidson of the Australian National University put their findings between hard covers at last.

NEW GUINEA, MICRONESIA, NAURU

It is my understanding that there is a rich literature on New Guinea in German, but because of the language barrier it has remained closed to me, and I have had to piece my historical notes together from such English language sources as I could find. Perhaps the richest single source of information I found was C. D. Rowley, *The Australians In German New Guinea 1914–1921* (Melbourne, 1958), which is a close study of the transition from German to Australian rule, while other books which served me well were S. S. Mackenzie, *The Australians at Rabaul* (Sydney, 1927 and later editions) (Vol. X of the *Official History of Australia in the War of 1914–1918*); S. W. Reed, *The Making of Modern New Guinea* (Philadelphia, 1943), which is mostly concerned with the Australian mandate up to World War II; and Anon., ed., *Official Handbook of the Territory of New Guinea* (Canberra, *c.* 1938). Additionally I profited a good deal from the "back references" in other of the books cited in this section. A classic missionary narrative covering the German period is Johann Flierl, *Forty Years in New Guinea,* translated by M. Wiedersenders (Columbus, Ohio, 1931). Frank Clune's *Somewhere in New Guinea* (Sydney, 1951) contains historical notes. Mr. Clune, a "dinkum Aussie" wielding a pen, was mentioned in the text above as a leading exponent of the genre, "internal travel," in Australia.

On the period of the Australian mandate, the S. W. Reed volume just cited is the principal book. The basic sources are the government papers, reports to the Mandates Commission, Commonwealth government papers, etc. To my knowledge nobody had yet worked these over in detail for the purpose of a historical narrative. Frankly, I have used only those which happen to be in my possession. A co-operative study of the mandate as it was in the late 1920's is contained in F. W. Eggleston, ed., *The Australian Mandate for New Guinea* (Melbourne, 1928); and an assessment of the situation as it appeared to a leader of the Methodist missionaries, Rev. J. Burton, is to be found in Campbell, Mills, and Portus, eds., *Studies in Australian Affairs* (Melbourne, 1928). Sir Thomas Henley's *New Guinea* (Sydney, 1927) is a slight, opinionated, sketch, not least interesting for its sideswipes at the Americans. The gold boom produced much popular literature. It is one of the topics treated in F. Clune's book, cited above. Mr. Clune also wrote a life of one of the pioneer aviators, *D'Air Devil: The Story of "Pard" Mustar* (Sydney, 1941). But the premier popular book on the gold boom is Ion Idries, *Gold Dust and Ashes* (19th ed.; Sydney, 1947). I understand that the matter is being restudied by an academic historian at the ANU. On the breakthrough into the "highlands" country, see Leahy and Crain, *The Land that*

Time Forgot: Adventures and Discoveries in New Guinea (New York, 1937). Australian writers themselves have often noted that there was remarkably little interest in the mandate in Australia and hence little writing about it. However, the periodicals should be scanned for the occasional articles, e.g., *The Australian Quarterly* (1929 ff.).

Although a writer trained in both history and anthropology has published a prospectus of a history of Papua, neither he nor anyone else has actually written one. In addition to official reports, Sir William Macgregor wrote and printed a number of essays, introductions to other people's books, etc., and a book of his own, *British New Guinea* (London, 1897). It is understood that Dr. R. B. Joyce of the University of Queensland has a comprehensive study of Macgregor's career in hand. An early description of the colony is J. P. Thomson, *British New Guinea* (London, 1892). C. A. W. Monckton's two volumes of reminiscences, *Taming New Guinea* (New York & London, 1921), also known as *Some Experiences of a New Guinea Resident Magistrate,* and *Last Days in New Guinea* (New York & London, 1922), refer to the period from Le Hunte's lieutenant-governorship to World War I. J. H. P. Murray, in addition to his annual reports and occasional papers, wrote two books, *Papua or British New Guinea* (London, 1912) and *Papua of Today* (London, 1925). A life of Murray is Lewis Lett, *Sir Hubert Murray* (Sydney & London, 1949), but it is considered unsatisfactory—altogether too hagiographic —even by Murray's warm friends. Mr. F. J. West of the ANU has a study in hand that will be better balanced and more perceptive. L. Lett also wrote *The Papuan Achievement* (Melbourne, 1942), but it is more interesting, apart from the factual material, for what it tells of Lett's and the Australian frame of mind than as an assessment of the Murray administration. J. D. Legge, *The Australian Colonial Policy* (Sydney, 1956) refers, in spite of the title, to Papuan policy only. It is a good and useful book. An *Official Handbook of Papua* was issued at Port Moresby (5th ed., 1938). On the search for oil in Papua (and the Territory), see the pamphlet, *Oil Exploration* (Melbourne, 1940). On gold hunting, L. Lett, *Papuan Gold* (Sydney, 1943). Among the books by patrol officers, the following stand out: W. R. Humphries, *Patrolling in Papua* (London, 1923); I. F. Champion, *Across New Guinea from the Fly to the Sepik* (London, 1932); and J. G. Hides, *Savage Patrol* (New York, 1936), also published as *In Wildest Papua* (London, 1935). It seems to me that the best missionary narratives are those of Father Andre Dupeyrat, *Papuan Conquest* (Melbourne, 1948) and *Savage Papua: A Missionary Among Cannibals* (New York, 1954). For Frank Clune at large in Papua, *Prowling Through Papua* (Sydney, 1942).

After World War II, books on New Guinea mostly dealt with both Papua and the Territory as Papua–New Guinea. In order of appearance, L. P. Mair, *Australia in New Guinea* (London, 1948); R. W. Robson and Judy Tudor, eds., *Handbook of Papua–New Guinea* (orig. ed.; Sydney, 1954; 3d, 1958); John Wilkes, ed., *New Guinea and*

Australia (Sydney: AIPS, 1958); Brian Essai, *Papua and New Guinea* (Melbourne, 1961); and Sir John Crawford, ed., *The Independence of Papua–New Guinea: What Are the Prerequisites?* (Sydney, 1962). In the postwar period, also, ministerial policy statements assumed great importance, through 1949 those of E. J. Ward for Labor, after that, Paul Hasluck for the Liberal-Country party coalition, as also did the papers emanating from the Trusteeship Council of the United Nations, while the volume of newspaper and periodical discussions of New Guinea rose to unprecedented heights.

The anthropological literature about New Guinea, which has been accumulating for seventy years, is voluminous. The classic studies of the Melanesians by Seligman, Codrington, Pitt-Rivers, etc., are of course relevant, but a general reader today is more likely to turn to Bronislaw Malinowski's writings about the natives of the islands off the eastern tip of Papua, e.g., *Argonauts of the Western Pacific* (ed. London, 1950); Margaret Mead's studies of the Manus Islands natives, *Growing Up in New Guinea* (New York, 1930), and *New Lives for Old* (New York, 1956); or her accounts of the "conditioning of the social personalities of the two sexes" among the Arapesh, Mundugumor, and Tchambuli on the mainland of New Guinea, collected in *Sex and Temperament* (New York, 1935); or Gregory Bateson's study of the Iatmul tribe in *Naven* (2d ed.; Stanford, Calif., 1958); C. S. Belshaw's study of Hanuabada in Papua, *The Great Village* (London, 1957); Marie Reay's *The Kuma* (Melbourne, 1959); K. O. L. Burridge's *Mambu,* a fascinating study of native "cultist" activity in particular situations on the north coast of the New Guinea mainland; or C. A. Valentin's short book, *Masks and Men in a Melanesian Society* (Lawrence, Kansas, 1961), dealing with tribes of New Britain. The difficulty is not to find something to read about the New Guinea natives, but rather to establish the relevance of what one reads to the history of the Europeans in New Guinea. Perhaps the best popular account of the New Guinea natives, not disregardful of anthropology, and well illustrated with color plates, is Colin Simpson, *Plumes and Arrows* (Sydney, 1962).

There are three books on the Japanese Mandate, one by a Japanese, two by Americans: P. H. Clyde, *Japan's Pacific Mandate* (New York, 1935); Willard Price, *Japan's Islands of Mystery* (New York, 1944); and Tadao Yanaihara, *Pacific Islands Under Japanese Mandate* (New York, 1940). On these islands under the Americans there is Robert Trumbull's *Paradise in Trust: A Report on Americans in Micronesia* (New York, 1959); the Annual Reports of the American administration, and a *Handbook of the Trust Territory of the Pacific Islands* (Washington, 1948). A geographer's account of Micronesia under the Americans is to be found in J. W. Coulter, *The Pacific Dependencies of the United States* (New York, 1957). Oliver's remarks in his *The Pacific Islands,* 1962 ed., are given special point if it is recalled that he had an association with the planning of the American approach to the problem these islands represent.

As far as I am aware, there is only one book available about Nauru —it also deals with Ocean Island: Sir Albert Ellis, *Ocean Island and Nauru* (Sydney, 1935). The Official Year Books of both Australia and New Zealand carry a note on Nauru and there are official annual reports.

The history of Dutch New Guinea is difficult to reconstruct from the materials available in English. Most of the books of substance on the Netherlands East Indies, published before World War II or after its outbreak, recognized that New Guinea was indeed part of the colony, but many of the best did precious little more than that and these limited and often opaque references are hard to "add up." Standard works thus described include Amry Vandenbosch, *The Dutch East Indies* (Berkeley, Calif., 1941); J. S. Furnivall, *Netherlands India* (New York, 1944); Raymond Kennedy, *The Ageless Indies* (New York, 1942); J. O. M. Broek, *Economic Development of the Netherlands Indies* (New York, 1942); J. H. Boeke, *The Structure of the Netherlands Indian Economy* (New York, 1942); and Emerson, Mills, and Thompson, *Government and Nationalism in South East Asia* (New York, 1942). The early postwar books were equally unsatisfactory in their treatment of New Guinea. Charles Wolf, Jr.'s, *The Indonesian Story* (New York, 1948) included no mention of New Guinea whatsoever; Soetan Sjahrir's *Out of Exile* (New York, 1949) dealt with it only as his place of exile in the 1930's; and while H. J. Van Mook, *The Stakes of Democracy in Southeast Asia* (New York, 1950) says something about New Guinea, it isn't too helpful. Even in B. H. M. Vlekke's *Nunsantara: A History of the East Indian Archipelago* (Cambridge, Mass., 1943) the references to New Guinea are sparse. It was only when New Guinea became a political issue between the Dutch and the Indonesians that the history of the territory began to be given some attention, more especially that aspect of it that contributed to clarifying the origin and evolution of the Dutch claim to it. The books on the New Guinea dispute I found most useful were R. C. Bone, *The Dynamics of the Western New Guinea (Irian Barat) Problem* (Ithaca, N.Y., 1958); Justus M. van der Kroef, *The West New Guinea Dispute* (New York, 1958); and Leslie Palmier, *Indonesia and the Dutch* (London, 1962). For the events that led up to the settlement of the question I relied on the *New York Times*. For the text of the settlement agreement arranged by Mr. Bunker, see the *New York Times,* August 16, 1962, p. 6. Along the way I accumulated a number of pamphlets and documents on Dutch New Guinea, but none was more comprehensive in coverage than *Handbook on Netherlands New Guinea,* printed in English in Rotterdam, 1958. An Australian effort to report what the Dutch were doing in New Guinea is G. T. Roscoe, *Our Neighbors in Netherlands New Guinea* (Brisbane, 1959). The Australian official view was several times clearly stated; and the Australian press carried many articles, chiefly of a political import, on the territory. An account of a famous exploratory journey across the territory is L. D. Brongersma and G. F. Venema, *To the Mountains of the Stars* (London, 1960). An account of an American anthropological expedition is Peter Matthiessen, *Under the Mountain Wall* (New York, 1962). A journalist's impression is Matthew Smedts, *No Tobacco, No Hallelujah* (London, 1955).

WORLD WAR I

For accounts of the German, British, Australian, and New Zealand moves in the Pacific during World War I, see the relevant volumes of the *Official History of Australia in the War of 1914–1918,* viz: IX, A. W. Jose, *The Royal Australian Navy* (1st ed., 1928; 9th, 1941); X, S. S. Mackenzie, *The Australians at Rabaul* (1st ed., 1927; 10th, 1941); and Ernest Scott, *Australia During the War* (1st ed., 1936),—which covers the Peace Conference. The most romantic German adventure in the Southwest Pacific during the war, save perhaps that of Captain Detzner mentioned in Chapter X, was that of Count Felix von Luckner which, unfortunately, I was unable to fit into my narrative. The von Luckner story is mentioned in Jose but the fullest popular account of it is Lowell Thomas and von Luckner, *Count Luckner: The Sea Devil* (1st ed., New York, 1927; paperback ed., 1962). The Luckner adventure took place in the Society, Cook, and Fiji islands and New Zealand. For the international political context of wartime and after, see for the American point of view, A. W. Griswold, *The Far Eastern Policy of the United States* (New York, 1938; reprinted 1962), and for the British point of view, the essay by J. W. Davidson, Chap. XV, "The Pacific in the First World War and in the Settlement," in David Thompson, ed., Vol. XII of *The New Cambridge Modern History* (Cambridge, Eng., 1960). A famous discussion of the naval-political situation in the Pacific as between United States and Japan was Hector C. Bywater, *Sea-Power in the Pacific* (Boston, 1921). Two books reflecting Australian opinion of the problem of the Pacific during and just after the war, C. Brunsdon Fletcher, *The New Pacific* (London, 1917) and *The Problem of the Pacific* (London, 1919). Fletcher was editor of the *Sydney Morning Herald*. Additional light on Australian opinion is given in the essay by H. S. Nicholas in M. Atkinson, ed., *Australia: Economic and Political Studies* (Melbourne, 1920). This seems as good a place as any to bring in the comprehensive studies of the mandate system which, of course, deal *inter alia* with the Pacific mandates. In order of appearance, E. van Maanin-Helmer, *The Mandates System* (London, 1929); Q. Wright, *Mandates under the League* (Chicago, 1930); and H. Duncan Hall, *Mandates, Dependencies and Trusteeship* (Washington & London, 1948), the latter dealing with the linkage between the mandate system of the League and the trusteeship system of the United Nations. An interesting statement of the attitude of the Australian pro-Leaguers toward mandates is to be found in J. C. Rookwood Proud, *World Peace, the League and Australia* (Melbourne, 1936).

THE SAMOAS:

(A) WESTERN SAMOA

First, see the references above under GENERAL. Because of my lack of German, my information about Samoa under Solf and Schultz-Ewarth has been gathered (and evaluated) where I could find it in English. Even those who had doubts about what the Germans had done in New Guinea agreed that they did a good job in Samoa. There is much valuable information about the acts in and attitudes toward Samoa of the New Zealanders in the books referred to in the forepart of the bibliography for Chapter VIII. An excellent essay on the origin and meaning of the argument that their experience with the Maoris gave New Zealanders a special competence for dealings with Polynesians, see Angus Ross, "Maori & Polynesian: The Racial Argument in Support of New Zealand's interests in Polynesia," in Freeman and Geddes, eds., *Anthropology in the South Seas* (New Plymouth, N.Z., 1959). My own attitude is that no *people* has any special competence in dealings with another race, but *individuals* may have such special competence. A book apparently designed to inform the New Zealanders about their new possession covering events through what is referred to as "The British (sic!) Military Occupation," which is disappointingly thin and unperceptive, is R. M. Watson, *History of Samoa* (Wellington, 1918). Harry Holland's pamphlet referred to in the text is *Samoa: A Story that Teems with Tragedy* (Wellington, n.d.; *c.* 1916?). In 1929 Holland, still speaking for Labour, published *The Revolt of the Samoans* (Wellington, 1929). These are, of course, propaganda exercises. An American book of comprehensive coverage permeated with pro-Mau and anti-New Zealand sentiments is N. A. Rowe, *Samoa Under the Sailing Gods* (London & New York, 1930). Quite the best on Samoa published during the interwar decades is F. M. Keesing, *Modern Samoa* (Stanford, Calif., 1934). V. D. Stace's *Western Samoa: An Economic Survey* (Nouméa: SPC, 1956) has valuable data on the 1920's and 1930's, even though focused in the mid-1950's. A good brief account of the changes in attitude of the New Zealanders toward Samoa is to be found in Wood (see Chapter VIII). On this subject see also A Study Group of NZIIA, *Western Samoa: Mandate or German Colony?* (Wellington, 1937). There are references to the mandate and defense in I. F. G. Milner, *New Zealand's Interests and Policies in the Far East* (New York, 1940). On developments after World War II, the material is scattered in the journals, official papers (N.Z. & U.N.), etc. Professor J. W. Davidson is, I believe, writing a book on the achievement of independence; meanwhile, see his article, "Transition to Independence," *Australian Journal of Politics and History,* May 1961. The New Zealand Department of Scientific and Industrial Research has published a number of technical studies of geology, hydrology, soils, etc., through the NZGPO, Wellington. Late in 1962 there was published at Wellington, Fox and Cumberland, eds., *Western Samoa: Land, Life and Agriculture in Tropical Polynesia,* but I had not seen it when I wrote my text.

(B) AMERICAN SAMOA

The single most important book (which carries the story forward to 1951) is Captain J. A. C. Gray, MC., USN, *Amerika Samoa: A History of American Samoa and its United States Naval Administration* (Annapolis, Md., 1960). Keesing in *Modern Samoa,* cited just above, deals with American Samoa as well as the mandate. Some rather cursory remarks about American Samoa are appended by J. W. Coulter to his essay on Hawaii in W. H. Haas, ed., *The American Empire: A Study of the Outlying Territories of the United States* (Chicago, 1940). Coulter also wrote the short monograph, *Land Utilization in American Samoa* (Honolulu, 1941) and included his most substantial account of American Samoa in his *The Pacific Dependencies of the United States* (New York, 1957). His point of view is that of a geographer. Margaret Mead's famous book, *Coming of Age in Samoa* (orig. pub.; New York, 1928; but subsequently in paperback) was based on observations in Manu'a where the Western impact was weaker than in Tutuila. After the change from naval administration to civilian rule in 1951, the principal reliance for information becomes the *Annual Report of the Governor of American Samoa* (GPO, Washington). Occasionally American Samoa breaks into the news (*New York Times, passim*), (*Pacific Islands Monthly, passim*), but discussions of substance by nonofficial persons are rare. Two exceptions are West as cited above under GENERAL and W. T. Perkins, *Denial of Empire* (Leyden, The Netherlands, 1962).

FIJI

First see the references above under GENERAL. Although we do not yet have Volume II of Derrick, there are many extremely useful historical notes referring to the period since 1900 in R. A. Derrick, *The Fiji Islands: A Geographical Handbook* (Suva, 1951). On Rotuma, W. J. E. Eason, *A Short History of Rotuma* (Suva, n.d.; c. 1951). A. G. Lowndes, ed., *South Pacific Enterprise* (Sydney, 1956), which deals with CSR, contains some history but not as much as one would like. So also do the government of Fiji publications called *The Colony of Fiji* (1st ed., 1924), the 3rd edition, 1931, of which covers the years 1874–1931, 4th ed., 1936, has notes on developments since 1931, while the 6th ed., 1957, does likewise for the years from 1936. (I have not seen the editions not named.) There are papers on history (and also anthropology, archeology, the natural sciences, etc.) in *Transactions and Proceedings of the Fiji Society,* vols. 2, 3, 4, 5, and 6 (vol. 1 is not available but will perhaps be printed soon), but few deal with the period since 1900. (Attention should be directed also to *Central Archives of Fiji and the Western Pacific High Commission:* No. 1 [1960], No. 2 [1961].) Books on the British colonies generally which contain valuable information about and observations on Fiji include Sir Alan Pim, *Colonial Agricultural Production* (London, 1946); C. K. Meek, *Land Law and Custom in the Colonies* (London, 1946); and G. B. Masefield, *A Short History of Agriculture in the British Colonies* (London, 1950). On the sugar industry, in addition to Lowndes above, see *The Sugar Industry of Fiji: Report by Dr. C. Y. Shephard* (London: HMSO, 1945); on the cane-carrying railways, Peter Dyer and Peter Hodge, *Balloon Stacks and Sugar Cane* (Wellington, N.Z., 1961); and the list of Fiji government papers below. On the Indians up to the end of indentures, K. L. Gillion, *Fiji's Indian Immigrants* (Melbourne, 1962), made from an ANU Ph.D. thesis, and at later stages, J. W. Coulter, *Fiji: Little India of the Pacific* (Chicago, 1942) and A. C. Mayer, *Peasants in the Pacific: A Study of Fiji Indian Rural Society* (Berkeley, Calif., 1961). On the Fijians, Basil Thompson, *The Fijians: A Study of the Decay of Custom* (London, 1908); Rev. Wallace Deane, *Fijian Society: Sociology and Psychology of the Fijians* (London, 1921); A. M. Hocart, *Lau Islands, Fiji* (Honolulu, 1929); Laura Thompson, *Southern Lau, Fiji: An Ethnology* (Honolulu, 1940) and *Fijian Frontier* (New York, 1940), the latter the "popular" account of the expedition that produced the former; Buell Quain, *Fijian Village* (Chicago, 1948)—a small village in the interior of Vanua Levu; G. K. Roth, *The Fijian Way of Life* (Melbourne, 1953), a most unsatisfactory and unsatisfying book; Howard Hayden, *Motukiri: A Pilot Project in Community Development* (Melbourne, 1954); M. D. Sahlins, *Moala: Culture and Nature on a Fijian Island* (Ann Arbor, 1962)—a small rather isolated island, that is. There is no single book on education in Fiji that is profitable, I fear. On the Rockefeller people and medical care and public health in the islands, see Lambert under GENERAL above; Victor Heiser, *An American Doctor's Odyssey* (New York, 1936); and R. B. Fosdick, *The Story of the Rockefeller Foundation* (New York, 1952). The government of Fiji probably publishes more "papers" each year than any other island government. The following appear to be the most important in recent years: Carleen O'Loughlin, *The Pattern of the Fiji Economy: The National Income 1950–1953* (Council Paper 44 of 1956); Norma McArthur, *Report on the Census of the Population, 1956* (Council Paper 1 of 1958); O. H. K. Spate, *The Fijian People: Economic Problems and Prospects* (Council Paper 13 of 1959); *Report of the Commission of Enquiry into the Natural Resources and Population Trends of the Colony of Fiji, 1959* (Council Paper 1 of 1960), popularly known as "the Burns report," after Sir Alan Burns, the Commission's chairman; and *Report of the Fiji Sugar Inquiry Commission* (Council Paper No. 20 of 1961), known as "the Eve report," after Chairman Sir Malcolm Trustram Eve. An enormous "secondary literature" goes on accumulating, which it would be profitless to list here but which must be burrowed through by scholars seeking to figure out where Fiji is going. While practically everything about the history of Fiji since 1900 is open for study, a most useful work would be a discerning account of the life and times of Ratu Sukuna, accompanied by a collection of his writings. Such a work, if properly done, would allow the writer to get to the heart of the Fijian problem, examine it from every possible angle, and lead to a conclusive assessment of Sukuna's contribution, about which there is today a good deal of dispute. Perhaps this will be done by the first Fijian to take a Ph.D. in the social sciences at ANU!

THE HIGH COMMISSION TERRITORIES

(A) TONGA

For information about Tonga since 1900 see under GENERAL above, the books by Lambert, Mander, and Robson. There are some useful references to Tonga in the essays in Katherine Luomala *et al.,* *Specialized Studies in Polynesian Anthropology* (Honolulu, 1947). A very good article is that by C. G. F. Simkin, "Modern Tonga," in *The New Zealand Geographer,* vol. 1, no. 2, October 1945. The best book on Tongan life in the interwar years is Ernest and Pearl Beaglehole, *Pangai: A Village in Tonga* (Wellington, 1944). For the situation after World War II see *Pacific Islands Monthly, passim* and the biennial Report on Tonga issued by HMSO, London.

(B) THE SOLOMON ISLANDS

It is especially difficult to get a perspective on what has gone on in the Solomons since 1900, for while there are a good many books about the protectorate, history has pretty uniformly been but an incidental concern of their authors. See under GENERAL above as indicating the best readily available, the books by Mander, Lambert, and Belshaw. Belshaw also wrote a good many journal articles, "data papers," etc., during the late 1940's and the 1950's which mostly refer to the periods just before and after World War II. Reference must be made to a book that described the situation in the 1880's, if only because it is a classic, H. B. Guppy, *The Solomon Islands and Their Natives* (London, 1887). An anthropological study from which a clear picture of the position of the natives in the interwar years emerges is H. Ian Hogbin, *Experiments in Civilization: The Effects of European Culture on a Native Community in the Solomon Islands* (London, 1939). Douglas L. Oliver's *A Solomon Island Society* (Cambridge, Mass., 1955) deals with Siuai natives of Bougainville, politically in the Territory of New Guinea. Raymond Firth's famous books, *We, The Tikopia* (2d ed.; London, 1957) and *Social Change in Tikopia* (London, 1959), deal with a Polynesian people living in the Solomons. The latter is a follow-up of the former and some readers may want to compare these works with Margaret Mead's pair on the Manus Island people of New

Guinea. Hector MacQuarrie's *Vouza and the Solomon Islands* (Sydney, 1946) tells rather more about the author than Vouza, and in any case deals only with Vouza's prewar career. His wartime and postwar activities are far more important. Nevertheless, the book gives a good picture of life in outlying portions of the protectorate, e.g., of timber getting on Vanikoro. Caroline Mytinger, *Headhunting in the Solomon Islands* (New York, 1942) is a superior example of the genus "travel book." Sir Harry Luke's *From A South Seas Diary* (London, 1945) can be noted here, since it has entries about the Solomons, but it is equally useful for all the High Commission territories, 1938–42, the period when Sir Harry was high commissioner.

(C) THE GILBERT AND ELLICE ISLANDS

A visit by Robert Louis Stevenson to this part of the Pacific three years before the British took over is reported in his *In the South Seas* (1890). The historical note in the *Report* (HMSO, London) on the G. & E's for 1958–59 is exceptionally good, far better than those in most of the colonial reports. In the *Report* specified there is a historical note on the British relation to the Line Islands at pp. 93–94. The paragraph on the history of the Tokelaus in the New Zealand government's annual *Report* on the Cook, Niue, and Tokelau islands is useful. What a complex history a not particularly "important" island can have is beautifully illustrated by Harry Maude's article on Christmas Island in *The Australian Outlook*. Two books that deal with the G. & E's are Sir Arthur Grimble's *We Chose the Islands* (New York, 1952) and *Return to the Islands* (New York, 1957), mostly about the situation in the 1920's and 1930's. Grimble tells the story of the Chinese-native riot. Dr. Lambert writes about these islands at this time also, not only in his *A Yankee Doctor* but also in his paper, *The Depopulation of Pacific Races* (Honolulu, 1934). Sir Harry Luke has entries about the G. & E's just before World War II in his *Diary*. On Ocean see Sir Albert Ellis, *Ocean Island and Nauru* (Sydney, 1935). On the islands of interest to the Americans see E. H. Bryan, Jr., *American Polynesia* (Honolulu, 1942). A list of the islands to which there is an American claim, a matter about which Bryan is not very specific, is to be found in *Nomenclature des Pays, Territoires, etc., du Monde, Avec Leur Situation Geographique* (Berne, Switzerland: Bureau International de l'Union Postale Universelle, 1956). See also the National Geographic map, Atlas Plate 61, April 1962. For the G. & E. Colony after World War II, in which it figured conspicuously, see, in addition to the colonial *Report,* the *Pacific Islands Monthly, passim.*

(D) NEW HEBRIDES

Here will be listed only those references which are in English. For French references see below under FRENCH ISLANDS. Attention is called to the following listed under GENERAL above: Robson, Mander, Belshaw, Lambert, and Oliver. See also Lambert's note in his *The Depopulation of Pacific Races* (Honolulu, 1934). Tom Harrison, *Savage Civilization* (New York, 1937) reflects the situation in the 1930's.

(E) PITCAIRN

Although the history of Pitcairn has not been developed in this book, it may be mentioned here because it was one of the high commissioner's responsibilities. I understand that one of Harry Maude's projects is a history of Pitcairn where at one stage he served as a High Commission officer. Pro tem, then, see Harry L. Shapiro, *Descendents of the Mutineers of the Bounty* (Honolulu, 1929) and Harry L. Shapiro, *Heritage of the Bounty* (rev. ed.; New York, 1962). For a grimly amusing and vastly illuminating "morality essay" on the history of Pitcairn, see "Politics in Pitcairn" in W. K. Hancock's book of the same title (London, 1947).

(F) EASTER ISLAND

Easter Island, which is a possession of Chile, has also figured only casually in this history. Probably no other island has had so much rubbish written about it. The classic archaeological investigation of Easter is Mrs. Scoresby Routledge, *The Mystery of Easter Island* (London, 1919). The best single book on Easter is, to my taste, Alfred Metraux, *Easter Island* (New York, 1957). It contains an illuminating sketch of the history of the island since European contacts began. Thor Heyerdahl's *Aku-Aku* (New York, 1958) is about Easter Island.

THE COOK ISLANDS

While information about the Cooks and Niue since 1900 that can be organized into a historical account is available, nobody seems to have attempted an historical narrative beyond 1900. Ernest Beaglehole's socio-anthropological study, *Social Change in the South Pacific* (London, 1957), dealing with Rarotonga and Aitutaki only, ceases to be historical at 1901 and becomes "contemporary analysis." Rarotonga is, of course, the principal island economically of all the Cooks. Beaglehole is also author of *Islands of Danger* (Wellington, 1944). This is a by-product of a stay on Pukapuka as an ethnologist and is a report of the situation between the wars. Edwin Loeb's *History and Traditions of Niue* (Honolulu, 1926) does not recount the history much beyond 1900. There are valuable notes on the Cooks in A. H. McLintock, ed., *A Descriptive Atlas of New Zealand* (Wellington, 1959); the government publicity publication *Introduction to New Zealand* (Wellington,

1945); *Contemporary New Zealand* (Wellington, 1938); *New Zealand Affairs* (Christchurch, 1929); and the annual *New Zealand Official Year-Book*. There is also the government annual, *Reports on the Cook, Niue and Tokelau Islands* (GPO, Wellington). For a survey of the N.Z. islands at the end of the war, see Ernest Beaglehole's essay "Trusteeship and New Zealand's Pacific Dependencies" in N.Z. Paper No. 1 for 10th Conference, IPR, 1947. There are also a number of polemics in book form against the administration from various points of view to the left of center, an accumulation of magazine articles of academic and left-journalistic origin, some special government reports, press releases, etc.

THE FRENCH ISLANDS

While the writing about the French islands, particularly Tahiti, is certainly copious, the bulk of it falls into the categories "travel" and "personal experience" and is only incidentally useful to anyone trying to write history. I regret that I have not explored the literature in French as fully as I would like. Ch.-Andre Julien's *Histoire de L'Océania* (Paris, 1951) skips very lightly and selectively over the period since 1900. When it comes to general surveys of the French empire, of which the Pacific islands are a part, the islands tend to be lightly and casually treated or omitted altogether. See, e.g., in English, H. I. Priestley, *France Overseas: A Study in Modern Imperialism* (New York, 1938) and Ellen Hammer's essay, "The French Empire Today" in E. M. Earle, ed., *Modern France* (Princeton, N.J., 1951); or in French, Henri Blet, *France D'Outre-Mer: L'Ouvre Coloniale de la Troisième République* (Paris, 1950); Hubert Deschamps, *Methodes et Doctrines Coloniales de la France* (Paris, 1953); and G. Hardy, *Histoire Sociale de la Colonization Française* (Paris, 1953). Beyond the writings referred to under GENERAL and for the New Hebrides in English, I have found most useful the following: in French, S. Ferdinand-Lop, *Les Possessions Françaises du Pacifique* (Paris, 1933); E. Aubert de la Rue, *Les Nouvelles-Hebrides* (Montreal, Canada, 1945); J. Bourgeau, *La France du Pacifique* (Paris, 1950); and H. Deschamps et Jean Guiart, *Tahiti, Nouvelle-Calédonie, Nouvelles-Hebrides* (Paris, 1957), in many ways the best book of all. The books in English, mostly about Tahiti, are of little use to a historian except as they depict the situation as of a given date (which they mostly do so selectively as to lower their value as history). A classic book on Tahiti, based on a visit in 1906, which contains a review of the early history, is "Tihoti" (George Calderon), *Tahiti* (New York, 1922). On Tahiti also, with pretensions to being history though the author barely knows what history is, is Robert Landon, *Island of Love* (London, 1959). The title is dreadful and the bibliography is far superior to the text. W. G. Burchett, *Pacific Treasure Island: New Caledonia* (Melbourne, 1942) is a useful book which is one of the few in English that regularly appears in the bibliographies

of French works. (At a later stage Burchett became a communist newspaper correspondent operating inside the Iron Curtain countries.) On
the anthropology of New Caledonia and the New Hebrides the best
French writers appear to be M. Leenhardt and Jean Guiart. Professor
Douglas Oliver of Harvard and associates are conducting a socio-
anthropological study of contemporary Tahiti, which if it does not
silence the romanticists will fortify the position of the realists.

WORLD WAR II

There was a good deal of writing, published in hardcovers or paperback, about the fighting and other activity in the islands during the
course of the war and some of it was quite properly avidly perused at
the time, but it is my experience that, because of foreshortened perspective, inadequate information, lack of any reasonable sense of the
island background, and censorship, little of such writing stands up to
critical reading twenty years after. Few titles of wartime origin will
be mentioned here: Richard Tregaskis' *Guadalcanal Diary* (orig. pub.
New York, 1943) of which the currently available edition (in paperback; New York, 1959) has been improved by the restoration of the
censor's cuts and the incorporation of information of Japanese origin;
Robert Sherrod's *Tarawa: The Story of a Battle* (New York, 1944);
W. G. Burchett's *Pacific Treasure Island: New Caledonia* (Melbourne,
1942) for its circumstantial account of the Vichy-Free French contention (though this episode has been traversed in the light of much
fuller information in the Australian war histories); H. E. L. Priday's
The War from Coconut Square (Wellington, 1945) for its review of
what went on in most of the islands other than New Guinea, including
those not the scene of fighting; and Hugh Buggy's *Pacific Victory:
A Short History of Australia's Part in the War Against Japan,* issued
by the Australian Ministry of Information either at the end of 1945
or early in 1946. On the Fijians in World War II, see Lt. R. A. Howlett,
The History of the Fiji Military Forces 1939–1945 (Suva: GPO,
1948). On the New Zealanders in the Pacific war see O. A. Gillespie,
The Pacific (Wellington, 1952), a volume of the *Official History of
New Zealand in the Second World War 1939–1945.* On the Australians
in the island fighting, see the following volumes in *Australia in the
War of 1939–1945:* Series 1 (Army), IV, Lionel Wigmore, *The Japa-
nese Thrust* (Canberra, 1957); V, Dudley McCarthy, *Southwest
Pacific Area—First Year* (Canberra, 1959); and VI, David Dexter,
The New Guinea Offensives (Canberra, 1961). Gavin Long, *The
Final Campaigns* is at this writing still to come. Series 2 (Navy) I,
G. Hermon Gill, *Royal Australian Navy* (Canberra, 1957), with Vol.
II, 1942–45 still to come. Series 3 (Air) II, George Odgers, *Air War
Against Japan 1943–1945* (Canberra, 1957). Of the available volumes
of Series 4 (Civil), only D. P. Mellor's *The Role of Science and In-
dustry* (Canberra, 1958) covers the years of the Pacific war. Series 5
(Medical) III, Allan S. Walker, *The Island Campaigns* (Canberra,

1957). For an interesting unofficial Australian account of a phase of the New Guinea fighting, see Raymond Paull, *Retreat from Kokoda* (London & Melbourne, 1958). On the coastwatchers, in addition to what is told in Gill, see E. A. Feldt, *The Coastwatchers* (orig. ed., New York, 1946; later in paperback). On the American participation in the island fighting the literature is almost excessively voluminous; see the relevant volumes in the various series issued through the Government Printing Office, Washington 25, by the historians of the Army and the Marines, the two-volume history of the Air Force issued by the University of Chicago Press, and for the Navy Samuel Eliot Morison's *History of the United States Naval Operations in World War II* (Boston, v.d.) *passim,* but particularly volumes III–VIII. Morison has also published, written in a strangely *en pantoufles* style to be affected by so elegant a Brahmin, *The Two-Ocean War: A Short History of the United States Navy in the Second World War* (Boston, 1963), essentially an epitome of his 15-volume history just mentioned. See also Morison's *Strategy and Compromise* (Boston, 1958), in which he points out firmly how much worse off the Australians and New Zealanders would have been had the British controlled strategy in the Pacific. On naval operations see also, E. P. Potter and Chester Nimitz, *The Great Sea War* (Englewood Cliffs, N.J., 1960). Douglas Oliver in his *The Pacific Islands,* 1961 edition, has an interesting discussion of World War II's impact. See also the references for Chapters IV and VIII above.

THE POSTWAR YEARS

Most of the bibliographies of the island groups given just above include books or other references which deal with the postwar period, some of them extensively or wholly. However, I know of no book on the impact of the war on the islands, physically or ideologically. An interesting early example of Australian reasoning about the probable effects of the Atlantic Charter is Julius Stone, *The Atlantic Charter* (Sydney, 1943). For early discussion of the islands and the future in pamphlet form, see A. P. Elkin, *Wanted—A Charter for the Native Peoples of the Southwest Pacific* (Sydney, 1943); H. I. Hogbin and C. Wedgwood, *Development and Welfare in the Western Pacific* (Sydney, 1943); Rev. J. W. Burton, *Brown and White in the Pacific* (Sydney, 1944); and Julius Stone, *Colonial Trusteeship in Transition* (Sydney, 1944). A later and fuller discussion of trusteeship with much material on the islands, A. H. McDonald, ed., *Trusteeship in the Pacific* (Sydney, 1949). There are interesting passages on the old colonial policy and the genesis and evolution of the United Kingdom's "development and welfare" line in W. K. Hancock. *Wealth of Colonies* (Cambridge, Eng., 1950). A short view of French, British, and Dutch colonial policies as they were just after the war, Anon. ed., *Colonial Administration by European Powers* (London, 1947). The best discussion of the recent background of South Pacific Regionalism is in

Chapter IX of L. A. Mander's *Some Dependent Peoples* (New York, 1954), but it only traces the idea from the end of World War I and it has much deeper roots. There are a number of discussions of the arrival on the scene of the South Pacific Commission, but no authoritative review of its progress during the last 15 years. A first-class discussion of the SPC when it was just an idea is Ernest Beaglehole, "The South Seas Regional Commission" in N.Z. Paper 3 for the 9th IPR Conference, January 1945. For an account almost at the moment of its actual birth, Roy E. James in *Pacific Affairs,* v. xx, no. 2, June 1947. The first secretary-general of the organization, W. D. Forsyth, printed a useful early statement of the Commission's plans in *Far Eastern Survey,* v. xvii, no. 5, March 9, 1949. Annually beginning in 1948 there has been a *Report of the South Pacific Commission for the Year....* Since the SPC represents the kind of co-operation in the islands R. W. Robson has promoted for thirty years, it gets both sympathetic support and stern criticism in *Pacific Islands Monthly.* Australian policy in the islands is reviewed in the quinquennial review of foreign policy, G. Greenwood and N. Harper, eds., *Australia in World Affairs 1950–1955* (Melbourne, 1957); the essays "The Southwest Pacific" by R. B. Joyce; and "New Guinea and Papua" by John Andrews. Since this review is the first of a series, similar essays will presumably be found in subsequent volumes. On Dr. Evatt and the islands in 1944 see F. L. W. Wood in the book on N.Z. in World War II cited in Chap. VIII. On the economic situation in the islands see the SPC studies cited above under GENERAL and Barrau on Melanesian subsistence agriculture, the late Horace Belshaw's excellent article, "Some Pacific Islands Problems" in *Pacific Viewpoint,* Vol. I, no. 2, September 1960, and E. K. Fisk's article "Planning a Primitive Economy," *The Economic Record,* Vol. 38, no. 84, Dec. 1962 as well as his essay in J. G. Crawford, ed., cited above under New Guinea. For the problems of calculating the national income of a mixed subsistence and commercial economy, see Carleen O'Loughlin's study of the Fiji economy cited above under Fiji. For a geographer's survey of the United States Trust Territory and its likely strategic importance today, Herold J. Wiens, *Pacific Island Bastions of the United States* (Princeton, N.J., 1962). For a dogma that is so frequently reiterated in one form or another, "the-islands-as-a-shield" has made a remarkable escape from reconsideration in the light of the vast changes in military technology. It seems to be assumed that only old-fashioned conventional wars are likely to be fought in future in the Southwest Pacific. Perhaps the liveliest critical inspection of the idea is A. J. Rose's essay, "Strategic Geography and the Northern Approaches" in *The Australian Outlook,* vol. 13, no. 4, December 1959. The final section of Douglas Oliver's 1961 edition is entitled "Cataclysm and Aftermath" and includes some rather apocalyptic reflections on what will happen if all of Asia goes communist. Having lived through two great wars and a great depression, I am more or less allergic to the apocalyptic approach. Walter Sullivan takes note of IGY in the islands in *Assault on the Unknown: The International Geophysical Year* (New York, 1961) and so does Sydney Chapman in

IGY: Year of Discovery (Ann Arbor, Mich., 1959). On the atomic tests the literature is now considerable, but see the *New York Times, passim.* For the "Agreements Regarding the Use of Eniwetock and Bikini Atolls," as fascinating island documents as have ever been prepared, see *Tenth Annual Report to the UN on the Administration of the Trust Territory of the Pacific Islands* (Washington, D.C., 1958), Appendix A.

ANTARCTICA

XII. THE HEROIC AGE

For an interesting study of adventure and its motivations, see Wilfred Noyce, *The Springs of Adventure* (New York, 1958). The literature of the Scott expeditions is enormous, especially that which relates to the second expedition. Scott's own narrative of the first expedition is excellent: R. F. Scott, *The Voyage of the Discovery,* 2 vols. (New York, 1905). See also A. B. Armitage, *Two Years in the Antarctic* (London, 1905). On the second expedition the basic book is Leonard Huxley, ed., *Scott's Last Expedition,* 2 vols. (New York, 1913), a rather indifferently edited work the core of which is Scott's diary. See also H. G. Ponting, *The Great White South* (New York, 1923); E. R. G. R. Evans, *South with Scott* (London, 1921); George Seaver, *Edward Wilson of the Antarctic* (London, 1933); and, above all, Apsley Cherry-Garrard, *The Worst Journey in the World: Antarctic 1910–1913,* 2 vols. (New York, 1922), to my taste the book about Antarctic exploration of the greatest *literary* value. Stephen Gwynn, *Captain Scott* (New York, 1930) is a rather syrupy "life." Griffith Taylor and Priestley also wrote books about the second Scott expedition. Taylor returns to it in his autobiography, *Journeyman Taylor* (London, 1958), and his *Antarctic Adventure and Research* (New York, 1930) is to a large extent based on what he learned at the time. A life of Bruce is R. N. Rudmose Brown, *A Naturalist at the Poles* (London, 1923). On the Shackleton expeditions see E. H. Shackleton, *The Heart of the Antarctic,* 2 vols. (Philadelphia, 1909) and E. H. Shakleton, *South!: Expedition of 1914–1917* (New York, 1920). Frank Hurley deals with his experiences with both Shackleton and Mawson in *Argonauts of the South* (New York, 1925) and abstracts from it his account of the drift on the ice in *Shackleton's Argonauts* (Sydney, 1948). Also on Shackleton see H. R. Mill, *The Life of Sir Ernest Shackleton* (Boston, 1923); Margery and James Fisher, *Shackleton and the Antarctic* (Boston, 1958); and, for the drift on the ice, Alfred Lansing, *Endurance* (New York, 1959). For the conquest of the South Pole, Roald Amundsen, *The South Pole,* 2 vols. (New York, 1913). Douglas Mawson's narrative is *The Home of the Blizzard: The Australasian Antarctic Expedition 1911–1914,* 2 vols. (Philadelphia, n.d.). See also C. F. Laserson, *South with Mawson* (Sydney, 1947). On the French expedition of 1908–1910, see Jean Charcot, *The Voyage of the 'Why Not?' in the Antarctic* (London, 1911). There appears to

be no good book on the history of Antarctic whaling, but see Paul Budker, *Whales and Whaling* (New York, 1959). In addition to the books
of general utility about Antarctica or portions thereof mentioned
earlier, there can be added here L. P. Kirwan, *The White Road: Polar
Exploration* (London, 1959), the merit of which is that it deals with
both the Arctic and Antarctica; W. Sullivan, *Quest for a Continent*
(New York, 1957); F. Debenham, *Antarctica* (London, 1959), not
one of the Professor Debenham's best books; and for Australian activities R. A. Swan, *Australia in the Antarctic* (Melbourne, 1961).

XIII. TEARING AT THE VEIL (1)

There are essays on the state of knowledge about Antarctica *circa*
the mid-1920's in W. L. G. Joerg, ed., *Problems of Polar Research*
(New York, 1928), an American Geographical Society publication. To
my mind the most useful account of Shackleton's last expedition is that
in the Fishers life of Shackleton. The material for an account of the
"Discovery" Committee's activities is scattered in many places. A
fascinating personal narrative of experience in Antarctica with the
Committee is F. D. Ommanney, *South Latitude* (London, 1938). It
includes an account of the "relief" of Ellsworth at Little America
(see the next chapter). The data about the Norwegian activities is
scattered in journal articles, etc., but there is Lars Chistensen's book,
Such is the Antarctic (London, 1935), rather lumpily written (or
translated) but full of interesting stuff. On whaling the information is
to be found in many places but the best single book reference seems to
be Budker. See also A. C. Bennett, *Whaling in the Antarctic* (New
York, 1932) and the personal narratives by Alan Villiers based upon
his participation in Captain Larsen's pioneering expedition into the
Ross Sea. Practically all general accounts of Antarctica include something about the politics but in my experience the best and most accurate discussions are by the international lawyers, most of whose
contributions are in the form of journal articles. These are fairly nu-
merous. The best single account in a separate book is in P. C. Jessup and
H. J. Taubenfeld, *Controls for Outer Space and the Antarctic Analogy*
(New York, 1959). The British presented their official case against the
Argentines and the Chileans in *I. C. J. Pleadings, Antarctica Cases
(United Kingdom v. Argentina; United Kingdom v. Chile)*. The
British case is presented more loosely in Christie. There are books in
Spanish presenting the Argentine and Chilean cases.

XIV. TEARING AT THE VEIL (2)

The material for this chapter was gathered from a wide variety of
sources including books devoted to the several expeditions, journal
articles, and the recapitulations (and sometimes evaluations) in such

books as those by Sullivan, Christie, Kirwan, Debenham, Swan, Lord Mountevans (*The Antarctic Challenged,* New York, 1958), W. L. G. Joerg (*Brief History of Polar Exploration since the Introduction of Flying,* New York, 1930), and J. G. Hayes (*Antarctica: A Treatise,* London, 1928). There is a biography of Wilkins, who died in Framingham, Massachusetts, in 1958, by Lowell Thomas (New York, 1961), in form an as-told-to narrative, excepting a final chapter by Lady Wilkins. It is not very satisfactory for it contains puzzling "holes" and some of the facts are off. Byrd wrote about his first and second expeditions, the quality of the second narrative much better than that of the first: *Little America* (New York, 1930) and *Discovery* (New York, 1935). Byrd also wrote an account of his isolation in the interest of meteorology called *Alone* (New York, 1938). Laurence Gould's story of Byrd I is *Cold* (New York, 1931). Siple's account of Byrd II in his book *90° South* (New York, 1959) is useful but not as solid as it should be. After I had prepared my text there came to hand A. G. Price, *The Winning of Australian Antarctica: Mawson's BANZARE Voyages 1929–1931* (Sydney, 1962). Meanwhile a valuable account of the expeditions was to be found in Swan. There is a book about the Rymill expedition, *Southern Lights* (London, 1938), but there is no closely circumstantial book-length account of the Ritscher expedition in English and, more surprisingly, no book describing the USAS expedition.

XV.   A SCIENTIFIC PRESERVE

On the United Kingdom-Argentina-Chile contention, see the references in Chap. XIII. For the Australian position, see Swan. My information about the outlooks of other claimants is from journal articles and documents. Data on the American proposal of 1948 and the reactions to it are to be found in most narratives about Antarctica. On Highjump see especially Sullivan and the stories of participants, Paul Siple, *90° South* and G. J. Dufek, *Operation Deepfreeze* (New York, 1957). On the Ronne expedition the principal reliance is Ronne's own book, *Antarctic Conquest* (New York, 1949). The Australian story is well told by Swan; the earlier stages are covered in Arthur Scholes *Seventh Continent* (London, 1953); a semi-official account covering more of the ground, beautifully illustrated, is Phillip Law and John Béchervaise, *ANARE: Australia's Antarctic Outposts* (Melbourne, 1957); and a personal reaction to Antarctica is John Béchervaise, *The Far South* (Sydney, 1961). There is a "portrait" of Law in John Hetherington, *Australians: Nine Profiles* (Melbourne, 1960). There are notes on Australian activity in Antarctica (and also New Zealand and South African) in the book edited by F. A. Simpson. There is a running account in the periodical publication, *Australia in Facts and Figures* (Canberra, 1943 *et seq.*). On the French return to Adélie Land see Sullivan, the official French pamphlet literature, and such personal narratives as Jean Rivolier, *Emperor Penguins* (New York, 1958).

The official narrative of the Norwegian-British-Swedish expedition is John Giaever, *The White Desert* (New York, 1955). On whaling post-World War II there is information in F. A. Simpson, ed., and in Swan, but the best single book reference remains Budker. Karl Brandt's pamphlet, *Whaling and Whale Oil During and After World War II* (Stanford, Calif., 1948) is very useful on the transitional period. A Russian account of a whaling season in Antarctica, printed in English, is A. Solyanik, *Cruising in the Antarctic* (Moscow, 1956). R. B. Robertson, *Of Whales and Men* (New York, 1954) makes fascinating reading but must be used with caution. On the Australian postwar adventure in whaling, see R. L. Wettenhall, "The Australian Whaling Commission in Retrospect" in *The Australian Quarterly,* December 1961, and the articles on whaling in the *Australian Encyclopedia.* On the International Geophysical Year the best accounts, which deal *inter alia* with Antarctica, are Walter Sullivan, *Assault on the Unknown* (New York, 1961) and S. Chapman, *IGY: Year of Discovery* (Ann Arbor, 1959). A symposium on the state of knowledge about Antarctica before the IGY is *Antarctica in the International Geophysical Year* (Washington, 1956), which is Geophysical Monograph, No. 1. On the state of knowledge a few years after the IGY see *Science in Antarctica:* Part I, *The Life Sciences,* Part II, *The Physical Sciences* (Washington, 1961). These volumes suggest research programs for the future. The Dufek and Siple volumes cited above deal chiefly with the IGY and its preliminaries. A Russian account of Antarctica, in English, which discusses the continent, runs over the history with the usual positive Russian claim for Bellingshausen's discovery of the continent, and gets down to the IGY is V. Lebedev, *Antarctica* (Moscow, 1959). An account of New Zealand's scientific contribution on the "continent" during IGY is T. Hatherton, *New Zealand's IGY Antarctic Expedition, Scott Base and Hallett Station* (N.Z. Dept. Scientific & Industrial Res., Bulletin 140; Wellington, 1961). On the Commonwealth Trans-Antarctic Expedition, see Sir V. Fuchs and Sir E. Hillary, *The Crossing of Antarctica* (London, 1958) and Hillary's personal narrative, *No Latitude for Error* (New York, 1961). Two interesting general surveys of the situation in the late 1950's are Laurence M. Gould, *The Polar Regions in their Relation to Human Affairs* (New York, 1958) and G. C. L. Bertram, *Antarctica Today and Tomorrow* (Dunedin, N.Z., 1958). On the Antarctic Treaty, 1959, see *The Conference on Antarctica,* Dept. of State Pub. 7060, September 1960, and H. J. Taubenfeld, *A Treaty for Antarctica,* International Conciliation, No. 531, January 1961. See also *Report of First Consultative Meeting* (Canberra, 1961). An exasperating paradox is that as the scientists gain in understanding of Antarctica, now peculiarly their province, the non-scientist laymen, not so badly off as long as it was mostly a matter of adventure and geography, are left with the feeling that there is more here than they can quite comprehend. Since the days of Ponting and Hurley professional photographers have worked in Antarctica and their pictures add a fascinating fillip to many of the narratives cited above. A most interesting recent book of photographs by a Swiss professional is Emil Schulthess, *Antarctica: A Photographic Survey* (New York, 1960), with accompanying brief texts by Sir Raymond Priestley, Rear Admiral Dufek, and Dr. H. M. Dater. A stylish photographic study of whaling is Christopher Ash's *Whaler's Eye* (New York, 1963), and a summary of what scientists know about whales is E. J. Slijper's *Whales* (New York, 1963).

DATE DUE

GAYLORD

PRINTED IN U.S.A.